THE BILL OF RIGHTS:
A DOCUMENTARY HISTORY

THE BILL OF RIGHTS:
A DOCUMENTARY HISTORY

BERNARD SCHWARTZ

Volume II

CHELSEA HOUSE PUBLISHERS in association with
McGRAW HILL BOOK COMPANY
New York, Toronto, London, Sydney
1971

MANAGING EDITOR: Leon Friedman
ASSISTANT EDITOR: Karyn Gullen Browne
EDITORIAL STAFF: Joan Tapper, Betsy Nicolaus,
Christine Pinches, Jeanne Brody

NOTE: The original spelling, grammar and style have been retained in all documentary material.

CONTENTS

Volume II

PART SIX
State Ratifying Conventions

PART SEVEN
Federal Bill of Rights: Legislative History

PART EIGHT
Ratification by the States

PART SIX
STATE RATIFYING CONVENTIONS

PENNSYLVANIA RATIFYING CONVENTION, 1787

Commentary

The first state to ratify the federal Constitution was Delaware, which acted by a unanimous vote on December 2, 1787. The second state to act was Pennsylvania, where the struggle between supporters and opponents of the Constitution was a closer one. The Pennsylvania Convention met on November 20, 1787. The principal speeches in favor of the motion to ratify were delivered by James Wilson, and extracts from his remarks in support of the Constitution are included in the materials that follow. Of particular interest to us are his answers to the Bill of Rights argument of the Antifederalists. Wilson states that the framers' Convention had not even considered the addition of a Bill of Rights until the subject was mentioned three days before adjournment ("such an idea never entered the mind of many of them"), though he errs in saying no motion was even offered (*supra* p. 435). He repeats the standard argument against a Bill of Rights (make famous by *The Federalist* [*supra* p. 578]), that a Bill of Rights was both unnecessary, since the Federal Government was not given authority over individual rights, and dangerous, since it implied possession of such power by the Federal Government. Wilson turns around a common claim in favor of a Bill of Rights: What harm could its addition do? "If it can do no good, I think that a sufficient reason to refuse having any thing to do with it."

The Antifederalists sought to answer Wilson on these points, for the lack of a Bill of Rights was one of their main issues throughout the Convention debate. Extracts from their speeches (as well as some by supporters of Wilson) are included in the materials that follow. The principal Antifederalist speaker was Robert Whitehill. He emulated Wilson in seeking to turn around his opponents' argument: "Truly, Sir, I will agree that a bill of rights may be a dangerous instrument, but it is to the views and projects of the aspiring ruler, and not the liberties of the citizen." In the Constitution, he asserted, there is no adequate security for the liberties of the people; therefore, a Bill of Rights is vitally necessary. Of particular interest is the interchange between Messrs. Smilie and Whitehill, on the one side, and Messrs. Wilson and M'Kean, on the other.

Acute lawyer that he was, Wilson raised a shrewd legal objection to any action by the Pennsylvania Convention on a federal Bill of Rights. "But to whom are we to report this bill of rights, if we should adopt it? Have we authority from those who sent us here to make one?"

Legally speaking, of course, the Pennsylvania delegates had no authority to adopt any federal Bill of Rights or to give effect to any such adoption by them. But they could recommend amendments containing guarantees for individual rights. Moreover, if their example in this respect were followed by the other ratifying states, it would be most difficult for the first Congress to meet under the Constitution (which would have the authority to propose constitutional amendments) to ignore the combined recommendations, though they were without legal effect, strictly speaking.

At any rate, the Antifederalists in the Pennsylvania Convention acted on the view just stated. On December 12, 1787, Whitehill introduced 15 proposed amendments for the Convention to recommend as part of its ratification action (*infra* p. 658). The Convention rejected the proposed amendments by a vote of 46 to 23 and, later on that day, ratified the Constitution itself by the same majority. The minority then issued "The Address and Reasons of Dissent of the Minority of the Convention" (from which follow extracts, [*infra* p. 662]). This gave wide dissemination to the proposed amendments which were intended to meet the need for a federal Bill of Rights, itself asserted as "indispensable to ascertain and establish 'those unalienable and personal' rights of man."

The amendments proposed by the Pennsylvania Convention minority are of great importance in the history of the federal Bill of Rights, for they pointed the way to be taken by states which desired to ratify the Constitution and, at the same time, wanted a Bill of Rights. Even the Federalist supporters of the Constitution (as we shall see in our discussion of the Massachusetts Convention) came to see that the Pennsylvania minority method was a means of defusing opposition to ratification. The example set by the Pennsylvania minority was soon followed by the Massachusetts Ratifying Convention itself, and then by the ratifying conventions of four other states (South Carolina, New Hampshire, Virginia, and New York).

The amendments proposed by the Pennsylvania minority bear a direct relation to those ultimately adopted as the federal Bill of Rights. Indeed, eight of the first 10 amendments were first suggested as amendments in the proposals of the Pennsylvania minority. These included the following Amendments ultimately adopted: the First (freedom of conscience, speech, and press—Pennsylvania's proposed amendments 1 and 6); Second (Pennsylvania's proposed amendment 7); Fourth (Pennsylvania's proposed amendment 5); Fifth (privilege against self-incrimination and right not to be deprived of life, liberty, or property "except by the law of the land or the judgment of his peers"—Pennsylvania's proposed amendment 3); Sixth (right to speedy and public jury trial, to accusation and confrontation, and counsel—Pennsylvania's proposed amendment 3); Seventh (Pennsylvania's proposed amendment 2); Eighth (Pennsylvania's proposed amendment 4); and Tenth (Pennsylvania's proposed amendment 15).

Pennsylvania Ratifying Convention, 1787*

Debates

[Monday, November 26]

Mr. M'Kean: . . . I now think it necessary, sir, to make you a motion—not that I apprehend it can be determined until a full investigation of the subject before us is had. The motion will be, sir, That this Convention do assent to, and ratify, the Constitution agreed to on the 17th of September last, by the Convention of the United States of America, held at Philadelphia.

Upon this motion being seconded, sir, the consideration of the Constitution will be necessarily drawn on. Every objection that can be suggested against the work will be listened to with attention, answered, and perhaps obviated; and finally, after a full discussion, the ground will be ascertained, on which we are to receive or reject the system now before you. I do not wish this question to be decided to-day; though perhaps it may be determined this day week. I offer you this for the sake of form, and shall hereafter trouble you with another motion, that may bring the particular parts of this Constitution before you, for a regular and satisfactory investigation.

In this motion, Mr. M'Kean was seconded by Mr. Allison.

Mr. Wilson: The system proposed, by the late Convention, for the government of the United States, is now before you. Of that Convention I had the honor to be a member. As I am the only member of that body who has the honor to be also a member of this, it may be expected that I should prepare the way for the deliberations of this assembly, by unfolding the difficulties which the late Convention were obliged to encounter; by pointing out the end which they proposed to accomplish; and by tracing the general principles which they have adopted for the accomplishment of that end.

To form a good system of government for a single city or state, however limited as to territory, or inconsiderable as to numbers, has been thought to require the strongest efforts of human genius. With what conscious diffidence, then, must the members of the Convention have revolved in their minds the immense undertaking which was before them. Their views could not be confined to a small or a single community, but were expanded to a great number of states; several of which contain an extent of territory, and resources of population, equal to those of some of the most respectable kingdoms on the other side of the Atlantic. Nor were even these the only objects to be comprehended within their deliberations. Numerous states yet unformed, myriads of the human race, who will inhabit regions hitherto

*J. Elliot, *The Debates in the Several State Conventions on the Adoption of the Constitution* (1836), Vol. 2, pp. 418–540.

uncultivated, were to be affected by the result of their proceedings. It was necessary, therefore, to form their calculations on a scale commensurate to a large portion of the globe.

For my own part, I have been often lost in astonishment at the vastness of the prospect before us. To open the navigation of a single river was lately thought, in Europe, an enterprise equal to imperial glory. But could the commercial scenes of the Scheldt be compared with those that, under a good government, will be exhibited on the Hudson, the Delaware, the Potomac, and the numerous other rivers, that water and are intended to enrich the dominions of the United States?

The difficulty of the business was equal to its magnitude. No small share of wisdom and address is requisite to combine and reconcile the jarring interests that prevail, or seem to prevail, in a single community. The United States contain already thirteen governments mutually independent. Those governments present to the Atlantic a front of fifteen hundred miles in extent. Their soil, their climates, their productions, their dimensions, their numbers, are different. In many instances, a difference, and even an opposition, subsists among their interests; and a difference, and even an opposition, is imagined to subsist in many more. An apparent interest produces the same attachment as a real one, and is often pursued with no less perseverance and vigor. When all these circumstances are seen, and attentively considered, will any member of this honorable body be surprised that such a diversity of things produced a proportionate diversity of sentiment? Will he be surprised that such a diversity of sentiment rendered a spirit of mutual forbearance and conciliation indispensably necessary to the success of the great work? And will he be surprised that mutual concessions and sacrifices were the consequences of mutual forbearance and conciliation? When the springs of opposition were so numerous and strong, and poured forth their waters in courses so varying, need we be surprised that the stream formed by their conjunction was impelled in a direction somewhat different from that which each of them would have taken separately?

*   *   *

[Wednesday, November 28]

Mr. Wilson: . . . Those who ordain and establish have the power, if they think proper, to repeal and annul. A proper attention to this principle may, perhaps, give ease to the minds of some who have heard much concerning the necessity of a bill of rights.

Its establishment, I apprehend, has more force than a volume written on the subject. It renders this truth evident—that the people have a right to do what they please with regard to the government. I confess I feel a kind of pride in considering the striking difference between the foundation on which the liberties of this country are declared to stand in this Constitution, and the footing on which the liberties of England are said to be placed. The Magna Charta of England is an instrument of high value to the people of that country. But, Mr. President, from what source does that instrument derive the liberties of the inhabitants of that kingdom? Let it speak for itself. The king says, "We have given and granted to all archbishops, bishops, abbots, priors, earls, barons, and to all the freemen of this our realm, these liberties following, to be kept in our kingdom of England forever." When this was assumed as the leading principle of that government, it was no wonder that the people were anxious to obtain bills of rights, and to take every opportunity of enlarging and securing their liberties. But here, sir, the fee-simple remains in the people at large, and by this Constitution they do not part with it.

I am called upon to give a reason why the Convention omitted to add a bill of rights to the work before you. I confess, sir, I did think that, in point of propriety, the honorable gentleman ought first to have furnished some reasons to show such an addition to be necessary; it is natural to prove the affirmative of a proposition; and, if he had established the propriety of this addition, he might then have asked why it was not made.

I cannot say, Mr. President, what were the reasons of every member of that Convention for not adding a bill of rights. I believe the truth is, that such an idea never entered the mind of many of them. I do not recollect to have heard the subject mentioned till within about three days of the time of our rising; and even then, there was no direct motion offered for any thing of the kind. I may be mistaken in this; but as far as my memory serves me, I believe it was the case. A proposition to adopt a measure that would have supposed that we were throwing into the general government every power not expressly reserved by the people, would have been spurned at, in that house, with the greatest indignation. Even in a single government, if the powers of the people rest on the same establishment as is expressed in this Constitution, a bill of rights is by no means a necessary measure. In a government possessed of enumerated powers, such a measure would be not only unnecessary, but preposterous and dangerous. Whence comes this notion, that in the United States there is no security without a bill of rights? Have the citizens of South Carolina no security for their liberties? They have no bill of rights. Are the citizens on the eastern side of the Delaware less free, or less secured in their liberties, than those on the western side? The state of New Jersey has no bill of rights. The state of New York has no bill of rights. The states of Connecticut and Rhode Island have no bill of rights. I know not whether I have exactly enumerated the states who have not thought it necessary to add a bill of rights to their constitutions; but this enumeration, sir, will serve to show by experience, as well as principle, that, even in single governments, a bill of rights is not an essential or necessary measure. But in a government consisting of enumerated powers, such as is proposed for the United States, a bill of rights would not only be unnecessary, but, in my humble judgment, highly imprudent. In all societies, there are many powers and rights which cannot be particularly enumerated. A bill of rights annexed to a constitution is an enumeration of the powers reserved. If we attempt an enumeration, every thing that is not enumerated is presumed to be given. The consequence is, that an imperfect enumeration would throw all implied power into the scale of the government, and the rights of the people would be rendered incomplete. On the other hand, an imperfect enumeration of the powers of government reserves all implied power to the people; and by that means the constitution becomes incomplete. But of the two, it is much safer to run the risk on the side of the constitution; for an omission in the enumeration of the powers of government is neither so dangerous nor important as an omission in the enumeration of the rights of the people.

Mr. President, as we are drawn into this subject, I beg leave to pursue its history a little farther. The doctrine and practice of declarations of rights have been borrowed from the conduct of the people of England on some remarkable occasions; but the principles and maxims, on which their government is constituted, are widely different from those of ours. I have already stated the language of Magna Charta. After repeated confirmations of that instrument, and after violations of it repeated equally often, the next step taken in this business was, when the petition of rights was presented to Charles I.

It concludes in this manner: "All of which they most humbly pray to be allowed, as their rights and liberties, according to the laws and statutes of this realm." (8th Par. Hist. 150.) One of the most material statutes of the realm was Magna Charta; so that we find they continue upon the old ground, as to the foundation on which they rest their liberties. It was not till the era of the revolution that the two houses assume a higher tone, and "demand and insist upon all the premises as their undoubted rights and liberties." (Par. Deb. 261.) But when the whole transaction is considered, we shall find that those rights and liberties are claimed only on the foundation of an original contract, supposed to have been made, at some former period, between the king and the people. (1 Blackstone, 233.)

But, in this Constitution, the citizens of the United States appear dispensing a part of their original power in what manner and what proportion they think fit. They never part with the whole; and they retain the right of recalling what they part with. When, therefore, they possess, as I have already mentioned, the fee-simple of authority, why should they have recourse to the minute and subordinate remedies, which can be necessary only to those who pass the fee, and reserve only a rent-charge?

To every suggestion concerning a bill of rights, the citizens of the United States may always say, We reserve the right to do what we please.

I concur most sincerely with the honorable gentleman who was last up in one sentiment—that if our liberties will be insecure under this system of government, it will become our duty not to adopt, but to reject it. On the contrary, if it will secure the liberties of the citizens of America,—if it will not only secure their liberties, but procure them happiness,—it becomes our duty, on the other hand, to assent to and ratify it. With a view to conduct us safely and gradually to the determination of that important question, I shall beg leave to notice some of the objections that have fallen from the honorable gentleman from Cumberland, (Whitehill.) But, before I proceed, permit me to make one general remark. Liberty has a formidable enemy on each hand; on one there is tyranny, on the other licentiousness. In order to guard against the latter, proper powers ought to be given to government: in order to guard against the former, those powers ought to be properly distributed. It has been mentioned, and attempts have been made to establish the position, that the adoption of this Constitution will necessarily be followed by the annihilation of all the state governments. If this was a necessary consequence, the objection would operate in my mind with exceeding great force. But, sir, I think the inference is rather unnatural, that a government will produce the annihilation of others, upon the very existence of which its own existence depends. Let us, sir, examine this Constitution, and mark its proportions and arrangements. It is composed of three great constituent parts—the legislative department, the executive department, and the judicial department. The legislative department is subdivided into two branches—the House of Representatives and the Senate. Can there be a House of Representatives in the general government, after the state governments are annihilated? Care is taken to express the character of the electors in such a manner, that even the popular branch of the general government cannot exist unless the governments of the states continue in existence.

*   *   *

[Tuesday, December 4]

Mr. Wilson: I shall take this opportunity of giving an answer to the objections already urged against the Constitution; I shall then point out some of those qualities that entitle it to the attention and approbation of this Convention; and, after having done this, I shall take a fit opportunity of stating the consequences which, I apprehend, will result from rejecting it, and those which will probably result from its adoption. I have given the utmost attention to the debates, and the objections that, from time to time, have been made by the three gentlemen who speak in opposition. I have reduced them to some order, perhaps not better than that in which they were introduced. I will state them; they will be in the recollection of the house, and I will endeavor to give an answer to them: in that answer, I will interweave some remarks, that may tend to elucidate the subject.

A good deal has already been said concerning a bill of rights. I have stated, according to the best of my recollection, all that passed in Convention relating to that business. Since that time, I have spoken with a gentleman, who has not only his memory, but full notes that he had taken in that body, and he assures me that, upon this subject, no direct motion was ever made at all; and certainly, before we heard this so violently supported out of doors, some pains ought to have been taken to have tried its fate within: but the truth is, a bill of rights would, as I have mentioned already, have been not only unnecessary, but improper. In some governments, it may come within the gentleman's idea, when he says it can do no harm; but even in these governments, you find bills of rights do not uniformly obtain; and do those states complain who have them not? Is it a maxim in forming governments, that not only all the powers which are given, but also that all those which are reserved, should be enumerated? I apprehend that the powers given and reserved form the whole rights of the people, as men and as citizens. I consider that there are very few who understand the whole of these rights. All the political writers, from Grotius and Puffendorf down to Vattel, have treated on this subject; but in no one of those books, nor in the aggregate of them all, can you find a complete enumeration of rights appertaining to the people as men and as citizens.

There are two kinds of government—that where general power is intended to be given to the legislature, and that where the powers are particularly enumerated. In the last case, the implied result is, that nothing more is intended to be given than what is so enumerated, unless it results from the nature of the government itself. On the other hand, when general legislative powers are given, then the people part with their authority, and, on the gentleman's principle of government, retain nothing. But in a government like the proposed one, there can be no necessity for a bill of rights for, on my principle, the people never part with their power. Enumerate all the rights of men! I am sure, sir that no gentleman in the late Convention would have attempted such a thing. I believe the honerable speakers in opposition on this floor were members of the assembly which appointed delegates to that Convention; if it had been thought proper to have sent them into that body, how luminous would the dark conclave have been!—so the gentleman has been pleased to denominate that body. Aristocrats as they were, they pretended not to define the rights of those who sent them there. We ask, repeatedly, What harm could the addition of a bill of rights do? If it can do no good, I think that a sufficient reason to refuse having any thing to do with it. But to whom are we to report this bill of rights, if we should adopt it? Have we authority from those who sent us here to make one?

It is true, we may propose as well as any other private persons: but how shall we know the sentiments of the citizens of this state and of the other states? Are we certain that any one of them will agree with our definitions and enumerations?

*   *   *

[Tuesday, December 11]

Mr. Wilson: Three weeks have now elapsed since this Convention met. Some of the delegates attended on Tuesday, the 20th November; a great majority within a day or two afterwards; and all but one on the 4th day. We have been since employed in discussing the business for which we are sent here. I think it will now become evident to every person who takes a candid view of our discussions, that it is high time our proceedings should draw towards a conclusion.

Perhaps our debates have already continued as long, nay, longer than is sufficient for every good purpose. The business which we were intended to perform is necessarily reduced to a very narrow compass. The single question to be determined is, Shall we assent to and ratify the Constitution proposed?

As this is the first state whose Convention has met on the subject, and as the subject itself is of very great importance, not only to Pennsylvania, but to the United States, it was thought proper fairly, openly, and candidly to canvass it. This has been done. You have heard, Mr. President, from day to day, and from week to week, the objections that could be offered from any quarter. We have heard these objections once: we have heard a great number of them repeated much oftener than once. Will it answer any valuable end, sir, to protract these debates longer? I suppose it will not. I apprehend it may serve to promote very pernicious and destructive purposes. It may, perhaps, be insinuated to other states, and even to distant parts of this state, by people in opposition to this system, that the expediency of adopting is at most very doubtful, and that the business lingers among the members of the Convention.

This would not be a true representation of the fact; for there is the greatest reason to believe that there is a very considerable majority who do not hesitate to ratify the Constitution. We were sent here to express the voice of our constituents on the subject, and I believe that many of them expected to hear the echo of that voice before this time.

When I consider the attempts that have been made on this floor, and the many misrepresentations of what has been said among us that have appeared in the public papers, printed in this city, I confess that I am induced to suspect that opportunity may be taken to pervert and abuse the principles on which the friends of this Constitution act. If attempts are made here, will they not be repeated when the distance is greater, and the means of information fewer? Will they not at length produce an uneasiness, for which there is, in fact, no cause? Ought we not to prohibit any such uses being made of the continuance of our deliberations? We do not wish to preclude debate: of this our conduct has furnished the most ample testimony. The members in opposition have not been prevented a repetition of all their objections that they could urge against this plan.

The honorable gentleman from Fayette, (Mr. Smilie,) the other evening, claimed for the minority the merit of contending for the rights of mankind; and he told us that it has been the practice of all ages to treat such minorities with contempt; he further took the liberty of observing, that, if the majority had the power, they do not want the inclination, to consign the minority to punishment. I know that claims, self-made, form no small part of the merit to which we have heard undisguised pretences; but it is one thing to claim, and it is another thing, very different indeed, to support that claim. The minority, sir, are contending for the rights of mankind; what, then, are the majority contending for? If the minority are contending for the rights of mankind, the majority must be contending for the doctrines of tyranny and slavery. Is it probable that that is the case? Who are the majority in this assembly? Are they not the people? are they not the representatives of the people, as well as the minority? Were they not elected by the people, as well as the minority? Were they not elected by the greater part of the people? Have we a single right separate from the rights of the people? Can we forge fetters for others that will not be clasped round our own limbs? Can we make heavy chains that shall not cramp the growth of our own posterity? On what fancied distinction shall the minority assume to themselves the merit of contending for the rights of mankind?

Sir, if the system proposed by the late Convention, and the conduct of its advocates who have appeared in this house, deserve the declarations and insinuations that have been made concerning them, well may we exclaim, "Ill-fated America! thy crisis was approaching! perhaps it was come! Thy various interests were neglected—thy most sacred rights were insecure. Without a government, without energy, without confidence internally, without respect externally, the advantages of society were lost to thee! In such a situation, distressed, but not despairing, thou desiredst to reassume thy native vigor, and to lay the foundation of future empire. Thou selectedst a number of thy sons, to meet together for the purpose. The selected and honored characters met; but, horrid to tell, they not only consented, but they combined in an aristocratic system, calculated and intended to enslave their country! Unhappy Pennsylvania! thou, as a part of the Union, must share in its unfortunate fate; for when this system, after being laid before thy citizens, comes before the delegates selected by them for its consideration, there are found but three of the numerous members that have virtue enough to raise their voices in support of the rights of mankind!" America, particularly Pennsylvania, must be ill-starred, indeed, if this is a true state of the case. I trust we may address our country in far other language.

"Happy America! thy crisis was indeed alarming, but thy situation was not desperate. We had confidence in our country; though, on whichever side we turned, we were presented with scenes of distress. Though the jarring interests of the various states, and the different habits and inclinations of their inhabitants, all lay in the way, and rendered our prospect gloomy and discouraging indeed, yet such were the generous and mutual sacrifices offered up, that, amidst forty-two members, who represented twelve of the

United States, there were only three who did not attest the instrument, as a confirmation of its goodness. Happy Pennsylvania! this plan has been laid before thy citizens for consideration; they have sent delegates to express their voice; and listen—with rapture listen!—from only three opposition has been heard against it."

The singular unanimity that has attended the whole progress of their business, will, in the minds of those considerate men who have not had opportunity to examine the general and particular interest of their country, prove, to their satisfaction, that it is an excellent Constitution, and worthy to be adopted, ordained, and established, by the people of the United States.

After having viewed the arguments drawn from probability, whether this is a good or a bad system, whether those who contend for it, or those who contend against it, contend for the rights of mankind, let us step forward and examine the fact.

We were told, some days ago, by the honorable gentleman from Westmoreland, (Mr. Findley,) when speaking of this system and its objects, that the Convention, no doubt, thought they were forming a compact, or contract, of the greatest importance. Sir, I confess I was much surprised, at so late a stage of the debate, to hear such principles maintained. It was a matter of surprise to see the great leading principle of this system still so very much misunderstood. "The Convention, no doubt, thought they were forming a contract!" I cannot answer for what every member thought; but I believe it cannot be said that they thought they were making a contract, because I cannot discover the least trace of a compact in that system. There can be no compact unless there are more parties than one. It is a new doctrine that one can make a compact with himself. "The Convention were forming compacts!" With whom? I know no bargains that were made there. I am unable to conceive who the parties could be. The state governments make a bargain with one another; that is the doctrine that is endeavored to be established by gentlemen in opposition, that state sovereignties wish to be represented! But far other were the ideas of the Convention, and far other are those conveyed in the system itself.

As this subject has been often mentioned, and as often misunderstood, it may not be improper to take some further notice of it. This, Mr. President, is not a government founded upon compact; it is founded upon the power of the people. They express in their name and their authority—"We, the people, do ordain and establish," &c.; from their ratification alone it is to take its constitutional authenticity; without that, it is no more than *tabula rasa.*

*   *   *

I shall now proceed, Mr. President, to notice the remainder of the objections that have been suggested by the honorable gentlemen who oppose the system now before you.

We have been told, sir, by the honorable member from Fayette, (Mr.

Smilie,) "that the trial by jury was intended to be given up, and the civil law was intended to be introduced into its place, in civil cases."

Before a sentiment of this kind was hazarded, I think, sir, the gentleman ought to be prepared with better proof in its support than any he has yet attempted to produce. It is a charge, sir, not only unwarrantable, but cruel: the idea of such a thing, I believe, never entered into the mind of a single member of that Convention; and I believe further, that they never suspected there would be found, within the United States, a single person that was capable of making such a charge. If it should be well founded, sir, they must abide by the consequences; but if (as I trust it will fully appear) it is ill founded, then he or they who make it ought to abide by the consequences.

Trial by jury forms a large field for investigation, and numerous volumes are written on the subject; those who are well acquainted with it may employ much time in its discussion; but in a country where its excellences are so well understood, it may not be necessary to be very prolix in pointing them out. For my part, I shall confine myself to a few observations in reply to the objections that have been suggested.

The member from Fayette (Mr. Smilie) has labored to infer that, under the Articles of Confederation, the Congress possessed no appellate jurisdiction; but this being decided against him by the words of that instrument, by which is granted to Congress the power of "establishing courts for receiving, and determining finally, appeals in all cases of capture, he next attempts a distinction, and allows the power of appealing from the decisions of the judges, but not from the verdict of a jury; but this is determined against him also by the practice of the states; for, in every instance which has occurred, this power has been claimed by Congress, and exercised by the Courts of Appeals. But what would be the consequence of allowing the doctrine for which he contends? Would it not be in the power of a jury, by their verdict, to involve the whole Union in a war? They may condemn the property of a neutral, or otherwise infringe the law of nations; in this case, ought their verdict to be without revisal? Nothing can be inferred from this to prove that trials by jury were intended to be given up. In Massachusetts, and all the Eastern States, their causes are tried by juries, though they acknowledge the appellate jurisdiction of Congress.

I think I am not now to learn the advantages of a trial by jury. It has excellences that entitle it to a superiority over any other mode, in cases to which it is applicable.

Where jurors can be acquainted with the characters of the parties and the witnesses,—where the whole cause can be brought within their knowledge and their view,—I know no mode of investigation equal to that by a jury: they hear every thing that is alleged; they not only hear the words, but they see and mark the features of the countenance; they can judge of weight due to such testimony; and moreover, it is a cheap and expeditious manner of distributing justice. There is another advantage annexed to the trial by jury;

the jurors may indeed return a mistaken or ill-founded verdict, but their errors cannot be systematical.

Let us apply these observations to the objects of the judicial department, under this Constitution. I think it has been shown, already, that they all extend beyond the bounds of any particular state; but further, a great number of the civil causes there enumerated depend either upon the law of nations, or the marine law, that is, the general law of mercantile countries. Now, sir, in such cases, I presume it will not be pretended that this mode of decision ought to be adopted for the law with regard to them is the same here as in every other country, and ought to be administered in the same manner. There are instances in which I think it highly probable that the trial by jury will be found proper; and if it is highly probable that it will be found proper, is it not equally probable that it will be adopted? There may be causes depending between citizens of different states; and as trial by jury is known and regarded in all the states, they will certainly prefer that mode of trial before any other. The Congress will have the power of making proper regulations on this subject, but it was impossible for the Convention to have gone minutely into it; but if they could, it must have been very improper, because alterations, as I observed before, might have been necessary; and whatever the Convention might have done would have continued unaltered, unless by an alteration of the Constitution. Besides, there was another difficulty with regard to this subject. In some of the states they have courts of chancery, and other appellate jurisdictions, and those states are as attached to that mode of distributing justice as those that have none are to theirs.

I have desired, repeatedly, that honorable gentlemen, who find fault, would be good enough to point out what they deem to be an improvement. The member from Westmoreland (Mr. Findley) tells us that the trial between citizens of different states ought to be by a jury of that state in which the cause of action rose. Now, it is easy to see that, in many instances, this would be very improper and very partial; for, besides the different manner of collecting and forming juries in the several states, the plaintiff comes from another state; he comes a stranger, unknown as to his character or mode of life, while the other party is in the midst of his friends, or perhaps his dependants. Would a trial by jury, in such a case, insure justice to the stranger? But again: I would ask that gentleman whether, if a great part of his fortune was in the hands of some person in Rhode Island, he would wish that his action to recover it should be determined by a jury of that country, under its present circumstances.

The gentleman from Fayette (Mr. Smilie) says that, if the Convention found themselves embarrassed, at least they might have done thus much—they should have declared that the substance should be secured by Congress. This would be saying nothing unless the cases were particularized.

Mr. Smilie: I said the Convention ought to have declared that the legislature should establish the trial by jury by proper regulations.

Mr. Wilson: The legislature shall establish it by proper regulations! So, after all, the gentleman has landed us at the very point from which we set out. He wishes them to do the very thing they have done—to leave it to the discretion of Congress. The fact, sir, is, nothing more could be done.

It is well known that there are some cases that should not come before juries; there are others, that, in some of the states, never come before juries, and in those states where they do come before them, appeals are found necessary, the facts reexamined, and the verdict of the jury sometimes is set aside; but I think, in all cases where the cause has come originally before a jury, that the last examination ought to be before a jury likewise.

The power of having appellate jurisdiction, as to facts, has been insisted upon as a proof, "that the Convention intended to give up the trial by jury in civil cases, and to introduce the civil law." I have already declared my own opinion on this point, and have shown not merely that it is founded on reason and authority;—the express declaration of Congress (*Journals of Congress,* March 6, 1779) is to the same purpose. They insist upon this power, as requisite to preserve the peace of the Union; certainly, therefore, it ought always to be possessed by the head of the confederacy. We are told, as an additional proof, that the trial by jury was intended to be given up; "that appeals are unknown to the common law; that the term is a civil-law term, and with it the civil law is intended to be introduced." I confess I was a good deal surprised at this observation being made; for Blackstone, in the very volume which the honorable member (Mr. Smilie) had in his hand, and read us several extracts from, has a chapter entitled "Of Proceeding in the Nature of Appeals,"—and in that chapter says, that the principal method of redress for erroneous judgments, in the king's courts of record, is by writ of error to some superior "court of appeal." (3 Blackstone, 406.) Now, it is well known that his book is a commentary upon the common law. Here, then, is a strong refutation of the assertion, "that appeals are unknown to the common law."

I think these were all the circumstances adduced to show the truth of the assertion, that, in this Constitution, the trial by jury was intended to be given up by the late Convention in framing it. Has the assertion been proved? I say not, and the allegations offered, if they apply at all, apply in a contrary direction. I am glad that this objection has been stated, because it is a subject upon which the enemies of this Constitution have much insisted. We have now had an opportunity of investigating it fully; and the result is, that there is no foundation for the charge, but it must proceed from ignorance, or something worse.

*   *   *

Mr. M'Kean: Sir, you have under your consideration a matter of very great weight and importance, not only to the present generation, but to posterity; for where the rights and liberties of the people are concerned, there certainly it is fit to proceed with the utmost caution and regard. You have done so hitherto. The power of this Convention being derived from the people of Pennsylvania, by a positive and voluntary grant, cannot be extended farther than what this positive grant hath conveyed. You have been chosen by the people for the sole purpose of "assenting to and ratifying the Constitution proposed for the future government of the United States, with respect to their general and common concerns," or of rejecting it. It is a sacred trust; and as, on the one hand, you ought to weigh well the innovations it will create in the governments of the individual states, and the dangers which may arise by its adoption, so, upon the other hand, you ought fully to consider the benefits it may promise, and the consequences of a rejection of it. You have hitherto acted strictly conformably to your delegated power; you have agreed that a single question can come before you; and it has been accordingly moved that you resolve "to assent to and ratify this Constitution." Three weeks have been spent in hearing the objections that have been made against it, and it is now time to determine whether they are of such a nature as to overbalance any benefits or advantages that may be derived to the state of Pennslyvania by your accepting it.

Sir, I have as yet taken up but little of your time; notwithstanding this, I will endeavor to contract what occurs to me on the subject. And in what I have to offer, I shall observe this method: I will first consider the arguments that may have been used against this Constitution, and then give my reasons why I am for the motion.

*   *   *

"That there is no bill or declaration of rights in this Constitution."

To this I answer, Such a thing has not been deemed essential to liberty, excepting in Great Britain, where there is a king and a House of Lords, quite distinct, with respect to power and interest, from the rest of the people; or, in Poland, the pacta conventus, which the king signs before he is crowned; and in six states of the American United States.

Again, because it is unnecessary; for the powers of Congress, being derived from the people in the mode pointed out by this Constitution, and being therein enumerated and positively granted, can be no other than what this positive grant conveys. (*Locke on Civil Government*, vol. ii, b. 2, chap. 2, sect. 140, and in the 13th chap., sect. 152.)

With respect to executive officers, they have no manner of authority, any of them, beyond what is by positive grant and commission delegated to them.

*   *   *

Pennsylvania Convention Debates, 1787*

[Wednesday, November 28]

Mr. Smilie: I expected, Mr. President, that the honorable gentleman would have proceeded to a full and explicit investigation of the proposed

*J. B. McMaster and F. D. Stone, *Pennsylvania and the Federal Constitution* (1888), pp. 249–426.

system, and that he would have made some attempts to prove that it was calculated to promote the happiness, power and general interests of the United States. I am sorry that I have been mistaken in this expectation, for surely the gentleman's talents and opportunities would have enabled him to furnish considerable information upon this important subject; but I shall proceed to make a few remarks upon those words in the preamble of this plan, which he has considered of so super-excellent a quality. Compare them, Sir, with the language used in forming the state constitution, and however superior they may be to the terms of the great charter of England; still, in common candor, they must yield to the more sterling expressions employed in this act. Let these speak for themselves:

"That all men are born equally free and independent, and have certain natural, inherent and unalienable rights, among which are the enjoying and defending life and liberty, acquiring possessing and protecting property, and pursuing and obtaining happiness and safety.

"That the people of this state have the sole, exclusive and inherent right of governing and regulating the internal police of the same.

"That all power being originally inherent in, and consequently derived from the people; therefore all officers of government, whether legislative or executive, are their trustees and servants, and at all times accountable to them.

"That government is, or ought to be, instituted for the common benefit, protection and security of the people, nation or community; and not for the particular emolument or advantage of any single man, family, or set of men, who are a part only of that community. And that the community hath an indubitable, unalienable, and indefeasible right to reform, alter or abolish government in such manner as shall be by that community judged most conducive to the public weal."

But the gentleman takes pride in the superiority of this short preamble when compared with Magna Charta—why, sir, I hope the rights of men are better understood at this day than at the framing of that deed, and we must be convinced that civil liberty is capable of still greater improvement and extension, than is known even in its present cultivated state. True, sir, the supreme authority naturally rests in the people, but does it follow, that therefore a declaration of rights would be superfluous? Because the people have a right to alter and abolish government, can it therefore be inferred that every step taken to secure that right would be superfluous and nugatory? The truth is, that unless some criterion is established by which it could be easily and constitutionally ascertained how far our governors may proceed, and by which it might appear when they transgress their jurisdiction, this idea of altering and abolishing government is a mere sound without substance. Let us recur to the memorable declaration of the 4th of July, 1776. Here it is said:

"When in the course of human events, it becomes necessary for one people to dissolve the political bands which have connected them with another, and to assume among the powers of the earth the separate and equal station to which the laws of nature's God entitle them, a decent respect to the opinions of mankind requires that they should declare the causes which impel them to the separation.

"We hold these truths to be self-evident; that all men are created equal; that they are endowed by their Creator with certain unalienable rights; that among these are life, liberty, and the pursuit of happiness. That to secure these rights, governments are instituted among men, deriving their just powers from the consent of the governed; that when any form of government becomes destructive of these ends, it is the right of the people to alter or to abolish it, and to institute a new government, laying its foundation on such principles, and organizing its powers in such form, as to them shall seem most likely to effect their safety and happiness."

Now, Sir, if in the proposed plan, the gentleman can show any similar security for the civil rights of the people, I shall certainly be relieved from a weight of objection to its adoption, and I sincerely hope, that as he has gone so far, he will proceed to communicate some of the reasons (and undoubtedly they must have been powerful ones) which induced the late federal convention to omit a bill of rights, so essential in the opinion of many citizens to a perfect form of government.

Mr. M'Kean: I conceived, Mr. President, that we were at this time to confine our reasoning to the first article, which relates to the legislative power composed of two branches, and the partial negative of the President. Gentlemen, however, have taken a more extensive field, and have employed themselves in animadverting upon what has been omitted, and not upon what is contained in the proposed system. It is asked, Sir, why a bill of rights is not annexed to the constitution? The origin of bills of rights has been referred to, and we find that in England they proceed upon the principle that the supreme power is lodged in the king and not in the people, so that their liberties are not claimed as an inherent right, but as a grant from the sovereign. The great charter rests on that footing, and has been renewed and broken above 30 times. Then we find the petition of rights in the reign of Charles I., and lastly, the declaration of rights on the accession of the Prince of Orange to the British throne. The truth is, Sir, that bills of rights are instruments of modern invention, unknown among the ancients, and unpractised but by the British nation, and the governments descended from them. For though it is said that Poland has a bill of rights, it must be remembered that the people have no participation in that government. Of the constitutions of the United States, there are but five out of the thirteen which have bills of rights. In short, though it can do no harm, I believe, yet it is an unnecessary instrument, for in fact the whole plan of government is nothing more than a bill of rights—a declaration of the people in what manner they choose to be governed. If, Sir, the people should at any time desire to alter and abolish their government, I agree with my honorable colleague that it is in their power to do so, and I am happy to observe, that the constitution before us provides a regular mode for that event. At present my chief object is to call upon those who deem a bill of rights so essential, to inform us if there are any other precedents than those I have alluded to, and if there is not, the sense of mankind and of nations will operate against the alleged necessity.

Mr. Wilson: Mr. President, we are repeatedly called upon to give some reason why a bill of rights has not been annexed to the proposed plan. I not only think that enquiry is at this time unnecessary and out of order, but I expect, at least, that those who desire us to show why it was omitted, will furnish some arguments to show that it ought to have been inserted; for the proof of the affirmative naturally falls upon them. But the truth is, Sir, that this circumstance; which has since occasioned so much clamor and debate, never struck the mind of any member in the late convention till, I believe, within three days of the dissolution of that body, and even then of so little account was the idea that it passed off in a short conversation, without introducing a formal debate or assuming the shape of a motion. For, Sir, the attempt to have thrown into the national scale an instrument in order to evince that any power not mentioned in the constitution was reserved, would have been spurned at as an insult to the common understanding of mankind. In civil government it is certain that bills of rights are unnecessary and useless, nor can I conceive whence the contrary notion has arisen. Virginia has no bill of rights, and will it be said that her constitution was the less free?

Mr. Smilie: I beg leave to observe, Mr. President, that although it has not been inserted in the printed volume of state constitution, yet I have been assured by Mr. Mason that Virginia has a bill of rights.

Mr. Wilson: I do not rely upon the information of Mr. Mason or of any other gentleman on a question of this kind, but I refer to the authenticity of the volume which contains the state constitutions, and in that Virginia has no bill of rights. But, Sir, has South Carolina no security for her liberties?—that state has no bill of rights. Are the citizens of the eastern shore of the Delaware more secured in their freedom, or more enlightened on the subject of government, than the citizens of the western shore? New Jersey has no bill of rights, New York has none, Connecticut has none, and Rhode Island has none. Thus, Sir, it appears from the example of other states, as well as from principle, that a bill of rights is neither an essential nor a necessary instrument in framing a system of government, since liberty may exist and be as well secured without it. But it was not only unnecessary, but on this occasion it was found impracticable—for who will be bold enough to undertake to enumerate all the rights of the people?—and when the attempt to enumerate them is made, it must be remembered that if the enumeration is not complete, everything not expressly mentioned will be presumed to be purposely omitted. So it must be with a bill of rights, and an omission in stating the powers granted to the government, is not so dangerous as an omission in recapitulating the rights reserved by the people. We have already seen the origin of magna charta, and tracing the subject still further we find the petition of rights claiming the liberties of the people, according to the laws and statutes of the realm, of which the great charter was the most material, so that here again recourse is had to the old source from which their liberties are derived, the grant of the king. It was not till the revolution that the subject was placed upon a different footing, and even then the people did not claim their liberties as an inherent right, but as the result of an original contract between them and the sovereign. Thus, Mr. President, an attention to the situation of England will show that the conduct of that country in respect to bills of rights, cannot furnish an example to the inhabitants of the United States, who by the revolution have regained all their natural rights, and possess their liberty neither by grant nor contract. In short, Sir, I have said that a bill of rights would have been improperly annexed to the federal plan, and for this plain reason that it would imply that whatever is not expressed was given, which is not the principle of the proposed constitution.

Mr. Smilie: The arguments which have been urged, Mr. President, have not, in my opinion, satisfactorily shown that a bill of rights would have been an improper, nay, that it is not a necessary appendage to the proposed system. As it has been denied that Virginia possesses a bill of rights, I shall on that subject only observe that Mr. Mason, a gentleman certainly of great information and integrity, has assured me that such a thing does exist, and I am persuaded I shall be able at a future period to lay it before the convention. But, Sir, the state of Delaware has a bill of rights, and I believe one of the honorable members (Mr. M'Kean) who now contests the necessity and propriety of that instrument, took a very conspicuous part in the formation of the Delaware government. It seems, however, that the members of the federal convention were themselves convinced, in some degree, of the expediency and propriety of a bill of rights, for we find them expressly declaring that the writ of habeas corpus and the trial by jury in criminal cases shall not be suspended or infringed. How does this indeed agree with the maxim that whatever is not given is reserved? Does it not rather appear from the reservation of these two articles that everything else, which is not specified, is included in the powers delegated to the government? This, Sir, must prove the necessity of a full and explicit declaration of rights; and when we further consider the extensive, the undefined powers vested in the administrators of this system, when we consider the system itself as a great political compact between the governors and the governed, a plain, strong, and accurate criterion by which the people might at once determine when, and in what instance their rights were violated, is a preliminary, without which, this plan ought not to be adopted. So loosely, so inaccurately are the powers which are enumerated in this constitution defined, that it will be impossible, without a test of that kind, to ascertain the limits of authority, and to declare when government has degenerated into oppression. In that event the contest will arise between the people and the rulers: "You have exceeded the powers of your office, you have oppressed us," will be the language of the suffering citizen. The answer of the government will be short—"We have not exceeded our power; you have no test by which you can prove it." Hence, Sir, it will be impracticable to stop the progress of tyranny, for there will be no check but the people, and their exertions must be futile and uncertain; since it will be difficult, indeed, to communicate to them the violation that has been committed, and their proceedings will be neither systematical nor unanimous. It is said, however, that the difficulty of framing a bill of rights was insurmountable; but, Mr. President, I cannot agree in this opinion. Our experience, and the numerous precedents before us, would have furnished a very sufficient guide. At present there is no security even for the rights of conscience, and under the sweeping force of the sixth article, every principle of a bill of rights, every stipulation for the most sacred and invaluable privileges of man, are left at the mercy of government.

Mr. Whitehill: I differ, Sir, from the honorable member from the city,[1] as to the impropriety or necessity of a bill of rights. If, indeed, the constitution itself so well defined the powers of the government that no mistake could arise, and we were well assured that our governors would always act right, then we might be satisfied without an explicit reservation of those rights with which the people ought not, and mean not to part. But, Sir, we know that it is the nature of power to seek its own augmentation, and thus the loss of liberty is the necessary consequence of a loose or extravagant delegation of authority. National freedom has been, and will be the sacrifice of ambition and power, and it is our duty to employ the present opportunity in stipulating such restrictions as are best calculated to protect us from oppression and slavery. Let us then, Mr. President, if other countries cannot supply an adequate example, let us proceed upon our own principles, and with the great end of government in view, the happiness of the people, it will be strange if we err. Government, we have been told, Sir, is yet in its infancy: we ought not therefore to submit to the shackles of foreign schools and opinions. In entering into the social compact, men ought not to leave their rulers at large, but erect a permanent land-mark by which they may learn the extent of their authority, and the people be able to discover the first encroachments on their liberties. But let us attend to the language of the system before us. "We the people of the United States," is a sentence that evidently shows the old foundation of the union is destroyed, the principle of confederation excluded, and a new and unwieldy system of consolidated empire is set up, upon the ruins of the present compact between the states. Can this be denied? No, Sir: It is artfully indeed, but it is incontrovertibly designed to abolish the independence and sovereignty of the states individu-

---

[1]Mr. Wilson.

ally, an event which cannot be the wish of any good citizen of America, and therefore it ought to be prevented, by rejecting the plan which is calculated to produce it.

*   *   *

. . . Let us, however, suppose what will be allowed to be at least possible, that the powers of this government should be abused, and the liberties of the people infringed; do any means of redress remain with the states or with the people at large, to oppose and counteract the influence and oppression of the general government? Secret combinations, partial insurrections, sudden tumults may arise; but these being easily defeated and subdued, will furnish a pretence for strengthening that power which they were intended to overthrow. A bill of rights, Mr. President, it has been said, would not only be unnecessary, but it would be dangerous, and for this special reason, that because it is not practicable to enumerate all the rights of the people, therefore it would be hazardous to secure such of the rights as we can enumerate! Truly, Sir, I will agree that a bill of rights may be a dangerous instrument, but it is to the views and projects of the aspiring ruler, and not the liberties of the citizen. Grant but this explicit criterion, and our governors will not venture to encroach; refuse it, and the people cannot venture to complain. From the formal language of magna charta we are next taught to consider a declaration of rights as superfluous; but, Sir, will the situation and conduct of Great Britian furnish a case parallel to that of America? It surely will not be contended that we are about to receive our liberties as a grant or concession from any power upon earth; so that if we learn anything from the English charter, it is this: that the people having negligently lost or submissively resigned their rights into the hands of the crown, they were glad to recover them upon any terms; their anxiety to secure the grant by the strongest evidence will be an argument to prove, at least, the expediency of the measure, and the result of the whole is a lesson instructing us to do by an easy precaution, what will hereafter be an arduous and perhaps insurmountable task. But even in Great Britain, whatever may be the courtesy of their expressions, the matter stands substantially on a different footing, for we know that the divine right of kings is there, as well as here, deemed an idle and chimerical tale. It is true, the preamble to the great charter declares the liberties enumerated in that instrument, to be the grant of the sovereign, but the hyperbolical language of the English law has likewise declared that "the king can do no wrong," and yet, from time to time, the people have discovered in themselves the natural source of power, and the monarchs have been made painfully responsible for their action. Will it still be said, that the state governments would be adequate to the task of correcting the usurpations of Congress? Let us not, however, give the weight of proof to the boldness of assertion; for, if the opposition is to succeed by force, we find both the purse and the sword are almost exclusively transferred to the general government; and if it is to succeed by legislative remonstrance, we shall find that expedient rendered nugatory by the law of Congress, which is to be the supreme law of the land. Thus, Mr. President, must the powers and sovereignty of the several states be eventually destroyed, and when, at last, it may be found expedient to abolish that connection which, we are told essentially exists between the federal and individual legislatures, the proposed constitution is amply provided with the means in that clause which assumes the authority to alter or prescribe the place and manner of elections. I feel, Mr. President, the magnitude of the subject in which I am engaged, and although I am exhausted with what I have already advanced, I am conscious that the investigation is infinitely far from being complete. Upon the whole, therefore, I wish it to be seriously considered, whether we have a right to leave the liberties of the people to such future constructions and expositions as may possibly be made upon this system; particularly when its advocates, even at this day, confess that it would be dangerous to omit anything in the enumeration of a bill of rights, and according to their principle, the reservation of the habeas corpus, and trial by jury in criminal cases, may hereafter be construed to be the only privileges reserved by the people. I am not anxious, Mr. President, about forms—it is the substance which I wish to obtain; and therefore I acknowledge, if our liberties are secured by the frame of government itself, the supplementary instrument of a declaration of rights may well be dispensed with. But, Sir, we find no security there . . . and it will not, I hope, any longer be alleged that no security is requisite, since those exceptions prove a contrary sentiment to have been entertained by the very framers of the proposed constitution.

*   *   *

Mr. M'Kean: The first objection offered, Mr. President, to the adoption of the proposed system, arises from the omission of a bill of rights, and the gentlemen in the opposition have gone (contrary, I think, to their former wishes, which were to discuss the plan minutely, section after section,) from the immediate objects of the first article into an investigation of the whole system. However, as they have taken this wide and extensive path, I shall, though reluctantly, pursue them. It appears then, Sir, that there are but seven nations in the world which have incorporated a bill or declaration of rights into their system of government. The ancients were unacquainted with any instrument of that kind and till the recent establishment of the thirteen United States, the moderns, except Great Britain and Poland (if the Pacta Conventa of that kingdom may be considered), have not recognized its utility. Hence, Sir, if any argument is to be drawn from the example of other countries, we find that far the greatest number, and those most eminent for their power and wisdom, have not deemed a declaration of rights in any degree essential to the institution of government or the preservation of civil liberty. But, Sir, it has already been incontrovertibly shown that on the present occasion a bill of rights was totally unnecessary, and that it might be accompanied with some inconveniency and danger, if there was any defect in the attempt to enumerate the privileges of the people. This system proposes a union of thirteen sovereign and independent states, in order to give dignity and energy to the transaction of their common concerns; it would be idle therefore to countenance the idea that any other powers were delegated to the general government than those specified in the constitution itself, which, as I have before observed, amounts in fact to a bill of rights—a declaration of the people in what manner they choose to be governed.

*　　　*　　　*

. . . Such, Mr. President, are the objects to which the powers of the proposed government extend. Nor is it entirely left to this evident principle, that nothing more is given than is expressed, to circumscribe the federal authority. For, in the ninth section of the first article, we find the powers so qualified that not a doubt can remain. In the first clause of that section, there is a provision made for an event which must gratify the feelings of every friend to humanity. The abolition of slavery is put within the reach of the federal government. And when we consider the situation and circumstances of the southern states, every man of candor will find more reason to rejoice that the power should be given at all, than to regret that its exercise should be postponed for twenty years. Though Congress will have power to declare war, it is here stipulated that "the privilege of the writ of habeas corpus shall not be suspended, unless when in cases of rebellion or invasion, the public safety may require it;" and men will not be exposed to have their actions construed into crimes by subsequent and retrospective laws, for it is expressly declared that "no bill of attainder or *ex post facto* law shall be passed." Though Congress will have the power to lay duties and taxes, yet, "no capitation or other direct tax shall be laid, unless in proportion to the census or actual enumeration of the states, nor can any tax or duty be laid on articles of exportation." This wise regulation, Sir, has been successfully practiced by England and Ireland, while the commerce of Spain by a different conduct has been weakened and destroyed. The next restriction on the powers of Congress respects the appropriation of the public funds. "For no money shall be drawn from the treasury, but in consequence of appropriations made by law; and a regular statement and account of the receipts and expenditures of all public money shall be published from time to time." What greater security could be required or given upon this important subject? First, the money must be appropriated by law, then drawn for according to that appropriation, and lastly, from time to time, an account of the receipts and expenditures must be submitted to the people, who will thus be enabled to judge of the conduct of their rulers, and, if they see cause to object to the use or the excess of the sums raised, they may express their wishes or disapprobation to the legislature in petitions or remonstrances, which, if just and reasonable, cannot fail to be effectual. Thus, Sir, if any power is given, you cannot in my opinion give less—for less would be inadequate to the great objects of the government, and would neither enable Congress to pay the debts, or provide for the common defence of the Union. The last restriction mentioned prohibits Congress "from granting titles of nobility, and the officers of the proposed government from accepting, without the consent of Congress, any present, emolument, office or title of any kind whatever, from any king, prince, or foreign State." The section which follows these qualifications of the powers of Congress, prescribes some necessary limits to the powers of the several States; among which, I find with particular satisfaction, it is declared that "no State shall emit bills of credit, or make anything but gold and silver coin a tender in payment of debts." By this means, Sir, some security will be offered for the discharge of honest contracts, and an end put to the pernicious speculation upon paper emissions—a medium which has undermined the morals, and relaxed the industry of the people, and from which one-half of the controversies in our courts of justice has arisen. Upon the whole, Mr. President, I must repeat, that I perceive nothing in this system which can alarm or intimidate the sincerest friend to the liberties of his country. The powers given to the government are necessary to its existence, and to the political happiness of the people—while the objections which are offered, arise from an evident perversion of its principles, and the presumption of a meaning which neither the framers of the system, nor the system itself, ever meant. True it is, Sir, that a form more pleasing, and more beneficial to the State of Pennsylvania, might be devised; but let it be remembered that this truth likewise applies to each of our sister States, whose separate interests have been proportionally sacrificed to the general welfare. And after all Mr. President, though a good system is certainly a blessing, yet the wealth, the prosperity, and the freedom of the people, must ultimately depend upon the administration of the best government. The wisdom, probity and patriotism of the rulers, will ever be the criterion of public prosperity; and hence it is, that despotism, if well administered, is the best form of government invented by human ingenuity. We have seen nations prosperous and happy under monarchies, aristocracies, and governments compounded of these, and to what can we ascribe their felicity, but the wise and prudent conduct of those who exercise the powers of government? For experience will demonstrate that the most perfect system may be so perverted as to produce poverty and misery, and the most despotic so executed as to disseminate affluence and happiness among the people. But, Sir, perfection is not to be expected in the business of this life, and it is so ordered by the wisdom of Providence, that as our stay in this world seldom exceeds three score and ten years, we may not become too reluctant to part with its enjoyments, but by reflecting upon the imperfections of the present, learn in time to prepare for the perfections of a future state. Let us then, Mr. President, be content to accept this system as the best which can be obtained. Every man may think, and many a man has said, that he could make it better; but, Sir, as I observed on a former occasion with respect to religion, this is nothing more than opinion, and every person being attached to his own, it will be difficult indeed to make any number of men correspond in the same objects of amendment. The excellent letter which accompanies the proposed system, will furnish a useful lesson upon this occasion. It deserves to be read with attention, and considered with candor. Allow me therefore, Sir, to close the trouble which I have given you in discussing the merits of the plan, with a perusal of this letter—in the second paragraph of which the reason is assigned for deviating from a single body for the federal government.

*   *   *

"Liberty and happiness (says Mr. Wilson) have a powerful enemy on each hand; on the one hand tyranny, on the other licentiousness. To guard against the latter, it is necessary to give the proper powers to government; and to guard against the former, it is necessary that those powers should be properly distributed."

"I agree (replies Mr. Smilie) that it is, or ought to be, the object of all governments to fix upon the intermediate point between tyranny and licentiousness; and I confess that the plan before us is perfectly armed to repel the latter; but I believe it has deviated too much on the left hand, and rather invites than guards against the approaches of tyranny."

*   *   *

[Friday, November 30]

The Convention met pursuant to adjournment.

Mr. Whitehill: I confess, Mr. President, that after the full exercise of his eloquence and ingenuity, the honorable delegate to the late convention has not removed those objections which I formerly submitted to your consideration, in hopes of striking, indeed, from his superior talents and information, a ray of wisdom to illuminate the darkness of our doubts, and to guide us in the pursuit of political truth and happiness. If the learned gentleman, however, with all his opportunities of investigating this particular system, and with all his general knowledge in the science of government, has not been able to convert or convince us, far be it from me to impute this failure to the defects of his elocution, or the languor of his disposition. It is no impeachment of those abilities which have been eminently distinguished in the abstruse disquisitions of law, that they should fail in the insidious task of supporting, on popular principles, a government which originates in mystery, and must terminate in despotism. Neither can the want of success, Sir, be ascribed to the want of zeal; for we have heard with our ears, and our eyes have seen, the indefatigable industry of the worthy member in advocating the cause which he has undertaken. But, Mr. President, the defect is in the system itself; there lies the evil which no argument can palliate, no sophistry can disguise. Permit me, therefore, Sir, again to call your attention to the princi-

ples which it contains, and for a moment to examine the ground upon which
those principles are defended. I have said, and with increasing confidence I
repeat, that the proposed constitution must eventually annihilate the independent sovereignty of the several states. In answer to this, the forms of
election for supplying the offices of the federal head have been recapitu-
lated; it has been thence inferred that the connection between the individual
and the general governments is of so indissoluble a nature, that they must
necessarily stand or fall together, and, therefore, it has been finally declared
to be impossible, that the framers of this constitution could have a premeditated design to sow, in the body of their work, the seeds of its own destruction. But, Sir, I think it may be clearly proved that this system contains the
seeds of self-preservation independent of all the forms referred to—seeds
which will vegetate and strengthen in proportion to the decay of state
authority, and which will ultimately spring up and overshadow the thirteen
commonwealths of America with a deadly shade. The honorable member
from the city has, indeed, observed that every government should possess the
means of its own preservation; and this constitution is possibly the result of
that proposition. For, Sir, the first article comprises the grants of powers so
superlative in their nature, and so unlimited in their extent, that without the
aid of any other branch of the system, a foundation rests upon this article
alone, for the extension of the federal jurisdiction to the most extravagant
degree of arbitrary sway.

*   *   *

. . . This, Mr. President, is but a slight view of the calamities that will be
produced by the exercise of those powers which the honorable members from
the city have endeavored to persuade us it is necessary to grant to the new
government in order to secure its own preservation and to accomplish the
objects of the Union. But in considering, Sir, what was necessary to the
safety and energy of the government, some attention ought surely to have
been paid to the safety and freedom of the people. No satisfactory reason
has yet been offered for the omission of a bill of rights; but on the contrary,
the honorable members are defeated in the only pretext which they have
been able to assign, that everything which is not given is excepted, for we
have shown that there are two articles expressly reserved, the writ of habeas
corpus and the trial by jury in criminal cases, and we have called upon them
in vain to reconcile this reservation with the tenor of their favorite proposition. For if there was danger in the attempt to enumerate the liberties of the
people, lest it should prove imperfect and destructive, how happens it that in
the instances I have mentioned, that danger has been incurred? Have the
people no other rights worth their attention, or is it to be inferred, agreeably
to the maxim of our opponents, that every other right is abandoned? Surely,
Sir, our language was competent to declare the sentiments of the people and
to establish a bar against the intrusion of the general government in other
respects as well as these; and when we find some privileges stipulated, the

argument of danger is effectually destroyed; and the argument of difficulty which has been drawn from the attempt to enumerate every right, cannot now be urged against the enumeration of more rights than this instrument contains. In short, Mr. President, it is our duty to take care that the foundation of this system is so laid that the superstructure, which is to be reared by other hands, may not cast a gloom upon the temple of freedom, the recent purchase of our toil and treasure. When, therefore, I consider it as the means of annihilating the constitutions of the several States, and consequently the liberties of the people, I should be wanting to my constituents, to myself and to posterity, did I not exert every talent with which heaven has endowed me to counteract the measures that have been taken for its adoption. That it was the design of the late federal convention to absorb and abolish the individual sovereignty of the States, I seek no other evidence but this system; for as the honorable delegate to that body has recommended, I am also satisfied to judge of the tree by its fruit. When, therefore, I behold it thus systematically constructed for the accomplishment of that object, when I recollect the talents of those who framed it, I cannot hesitate to impute to them an intention corresponding with the principles and operation of their own work. Finally, Sir, that the dissolution of our State constitutions will produce the ruin of civil liberty is a proposition easy to be maintained, and which I am persuaded in the course of these debates will be incontrovertibly established in the mind of every member whose judgment is open to conviction, and whose vote has not been conclusively pledged for the ratification of this constitution before its merits were discussed.

*   *   *

Mr. Hartley: It has been uniformly admitted, Sir, by every man who has written or spoken upon the subject, that the existing confederation of the States is inadequate to the duties of a general government. The lives, the liberties and the property of the citizens are no longer protected and secured, so that necessity compels us to seek beneath another system, some safety for our most invaluable rights and possessions. It is then the opinion of many wise and good men, that the constitution presented by the late federal convention, will in a great measure afford the relief which is required by the wants and weakness of our present situation, but, on the other hand, it has been represented as an instrument to undermine the sovereignty of the States and destroy the liberties of the people. It is the peculiar duty of this convention to investigate the truth of those opinions, and to adopt or reject the proposed constitution, according to the result of that investigation. For my part I freely acknowledge, Mr. President, that impressed with a strong sense of the public calamities, I regard the system before us as the only prospect which promises to relieve the distresses of the people and to advance the national honor and interests of America. I shall therefore offer such arguments in opposition to the objections raised by the honorable delegates from Cumberland and Fayette, as have served to establish my judgment, and will, I hope, communicate some information to the judgment of the worthy members who shall favor me with a candid attention. The first objection is, that the proposed system is not coupled with a bill of rights, and therefore, it is said, there is no security for the liberties of the people. This objection, Sir, has been ably refuted by the honorable members from the city, and will admit of little more animadversion than has already been bestowed upon it, in the course of their arguments. It is agreed, however, that the situation of a British subject, and that of an American citizen in the year 1776, were essentially different; but it does not appear to be accurately understood in what manner the people of England became enslaved before the reign of King John. Previously to the Norman conquest, that nation certainly enjoyed the greatest portion of civil liberty then known in the world. But when William, accompanied by a train of courtiers and dependents, seized upon the crown, the liberties of the vanquished were totally disregarded and forgotten, while titles, honors and estates, were distributed with a liberal hand among his needy and avaricious followers. The lives and fortunes of the ancient inhabitants became thus subject to the will of the usurper, and no stipulations were made to protect and secure them from the most wanton violations. Hence, Sir, arose the successful struggles in the reign of John, and to this source may be traced the subsequent exertions of the people for the recovery of their liberties, when Charles endeavored totally to destroy, and the Prince of Orange at the celebrated era of British revolution, was invited to support them, upon the principles declared in the bill of rights. Some authors, indeed, have argued that the liberties of the people were derived from the prince, but how they came into his hands is a mystery which has not been disclosed. Even on that principle, however, it has occasionally been found necessary to make laws for the security of the subject—a necessity that has produced the writ of habeas corpus, which affords an easy and immediate redress for the unjust imprisonment of the person, and the trial by jury, which is the fundamental security for every enjoyment that is valuable in the contemplation of a freeman. These advantages have not been obtained by the influence of a bill of rights, which after all we find is an instrument that derives its validity only from the sanction and ratification of the prince. How different then is our situation from the circumstances of the British nation?

As soon as the independence of America was declared, in the year 1776, from that instant all our natural rights were restored to us, and we were at liberty to adopt any form of government to which our views or our interest might incline us. This truth, expressly recognized by the act declaring our independence, naturally produced another maxim, that whatever portion of those natural rights we did not transfer to the government, was still reserved and retained by the people; for, if no power was delegated to the government, no right was resigned by the people; and if a part only of our natural rights was delegated, is it not absurd to assert that we have relinquished the whole? Where then is the necessity of a formal declaration, that those rights are still retained, of the resignation of which no evidence can possibly be produced? Some articles, indeed from their pre-eminence in the scale of political security, deserve to be particularly specified, and these have not been omitted in the system before us.

The definition of treason, the writ of habeas corpus, and the trial by jury in criminal cases, are here expressly provided for; and in going thus far, solid foundation has been laid.

The ingenuity of the gentlemen who are inimical to the proposed constitution may serve to detect an error, but can it furnish a remedy? They have told us that a bill of rights ought to have been annexed; but, while some are for this point, and others for that, is it not evidently impracticable to frame an instrument which will be satisfactory to the wishes of every man who thinks himself competent to propose and obviate objections? Sir, it is enough for me that the great cardinal points of a free government are here secured without the useless enumeration of privileges, under the popular appellation of a bill of rights.

*   *   *

Doctor Rush: I believe, Mr. President, that of all the treaties which have ever been made, William Penn's was the only one, which was contracted without parchment; and I believe, likewise, it is the only one that has ever been faithfully adhered to. As it has happened with treaties, so, Sir, has it happened with bills of rights, for never yet has one been made which has not, at some period or other, been broken. The celebrated magna charta of England was broken over and over again, and these infractions gave birth to the petition of rights. If, indeed, the government of that country has not been violated for the last hundred years, as some writers have said, it is not owing to charters or declarations of rights, but to the balance which has been introduced and established in the legislative body. The constitution, of Pennsylvania, Mr. President, is guarded by an oath, which every man employed in the administration of the public business is compelled to take; and yet, Sir, examine the proceedings of the council of censors, and you will find innumerable instances of the violation of that constitution, committed equally by its friends and enemies. In truth, then, there is no security but in a pure and adequate representation; the checks and all the other desiderata of government are nothing but political error without it, and with it, liberty can never be endangered. While the honorable convention, who framed this system, were employed in their work, there are many gentlemen who can bear testimony that my only anxiety was upon the subject of representation; and when I beheld a legislature constituted of three branches, and in so excellent a manner, either directly or indirectly, elected by the people, and amenable to them, I confess, Sir, that here I cheerfully reposed all my hopes and confidence of safety. Civilians having taught us, Mr. President, that occupancy was the origin of property, I think it may likewise be considered as the origin of liberty; and as we enjoy all our natural rights from a pre-occupancy, antecedent to the social state, in entering into that state, whence shall they be said to be derived? Would it not be absurd to frame a formal declaration that our natural rights are acquired from ourselves? and would it not be a more ridiculous solecism to say, that they are the gift of those rulers whom we have created, and who are invested by us with every power they possess? Sir, I consider it as an honor to the late convention, that this system has not been disgraced with a bill of rights; though I mean not to blame or reflect upon those States which have encumbered their constitutions with that idle and superfluous instrument. One would imagine, however, from the arguments of the opposition, that this government was immediately to be administered by foreigners—strangers to our habits and opinions, and unconnected with our interests and prosperity. These apprehensions, Sir, might have been excused while we were contending with Great Britain; but at this time they are applicable to all governments, as well as that under consideration; and the arguments of the honorable member are, indeed, better calculated for an Indian council-fire, than the meridian of this refined and enlightened convention.

Mr. Yeates: The objections hitherto offered to this system, Mr. President, may, I think, be reduced to these general heads: first, that there is no bill of rights, and secondly, that the effect of the proposed government will be a consolidation and not a confederation of the States. Upon the first head it appears to me that great misapprehension has arisen, from considering the situation of Great Britain to be parallel to the situation of this country; whereas the difference is so essential, that a bill of rights which was there both useful and necessary, becomes here at once useless and unnecessary. In England a power (by what means it signifies little) was established paramount to that of the people, and the only way which they had to secure the remnant of their liberties, was, on every opportunity, to stipulate with that power for the uninterrupted enjoyment of certain enumerated privileges. But our case is widely different, and we find that upon the opinion of this difference, seven of the thirteen United States have not added a bill of rights to their respective constitutions. Nothing, indeed, seems more clear to my judgment than this, that in our circumstances, every power which is not expressly given is in fact reserved. But it is asked, as some rights are here expressly provided for, why should not more? In truth, however, the writ of habeas corpus, and the trial by jury in criminal cases, cannot be considered as a bill of rights, but merely as a reservation on the part of the people, and a restriction on the part of their rulers. And I agree with those gentlemen who conceive that a bill of rights, according to the ideas of the opposition, would be accompanied with considerable difficulty and danger; for it might be argued at a future day by the persons then in power, You undertook to enumerate the rights which you meant to reserve; the pretension which you now make is not comprised in that enumeration, and consequently our jurisdiction is not circumscribed. The second general head respects the consolidation of the States; but I think, Sir, candor will forbid us to impute that design to the late convention, when we review the principles and texture of their work. Does it not appear that the organization of the new government must originate with the States? Is not the whole system of federal representation dependent upon the individual governments? For we find that those persons who are qualified to vote for the most numerous branch of the State legislatures, are alone qualified to vote for delegates to the house of representatives: the senators are to be chosen immediately by the legislatures of the States; and those legislatures likewise are to prescribe the manner for the appointment of electors who are to elect the President. Thus, Sir, is the connection between the States in their separate and aggregate capacity preserved, and the existence of the Federal government made necessarily dependant upon the existence and actual operation of its constituent members. Lest anything, indeed, should be wanting to assure us of the intention of the framers of this constitution to preserve the individual sovereignty and independence of the States inviolate, we find it expressly declared by the 4th section of the 4th article, that "the United States shall guarantee to every State in this Union, a republican form of government"—a constitutional security far superior to the fancied advantages of a bill of rights.

[Wednesday, December 12]

Doctor Rush then proceeded to consider the origin of the proposed system, and fairly deduced it from heaven, asserting that he as much believed the hand of God was employed in this work, as that God had divided the Red Sea to give a passage to the children of Israel, or had fulminated the ten commandments from Mount Sinai! Dilating sometime upon this new species of divine right, thus transmitted to the future governors of the Union, he made a pathetic appeal to the opposition, in which he deprecated the consequences of any further contention, and pictured the honorable and endearing effects of an unanimous vote, after the full and fair investigation which the great question had undergone. . "It is not, Sir, a majority, (continued the Doctor) however numerous and respectable, that can gratify my wishes—nothing short of an unanimous vote can indeed complete my satisfaction. And, permit me to add, were that event to take place, I could not preserve the strict bounds of decorum, but, flying to the other side of this room, cordially embrace every member, who has hitherto been in opposition, as a brother and a patriot. Let us then, Sir, this night bury the hatchet, and smoke the calumet of peace!" When Dr. Rush had concluded, Mr. Chambers remarked upon the Doctor's wish of conciliation and unanimity, that it was an event which he neither expected nor wished for. Mr. Whitehill now rose, and having animadverted upon Dr. Rush's metaphysical arguments, and regretted that so imperfect a work should have been ascribed to God, he presented several petitions from 750 inhabitants of Cumberland county, praying, for the reasons therein specified, that the proposed Constitution should not be adopted without amendments, and particularly, without a bill of rights. The petitions being read from the chair, Mr. M'Kean said he was sorry at this stage of the business so improper an attempt should be made. He repeated that the duty of the Convention was circumscribed to the adoption or rejection of the proposed plan, and such had certainly been the sense of the members, when it was agreed that only one question could be taken on the important subject before us. He hoped, therefore, that the petitions would not be attended to. Mr. Whitehill then read, and offered as the ground of a motion for adjourning to some remote day the consideration of the following articles, which, he said, might either be taken collectively, as a bill of rights, or, separately, as amendments to the general form of government proposed.

1. The rights of conscience shall be held inviolable, and neither the legislative, executive nor judicial powers of the United States shall have authority to alter, abrogate or infringe any part of the constitutions of the several States, which provide for the preservation of liberty in matters of religion.

2. That in controversies respecting property and in suits between man and man, trial by jury shall remain as heretofore, as well in the federal courts, as in those of the several States.

3. That in all capital and criminal prosecutions, a man has a right to demand the cause and nature of his accusation, as well in the federal courts, as in those of the several States; to be heard by himself or his counsel; to be confronted with the accusers and witnesses; to call for evidence in his favor, and a speedy trial, by an impartial jury of the vicinage, without whose unanimous consent he cannot be found guilty, nor can he be compelled to give evidence against himself; that no man be deprived of his liberty, except by the law of the land or the judgment of his peers.

4. That excessive bail ought not to be required, nor excessive fines imposed, nor cruel or unusual punishments inflicted.

5. That warrants unsupported by evidence, whereby any officer or messenger may be commanded or required to search suspected places, or to seize any person or persons, his or their property, not particularly described, are grievous and oppressive, and shall not be granted either by the magistrates of the federal government or others.

6. That the people have a right to the freedom of speech, of writing and of publishing their sentiments; therefore, the freedom of the press shall not be restrained by any law of the United States.

7. That the people have a right to bear arms for the defence of themselves and their own State, or the United States, or for the purpose of killing game; and no law shall be passed for disarming the people or any of them, unless for crimes committed, or real danger of public injury from individuals; and as

standing armies in the time of peace are dangerous to liberty, they ought not to be kept up; and that the military shall be kept under strict subordination to and be governed by the civil power.

8. The inhabitants of the several States shall have liberty to fowl and hunt in seasonable times on the lands they hold, and on all other lands in the United States not inclosed, and in like manner to fish in all navigable waters, and others not private property, without being restrained therein by any laws to be passed by the legislature of the United States.

9. That no law shall be passed to restrain the legislatures of the several States from enacting laws for imposing taxes, except imposts and duties on goods exported and imported, and that no taxes, except imposts and duties upon goods imported and exported and postage on letters, shall be levied by the authority of Congress.

10. That elections shall remain free, that the house of representatives be properly increased in number, and that the several States shall have power to regulate the elections for senators and representatives, without being controlled either directly or indirectly by any interference on the part of Congress, and that elections of representatives be annual.

11. That the power of organizing, arming and disciplining the militia, (the manner of disciplining the militia to be prescribed by Congress) remain with the individual States, and that Congress shall not have authority to call or march any of the militia out of their own State, without the consent of such State, and for such length of time only as such State shall agree.

12. That the legislative, executive, and judicial powers be kept separate, and to this end, that a constitutional council be appointed to advise and assist the President, who shall be responsible for the advice they give (hereby, the senators would be relieved from almost constant attendance); and also that the judges be made completely independent.

13. That no treaties which shall be directly opposed to the existing laws of the United States in Congress assembled, shall be valid until such laws shall be repealed or made conformable to such treaty, neither shall any treaties be valid which are contradictory to the constitution of the United States, or the constitutions of the individual States.

14. That the judiciary power of the United States shall be confined to cases affecting ambassadors, other public ministers and consuls, to cases of admiralty and maritime jurisdiction, to controversies to which the United States shall be a party, to controversies between two or more States— between a State and citizens of different States—between citizens claiming lands under grants of different States, and between a State or the citizens thereof and foreign States, and in criminal cases, to such only as are expressly enumerated in the constitution, and that the United States in Congress assembled, shall not have power to enact laws, which shall alter the laws of descents and distributions of the effects of deceased persons, the title of lands or goods, or the regulation of contracts in the individual States.

15. That the sovereignty, freedom and independency of the several

States shall be retained, and every power, jurisdiction and right which is not by this constitution expressly delegated to the United States in Congress assembled.

Some confusion arose on these articles being presented to the chair, objections were made by the majority to their being officially read, and, at last, Mr. Wilson desired that the intended motion might be reduced to writing, in order to ascertain its nature and extent. Accordingly, Mr. Whitehill drew it up, and it was read from the chair in the following manner:

"That this Convention do adjourn to the   day of   next, then to meet in the city of Philadelphia, in order that the propositions for amending the proposed constitution may be considered by the people of this State; that we may have an opportunity of knowing what amendments or alterations may be proposed by other States, and that these propositions, together with such other amendments as may be proposed by other States, may be offered to Congress, and taken into consideration by the United States, before the proposed constitution shall be finally ratified."

As soon as the motion was read, Mr. Wilson said he rejoiced that it was by this means ascertained upon what principles the opposition proceeded, for, he added, the evident operation of such a motion would be to exclude the people from the government and to prevent the adoption of this or any other plan of confederation. For this reason he was happy to find the motion reduced to certainty, that it would appear upon the journals, as an evidence of the motives that prevailed with those who framed and supported it, and that its merited rejection would permanently announce the sentiments of the majority respecting so odious an attempt. Mr. Smilie followed Mr. Wilson, declaring that he too rejoiced that the motion was reduced to a certainty, from which it might appear to their constituents that the sole object of the opposition was to consult with and obtain the opinions of the people upon a subject, which they had not yet been allowed to consider. "If," exclaimed Mr. Smilie, "those gentlemen who have affected to refer all authority to the people, and to act only for the common interest, if they are sincere, let them embrace this last opportunity to envince that sincerity. They all know the precipitancy with which the measure has hitherto been pressed upon the State, and they must be convinced that a short delay cannot be injurious to the proposed government, if it is the wish of the people to adopt it; if it is not their wish, a short delay, which enables us to collect their real sentiments, may be the means of preventing future contention and animosity in a community, which is, or ought to be, equally dear to us." The question being taken on the motion, there appeared for it 23, against it 46. The great and conclusive question was then taken, that "this convention do assent to and ratify the plan of federal government, agreed to and recommended by the late federal convention?" when the same division took place, and the yeas and nays being called by Mr. Smilie and Mr. Chambers, were as given in our paper of Thursday last. Yeas 46. Nays 23.

This important decision being recorded, Mr. M'Kean moved that the convention do to-morrow proceed in a body to the Court House, there to proclaim the ratification, and that the supreme executive council be requested to make the necessary arrangements for the procession on that occasion, which motion was agreed to, and the convention adjourned till the next morning at half-past nine o'clock.

From the minutes of the convention it appears that the vote of each member was,

Yeas

George Latimer,
Benjamin Rush,
Hilary Baker,
James Wilson,
Thomas M'Kean,
William Macpherson,
John Hunn,
George Gray,
Samuel Ashmead,
Enoch Edwards,
Henry Wynkoop,
John Barclay,
Thomas Yardley,
Abraham Stout,
Thomas Bull,
Anthony Wayne,
William Gibbons,
Richard Downing,
Thomas Cheyney,
John Hannum,
Stephen Chambers,
Robert Coleman,
Sebastian Graff,

John Hubley,
Jasper Yeates,
Henry Slagle,
Thomas Campbell,
Thomas Hartley,
David Grier,
John Black,
Benjamin Pedan,
John Arndt,
Stephen Balliet,
Joseph Horsfield,
David Deshler,
William Wilson,
John Boyd,
Thomas Scott,
John Neville,
John Allison,
Jonathan Roberts,
John Richards,
F. A. Muhlenberg,
James Morris,
Timothy Pickering,
Benjamin Elliot.

Nays

John Whitehill,
John Harris,
John Reynolds,
Robert Whitehill,
Jonathan Hoge,
Nicholas Lutz,
John Ludwig,
Abraham Lincoln,
John Bishop,
Joseph Hiester,
James Martain,
Joseph Powell,

William Findley,
John Bard,
William Todd,
James Marshall,
James Edgar,
Nathaniel Breading,
John Smilie,
Richard Baird,
William Brown,
Adam Orth,
John Andre Hannah.

[Thursday, December 13]

On Thursday, the convention being assembled, Mr. Whitehill remarked that the bill of rights, or articles of amendment, which he had the day before presented to the chair, were not inserted upon the journals, together with the resolution which referred to them. This he declared an improper omission, and desired they might be inserted. This was opposed by the majority, but as there was no motion before the convention, the president did not see how a determination could take place, though he wished to know the sense of the members upon this occasion. Mr. Smilie, in consequence of this intimation, moved for the insertion of Mr. Whitehill's articles. Mr. Wilson continued his opposition, and called upon Mr. Smilie to reduce his motion to writing. "Indeed, sir," observed Mr. Smilie, "I know so well that if the honorable member from the city says the articles shall not, they will not be admitted, that I am not disposed to take the useless trouble of reducing my motion to writing, and therefore I withdraw it."

*   *   *

The Address and Reasons of Dissent of the Minority of the Convention of the State of Pennsylvania to Their Constituents, 1787*

It was not until after the termination of the late glorious contest, which made the people of the United States an independent nation, that any defect was discovered in the present confederation. It was formed by some of the ablest patriots in America. It carried us successfully through the war, and the virtue and patriotism of the people, with their disposition to promote the common cause, supplied the want of power in Congress.

The requisition of Congress for the five percent. impost was made before the peace, so early as the first of February, 1781, but was prevented taking effect by the refusal of one State; yet it is probable every State in the Union would have agreed to this measure at that period, had it not been for the extravagant terms in which it was demanded. The requisition was new moulded in the year 1783, and accompanied with an additional demand of certain supplementary funds for twenty-five years. Peace had now taken place, and the United States found themselves laboring under a considerable foreign and domestic debt, incurred during the war. The requisition of 1783 was commensurate with the interest of the debt, as it was then calculated; but it has been more accurately ascertained since that time. The domestic debt has been found to fall several millions of dollars short of the calculation, and it has lately been considerably diminished by large sales of the Western lands. The States have been called on by Congress annually for supplies until the general system of finance proposed in 1783 should take place.

It was at this time that the want of an efficient federal government was first complained of, and that the powers vested in Congress were found to be

*Pennsylvania and the Federal Constitution, pp. 454–83.

inadequate to the procuring of the benefits that should result from the union. The impost was granted by most of the States, but many refused the supplementary funds; the annual requisitions were set at naught by some of the States, while others complied with them by legislative acts, but were tardy in their payments, and Congress found themselves incapable of complying with their engagements and supporting the federal government. It was found that our national character was sinking in the opinion of foreign nations. The Congress could make treaties of commerce, but could not enforce the observance of them. We were suffering from the restrictions of foreign nations, who had suckled our commerce while we were unable to retaliate, and all now agreed that it would be advantageous to the union to enlarge the powers of Congress, that they should be enabled in the amplest manner to regulate commerce and to lay and collect duties on the imports throughout the United States. With this view, a convention was first proposed by Virginia, and finally recommended by Congress for the different States to appoint deputies to meet in convention, "for the purposes of revising and amending the present articles of confederation, so as to make them adequate to the exigencies of the union." This recommendation the legislatures of twelve States complied with so hastily as not to consult their constituents on the subject; and though the different legislatures had no authority from their constituents for the purpose, they probably apprehended the necessity would justify the measure, and none of them extended their ideas at that time further than "revising and amending the present articles of confederation." Pennsylvania, by the act appointing deputies, expressly confined their powers to this object, and though it is probable that some of the members of the assembly of this State had at that time in contemplation to annihilate the present confederation, as well as the constitution of Pennsylvania, yet the plan was not sufficiently matured to communicate it to the public.

*   *   *

Affairs were in this situation, when on the 28th of September last, a resolution was proposed to the assembly by a member of the house, who had been also a member of the federal convention, for calling a State convention to be elected within ten days for the purpose of examining and adopting the proposed Constitution of the United States, though at this time the house had not received it from Congress. This attempt was opposed by a minority, who after offering every argument in their power to prevent the precipitate measure, without effect, absented themselves from the house as the only alternative left them, to prevent the measures taking place previous to their constituents being acquainted with the business. That violence and outrage which had been so often threatened was now practised; some of the members were seized the next day by a mob collected for the purpose, and forcibly dragged to the house, and there detained by force whilst the quorum of the legislature so formed, completed their resolution. We shall dwell no longer on this subject: the people of Pennsylvania have been already acquainted therewith.

*   *   *

In the city of Philadelphia and some of the eastern counties the junto that took the lead in the business agreed to vote for none but such as would solemnly promise to adopt the system *in toto,* without exercising their judgment. In many of the counties the people did not attend the elections, as they had not an opportunity of judging of the plan. Others did not consider themselves bound by the call of a set of men who assembled at the State-house in Philadelphia and assumed the name of the legislature of Pennsylvania; and some were prevented from voting by the violence of the party who were determined at all events to force down the measure. To such lengths did the tools of despotism carry their outrage, that on the night of the election for members of convention, in the city of Philadelphia, several of the subscribers (being then in the city to transact your business) were grossly abused, ill-treated and insulted while they were quiet in their lodgings, though they did not interfere nor had anything to do with the said election, but, as they apprehend, because they were supposed to be adverse to the proposed constitution, and would not tamely surrender those sacred rights which you had committed to their charge.

The convention met, and the same disposition was soon manifested in considering the proposed constitution, that had been exhibited in every other stage of the business. We were prohibited by an express vote of the convention from taking any questions on the separate articles of the plan, and reduced to the necessity of adopting or rejecting *in toto.* 'Tis true the majority permitted us to debate on each article, but restrained us from proposing amendments. They also determined not to permit us to enter on the minutes our reasons of dissent against any of the articles, nor even on the final question our reasons of dissent against the whole. Thus situated we entered on the examination of the proposed system of government, and found it to be such as we could not adopt, without, as we conceived, surrendering up your dearest rights. We offered our objections to the convention, and opposed those parts of the plan which, in our opinion, would be injurious to you, in the best manner we were able; and closed our arguments by offering the following propositions to the convention.

1. The right of conscience shall be held inviolable; and neither the legislative, executive nor judicial powers of the United States shall have authority to alter, abrogate or infringe any part of the constitution of the several States, which provide for the preservation of liberty in matters of religion.

2. That in controversies respecting property, and in suits between man and man, trial by jury shall remain as heretofore, as well in the federal courts as in those of the several States.

3. That in all capital and criminal prosecutions, a man has a right to

demand the cause and nature of his accusation, as well in the federal courts as in those of the several States; to be heard by himself and his counsel; to be confronted with the accusers and witnesses; to call for evidence in his favor, and a speedy trial by an impartial jury of his vicinage, without whose unanimous consent he cannot be found guilty, nor can he be compelled to give evidence against himself; and, that no man be deprived of his liberty, except by the law of the land or the judgment of his peers.

4. That excessive bail ought not to be required, nor excessive fines imposed, nor cruel nor unusual punishments inflicted.

5. That warrants unsupported by evidence, whereby any officer or messenger may be commanded or required to search suspected places; or to seize any person or persons, his or their property not particularly described, are grievous and oppressive, and shall not be granted either by the magistrates of the federal government or others.

6. That the people have a right to the freedom of speech, of writing and publishing their sentiments; therefore the freedom of the press shall not be restrained by any law of the United States.

7. That the people have a right to bear arms for the defence of themselves and their own State or the United States, or for the purpose of killing game; and no law shall be passed for disarming the people or any of them unless for crimes committed, or real danger of public injury from individuals; and as standing armies in the time of peace are dangerous to liberty, they ought not to be kept up; and that the military shall be kept under strict subordination to, and be governed by the civil powers.

8. The inhabitants of the several States shall have liberty to fowl and hunt in seasonable time on the lands they hold, and on all other lands in the United States not inclosed, and in like manner to fish in all navigable waters, and others not private property, without being restrained therein by any laws to be passed by the legislature of the United States.

9. That no law shall be passed to restrain the legislatures of the several States from enacting laws for imposing taxes, except imposts and duties on goods imported or exported, and that no taxes, except imposts and duties upon goods imported and exported, and postage on letters, shall be levied by the authority of Congress.

10. That the house of representatives be properly increased in number; that elections shall remain free; that the several States shall have power to regulate the elections for senators and representatives, without being controlled either directly or indirectly by any interference on the part of the Congress; and that the elections of representatives be annual.

11. That the power of organizing, arming and disciplining the militia (the manner of disciplining the militia to be prescribed by Congress), remain with the individual States, and that Congress shall not have authority to call or march any of the militia out of their own State, without the consent of such State, and for such length of time only as such State shall agree.

That the sovereignty, freedom and independency of the several States shall be retained, and every power, jurisdiction and right which is not by this Constitution expressly delegated to the United States in Congress assembled.

12. That the legislative, executive and judicial powers be kept separate; and to this end that a constitutional council be appointed to advise and assist the President, who shall be responsible for the advice they give—hereby the senators would be relieved from almost constant attendance; and also that the judges be made completely independent.

13. That no treaty which shall be directly opposed to the existing laws of the United States in Congress assembled, shall be valid until such laws shall be repealed or made conformable to such treaty; neither shall any treaties be valid which are in contradiction to the Constitution of the United States, or the constitution of the several States.

14. That the judiciary power of the United States shall be confined to cases affecting ambassadors, other public ministers and consuls, to cases of admiralty and maritime jurisdiction; to controversies to which the United States shall be a party; to controversies between two or more States—between a State and citizens of different States—between citizens claiming lands under grants of different States, and between a State or the citizens thereof and foreign States; and in criminal cases to such only as are expressly enumerated in the constitution; and that the United States in Congress assembled shall not have power to enact laws which shall alter the laws of descent and distribution of the effects of deceased persons, the titles of lands or goods, or the regulation of contracts in the individual States.

After reading these propositions, we declared our willingness to agree to the plan, provided it was so amended as to meet those propositions or something similar to them, and finally moved the convention to adjourn, to give the people of Pennsylvania time to consider the subject and determine for themselves; but these were all rejected and the final vote taken, when our duty to you induced us to vote against the proposed plan and to decline signing the ratification of the same.

During the discussion we met with many insults and some personal abuse. We were not even treated with decency, during the sitting of the convention, by the persons in the gallery of the house. However, we flatter ourselves that in contending for the preservation of those invaluable rights you have thought proper to commit to our charge, we acted with a spirit becoming freemen; and being desirous that you might know the principles which actuated our conduct, and being prohibited from inserting our reasons of dissent on the minutes of the convention, we have subjoined them for your consideration, as to you alone we are accountable. It remains with you whether you will think those inestimable privileges, which you have so ably contended for, should be sacrificed at the shrine of despotism, or whether you mean to contend for them with the same spirit that has so often baffled the attempts of an aristocratic faction to rivet the shackles of slavery on you and your unborn posterity.

Our objections are comprised under three general heads of dissent, viz.:

We dissent, first, because it is the opinion of the most celebrated writers on government, and confirmed by uniform experience, that a very extensive territory cannot be governed on the principles of freedom, otherwise than by a confederation of republics, possessing all the powers of internal government, but united in the management of their general and foreign concerns.

If any doubt could have been entertained of the truth of the foregoing principle, it has been fully removed by the concession of Mr. Wilson, one of the majority on this question, and who was one of the deputies in the late general convention. In justice to him, we will give his own words; they are as follows, viz.: "The extent of country for which the new constitution was required, produced another difficulty in the business of the federal convention. It is the opinion of some celebrated writers, that to a small territory, the democratical; to a middling territory (as Montesquieu has termed it), the monarchical; and to an extensive territory, the despotic form of government is best adapted. Regarding then the wide and almost unbounded jurisdiction of the United States, at first view, the hand of despotism seemed necessary to control, connect and protect it; and hence the chief embarrassment rose. For we know that although our constituents would cheerfully submit to the legislative restraints of a free government, they would spurn at every attempt to shackle them with despotic power." And again, in another part of his speech, he continues: "Is it probable that the dissolution of the State governments, and the establishment of one consolidated empire would be eligible in its nature, and satisfactory to the people in its administration? I think not, as I have given reasons to show that so extensive a territory could not be governed, connected and preserved, but by the supremacy of despotic power. All the exertions of the most potent emperors of Rome were not capable of keeping that empire together, which in extent was far inferior to the dominion of America."

We dissent, secondly, because the powers vested in Congress by this constitution, must necessarily annihilate and absorb the legislative, executive, and judicial powers of the several States, and produce from their ruins one consolidated government, which from the nature of things will be an iron handed despotism, as nothing short of the supremacy of despotic sway could connect and govern these United States under one government.

*   *   *

3. We dissent, thirdly, because if it were practicable to govern so extensive a territory as these United States include, on the plan of a consolidated government, consistent with the principles of liberty and the happiness of the people, yet the construction of this Constitution is not calculated to attain the object; for independent of the nature of the case, it would of itself necessarily produce a despotism, and that not by the usual gradations, but with the celerity that has hitherto only attended revolutions effected by the sword.

To establish the truth of this position, a cursory investigation of the principles and form of this constitution will suffice.

The first consideration that this review suggests, is the omission of a Bill of Rights ascertaining and fundamentally establishing those unalienable and personal rights of men, without the full, free and secure enjoyment of which there can be no liberty, and over which it is not necessary for a good government to have the control—the principal of which are the rights of conscience, personal liberty by the clear and unequivocal establishment of the writ of habeas corpus, jury trial in criminal and civil cases, by an impartial jury of the vicinage or county, with the common law proceedings for the safety of the accused in criminal prosecutions; and the liberty of the press, that scourge of tyrants, and the grand bulwark of every other liberty and privilege. The stipulations heretofore made in favor of them in the State constitutions, are entirely superseded by this Constitution.

The legislature of a free country should be so formed as to have a competent knowledge of its constitutents, and enjoy their confidence. To produce these essential requisites, the representation ought to be fair, equal and sufficiently numerous to possess the same interests, feelings, opinions and views which the people themselves would possess, were they all assembled; and so numerous as to prevent bribery and undue influence, and so responsible to the people, by frequent and fair elections, as to prevent their neglecting or sacrificing the views and interests of their constituents to their own pursuits.

We will now bring the legislature under this Constitution to the test of the foregoing principles, which will demonstrate that it is deficient in every essential quality of a just and safe representation.

The House of Representatives is to consist of sixty-five members; that is one for about every 50,000 inhabitants, to be chosen every two years. Thirty-three members will form a quorum for doing business, and seventeen of these, being the majority, determine the sense of the house.

The Senate, the other constituent branch of the legislature, consists of twenty-six members, being two from each State, appointed by their legislatures every six years; fourteen senators make a quorum—the majority of whom, eight, determines the sense of that body, except in judging on impeachments, or in making treaties, or in expelling a member, when two-thirds of the senators present must concur.

The president is to have the control over the enacting of laws, so far as to make the concurrence of two-thirds of the representatives and senators present necessary, if he should object to the laws.

Thus it appears that the liberties, happiness, interests, and great concerns of the whole United States, may be dependent upon the integrity, virtue, wisdom, and knowledge of twenty-five or twenty-six men. How inadequate and unsafe a representation! Inadequate, because the sense and views of three or four millions of people, diffused over so extensive a territory, comprising such various climates, products, habits, interests, and opinions, cannot be collected in so small a body; and besides, it is not a fair and equal representation of the people even in proportion to its number, for the smallest State has as much weight in the Senate as the largest; and from the smallness of the number to be chosen for both branches of the legislature, and from the mode of election and appointment, which is under the control of Congress, and from the nature of the thing, men of the most elevated rank in life will alone be chosen. The other orders in the society, such as farmers, traders, and mechanics, who all ought to have a competent number of their best informed men in the legislature, shall be totally unrepresented.

The representation is unsafe, because in the exercise of such great powers and trusts, it is so exposed to corruption and undue influence, by the gift of the numerous places of honor and emolument at the disposal of the executive, by the arts and address of the great and designing, and by direct bribery.

The representation is moreover inadequate and unsafe, because of the long terms for which it is appointed, and the mode of its appointment, by which Congress may not only control the choice of the people, but may so manage as to divest the people of this fundamental right, and become self-elected.

The number of members in the House of Representatives may be increased to one for every 30,000 inhabitants. But when we consider that this cannot be done without the consent of the Senate, who from their share in the legislative, in the executive, and judicial departments, and permanency of appointment, will be the great efficient body in this government, and whose weight and predominancy would be abridged by an increase of the representatives, we are persuaded that this is a circumstance that cannot be expected. On the contrary, the number of representatives will probably be continued at sixty-five, although the population of the country may swell to treble what it now is, unless a revolution should effect a change.

We have before noticed the judicial power as it would affect a consolidation of the States into one government; we will now examine it as it would affect the liberties and welfare of the people, supposing such a government were practicable and proper.

The judicial power, under the proposed constitution, is founded on well-known principles of the civil law, by which the judge determines both on law and fact, and appeals are allowed from the inferior tribunals to the superior, upon the whole question; so that facts as well as law, would be re-examined, and even new facts brought forward in the court of appeals; and to use the words of a very eminent civilian—"The cause is many times another thing before the court of appeals, than what it was at the time of the first sentence."

That this mode of proceeding is the one which must be adopted under this constitution, is evident from the following circumstances: 1st. That the trial by jury, which is the grand characteristic of the common law, is secured by the constitution only in criminal cases. 2d. That the appeal from both law and fact is expressly established, which is utterly inconsistent with the principles of the common law and trials by jury. The only mode in which an appeal from law and fact can be established, is by adopting the principles and practice of the civil law, unless the United States should be drawn into the absurdity of calling and swearing juries, merely for the purpose of contradicting their verdicts, which would render juries contemptible and worse than useless. 3d. That the courts to be established would decide on all cases of law and equity, which is a well-known characteristic of the civil law, and these courts would have conusance not only of the laws of the United States, and of treaties, and of cases affecting ambassadors, but of all cases of admiralty and maritime jurisdiction, which last are matters belonging exclusively to the civil law, in every nation in Christendom.

Not to enlarge upon the loss of the invaluable right of trial by an unbiased jury, so dear to every friend of liberty, the monstrous expense and inconveniences of the mode of proceeding to be adopted, are such as will prove intolerable to the people of this country.

*   *   *

For the moderate exercise of this power, there is no control left in the State governments, whose intervention is destroyed. No relief, or redress of grievances, can be extended as heretofore by them. There is not even a declaration of rights to which the people may appeal for the vindication of their wrongs in the court of justice. They must therefore, implicitly obey the most arbitrary laws, as the most of them will be pursuant to the principles and form of the constitution, and that strongest of all checks upon the conduct of administration, responsibility to the people, will not exist in this government. The permanency of the appointments of senators and representatives, and the control the congress have over their election, will place them independent of the sentiments and resentment of the people, and the administration having a greater interest in the government than in the community, there will be no consideration to restrain them from oppression and tyranny. In the government of this State, under the old confederation, the members of the legislature are taken from among the people, and their interests and welfare are so inseparably connected with those of their constituents, that they can derive no advantage from oppressive laws and taxes; for they would suffer in common with their fellow-citizens, would participate in the burthens they impose on the community as they must return to the common level, after a short period; and notwithstanding every exertion of influence, every means of corruption, a necessary rotation excludes them from permanency in the legislature.

This large State is to have but ten members in that Congress which is to have the liberty, property and dearest concerns of every individual in this vast country at absolute command, and even these ten persons, who are to be our only guardians, who are to supersede the legislature of Pennsylvania, will not be of the choice of the people, nor amenable to them. From the mode of their election and appointment they will consist of the lordly and high minded; of men who will have no congenial feelings with the people, but a perfect indifference for, and contempt of them; they will consist of those harpies of power that prey upon the very vitals, that riot on the miseries of the community. But we will suppose, although in all probability it may never be realized in fact, that our deputies in Congress have the welfare of their constituents at heart, and will exert themselves in their behalf, what security could even this afford? what relief could they extend to their oppressed constitutents? To attain this, the majority of the deputies of the twelve other States in Congress must be alike well disposed; must alike forego the sweets of power, and relinquish the pursuits of ambition, which, from the nature of things, is not to be expected. If the people part with a responsible representation in the legislature, founded upon fair, certain and frequent elections, they have nothing left they can call their own. Miserable is the lot of that people whose every concern depends on the will and pleasure of their rulers. Our soldiers will become Janissaries, and our officers of government Bashaws; in short, the system of despotism will soon be completed.

From the foregoing investigation, it appears that the Congress under this constitution will not possess the confidence of the people, which is an essential requisite in a good government; for unless the laws command the confidence and respect of the great body of the people, so as to induce them to support them when called on by the civil magistrate, they must be executed by the aid of a numerous standing army, which would be inconsistent with every idea of liberty; for the same force that may be employed to compel obedience to good laws, might and probably would be used to wrest from the people their constitutional liberties. The framers of this constitution appear to have been aware of this great deficiency—to have been sensible that no dependence could be placed on the people for their support: but on the contrary, that the government must be executed by force. They have therefore made a provision for this purpose in a permanent standing army and a militia that may be objected to as strict discipline and government.

A standing army in the hands of a government placed so independent of the people, may be made a fatal instrument to overturn the public liberties; it may be employed to enforce the collection of the most oppressive taxes, and to carry into execution the most arbitrary measures. An ambitious man who may have the army at his devotion, may step up into the throne, and seize upon absolute power.

The absolute unqualified command that Congress have over the militia may be made instrumental to the destruction of all liberty, both public and private; whether of a personal, civil or religious nature.

First, the personal liberty of every man, probably from sixteen to sixty years of age, may be destroyed by the power Congress have in organizing and governing of the militia. As militia they may be subjected to fines to any amount, levied in a military manner; they may be subjected to corporal punishments of the most disgraceful and humiliating kind; and to death itself, by the sentence of a court martial. To this our young men will be more immediately subjected, as a select militia, composed of them, will best answer the purposes of government.

Secondly, the rights of conscience may be violated, as there is no exemption of those persons who are conscientiously scrupulous of bearing arms. These compose a respectable proportion of the community in the State. This is the more remarkable, because even when the distresses of the late war, and the evident disaffection of many citizens of that description, inflamed our passions, and when every person who was obliged to risk his own life, must have been exasperated against such as on any account kept back from the common danger, yet even then, when outrage and violence might have been expected, the rights of conscience were held sacred.

At this momentous crisis, the framers of our State Constitution made the most express and decided declaration and stipulations in favor of the rights of conscience; but now, when no necessity exists, those dearest rights of men are left insecure.

Thirdly, the absolute command of Congress over the militia may be destructive of public liberty; for under the guidance of an arbitrary government, they may be made the unwilling instruments of tyranny. The militia of Pennsylvania may be marched to New England or Virginia to quell an insurrection occasioned by the most galling oppression, and aided by the standing army, they will no doubt be successful in subduing their liberty and independency; but in so doing, although the magnanimity of their minds will be extinguished, yet the meaner passions of resentment and revenge will be increased, and these in turn will be the ready and obedient instruments of despotism to enslave the others; and that with an irritated vengeance. Thus may the militia be made the instruments of crushing the last efforts of expiring liberty, of riveting the chains of despotism on their fellow-citizens, and on one another. This power can be exercised not only without violating the Constitution, but in strict conformity with it; it is calculated for this express purpose, and will doubtless be executed accordingly.

As this government will not enjoy the confidence of the people, but be executed by force, it will be a very expensive and burthensome government. The standing army must be numerous, and as a further support, it will be the policy of this government to multiply officers in every department; judges, collectors, tax-gatherers, excisemen and the whole host of revenue officers, will swarm over the land, devouring the hard earnings of the industrious—like the locusts of old, impoverishing and desolating all before them.

We have not noticed the smaller, nor many of the considerable blemishes, but have confined our objections to the great and essential defects, the main pillars of the constitution; which we have shown to be inconsistent with the liberty and happiness of the people, as its establishment will annihilate the State governments, and produce one consolidated government that will eventually and speedily issue in the supremacy of despotism.

In this investigation we have not confined our views to the interests or welfare of this State, in preference to the others. We have overlooked all local circumstances—we have considered this subject on the broad scale of the general good; we have asserted the cause of the present and future ages—the cause of liberty and mankind.

Nathaniel Breading,
John Smilie,
Richard Baird,
Adam Orth,
John A. Hannah,
John Whitehill,
John Harris,
Robert Whitehill,
John Reynolds,
Jonathan Hoge,
Nicholas Lutz,

John Ludwig,
Abraham Lincoln,
John Bishop,
Joseph Hiester,
Joseph Powell,
James Martin,
William Findley,
John Bard,
James Edgar,
William Todd.

MASSACHUSETTS RATIFYING CONVENTION, 1788

Commentary

New Jersey and Georgia speedily followed Pennsylvania in ratifying the federal Constitution (each by unanimous votes) on December 18, 1787, and January 2, 1788 respectively. On January 9, Connecticut ratified by a large majority (128 to 40). In none of the three Ratifying Conventions (so far as we know from the skimpy records available) was there express attack upon the absence of a Bill of Rights. The same was not true in Massachusetts—the next state to ratify. Its Convention was sharply divided between the Federalists and Antifederalists and it was only after a month of debate (much of it devoted to the Bill of Rights issue) that Massachusetts was able to vote ratification.

The Massachusetts ratification was in many ways, the key action in the post-Philadelphia Convention movement to secure a federal Bill of Rights. Massachusetts was the first state officially to propose ratificatory amendments, which were transmitted to Congress together with the state's ratification (thus adopting the method proposed by the Pennsylvania minority, but turned down by that state's Convention majority). It is not known whether the Massachusetts delegates were directly influenced by the Pennsylvania minority example. There is evidence that the Philadelphia newspapers containing the Address of the Pennsylvania minority did not reach Boston until after the Massachusetts Ratifying Convention adjourned. (Antifederalists saw this as evidence of a conspiracy among Federalists in the post offices). It is nevertheless all but inconceivable (bearing in mind the intense interest in the result of the ratification contest in the crucial states like Pennsylvania) that some news of the Pennsylvania minority proposals did not reach the Massachusetts delegates.

What is particularly noteworthy about the Massachusetts ratificatory amendments is that they were drafted by the Federalist leaders in the Convention themselves. When the delegates convened, on January 9, 1788, it soon became apparent that the Convention was closely divided between supporters and opponents of the Constitution. (As the debate went on, indeed, it even seemed that the Antifederalists had a narrow margin.) Without some concession to the widespread feeling that a Bill of Rights was necessary, the Massachusetts ratification itself might be in danger. The Federalist leaders decided upon the introduction of proposed amendments to be sent with the ratification as a compromise. The amendments were drafted by Theophilus Parsons (who had also written the *Essex Result*, [*supra* p. 344]). The shrewd move was then made of allowing John Hancock, the Convention president, to introduce them as his own handiwork. Hancock had been reputed to be an Antifederalist and getting him to sponsor the amendments dissipated much of the opposition, particularly since the motion to consider the Hancock amendments was made by Samuel Adams who was also considered an Antifederalist. Adams and other Antifederalists joined in praising the proposed amendments. As Dr. Jarvis summed it up, "The amendments have a tendency to remove many objections which have been made to it"—i.e., the Constitution.

Some of the Antifederalists objected that the Hancock amendments were far from the Bill of Rights that was necessary. Nor would it be as difficult as the Federalists claimed to draw up a Bill of Rights: "any gentlemen in that Convention could form one in a few hours, as he might take the bill of rights of Massachusetts for a guide." Parsons made the standard answer, "that no power was given to Congress to infringe on any one of the natural rights of the people." Apparently this was not enough for some delegates and Adams then introduced amendments to be added to the Hancock proposals. These would have gone far in the direction of a Bill of Rights, since they included (as the Convention *Journal* for February 6 tells us) guarantees of freedom of the press and conscience, right to bear arms, to petition for redress of grievances, and against unreasonable searches and seizures. We do not have any report of the debate on the Adams motion, only the statement in the *Journal* that "the question being put was determined in the negative." (The report of the debates erroneously states that Adams withdrew his amendments.)

Defeat of Adams' additional amendments marked the real end of the ratification debate. Later on the same day, the Convention voted to ratify the Constitution and, at the same time, to "remove the fears and quiet the apprehensions of many of the good people of this Commonwealth," recommended to Congress the amendments proposed by Hancock. The final vote was surprisingly close (187 to 168), indicating the wisdom of the Federalists in appropriating the amendment issue for themselves.

As the letter from Benjamin Lincoln to Washington points out, after Hancock introduced his proposed amendments, the Antifederalists wanted the ratification to be upon condition that the amendments be adopted. Such a ratification would have been equivalent to none at all, since it would have required a Second Constitutional Convention to make the amendments. At the same time, when Massachusetts and four other states recommended amendments as part of their ratifications, it placed almost irresistible pressure on the first Congress elected under the Constitution to initiate the amending process. The proposed amendments introduced by Hancock thus led directly to the federal Bill of Rights.

The Massachusetts proposed amendments themselves consisted of nine articles. Four of them were included in the 12 amendments approved by Congress in 1789: the first, that all powers not expressly delegated to the Federal Government be reserved to the states (later guaranteed in the Tenth Amendment); the second governing representation in the House (a similar provision in the first of the amendments approved by Congress in 1789 was not ratified); the sixth, providing for a right to a grand jury indictment (the direct source of the right later included in the Fifth Amendment); and the eighth, providing for jury trial in civil cases (later guaranteed in the Seventh Amendment).

The Massachusetts-proposed amendments were themselves but a mild version of a Bill of Rights, since they did not cover any of the basic rights already protected in the state Declarations of Rights, such as that in Massachusetts itself. The key rights of freedom of speech, press, and conscience (which had been included, in part, in Sam Adams' abortive amendments) were left unprotected. More important, however, than the details of the Massachusetts-proposed amendments was the fact that they were officially recommended by the state. Madison may (as the letters which follow show) have considered the Massachusetts amendments "a blemish." But Jefferson acutely recognized the merits of the Massachusetts plan, which "will I hope be followed by those who are yet to decide." Jefferson's hope was borne out by the event. The other states which followed the Massachusetts example were far bolder in protecting individual rights and, between them, included all of the rights later guaranteed in the federal Bill of Rights.

Massachusetts Ratifying Convention, 1788*

Journal of Proceedings

[Thursday, January 31]

Met according to adjournment.

The Convention proceeded in the consideration of the Constitution or Frame of Government reported by the Convention held at Philadelphia, and, having debated upon all the paragraphs thereof, a motion was made and seconded, that this Convention assent to and ratify the Constitution agreed upon by the Convention of Delegates from the United States, at Philadelphia, on the 17th day of September, 1787, and, after debate on the said motion.

Adjourned to 3 o'clock, P.M.

Met according to adjournment. . . .

The Convention proceeded in the consideration of the motion that this Convention do assent to and ratify the Constitution agreed upon by the Convention of Delgates from the United States, at Philadelphia, on the 17th day of September, 1787.

The following was proposed to the Convention by his Excellency the President, viz.:

*Debates and Proceedings in the Convention of the Commonwealth of Massachusetts Held in the Year 1788 (1856), pp. 78–92.

Commonwealth of Massachusetts

The Convention having impartially discussed and fully considered the Constitution for the United States of America, reported to Congress by the Convention of Delegates from the United States of America, and submitted to us by a Resolution of the General Court of the said Commonwealth, passed the twenty-fifth day of October last past; and acknowledging, with grateful hearts, the goodness of the Supreme Ruler of the Universe, in affording the people of the United States, in the course of his providence, an opportunity, deliberately and peaceably, without fraud or surprise, of entering into an explicit and solemn compact with each other, by assenting to and ratifying a new constitution, in order to form a more perfect union, establish justice, insure domestic tranquillity, provide for the common defence, promote the general welfare, and secure the blessings of liberty to themselves and their posterity; do, in the name, and in behalf of the people of the Commonwealth of Massachusetts, assent to and ratify the said Constitution for the United States of America.

And as it is the opinion of this Convention that certain amendments and alterations in the said Constitution would remove the fears and quiet the apprehensions of many of the good people of this Commonwealth, and more effectually guard against an undue administration of the federal government; the Convention do therefore recommend that the following alterations and provisions be introduced into the said Constitution:

First. That it be explicitly declared that all powers not expressly delegated to Congress, are reserved to the several States, to be by them exercised.

Secondly. That there shall be one representative to every thirty thousand persons, until the whole number of representatives amount to

Thirdly. That Congress do not exercise the powers vested in them by the fourth section of the first article, but in cases where a State shall neglect or refuse to make adequate provision for an equal representation of the people, agreeably to this Constitution.

Fourthly. That Congress do not lay direct taxes, but when the moneys arising from the impost and excise are insufficient for the public exigencies.

Fifthly. That Congress erect no company of merchants with exclusive advantages of commerce.

Sixthly. That no person shall be tried for any crime, by which he may incur an infamous punishment, or loss of life, until he be first indicted by a grand jury, except in such cases as may arise in the government and regulation of the land and naval forces.

Seventhly. The Supreme Judicial Federal Court shall have no jurisdiction of causes between citizens of different States, unless the matter in dispute be of the value of   dollars, at the least.

Eightly. In civil actions between citizens of different States, every issue of fact arising in actions at common law, shall be tried by a jury, if the parties, or either of them, request it.

Ninthly. That the words, "without the consent of the Congress," in the last paragraph of the ninth section of the first article, be stricken out.

And the Convention do, in the name and in behalf of the people of this Commonwealth, enjoin it upon their Representatives in Congress, at all times, until the alterations and provisions aforesaid have been considered, agreeably to the fifth article of the said Constitution, to exert all their influence, and use all reasonable and legal methods to obtain a ratification of the said alterations and provisions, in such manner as is provided in the said article.

And that the United States, in Congress assembled, may have due notice of the assent and ratification of the said Constitution, by this Convention, it is

Resolved, That the assent and ratification aforesaid be engrossed on parchment, together with the recommendation and injunction aforesaid, and with this Resolution, and that his Excellency John Hancock, Esquire, President, and the Honorable William Cushing, Esquire, Vice-President of this Convention, transmit the same, countersigned by the Secretary of the Convention, under their hands and seals, to the United States, in Congress assembled.

[Saturday, February 2]

Met according to adjournment.

The Convention proceeded in the consideration of the motion that this Convention do assent to and ratify the Constitution agreed upon by the Convention of Delegates from the United States, at Philadelphia, on the 17th day of September, 1787, and of the propositions made by his Excellency the President, the 31st ultimo. After debate,

Voted, That a Committee, consisting of members from each county, be appointed to take into consideration the subject of the propositions of his Excellency the President, of the 31st ultimo, at large, and report.

The following gentlemen were then appointed on the said committee, viz.:

Hon. Mr. Bowdoin, Mr. Southworth, Mr. Parsons, Hon. Mr. Hutchinson, Hon. Mr. Dana, Mr. Winn, Hon. Mr. Strong, Mr. Bodman, Hon. Mr. Turner, Mr. Thomas, of Plymouth, Dr. Smith, Mr. Bourn, Hon. Mr. Spooner, Mr. Bishop, Rev. Dr. Hemmenway, Mr. Barrell, Mr. Mayhew, Hon. Mr. Taylor, Hon. Mr. Sprague, Mr. Fox, Mr. Longfellow, Mr. Sewall, Mr. Sylvester, Mr. Lusk, Hon. Mr. Sedgwick.

Adjourned to Monday next, 3 o'clock, P.M.

[Monday, February 4]

Met according to adjournment.

The Committee appointed on the subject of the propositions of his Excellency the President, on Saturday last, reported as follows, viz.:

The Committee appointed by the Convention to take into consideration the subject of the propositions of his Excellency the President, of the 31st ultimo, at large, and report, beg leave to report the alterations hereafter mentioned, to the said propositions, and that the whole of the said propositions, so altered, be accepted and passed by the Convention, viz.:

Commonwealth of Massachusetts

The Convention having impartially discussed and fully considered the Constitution for the United States of America, reported to Congress by the Convention of Delegates from the United States of America, and submitted to us by a Resolution of the General Court of the said Commonwealth, passed the twenty-fifth day of October last past; and acknowledging with grateful hearts the goodness of the Supreme Ruler of the Universe, in affording the people of the United States, in the course of his providence, an opportunity, deliberately and peaceably, without fraud or surprise, of entering into an explicit and solemn compact with each other, by assenting to and ratifying a new Constitution, in order to form a more perfect union, establish justice, insure domestic tranquillity, provide for the common defence, promote the general welfare, and secure the blessings of liberty to themselves and their posterity; do, in the name and in behalf of the people of the Commonwealth of Massachusetts, assent to and ratify the said Constitution for the United States of America.

And as it is the opinion of this Convention, that certain amendments and alterations in the said Constitution would remove the fears and quiet the apprehensions of many of the good people of this Commonwealth, and more effectually guard against an undue administration of the federal government, the Convention do therefore recommend that the following alterations and provisions be introduced into the said Constitution.

First. That it be explicitly declared, that all powers not expressly delegated by the aforesaid Constitution, are reserved to the several States, to be by them exercised.

Secondly. That there shall be one representative to every thirty thousand persons, according to the census mentioned in the Constitution, until the whole number of representatives amounts to two hundred.

Thirdly. That Congress do not exercise the power vested in them by the fourth section of the first article, but in cases when a State shall neglect or refuse to make the regulations therein mentioned, or shall make regulations subversive of the rights of the people to a free and equal representation in Congress, agreeably to the Constitution.

Fourthly. That Congress do not lay direct taxes but when the moneys arising from the impost and excise are insufficient for the public exigencies, nor then, until Congress shall have first made a requisition upon the States, to assess, levy and pay their respective proportions of such requisition, agreeably to the census fixed in the said constitution, in such way and manner as the legislatures of the States shall think best; and, in such case, if any State shall neglect or refuse to pay its proportion, pursuant to such requisition, then Congress may assess and levy such State's proportion, together with interest thereon, at the rate of six per cent. per annum, from the time of payment prescribed in such requisition.

Fifthly. That Congress erect no company with exclusive advantages of commerce.

Sixthly. That no person shall be tried for any crime, by which he may incur an infamous punishment, or loss of life, until he be first indicted by a grand jury, except in such cases as may arise in the government and regulation of the land and naval forces.

Seventhly. The supreme judicial federal court shall have no jurisdiction of causes between citizens of different States, unless the matter in dispute, whether it concern the realty or personalty, be of the value of three thousand dollars, at the least; nor shall the federal judicial powers extend to any actions between citizens of different States, where the matter in dispute, whether it concerns the realty or personalty, is not of the value of fifteen hundred dollars, at the least.

Eighthly. In civil actions between citizens of different States, every issue of fact arising in actions at common law, shall be tried by a jury, if the parties, or either of them, request it.

Ninthly. Congress shall at no time consent that any person holding an office of trust or profit under the United States, shall accept of a title of nobility, or any other title or office, from any king, prince, or foreign state.

And the Convention do, in the name and in behalf of the people of this Commonwealth, enjoin it upon their representatives in Congress, at all times, until the alterations and provisions aforesaid have been considered, agreeably to the fifth article of the said Constitution; to exert all their influence, and use all reasonable and legal methods to obtain a ratification of the said alterations and provisions, in such manner as is provided in the said article.

And that the United States, in Congress assembled, may have due notice of the assent and ratification of the said constitution, by this Convention, it is

Resolved, That the assent and ratification aforesaid be engrossed on parchment, together with the recommendation and injunction aforesaid, and with this Resolution; and that his Excellency John Hancock, Esquire, President, and the Honorable William Cushing, Esquire, Vice-President of this Convention, transmit the same, countersigned by the Secretary of the Convention, under their hands and seals, to the United States, in Congress assembled.

Adjourned. . . .

[Wednesday, February 6]

Met according to adjournment.

The Convention proceeded in the consideration of the motion that tomorrow, 11 o'clock, A.M., be assigned to take the question, by yeas and nays, whether this Convention will accept of the report of the Committee made on Monday last; and, the question being put, passed in the negative.

It was then voted that 4 o'clock, P.M., be assigned for that purpose.

A motion was made and seconded, that the report of the Committee made on Monday last, be amended, so far as to add the following to the first article therein mentioned, viz.: "And that the said Constitution be never construed to authorize Congress to infringe the just liberty of the press, or the rights of conscience; or to prevent the people of the United States, who are peaceable citizens, from keeping their own arms; or to raise standing armies, unless when necessary for the defence of the United States, or of some one or more of them; or to prevent the people from petitioning, in a peaceable and orderly manner, the federal legislature, for a redress of grievances; or to subject the people to unreasonable searches and seizures of their persons, papers or possessions." And the question being put, was determined in the negative.

Adjourned to 3 o'clock, P.M.

Met according to adjournment.

The Convention proceeded to the consideration of the report of the Committee on the subject of the propositions of his Excellency the President, of the 31st ultimo, made on Monday last, and the question, whether this Convention will accept of the said report, being put, was determined by yeas and nays, as follows, viz.:

[Yeas, 187–Nays, 168—for the actual vote, see *infra* p. 714].

Massachusetts Convention Debates, 1788*

[Wednesday, January 23]

Col. Varnum, in answer to an inquiry, why a bill of rights was not annexed to this Constitution, said, that, by the constitution of Massachusetts, the legislature have a right to make all laws not repugnant to the Constitution. Now, said he, if there is such a clause in the Constitution under consideration, then there would be a necessity for a bill of rights. In the section under debate, Congress have an expressed power to levy taxes, &c., and to pass laws to carry their requisitions into execution: this, he said, was express, and required no bill of rights. After stating the difference between delegated power and the grant of all power, except in certain cases, the colonel proceeded to controvert the idea that this Constitution went to a consolidation of the Union. He said it was only a consolidation of strength, and that it was apparent Congress had no right to alter the internal relations

*The Debates in the Several State Conventions on the Adoption of the Constitution, Vol. 2, pp. 78–183.

of a state. The design in amending the Confederation, he said, was to remedy its defects. It was the interest of the whole to confederate against a foreign enemy, and each was bound to exert its utmost ability to oppose that enemy; but it had been done at our expense in a great measure, and there was no way to provide for a remedy, because Congress had not the power to call forth the resources of every state, nor to coerce delinquent states. But under the proposed government, those states which will not comply with equal requisitions, will be coerced; and this, he said, is a glorious provision. In the late war, said the colonel, the states of New Hampshire and Massachusetts, for two or three years, had in the field half the Continental army under General Washington. Who paid those troops? The states which raised them were called on to pay them. How, unless Congress have a power to levy taxes, can they make the states pay their proportion? In order that this and some other states may not again be obliged to pay eight or ten times their proportion of the public exigencies, he said, this power is highly necessary to be delegated to the federal head. He showed the necessity of Congress being enabled to prepare against the attacks of a foreign enemy; and he called upon the gentleman from Andover, (Mr. Symmes,) or any other gentleman, to produce an instance where any government, consisting of three branches, elected by the people, and having checks on each other, as this has, abused the power delegated to them.

Mr. Choate said, that this clause gives power to Congress to levy duties, excises, imposts, &c., considering the trust delegated to Congress, that they are to "provide for the common defence, promote the general welfare," &c. If this is to be the object of their delegation, the next question is, whether they shall not be vested with powers to prosecute it. And this can be no other than an unlimited power of taxation, if that defence requires it. Mr. C. contended that it was the power of the people concentred to a point; that, as all power is lodged in them, this power ought to be supreme. He showed the necessity of its being so, not only for our common defence, but for our advantage in settling commercial treaties. Do we wish to make a treaty with any nation of Europe, we are told we have no stability as a nation. As Congress must provide for the common defence, shall they, asked Mr. C., be confined for the impost and excise? They are alone the judges whether five or one per cent. is necessary or convenient. It has been the practice of all nations to anticipate their resources by loans; this will be the case of the United States in war; and he asked, if our resources are competent and well established, and that no doubt remained of them, whether, in that case, the individuals who have property will not cheerfully offer it for the general defence. After adverting to the idea of some, of its being a consolidation of the Union, Mr. Choate concluded by a brief display of the several checks contained, and securities for the people to be found, in this system.

Gen. Thompson: Sir, the question is, whether Congress shall have power. Some say that, if this section was left out, the whole would fall to the ground.

I think so too, as it is all of a piece. We are now fixing a national consolidation. This section, I look upon it, is big with mischiefs. Congress will have power to keep standing armies. The great Mr. Pitt says, standing armies are dangerous—keep your militia in order—we don't want standing armies. A gentleman said, We are a rich state: I say so too. Then why shall we not wait five or six months, and see what our sister states do? We are able to stand our ground against a foreign power; they cannot starve us out; they cannot bring their ships on the land; we are a nation of healthy and strong men; our land is fertile, and we are increasing in numbers. It is said we owe money: no matter if we do; our safety lies in not paying it—pay only the interest. Don't let us go too fast. Shall not Massachusetts be a mediator? It is my wish she may be one of the four dissenting states; then we shall be on our old ground, and shall not act unconstitutionally. Some people cry, It will be a great charge; but it will be a greater charge, and be more dangerous, to make a new one. Let us amend the old Confederation. Why not give Congress power only to regulate trade? Some say, that those we owe will fall upon us; but it is no such thing: the balance of power in the old countries will not permit it; the other nations will protect us. Besides, we are a brave and happy people. Let us be cautious how we divide the states. By uniting we stand, by dividing we fall. We are in our childhood yet: don't let us grow too fast, lest we grow out of shape. I have proved that we are a respectable people, in possession of liberty, property, and virtue, and none in a better situation to defend themselves. Why all this racket? Gentlemen say we are undone if we cannot stop up the Thames; but, Mr. President, nations will mind their own interest, and not ours. Great Britain has found out the secret to pick the subjects' pockets, without their knowing of it: that is the very thing Congress is after. Gentlemen say this section is as clear as the sun, and that all power is retained which is not given. But where is the bill of rights which shall check the power of this Congress; which shall say, Thus far shall ye come, and no farther. The safety of the people depends on a bill of rights. If we build on a sandy foundation, is it likely we shall stand? I apply to the feelings of the Convention. There are some parts of this Constitution which I cannot digest; and, sir, shall we swallow a large bone for the sake of a little meat? Some say, Swallow the whole now, and pick out the bone afterwards. But I say, Let us pick off the meat, and throw the bone away.

This section, sir, takes the purse-strings from the people. England has been quoted for their fidelity; but did their constitution ever give such a power as is contained in this Constitution? Did they ever allow Parliament to vote an army but for one year? But here we are giving Congress power to vote an army for two years—to tax us without limitation; no one to gainsay them, and no inquiry yearly, as in Britain; therefore, if this Constitution is got down, we shall alter the system entirely, and have no checks upon Congress.

Rev. Mr. Niles wished the honorable gentleman would point out the limits to be prescribed to the powers given in this section.

Hon. Mr. Bowdoin: Mr. President, on the subject of government, which admits of so great a variety in its parts and combinations, a diversity of opinions is to be expected; and it was natural to suppose that, in this Convention, respectable for its numbers, but much more so for the characters which compose it, there would be a like diversity concerning the federal Constitution, that is now the subject of our consideration.

*   *   *

There have been many objections offered against the Constitution; and of these the one most strongly urged has been, the great power vested in Congress. On this subject, I beg leave to make a few general observations, which ought to be attended to, as being applicable to every branch of that power.

It may, therefore, be observed, that the investiture of such power, so far from being an objection, is a most cogent reason for accepting the Constitution. The power of Congress, both in the legislative and executive line, is the power of the people, collected through a certain medium, to a focal point, at all times ready to be exerted for the general benefit, according as circumstances or exigencies may require. If you diminish or annihilate it, you diminish or annihilate the means of your own safety and prosperity; which means, if they were to be measured like mathematical quantities, would be in exact proportion, as the power is greater or less. But this is not the case; for power that does not reach, or is inadequate to the object, is worse than none. An exertion of such power would increase the evil it was intended to remove, and at the same time create a further evil, which might be a very great one—the expense of a fruitless exertion.

If we consider the objects of the power, they are numerous and important; and as human foresight cannot extend to many of them, and all of them are in the womb of futurity, the quantum of the power cannot be estimated.

*   *   *

. . . In short, the commercial and political happiness, the liberty and property, the peace, safety, and general welfare, both internal and external, of each and all the states, depend on that power; which, as it must be applied to a vast variety of objects, and to cases and exigencies beyond the ken of human prescience, must be very great; and which cannot be limited without endangering the public safety.

It will be, and has been said, this great power may be abused, and, instead of protecting, may be employed by Congress in oppressing, their constituents. A possibility of abuse, as it may be affirmed of all delegated power whatever, is by itself no sufficient reason for withholding the delegation. If it were a sufficient one, no power could be delegated; nor could government of any sort subsist. The possibility, however, should make us careful, that, in all delegations of importance, like the one contained in the proposed Constitution, there should be such checks provided as would not frustrate the end and intention of delegating the power, but would, as far as it could be safely done, prevent the abuse of it; and such checks are provided in the Constitution. . . .

The two capital departments of government, the legislative and executive, in which the delegated power resides, consisting of the President, Vice-President, Senate and Representatives, are directly, and by the respective legislatures and delegates, chosen by the people.

The President, and also the Vice-President, when acting as President, before they enter on the execution of the office, shall each "solemnly swear or affirm, that he will faithfully execute the office of President of the United States, and will, to the best of his ability, preserve, protect, and defend, the Constitution of the United States."

"The senators and representatives before mentioned and the members of the state legislatures, and all executive and judicial officers, both of the United States and of the several states, shall be bound, by oath or affirmation, to support this Constitution."

"The President and Vice-President, and all civil officers of the United States, shall be removed from office, on impeachment for, and conviction of, treason, bribery, or other high crimes or misdemeanors."

"No senator or representative shall, during the time for which he was elected, be appointed to any civil office, which shall have been created, or the emoluments whereof shall have been increased, during such time; and no person holding any office under the United States shall be a member of either house, during his continuance in office."

"No title of nobility shall be granted by the United States, or by any particular state; and no person holding any office of profit or trust under the United States shall, without the consent of the Congress, accept of any present, emolument, office, or title, of any kind whatever, from any king, prince, or foreign state."

"The United States shall guaranty to every state in this Union a republican form of government, and shall protect each of them against invasion and domestic violence."

To these great checks may be added several other very essential ones, as, the negative which each house has upon the acts of the other; the disapproving power of the President, which subjects those acts to a revision by the two houses, and to a final negative, unless two thirds of each house shall agree to pass the returned acts, notwithstanding the President's objections; the printing the journals of each house, containing their joint and respective proceedings; and the publishing, from time to time, a regular statement and account of receipts and expenditures of all public money, none of which shall be drawn from the treasury but in consequence of appropriations made by law.

All these checks and precautions, provided in the Constitution, must, in a great measure, prevent an abuse of power, at least in all flagrant instances, even if Congress should consist wholly of men who were guided by no other principle than their own interest. Under the influence of such checks, this would compel them to a conduct which, in the general, would answer the intention of the Constitution. But the presumption is,—and, if the people duly attend to the objects of their choice, it would be realized,—that the President of the United States and the members of Congress would, for the most part, be men, not only of ability, but of a good moral character; in which case, an abuse of power is not to be apprehended, nor any error in the government, but such as every human institution is subject to.

There is a further guard against the abuse of power, which, though not expressed, is strongly implied in the federal Constitution, and, indeed, in the constitution of every government founded on the principles of equal liberty; and that is, that those who make the laws, and particularly laws for the levying of taxes, do, in common with their fellow-citizens, fall within the power and operation of those laws.

As, then, the individuals in Congress will all share in the burdens they impose, and be personally affected by the good or bad laws they make for the Union, they will be under the strongest motives of interest to lay the lightest burdens possible, and to make the best laws, or such laws as shall not unnecessarily affect either the property or the personal rights of their fellow-citizens.

With regard to rights, the whole Constitution is a declaration of rights, which primarily and principally respect the general government intended to be formed by it. The rights of particular states, or private citizens, not being the object or subject of the Constitution, they are only incidentally mentioned. In regard to the former, it would require a volume to describe them, as they extend to every subject of legislation, not included in the powers vested in Congress; and, in regard to the latter, as all governments are founded on the relinquishment of personal rights in a certain degree, there was a clear impropriety in being very particular about them. By such a particularity the government might be embarrassed, and prevented from doing what the private, as well as the public and general, good of the citizens and states might require.

The public good, in which private is necessarily involved, might be hurt by too particular an enumeration; and the private good could suffer no injury from a deficient enumeration, because Congress could not injure the rights of private citizens without injuring their own, as they must, in their public as well as private character, participate equally with others in the consequences of their own acts. And by this most important circumstance, in connection with the checks above mentioned, the several states at large, and each citizen in particular, will be secured, as far as human wisdom can secure them, against the abuse of the delegated power.

In considering the Constitution, we shall consider it, in all its parts, upon those general principles which operate through the whole of it, and are equivalent to the most extensive bill of rights that can be formed.

These observations, which are principally of a general nature, but will apply to the most essential parts of the Constitution, are, with the utmost deference and respect, submitted to your candid consideration; with the hope that, as they have influenced my own mind decidedly in favor of the Constitution, they will not be wholly unproductive of a like influence on the minds of the gentlemen of the Convention.

If the Constitution should be finally accepted and established, it will complete the temple of American liberty, and, like the keystone of a grand and magnificent arch, be the bond of union to keep all the parts firm and compacted together. May this temple, sacred to liberty and virtue, sacred to justice, the first and greatest political virtue, and built upon the broad and solid foundation of perfect union, be dissoluble only by the dissolution of nature; and may this Convention have the distinguished honor of erecting one of its pillars on that lasting foundation!

Dr. Taylor said, the consideration of the 8th section had taken up a great deal of time; that gentlemen had repeated the same arguments over and over again; and, although the order of the Convention was, that the proposed Constitution should be considered by paragraphs, he was pleased, he said, to observe that the honorable gentleman last speaking had gone into the matter at large, and therefore he hoped that other gentlemen would take the same liberty, and that all further observations might be on the system at large.

Mr. Parsons: Mr. President, a great variety of supposed objections have been made against vesting Congress with some of the powers defined in the 8th section. Some of the objectors have considered the powers as unnecessary, and others, that the people have not the proper security that these powers will not be abused. To most of these objections, answers, convincing, in my opinion, to a candid mind, have been given. But as some of the objections have not been noticed, I shall beg the indulgence of the Convention, while I briefly consider them. And, as it is my intention to avoid all repetition, my observations will necessarily be unconnected and desultory.

It has been said that the grant in this section includes all the possessions of the people, and divests them of every thing; that such a grant is impolitic; for, as the poverty of an individual guards him against luxury and extravagance, so poverty in a ruler is a fence against tyranny and oppression. Sir, gentlemen do not distinguish between the government of an hereditary aristocracy, where the interest of the governors is very different from that of the subjects, and a government to be administered for the common good by the servants of the people, vested with delegated powers by popular elections at stated periods. The federal Constitution establishes a government of the last description, and in this case the people divest themselves of nothing; the government and powers which the Congress can administer, are the mere result of a compact made by the people with each other, for the common defence and general welfare. To talk, therefore, of keeping the Congress poor, if it means anything, must mean a depriving the people themselves of their own resources. But if gentlemen will still insist that these powers are a grant from the people, and consequently improper, let it then be observed, that it is now too late to impede the grant; it is already completed; the Congress, under the Confederation, are invested with it by solemn compact; they have powers to demand what moneys and forces they judge necessary for the common defence and general welfare—powers as extensive as those proposed in this Constitution. But it may be said, as the ways and means are reserved to the several states, they have a check upon Congress, by refusing a compliance with the requisitions. Sir, is this the boasted check?—a check that can never be exercised but by perfidy and a breach of public faith; by a violation of the most solemn stipulations? It is this check that has embarrassed at home, and made us contemptible abroad; and will any honest man plume himself upon a check which an honest man would blush to exercise?

It has been objected that the Constitution provides no religious test by oath, and we may have in power unprincipled men, atheists and pagans. No man can wish more ardently than I do that all our public offices may be filled by men who fear God and hate wickedness; but it must remain with the electors to give the government this security. An oath will not do it. Will an unprincipled man be entangled by an oath? Will an atheist or a pagan dread the vengeance of the Christian's God, a being, in his opinion, the creature of fancy and credulity? It is a solecism in expression. No man is so illiberal as to wish the confining places of honor or profit to any one sect of Christians; but what security is it to government, that every public officer shall swear that he is a Christian? For what will then be called Christianity? One man will declare that the Christian religion is only an illumination of natural religion, and that he is a Christian; another Christian will assert that all men must be happy hereafter in spite of themselves; a third Christian reverses the image, and declares that, let a man do all he can, he will certainly be punished in another world; and a fourth will tell us that, if a man use any force for the common defence, he violates every principle of Christianity. Sir, the only evidence we can have of the sincerity of a man's religion is a good life; and I trust that such evidence will be required of every candidate by every elector. That man who acts an honest part to his neighbor, will, most probably, conduct honorably towards the public.

*   *   *

It has been objected that we have no bill of rights. If gentlemen who make this objection would consider what are the supposed inconveniences resulting from the want of a declaration of rights, I think they would soon satisfy themselves that the objection has no weight. Is there a single natural right we enjoy, uncontrolled by our own legislature, that Congress can infringe? Not one. Is there a single political right secured to us by our constitution, against the attempts of our own legislature, which we are deprived of by this Constitution? Not one, that I recollect. All the rights Congress can control we have surrendered to our own legislature; and the only question is, whether the people shall take from their own legislatures a certain portion of the several sovereignties, and unite them in one head, for the more effectual securing of the national prosperity and happiness.

The honorable gentleman from Boston has stated at large most of the checks the people have against usurpation, and the abuse of power, under the proposed Constitution; but from the abundance of his matter, he has, in my opinion, omitted two or three, which I shall mention. The oath the several legislative, executive, and judicial officers of the several states take to support the federal Constitution, is as effectual a security against the usurpation of the general government as it is against the encroachment of the state governments. For an increase of the powers by usurpation is as clearly a violation of the federal Constitution as a diminution of these powers by private encroachment; and that the oath obliges the officers of the several states as vigorously to oppose the one as the other. But there is another check, founded in the nature of the Union, superior to all the parchment checks that can be invented. If there should be a usurpation, it will not be on the farmer and merchant, employed and attentive only to their several occupations; it will be upon thirteen legislatures, completely organized, possessed of the confidence of the people, and having the means, as well as inclination, successfully to oppose it. Under these circumstances, none but madmen would attempt a usurpation. But, sir, the people themselves have it in their power effectually to resist usurpation, without being driven to an appeal to arms. An act of usurpation is not obligatory; it is not law; and any man may be justified in his resistance. Let him be considered as a criminal by the general government, yet only his own fellow-citizens can convict him; they are his jury, and if they pronounce him innocent, not all the powers of Congress can hurt him; and innocent they certainly will pronounce him, if the supposed law he resisted was an act of usurpation.

*   *   *

[Wednesday, January 30]

Mr. Holmes: Mr. President, I rise to make some remarks on the paragraph under consideration, which treats of the judiciary power.

It is a maxim universally admitted, that the safety of the subject consists in having a right to a trial as free and impartial as the lot of humanity will admit of. Does the Constitution make provision for such a trial? I think not; for in a criminal process, a person shall not have a right to insist on a trial in the vicinity where the fact was committed, where a jury of the peers would, from their local situation, have an opportunity to form a judgment of the character of the person charged with the crime, and also to judge of the credibility of the witnesses. There a person must be tried by a jury of strangers; a jury who may be interested in his conviction; and where he may, by reason of the distance of his residence from the place of trial, be incapable of making such a defence as he is, in justice, entitled to, and which he could avail himself of, if his trial was in the same county where the crime is said to have been committed.

These circumstances, as horrid as they are, are rendered still more dark and gloomy, as there is no provision made in the Constitution to prevent the attorney-general from filing information against any person, whether he is indicted by the grand jury or not; in consequence of which the most innocent person in the commonwealth may be taken by virtue of a warrant issued in consequence of such information, and dragged from his home, his friends, his acquaintance, and confined in prison, until the next session of the court, which has jurisdiction of the crime with which he is charged, (and how frequent those sessions are to be we are not yet informed of,) and after long, tedious, and painful imprisonment, though acquitted on trial, may have no possibility to obtain any kind of satisfaction for the loss of his liberty, the loss of his time, great expenses, and perhaps cruel sufferings.

But what makes the matter still more alarming is, that the mode of criminal process is to be pointed out by Congress, and they have no constitutional check on them, except that the trial is to be by a jury: but who this jury is to be, how qualified, where to live, how appointed, or by what rules to regulate their procedure, we are ignorant of as yet: whether they are to live in the county where the trial is; whether they are to be chosen by certain districts, or whether they are to be appointed by the sheriff ex officio; whether they are to be for one session of the court only, or for a certain term of time, or for good behavior, or during pleasure, are matters which we are entirely ignorant of as yet.

The mode of trial is altogether indetermined; whether the criminal is to be allowed the benefit of counsel; whether he is to be allowed to meet his accuser face to face; whether he is to be allowed to confront the witnesses, and have the advantage of cross-examination, we are not yet told.

These are matters of by no means small consequence, yet we have not the smallest constitutional security that we shall be allowed the exercise of these privileges, neither is it made certain, in the Constitution, that a person charged with the crime shall have the privilege of appearing before the court or jury which is to try him.

On the whole, when we fully consider this matter, and fully investigate the powers granted, explicitly given, and specially delegated, we shall find Congress possessed of powers enabling them to institute judicatories little less inauspicious than a certain tribunal in Spain, which has long been the disgrace of Christendom: I mean that diabolical institution, the Inquisition.

What gives an additional glare of horror to these gloomy circumstances is the consideration, that Congress have to ascertain, point out, and determine, what kind of punishments shall be inflicted on persons convicted of crimes. They are nowhere restrained from inventing the most cruel and unheard-of punishments, and annexing them to crimes; and there is no constitutional check on them, but that racks and gibbets may be amongst the most mild instruments of their discipline.

There is nothing to prevent Congress from passing laws which shall compel a man, who is accused or suspected of a crime, to furnish evidence against himself, and even from establishing laws which shall order the court to take the charge exhibited against a man for truth, unless he can furnish evidence of his innocence.

I do not pretend to say Congress will do this; but, sir, I undertake to say that Congress (according to the powers proposed to be given them by the Constitution) may do it; and if they do not, it will be owing entirely—I repeat it, it will be owing entirely—to the goodness of the men, and not in the least degree owing to the goodness of the Constitution.

The framers of our state constitution took particular care to prevent the General Court from authorizing the judicial authority to issue a warrant against a man for a crime, unless his being guilty of the crime was supported by oath or affirmation, prior to the warrant being granted; why it should be esteemed so much more safe to intrust Congress with the power of enacting laws, which it was deemed so unsafe to intrust our state legislature with, I am unable to conceive.

Mr. Gore observed, in reply to Mr. Holmes, that it had been the uniform conduct of those in opposition to the proposed form of government, to determine, in every case where it was possible that the administrators thereof could do wrong, that they would do so, although it were demonstrable that such wrong would be against their own honor and interest, and productive of no advantage to themselves. On this principle alone have they determined that the trial by jury would be taken away in civil cases; when it had been clearly shown, that no words could be adopted, apt to the situation and customs of each state in this particular. Jurors are differently chosen in different states, and in point of qualification the laws of the several states are very diverse; not less so in the causes and disputes which are entitled to trial by jury. What is the result of this? That the laws of Congress may and will be conformable to the local laws in this particular, although the Constitution could not make a universal rule equally applying to the customs and statutes of the different states. Very few governments (certainly not this) can be interested in depriving the people of trial by jury, in questions of *meum et tuum*. In criminal cases alone are they interested to have the trial under their own control; and, in such cases, the Constitution expressly stipulates for trial by jury; but then, says the gentleman from Rochester, (Mr. Holmes,) to the safety of life it is indispensably necessary the trial of crimes should be in the vicinity; and the vicinity is construed to mean county; this is very incorrect, and gentlemen will see the impropriety, by referring themselves to the different local divisions and districts of the several states. But further, said the gentleman, the idea that the jury coming from the neighborhood, and knowing the character and circumstances of the party in trial, is promotive of justice, on reflection will appear not founded in truth. If the jury judge from any other circumstances but what are part of the cause in question, they are not impartial. The great object is to determine on the real merits of the cause, uninfluenced by any personal considerations; if, therefore, the jury could be perfectly ignorant of the person in trial, a just decision would be more probable. From such motives did the wise Athenians so constitute the famed Areopagus, that, when in judgment, this court should sit at midnight, and in total darkness, that the decision might be on the thing, and not on the person. Further, said the gentleman, it has been said, because the Constitution does not expressly provide for an indictment by grand jury in criminal cases, therefore some officer under this government will be authorized to file informations, and bring any man to jeopardy of his life, and indictment by grand jury will be disused. If gentlemen who pretend such fears will look into the constitution of Massachusetts, they will see that no provision is therein made for an indictment by grand jury, or to oppose the danger of an attorney-general filing informations; yet no difficulty or danger has arisen to the people of this commonwealth from this defect, if gentlemen please to call it so. If gentlemen would be candid, and not consider that, wherever Congress may possibly abuse power, they certainly will, there would be no difficulty in the minds of any in adopting the proposed Constitution.

Mr. Dawes said, he did not see that the right of trial by jury was taken away by the article. The word court does not, either by a popular or technical construction, exclude the use of a jury to try facts. When people, in common language, talk of a trial at the Court of Common Pleas, or the Supreme Judicial Court, do they not include all the branches and members of such court—the jurors as well as the judges? They certainly do, whether they mention the jurors expressly or not. Our state legislators have construed the word court in the same way; for they have given appeals from a justice of peace to the Court of Common Pleas, and from thence to the Supreme Court, without saying any thing of the jury; but in cases which, almost time out of mind, have been tried without jury, there the jurisdiction is given expressly to the justices of a particular court, as may be instanced by suits upon the absconding act, so called.

Gentlemen have compared the article under consideration to that power which the British claimed, and we resisted, at the revolution; namely, the power of trying the Americans without a jury. But surely there was no parallel in the cases; it was criminal cases in which they attempted to make this abuse of power. Mr. D. mentioned one example of this, which, though young, he well remembered; and that was the case of Nickerson, the pirate, who was tried without a jury, and whose judges were the governors of Massachusetts and of some neighboring provinces, together with Admiral Montague, and some gentlemen of distinction. Although this trial was without a jury, yet, as it was a trial upon the civil law, there was not so much clamor about it as otherwise there might have been; but still it was disagreeable to the people, and was one of the then complaints. But the trial by jury was not attempted to be taken from civil causes. It was no object of power, whether one subject's property was lessened, while another's was increased; nor can it be now an object with the federal legislature. What interest can they have in constituting a judiciary, to proceed in civil causes without a trial by jury? In criminal causes, by the proposed government, there must be a jury. It is asked, Why is not the Constitution as explicit in securing the right of jury in civil as in criminal cases? The answer is, Because it was out of the power of the Convention. The several states differ so widely in their modes of trial, some states using a jury in causes wherein other states employ only their judges, that the Convention have very wisely left it to the federal legislature to make such regulations as shall, as far as possible, accommodate the whole. Thus our own state constitution authorizes the General Court to erect judicatories, but leaves the nature, number, and extent of them, wholly to the discretion of the legislature. The bill of rights, indeed, secures the trial by jury, in civil causes, except in cases where a contrary practice has obtained. Such a clause as this some gentlemen wish were inserted in the proposed Constitution, but such a clause would be abused in that Constitution, as has been clearly stated by the Honorable gentleman from Charlestown, (Mr. Gorham,) because the "exception of all cases where a jury have not heretofore been used," would include almost all cases that could be mentioned, when applied to all the states, for they have severally differed in the kinds of causes where they have tried without a jury.

$$*\qquad *\qquad *$$

Gen. Heath: . . . many gentlemen appear opposed to the system; and this, I apprehend, arises from their objections to some particular parts of it. Is there not a way in which their minds may be relieved from embarrassment? I think there is; and if there is, no exertions should be spared in endeavoring to do it.

If we should ratify the Constitution, and instruct our first members to Congress to exert their endeavors to have such checks and guards provided as appear to be necessary in some of the paragraphs of the Constitution, communicate what we may judge proper to our sister states, and request their concurrence, is there not the highest probability that every thing which we wish may be effectually secured? I think there is; and I cannot but flatter myself that in this way the gentlemen of the Convention will have the difficulties under which they now labor removed from their minds. We shall be united: the people of this commonwealth and our sister states may be united. Permit me, therefore, most earnestly to recommend it to the serious consideration of every gentleman in this honorable Convention.

After Gen. Heath sat down, his excellency, the President, rose, and observed, that he was conscious of the impropriety, situated as he was, of his entering into the deliberations of the Convention; that, unfortunately, through painful indisposition of body, he had been prevented from giving his attendance in his place, but, from the information he had received, and from the papers, there appeared to him to be a great dissimilarity of sentiments in the Convention. To remove the objections of some gentlemen, he felt himself induced, he said, to hazard a proposition for their consideration; which, with the permission of the Convention, he would offer in the afternoon.

When the Convention met in the afternoon, his excellency, the President, observed, that a motion had been made and seconded, that this Convention do assent to and ratify the Constitution which had been under consideration; and that he had, in the former part of the day, intimated his intention of submitting a proposition to the Convention. My motive, says he, arises from my earnest desire to this Convention, my fellow-citizens, and the public at large, that this Convention may adopt such a form of government as may extend its good influence to every part of the United States, and advance the prosperity of the whole world. His situation, his excellency said, had not permitted him to enter into the debates of this Convention: it, however, appeared to him necessary, from what had been advanced in them, to adopt the form of government proposed; but, observing a diversity of sentiment in the gentlemen of the Convention, he had frequently had conversation with them on the subject, and from this conversation he was induced to propose to them, whether the introduction of some general amendments would not be attended with the happiest consequences. For that purpose, he should, with the leave of the honorable Convention, submit to their consideration a proposition, in order to remove the doubts and quiet the apprehensions of gentlemen; and if, in any degree, the object should be acquired, he should feel himself perfectly satisfied. He should therefore submit them; for he was, he said, unable to go more largely into the subject, if his abilities would permit him; relying on the candor of the Convention to bear him witness that his wishes for a good constitution were sincere. [His excellency then read his proposition.] This, gentlemen, concluded his excellency, is the proposition which I had to make; and I submit it to your consideration, with the sincere wish that it may have a tendency to promote a spirit of union.

[The proposition submitted by his excellency having been committed to a large committee, who reported some amendments, we think it expedient to refer the reader to the form of ratification for it.]

Hon. Mr. Adams: Mr. President, I feel myself happy in contemplating the idea that many benefits will result from your excellency's conciliatory proposition to this commonwealth and to the United States; and I think it ought to precede the motion made by the gentleman from Newburyport, and to be at this time considered by the Convention I have said that I have had my doubts of this Constitution. I could not digest every part of it as readily as some gentlemen; but this, sir, is my misfortune, not my fault. Other gentlemen have had their doubts; but, in my opinion, the proposition submitted will have a tendency to remove such doubts, and to conciliate the minds of the Convention, and the people without doors. This subject, sir, is of the greatest magnitude, and has employed the attention of every rational man in the United States; but the minds of the people are not so well agreed on it as all of us could wish. A proposal of this sort, coming from Massachusetts, from her importance, will have its weight. Four or five states have considered and ratified the Constitution as it stands; but we know there is a diversity of opinion even in these states, and one of them is greatly agitated. If this Convention should particularize the amendments necessary to be proposed, it appears to me it must have weight in other states, where Conventions have not yet met. I have observed the sentiments of gentlemen on the subject as far as Virginia, and I have found that the objections were similar, in the newspapers, and in some of the Conventions. Considering these circumstances, it appears to me that such a measure will have the most salutary effect throughout the Union. It is of the greatest importance that America should still be united in sentiment. I think I have not, heretofore, been unmindful of the advantage of such a union. It is essential that the people should be united in the federal government, to withstand the common enemy, and to preserve their valuable rights and liberties. We find, in the great state of Pennsylvania, one third of the Convention are opposed to it: should, then, there be large minorities in the several states, I should fear the consequences of such disunion.

Sir, there are many parts of it I esteem as highly valuable, particularly the article which empowers Congress to regulate commerce, to form treaties, &c. For want of this power in our national head, our friends are grieved, and our enemies insult us. Our ambassador at the court of London is considered as a mere cipher, instead of the representative of the United States. Therefore it appears to me, that a power to remedy this evil should be given to Congress, and the remedy applied as soon as possible.

The only difficulty on gentlemen's minds is, whether it is best to accept this Constitution on conditional amendments, or to rely on amendments in future, as the Constitution provides. When I look over the article which provides for a revision, I have my doubts. Suppose, sir, nine states accept the Constitution without any conditions at all, and the four states should wish to have amendments,—where will you find nine states to propose, and the legislatures of nine states to agree to, the introduction of amendments? Therefore it seems to me that the expectation of amendments taking place at some future time, will be frustrated. This method, if we take it, will be the most likely to bring about the amendments, as the Conventions of New Hampshire, Rhode Island, New York, Maryland, Virginia, and South Carolina, have not yet met. I apprehend, sir, that these states will be influenced by the proposition which your excellency has submitted, as the resolutions of Massachusetts have ever had their influence. If this should be the case, the necessary amendments would be introduced more early and more safely. From these considerations, as your excellency did not think it proper to make a motion, with submission, I move that the paper read by your excellency be now taken under consideration by the Convention.

The motion being seconded, the proposition was read by the secretary at the table.

Dr. Taylor liked the idea of amendments; but, he said, he did not see any constitutional door open for the introduction of them by the Convention. He read the several authorities which provided for the meeting of Conventions, but did not see in any of them any power given to propose amendments. We are, he said, therefore, treading on unsafe ground to propose them; we must take the whole, or reject the whole. The honorable gentleman was in favor of the adjournment, and, in a speech of some length, deprecated the consequences, which, he said, must arise, if the Constitution was adopted or rejected by a small majority; and that the expenses which would accrue from the adjournment would not exceed fourpence per poll throughout the commonwealth.

Hon. Mr. Cabot rose, and observed, on what fell from the honorable gentleman last speaking, that the reason why no provision for the introduction of amendments was made in the authorities quoted by the honorable gentleman, was, that they were provided for in the 5th article of the Constitution.

[Friday, February 1]

Mr. Bowdoin (of Dorchester) observed, that he could not but express his hearty approbation of the propositions made by his excellency, as they would have a tendency to relieve the fears, and quiet the apprehensions of some very respectable and worthy gentlemen, who had expressed their doubts whether some explanation of certain clauses in the Constitution, and some additional reflections on Congress, similar to those proposed by his excellency, were not necessary. . . . propositions were incorporated with the great and important question, whether this Convention will adopt and ratify the Constitution. . . .

Hon. Mr. Adams: As your excellency was pleased yesterday to offer, for the consideration of this Convention, certain propositions intended to accompany the ratification of the Constitution before us, I did myself the honor to bring them forward by a regular motion, not only from the respect due to your excellency, but from a clear conviction, in my own mind, that they would tend to effect the salutary and important purposes which you had in view—"the removing the fears and quieting the apprehensions of many of the good people of this commonwealth, and the more effectually guarding against an undue administration of the federal government."

I beg leave, sir, more particularly to consider those propositions, and, in a very few words, to express my own opinion, that they must have a strong tendency to ease the minds of gentlemen, who wish for the immediate operation of some essential parts of the proposed Constitution, as well as the most speedy and effectual means of obtaining alterations in some other parts of it, which they are solicitous should be made. I will not repeat the reasons I offered when the motion was made, which convinced me that the measure now under consideration will have a more speedy as well as a more certain influence, in effecting the purpose last mentioned, than the measure proposed in the Constitution before us.

Your excellency's first proposition is, "that it be explicitly declared, that all powers not expressly delegated to Congress are reserved to the several states, to be by them exercised." This appears, to my mind, to be a summary of a bill of rights, which gentlemen are anxious to obtain. It removes a doubt which many have entertained respecting the matter, and gives assurance that, if any law made by the federal government shall be extended beyond the power granted by the proposed Constitution, and inconsistent with the constitution of this state, it will be an error, and adjudged by the courts of law to be void. It is consonant with the second article in the present Confederation, that each state retains its sovereignty, freedom, and independence, and every power, jurisdiction, and right, which is not, by this Confederation, expressly delegated to the United States in Congress assembled. I have long considered the watchfulness of the people over the conduct of their rulers the strongest guard against the encroachments of power; and I hope the people of this country will always be thus watchful.

Another of your excellency's propositions is calculated to quiet the apprehensions of gentlemen lest Congress should exercise an unreasonable control over the state legislatures, with regard to the time, place, and manner of holding elections, which, by the 4th section of the 1st article, are to be prescribed in each state by the legislature thereof, subject to the control of Congress. I have had my fears lest this control should infringe the freedom of elections, which ought ever to be held sacred. Gentlemen who have objected to this controlling power in Congress have expressed their wishes that it had been restricted to such states as may neglect or refuse that power vested in them, and to be exercised by them if they please. Your excellency proposes, in substance, the same restriction, which, I should think, cannot but meet with their full approbation.

The power to be given to Congress to lay and collect taxes, duties, imposts, and excises, has alarmed the minds of some gentlemen. They tell you, sir, that the exercise of the power of laying and collecting direct taxes might greatly distress the several states, and render them incapable of raising moneys for the payment of their respective state debts, or for any purpose. They say the impost and excise may be made adequate to the public emergencies in the time of peace, and ask why the laying direct taxes may not be confined to a time of war. You are pleased to propose to us that it be a recommendation, that "Congress do not lay direct taxes, but when the moneys arising from the impost and excise shall be insufficient for the public exigencies." The prospect of approaching war might necessarily create an expense beyond the productions of impost and excise. How, then, would the government have the necessary means of providing for the public defence? Must they not have recourse to other resources besides impost and excise? The people, while they watch for their own safety, must and will have a just confidence in a legislature of their own election. The approach of war is seldom, if ever, without observation: it is generally observed by the people at large; and I believe no legislature of a free country would venture a measure which should directly touch the purses of the people, under a mere pretence, or unless they could show, to the people's satisfaction, that there had been, in fact, a real public exigency to justify it.

Your excellency's next proposition is, to introduce the indictment of a grand jury, before any person shall be tried for any crime, by which he may incur infamous punishment, or loss of life; and it is followed by another, which recommends a trial by jury in civil actions between citizens of different states, if either of the parties shall request it. These, and several others which I have mentioned, are so evidently beneficial as to need no comment of mine. And they are all, in every particular, of so general a nature, and so equally interesting to every state, that I cannot but persuade myself to think they would all readily join with us in the measure proposed by your excellency, if we should now adopt it. Gentlemen may make additional propositions if they think fit. It is presumed that we shall exercise candor towards each other; and that whilst, on the one hand, gentlemen will cheerfully agree to any proposition intended to promote a general union, which may not be inconsistent with their own mature judgment, others will avoid the making such as may be needless, or tend to embarrass the minds of the people of this commonwealth and our sister states, and thereby not only frustrate your excellency's wise intention, but endanger the loss of that degree of reputation, which, I flatter myself, this commonwealth has justly sustained.

*   *   *

Judge Sumner, adverting to the pathetic apostrophe of the gentleman last speaking, said, he could with as much sincerity apostrophize—O Government! thou greatest good! thou best of blessings! with thee I wish to live—with thee I wish to die! Thou art as necessary to the support of the political body as meat and bread are to the natural body. The learned judge then turned his attention to the proposition submitted by the president, and said, he sincerely hoped that it would meet the approbation of the Convention, as it appeared to him a remedy for all the difficulties which gentlemen, in the course of the debates, had mentioned. He particularized the objections which had been started, and showed that their removal was provided for in the

STATE RATIFYING CONVENTIONS

proposition; and concluded by observing, that the probability was very great, that, if the amendments proposed were recommended by this Convention, they would, on the meeting of the first Congress, be adopted by the general government.

Mr. Widgery said, he did not see the probability that these amendments would be made, if we had authority to propose them. He considered, he said, that the Convention did not meet for the purpose of recommending amendments, but to adopt or reject the Constitution. He concluded by asking, whether it was probable that those states who had already adopted the Constitution would be likely to submit to amendments.

[When the Convention met, a short conversation ensued on the time when the grand question should be taken. It was agreed that it should not be until Tuesday. After this conversation subsided, another took place on the division of the motion, in order that the question of ratifying might be considered separately from the amendments; but nothing final was determined upon.]

Judge Dana advocated the proposition submitted by his excellency, the president. It contained, he said, the amendments generally wished for, as they were not of a local nature, but extended to every part of the Union. If they were recommended to be adopted by this Convention, it was very probable that two thirds of the Congress would concur in promising them; or that two thirds of the legislatures of the several states would apply for the call of a convention to consider them, agreeably to the mode pointed out in the Constitution; and said he did not think that gentlemen would wish to reject the whole of the system, because some part of it did not please them. He then went into consideration of the advantages which would ensue, from its adoption, to the United States, to the individual states, and to the several classes of citizens, and concluded by representing, in a lively manner, the evils to the whole continent, and to the Northern States in particular, which must be the unavoidable attendants on the present system of general government.

*　　　*　　　*

Mr. Pierce: Mr. President, the amendments proposed by your excellency are very agreeable to my opinion, and I should wish to add several more, but will mention but one; and that is, that the Senate should not continue in office more than two years. But, sir, I think that, if the want of these amendments were sufficient for me to vote against the Constitution, the addition, in the manner proposed by your excellency, will not be sufficient for me to vote for it, as it appears to me to be very uncertain whether they ever are a part of the Constitution.

Several gentlemen said a few words each, on the proposition of amendments, which it was acceded to, by gentlemen opposed to the Constitution, was good, but that it was not probable it would be interwoven in the

Constitution. Gentlemen on the other side said there was a great probability that it would, from its nature, be also recommended by the several conventions which have not yet convened.

[Saturday, February 2]

The Hon. Mr. Strong went into a particular discussion of the several amendments recommended in the proposition submitted by his excellency, each of which he considered with much attention. He anticipated the good effect it must have in conciliating the various sentiments of gentlemen on the subject, and expressed his firm belief that, if it was recommended by the Convention it would be inserted in the Constitution.

Gen. Thompson said, we have no right to make amendments. It was not, he said, the business we were sent for. He was glad, he said, that gentlemen were now convinced it was not a perfect system, and that it wanted amendments. This, he said, was different from the language they had formerly held. However, as to the amendments, he could not say amen to them, but they might be voted for by some men—he did not say Judases.

Mr. Parsons, Col. Orne, Mr. Phillips, the Rev. Mr. Niles, and several other gentlemen, spoke in favor of the proposition, as a conciliatory measure, and the probability of the amendments being adopted. Mr. Nasson, Dr. Taylor, Mr. Thomas, (of Middleboro',) and others, though in sentiment with gentlemen on the propriety of their being admitted into the Constitution, did not think it was probable they would be inserted.

Before the Convention adjourned, Gen. Whitney moved that a committee, consisting of two from each county, should be raised, to consider the amendments, or any other that might be proposed, and report thereon. Hon. Mr. Sedgwick seconded the motion.

Hon. Mr. Dalton: Mr. President, I am not opposed to the motion; but, sir, that gentlemen may not again say, as has been the case this day, that the gentlemen who advocate the measure of the proposition were now convinced that amendments to the Constitution are indispensable, I, sir, in my place, say, that I am willing to accept the Constitution as it is; and I am in favor of the motion of proposing amendments, only as it is of a conciliating nature, and not as a concession that amendments are necessary.

The motion was put, and carried unanimously. The following gentlemen were then appointed on the said committee, viz.:

Hon. Mr. Bowdoin, Mr. Southworth, Mr. Parsons, Hon Mr. Hutchinson—Hon. Mr. Dana, Mr. Winn—Hon. Mr. Strong, Mr. Bodman—Hon. Mr. Turner, Mr. Thomas, of Plymouth—Dr. Smith, Mr. Bourn—Hon. Mr. Spooner, Mr. Bishop—Rev. Dr. Hemmenway, Mr. Barrell—Mr. Mayhew, Hon. Mr. Taylor, Hon. Mr. Sprague—Mr. Fox, Mr. Longfellow—Mr. Sewall, Mr. Sylvester—Mr. Lusk, Hon. Mr. Sedgwick.

*　　　*　　　*

[The committee appointed, on Saturday, to consider his excellency's propositions, by their chairman, honorable Mr. Bowdoin, reported a few alterations to the amendments submitted to them; and that, at the decision, the
committee consisted of twenty-four, fifteen of whom agreed in the report,
seven were against it, one was absent, and one declined giving his opinion.
For the report, see the form of ratification, at the end of the debates.]

Major Lusk concurred in the idea already thrown out in the debate, that,
although the insertion of the amendments in the Consitution was devoutly
wished, yet he did not see any reason to suppose they ever would be
adopted. Turning from the subject of amendments, the major entered largely
into the consideration of the 9th section, and, in the most pathetic and
feeling manner, described the miseries of the poor natives of Africa, who are
kidnapped and sold for slaves. With the brightest colors he painted their
happiness and ease on their native shores, and contrasted them with their
wretched, miserable, and unhappy condition, in a state of slavery. From this
subject he passed to the article dispensing with the qualification of a religious
test, and concluded by saying, that he shuddered at the idea that Roman
Catholics, Papists, and Pagans might be introduced into office, and that
Popery and the Inquisition may be established in America.

*   *   *

Dr. Jarvis: Mr. President, the objections which gentlemen have made to
the form of ratification which has been submitted by your excellency, have
arisen either from a doubt of our having a right to propose alterations, or
from the supposed improbability that any amendments recommended by this
assembly will ever become a part of the federal system If we have no right,
sir, to propose alterations, there remains nothing further to be attempted, but
to take the final question, independent of the propositions for amendment.
But I hope the mere assertion of any one is not to operate as an argument in
this assembly; and we are not yet waiting for evidence to prove this very
singular position, which has been so often repeated. If we have a right, sir, to
receive or reject the Constitution, surely we have an equal authority to
determine in what way this right shall be exercised. It is a maxim, I believe,
universally admitted, that, in every instance, the manner in which every
power is to be exerted, must be in its nature discretionary with that body to
which this power is delegated. If this principle be just, sir, the ground which
has been taken to oppose your excellency's proposals, by disputing the right
of recommending alterations, must be necessarily relinquished. But gentlemen say, that they find nothing about amendments in the commission under
which they are acting, and they conceive it neither agreeable to the resolution of the legislature, nor to the sense of their constituents, that such a
scheme should be adopted. Let us inquire, then, sir, under what authority we
are acting, and to what tribunal we are amenable. Is it, then, sir, from the
late federal Convention that we derive that authority? Is it from Congress, or
is it even from the legislature itself? It is from neither, sir. We are convened

in right of the people, as their immediate representatives, to execute the most important trust which it is possible to receive; we are accountable, in its execution, to God only, and our own consciences. When gentlemen assert, then, that we have no right to recommend alterations, they must have ideas strangely derogatory to the influence and authority of our constituents, whom we have the honor of representing. But should it be thought there was even a part of the people who conceived we were thus restricted as to the forms of our proceedings, we are still to recollect that their aggregate sense, on this point, can only be determined by the voices of the majority in this Convention. The arguments of those gentlemen who oppose any propositions of amendments, amount simply to this, sir,—that the whole people of Massachusetts, assembled by their delegates, on the most solemn and interesting occasion, are not at liberty to resolve in what form this trust shall be executed. When we reflect seriously and coolly on this point, I think, sir, we shall doubt no longer.

But, with respect to the prospect of these amendments, which are the subject of discussion, being adopted by the first Congress which shall be appointed under the new Constitution, I really think, sir, that it is not only far from being improbable, but is in the highest degree likely. I have thought long and often on the subject of amendments, and I know no way in which they would be more likely to succeed. If they were made conditional to our receiving the proposed Constitution, it has appeared to me that a conditional amendment must operate as a total rejection. As so many other states have received the Constitution as it is, how can it be made to appear that they will not adhere to their own resolutions? and should they remain as warmly and pertinaciously attached to their opinion as we might be decidedly in favor of our own sentiments, a long and painful interval might elapse before we should have the benefit of a federal Constitution. I have never yet heard an argument to remove this difficulty. Permit me to inquire of gentlemen what reason we have to suppose that the states which have already adopted the Constitution will suddenly consent to call a new convention at the request of this state. Are we going to expose the commonwealth to the disagreeable alternative of being forced into a compliance, or of remaining in opposition, provided nine others should agree to receive it? As highly as some persons talk of the force of this state, I believe we should be but a feeble power, unassisted by others, and detached from the general benefit of a national government. We are told that, under the blessing of Providence, we may do much. It is very true, sir, but it must be proved that we shall be most likely to securre the approbation of Heaven by refusing the proposed system.

It has been insinuated, sir, that these amendments have been artfully introduced to lead to a decision which would not otherwise be had. Without stopping to remark on the total want of candor in which such an idea has arisen, let us inquire whether there is even the appearance of reason to support this insinuation. The propositions are annexed, it is true, to the ratification; but the assent is complete and absolute without them. It is not possible it can be otherwise understood by a single member in this honorable body. Gentlemen, therefore, when they make such an unjust observation, do no honor to the sagacity of others. Supposing it possible that any single member can be deceived by such a shallow artifice, permit me to do justice to the purity of intention in which they have arisen, by observing, that I am satisfied nothing can be farther from your excellency's intentions. The propositions are general, and not local; they are not calculated for the peculiar interest of this state, but, with indiscriminate justice, comprehend the circumstances of the individual on the banks of the Savannah, as well as the hardy and industrious husbandman on the margin of the Kennebeck. Why, then, they should not be adopted, I confess I cannot conceive. There is one of them, in a particular manner, which is very agreeable to me. When we talk of our wanting a bill of rights to the new Constitution, the first article proposed must remove every doubt on this head; as, by positively securing what is not expressly delegated, it leaves nothing to the uncertainty of conjecture, or to the refinements of implication, but is an explicit reservation of every right and privilege which is nearest and most agreeable to the people. There has been scarcely an instance where the influence of Massachusetts has not been felt and acknowledged in the Union. In such a case, her voice will be heard, sir, and I am fully in sentiment, if these amendments are not ingrafted on the Constitution, it will be our own fault. The remaining seven states will have our example before them; and there is a high probability that they, or at least some of them, will take our conduct as a precedent, and will perhaps assume the same mode of procedure. Should this be the fact, their influence will be united to ours. But your delegates will, besides, be subjected to a perpetual instruction, until its object is completed; and it will be always in the power of the people and legislature to renew those instructions. But, if they should fall, we must then acquiesce in the decision of the majority; and this is the known condition on which all free governments depend.

Would gentlemen who are opposed to the Constitution wish to have no amendments? This does not agree with their reiterated objections to the proposed system. Or are they afraid, sir, that these propositions will secure a larger majority? On such an occasion we cannot be too generally united. The Constitution is a great political experiment. The amendments have a tendency to remove many objections which have been made to it; and I hope, sir, when it is adopted, they will be annexed to the ratification, in the manner which your excellency has proposed.

[Tuesday, February 5]

Mr. Ames observed that, at length, it is admitted that the Constitution, connected with the amendments, is good. Almost every one, who has appeared against the Constitution, has declared that he approves it, with the amendments. One gentleman, who has been distinguished by his zealous opposition, has declared that he would hold up both hands for it, if they could be adopted. I admire this candid manner of discussing the subject, and will endeavor to treat it myself with equal care and fairness. The only question which seems to labor is this: the amendments are not a part of the Constitution, and there is nothing better than a probability to trust to, that they will ever be adopted, The nature of the debate is totally shifted, and the inquiry is now, not what the Constitution is, but what degree of probability there is that the amendments will hereafter be incorporated into it.

Before he proceeded to discuss this question, he wished to notice two objections, which had been urged against his excellency's proposition—that this Convention, being confined in their powers to reject or ratify the Constitution as it is, have no right to propose amendments; and that the very propositions imply the Constitution is not perfect, and amount to a confession that it ought to be rejected. It is well that these objections were not made by a lawyer: they would have been called quibbles, and he would have been accused of having learned them at the bar. Have we no right to propose amendments? This is the fullest representation of the people ever known, and if we may not declare their opinion, and upon a point for which we have been elected, how shall it ever be known? A majority may not fully approve the Constitution, and yet they may think it unsafe to reject it; and they may fully approve his excellency's propositions. What shall they say? That they accept, or reject, and no more?—that they be embarrassed, perhaps, to do either. But let them say the truth, that they accept it, in the hope that amendments will obtain. We are chosen to consider the Constitution, and it is clearly incident to our appointment to declare the result of our deliberations. This very mode of obtaining amendments is pointed out in the Constitution itself. How can it be said that we have no right to propose them? If, however, there was any irregularity in this proceeding, the General Court would not delay to conform it.

If it is insisted that the Constitution is admitted to be imperfect, let those objectors consider the nature of their own argument. Do they expect a perfect constitution? Do they expect to find that perfection in government which they well know is not to be found in nature? There is not a man who is not more or less discontented with his condition in life, and who does not experience a mixture of good and evil; and will he expect that a whole society of men can exclude that imperfection which is the lot of every individual in it? The truth is, we call that condition good and happy, which is so upon the whole. But this Constitution may be good without any amendments, and yet the amendments may be good; for they are not repugnant to the Constitution. It is a gratification to observe how little we disagree in our sentiments; but it is not my purpose to compare the amendments with the Constitution. Whatever opinion may be formed of it by others, Mr. Ames professed to think it comparatively perfect. There was not any government which he knew to subsist, or which he had ever heard of, that would bear a comparison with the new Constitution. Considered merely as a literary performance, it was an honor to our country: legislators have at length condescended to speak the language of philosophy; and if we adopt it, we shall demonstrate to the sneering world, who deride liberty because they have lost it, that the principles of our government are as free as the spirit of our people.

I repeat it, our debates have been profitable, because, upon every leading point, we are at last agreed. Very few among us now deny that a federal government is necessary to save us from ruin; that the Confederation is not that government; and that the proposed Constitution, connected with the amendments, is worthy of being adopted. The question recurs, Will the amendments prevail, and become part of the system? In order to obtain such a system as the Constitution and the amendments, there are but three ways of proceeding—to reject the whole, and begin anew, to adopt this plan upon condition that the amendments be inserted into it; or to adopt his excellency's proposition.

Those who propose to reject the whole, are bound to show that we shall possess some advantage in forming a system which we do not enjoy at present, or that some obstacles will be removed which impede us now. But will that be the case? Shall we adopt another constitution with more unanimity than we expect to find in this Convention? Do gentlemen so soon forget their own arguments? We have been told that the new Constitution will be rebellion against the Confederation; that the interests of the states are too dissimilar for a union; and that Massachusetts can do without the union, and is a match for all the world. We have been warned of the tendency of all power towards tyranny, and of the danger of trusting Congress with the power of the purse and of the sword; that the system is not perfect; there is no religious test, and slavery is not abolished. Now, sir, if we reject the Constitution, and, after two or three years' exertion, another constitution should be submitted to another convention of Massachusetts, shall we escape the opposition which is made in this assembly? Will not the same objections then apply with equal force to another system? Or do gentlemen expect that a constitution may be formed which will not be liable to those objections? Do they expect one which will not annul the Confederation, or that the persons and properties of the people shall not be included in the compact, and that we shall hear no more about armies and taxes? But suppose that it was so framed, who is there, even amongst the objectors, who would give his vote for so paltry a system? If we reject, we are exposed to the risk of having no constitution, of being torn with factions, and at last divided into distinct confederacies.

If we accept upon condition, shall we have a right to send members to the new Congress? We shall not; and, of course, this state would lose its voice and influence in obtaining the adoption of the amendments. This is too absurd to need any further discussion.

But, in objection to your excellency's propositions, it is said that it is no more than probable that they will be agreed to by the other states. I ask, What is any future thing that we devise more than probable? What more is another constitution? All agree that we must have one; and it is easy to perceive that such a one as the majority of the people approve must be submitted to by this state; for what right have an eighth or tenth part of the people to dictate a government for the whole? It comes to this point, therefore: Is any method more likely to induce the people of the United States to concur with Massachusetts, than that proposed by your excellency? If it is answered that there is none, as I think it must be, then the objection, that the chance of obtaining the amendments is no more than probable, will come to the ground, and it will appear that, of all chances, we depend upon that which is the safest. For when will the voice of Massachusetts have so powerful an influence as at present? There is not any government now to counteract or awe the people. The attention of the people is excited from one end of the states to the other, and they will watch and control the conduct of their members in Congress. Such amendments as afford better security to liberty will be supported by the people. There will be a Congress in existence to collect their sentiments, and to pursue the objects of their wishes. Nine states may insert amendments into the Constitution; but if we reject it, the vote must be unanimous. Our state, in that case, would lose the advantage of having representatives according to numbers, which is allowed by the Constitution. Upon a few points, and those not of a local nature, unanimity may be expected; but, in discussing a whole Constitution, in which the very amendments, that, it is said, will not be agreed to by the states, are to be inserted, unanimity will be almost a miracle. Either the amendments will be agreed to by the Union, or they will not. If it is admitted that they will be agreed to, there is an end of the objection to your excellency's propositions, and we ought to be unanimous for the Constitution. If it is said that they will not be agreed to, then it must be because they are not approved by the United States, or at least nine of them. Why shall we reject the Constitution, then, for the sole purpose of obtaining that unanimous vote of thirteen states, which, it is confidently said, it is impossible we ever shall obtain from nine only? An object which is impossible is out of the question. The argument that the amendments will not prevail, is not only without force, but directly against those who use it, unless they admit that we have no need of a government, or assert that, by ripping up the foundations of the compact, upon which we now stand, and setting the whole Constitution afloat, and introducing an infinity of new subjects of controversy, we pursue the best method to secure the entire unanimity of thirteen states.

But shall we put every thing that we hold precious to the hazard by rejecting this Constitution? We have great advantages by it in respect of navigation; and it is the general interest of the states that we should have them. But if we reject it, what security have we that we shall obtain them a second time, against the local interests and prejudices of the other states? Who is there, that really loves liberty, that will not tremble for its safety, if the federal government should be dissolved. Can liberty be safe without government?

* * *

Dr. Taylor examined the observations of several gentlemen, who had said, that, had the Constitution been so predicated as to require a bill of rights to be annexed to it, it would have been the work of a year, and could not be contained but in volumes. This, if true, he said, was an argument in favor of one being annexed; but so far from its being the case, he believed any gentleman in that Convention could form one in a few hours, as he might take the bill of rights of Massachusetts for a guide. He concluded by objecting to the amendments, because no assurance was given that they ever would become a part of the system.

Mr. Parsons demonstrated the impracticability of forming a bill, in a national constitution, for securing individual rights, and showed the inutility of the measure, from the ideas, that no power was given to Congress to infringe on any one of the natural rights of the people by this Constitution; and, should they attempt it without constitutional authority, the act would be a nullity, and could not be enforced.

Several other gentlemen spoke in a desultory conversation on the amendments. It was urged again and again, on one side, that it was uncertain whether they ever would be interwoven in the Constitution, and that, therefore, they could not vote for it, on that precarious condition. On the other side, the importance of the opinion of Massachusetts, in other states, in determining on great political questions, the general nature of the amendments proposed, &c., were repeatedly urged in favor of their being a part of the ratification.

* * *

[Wednesday, February 6]

[The Hon. Mr. Adams introduced some amendments, to be added to those reported by the committee; but, they not meeting the approbation of those gentlemen whose minds they were intended to ease, after they were debated a considerable time, the honorable gentleman withdrew them.]

* * *

Hon. Mr. Turner: Mr. President, being advanced in life, and having endeavored, I hope, with a faithful attention, according to my ability, to assist my country in their trying difficulties and dangers for more than twenty years; and as, for three weeks past, my state of health has been such as to render me unable to speak in this assembly,—I trust I shall be heard with some indulgence, while I express a few sentiments at this solemn crisis. I have been averse to the reception of this Constitution, while it was considered merely in its original form; but since the honorable Convention have pleased to agree to the recommendation of certain amendments, I acknowledge my mind is reconciled. But even thus amended, I still see, or think I see, several imperfections in it, and some which give me pain. Indeed, I never expect to see a constitution free from imperfections; and, considering the great diversity of local interests, views, and habits,—considering the unparalleled variety of sentiments among the citizens of the United States,— I despair of obtaining a more perfect constitution than this, at present. And a constitution preferable to the Confederation must be obtained, and obtained soon, or we shall be an undone people. In my judgment, there is a rational probability, a moral certainty, that the proposed amendments will meet the approbation of the several states in the Union. If there is any respect due to the hoary head of Massachusetts, it will undoubtedly have its proper influence in this case. The minds of gentlemen, throughout the nation, must be impressed with such a sense of the necessity of all-important union, especially in our present circumstances, as must strongly operate in favor of a concurrence. The proposed amendments are of such a liberal, such a generous, and such a catholic nature and complexion,—they are so congenial to the soul of every man who is possessed of patriotic regard to the preservation of the just rights and immunities of his country, as well as to the institution of a good and necessary government,—that I think they must, they will, be universally accepted. When, in connection with this confidence, I consider the deplorable state of our navigation and commerce, and various branches of business thereon dependent; the inglorious and provoking figure we make in the eyes of our European creditors; the degree in which the landed interest is burdened and depreciated; the tendency of depreciating paper, and tender acts, to destroy mutual confidence, faith, and credit, to prevent the circulation of specie, and to overspread the land with an inundation, a chaos of multiform injustice, oppression, and knavery; when I consider what want of efficiency there is in our government, as to obliging people seasonably to pay their dues to the public, instead of spending their money in support of luxury and extravagance, of consequence the inability of government to satisfy the just demands of its creditors, and to do it in season, so as to prevent their suffering amazingly by depreciation; in connection with my anxious desire that my ears may be no longer perstringed, nor my heart pained, with the cries of the injured widow and orphans; when I also consider that state of our finances which daily exposes us to become a prey to the despotic humor even of an impotent invader,—I find myself constrained to say, before this assembly, and before God, that I think it my duty to give my vote in favor of this Constitution, with the proposed amendments; and, unless some further light shall be thrown in my way to influence my opinion, I shall conduct accordingly. I know not whether this Convention will vote a ratification of this Constitution, or not. If they should do it, and have the concurrence of the other states may that God, who has always, in a remarkable manner watched over us and our fathers for good, in all difficulties, dangers, and distresses, be pleased to command his almighty blessing upon it, and make it instrumental of restoring justice, honor, safety, support, and salvation, to a sinking land! But I hope it will be considered, by persons of all orders, ranks, and ages, that, without the prevalence of Christian piety and morals, the best republican constitution can never save us from slavery and ruin. If vice is predominant, it is to be feared we shall have rulers whose grand object will be (slyly evading the spirit of the Constitution) to enrich and aggrandize themselves and their connections, to the injury and oppression of the laborious part of the community; while it follows, from the moral constitution of the Deity, that prevalent iniquity must be the ruin of any people. The world of mankind have always, in general, been enslaved and miserable, and always will be, until there is a greater prevalence of Christian moral principles; nor have I any expectation of this, in any great degree, unless some superior mode of education shall be adopted. It is education which almost entirely forms the character, the freedom or slavery, the happiness or misery, of the world. And if this Constitution shall be adopted, I hope the Continental legislature will have the singular honor, the indelible glory, of making it one of their first acts, in their first session, most earnestly to recommend to the several states in the Union the institution of such means of education as shall be adequate to the divine, patriotic purpose of training up the children and youth at large in that solid learning, and in those pious and moral principles, which are the support, the life and soul, of republican government and liberty, of which a free constitution is the body; for, as the body, without the spirit, is dead, so a free form of government, without the animating principles of piety and virtue, is dead also, being alone. May religion, with sanctity of morals, prevail and increase, that the patriotic civilian and ruler may have the sublime, parental satisfaction of eagerly embracing every opportunity of mitigating the rigors of government, in proportion to that increase of morality which may render the people more capable of being a law to themselves! How much more blessed this than to be employed in fabricating constitutions of a higher tone, in obedience to necessity, arising from an increase of turbulent vice and injustice in society! I believe your excellency's patience will not be further exercised by hearing the sound of my voice on the occasion, when I have said, May the United States of America live before God! May they be enlightened, pious, virtuous, free, and happy, to all generations!

*   *   *

Sir, it never was my opinion that we ought, entirely, to abandon this Constitution. I thought it had great defects, and I still think it by no means free from blemishes; but I ever expected the worst consequences to follow a total rejection of it. I always intended to urge amendments, and was in hopes that the wisdom of this assembly would devise a method to secure their adoption. Therefore, when your excellency came forward, as well became your high office, in the character of a mediator, a ray of hope shone in upon the gloom that overspread my heart—of hope that we should still be united in the grand decision.

Sir, a mortal hatred, a deadly opposition, can be deserved by no government but the tyranny of hell, and perhaps a few similar forms on earth. A government of that complexion, in the present enlightened age, could never enter the heart of man; and if it could, and impudence enough were found to propose it,—nay, if it should be accepted,—I affirm, sir, that in America it would never operate a moment. I should glory in debating on my grounds for this assertion; but who will dare to question the truth of it?

Mr. President, so ample have been the arguments drawn from our national distress, the weakness of the present Confederation, the danger of instant disunion, and perhaps some other topics not included in these, that a man must be obstinate indeed, to say, at this period, that a new government is needless. One is proposed. Shall we reject it totally, or shall we amend it? Let any man recollect or peruse the debates in this assembly, and I venture to say, he shall not be a moment, if he loves his country, in making his election. He would contemplate the idea of rejection with horror and detestation. But, sir, it has been alleged that the necessary amendments cannot be obtained in the way your excellency has proposed. This matter has been largely debated. I beg a moment to consider it. Our committee, sir, were pretty well agreed to the amendments necessary to be made, and, in their report, it appears that these amendments are equally beneficial to all the citizens of America. There is nothing local in them, Shall we, then, totally reject the Constitution, because we are only morally certain that they will be adopted? Shall we choose certain misery in one way, when we have the best human prospect of enjoying our most sanguine wishes in another? God forbid!

But, sir, a great deal has been said about the amendments. Here again I refer to the debates. Such has been said to have been the past prevalence of the Northern States in Congress, the sameness of interest in a majority of the states, and their necessary adhesion to each other, that I think there can be no reasonable doubt of the success of any amendments proposed by Massachusetts. Sir, we have, we do, and we shall, in a great measure, give birth to all events, and hold the balance among the United States. . . .

Upon the whole, Mr. President, approving the amendments, and firmly believing that they will be adopted, I recall my former opposition, such as it was, to this Constitution, and shall—especially as the amendments are a standing instruction to our delegates until they are obtained—give it my unreserved assent.

In so doing, I stand acquitted to my own conscience; I hope and trust I shall to my constituents, and [laying his hand on his breast] I know I shall before God.

The time agreed upon for taking the question being arrived and the same being called for from every quarter,

John Hancock, the President, rose, and addressed the honorable Convention as follows:

Gentlemen, being now called upon to bring the subject under debate to a decision, by bringing forward the question, I beg your indulgence to close the business with a few words. I am happy that my health has been so far restored, that I am rendered able to meet my fellow-citizens as represented in this Convention. I should have considered it as one of the most distressing misfortunes of my life to be deprived of giving my aid and support to a system which, if amended (as I feel assured it will be) according to your proposals, cannot fail to give the people of the United States a greater degree of political freedom, and eventually as much national dignity, as falls to the lot of any nation on earth. I have not, since I had the honor to be in this place, said much on the important subject before us. All the ideas appertaining to the system, as well those which are against as for it, have been debated upon with so much learning and ability, that the subject is quite exhausted.

But you will permit, me, gentlemen, to close the whole with one or two general observations. This I request, not expecting to throw any new light on the subject, but because it may possibly prevent uneasiness and discordance from taking place amongst us and amongst our constituents.

That a general system of government is indispensably necessary to save our country from ruin, is agreed upon all sides. That the one now to be decided upon has its defects, all agree; but when we consider the variety of interests, and the different habits of the men it is intended for, it would be very singular to have an entire union of sentiment respecting it. Were the people of the United States to delegate the powers proposed to be given, to men who were not dependent on them frequently for elections—to men whose interest, either from rank or title, would differ from that of their fellow-citizens in common—the task of delegating authority would be vastly more difficult; but, as the matter now stands, the powers reserved by the people render them secure, and, until they themselves become corrupt, they will always have upright and able rulers. I give my assent to the Constitution, in full confidence that the amendments proposed will soon become a part of the system. These amendments being in no wise local, but calculated to give security and ease alike to all the states, I think that all will agree to them.

Suffer me to add, that, let the question be decided as it may, there can be no triumph on the one side or chagrin on the other. Should there be a great division, every good man, every man who loves his country, will be so far from exhibiting extraordinary marks of joy, that he will sincerely lament the

want of unanimity, and strenuously endeavor to cultivate a spirit of conciliation, both in Convention and at home. The people of this commonwealth are
a people of great light—of great intelligence in public business. They know
that we have none of us an interest separate from theirs: that it must be our
happiness to conduce to theirs; and that we must all rise or fall together.
They will never, therefore, forsake the first principle of society—that of
being governed by the voice of the majority; and should it be that the
proposed form of government should be rejected, they will zealously attempt
another. Should it, by the vote now to be taken, be ratified, they will quietly
acquiesce, and where they see a want of perfection in it, endeavor, in a
constitutional way, to have it amended.

The question now before you is such as no nation on earth, without the
limits of America, has ever had the privilege of deciding upon. As the
Supreme Ruler of the universe has seen fit to bestow upon us this glorious
opportunity, let us decide upon it; appealing to him for the rectitude of our
intentions, and in humble confidence that he will yet continue to bless and
save our country.

The question being put, whether this Convention will accept of the report
of the committee, as follows,

Commonwealth of Massachusetts

The Convention, having impartially discussed and fully considered the
Constitution for the United States of America, reported to Congress by the
Convention of delegates from the United States of America, and submitted to
us by a resolution of the General Court of the said commonwealth, passed
the twenty-fifth day of October last past; and acknowledging, with grateful
hearts, the goodness of the Supreme Ruler of the universe in affording the
people of the United States, in the course of his providence, an opportunity,
deliberately and peaceably, without fraud or surprise, of entering into an
explicit and solemn compact with each other, by assenting to and ratifying a
new Constitution, in order to form a more perfect union, establish justice,
insure domestic tranquillity, provide for the common defence, promote the
general welfare, and secure the blessings of liberty to themselves and their
posterity, Do, in the name and in behalf of the people of the commonwealth
of Massachusetts, assent to and ratify the said Constitution for the United
States of America.

And, as it is the opinion of this Convention, that certain amendments and
alterations in the said Constitution would remove the fears and quiet the
apprehensions of many of the good people of the commonwealth, and more
effectually guard against an undue administration of the federal government,
the Convention do therefore recommend that the following alterations and
provisions be introduced into the said Constitution:

First. That it be explicitly declared, that all powers not expressly delegated
by the aforesaid Constitution are reserved to the several states, to be by them
exercised.

Secondly. That there shall be one representative to every thirty thousand persons, according to the census mentioned in the Constitution, until the whole number of representatives amounts to two hundred.

Thirdly. That Congress do not exercise the powers vested in them by the 4th section of the 1st article, but in cases where a state shall neglect or refuse to make the regulations therein mentioned, or shall make regulations subversive of the rights of the people to a free and equal representation in Congress, agreeably to the Constitution.

Fourthly. That Congress do not lay direct taxes, but when the moneys arising from the impost and excise are insufficient for the public exigencies, nor then, until Congress shall have first made a requisition upon the states, to assess, levy, and pay their respective proportion of such requisitions, agreeably to the census fixed in the said Constitution, in such way and manner as the legislatures of the states shall think best, and, in such case, if any state shall neglect or refuse to pay its proportion, pursuant to such requisition, then Congress may assess and levy such state's proportion, together with interest thereon, at the rate of six per cent, per annum, from the time of payment prescribed in such requisitions.

Fifthly. That Congress erect no company with exclusive advantages of commerce.

Sixthly. That no person shall be tried for any crime, by which he may incur an infamous punishment, or loss of life, until he be first indicted by a grand jury, except in such cases as may arise in the government and regulation of the land and naval forces.

Seventhly. The Supreme Judicial Federal Court shall have no jurisdiction of causes between citizens of different states, unless the matter in dispute, whether it concern the realty or personalty, be of the value of three thousand dollars at the least; nor shall the federal judicial powers extend to any action between citizens of different states, where the matter in dispute, whether it concern the realty or personalty, is not of the value of fifteen hundred dollars at the least.

Eighthly. In civil actions between citizens of different states, every issue of fact, arising in actions at common law, shall be tried by a jury, if the parties, or either of them, request it.

Ninthly. Congress shall at no time consent that any person holding an office of trust or profit, under the United States, shall accept of a title of nobility, or any other title or office, from any king, prince, or foreign state.

And the Convention do, in the name and in the behalf of the people of this commonwealth, enjoin it upon their representatives in Congress, at all times, until the alterations and provisions aforesaid have been considered, agreeably to the 5th article of the said Constitution, to exert all their influence, and use all reasonable and legal methods, to obtain a ratification of the said alterations and provisions, in such manner as is provided in the said article.

And, that the United States, in Congress assembled, may have due notice of the assent and ratification of the said Constitution by this Convention, it is

Resolved, That the assent and ratification aforesaid be engrossed on parchment, together with the recommendation and injunction aforesaid, and with this resolution; and that his excellency, John Hancock, President, and the Hon. William Cushing, Esq., Vice-President of this Convention, transmit the same, countersigned by the Secretary of the Convention, under their hands and seals, to the United States in Congress assembled.

The question was determined by yeas and nays, as follows:

County of Suffolk

Boston—His Ex. John Hancock,	Yea.
Hon. James Bowdoin,	Yea.
Hon. Samuel Adams,	Yea.
Hon. William Phillips,	Yea.
Hon. Caleb Davis,	Yea.
Charles Jarvis, Esq.,	Yea.
John Coffin Jones, Esq.,	Yea.
John Winthrop, Esq.,	Yea.
Thomas Dawes, Jun.,	Yea.
Rev. Samuel Stillman,	Yea.
Thomas Russell, Esq.,	Yea.
Christopher Gore, Esq.,	Yea.
Roxbury—Hon. William Heath,	Yea.
Hon. Increase Sumner,	Yea.
Dorchester—James Bowdoin, Jun.,	Yea.
Ebenezer Wales, Esq.,	Yea.
Milton—Rev. Nathaniel Robbins,	Yea.
Weymouth—Hon. Cotton Tufts,	Yea.
Hingham—Hon. Benj. Lincoln,	Yea.
Rev. Daniel Shute,	Yea.
Braintree—Hon. Richard Cranch,	Yea.
Rev. Anthony Wibird,	Yea.
Brookline—Rev. Joseph Jackson,	Yea.
Dedham—Rev. Thomas Thacher,	Yea.
Fisher Ames, Esq.,	Yea.
Needham—Col. William M'Intosh,	Yea.
Medfield—John Baxter, Jun.,	Yea.
Stoughton—Hon. Elijah Dunbar,	Yea.
Capt. Jedediah Southworth,	Nay.
Wretham—Mr. Thomas Man,	Yea.
Mr. Nathan Comstock,	Nay.
Walpole—Mr. George Payson,	Yea.
Sharon—Mr. Benjamin Randall,	Nay.
Franklin—Hon. J. Fisher,	Yea.
Medway—M. Richardson, Jun.,	Nay.
Bellingham—Rev. Noah Alden,	Nay.
Chelsea—Rev. Phillips Payson,	Yea.
Foxboro'—Mr. Ebenezer Warren,	Yea.
Hull—Mr. Thomas Jones,	Yea.

Yeas, 34. Nays, 5.

County of Essex

Salem—Richard Manning, Esq.,	Yea.
Edward Pulling Esq.,	Yea.
Mr. William Gray, Jun.,	Yea.
Mr. Francis Cabot,	Yea.
Danvers—Hon. Is. Hutchinson,	Nay.
Newbury—Hon. Tristam Dalton,	Yea.
Enos Sawyer, Esq.,	Yea.
E. March, Esq.,	Yea.
Newburyport—Hon. Rufus King,	Yea.
Hon. Benjamin Greenleaf,	Yea.
Theophilus Parsons, Esq.,	Yea.
Hon. Jonathan Titcomb,	Yea.
Beverly—Hon. G. Cabot,	Yea.
Mr. Joseph Wood,	Yea.
Capt. Israel Thorndike,	Yea.
Ipswich—Hon. Michael Farley,	Yea.
J. Choate, Esq.,	Yea.
Daniel Noyes, Esq.,	Yea.
Col. Jonathan Cogswell,	Yea.
Marblehead—Isaac Mansfield,	Yea.
J. Glover, Esq.,	Yea.
Hon. Azor Orne,	Yea.
John Glover, Esq.,	Yea.
Gloucester—Daniel Rodgers, Esq.,	Yea.
John Low, Esq.,	Yea.
Capt. W. Pearson,	Yea.
Lynn and Lynnfield—J. Carnes,	Yea.
Capt. John Burnham,	Yea.
Andover—Peter Osgood, Jun.,	Nay.
Dr. Thomas Kittridge,	Nay.
William Symmes, Jun.,	Yea.
Rowley—Capt. Thomas Mighill,	Nay.
Haverhill—Bailey Bartlett, Esq.,	Yea.
Capt. Nathaniel Marsh,	Nay.
Topsfield—Mr. Israel Clark,	Yea.
Salisbury—Dr. Samuel Nyre,	Yea.
Mr. Enoch Jackman,	Yea.
Amesbury—Capt. Benj. Lurvey,	Yea.
Mr. Willis Patten,	Yea.
Boxford—Hon. Aaron Wood,	Nay.
Bradford—Daniel Thruston, Esq.,	Yea.
Methuen—Capt. E. Carlton,	Nay.
Wenham—Mr. Jacob Herrick,	Yea.
Manchester—Mr. Simeon Miller,	Yea.

Yeas, 38. Nays. 6.

County of Middlesex

Cambridge—Hon. Francis Dana,	Yea.
Stephen Dana, Esq.,	Yea.
Charlestown—Hon. N. Gorham,	Yea.

Watertown—Dr. Marshal Spring,	Nay.
Woburn—Capt. Timothy Winn,	Nay.
Concord—Hon. Joseph Hosmer,	Yea.
Newtown—Hon. A. Fuller,	Yea.
Reading—Mr. William Flint,	Nay.
Mr. Peter Emerson,	Nay.
Marlborough—Mr. Jonas Morse,	Nay.
Maj. Benjamin Sawin,	Nay.
Billerica—Wm. Thompson, Esq.,	Nay.
Framingham—Capt. L. Buckminster,	Yea.
Lexington—Benj. Browne, Esq.,	Yea.
Chelmsford—Maj. John Minot,	Nay.
Sherburne—Daniel Whitney, Esq.,	Yea.
Sudbury—Capt. Asahel Wheeler,	Yea.
Malden—Capt. Benjamin Blaney,	Yea.
Weston—Capt. Abraham Bigelow,	Yea.
Medford—Maj. Gen. John Brooks,	Yea.
Hopkinton—Capt. Gilbert Dench,	Yea.
Westford—Mr. Jonathan Keep,	Nay.
Stow—Dr. Charles Whitman,	Yea.
Groton—Dr. Benjamin Morse,	Nay.
Joseph Sheple, Esq.,	Nay.
Shirley—Mr. Obadiah Sawtell,	Nay.
Pepperell—Mr. Daniel Fisk,	Nay.
Waltham—Leonard Williams, Esq.,	Yea.
Townsend—Capt. Daniel Adams,	Nay.
Dracut—Hon. Joseph B. Varnum.	Yea.
Bedford—Capt. John Webber,	Nay.
Holliston—Capt. St. Chamberlain,	Nay.
Acton and Carlisle—Mr. A. Parlin	Nay.
Dunstable—Hon. J. Pitts,	Yea.
Lincoln—Hon. E. Brooks,	Yea.
Wilmington—Capt. J. Harnden,	Nay.
Tewksbury—Mr. Newman Scarlet,	Nay.
Littleton—Mr. Samuel Reed,	Nay.
Ashby—Mr. Benjamin Adams,	Nay.
Natick—Maj. Hezekiah Broad,	Nay.
Stoneham—Capt. Jonathan Green,	Nay.
East Sudbury—Mr. Phi. Gleason,	Nay.

Yeas, 17. Nays, 25.

County of Hampshire

Springfield—Wm. Pynchon, Esq.,	Yea.
West Springfield—Col. Benj. Ely,	Nay.
Capt. John Williston,	Nay.
Wilbraham—Capt. Phin. Stebbins,	Nay.
Northampton and Easthampton—	
Hon. Caleb Strong,	Yea.
Benjamin Sheldon,	Yea.
Southampton—Capt. L. Pomeroy,	Yea.
Hadley—Brig. Gen. Elisha Porter,	Yea.
South Hadley—Hon. N. Goodman,	Yea.

Amherst—Mr. Daniel Cooly,	Nay.
Granby—Mr. Benjamin Eastman,	Nay.
Hatfield—Hon. J. Hastings,	Yea.
Whately—Mr. Josiah Allis,	Nay.
Williamsburg—Mr. W. Bodman,	Nay.
Westfield—John Ingersoll, Esq.,	Yea.
Deerfield—Mr. Samuel Field,	Nay.
Greenfield—Mr. Moses Bascum,	Nay.
Shelburne—Mr. Robert Wilson,	Nay.
Conway—Capt. Consider Arms,	Nay.
Mr. Malachi Maynard,	Nay.
Sunderland—Capt. Z. Crocker,	Nay.
Montague—Mr. M. Severance,	Nay.
Northfield—Mr. Eben James,	Yea.
Brimfield—Abner Morgan, Esq.,	Yea.
South Brimfield—Capt. A. Fisk,	Nay.
Monson—Mr. Phineas Merrick,	Nay.
Pelham—Mr. Adam Clark,	Nay.
Greenwich—Capt. N. Whitcomb,	Nay.
Blandford—Mr. Timothy Blair,	Nay.
Palmer—Mr. Aaron Merrick,	Nay.
Granville—Mr. John Hamilton,	Nay.
Mr. Clark Cooley,	Nay.
New Salem—Mr. J. Chamberlin,	Nay.
Belchertown—Mr. Justus Dwight,	Nay.
Coleraine—Mr. Samuel Eddy,	Nay.
Ware—Mr. Isaac Pepper,	Nay.
Warwick and Orange—	
Capt. John Goldsborough,	Nay.
Chester—Capt. David Shepard,	Yea.
Charlemont—Mr. Jesse Reed,	Yea.
Ashfield—Mr. Ephraim Williams,	Nay.
Worthington—Nahum Eager, Esq.,	Yea.
Shutesbury—Mr. Asa Powers,	Nay.
Chesterfield—Col. Benj. Bonney,	Yea.
Southwick—Capt. Silas Fowler,	Nay.
Northwick—Maj. T. J. Doglass,	Yea.
Ludlow—Mr. John Jennings,	Nay.
Leverett—Mr. Jonathan Hubbard,	Nay.
West Hampton—Mr. A. Fisher,	Yea.
Cunningham and Plainfield—	
Mr. Edmund Lazell,	Yea.
Buckland—Capt. T. Maxwell,	Yea.
Long Meadows—Mr. E. Colton,	Yea.
Yeas, 33. Nays, 19.	

County of Plymouth

Plymouth—Joshua Thomas, Esq.,	Yea.
Thomas Davis,	Yea.
John Davis,	Yea.
Scituate—Hon. William Cushing,	Yea.
Hon. Nathan Cushing,	Yea.
Hon. Charles Turner, Esq.,	Yea.

Marshfield—Rev. William Shaw,	Yea.
Bridgewater—D. Howard, Esq.,	Yea.
Mr. Hezekiah Hooper,	Yea.
Capt. Elisha Mitchell,	Yea.
Mr. Daniel Howard, Jun.,	Yea.
Middleboro'—Rev. Isaac Backus,	Yea.
Mr. Benjamin Thomas,	Nay.
Isaac Thompson, Esq.,	Yea.
Mr. Isaac Soule,	Nay.
Duxbury—Hon. G. Partridge,	Yea.
Rochester—Mr. N. Hammond,	Nay.
Mr. Abraham Holmes,	Nay.
Plympton—Capt. F. Shurtliff,	Nay.
Mr. Elisha Bisbee, Jun.,	Nay.
Pembroke—Capt. John Turner,	Yea.
Mr. Josiah Smith,	Yea.
Kingston—W. Sever, Jun., Esq.,	Yea.
Hanover—Hon. Joseph Cushing,	Yea.
Abington—Rev. Samuel Niles,	Yea.
Halifax—Mr. F. Waterman,	Yea.
Wareham—Col. Israel Fearing,	Yea.

Yeas, 22. Nays, 6.

County of Barnstable

Barnstable—Shear. Browne, Esq.,	Yea.
Sandwich—Dr. Thomas Smith,	Nay.
Mr. Thomas Nye,	Nay.
Yarmouth—D. Thatcher, Esq.,	Yea.
Capt. Jonathan Howes,	Yea.
Harwich—Hon. Solomon Freeman,	Yea.
Capt Kimball Clark,	Yea.
Wellfleet—Rev. Levi Whitman,	Yea.
Falmouth—Capt. Joseph Palmer,	Yea.

Yeas, 7. Nays, 2.

County of Bristol

Taunton—James Williams, Esq.,	Yea.
Col. Nathaniel Leonard,	Nay.
Mr. Aaron Pratt,	Nay.
Rehoboth—Capt. Phan. Bishop,	Nay.
Maj. Frederick Brown,	Nay.
William Windsor, Esq.,	Nay.
Swansey—Mr. Christopher Mason,	Nay.
Mr. David Brown,	Nay.
Dartmouth—Hon. Hol'r Slocum,	Nay.
Mr. Melatiah Hathaway,	Nay.
Norton—Hon. Abraham White,	Nay.
Attleboro'—Hon. Elisha May,	Yea.
Capt. Moses Wilmarth,	Yea.
Dighton—Col. Sylvester Richmond,	Yea.
Hon. William Baylies,	Yea.
Freetown—Hon. Thomas Durfee,	Yea.
Israel Washburn, Esq.,	Yea.

Easton—Capt. Eben Tisdell,	Nay.
Mansfield—Capt. John Pratt,	Nay.
New Bedford—Hon. W. Spooner,	Yea.
Rev. Samuel West.	Yea.
Westport—Mr. William Almy,	Yea.
Yeas, 10. Nays, 12.	

County of York

York—Capt. Esaias Preble,	Nay.
Nathaniel Barrell, Esq.,	Yea.
Kittery—Mr. Mark Adams,	Nay.
Mr. James Neal,	Nay.
Wells—Rev. Mr. Hemmenway,	Yea.
Hon. Nathaniel Wells,	Yea.
Berwick—Dr. Nathaniel Low,	Nay.
Mr. Richard F. Cutts,	Nay.
Mr. Elijah Hays,	Nay.
Pepperelboro'—T. Cutts, Esq.,	Yea.
Lebanon—Mr. T. M. Wentworth,	Nay.
Sanford—Maj. Samuel Nason,	Nay.
Buxton—Jacob Bradbury, Esq.,	Yea.
Fryeburg—Mr. Moses Ames,	Nay.
Coxhall—Capt. John Low,	Yea.
Shapleigh—Mr. Jeremiah Emery,	Nay.
Waterboro'—Rev. Pel. Tingley,	Nay.
Yeas, 6. Nays, 11.	

County of Dukes

Edgartown—Mr. Wm Mayhew,	Yea.
Tisbury—Mr. C. Dunham,	Yea.
Yeas, 2.	

County of Worcester

Worcester—Mr. David Bigelow,	Nay.
Lancaster—Hon. John Sprague,	Yea.
Mendon—Ed. Thompson, Esq.,	Nay.
Brookfield—Mr. Daniel Forbes,	Nay.
Mr. N. Jenks,	Nay.
Oxford—Capt. Jeremiah Learned,	Nay.
Charlton—Mr. Caleb Curtiss,	Nay.
Mr. Ezra M'Intier,	Nay.
Sutton—Mr. David Harwood,	Nay.
Hon. Amos Singletary,	Nay.
Leicester—Col. Samuel Denny,	Nay.
Spencer—Mr. James Hathun,	Nay.
Rutland—Mr. Asapu Sherman,	Nay.
Paxton—Mr. Abraham Smith,	Nay.
Oakham—Capt. Jonathan Bullard,	Nay.
Barre—Capt. John Black,	Nay.
Hubbardston—Capt. J. Woods,	Nay.
New Braintree—Capt. B. Joslyn,	Nay.
Southboro'—Capt. Seth Newton,	Yea.
Westboro'—Capt. S. Maynard,	Nay.

Northboro'—Mr. Art. Brigham,	Nay.
Shrewsbury—Capt. I. Harrington,	Nay.
Lunenburg—Capt. John Fuller,	Nay.
Fitchburg—Mr. Daniel Putman,	Nay.
Uxbridge—Dr. Samuel Willard,	Nay.
Harvard—Joshua Whitney, Esq.,	Nay.
Dudley—Mr. Jonathan Day,	Nay.
Bolton—Hon. Samuel Baker,	Yea.
Upton—Capt. T. M. Baker,	Nay.
Sturbridge—Capt. Timothy Parker,	Nay.
Leominster—Maj. D. Wilder,	Yea.
Hardwick—Maj. M. Kinsley,	Nay.
Holden—Rev. Joseph Davi,	Nay.
Western—Mr. Mat. Patrick,	Yea.
Douglass—Hon. John Taylor,	Nay.
Grafton—Dr. Joseph Wood,	Nay.
Petersham—Jonathan Grout, Esq.,	Nay.
Capt. Samuel Peckham,	Nay.
Royalston—John Frye, Esq.,	Nay.
Westminster—Mr. Stephen Holden,	Nay.
Templeton—Capt. J. Fletcher,	Nay.
Princeton—Mr. Timothy Fuller,	Nay.
Ashburnham—Mr. Jacob Willard,	Nay.
Winchendon—Mr. Moses Rale,	Nay.
Northbridge—Capt. J. Wood,	Nay.
Ward—Mr. Joseph Stone,	Nay.
Athol—Mr. Josiah Goddard,	Yea.
Milford—Mr. David Stearns,	Nay.
Sterling—Mr. Ephraim Wilder,	Yea.
Boylston—Mr. Jonas Temple,	Nay.
Yeas, 8. Nays, 43.	

County of Cumberland

Falmouth—Daniel Isley, Esq.,	Nay.
John K. Smith, Esq.,	Yea.
Portland—Mr. John Fox,	Yea.
Capt. Joseph M'Lellen,	Yea.
North Yarmouth—D. Mitchell,	Yea.
Samuel Merrill, Esq.,	Yea.
Scarboro'—W. Thompson, Esq.,	Yea.
Brunswick—Capt. John Dunlap,	Yea.
Harpswell—Capt. Isaac Snow,	Yea.
Cape Elizabeth—Mr. Joshua Dyer,	Yea.
Gorham—Mr. S. Longfellow, Jun.,	Nay.
New Gloucester—Mr. Widgery,	Nay.
Gray—Rev. Samuel Perley,	Yea.
Yeas, 10. Nays, 3.	

County of Lincoln

Pownalboro'—Thomas Rice, Esq.,	Yea.
Mr. David Sylvester,	Yea.
Georgetown—Mr. N. Wyman,	Yea.

Newcastle—Mr. David Murray,	Nay.
Woolwich—Mr. David Gilmore,	Yea.
Topsham—Hon. S. Thompson,	Nay.
Winslow—Mr. Jonah Crosby,	Nay.
Bowdoinham—Mr. Zach. Beal,	Nay.
Boothbay—William M'Cobb, Esq.,	Yea.
Bristol—William Jones, Esq.,	Nay.
Vassalboro'—Capt. Samuel Grant,	Yea.
Edgecomb—Moses Davis, Esq.,	Yea.
Hallowell—Capt. James Carr,	Nay.
Thomaston—David Fayles, Esq.,	Yea.
Bath—Dummer Sewall, Esq.,	Yea.
Winthrop—Mr. Joshua Bean,	Nay.

Yeas, 9. Nays, 7.

County of Berkshire

Sheffield and Mount Washington—	
John Ashley, Jun., Esq.,	Yea.
Great Barrington—Hon. E. Dwight,	Yea.
Stockbridge—Hon. T. Sedgwick,	Yea.
Pittsfield—Mr. Val. Rathburn,	Nay.
Richmond—Mr. Comstock Betts,	Nay.
Lenox—Mr. Lemuel Collins,	Nay.
Lanesboro'—Hon. Jona. Smith,	Nay.
Williamstown—Hon. T. J. Skinner,	Yea.
Adams—Capt. J. Pleroe,	Nay.
Egremont—Ephraim Fitch, Esq.,	Nay.
Becket—Mr. Elisha Carpenter,	Yea.
West Stockbridge—Maj. T. Lusk,	Nay.
Alford—Mr. John Hulbert,	Nay.
New Marlborough—D. Taylor,	Yea.
Tyringham—Capt. E. Herrick,	Nay.
Loudon—Mr. Joshua Lawton,	Nay.
Windsor—Mr. Timothy Mason,	Nay.
Partridgefield—E. Peirce, Esq.,	Nay.
Hancock—Mr. David Vaughan,	Nay.
Lee—Capt. Jesse Bradley,	Nay.
Washington—Mr. Zenas Noble,	Nay.
Sandisfield—Mr. J. Picket, Jun.,	Nay.

Yeas, 6. Nays, 16.

Total—Yeas, 187. Nays, 168.

On the motion for ratifying being declared in the affirmative, by a majority of nineteen, the

Hon. Mr. White rose, and said that, notwithstanding he had opposed the adoption of the Constitution, upon the idea that it would endanger the liberties of his country, yet, as a majority had seen fit to adopt it, he should use his utmost exertions to induce his constituents to live in peace under and cheerfully submit to it.

He was followed by Mr. Widgery, who said, that he should return to his constituents, and inform them that he had opposed the adoption of this Constitution; but that he had been overruled, and that it had been carried by a majority of wise and understanding men; that he should endeavor to sow the seeds of union and peace among the people he represented; and that he hoped, and believed, that no person would wish for, or suggest, the measure of a protest; for, said he, we must consider that this body is as full a representation of the people as can be convened. After expressing his thanks for the civility which the inhabitants of this town have shown to the Convention, and declaring, as his opinion, that they had not in the least influenced the decision, he concluded by saying, that he should support, as much as in him lay, the Constitution, and that he believed, as this state had adopted it, that not only nine, but the whole thirteen, would come into the measure.

Mr. Whitney said that, though he had been opposed to the Constitution, he should support it as much as if he had voted for it.

Mr. Cooley (Amherst) said, that he endeavored to govern himself by the principles of reason; that he was directed to vote against the adoption of the Constitution, and that, in so doing, he had not only complied with his directions, but had acted according to the dictates of his own conscience; and that, as it had been agreed to by a majority, he should endeavor to convince his constituents of the propriety of its adoption.

Dr. Taylor also said, he had uniformly opposed the Constitution; that he found himself fairly beaten, and expressed his determination to go home and endeavor to infuse a spirit of harmony and love among the people.

Other gentlemen expressed their inclination to speak; but, it growing late, the Convention adjourned to the next morning.

[Thursday, February 7]

The Convention met, when Major Nason, in a short address, intimated his determination to support the Constitution, and to exert himself to influence his constituents to do the same.

Mr. Randal said, he had been uniformly opposed to the Constitution. He had, he said, fought like a good soldier; but, as he was beaten, he should sit down contented, hoping the minority may be disappointed in their fears, and that the majority may reap the full fruition of the blessings they anticipate. In the hope that the amendments recommended by his excellency, the president, will take place, I shall, says he, go home and endeavor to satisfy those that have honored me by their choice, so that we may all live in peace.

Major Swain declared, that the Constitution had had a fair trial, and that there had not, to his knowledge, been any undue influence exercised to obtain the vote in its favor; that many doubts which lay on his mind had been removed, and that, although he was in the minority, he should support the Constitution as cheerfully and as heartily as though he had voted on the other side of the question.

Benjamin Lincoln to Washington, 1788*

Feb. 3, 1788

My Dear General:

Your Excellency will find, by the papers of yesterday, which I do myself the pleasure to inclose, that the Governor has taken his seat as President of the Convention; and that he came forward with a motion for the adoption of the Constitution, and subjoined a recommendation that some alterations may take place in it. The motion has taken up a considerable time. Those in the opposition want the Constitution to be accepted upon condition that the alterations be made. This they will not be able to carry.

Yesterday noon, a motion was made that the motion under consideration should be committed. This was agreed to, and a large committee was raised, consisting of two members from each of the large counties, and of one for two small ones. It was also agreed that each county should nominate their own members, and that they should take one who had given his opinion for, and one who had given his opinion against, the Constitution, in each county wherein two were chosen. I expect they will report to-morrow afternoon, to which time the Convention stands adjourned. I hope good will arise from the measure, and that the main question will be taken by Wednesday next. The gentlemen in the opposition urge that the Governor's motion ought to be divided, and that the first question be taken simply, "Whether they will or will not accept the Constitution?" They are opposed in this, and I hope the large committee will adjust the matter, and put an end to any further dispute upon the question.

We find ourselves exceedingly embarrassed by the temper which raged the last winter in some of the counties. Many of the insurgents are in the Convention; even some of Shays's officers. A great proportion of those men are high in the opposition. We could hardly expect any thing else; nor could we, I think, justly suppose that those men who were so lately intoxicated with large draughts of liberty, and who were thirsting for more, would, in so short a time, submit to a Constitution which would further take up the reins of government which, in their opinion, were too strait before. I hope people abroad will consider this matter, and make proper allowances for a clog of this kind. I think the Constitution will pass. I have the honor of being, my dear General, With perfect esteem, &c.,

---

*Debates and Proceedings in the Convention of the Commonwealth of Massachusetts Held in the Year 1788, pp. 404–5.

Madison to Washington, 1788*

Feb. 11, 1788

Dear Sir,

The newspaper inclosed with the letter which follows, comprises the information brought me by the mail of yesterday

Boston, Feby. 3d.

I inclose a newspaper containing the propositions communicated by Mr. Hancock to the Convention on thursday last. Mr. Adams who contrary to his own sentiments has been hitherto silent in Convention, has given his Public and explicit approbation of Mr. Hancock's propositions. We flatter ourselves that the weight of these two characters will ensure our success; but the event is not absolutely certain. Yesterday a committee was appointed on the motion of a doubtful character to consider the propositions submitted by Mr. Hancock and to report to-morrow afternoon. We have a majority of federalists on this Committee and flatter ourselves the result will be favorable. P. S. We shall probably decide on thursday or friday next, when our numbers will amount to about 363. Gerry has kept at Cambridge & our opponents say nothing of his reinvitation.

With greatest esteem & attachment, I am Dear Sir, Yr. Obedt. & affe. Servt.

Madison to Washington, 1788†

Feb. 15, 1788

Dear Sir,

I have at length the pleasure to inclose you the favorable result of the Convention at Boston. The amendments are a blemish, but are in the least offensive form. The minority also is very disagreeably large, but the temper of it is some atonement. I am assured by Mr. King that the leaders of it as well as the members of it in general are in good humor; and will countenance no irregular opposition there or elsewhere. The Convention of New Hampshire is now sitting. There seems to be no question that the issue there will add a seventh pillar, as the phrase now is, to the federal Temple.

With the greatest respect & attachment, I am, Dr. Sir Yrs.

Madison to Jefferson, 1788††

Feb. 19, 1788

Dear Sir,

By the Count de Moustier I received your favour of the 8th. of October. I rec'd by his hands also the watch which you have been so good as to provide

*G. Hunt, ed., *The Writings of James Madison* (1904), Vol. 5, pp. 99–100.
†*The Writings of James Madison,* p. 100.
††*The Writings of James Madison,* p. 100.

for me, and for which I beg you to accept my particular thanks. During the short trial I have made she goes with great exactness. Since the arrival of the Count de Moustier, I have rec'd also by the Packet Mr. Calonui's publication for myself, and a number of the Mercuries for Mr. Banister. The bearer was a Mr. Stuart. I had a conveyance to Mr. Banister a few days after the Mercuries came to hand.

The Public here continues to be much agitated by the proposed feder Constitution and to be attentive to little else. At the date of my last, Delaware Pennsylvania, and New Jersey, had adopted it. It has been since adopted by Connecticut, Georgia, and Massachusetts. In the first the minority consisted of 40 against 127. In Georgia, the adoption was unanimous. In Massachusetts the conflict was tedious and the event extremely doubtful. On the final question the vote stood 187 against 168; a majority of 19 only being in favor of the Constitution.

The prevailing party comprized however all the men of abilities, of property, and of influence. In the opposite multitude there was not a single character capable of uniting their wills or directing their measures. It was made up partly of deputies from the province of Maine, who apprehended difficulties from the New Government to their scheme of separation, partly of men who had espoused the disaffection of Shay's; and partly of ignorant and jealous men, who had been taught or had fancied, that the Convention at Philada. had entered into a conspiracy against the liberties of the people at large, in order to erect an aristocracy for the rich the well born, and the men of Education. They had no plan whatever. They looked no farther than to put a negative on the Constitution and return home. The amendments as recommended by the Convention, were as I am well informed not so much calculated for the minority in the Convention, on whom they had little effect, as for the people of the State. You will find the amendments in the Newspapers which are sent from the office of foreign affairs. It appears from a variety of circumstances that disappointment had produced no asperity in the minority, and that they will probably not only acquiesce in the event, but endeavour to reconcile their constituents to it. This was the public declaration of several who were called the leaders of the party. The minority of Connecticut behaved with equal moderation. That of Pennsylvania has been extremely intemperate and continues to use a very bold and menacing language. Had the decision in Massachusetts been averse to the Constitution, it is not improbable that some very violent measures would have followed in that State. The cause of the inflammation however is much more in their State factions, than in the system proposed by the Convention. New Hampshire is now deliberating on the Constitution. It is generally understood that an adoption is a matter of certainty. South Carolina & Maryland have fixed on April or May for their Conventions. The former it is currently said will be one of the ratifying States. Mr. Chace and a few others will raise a considerable opposition in the latter. But the weight of personal influence is on the side of the Constitution, and the present expectation is that the opposition will be outnumbered by a great majority. This State is much divided in its sentiment. Its Convention is to be held in June. The decision of Massts. will give the turn in favor of the Constitution unless an idea should prevail or the fact should appear, that the voice of the State is opposed to the result of its Convention. North Carolina has put off her Convention till July. The State is much divided, it is said. The temper of Virginia, as far as I can learn, has undergone but little change of late. At first there was an enthusiasm for the Constitution. The tide next took a sudden and strong turn in the opposite direction. The influence and exertions of Mr. Henry and Col. Mason and some others will account for this. Subsequent information again represented the Constitution as regaining in some degree its lost ground. The people at large have been uniformly said to be more friendly to the Constitution than the Assembly. But it is probable that the dispersion of the latter will have a considerable influence on the opinions of the former. The previous adoption of nine States must have a very persuasive effect on the minds of the opposition, though I am told that a very bold language is held by Mr. H——y and some of his partizans. Great stress is laid on the self-sufficiency of that State, and the prospect of external props is alluded to.

Congress have done no business of consequence yet, nor is it probable that much more of any sort will precede the event of the great question before the public.

The Assembly of Virginia have passed the district Bill of which I formerly gave you an account. There are 18 districts, with 4 new Judges, Mr. Gabl. Jones, Richd. Parker, St. George Tucker and Jos. Prentis. They have reduced much the taxes, and provided some indulgences for debtors. The question of British debts underwent great vicissitudes. It was, after long discussion resolvd. by a majority of 30 agst. the utmost exertions of Mr. Henry that they shd. be paid as soon as the other States shd. have complied with the treaty. A few days afterwards he carried his point by a majority of 50 that G. B. should first comply. Adieu. Yrs. affecty.

P. S. Mr. St. John has given me a very interesting description of a System of Nature, lately published at Paris. Will you add it for me. The Boxes which were to have come for myself G. W. & [illegible] have not yet arrived.

Madison to Edmund Randolph, 1788*

Apr. 10, 1788

My dear Friend,

Since I got home which was on the day preceding our election, I have received your favor of the 29th of Feby., which did not reach New York before I had left it.

*The Writings of James Madison, pp. 117–18.

I view the amendments of Massachusetts pretty nearly in the same light that you do. They were meant for the people at large, not for the minority in the Convention. The latter were not affected by them; their objections being levelled against the very essence of the proposed Government. I do not see that the 2d amendment,[1] if I understand its scope, can be more exceptionable to the S. Sts than the others. I take it to mean that the number of Reps shall be limited to 200. who will be apportioned from time to time according to a census; not that the apportionment first made when the Reps. amount to that number shall be perpetual. The 9th. amendment[2] I have understood was made a very serious point of by S. Adams.

I do not know of anything in the new Constitution that can change the obligations of the public with regard to the old money. The principle on which it is to be settled, seems to be equally in the power of that as of the existing one. The claim of the Indiana Company cannot I should suppose be any more validated by the new System, than that of all the creditors and others who have been aggrieved by unjust laws. You do not mention what part of the Constitution, could give colour to such a doctrine. The condemnation of retrospective laws, if that be the part, does not appear to me, to admit on any principle of such a retrospective construction. As to the religious test, I should conceive that it can imply at most nothing more than that without that exception, a power would have been given to impose an oath involving a religious test as a qualification for office. The constitution of necessary offices being given to the Congress, the proper qualifications seem to be evidently involved. I think too there are several other satisfactory points of view in which the exception might be placed.

Madison to Randolph, 1788*

July 2, 1788

My dear Friend,

Some of the letters herewith enclosed have been here for some time without my knowing it. The others came to hand yesterday. I have also in hand for you the Marquis Condorcet's essai on the probability of decisions resulting from plurality of voices, which I understand from Mazzei is a gift from the author. I shall forward it by the first conveyance.

There are public letters just arrived from Jefferson. The contents are not

[1]"That there shall be one representative to every thirty thousand persons according to the Census mentioned in the Constitution until the whole number of Representatives amounts to two hundred."

[2]"Congress shall at no time consent that any person holding an office of trust or profit under the United States shall accept of a title of nobility or any other title or office from any King, prince or foreign state."

*The Writings of James Madison, pp. 235–36.

yet known. His private letters to me & others refer to his public political views. I find that he is becoming more and more a friend to the new Constitution, his objections being gradually dispelled by his own further reflections on the subject. He particularly renounces his opinion concerning the expediency of a ratification by 9 & a refusal by 4 States, considering the mode pursued by Massts. as the only rational one, but disapproving some of the alterations recommended by that State. He will see still more room for disapprobation in the reconsideration of other States. The defects of the Constitution which he continues to criticize are the omission of a bill of right, and of the principle of rotation at least in the Ex. Departmt.

Congress have been some days on the question where the first meeting of the new Congs. shall be placed. Philada. failed by a single voice from Delaware which ultimately aimed at that place, but wished to bring Wilmington into view. In that vote N. Hampshire & Connecticut both concurred. N. York is now in nomination and if those States accede which I think probable, and Rhode Island which has as yet refused to sit in the Question can be prevailed on to vote which I also think probable, the point will be carried. In this event a great handle I fear will be given to those who have opposed the new Govt. on account of the Eastern preponderancy in the federal system. I enclose a copy of the ratification as proposed of N. York. What think you of some of the expository articles?

MARYLAND RATIFYING CONVENTION, 1788

Commentary

Maryland, the seventh state to ratify the Constitution, did so on April 26, 1788. Although Maryland was the home state of Luther Martin, its Ratifying Convention contained a large Federalist majority. They were determined to ratify, and shouted down a motion made by William Paca to adopt proposed amendments to accompany the ratification: "Mr. Paca was not even permitted to read his amendments." Ratification was then voted 63 to 11. Paca renewed his proposition for amendments, saying he had voted for ratification "only . . . under the firm persuasion, and in full confidence that such amendments would be peacably obtained so as to enable the people to live happy under the government." A committee was appointed to draft "such amendments and alterations as may be thought necessary, in the proposed Constitution."

The committee recommended 13 proposed amendments. Fifteen others were rejected by the committee majority. The minority insisted on their right to present some of their amendments to the Convention, but the majority then decided to make no report of any amendments. The Convention majority voted not to consider any amendments and voted not even to record the yeas and nays. The minority, however, appealed to the court of public opinion and issued all 28 proposed amendments in pamphlet form. (The extracts which follow are from this minority Address, which appears to have been widely distributed. We know, for example, that a copy reached Jefferson.)

Though not officially adopted by the Maryland Convention, the proposed amendments of the Maryland committee were of great consequence. The proposals of the committee, as well as those of the minority, were another step in the direction of a federal Bill of Rights, for they went far beyond the minimal provisions contained in the Massachusetts proposed amendments. Most important, they apparently directly influenced the proposed amendments later recommended by Virginia, upon which Madison drew in writing his draft of the Bill of Rights. According to Judge Edward Dumbauld, the only Maryland proposals that were put forward for the first time (i.e., that were not taken from the Pennsylvania and Massachusetts proposals) and which were not included in those of Virginia were amendments 4, 6, 7 and 11 of the committee, and 1, 5 and 13 of the minority of the committee.

The Maryland-proposed amendments (both those accepted by the committee and those of the minority) appear adequately in the extracts which follow. Among them are the following guarantees later included in the federal Bill of Rights: A) Committee amendments— 1) limiting Congress to powers expressly delegated (another version of the Tenth Amendment); 2) providing trial by jury and against double jeopardy (the first protection against double jeopardy in the state-proposed amendments); 8) insuring against oathless warrants and general warrants (part of the guarantees included in the Fourth Amendment); 10) insuring against quartering of soldiers (the first guarantee in the state-proposed amendments of the right protected by the Third Amendment); 12) providing freedom of the press. B) Minority amendments—12) prohibiting the establishment of "national religion" and guaranteeing religious liberty (the first attempt to include a prohibition against establishment of religion in the state amendments); 14) insuring the right to petition for redress of grievances (again the first effort to include this right later protected by the First Amendment in a proposed state amendment).

Maryland Ratifying Convention, 1788*

Address to the People of Maryland.

The following facts, disclosing the conduct of the late Convention of Maryland, are submitted to the serious consideration of the citizens of the state.

On Monday, the 21st of April, the Convention met in Annapolis, and elected the Hon. George Plater, Esq., president. On Tuesday, they established rules for the conduct of business; and, on the same day, the following question was propounded to the Convention:

> When a motion is made and seconded, the matter of the motion shall receive a determination by the question, or be postponed, by general consent, or the previous question, before any other motion shall be received.

And the following question, viz.,

> Every question shall be entered on the journal; and the yeas and nays may be called for, by any member, on any question, and the name of the member requiring them shall be entered on the journal.

Which two questions the Convention determined in the negative.

On Wednesday, the proposed plan of government was read the first time, and thereupon it was resolved, "That this Convention will not enter into any resolution upon any particular part of the proposed plan of federal government for the United States; but that the whole thereof shall be read through a second time, after which the subject may be fully debated and considered; and then the president shall put the question, That this Convention do assent to and ratify the same Constitution." On which question, the yeas and nays shall be taken.

*The Debates in the Several State Conventions on the Adoption of the Constitution, Vol. 2, pp. 547–56.

On Thursday, the members who were opposed to the ratification of the Constitution, without such previous amendments could be obtained as they thought essentially necessary to secure the liberty and happiness of the people, (being confined, by the last resolution, to consider, in one view, the whole of the plan of government,) stated some of their objections to the Constitution. The Convention met in the evening, when Mr. Paca, member from Hartford, having just taken his seat, rose, and informed the president that he had great objections to the Constitution proposed, in its present form, and meant to propose a variety of amendments, not to prevent, but to accompany the ratification; but, having just arrived, he was not ready to lay them before the house; and requested indulgence, until the morning, for that purpose. The proposal being seconded, and the house asked if they would give the indulgence, it was granted without a division; and they adjourned for that purpose. On Friday, at the meeting of the house, Mr. Paca rose, and informed the president, that, in consequence of the permission of the house, given him the preceding evening, he had prepared certain amendments, which he would read in his place, and then lay on the table; when he was interrupted, and one member from each of the following counties, viz., Frederic, Talbot, Charles, Kent, Somerset, Prince George's, Worcester, Queen Anne's, Dorchester, Calvert, and Caroline, and one member from the city of Annapolis, and one from Baltimore town, arose in their places, and declared, for themselves and their colleagues, "that they were elected and instructed, by the people they represented, to ratify the proposed Constitution, and that as speedily as possible, and to do no other act; that, after the ratification, their power ceased, and they did not consider themselves as authorized by their constituents to consider any amendments." After this, Mr. Paca was not permitted even to read his amendments. The opponents continued to make their objections to the Constitution until Saturday noon. The advocates of the government, although repeatedly called on, and earnestly requested, to answer the objections, if not just, remained inflexibly silent, and called for the question, that "the Convention assent to and ratify the proposed plan of federal government for the United States;" which was carried in the affirmative, by sixty-three to eleven.

The vote of ratification having thus passed, Mr. Paca again rose, and laid before the Convention his propositions for amending the Constitution thus adopted, which he had prepared by leave of the house; declaring that he had only given his assent to the government under the firm persuasion, and in full confidence that such amendments would be peaceably obtained so as to enable the people to live happy under the government; that the people of the county he represented, and that he himself, would support the government, with such amendments; but, without them, not a man in the state, and no people, would be more firmly opposed to it than himself and those he represented. Sentiments highly favorable to amendments were expressed, and a general murmur of approbation seemed to arise from all parts of the

house, expressive of a desire to consider amendments, either in their characters as members of convention, or in their individual capacities as citizens;
and the question was put on the following motion:

> Resolved, That a committee be appointed to take into consideration,
> and report to this house on Monday morning next, a draught of such
> amendments and alterations as may be thought necessary, in the proposed
> Constitution for the United States, to be recommended to the consider-
> ation of the people of this state, if approved of by this Convention; and
> Mr. Paca, Mr. Johnson, Mr. S. Chase, Mr. Potts, Mr. Mercer, Mr.
> Goldsborough, Mr. Tilghman, Mr. Hanson, Mr. J. T. Chase, Mr. Lee,
> Mr. W. Tilghman, Mr. M'Henry, and Mr. G. Gale, be appointed a
> committee for that purpose.

A division was called for on this resolution, when there appeared sixty-six
members for, and not more than seven against it.

And then it was resolved, "That the amendments proposed to the Constitution by the delegate from Hartford county should be referred to the above
committee."

The committee thus appointed, the Convention adjourned to give them
time to prepare their propositions; and they proceeded, with every appearance of unanimity, to execute the trust reposed in them.

The following amendments to the proposed Constitution were separately
agreed to by the committee, most of them by a unanimous vote, and all of
them by a great majority.

1. That Congress shall exercise no power but what is expressly delegated
by this Constitution.

By this amendment, the general powers given to Congress by the first and
last paragraphs of the 8th sect. of art. 1, and the 2d paragraph of the 6th
article, would be in a great measure restrained; those dangerous expressions,
by which the bills of rights, and constitutions, of the several states may be
repealed by the laws of Congress, in some degree moderated; and the
exercise of constructive powers wholly prevented.

2. That there shall be a trial by jury in all criminal cases, according to the
course of proceeding in the state where the offence is committed; and that
there be no appeal from matter of fact, or second trial after acquittal; but
this provision shall not extend to such cases as may arise in the government
of the land or naval forces.

3. That, in all actions on debts or contracts, and in all other controversies
respecting property, of which the inferior federal courts have jurisdiction, the
trial of facts shall be by jury, if required by either party; and that it be
expressly declared that the state courts, in such cases, have a concurrent
jurisdiction with the federal courts, with an appeal from either, only as to
matter of law, to the Supreme Federal Court, if the matter in dispute be of
the value of   dollars.

4. That the inferior federal courts shall not have jurisdiction of less than   dollars; and there may be an appeal, in all cases of revenue, as well to matter of fact as law; and Congress may give the state courts jurisdiction of revenue cases, for such forms, and in such manner, as they may think proper.

5. That, in all cases of trespasses done within the body of a county, and within the inferior federal jurisdiction, the party injured shall be entitled to trial by jury in the state where the injury shall be committed; and that it be expressly declared that the state courts, in such cases, shall have concurrent jurisdiction with the federal courts, and there shall be no appeal from either, except on matter of law; and that no person be exempt from such jurisdiction and trial but ambassadors and ministers privileged by the law of nations.

6. That the federal courts shall not be entitled to jurisdiction by fictions or collusion.

7. That the federal judges do not hold any other office of profit, or receive the profits of any other office under Congress, during the time they hold their commission.

The great objects of these amendments were, 1st. To secure the trial by jury in all cases, the boasted birthright of Englishmen and their descendants, and the palladium of civil liberty; and to prevent the appeal from fact, which not only destroys that trial in civil cases, but, by construction, may also elude it in criminal cases—a mode of proceeding both expensive and burdensome, and which, by blending law with fact, will destroy all check on the judiciary authority, render it almost impossible to convict judges of corruption, and may lay the foundation of that gradual and silent attack on individuals, by which the approaches of tyranny become irresistible. 2d. To give a concurrent jurisdiction to the state courts, in order that Congress may not be compelled, as they will be under the present form, to establish inferior federal courts, which, if not numerous, are very expensive; the circumstances of the people being unequal to the increased expense of double courts and double officers—an arrangement that will render the law so complicated and confused, that few men can know how to conduct themselves with safety to their persons or property, the great and only security of freemen. 3d. To give such jurisdiction to the state courts that transient foreigners, and persons from other states, committing injuries in this state, may be amenable to the state whose laws they violate and whose citizens they injure. 4th. To prevent an extension of the federal jurisdiction, which may, and in all probability will, swallow up the state jurisdictions, and consequently sap those rules of descent and regulations of personal property, by which men hold their estates. And lastly, to secure the independence of the federal judges, to whom the happiness of the people of this great continent will be so greatly committed by the extensive powers assigned them.

8. That all warrants without oath, or affirmation of a person conscientiously scrupulous of taking an oath, to search suspected places, or seize any

person or his property, are grievous and oppressive; and all general warrants to search suspected places, or to apprehend any person suspected, without naming or describing the place or person in special, are dangerous, and ought not to be granted.

This amendment was considered indispensable by many of the committee; for, Congress having the power of laying excises, (the horror of a free people,) by which our dwelling houses, those castles considered so sacred by the English law, will be laid open to the insolence and oppression of office, there could be no constitutional check provided that would prove so effectual a safeguard to our citizens. General warrants, too, the great engine by which power may destroy those individuals who resist usurpation, are also hereby forbidden to those magistrates who are to administer the general government.

9. That no soldier be enlisted for a longer time than four years, except in time of war, and then only during the war.

10. That soldiers be not quartered, in time of peace, upon private houses, without the consent of the owners.

11. That no mutiny bill continue in force longer than two years.

These were the only checks that could be obtained against the unlimited power of raising and regulating standing armies, the natural enemies to freedom; and even with these restrictions, the new Congress will not be under such constitutional restraints as the Parliament of Great Britain—restraints which our ancestors have bled to establish, and which have hitherto preserved the liberty of their posterity.

12. That the freedom of the press be inviolably preserved.

In prosecutions in the federal courts for libels, the constitutional preservation of this great and fundamental right may prove invaluable.

13. That the militia shall not be subject to martial law, except in time of war, invasion, or rebellion.

This provision to restrain the powers of Congress over the militia, although by no means so ample as that provided by Magna Charta, and the other great fundamental and constitutional laws of Great Britain, (it being contrary to Magna Charta to punish a freeman by martial law, in time of peace, and murder to execute him,) yet it may prove an inestimable check; for all other provisions in favor of the rights of men would be vain and nugatory, if the power of subjecting all men, able to bear arms, to martial law at any moment should remain vested in Congress.

Thus far the amendments were agreed to.

The following amendments were laid before the committee, and negatived by a majority.

1. That the militia, unless selected by lot, or voluntarily enlisted, shall not be marched beyond the limits of an adjoining state, without the consent of their legislature or executive.

2. That the Congress shall have no power to alter or change the time,

place, or manner of holding elections for senators or representatives, unless a state shall neglect to make regulations, or to execute its regulations, or shall be prevented by invasion or rebellion; in which cases only, Congress may interfere, until the cause be removed.

3. That, in every law of Congress imposing direct taxes, the collection thereof shall be suspended for a certain reasonable time, therein limited and on payment of the sum by any state, by the time appointed, such taxes shall not be collected.

4. That no standing army shall be kept up in time of peace, unless with the consent of two thirds of the members present of each branch of Congress.

5. That the President shall not command the army in person, without the consent of Congress.

6. That no treaty shall be effectual to repeal or abrogate the constitutions or bills of rights of the states, or any part of them.

7. That no regulation of commerce, or navigation act, shall be made, unless with the consent of two thirds of the members of each branch of Congress.

8. That no member of Congress shall be eligible to any office of profit under Congress, during the time for which he shall be appointed.

9. That Congress shall have no power to lay a poll tax.

10. That no person conscientiously scrupulous of bearing arms, in any case, shall be compelled personally to serve as a soldier.

11. That there be a responsible council to the President.

12. That there be no national religion established by law; but that all persons be equally entitled to protection in their religious liberty.

13. That all imposts and duties laid by Congress shall be placed to the credit of the state in which the same shall be collected, and be deducted out of such state's quota of the common or general expenses of government.

14. That every man hath a right to petition the legislature for the redress of grievances, in a peaceable and orderly manner.

15. That it be declared, that all persons intrusted with the legislative or executive powers of government are the trustees and servants of the public; and, as such, accountable for their conduct. Wherefore, whenever the ends of government are perverted, and public liberty manifestly endangered, and all other means of redress are ineffectual, the people may, and of right ought to, reform the old, or establish a new government. The doctrine of non-resistance against arbitrary power and oppression is absurd, slavish, and destructive of the good and happiness of mankind.

The committee having proceeded thus far, all the members who voted for the ratification declared that they would engage themselves, under every tie of honor, to support the amendments they had agreed to, both in their public and private characters, until they should become a part of the general government; but a great majority of them insisted on this express condition, that none of the propositions rejected, or any others, should be laid before the Convention for their consideration, except those the committee had so agreed to.

The gentlemen of the minority, who had made the propositions which had been rejected, reduced to the necessity of accommodating their sentiments to the majority, through fear of obtaining no security whatever for the people, not withstanding they considered all the amendments as highly important to the welfare and happiness of the citizens of the states,—yet, to conciliate, they agreed to confine themselves to the first three of those propositions, and solemnly declared and pledged themselves, that, if these were added, and supported by other gentlemen, they would not only cease to oppose the government, but give all their assistance to carry it into execution so amended. Finally, they only required liberty to take the sense of the Convention on the first three propositions, agreeing that they would hold themselves bound by the decision of a majority of that body.

The first of these objections, concerning the militia, they considered as essential; for, to march beyond the limits of a neighboring state the general militia, which consists of so many poor people that can illy be spared from their families and domestic concerns, by power of Congress, (who could know nothing of their circumstances,) without consent of their own legislature or executive, ought to be restrained.

The second objection, respecting the power of Congress to alter elections, they thought indispensable. Montesquieu says that the rights of elections should be established unalterably by fundamental laws, in a free government.

The third objection, concerning previous requisitions, they conceived highly important: they thought, if the money required by direct taxation could be paid with certainty, and in due time, to Congress, that every good consequence would be secured to the Union, and the people of the state thereby relieved from the great inconvenience and expense of a double collection, and a double set of tax-gatherers, and they might also get rid of those odious taxes by excise and poll, without injury to the general government.

They were, however, again proposed and rejected.

> *Affirmative.* Mr. Paca, Mr. Johnson, Mr. Mercer, Mr. J. T. Chase, Mr. S. Chase.
> *Negative.* Mr. Lee, Mr. Potts, Mr. Goldsborough, Mr. J. T. Tilghman, Mr. W. Tilghman, Mr. Hanson, Mr. G. Gale, Mr. M'Henry.

Previous to this, a motion was made on Monday, the 29th, in the Convention, while the committee were sitting, in the following words, to wit:

> *Resolved,* That this Convention will consider of no propositions for amendment of the federal government, except such as shall be submitted to them by the committee of thirteen.

The committee being sent for by the Convention, the gentlemen of the majority in committee then determined that they would make no report of any amendments whatever, not even of those which they had almost unanimously agreed to; and the committee, under those circumstances, attended the house. Mr. Paca, as chairman, stated to the Convention what had passed in the committee, read the amendments which had there been agreed to, and assigned the reason why no report had been formally made. A member then rose, and proposed that a vote of thanks to the president, which had been once read before the attendance of the committee, should have a second reading; and upon the second reading thereof, the previous question was called for by the members who wished to consider the amendments agreed to by the committee, and such other amendments as might be proposed. The house thereupon divided, and the yeas and nays were called for by the minority; the sense of the Convention was taken thereon; and a majority determined that the yeas and nays should not be taken, nor would they permit the vote to be entered on the journal, by which the yeas and nays were prohibited; to preclude the consideration of any amendments.

A motion was then made, "that the Convention adjourn without day," on which the yeas and nays were taken, and appeared as follows:

> *Affirmative.* The Hon. the President, Messrs. Barns, Chilton, Sewel, W. Tilghman, Yates, Granger, Chesly, Smith, Brown, Turner, Stone, Goldsborough, Stevens, G. Gale, Waggaman, Stewart, J. Gale, Sulivane, Shaw, Gilpin, Hollingsworth, Heron, Evans, O. Sprigg, Hall, Digges, Hanson, J. Tilghman, Hollidat, Hemsley, Morris, Lee, Potts, Faw, J. Richardson, Edmondson, M'Henry, Coulter, T. Sprigg, Stull, Rawlins, Shryoch, Cramphin, Thomas, Deakins, Edwards. 47.
>
> *Negative.* Messrs. Perkins, J. T. Chase, S. Chase Mercer, Wilkinson, Grahame, Parnham, Ridgely, Cockey, Cromwell, Lloyd, Hammond, Bowie, Carroll, Seney, Chaile, Martin, Done, Johnson, Paca, Love, Pinckney, L. Martin, W. Richardson, Driver, and Harrison. 27.

We consider the proposed form of national government as very defective, and that the liberty and happiness of the people will be endangered if the system be not greatly changed and altered. The amendments agreed to by the committee, and those proposed by the minority, are now laid before you for your consideration, that you may express your sense as to such alterations as you may think proper to be made in the new Constitution.

We remain persuaded that the importance of the alterations proposed, calculated to preserve public liberty by those checks on power which the experience of ages has rendered venerable, and to promote the happiness of the people, by a due attention to their ease and convenience, will justify the steps we have taken, to obtain them, to our constituents and the world.

Having no interest that can distinguish us from the rest of the community, we neither fear censure nor wish applause. Having thus discharged the duty of citizens and trustees of the public, we shall now submit to the people those precautions and securities, which, on mature reflection on this momentous subject, we deem necessary for that safety and happiness.

May the all-wise and omnipotent Being, who made us masters of a fair and fruitful empire, inspire us with wisdom and fortitude to perpetuate to posterity that freedom which we received from our fathers!

Members of the Committee. William Paca, Samuel Chase, John F. Mercer, Jeremiah T. Chase.

Members of the Convention. John Love, Charles Ridgely, Edward Cockey, Nathan Cromwell, Charles Ridgely, of Wm., Luther Martin, Benjamin Harrison, Wm. Pinckney.

SOUTH CAROLINA RATIFYING CONVENTION, 1788

Commentary

South Carolina (the eighth state to ratify the federal Constitution) did so on May 23, 1788. The extracts which follow are from the debates in both the Legislature which called the Convention and the Ratifying Convention itself. The principal speaker for the Constitution in both debates was Charles Pinckney, who had (*supra* p. 437) attempted to provide specific protections for freedom of the press and from troop quartering in the framers' Convention. Little was said about the Bill of Rights issue (aside from some reference to trial by jury) until James Lincoln rose in the legislature and asked, "Why was not the Constitution ushered in with the bill of rights?" There was a total silence in the Constitution on fundamental rights—notably liberty of the press. "Are the people to have no rights?" Charles Cotesworth Pinckney answered with the familiar Federalist argument that a Bill of Rights was unnecessary, since the Federal Government had no power to infringe upon individual rights. He also made the shrewd argument (in a slaveholding state) that Bills of Rights "generally begin with declaring that all men are by nature born free. Now, we should make that declaration with a very bad grace, when a large part of our property consists in men who are actually born slaves."

Despite strong opposition, the South Carolina Convention voted for ratification by 149 to 73. As had been true in Massachusetts, the Federalists made the concession of adopting four recommendatory amendments. The only one which bears upon the federal Bill of Rights is another version of what later became the Tenth Amendment. The importance of the South Carolina proposals is not their substance (which was negligible) but the fact that they gave further impetus to the movement to have ratification accompanied by recommendatory amendments.

South Carolina Ratyfying Convention, 1788*

Debates

[Wednesday, January 16]

Read the proposed Federal Constitution, after which the house resolved itself into a committee of the whole. Hon. Thomas Bee in the chair.

*The Debates in the Several State Conventions on the Adoption of the Constitution, Vol. 4, pp. 253–340.

Hon. Charles Pinckney (one of the delegates of the Federal Convention) rose in his place, and said that, although the principles and expediency of the measures proposed by the late Convention will come more properly into discussion before another body, yet, as their appointment originated with them, and the legislatures must be the instrument of submitting the plan to the opinion of the people, it became a duty in their delegates to state with conciseness the motives which induced it.

*   *   *

For his part, he confessed that he ever treated all fears of aristocracies or despotisms, in the federal head, as the most childish shimeras that could be conceived. In a Union extensive as this is, composed of so many state governments, and inhabited by a people characterized, as our citizens are, by an impatience under any act which even looks like an infringement of their rights, an invasion of them by the federal head appeared to him the most remote of all our public dangers. So far from supposing a change of this sort at all probable, he confessed his apprehensions were of a different kind: he rather feared that it was impossible, while the state systems continue—and continue they must—to construct any government upon republican principles sufficiently energetic to extend its influence through all its parts. Near the federal seat, its influence may have complete effect; but he much doubted its efficacy in the more remote districts. The state governments will too naturally slide into an opposition against the general one, and be easily induced to consider themselves as rivals. They will, after a time, resist the collection of a revenue; and if the general government is obliged to concede, in the smallest degree, on this point, they will of course neglect their duties, and despise its authority: a great degree of weight and energy is necessary to enforce it; nor is any thing to be apprehended from them. All power being immediately derived from the people, and the state governments being the basis of the general one, it will easily be in their power to interfere, and to prevent its injuring or invading their rights. Though at first he considered some declaration on the subject of trial by jury in civil causes, and the freedom of the press, necessary, and still thinks it would have been as well to have had it inserted, yet he fully acquiesced in the reasoning which was used to show that the insertion of them was not essential. The distinction which has been taken between the nature of a federal and state government appeared to be conclusive—that in the former, no powers could be executed, or assumed, but such as were expressly delegated; that in the latter, the indefinite power was given to the government, except on points that were by express compact reserved to the people.

On the subject of juries, in civil cases, the Convention were anxious to make some declaration; but when they reflected that all courts of admiralty and appeals, being governed in their propriety by the civil law and the laws of nations, never had, or ought to have, juries, they found it impossible to make any precise declaration upon the subject; they therefore left it as it was, trusting that the good sense of their constituents would never induce them to suppose that it could be the interest or intention of the general government to abuse one of the most invaluable privileges a free country can boast; in the loss of which, themselves, their fortunes and connections, must be so materially involved, and to the deprivation of which, except in the cases alluded to, the people of this country would never submit.

*   *   *

Mr. Lowndes: . . . It was true, no article of the Constitution declared there should not be jury trials in civil cases; yet this must be implied, because it stated that all crimes, except in cases of impeachment, shall be tried by a jury. But even if trials by jury were allowed, could any person rest satisfied with a mode of trial which prevents the parties from being obliged to bring a cause for discussion before a jury of men chosen from the vicinage, in a manner comformable to the present administration of justice, which had stood the test of time and experience, and ever been highly approved of? Mr. Lowndes expatiated some time on the nature of compacts, the sacred light in which they were held by all nations, and solemnly called on the house to consider whether it would not be better to add strength to the old Confederation, instead of hastily adopting another; asking whether a man could be looked on as wise, who, possessing a magnificent building, upon discovering a flaw, instead of repairing the injury, should pull it down, and build another. Indeed, he could not understand with what propriety the Convention proceeded to change the Confederation; for every person with whom he had conversed on this subject concurred in opinion that the sole object of appointing a convention was to inquire what alterations were necessary in the Confederation, in order that it might answer those salutary purposes for which it was originally intended.

*   *   *

Mr. Barnwell: . . . The honorable gentleman asks why the trial by jury was not established in every instance. Mr. Barnwell considered this right of trial as the birthright of every American, and the basis of our civil liberty; but still most certainly particular circumstances may arise, which would induce even the greatest advocates for this right to yield it for a time. In his opinion, the circumstances that would lead to this point were those which are specified by the Constitution. Mr. Barnwell said, Suffer me to state a case, and let every gentleman determine whether, in particular instances, he would not rather resign than retain this right of trial. A suit is depending between a citizen of Carolina and Georgia, and it becomes necessary to try it in Georgia. What is the consequence? Why, the citizen of this state must rest his cause upon the jury of his opponent's vicinage, where, unknown and unrelated, he stands a very poor chance for justice against one whose neighbors, whose friends and relations, compose the greater part of his judges. It is in this case, and only in cases of a similar nature with this, that the right of trial by jury is not established; and judging from myself, it is in this instance only that every man would wish to resign it, not to a jury with whom he is unacquainted, but to an impartial and responsible individual.

*   *   *

Mr. Pinckney: . . . As to the judiciary department, General Pinckney observed, that trial by jury was so deservedly esteemed by the people of America, that it is impossible for their representatives to omit introducing it whenever it can with propriety be done. In appeals from courts of chancery, it surely would be improper. In a dispute between a citizen of Carolina and a citizen of Georgia, if a jury was to try the case, from which state are they to be drawn? If from both or either, would the citizens of Carolina and Georgia choose to be summoned to attend on juries eight hundred miles from their home? and if the jury is to be drawn from the state in which Congress shall sit, would these citizens wish that a cause relative to negro property should be tried by the Quakers of Pennsylvania, or by the freeholders of those states that have not that species of property amongst them? Surely not. Yet it is necessary, when a citizen of one state cannot obtain an impartial trial in another, that, for the sake of justice, he should have a right to appeal to the supreme judiciary of the United States to obtain redress; and as this right of appeal does not extend to citizens of the same state, (unless they claim under grants of different states,) but only to the causes and persons particularly mentioned in the Constitution, and Congress have power to make such regulations and impose such restrictions relative to appeals as they think proper, it can hardly be supposed that they will exercise it in a manner injurious to their constituents.

Trials by jury are expressly secured in all criminal cases, and not excluded in any civil cases whatsoever. But experience had demonstrated that it was impossible to adhere to them in all civil cases: for instance, on the first establishment of the admiralty jurisdiction, Congress passed an ordinance requiring all causes of capture to be decided by juries: this was contrary to the practice of all nations, and we knew it; but still an attachment to a trial by jury induced the experiment. What was the consequence? The property of our friends was, at times, condemned indiscriminately with the property of our enemies, and the property of our citizens of one state by the juries of another. Some of our citizens have severely felt these inconveniences. Citizens of other states and other powers experienced similar misfortunes from this mode of trial. It was, therefore, by universal consent and approbation, laid aside in cases of capture. As the ordinance which regulated these trials was passed by Congress, they had the power of altering it, and they exercised that power; but had that ordinance been part of the Confederation, it could not then have been repealed in the then situation of America; and had a clause of a similar tendency been inserted in this Constitution, it could only be altered by a convention of the different states. This shows at once how improper it would have been to have descended to *minutiae* in this particular; and he trusted it was unnecessary, because the laws which are to regulate trials must be made by the representatives of the people chosen as this house are, and as amenable as they are for every part of their conduct. The honorable gentleman says, compacts should be binding, and that the Confederation was a compact. It was so; but it was a compact that had been repeatedly broken by every state in the Union; and all the writers on the laws of nations agree that, when the parties to a treaty violate it, it is no longer binding. This was the case with the old Confederation; it was virtually dissolved, and it became necessary to form a new constitution, to render us secure at home, respectable abroad, and to give us that station among the nations of the world, to which, as free and independent people, we are justly entitled.

*   *   *

Hon. James Lincoln, of Ninety-six, declared, that if ever any person rose in a public assembly with diffidence, he then did; if ever any person felt himself deeply interested in what he thought a good cause, and at the same time lamented the want of abilities to support it, it was he. On a question on which gentlemen, whose abilities would do honor to the senate of ancient Rome, had enlarged with so much eloquence and learning, who could venture without anxiety and diffidence? He had not the vanity to oppose his opinion to such men; he had not the vanity to suppose he could place this business in any new light; but the justice he owed to his constituents—the justice he owed to his own feelings, which would perhaps upbraid him hereafter, if he indulged himself so far as to give merely a silent vote on this great question—impelled him, reluctantly impelled him, to intrude himself on the house. He had, for some years past, turned his thoughts towards the politics of this country; he long since perceived that not only the federal but the state Constitution required much the hand of correction and revision. They were both formed in times of confusion and distress, and it was a matter of wonder they were so free from defects as we found them. That they were imperfect, no one would deny; and that something must be done to remedy those imperfections, was also evident; but great care should be taken that, by endeavoring to do some good, we should not do an infinite deal of mischief. He had listened with eager attention to all the arguments in favor of the Constitution; but he solemnly declared that the more he heard, the more he was persuaded of its evil tendency. What does this proposed Constitution do? It changes, totally changes, the form of your present government. From a well-digested, well-formed democratic, you are at once rushing into an aristocratic government. What have you been contending for these ten years past? Liberty! What is liberty? The power of governing yourselves. If you adopt this Constitution, have you this power? No: you give it into the hands of a set of men who live one thousand miles distant from you. Let the people but once trust their liberties out of their own hands, and what will be the consequence? First, a haughty, imperious aristocracy; and ultimately, a tyrannical monarchy. No people on earth are, at this day, so free as the people of America. All other nations are, more or less, in a state of slavery. They owe their constitutions partly to chance, and partly to the sword; but that of America is the offspring of their choice—the darling of their bosom: and was there ever an instance in the world that a people in this situation, possessing all that Heaven could give on earth, all that human wisdom and valor could procure—was there ever a people so situated, as calmly and deliberately to convene themselves together for the express purpose of considering whether they should give away or retain those inestimable blessings? In the name of God, were we a parcel of children, who would cry and quarrel for a hobbyhorse, which, when we were once in possession of, we quarrel with and throw it away? It is said this Constitution is an experiment; but all regular-bred physicians are cautious of experiments. If the constitution be crazed a little, or somewhat feeble, is it therefore necessary to kill it in order to cure it? Surely not. There are many parts of this Constitution he objected to: some few of them had not been mentioned; he would therefore request some information thereon. The President holds his employment for four years; but he may hold it for fourteen times four years: in short, he may hold it so long that it will be impossible, without another revolution, to displace him. You do not put the same check on him that you do on your own state governor—a man born and bred among you; a man over whom you have a continual and watchful eye; a man who, from the very nature of his situation, it is almost impossible can do you any injury: this man, you say, shall not be elected for more than four years; and yet this mighty, this omnipotent governor-general may be elected for years and years.

He would be glad to know why, in this Constitution, there is a total silence with regard to the liberty of the press. Was it forgotten? Impossible! Then it must have been purposely omitted; and with what design, good or bad, he left the world to judge. The liberty of the press was the tyrant's scourge—it was the true friend and firmest supporter of civil liberty; therefore why pass it by in silence? He perceived that not till almost the very end of the Constitution was there any provision made for the nature or form of government we were to live under: he contended it should have been the very first article; it should have been, as it were, the groundwork or foundation on which it should have been built. But how is it? At the very end of the Constitution, there is a clause which says,—"The Congress of the United States shall guaranty to each state a republican form of government." But pray, who are the United States?—A President and four or five senators? Pray, sir, what security have we for a republican form of government, when it depends on the mere will and pleasure of a few men, who, with an army, navy, and rich treasury at their back, may change and alter it as they please? It may be said they will be sworn. Sir, the king of Great Britain, at his coronation, swore to govern his subjects with justice and mercy. We were then his subjects, and continued so for a long time after. He would be glad to know how he observed his oath. If, then, the king of Great Britain forswore himself, what security have we that a future President and four or five senators—men like himself—will think more solemnly of so sacred an obligation than he did?

Why was not this Constitution ushered in with the bill of rights? Are the people to have no rights? Perhaps this same President and Senate would, by and by, declare them. He much feared they would. He concluded by returning his hearty thanks to the gentleman who had so nobly opposed this Constitution: it was supporting the cause of the people; and if ever any one deserved the title of man of the people, he, on this occasion, most certainly did.

Gen. Charles Cotesworth Pinckney answered Mr. Lincoln on his objections. He said, that the time for which the President should hold his office, and whether he should be reeligible, had been fully discussed in the Convention. It had been once agreed to by a majority, that he should hold his office for the term of seven years, but should not be reelected a second time. But upon reconsidering that article, it was thought that to cut off all hopes from a man of serving again in that elevated station, might render him dangerous, or perhaps indifferent to the faithful discharge of his duty. His term of service might expire during the raging of war, when he might, perhaps, be the most capable man in America to conduct it; and would it be wise and prudent to declare in our Constitution that such a man should not again direct our military operations, though our success might be owing to his abilities? The mode of electing the President rendered undue influence almost impossible; and it would have been imprudent in us to have put it out of our power to reelect a man whose talents, abilities, and integrity, were such as to render him the object of the general choice of his country. With regard to the liberty of the press, the discussion of that matter was not forgotten by the members of the Convention. It was fully debated, and the impropriety of saying any thing about it in the Constitution clearly evinced. The general government has no powers but what are expressly granted to it; it therefore has no power to take away the liberty of the press. That invaluable blessing, which deserves all the encomiums the gentleman has justly bestowed upon it, is secured by all our state constitutions; and to have mentioned it in our general Constitution would perhaps furnish an argument, hereafter, that the general government had a right to exercise powers not expressly delegated to it. For the same reason, we had no bill of rights inserted in our Constitution; for, as we might perhaps have omitted the enumeration of some of our rights, it might hereafter be said we had delegated to the general government a power to take away such of our rights as we had not enumerated; but by delegating express powers, we certainly reserve to ourselves every power and right not mentioned in the Constitution. Another reason weighed particularly, with the members from this state, against the insertion of a bill of rights. Such bills generally begin with declaring that all men are by nature born free. Now, we should make that declaration with a very bad grace, when a large part of our property consists in men who are actually born slaves. As to the clause guarantying to each state a republican form of government being inserted near the end of the Constitution, the general observed that it was as binding as if it had been inserted in the first article. The Constitution takes its effect from the ratification, and every part of it is to be ratified at the same time, and not one clause before the other; but he thought there was a peculiar propriety in inserting it where it was, as it was necessary to form the government before that government could guaranty any thing.

Col. Mason thanked Mr. Lowndes for his opposition, by the desire of several gentlemen, members of that house. It had drawn forth from the other side most valuable information, and he thanked those gentlemen for the willingness with which they had given it, with so much good-nature. Those gentlemen who lived in the country were now enabled to satisfy their constituents.

The question being put, that a convention of the people should be called for the purpose of considering, and of ratifying or rejecting, the Constitution framed for the United States by a Convention of delegates assembled at Philadelphia in May last, it was unanimously agreed to.

[There will appear some omissions in what fell from Mr. Lowndes, which could not be supplied, owing to the loss of a note-book in the fire which consumed the State-House.]

[Saturday, January 19]

On the question being put for the Convention to assemble in Charleston on Monday, the 12th day of May next, the ayes and nays were as follows, viz.: Ayes, 76; Nays, 75.

So it was resolved in the affirmative.

[Monday, May 12]

This day being appointed for the meeting of the state Convention, (Mr. Thomas Bee, in the chair, *pro tem.*,) the returns were read, and there not being a majority, adjourned until Tuesday, the 13th.

[Tuesday, May 13]

On this day the Convention met, and the names being called over, there appeared to be present one hundred and seventy-three members; upon which they proceeded to ballot, when

His excellency, Governor Thomas Pinckney, was elected President.

Colonel John Sandford Dart was elected Secretary.

Mr. Atmore, Messenger. Mr. Athwell, Door-keeper. Mr. John Bounetheau, Bar-keeper. Mr. Stevens, Cashier. Colonel Lushington, Assistant-Cashier.

[Wednesday, May 14]

Speech of Charles Pinckney

Mr. President, after so much has been said with respect to the powers possessed by the late Convention to form and propose a new system—after so many observations have been made on its leading principles, as well in the House of Representatives as in the conventions of other states, whose proceedings have been published—it will be as unnecessary for me again minutely to examine a subject which has been so thoroughly investigated, as it would be difficult to carry you into a field that has not been sufficiently explored.

Having, however, had the honor of being associated in the delegation from this state, and presuming upon the indulgence of the house, I shall proceed to make some observations which appear to me necessary to a full and candid discussion of the system now before us.

It seems to be generally confessed that, of all sciences, that of government, or politics, is the most difficult. In the old world, as far as the lights of history extend, from the earliest ages to our own, we find nations in the constant exercise of all the forms with which the world is at present furnished. We have seen among the ancients, as well as the moderns, monarchies, limited and absolute, aristocracies, republics of a single state, and federal unions. But notwithstanding all their experience, how confined and imperfect is their knowledge of government! how little is the true doctrine of representation understood! how few states enjoy what we call freedom! how few governments answer those great ends of public happiness which we seem to expect from our own!

In reviewing such of the European states as we are best acquainted with, we may with truth assert that there is but one among the most important which confirms to its citizens their civil liberties, or provides for the security of private rights. But as if it had been fated that we should be the first perfectly free people the world had ever seen, even the government I have alluded to withholds from a part of its subjects the equal enjoyment of their religious liberties. How many thousands of the subjects of Great Britain at this moment labor under civil disabilities, merely on account of their religious persuasions! To the liberal and enlightened mind, the rest of Europe affords a melancholy picture of the depravity of human nature, and of the total subversion of those rights, without which we should suppose no people could be happy or content.

We have been taught here to believe that all power of right belongs to the people; that it flows immediately from them, and is delegated to their officers for the public good; that our rulers are the servants of the people, amenable to their will, and created for their use. How different are the governments of Europe! There the people are the servants and subjects of their rulers; there merit and talents have little or no influence; but all the honors and offices of government are swallowed up by birth, by fortune, or by rank.

From the European world are no precedents to be drawn for a people who think they are capable of governing themselves. Instead of receiving instruction from them, we may, with pride, affirm that, new as this country is in point of settlement, inexperienced as she must be upon questions of government, she still has read more useful lessons to the old world, she has made them more acquainted with their own rights, than they had been otherwise for centuries. It is with pride I repeat that, old and experienced as they are, they are indebted to us for light and refinement upon points of all others the most interesting.

*   *   *

. . . We know that all the states have adhered, in their forms, to the republican principle, though they have differed widely in their opinions of the mode best calculated to preserve it.

In Pennsylvania and Georgia, the whole powers of government are lodged in a legislative body, of a single branch, over which there is no control; nor are their executives or judicials, from their connection and necessary dependence on the legislature, capable of strictly executing their respective offices. In all the other states, except Maryland, Massachusetts, and New York, they are only so far improved as to have a legislature with two branches, which completely involve and swallow up all the powers of their government. In neither of these are the judicial or executive placed in that firm or independent situation which can alone secure the safety of the people or the just administration of the laws. In Maryland, one branch of their legislature is a Senate, chosen, for five years, by electors chosen by the people. The knowledge and firmness which this body have, upon all occasions, displayed, not only in the exercise of their legislative duties, but in withstanding and defeating such of the projects of the other house as appeared to them founded in local and personal motives, have long since convinced me that the Senate of Maryland is the best model of a senate that has yet been offered to the Union; that it is capable of correcting many of the vices of the other parts of their Constitution, and, in a great measure, atoning for those defects which, in common with the states I have mentioned, are but too evident in their execution—the want of stability and independence in the judicial and executive departments.

In Massachusetts, we find the principle of legislation more improved by the revisionary power which is given to their governor, and the independence of their judges.

In New York, the same improvement in legislation has taken place as in Massachusetts; but here, from the executive's being elected by the great body of the people; holding his office for three years, and being reeligible; from the appointment to offices being taken from the legislature and placed in a select council,—I think their Constitution is, upon the whole, the best in the Union. Its faults are the want of permanent salaries to their judges, and giving to their executive the nomination to offices, which is, in fact, giving him the appointment.

It does not, however, appear to me, that this can be called a vice of their system, as I have always been of opinion that the insisting upon the right to nominate was a usurpation of their executive's, not warranted by the letter or meaning of their Constitution.

These are the outlines of their various forms, in few of which are their executive or judicial departments wisely constructed, or that solid distinction adopted between the branches of their legislative which can alone provide for the influence of different principles in the operation.

In every government there necessarily exists a power from which there is no appeal, and which, for that reason, may be formed absolute and uncontrollable.

The person or assembly in whom this power resides is territory. We know of none a tenth part so large as the United States; indeed, we are hardly able to determine, from the lights we are furnished with, whether the governments we have heard of under the names of republics really deserved them, or whether the ancients ever had any just or proper ideas upon the subject. Of the doctrine of representation, the fundamental of a republic, they certainly were ignorant. If they were in possession of any other safe or practicable principles, they have long since been lost and forgotten to the world. Among the other honors, therefore, that have been reserved for the American Union, not the least considerable of them is that of defining a mixed system, by which a people may govern themselves, possessing all the virtues and benefits, and avoiding all the dangers and inconveniences, of the three simple forms.

*   *   *

I trust that, when we proceed to review the system by sections, it will be found to contain all those necessary provisions and restraints, which, while they enable the general government to guard and protect our common rights as a nation, to restore to us those blessings of commerce and mutual confidence which have been so long removed and impaired, will secure to us those rights, which, as the citizens of a state, will make us happy and content at home—as the citizens of the Union, respectable abroad.

How different, Mr. President, is this government constructed from any we have known among us!

In their individual capacities as citizens, the people are proportionably represented in the House of Representatives. Here they who are to pay to support the expenses of government, have the purse-strings in their hands; here the people hold, and feel that they possess, an influence sufficiently powerful to prevent every undue attempt of the other branches, to maintain that weight in the political scale which, as the source of all authority, they should ever possess; here, too, the states, whose existence as such we have often heard predicted as precarious, will find, in the Senate, the guards of their rights as political associations.

On them (I mean the state systems) rests the general fabric: on their foundation is this magnificent structure of freedom erected, each depending upon, supporting, and protecting the other: nor—so intimate is the connection—can the one be removed without prostrating the other in ruin: like the head and the body, separate them and they die.

Far be it from me to suppose that such an attempt should ever be made, the good sense and virtue of our country forbid the idea. To the Union we will look up, as to the temple of our freedom—a temple founded in the affections, and supported by the virtue, of the people. Here we will pour out our gratitude to the Author of all good, for suffering us to participate in the rights of a people who govern themselves.

Is there, at this moment, a nation upon earth that enjoys this right, where the true principles of representation are understood and practised, and where all authority flows from and returns at stated periods to, the people? I answer, there is not. Can a government be said to be free where these rights do not exist? It cannot. On what depends the enjoyment of these rare, these inestimable privileges? On the firmness, on the power, of the Union to protect and defend them.

How grateful, then, should we be, that, at this important period,—a period important, not to us alone, but to the general rights of mankind,—so much harmony and concession should prevail throughout the states; that the public opinion should be so much actuated by candor, and an attention to their general interests; that, disdaining to be governed by the narrow motives of state policy, they have liberally determined to dedicate a part of their advantages to the support of that government from which they received them! To fraud, to force, or accident, all the governments we know have owed their births. To the philosophic mind, how new and awful an instance do the United States at present exhibit in the political world! They exhibit, sir, the first instance of a people, who, being dissatisfied with their government,—unattacked by foreign force, and undisturbed by domestic uneasiness,—coolly and deliberately resort to the virtue and good sense of their country, for a correction of their public errors.

It must be obvious that, without a superintending government, it is impossible the liberties of this country can long be secured.

Single and unconnected, how weak and contemptible are the largest of our states!—how unable to protect themselves from external or domestic insult! How incompetent to national purposes would even partial union be!—how liable to intestine wars and confusion!—how little able to secure the blessings of peace!

Let us, therefore, be careful in strengthening the Union. Let us remember that we are bounded by vigilant and attentive neighbors, who view with a jealous eye our rise to empire.

Let us remember that we are bound, in gratitude to our northern brethren, to aid them in the recovery of those rights which they have lost in obtaining for us an extension of our commerce, and the security of our liberties. Let us not be unmindful that those who are weak, and may expect support, must, in their turn, be ready to afford it.

We are called upon to execute an important trust—to examine the principles of the Constitution now before you, and, in the name of the people, to receive or reject it.

I have no doubt we shall do this with attention and harmony; and flatter myself that, at the conclusion of our discussion, we shall find that it is not only expedient, but safe and honorable, to adopt it.

[Tuesday, May 20]

This day the Convention went through the discussion of the Federal Constitution by paragraphs.

Mr. Alexander Tweed, of Prince Frederick, said: Since I came to town, I have more than once heard it asserted, that the representatives of the parish of Prince Frederick were, prior to their election, put under promise to their constituents, that they should by no means give their sanction to the adoption of the new Constitution. Any such restriction, sir, on my own part, I deny. Had they taken upon them so far as to dictate for me, I should have spurned at the idea, and treated such proposals with that contempt they would have justly merited; and I am clearly of opinion, and I think warranted to say, that these are the sentiments and situation of (at least) some others of my colleagues. Notwithstanding, sir, from all I have heard or can learn, the general voice of the people is against it. For my own part, Mr. President, I came not here to echo the voice of my constituents, nor determined to approve or put a negative upon the Constitution proposed. I came with a mind open to conviction, in order to hear what, in the course of the debates of this house, might be said for and against it. Much, very much, sir, has been advanced on both sides. The matter in hand I look upon to be the most important and momentous that ever came before the representatives of the people of South Carolina. We were told, sir, some days ago, by a learned and honorable gentleman now on the floor, that, as our case at present stood, we must adopt the Constitution proposed; for, if we did not, in all probability some powerful despot might start up and seize the reins of government. Another learned and honorable gentleman on my left hand said, we must look up to it as the rock of our salvation. To make short, sir, *necessitas non habet legem* was the word.

Those gentlemen, Mr. President, and some others, members of this respectable Convention,—whose profound oratory and elocution would, on the journals of a British House of Commons, stand as lasting monuments of their great abilities,—a man of my circumscribed scale of talents is not adequate to the task of contending with; nor have I a turn for embellishing my language, or bedecking it with all the flowers of rhetoric. In a word, Mr. President, my idea of the matter now under our consideration is, that we very much stand in need of a reform of government, as the very sinews of our present constitution are relaxed. But, sir, I would fondly hope that our case is not so bad as represented. Are we invaded by a foreign enemy? Or are the bowels of our country torn to pieces by insurrections and intestine broils? I answer, No.

Sir, admit but this, and then allow me to ask if history furnishes us with a single instance of any nation, state, or people, who had it more in their power than we at present have to frame for ourselves a perfect, permanent, free, and happy constitution. The Constitution, sir, now under consideration, was framed (I shall say) by the wisdom of a General Convention of the United States; it now lies before us to wait our concurrence or disapprobation. We, sir, as citizens and freemen, have an undoubted right of judging for ourselves; it therefore behoves us most seriously to consider, before we determine a matter of such vast magnitude. We are not acting for ourselves alone, but to all appearance, for generations unborn.

Mr. Dollard: . . . They are nearly all, to a man, opposed to this new Constitution, because, they say, they have omitted to insert a bill of rights therein, ascertaining and fundamentally establishing, the unalienable rights of men, without a full, free, and secure enjoyment of which there can be no liberty, and over which it is not necessary that a good government should have the control. They say that they are by no means against vesting Congress with ample and sufficient powers; but to make over to them, or any set of men, their birthright, comprised in Magna Charta, which this new Constitution absolutely does, they can never agree to. Notwithstanding this, they have the highest opinion of the virtues and abilities of the honorable gentlemen from this state, who represented us in the General Convention; and also a few other distinguished characters, whose names will be transmitted with honor to future ages; but I believe, at the same time, they are but mortal, and, therefore, liable to err; and as the virtue and abilities of those gentlemen will consequently recommend their being first employed in jointly conducting the reins of this government, they are led to believe it will

commence in a moderate aristocracy: but, that it will, in its future operations, produce a monarchy, or a corrupt and oppressive aristocracy, they
have no manner of doubt. Lust of dominion is natural in every soil, and the
love of power and superiority is as prevailing in the United States, at
present, as in any part of the earth; yet in this country; depraved as it is,
there still remains a strong regard for liberty: an American bosom is apt to
glow at the sound of it, and the splendid merit of preserving that best gift of
God, which is mostly expelled from every country in Europe, might stimulate
Indolence, and animate even Luxury to consecrate herself at the altar of
freedom.

My constituents are highly alarmed at the large and rapid strides which
this new government has taken towards despotism. They say it is big with
political mischiefs, and pregnant with a greater variety of impending woes to
the good people of the Southern States, especially South Carolina, than all
the plagues supposed to issue from the poisonous box of Pandora. They say
it is particularly calculated for the meridian of despotic aristocracy; that it
evidently tends to promote the ambitious views of a few able and designing
men, and enslave the rest; that it carries with it the appearance of an old
phrase, formerly made use of in despotic reigns, and especially by Archbish-
op Laud, in the reign of Charles I., that is, "non-resistance." They say they
will resist against it; that they will not accept of it unless compelled by force
of arms, which this new Constitution plainly threatens; and then, they say,
your standing army, like Turkish janizaries enforcing despotic laws, must
ram it down their throats with the points of bayonets. They warn the
gentlemen of this Convention, as the guardians of their liberty, to beware
how they will be accessory to the disposal of, or rather sacrificing, their
dear-bought rights and privileges. This is the sense and language, Mr.
President, of the people; and it is an old saying, and I believe a very true
one, that the general voice of the people is the voice of God. The general
voice of the people to whom I am responsible, is against it. I shall never betray the trust resposed in me by them; therefore, shall give my hearty dissent.

[Wednesday, May 21]

Gen. Sumpter, agreeably to notice given yesterday, (Tuesday, 20th,)
moved for an adjournment of the Convention to the (20th October) twentieth day of October next, in order to give time for the further consideration of
the Federal Constitution. After considerable debate, it was rejected by a
majority of (46) forty-six—yeas, eighty-nine, (89;) nays, one hundred and
thirty-five (135).

[Friday, May 23]

On motion, Resolved, That this Convention do assent to and ratify the

Constitution agreed to on the 17th day of September last, by the Convention of the United States of America, held at Philadelphia.

On the question being put to agree to the same, the yeas and nays were called for by the unanimous voice of the Convention, and are as follows.

For the Parishes of St. Philip and St. Michael, Charleston.—Yeas: His excellency, Governor Thomas Pinckney, did not vote. Lieutenant-Governor Thomas Gadsden, C. C. Pinckney, (general,) Christopher Gadsden, (general—member of Congress of '65, at New York,) Edward Rutledge, (governor—one of the Congress of '76,) David Ramsay, (Dr.,) Thomas Heyward, Jun., (judge—and one of the Congress of '76,) Edward Darrell, Isaac Motte, John Mathews, (governor,) Edward Blake, Thomas Bee, (judge,) Daniel De Soussure, Thomas Jones, John F. Grimke (judge,) William Johnson, John J. Pringle, (attorney-general,) John Blake, Daniel Stevens, Daniel Cannon, Anthony Toomer, Hugh Rutledge, (judge,) John Budd, (Dr.,) Francis Kinloch, Thomas Sommersall, Michael Kalteisen, (captain of Fort Johnson,) Richard Lushington, (colonel,) Nathaniel Russel, Josiah Smith, Lewis Morris, Edward Lightwood, John Edwards. 31

Christ Church.—Yeas: Hon. Charles Pinckney, Hon. John Rutledge, Hon. A. Vanderhorst, William Read, Joseph Manigault, Jacob Read, Joshua Toomer. 7.

St. John's, Berkley.—Yeas: Hon. Henry Laurens, Gen. William Moultrie, Henry Laurens, Jun. 3.—Nays: Peter Fayssoux, Keating Simons, Thomas Walter. 3.—Absent: Francis Marion. 1.

St. Andrew's.—Yeas: Glen Drayton, Hon. Richard Hutson, Thomas Fuller, James Ladson, Ralph Izard, Jun., Charles Drayton, Hon. William Scott. 7.—Nays: none.

St. George's, Dorchester.—Yeas: John Glaze, Morton Waring, Thomas Warring, Maj. J. Postell, William Postell, Mathias Hutchinson, John Dawson. 7.—Nays: none.

St. James's, Goose Creek.—Yeas: Hon. Ralph Izard, Peter Smith, Hon. Benjamin Smith, Gabriel Manigault, William Smith, J. Parker, Jun., J. Deas, Jun. 7.—Nays: none.

St. Thomas and St. Dennis.—Yeas: Hon. John Huger, Thomas Karwon, Thomas Screven, Robert Daniel, Lewis Fogartie, Issac Harleston, Issac Parker.—Nays: none.

St. Paul's Parish.—Yeas. Paul Hamilton, George Haig, Joseph Slann, Roger Parker Saunders, William Washington, (hero of Eutaw and Cowpens.)—Nays: John Wilson, Hon. Melcher Garner. 2.

St. Bartholomew's.—Yeas: Hon. John Lloyd, John Crosskeys.—Nays: Benjamin Postell, William Clay Snipes, O'Brien Smith, Paul Walter, Edmund Bellinger. 5.

St. Helena's.—Yeas: Hon. John Barnwell, Hon. John Joyner, Hon. John Kean, Hon. William H. Wigg, Hon. Robert Barnwell, Hon. William Elliott, Hon. James Stuart. 7.—Nays: none.

St. James's, Santee.—Yeas. Isaac Dubose, Lewis Miles, Samuel Warren, Richard Withers, John Mayrant, Thomas Horry. 6.—Nay: John Bowman. 1.

Prince George's, Winyaw.—Yeas: Hon. Thomas Waties, (judge of C. C. P., and chancellor,) Samuel Smith, Cleland Kinloch, Hon. William Allston, Jun. 4.—Nays: none.—Absent: Peter Horry. 1.

All Saints'.—Yeas: Daniel Morral, Thomas Allston. 2.—Nays: none.

Prince Frederick's.—Yeas: William Wilson, Alexander Tweed, William Frierson, James Pettigrew. 4.—Nays: Patrick Dollard, William Read, J. Burges, Jun. 3.

St. John's, Colleton County.—Yeas: Thomas Legare, Richard Muncreef, Jun., Hon. Daniel Jenkins, Hugh Wilson, Isaac Jenkins, Ephraim Mikel, William Smelie.—Nays: none.

St. Peter's.—Yeas: John Fenwick, Joachin Hartstone, Seth Stafford, Rev. Henry Holcom. 4.—Nays: John Chisholm, John Lewis Bourjin, Jun. 2.—Absent: William Stafford. 1.

Prince William's.—Yeas: Thomas Hutson, John M'Pherson, James Maine, John A. Cuthbert, John Lightwood, John Simmons, Stephen Devaux. 7.—Nays: none.

St. Stephen's.—Yeas: John Palmer, Hon. Hezekiah Mahams, Samuel Dubose, John Peyre. 4.—Nays: none.—Absent: Thomas Cooper, Thomas Palmer. 1 vacant.

District Eastward of the Wateree.—Yea: John Chesnut. 1.—Nays: Thomas Sumter, Andrew Baskins, John Lowry, Benjamin Cudworth, William Massay, Hugh White, Thomas Dunlap, Samuel Dunlap, John Montgomery. 9.—Absent: S. Boykin.

District of Ninety-six.—Yea: Dr. John Harris. 1.—Nays: James Lincoln, Adam Crain Jones, Edmond Martin, Andrew Hamilton, Joseph Calhoun, William Butler, John Bowie, Hon. John L. Gervais. 8.—Absent: John Ewing Calhoun, Charles Davenport. 2.

North Side of Saluda.—Yeas: Samuel Earle, Lemuel J. Allstone, John Thomas, Jun. 3.—Nays: none.

South Side of Saluda.—Yeas: John Miller, William M'Caleb. 2.—Nays: none.—Absent: Robert Anderson. 1.

District of Saxe Gotha.—Yea: Hon. Henry Pendleton. 1.—Nays: Hon. Richard Hampton, J. Culpeper, William Fitzpatrick, Llewellen Threewits, John Threewits, Wade Hampton. 6.

Lower Districts between Broad and Saluda Rivers.—Yeas: none.—Nays: Hon. Edanus Burke, J. Lindsay, Philemon Waters, Robert Ruthford, Hon. J. Hampton. 5.

Little River District.—Yeas: John Hunter, Thomas Wadsworth. 2.—Nays: Samuel Saxon, Joshua Saxon. 2.—Absent: James Mayson. 1.

Upper or Spartan District.—Yeas: none. Nays: William Kennedy, James Jourdon, Charles Sims, Thomas Brandon, Hon. Zacariah Bullock. 5.

District between Broad and Catawba Rivers, Richland County.—Yeas: none.—Nays: Hon. Thomas Taylor, William Meyer, Thomas Howell. 3.

Fairfield County.—Nays: James Craig, Jacob Brown, John Gray, John Cook. 4.

Chester District.—Yeas: none.—Nays: Edward Lacy, Joseph Brown, William Miles, James Knox. 4.

District called the New Acquisition.—Yea: Rev. Francis Cummins. 1.—Nays: Hon. William Hill, Robert Patton, Samuel Watson, James Martin, James G. Hunt. Samuel Lowry, Andrew Love, John M'Caw, Adam Meek, Abraham Smith. 10.

St. Matthew's.—Yeas: Hon. William Thompson, Hon. Paul Warley. 2.—Nay: Hon. John Linton. 1.

Orange.—Yeas: Lewis Lesterjette, Jacob Rumph, Donald Bruce. 3.—Nays: none.—Absent: Lewis Golsan. 1.

St. David's.—Yeas: Lemuel Benton, William Dewitt, Calvin Spencer, Samuel Taylor, R. Brownfield, Benjamin Hicks, Jun. 6.—Nays: none.— Absent: Trist Thomas. 1.

District between Savannah River, and the North Fork of Edisto.— Yeas: Stephen Smith, Hon. William Dunbar, Joseph Vince, William Robison, John Collins, Jonathan Clark. 6.—Nays: none.—Absent: William Buford. 1.

Yeas,——149. | Nays,——73. | Majority,——76 | Absent,——15.

So it was resolved in the affirmative.

John S. Dart
Secretary of Convention

South Carolina Proposed Amendments, 1788*

In Convention of the people of the state of South Carolina by their Representatives held in the city of Charleston on Monday the twelfth day of May and continued by divers Adjournments to friday the twenty third day of May Anno Domini One thousand seven hundred and eighty eight, and in the twelfth Year of the Independence of the United States of America.

The Convention having maturely considered the constitution or form of Government reported to Congress by the Convention of Delegates from the United states of America and submitted to them by a Resolution of the Legislature of this State passed the seventeenth and eighteenth days of February last in order to form a more perfect Union, establish Justice, ensure Domestic tranquillity, provide for the common defence, promote the general Welfare and secure the blessings of Liberty to the people of the said United States and their posterity do in the name and behalf of the people of this State hereby assent to and ratify the said Constitution.

Done in Convention the twenty third day of May in the Year of our Lord One thousand seven hundred and eighty eight, and of the Independence of the United States of America the twelfth.

Thomas Pinckney
President
Attest
John Sandford Dart
Secretary

And Whereas it is essential to the preservation of the rights reserved to the several states, and the freedom of the people under the operations of a General government that the right of prescribing the manner time and places of holding the Elections to the Federal Legislature, should be for ever inseperably annexed to the sovereignty of the several states. This convention

Documentary History of the Constitution of the United States (1905), Vol. 2, pp. 138–40.

doth declare that the same ought to remain to all posterity a perpetual and fundamental right in the local, exclusive of the interference of the General Government except in cases where the Legislatures of the States, shall refuse or neglect to perform and fulfil the same according to the tenor of the said Constitution.

This Convention doth also declare that no Section or paragraph of the said Constitution warrants a Construction that the states do not retain every power not expressly relinquished by them and vested in the General Government of the Union.

Resolved that the general Government of the United States ought never to impose direct taxes, but where the monies arising from the duties, imposts and excise are insufficient for the public exigencies nor then until Congress shall have made a requisition upon the states to Assess levy and pay their respective proportions of such requisitions. And in case any state shall neglect or refuse to pay its proportion pursuant to such requisition then Congress may assess and levy such state's proportion together with Interest thereon at the rate of six per centum per annum from the time of payment prescribed by such requisition—

Resolved that the third section of the Sixth Article ought to be amended by inserting the word "other" between the words "no" and "religious"

Resolved that it be a standing instruction to all such delegates as may hereafter be elected to represent this State in the general Government to exert their utmost abilities and influence to effect an Alteration of the Constitution conformably to the foregoing Resolutions.

Done in Convention the twenty third day of May in the year of our Lord One thousand Seven hundred and eighty eight and of the Independence of the United States of America the twelfth

Thomas Pinckney
President
Attest
John Sandford Dart
Secretary

NEW HAMPSHIRE RATIFYING CONVENTION, 1788

Commentary

New Hampshire ratified the Constitution on June 21, 1788, the ninth state to ratify—thus bringing the new Constitution into effect according to its terms. The Antifederalists had at first appeared so strong in New Hampshire's Convention that the supporters of the Constitution had had to secure a temporary adjournment to ward off defeat. When the Convention met again in June, the Antifederalist sentiment was weaker. A committee was appointed to draft recommendatory amendments. Despite the strong opposition of men like Joshua Atherton (the extract from his speech that follows, based upon his hostility to the slave trade, is the only fragment we have from the New Hampshire debates), the amendments were approved. The effort of the Antifederalists to make ratification conditional until the amendments went into effect was defeated. Ratification was then voted by an 11-man majority.

The New Hampshire Ratifying Convention recommended 12 proposed amendments. The first nine were taken almost verbatim from those proposed by Massachusetts. The last three were added by the New Hampshire drafting committee: 10) no standing army without a three-fourths vote and a ban on troop quartering (the latter the first official state recommendation of what became the Third Amendment); 11) "Congress shall make no laws touching Religion, or to infringe the rights of Conscience" (the first official state recommendation of the freedom of conscience guaranteed by the First Amendment and, most important, the first use of the actual prohibitory language with which the First Amendment starts—a vast improvement, from a legal point of view, in the language of the freedom of religion guarantee); 12) right to bear arms (the first official state recommendation to protect the right guaranteed by the Second Amendment).

New Hampshire Ratifying Convention, 1788*

Page 7, Sec. 9th. "The migration or importation of such persons as any of the states now existing shall think proper to admit, shall not be prohibited by Congress prior to the year 1808; but a tax or duty may be imposed on such importation, not exceeding ten dollars for each person."

The Hon. Mr. Dow, from Weare, spoke very sensibly and feelingly against this paragraph.

Several members, on the other side, spoke in favor of it, with remarks on what Mr. Dow had said; after which, the Hon. Joshua Atherton, from Amherst, spoke as follows:

*The Debates in the Several State Conventions on the Adoption of the Constitution, Vol. 2, pp. 203–04.

Mr. President, I cannot be of the opinion of the honorable gentlemen who last spoke, that this paragraph is either so useful or so inoffensive as they seem to imagine, or that the objections to it are so totally void of foundation. The idea that strikes those, who are opposed to this clause, so disagreeably and so forcibly, is, hereby it is conceived (if we ratify the Constitution) that we become consenters to, and partakers in, the sin and guilt of this abominable traffic, at least for a certain period, without any positive stipulation that it should even then be brought to an end. We do not behold in it that valuable acquisition so much boasted of by the honorable member from Portsmouth, "that an end is then to be put to slavery " Congress may be as much, or more, puzzled to put a stop to it then, than we are now. The clause has not secured its abolition.

We do not think ourselves under any obligation to perform works of supererogation in the reformation of mankind; we do not esteem ourselves under any necessity to go to Spain or Italy to suppress the inquisition of those countries, or of making a journey to the Carolinas to abolish the detestable custom of enslaving the Africans; but, sir, we will not lend the aid of our ratification to this cruel and inhuman merchandise, not even for a day. There is a great distinction in not taking a part in the most barbarous violation of the sacred laws of God and humanity, and our becoming guaranties for its exercise for a term of years. Yes, sir, it is our full purpose to wash our hands clear of it; and, however unconcerned spectators we may remain of such predatory infractions of the laws of our nature, however unfeelingly we may subscribe to the ratification of manstealing, with all its baneful consequences, yet I cannot but believe, in justice to human nature, that, if we reserve the consideration, and bring this claimed power somewhat nearer to our own doors, we shall form a more equitable opinion of its claim to this ratification. Let us figure to ourselves a company of these manstealers, well equipped for the enterprise, arriving on our coast. They seize and carry off the whole or a part of the inhabitants of the town of Exeter. Parents are taken, and children left; or possibly they may be so fortunate as to have a whole family taken and carried off together by these relentless robbers. What must be their feelings in the hands of their new and arbitrary masters? Dragged at once from every thing they held dear to them—stripped of every comfort of life, like beasts of prey—they are hurried on a loathsome and distressing voyage to the coast of Africa, or some other quarter of the globe, where the greatest price may await them; and here, if any thing can be added to their miseries, comes on the heart-breaking scene! A parent is sold to one, a son to another, and a daughter to a third! Brother is cleft from brother, sister from sister, and parents from their darling offspring! Broken with every distress that human nature can feel, and bedewed with tears of anguish, they are dragged into the last stage of depression and slavery, never, never to behold the faces of one another again! The scene is too affecting. I have not fortitude to pursue the subject!

*   *   *

New Hampshire Proposed Amendments, 1788*

The Convention haveing Impartially discussed and fully considered the Constitution for the United States of America, reported to Congress by the Convention of Delegates from the United States of America & submitted to us by a Resolution of the General Court of said State passed the fourteenth Day of December last past and acknowledgeing with gratefull Hearts the goodness of the Supreme ruler of the Universe in affording the People of the United States in the Course of his Providence an Opportunity, deliberately & peaceably without fraud or surprize of entering into an Explicit and solemn compact with each other by assenting to & ratifying a new Constitution, in Order to form a more perfect Union, establish Justice, Insure domestick Tranquility, provide for the common defence, promote the general welfare and secure the Blessings of Liberty to themselves & their Posterity—Do In the Name & behalf of the People of the State of New-Hampshire assent to & ratify the said Constitution for the United States of America. And as it is the Opinion of this Convention that certain amendments & alterations in the said Constitution would remove the fears & quiet the apprehensions of many of the good People of this State & more Effectually guard against an undue Administration of the Federal Government—The Convention do therefore recommend that the following alterations & provisions be introduced into the said Constitution.

First, That it be Explicitly declared that all Powers not expressly & particularly Delegated by the aforesaid Constitution are reserved to the several States to be, by them Exercised.

Secondly, That there shall be one Representative to every Thirty thousand Persons according to the Census mentioned in the Constitution, untill the whole number of Representatives amount to Two hundred.

Thirdly, That Congress do not Exercise the Powers vested in them, by the fourth Section of the first Article, but in Cases when a State shall neglect or refuse to make the Regulations therein mentioned, or shall make regulations Subversive of the rights of the People to a free and equal Representation in Congress. Nor shall Congress in any Case make regulations contrary to a free and equal Representation.

Fourthly, That Congress do not lay direct Taxes but when the money arising from Impost, Excise and their other resources are insufficient for the Publick Exigencies; nor then, untill Congress shall have first made a Requisition upon the States, to Assess, Levy, & pay their respective proportions, of such requisition agreeably to the Census fixed in the said Constitution in such way & manner as the Legislature of the State shall think best and in such Case if any State shall neglect, then Congress may Assess & Levy such States proportion together with the Interest thereon at the rate of six per Cent per Annum from the Time of payment prescribed in such requisition.

Documentary History of the Constitution of the United States, Vol. 2, pp. 141–44.

Fifthly, That Congress shall erect no Company of Merchants with exclusive advantages of Commerce.

Sixthly, That no Person shall be Tryed for any Crime by which he may incur an Infamous Punishment, or loss of Life, untill he first be indicted by a Grand Jury except in such Cases as may arise in the Government and regulation of the Land & Naval Forces.

Seventhly, All Common Law Cases between Citizens of different States shall be commenced in the Common Law-Courts of the respective States & no appeal shall be allowed to the Federal Court in such Cases unless the sum or value of the thing in Controversy amount to three Thousand Dollars.

Eighthly, In Civil Actions between Citizens of different States every Issue of Fact arising in Actions at Common Law shall be Tryed by Jury, if the Parties, or either of them request it.

Ninthly, Congress shall at no Time consent that any Person holding an Office of Trust or profit under the United States shall accept any Title of Nobility or any other Title or Office from any King, Prince, or Foreign State.

Tenth, That no standing Army shall be Kept up in time of Peace unless with the consent of three fourths of the Members of each branch of Congress, nor shall Soldiers in Time of Peace be quartered upon private Houses without the consent of the Owners.

Eleventh, Congress shall make no Laws touching Religion, or to infringe the rights of Conscience.

Twelfth, Congress shall never disarm any Citizen unless such as are or have been in Actual Rebellion.

And the Convention Do. In the Name & behalf of the People of this State enjoin it upon their Representatives in Congress, at all Times untill the alterations and provisions aforesaid have been Considered agreeably to the fifth Article of the said Constitution to exert all their Influence & use all reasonable & Legal methods to obtain a ratification of the said alterations & Provisions, in such manner as is provided in the said article—And That the United States in Congress Assembled may have due notice of the assent & Ratification of the said Constitution by this Convention.—It is resolved that the Assent & Ratification aforesaid be engrossed on Parchment, together with the Recommendation & injunction aforesaid & with this Resolution—And that John Sullivan Esquire President of Convention, & John Langdon Esquire President of the State Transmit the same Countersigned by the Secretary of Convention & the Secretary of the State under their hands & Seals to the United States in Congress Assembled.

Jn. Sullivan, Presidt of the Convention
John Langdon, Presidt of State
By order
John Calfe, Secy of Convention
Joseph Pearson, Secy of State

VIRGINIA RATIFYING CONVENTION, 1788

Commentary

For both supporters and opponents of the federal Constitution, Virginia was the crucial state in the ratification contest. Though the Constitution technically went into operation upon ratification by New Hampshire (the ninth state to ratify), everyone knew that the new Union could scarcely prove effective without the adherence of Virginia, at the time the largest and most important state. Moreover, Virginia was closely divided, with its Antifederalist leaders among the best known men in the country: Patrick Henry, George Mason, and Richard Henry Lee. In no state was the opposition to the Constitution led by men of such caliber—but then in no state were the stakes so high or the debate so thorough.

The Virginia Ratifying Convention assembled at Richmond on June 2, 1788. The record which we have of its debates is the most complete of any of the state Conventions. The extracts that follow contain the discussions which bear upon the Bill of Rights issue—an issue which was (even more than in other states) a principal point of difference between the Federalists and Antifederalists in the state. This was only natural in the state which was the first to have its own Bill of Rights. All those who had been responsible for including the pioneer Declaration of Rights in the Virginia Constitution of 1776 were members of the 1788 Convention (particularly George Mason). They emphasized the lack of a similar Bill of Rights in the federal Constitution and argued against ratification until adequate protections for individual rights were included in it.

As it turned out, this demand of the Antifederalists became the nub of the Bill of Rights debate in the Virginia Convention. In the debate, the issue resolved itself into the question of prior versus subsequent amendments. Federalists like Madison had, as his letters show, originally opposed amendments and had (*supra* p. 724) characterized the Massachusetts proposed amendments as "a blemish." As had been the case in Massachusetts, however, the closeness of the division in the Richmond Convention forced the Virginia Federalists to reconsider. Even Madison, in an April letter to Edmund Randolph (*supra* p. 727) conceded that "Recommendatory alteration" might be necessary. By the time of the Convention, the Federalist leaders were willing to concede on the issue of following the example of the Massachusetts proposed amendments. This is clearly shown in Madison's June 22 letter to Hamilton (*infra* p. 848).

The Federalist concession was nevertheless, not enough for the Antifederalist leaders. They insisted upon prior amendments protecting basic individual rights as a condition for ratification. Their views were expressed again and again by Henry who was the principal speaker against ratification throughout the month-long debate. One who reads Henry's speeches is bound to have renewed respect for him as one of the greatest orators in our history. To be sure, every schoolboy knows of Henry's "liberty or death" speech before the Virginia House of Burgesses in 1765. But we tend to think of him only as a fiery young orator, with the bloom wearing off in the transition to a mature politician. Reading the reports of the Virginia Ratifying Convention debates makes one realize the shallowness of this conception.

Of course, Henry's oratory was delivered in support of what we now consider the *wrong* side, and advocates of lost causes (however close they were at the time) have not fared well at the hands of American historians. But that scarcely dims the brilliance of Henry's performance in 1788. By force of his personality and oratorical ability (and we must remember that the reports we have of his speeches must be only a pale shadow of the reality), he completely dominated a Convention composed of some of the greatest men in our political history.

In the Virginia Convention itself, the most important early development was Edmund Randolph's open avowal of the Federalist cause. Randolph (then Governor of Virginia) was one of the delegates at Philadelphia who had refused to sign the federal Constitution, and the Virginia Antifederalists counted upon his leadership. Instead, after Henry opened the case for the opposition on June 4 with his famous attack upon the Constitution: "Who authorized them to speak the language of, *We, the people,* instead of, *We, the states?*" Randolph answered for the Federalists. On June 16, he renewed the matter with a personal attack upon Henry, charging that the attainder of Josiah Philips in 1778 had been moved by Henry himself, and the Virginia Declaration of Rights had not been able to prevent the execution.

The Randolph attack was unfair, as the Virginia Declaration of Rights did not contain any prohibition against bills of attainder. Nor was it accurate to say, as Randolph did, that the Declaration of Rights "has never secured us against any danger." As the *Caton* case (*supra* p. 410) shows, the provisions of the Virginia Constitution were enforceable by the courts; when the delegates at the Richmond Convention fought for amendments protecting individual rights, they well understood that the amendments would be enforced by the power of judicial review. As Madison put it in his 1788 *Observations on the Draught of a Constitution for Virginia,* "as the Courts are generally the last in making ye decision, it results to them by refusing or not refusing to execute a law, to stamp it with its final character."

As already indicated, the chief issue between the Federalists and Antifederalists in the Virginia Convention was that of whether there should be prior or subsequent amendments protecting individual rights: as Madison summarized it (in his July 24 letter to Jefferson), "whether previous amendments should be made a condition of ratification." Henry and his followers rejected the notion that the Convention "should . . . follow the conduct of Massachusetts," saying, "I can never . . . consent to hazard our most unalienable rights on an absolute uncertainty. . . . Let us not adopt this system till we see them secure"—i.e., by prior amendments.

Madison and the other Federalist leaders strongly challenged "the probability of obtaining previous amendments." To condition ratification by prior amendments would be too great a risk; in Randolph's query, "am I therefore obliged to run the risk of losing the Union, by proposing amendments previously, when amendments without that risk can be obtained afterwards?" Among the most effective Federalist speakers was the young John Marshall. He noted acutely that Henry's argument could be used against him: "for, sir, if subsequent amendments cannot be obtained, shall we get amendments before we ratify?"

Thus, the debate went on, with Henry coming back to the Bill of Rights issue virtually every day—one of his speeches on the matter lasting seven hours. He kept insisting on prior amendments and referred as authority to Jefferson, saying, "His amendments go to that despised thing, called a *bill of rights,* and all the rights which are dear to human nature—trial by jury, the liberty of religion and the press, etc." As shown by Madison's letter to Randolph, Jefferson's switch to support of the Massachusetts approach (*supra* p. 727) was not known until later. The Federalists then repeated the view asserted in other Conventions that a Bill of Rights was not necessary, and even that it was no security at all. Surprisingly, Madison, speaking of freedom of religion, asserted that "a bill of rights would be a poor protection for liberty." Marshall (who was to make judicial review the cornerstone of the constitutional edifice in *Marbury* v. *Madison*) declared, "The bill of rights is merely recommendatory." These were, however, only statements made in the heat of debate. As previously indicated, the Federalist leaders had already decided upon recommendatory amendments as a concession to the popular sentiment for a Bill of Rights.

On June 24, George Wythe (one of the judges in the *Caton* case [*supra* p. 410] and a leading Federalist) spoke in favor of amendments to be recommended after ratification—and mentioned specifically guarantees of freedom of the press and religion, and trial by jury. Henry remained obdurate and moved a Declaration of Rights and other amendments to be referred "to the other states in the confederacy, for their consideration, previous to its ratification." Madison replied that those of Henry's amendments which "are not objectionable, or unsafe . . . may be subsequently recommended—not because they are necessary, but because they can produce no possible danger, and may gratify some gentlemen's wishes. But I never can consent to his previous amendments." The Federalist effort was then devoted to defeating the Henry motion for prior amendments—though only by the narrow vote of 88 to 80. The vote on the motion to ratify quickly followed and carried by 89 to 79. Both votes took place on June 25, 1788.

The next day, a committee was appointed "to prepare and report such amendments as by them shall be deemed necessary, to be recommended."

Both Mason and Henry were placed on the drafting committee (along with Madison, Marshall, and Wythe) and were able to secure many of the original Henry proposals, though only by way of recommendation for subsequent amendments. On June 27, the committee reported a proposed federal Declaration or Bill of Rights of 20 articles to be added to the Constitution, as well as 20 other amendments to the constitutional text. The Convention agreed to the committee report, and enjoined "it upon their representatives in Congress to exert all their influence, and use all reasonable and legal methods, to obtain a ratification of the foregoing alterations and provisions."

The Virginia-proposed Bill of Rights and other amendments follow, starting on p. 840 . They are of crucial importance to the history of the federal Bill of Rights, both because they were the first state proposal for a specific Bill of Rights and because they were recommended by Virginia itself. Though Madison wrote to Washington in the heat of the Convention struggle with regard to the just-adopted recommendatory amendments, "several of them highly objectionable, but which could not be parried," when the time came for him to draft his amendments in the first Congress, he naturally chose as his model the Bill of Rights recommended by the Convention of which he had been an active member.

As Judge Dumbauld tells us, the importance of the Virginia Ratifying Convention's proposed Bill of Rights is shown by the fact that (apart from the "political generalities" contained in the first seven articles and in the tenth and twelfth), every specific guarantee in the Virginia-proposed Bill of Rights later found a place in the federal Bill of Rights, except for Article 19, allowing conscientious objectors to hire substitutes (and even that was included in the amendments which Madison proposed to Congress).

The following are the guarantees contained in the Virginia-proposed Bill of Rights which were later included in the federal Bill of Rights: Article 8: right to nature and cause of accusation, confrontation, evidence, counsel, trial by jury of vicinage, (i.e. all of the rights included in the Sixth Amendment) and privilege against self-incrimination (later protected by Fifth Amendment); Article 9: no deprivation of life, liberty, or property "but by the law of the land" (another precursor of the Fifth Amendment's Due Process Clause); Article 11: trial by jury in civil cases (included in the Seventh Amendment); Article 13: prohibition against excessive bail or fines and cruel and unusual punishment (later the Eighth Amendment); Article 14: right against unreasonable searches and seizures (later the Fourth Amendment); Article 15: right to assemble and petition for redress of grievances (the last right later secured by the First Amendment); Article 16: freedom of speech and press (the core rights protected by the First Amendment); Article 17: right to bear arms (later guaranteed by the Second Amendment); Article 18: prohibition against quartering of soldiers (later the Third Amendment); Article 20: freedom of religion (both guaranteeing free exercise and prohibiting establishment, as was later to be done by the First

Amendment). In addition, the first of the proposed Virginia amendments anticipated the guarantee of reserved powers contained in the Tenth Amendment.

We can best estimate the importance of the Virginia-proposed Bill of Rights and amendments by comparing them with the sketchy proposals recommended by Massachusetts, South Carolina, and New Hampshire—the states which had previously adopted recommendatory amendments. In place of the rudimentary protections suggested by the other states, Virginia recommended a complete Bill of Rights—and one which covered all the essential guarantees later included in the federal Bill of Rights, except for the right to a grand jury indictment and the guarantee contained in the Ninth Amendment (and even it was stated, though in different language, in the seventeenth Virginia-proposed amendment).

Virginia Ratifying Convention, 1788*

[Wednesday, June 4]

Mr. Henry: Mr. Chairman, the public mind, as well as my own, is extremely uneasy at the proposed change of government. Give me leave to form one of the number of those who wish to be thoroughly acquainted with the reasons of this perilous and uneasy situation, and why we are brought hither to decide on this great national question. I consider myself as the servant of the people of this commonwealth, as a sentinel over their rights, liberty, and happiness. I represent their feelings when I say that they are exceedingly uneasy at being brought from that state of full security, which they enjoyed, to the present delusive appearance of things. A year ago, the minds of our citizens were at perfect repose. Before the meeting of the late federal Convention at Philadelphia, a general peace and a universal tranquillity prevailed in this country; but, since that period, they are exceedingly uneasy and disquieted. When I wished for an appointment to this Convention, my mind was extremely agitated for the situation of public affairs. I conceived the republic to be in extreme danger. If our situation be thus uneasy, whence has arisen this fearful jeopardy? It arises from this fatal system; it arises from a proposal to change our government—a proposal that goes to the utter annihilation of the most solemn engagements of the states—a proposal of establishing nine states into a confederacy, to the eventual exclusion of four states. It goes to the annihilation of those solemn treaties we have formed with foreign nations.

*The Debates in the Several State Conventions on the Adoption of the Constitution, Vol. 3, pp. 21–663.

Make the best of this new government—say it is composed by any thing but inspiration—you ought to be extremely cautious, watchful, jealous of your liberty; for, instead of securing your rights, you may lose them forever. If a wrong step be now made, the republic may be lost forever. If this new government will not come up to the expectation of the people, and they shall be disappointed, their liberty will be lost, and tyranny must and will arise. I repeat it again, and I beg gentlemen to consider, that a wrong step, made now, will plunge us into misery, and our republic will be lost. It will be necessary for this Convention to have a faithful historical detail of the facts that preceded the session of the federal Convention, and the reasons that actuated its members in proposing an entire alteration of government, and to demonstrate the dangers that awaited us. If they were of such awful magnitude as to warrant a proposal so extremely perilous as this, I must assert, that this Convention has an absolute right to a thorough discovery of every circumstance relative to this great event. And here I would make this inquiry of those worthy characters who composed a part of the late federal Convention. I am sure they were fully impressed with the necessity of forming a great consolidated government, instead of a confederation. That this is a consolidated government is demonstrably clear; and the danger of such a government is, to my mind, very striking. I have the highest veneration for those gentlemen; but, sir, give me leave to demand, What right had they to say, We, the people? My political curiosity, exclusive of my anxious solicitude for the public welfare, leads me to ask, Who authorized them to speak the language of, We, the people, instead of, We, the states? States are the characteristics and the soul of a confederation. If the states be not the agents of this compact, it must be one great, consolidated, national government, of the people of all the states. I have the highest respect for those gentlemen who formed the Convention, and, were some of them not here, I would express some testimonial of esteem for them. America had, on a former occasion, put the utmost confidence in them—a confidence which was well placed; and I am sure, sir, I would give up any thing to them; I would cheerfully confide in them as my representatives. But, sir, on this great occasion, I would demand the cause of their conduct Even from that illustrious man who saved us by his valor, I would have a reason for his conduct: that liberty which he has given us by his valor, tells me to ask this reason; and sure I am, were he here, he would give us that reason. But there are other gentlemen here, who can give us this information. The people gave them no power to use their name. That they exceeded their power is perfectly clear. It is not mere curiosity that actuates me: I wish to hear the real, actual, existing danger, which should lead us to take those steps, so dangerous in my conception. Disorders have arisen in other parts of America; but here, sir, no dangers, no insurrection or tumult have happened; every thing has been calm and tranquil. But, notwithstanding this, we are wandering on the great ocean of human affairs. I see no landmark to guide us. We are running we know not whither. Difference of opinion has gone to a degree of inflammatory resentment in different parts of the country which has been occasioned by this perilous innovation. The federal Convention ought to have amended the old system; for this purpose they were solely delegated; the object of their mission extended to no other consideration. You must, therefore, forgive the solicitation of one unworthy member to know what danger could have arisen under the present Confederation, and what are the causes of this proposal to change our government.

Gov. Randolph: Mr. Chairman, had the most enlightened statesman whom America has yet seen, foretold, but a year ago, the crisis which has now called us together, he would have been confronted by the universal testimony of history; for never was it yet known, that, in so short a space, by the peaceable working of events, without a war, or even the menace of the smallest force, a nation has been brought to agitate a question, an error in the issue of which may blast their happiness. It is, therefore, to be feared, lest to this trying exigency the best wisdom should be unequal; and here (if it were allowable to lament any ordinance of nature) might it be deplored that, in proportion to the magnitude of a subject, is the mind intemperate. Religion, the dearest of all interests, has too often sought proselytes by fire rather than by reason; and politics, the next in rank, is too often nourished by passion, at the expense of the understanding. Pardon me, however, for expecting one exception to the tendency of mankind from the dignity of this Convention—a mutual toleration, and a persuasion that no man has a right to impose his opinions on others. Pardon me, too, sir, if I am particularly sanguine in my expectations from the chair: it well knows what is order, how to command obedience, and that political opinions may be as honest on one side as on the other. Before I press into the body of the argument, I must take the liberty of mentioning the part I have already borne in this great question; but let me not here be misunderstood. I come not to apologize to any individual within these walls, to the Convention as a body, or even to my fellow-citizens at large. Having obeyed the impulse of duty, having satisfied my conscience, and, I trust, my God, I shall appeal to no other tribunal: nor do I come a candidate for popularity; my manner of life has never yet betrayed such a desire. The highest honors and emoluments of this commonwealth are a poor compensation for the surrender of personal independence. The history of England from the revolution, and that of Virginia for more than twenty years past, show the vanity of a hope that general favor should ever follow the man who, without partiality or prejudice, praises or disapproves the opinions of friends or of foes: nay, I might enlarge the field, and declare, from the great volume of human nature itself, that to be moderate in politics forbids an ascent to the summit of political fame. But I come hither, regardless of allurements, to continue as I have begun; to repeat my earnest endeavors for a firm, energetic government; to enforce my objections to the Constitution, and to concur in any practical scheme of amendments; but I never will assent to any scheme that will operate a dissolution of the Union, or any measure which may lead to it.

This conduct may possibly be upbraided as injurious to my own views; if it be so, it is, at least, the natural offspring of my judgment. I refused to sign, and if the same were to return, again would I refuse. Wholly to adopt, or wholly to reject, as proposed by the Convention, seemed too hard an alternative to the citizens of America, whose servants we were, and whose pretensions amply to discuss the means of their happiness were undeniable. Even if adopted under the terror of impending anarchy, the government must have been without the safest bulwark—the hearts of the people; and, if rejected because the chance for amendments was cut off the Union would have been irredeemably lost. This seems to have been verified by the event in Massachusetts, but our Assembly have removed these inconveniences, by propounding the Constitution to our full and free inquiry. When I withheld my subscription, I had not even the glimpse of the genius of America, relative to the principles of the new Constitution. Who, arguing from the preceding history of Virginia, could have divined that she was prepared for the important change? In former times, indeed, she transcended every colony in professions and practices of loyalty; but she opened a perilous war, under a democracy almost as pure as representation would admit; she supported it under a constitution which subjects all rule, authority, and power, to the legislature; every attempt to alter it had been baffled: the increase of Congressional power had always excited an alarm. I therefore would not bind myself to uphold the new Constitution, before I had tried it by the true touchstone; especially, too, when I foresaw that even the members of the general Convention might be instructed by the comments of those who were without doors. But I had, moreover, objections to the Constitution, the most material of which, too lengthy in detail, I have as yet barely stated to the public, but shall explain when we arrive at the proper points. Amendments were consequently my wish; these were the grounds of my repugnance to subscribe, and were perfectly reconcilable with my unalterable resolution to be regulated by the spirit of America, if, after our best efforts for amendments, they could not be removed. I freely indulge those who may think this declaration too candid, in believing that I hereby depart from the concealment belonging to the character of a statesman. Their censure would be more reasonable, were it not for an unquestionable fact, that the spirit of America depends upon a combination of circumstances which no individual can control, and arises not from the prospect of advantages which may be gained by the arts of negotiation, but from deeper and more honest causes.

As with me the only question has ever been between previous and subsequent amendments, so will I express my apprehensions, that the postponement of this Convention to so late a day has extinguished the probability of the former without inevitable ruin to the Union, and the Union is the anchor of our political salvation.

*   *   *

The gentleman then proceeds, and inquires why we assumed the language of "We, the people." I ask, Why not? The government is for the people; and the misfortune was, that the people had no agency in the government before. The Congress had power to make peace and war under the old Confederation. Granting passports, by the law of nations, is annexed to this power; yet Congress was reduced to the humiliating condition of being obliged to send deputies to Virginia to solicit a passport. Notwithstanding the exclusive power of war given to Congress, the second article of the Confederation was interpreted to forbid that body to grant a passport for tobacco, which, during the war, and in pursuance of engagements made at Little York, was to have been sent into New York. What harm is there in consulting the people on the construction of a government by which they are to be bound? Is it unfair? Is it unjust? If the government is to be binding on the people, are not the people the proper persons to examine its merits or defects? I take this to be one of the least and most trivial objections that will be made to the Constitution; it carries the answer with itself. In the whole of this business, I have acted in the strictest obedience to the dictates of my conscience, in discharging what I conceive to be my duty to my country. I refused my signature, and if the same reasons operated on my mind, I would still refuse; but as I think that those eight states which have adopted the Constitution will not recede, I am a friend to the Union.

Mr. George Mason: Mr. Chairman, whether the Constitution be good or bad, the present clause clearly discovers that it is a national government, and no longer a Confederation.

*   *   *

If such amendments be introduced as shall exclude danger, I shall most gladly put my hand to it. When such amendments as shall, from the best information, secure the great essential rights of the people, shall be agreed to by gentlemen, I shall most heartily make the greatest concessions, and concur in any reasonable measure to obtain the desirable end of conciliation and unanimity. An indispensable amendment in this case is, that Congress shall not exercise the power of raising direct taxes till the states shall have refused to comply with the requisitions of Congress. On this condition it may be granted; but I see no reason to grant it unconditionally, as the states can raise the taxes with more ease, and lay them on the inhabitants with more propriety, than it is possible for the general government to do. If Congress hath this power without control, the taxes will be laid by those who have no fellow-feeling or acquaintance with the people. This is my objection to the article now under consideration. It is a very great and important one. I therefore beg gentlemen to consider it. Should this power be restrained, I shall withdraw my objections to this part of the Constitution; but as it stands, it is an objection so strong in my mind, that its amendment is with me a *sine qua non* of its adoption. I wish for such amendments, and such only, as are necessary to secure the dearest rights of the people.

*   *   *

[Thursday, June 5]

Mr. Henry: . . . The question turns, sir, on that poor little thing—the expression, We, the people, instead of the states, of America. I need not take much pains to show that the principles of this system are extremely pernicious, impolitic, and dangerous. Is this a monarchy, like England—a compact between prince and people, with checks on the former to secure the liberty of the latter? Is this a confederacy, like Holland—an association of a number of independent states, each of which retains its individual sovereignty? It is not a democracy, wherein the people retain all their rights securely. Had these principles been adhered to, we should not have been brought to this alarming transitition, from a confederacy to a consolidated government. We have no detail of these great considerations, which, in my opinion, ought to have abounded before we should recur to a government of this kind. Here is a resolution as radical as that which separated us from Great Britain. It is radical in this transition; our rights and privileges are endangered, and the sovereignty of the states will be relinquished: and cannot we plainly see that this is actually the case? The rights of conscience, trial by jury, liberty of the press, all your immunities and franchises, all pretensions to human rights and privileges, are rendered insecure, if not lost, by this change, so loudly talked of by some, and inconsiderately by others. Is this tame relinquishment of rights worthy of freemen? Is it worthy of that manly fortitude that ought to characterize republicans? It is said eight states have adopted this plan. I declare that if twelve states and a half had adopted it, I would, with manly firmness, and in spite of an erring world, reject it. You are not to inquire how your trade may be increased, nor how you are to become a great and powerful people, but how your liberties can be secured; for liberty ought to be the direct end of your government.

Having premised these things, I shall, with the aid of my judgment and information, which I confess, are not extensive, go into the discussion of this system more minutely. Is it necessary for your liberty that you should abandon those great rights by the adoption of this system? Is the relinquishment of the trial by jury and the liberty of the press necessary for your liberty? Will the abandonment of your most sacred rights tend to the security of your liberty? Liberty, the greatest of all earthly blessings—give us that precious jewel, and you may take every thing else! But I am fearful I have lived long enough to become an old-fashioned fellow. Perhaps an invincible attachment to the dearest rights of man may, in these refined, enlightened days, be deemed old-fashioned; if so, I am contented to be so. I say, the time has been when every pulse of my heart beat for American liberty, and which, I believe, had a counterpart in the breast of every true American; but suspicions have gone forth—suspicions of my integrity—publicly reported that my professions are not real. Twenty-three years ago was I supposed a traitor to my country? I was then said to be the bane of sedition, because I supported the rights of my country. I may be thought suspicious when I say our privileges and rights are in danger. But, sir, a number of the people of this country are weak enough to think these things are too true. I am happy to find that the gentleman on the other side declares they are groundless. But, sir, suspicion is a virtue as long as its object is the preservation of the public good, and as long as it stays within proper bounds: should it fall on me, I am contented: conscious rectitude is a powerful consolation. I trust there are many who think my professions for the public good to be real. Let your suspicion look to both sides. There are many on the other side, who possibly may have been persuaded to the necessity of these measures, which I conceive to be dangerous to your liberty. Guard with jealous attention the public liberty. Suspect every one who approaches that jewel. Unfortunately, nothing will preserve it but downright force. Whenever you give up that force, you are inevitably ruined. I am answered by gentlemen, that, though I might speak of terrors, yet the fact was, that we were surrounded by none of the dangers I apprehended. I conceive this new government to be one of those dangers: it has produced those horrors which distress many of our best citizens. We are come hither to preserve the poor commonwealth of Virginia, if it can be possibly done: something must be done to preserve your liberty and mine. The Confederation, this same despised government, merits, in my opinion, the highest encomium: it carried us through a long and dangerous war; it rendered us victorious in that bloody conflict with a powerful nation; it has secured us a territory greater than any European monarch possesses: and shall a government which has been thus strong and vigorous, be accused of imbecility, and abandoned for want of energy? Consider what you are about to do before you part with the government. Take longer time in reckoning things; revolutions like this have happened in almost every country in Europe; similar examples are to be found in ancient Greece and ancient Rome—instances of the people losing their liberty by their own carelessness and the ambition of a few. We are cautioned by the honorable gentleman, who presides, against faction and turbulence. I acknowledge that licentiousness is dangerous, and that it ought to be provided against: I acknowledge, also, the new form of government may effectually prevent it: yet there is another thing it will as effectually do—it will oppress and ruin the people.

There are sufficient guards placed against sedition and licentiousness; for, when power is given to this government to suppress these, or for any other purpose, the language it assumes is clear, express, and unequivocal; but when this Constitution speaks of privileges, there is an ambiguity, sir, a fatal ambiguity—an ambiguity which is very astonishing.

*   *   *

. . . I shall be told I am continually afraid: but, sir, I have strong cause of apprehension. In some parts of the plan before you, the great rights of freemen are endangered; in other parts, absolutely taken away. How does your trial by jury stand? In civil cases gone—not sufficiently secured in criminal—this best privilege is gone. But we are told that we need not fear; because those in power, being our representatives, will not abuse the powers we put in their hands. I am not well versed in history, but I will submit to your recollection, whether liberty has been destroyed most often by the licentiousness of the people, or by the tyranny of rulers. I imagine, sir, you will find the balance on the side of tyranny. Happy will you be if you miss the fate of those nations, who, omitting to resist their oppressors, or negligently suffering their liberty to be wrested from them, have groaned under intolerable despotism! Most of the human race are now in this deplorable condition; and those nations who have gone in search of grandeur, power, and splendor, have also fallen a sacrifice, and been the victims of their own folly. While they acquired those visionary blessings, they lost their freedom. My great objection to this government is, that it does not leave us the means of defending our rights, or of waging war against tyrants. It is urged by some gentlemen, that this new plan will bring us an acquisition of strength—an army, and the militia of the states. This is an idea extremely ridiculous; gentlemen cannot be earnest. This acquisition will trample on our fallen liberty. Let my beloved Americans guard against that fatal lethargy that has pervaded the universe. Have we the means of resisting disciplined armies, when our only defence, the militia, is put into the hands of Congress? The honorable gentleman said that great danger would ensue if the Convention rose without adopting this system. I ask, Where is that danger? I see none. Other gentlemen have told us, within these walls, that the union is gone, or that the union will be gone. Is not this trifling with the judgment of their fellow-citizens? Till they tell us the grounds of their fears, I will consider them as imaginary. I rose to make inquiry where those dangers were; they could make no answer: I believe I never shall have that answer. Is there a disposition in the people of this country to revolt against the dominion of laws? Has there been a single tumult in Virginia? Have not the people of Virginia, when laboring under the severest pressure of accumulated distresses, manifested the most cordial acquiescence in the execution of the laws? What could be more awful than their unanimous acquiescence under general distresses? Is there any revolution in Virginia? Whither is the spirit of America gone? Whither is the genius of America fled? It was but yesterday, when our enemies marched in triumph through our country. Yet the people of this country could not be appalled by their pompous armaments: they stopped their career, and victoriously captured them. Where is the peril, now, compared to that? Some minds are agitated by foreign alarms. Happily for us, there is no real danger from Europe; that country is engaged in more arduous business: from that quarter there is no cause of fear: you may sleep in safety forever for them.

Where is the danger? If, sir, there was any, I would recur to the American spirit to defend us; that spirit which has enabled us to surmount the greatest difficulties: to that illustrious spirit I address my most fervent prayer to prevent our adopting a system destructive to liberty. Let not gentlemen be told that it is not safe to reject this government. Wherefore is it not safe? We are told there are dangers, but those dangers are ideal; they cannot be demonstrated. To encourage us to adopt it, they tell us that there is a plain, easy way of getting amendments. When I come to contemplate this part, I suppose that I am mad, or that my countrymen are so. The way to amendment is, in my conception, shut. Let us consider this plain, easy way. "The Congress, whenever two thirds of both houses shall deem it necessary, shall propose amendments to this Constitution, or on the application of the legislatures of two thirds of the several states, shall call a Convention for proposing amendments, which, in either case, shall be valid to all intents and purposes, as part of this Constitution, when ratified by the legislatures of three fourths of the several states, or by the Conventions in three fourths thereof, as the one or the other mode of ratification may be proposed by the Congress. Provided, that no amendment which may be made prior to the year 1808, shall in any manner affect the 1st and 4th clauses in the 9th section of the 1st article; and that no state, without its consent, shall be deprived of its equal suffrage in the Senate."

Hence it appears that three fourths of the states must ultimately agree to any amendments that may be necessary. Let us consider the consequence of this. However uncharitable it may appear, yet I must tell my opinion—that the most unworthy characters may get into power, and prevent the introduction of amendments. Let us suppose—for the case is supposable, possible, and probable—that you happen to deal those powers to unworthy hands; will they relinquish powers already in their possession, or agree to amendments? Two thirds of the Congress, or of the state legislatures, are necessary even to propose amendments. If one third of these be unworthy men, they may prevent the application for amendments; but what is destructive and mischievous, is, that three fourths of the state legislatures, or of the state conventions, must concur in the amendments when proposed! In such numerous bodies, there must necessarily be some designing, bad men. To suppose that so large a number as three fourths of the states will concur, is to suppose that they will possess genius, intelligence, and integrity, approaching to miraculous. It would indeed be miraculous that they should concur in the same amendments, or even in such as would bear some likeness to one another; for four of the smallest states, that do not collectively contain one tenth part of the population of the United States, may obstruct the most salutary and necessary amendments. Nay, in these four states, six tenths of the people may reject these amendments; and suppose that amendments shall be opposed to amendments, which is highly probable,—is it possible that three fourths can ever agree to the same amendments? A bare majority in these four small states may hinder the adoption of amendments; so that we may fairly and justly conclude that one twentieth part of the American people may prevent the removal of the most grievous inconveniences and oppression, by refusing to accede to amendments. A trifling minority may reject the most salutary amendments. Is this an easy mode of securing the public liberty? It is, sir, a most fearful situation, when the most contemptible minority can prevent the alteration of the most oppressive government; for it may, in many respects, prove to be such. Is this the spirit of republicanism?

What, sir, is the genius of democracy? Let me read that clause of the bill of rights of Virginia which relates to this: 3d clause: —that government is, or ought to be, instituted for the common benefit, protection, and security of the people, nation, or community. Of all the various modes and forms of government, that is best, which is capable of producing the greatest degree of happiness and safety, and is most effectually secured against the danger of mal-administration; and that whenever any government shall be found inadequate, or contrary to those purposes, a majority of the community hath an indubitable, unalienable, and indefeasible right to reform, alter, or abolish it, in such manner as shall be judged most conducive to the public weal.

This, sir, is the language of democracy—that a majority of the community have a right to alter government when found to be oppressive. But how different is the genius of your new Constitution from this! How different from the sentiments of freemen, that a contemptible minority can prevent the good of the majority! If, then, gentlemen, standing on this ground, are come to that point, that they are willing to bind themselves and their posterity to be oppressed, I am amazed and inexpressibly astonished.

*   *   *

[Friday, June 16]

The Convention, according to the order of the day, again resolved itself into a committee of the whole Convention, to take into further consideration the proposed plan of government. Mr. Wythe in the chair.

Gov. Randolph: Mr. Chairman, I am a child of the revolution. My country, very early indeed, took me under its protection, at a time when I most wanted it, and, by a succession of favors and honors, gratified even my most ardent wishes. I feel the highest gratitude and attachment to my country; her felicity is the most fervent prayer of my heart. Conscious of having exerted my faculties to the utmost in her behalf, if I have not succeeded in securing the esteem of my countrymen, I shall reap abundant consolation from the rectitude of my intentions: honors, when compared to the satisfaction accruing from a conscious independence and rectitude of conduct, are no equivalent. The unwearied study of my life shall be to promote her happiness. As a citizen, ambition and popularity are no objects with me. I expect, in the course of a year, to retire to that private station which I most sincerely and cordially prefer to all others. The security of public justice, sir, is what I most fervently wish, as I consider that object to be the primary step to the attainment of public happiness. I can declare to the whole world, that, in the part I take in this very important question, I am actuated by a regard for what I conceive to be our true interest. I can also, with equal sincerity, declare that I would join heart and hand in rejecting this system, did I not conceive it would promote our happiness; but, having a strong conviction on my mind, at this time, that by a disunion we shall throw away all those blessings we have so earnestly fought for, and that a rejection of the Constitution will operate disunion, pardon me if I discharge the obligation I owe to my country, by voting for its adoption. We are told that the report of dangers is false. The cry of peace, sir, is false: say peace, when there is peace; it is but a sudden calm. The tempest growls over you: look round—wheresoever you look, you see danger. Where there are so many witnesses in many parts of America, that justice is suffocated, shall peace and happiness still be said to reign? Candor, sir, requires an undisguised representation of our situation. Candor, sir, demands a faithful exposition of facts. Many citizens have found justice strangled and trampled under foot, through the course of jurisprudence in this country. Are those who have debts due to them satisfied with your government? Are not creditors wearied with the tedious procrastination of your legal process—a process obscured by legislative mists? Cast your eyes to your seaports; see how commerce languishes. This country, so blessed, by nature, with every advantage that can render commerce profitable, through defective legislation is deprived of all the benefits and emoluments she might otherwise reap from it. We hear many complaints on the subject of located lands; a variety of competitors claiming the same lands under legislative acts, public faith prostrated, and private confidence destroyed. I ask you if your laws are reverenced. In every well-regulated community, the laws command respect. Are yours entitled to reverence? We not only see violations of the constitution, but of national principles in repeated instances. How is the fact? The history of the violations of the consitution extends from the year 1776 to this present time— violations made by formal acts of the legislature: everything has been drawn within the legislative vortex.

There is one example of this violation in Virginia, of a most striking and shocking nature—an example so horrid, that, if I conceived my country would passively permit a repetition of it, dear as it is to me, I would seek means of expatriating myself from it. A man, who was then a citizen, was deprived of his life thus: from a mere reliance on general reports, a gentleman in the House of Delegates informed the house, that a certain man (Josiah Philips) had committed several crimes, and was running at large, perpetrating other crimes. He therefore moved for leave to attaint him; he obtained that leave instantly; no sooner did he obtain it, than he drew from his pocket a bill ready written for that effect; it was read three times in one day, and carried to the Senate. I will not say that it passed the same day through the Senate; but he was attainted very speedily and precipitately, without any proof better than vague reports. Without being confronted with his accusers and witnesses, without the privilege of calling for evidence in his behalf, he was sentenced to death, and was afterwards actually executed. Was this arbitrary deprivation of life, the dearest gift of God to man, consistent with the genius of a republican government? Is this compatible with the spirit of freedom? This, sir, has made the deepest impression on my heart, and I cannot contemplate it without horror. There are still a multiplicity of complaints of the debility of the laws. Justice, in many instances, is so unattainable that commerce may, in fact, be said to be stopped entirely. There is no peace, sir, in this land. Can peace exist with injustice, licentiousness, insecurity, and oppression? These considerations, independent of many others which I have not yet enumerated, would be a sufficient reason for the adoption of this Constitution, because it secures the liberty of the citizen, his person and property, and will invigorate and restore commerce and industry. An additional reason to induce us to adopt it is that excessive licentiousness which has resulted from the relaxation of our laws, and which will be checked by this government. Let us judge from the fate of more ancient nations: licentiousness has produced tyranny among many of them: it has contributed as much (if not more) as any other cause whatsoever to the loss of their liberties. I have respect for the integrity of our legislatures; I believe them to be virtuous; but as long as the defects of the Constitution exist, so long will laws be imperfect.

The honorable gentleman went on further, and said that the accession of eight states is not a reason for our adoption. Many other things have been alleged out of order; instead of discussing the system regularly, a variety of points are promiscuously debated, in order to make temporary impression on the members. Sir, were I convinced of the validity of their arguments, I would join them heart and hand. Were I convinced that the accession of eight states did not render our accession also necessary to preserve the Union, I would not accede to it till it should be previously amended; but, sir, I am convinced that the Union will be lost by our rejection. Massachusetts has adopted it: she has recommended subsequent amendments; her influence must be very considerable to obtain them. I trust my countrymen have sufficient wisdom and virtue to entitle them to equal respect. Is it urged that, being wiser, we ought to prescribe amendments to the other states? I have considered this subject deliberately; wearied myself in endeavoring to find a possibility of preserving the Union, without our unconditional ratification; but, sir, in vain; I find no other means. I ask myself a variety of questions applicable to the adopting states, and I conclude, Will they repent of what they have done? Will they acknowledge themselves in an error? Or will they recede, to gratify Virginia? My prediction is, that they will not. Shall we stand by ourselves, and be severed from the Union, if amendments cannot be had? I have every reason for determining within myself that our rejection must dissolve the Union; and that that dissolution will destroy our political happiness. The honorable gentleman was pleased to draw out several other arguments out of order, that this government would destroy the state governments, the trial by jury, &c. &c., and concluded by an illustration of his opinion by a reference to the confederacy of the Swiss. Let us argue with unprejudiced minds. They say that the trial by jury is gone. Is this so? Although I have declared my determination to give my vote for it, yet I shall freely censure those parts which appear to me reprehensible.

The trial by jury in criminal cases is secured; in civil cases it is not so expressly secured as I should wish it; but it does not follow that Congress has the power of taking away this privilege, which is secured by the constitution of each state, and not given away by this Constitution. I have no fear on this subject. Congress must regulate it so as to suit every state. I will risk my property on the certainty that they will institute the trial by jury in such manner as shall accommodate the conveniences of the inhabitants in every state. The difficulty of ascertaining this accommodation was the principal cause of its not being provided for. It will be the interest of the individuals composing Congress to put it on this convenient footing. Shall we not choose men respectable for their good qualities? Or can we suppose that men tainted with the worst vices will get into Congress?

*   *   *

. . . The honorable gentleman attacks the Constitution, as he thinks it is contrary to our bill of rights. Do we not appeal to the people, by whose authority all government is made? That bill of rights is of no validity, because, I conceive, it is not formed on due authority. It is not a part of our Constitution; it has never secured us against any danger; it has been repeatedly disregarded and violated. But we must not discard the Confederation, for the remembrance of its past services. I am attached to old servants. I have regard and tenderness for this old servant; but when reason tells us, that it can no longer be retained without throwing away all that it has gained us, and running the risk of losing every thing dear to us, must we still continue our attachment? Reason and my duty tell me not. Other gentlemen may think otherwise.

Mr. Madison then arose [but he spoke so low that his exordium could not be heard distinctly.] I shall not attempt to make impressions by any ardent professions of zeal for the public welfare. We know the principles of every man will, and ought to be, judged, not by his professions and declarations, but by his conduct; by that criterion I mean, in common with every other member, to be judged; and should it prove unfavorable to my reputation, yet it is a criterion from which I will by no means depart. Comparisons have been made between the friends of this Constitution and those who oppose it: although I disapprove of such comparisons, I trust that, in point of truth, honor, candor, and rectitude of motives, the friends of this system, here and in other states, are not inferior to its opponents. But professions of attachment to the public good, and comparisons of parties, ought not to govern or influence us now. We ought, sir, to examine the Constitution on its own merits solely: we are to inquire whether it will promote the public happiness: its aptitude to produce this desirable object ought to be the exclusive subject of our present researches. In this pursuit, we ought not to address our arguments to the feelings and passions, but to those understandings and judgments which were selected by the people of this country, to decide this great question by a calm and rational investigation. I hope that gentlemen, in displaying their abilities on this occasion, instead of giving opinions and making assertions, will condescend to prove and demonstrate, by a fair and regular discussion. It gives me pain to hear gentlemen continually distorting the natural construction of language, for it is sufficient if any human production can stand a fair discussion. Before I proceed to make some additions to the reasons which have been adduced by my honorable friend over the way, I must take the liberty to make some observations on what was said by another gentleman, (Mr. Henry.) He told us that this Constitution ought to be rejected because it endangered the public liberty, in his opinion, in many instances. Give me leave to make one answer to that observation: Let the dangers which this system is supposed to be replete with be clearly pointed out: if any dangerous and unnecessary powers be given to the general legislature, let them be plainly demonstrated, and let us not rest satisfied with general assertions of danger, without examination. If powers be necessary, apparent danger is not a sufficient reason against conceding them. He has suggested that licentiousness has seldom produced the loss of liberty; but that the tyranny of rulers has almost always effected it. Since the general civilization of mankind, I believe there are more instances of the abridgment of the freedom of the people by gradual and silent encroachments of those in power, than by violent and sudden usurpations; but, on a candid examination of history, we shall find that turbulence, violence, and abuse of power, by the majority trampling on the rights of the minority, have produced factions and commotions, which, in republics, have, more frequently than any other cause, produced despotism. If we go over the whole history of ancient and modern republics, we shall find their destruction to have generally resulted from those causes. If we consider the peculiar situation of the United States, and what are the sources of that diversity of sentiment which pervades its inhabitants, we shall find great danger to fear that the same causes may terminate here in the same fatal effects which they produced in those republics. This danger ought to be wisely guarded against. Perhaps, in the progress of this discussion, it will appear that the only possible remedy for those evils, and means of perserving and protecting the principles of republicanism, will be found in that very system which is now exclaimed against as the parent of oppression.

I must confess I have not been able to find his usual consistency in the gentleman's argument on this occasion. He informs us that the people of the country are at perfect repose, that is, every man enjoys the fruits of his labor peaceably and securely, and that every thing is in perfect tranquility and safety. I wish sincerely, sir, this were true. If this be their happy situation, why has every state acknowledged the contrary? Why were deputies from all the states sent to the general Convention? Why have complaints of national and individual distresses been echoed and reechoed throughout the continent? Why has our general government been so shamefully disgraced, and our Constitution violated? Wherefore have laws been made to authorize a change, and wherefore are we now assembled here? A federal government is formed for the protection of its individual members. Ours has attacked itself with impunity. Its authority has been disobeyed and despised. I think I perceive a glaring inconsistency in another of his arguments. He complains of this Constitution, because it requires the consent of at least three fourths of the states to introduce amendments which shall be necessary for the happiness of the people. The assent of so many he urges as too great an obstacle to the admission of salutary amendments, which, he strongly insists, ought to be at the will of a bare majority. We hear this argument, at the very moment we are called upon to assign reasons for proposing a constitution which puts it in the power of nine states to abolish the present inadequate, unsafe, and pernicious Confederation! In the first case, he asserts that a majority ought to have the power of altering the government, when found to be inadequate to the security of public happiness. In the last case, he affirms that even three fourths of the community have not a right to alter a government which experience has proved to be subversive of national felicity! nay, that the most necessary and urgent alterations cannot be made without the absolute unanimity of all the states! Does not the thirteenth article of the Confederation expressly require that no alteration shall be made without the unanimous consent of all the states? Could anything in theory of the Confederation expressly require that no alteration shall be made without the unanimous consent of all the states? Could anything in theory be more perniciously improvident and injudicious than this submission of the will of the majority to the most trifling minority?

*   *   *

I confess to you, sir, were uniformity of religion to be introduced by this system, it would, in my opinion, be ineligible; but I have no reason to conclude that uniformity of government will produce that of religion. This subject is, for the honor of America, perfectly free and unshackled. The government has no jurisdiction over it: the least reflection will convince us there is no danger to be feared on this ground.

But we are flattered with the probability of obtaining previous amendments. This calls for the most serious attention of this house. If amendments are to be proposed by one state, other states have the same right, and will also propose alterations. These cannot but be dissimilar, and opposite in their nature. I beg leave to remark, that the governments of the different states are in many respects dissimilar in their structure; their legislative bodies are not similar; their executive are more different. In several of the states, the first magistrate is elected by the people at large; in others, by joint ballot of the members of both branches of the legislature; and in others, in other different manners. This dissimilarity has occasioned a diversity of opinion on the theory of government, which will, without many reciprocal concessions, render a concurrence impossible.

*   *   *

[Saturday, June 7]

Mr. Henry: I have thought, and still think, that a full investigation of the actual situation of America ought to precede any decision on this great and important question. That government is no more than a choice among evils, is acknowledged by the most intelligent among mankind, and has been a standing maxim for ages. If it be demonstrated that the adoption of the new plan is a little or a trifling evil, then, sir, I acknowledge that adoption ought to follow; but, sir, if this be a truth, that its adoption may entail misery on the free people of this country, I then insist that rejection ought to follow. Gentlemen strongly urge, its adoption will be a mighty benefit to us; but, sir, I am made of so incredulous materials, that assertions and declarations do not satisfy me. I must be convinced, sir. I shall retain my infidelity on that subject till I see our liberties secured in a manner perfectly satisfactory to my understanding.

There are certain maxims by which every wise and enlightened people will regulate their conduct. There are certain political maxims which no free people ought ever to abandon—maxims of which the observance is essential to the security of happiness. It is impiously irritating the avenging hand of Heaven, when a people, who are in the full enjoyment of freedom, launch out into the wide ocean of human affairs, and desert those maxims which alone can preserve liberty. Such maxims, humble as they are, are those only which can render a nation safe or formidable. Poor little humble republican maxims have attracted the admiration, and engaged the attention, of the virtuous and wise in all nations, and have stood the shock of ages. We do not now admit the validity of maxims which we once delighted in. We have since adopted maxims of a different, but more refined nature—new maxims, which tend to the prostration of republicanism.

We have one, sir, that all men are by nature free and independent, and have certain inherent rights, of which, when they enter into society, they cannot by any compact deprive or divest their posterity. We have a set of maxims of the same spirit, which must be beloved by every friend to liberty, to virtue, to mankind: our bill of rights contains those admirable maxims.

Now, sir, I say, let us consider whether the picture given of American affairs ought to drive us from those beloved maxims.

The honorable gentleman, Governor Randolph, has said that it is too late in the day for us to reject this new plan. That system which was once execrated by the honorable member must now be adopted, let its defects be ever so glaring. . . . It seems to me very strange and unaccountable that that which was the object of his execration should now receive his encomiums. Something extraordinary must have operated so great a change in his opinion. It is too late in the day! Gentlemen must excuse me if they should declare, again and again, that it was too late, and I should think differently. I never can believe, sir, that it is too late to save all that is precious: if it be proper, and, independently of every external consideration, wisely constructed, let us receive it: but, sir, shall its adoption by eight states induce us to receive it, if it be replete with the most dangerous defects? They urge that subsequent amendments are safer than previous amendments, and that they will answer the same ends.

At present we have our liberties and privileges in our own hands. Let us not relinquish them. Let us not adopt this system till we see them secure. There is some small possibility that, should we follow the conduct of Massachusetts, amendments might be obtained. There is a small possibility of amending any government; but, sir, shall we abandon our most inestimable rights, and rest their security on a mere possibility? The gentleman fears the loss of the Union. If eight states have ratified it unamended, and we should rashly imitate their precipitate example, do we not thereby disunite from several other states? Shall those who have risked their lives for the sake of the Union be at once thrown out of it? If it be amended, every state will accede to it; but by an imprudent adoption in its defective and dangerous state, a schism must inevitably be the consequence. I can never, therefore, consent to hazard our most unalienable rights on an absolute uncertainty.

*   *   *

. . . We are giving power; they are getting power; judge, then, on which side the implication will be used! When we once put it in their option to assume constructive power, danger will follow. Trial by jury, and liberty of the press, are also on this foundation of implication. If they encroach on these rights, and you give your implication for a plea, you are cast; for they will be justified by the last part of it, which gives them full power "to make all laws which shall be necessary and proper to carry their power into execution." Implication is dangerous, because it is unbounded: if it be admitted at all, and no limits be prescribed, it admits of the utmost extension. They say that every thing that is not given is retained. The reverse of the proposition is true by implication. They do not carry their implication so far when they speak of the general welfare—no implication when the sweeping clause comes. Implication is only necessary when the existence of privileges is in dispute. The existence of powers is sufficiently established. If we trust our dearest rights to implication, we shall be in a very unhappy situation.

Implication, in England, has been a source of dissension. There has been a war of implication between the king and people. For a hundred years did the mother country struggle under the uncertainty of implication. The people insisted that their rights were implied; the monarch denied the doctrine. The Bill of Rights, in some degree, terminated the dispute. By a bold implication, they said they had a right to bind us in all cases whatsoever. This constructive power we opposed, and successfully. Thirteen or fourteen years ago, the most important thing that could be thought of was to exclude the possibility of construction and implication. These, sir, were then deemed perilous. The first thing that was thought of was a bill of rights. We were not satisfied with your constructive, argumentative rights.

Mr. Henry then declared a bill of rights indispensably necessary; that a general positive provision should be inserted in the new system, securing to the states and the people every right which was not conceded to the general government; and that every implication should be done away. It being now late, he concluded by observing, that he would resume the subject another time.

* * *

[Monday, June 9]

Gov. Randolph: Having consumed heretofore so much of your time, I did not intend to trouble you again so soon. But now I call on this committee, by way of right, to permit me to answer some severe charges against the friends of the new Constitution. It is a right I am entitled to, and shall have. I have spoken twice in this committee. I have shown the principles which actuated the general Convention; and attempted to prove that, after the ratification of the proposed system by so many states, the preservation of the Union depended on its adoption by us. I find myself attacked in the most illiberal manner by the honorable gentleman, (Mr. Henry.) I disdain his aspersions and his insinuations. His asperity is warranted by no principle of parliamentary decency, nor compatible with the least shadow of friendship; and if our friendship must fall, let it fall, like Lucifer, never to rise again! Let him remember that it is not to answer him, but to satisfy his respectable audience, that I now get up. He has accused me of inconsistency in this very respectable assembly. Sir, if I do not stand on the bottom of integrity, and pure love for Virginia, as much as those who can be most clamorous, I wish to resign my existence. Consistency consists in actions, and not in empty, specious words. Ever since the first entrance into that federal business, I have been inevitably governed by an invincible attachment to the happiness of the people of America. Federal measures had been before that time repudiated. The augmentation of congressional powers was dreaded. The imbecility of the Confederation was proved and acknowledged. When I had the honor of being deputed to the federal Convention, to revise the existing system, I was impressed with the necessity of a more energetic government, and thoroughly persuaded that the salvation of the people of America depended on an intimate and firm union. The honorable gentlemen there can say, that, when I went thither, no man was a stronger friend to such a union than myself. I informed you why I refuse to sign.

I understand not him who wishes to give a full scope to licentiousness and dissipation—who would advise me to reject the proposed plan, and plunge us into anarchy.

*   *   *

He said that Magna Charta destroyed all implication. This was not the object of Magna Charta, but to destroy the power of the king, and secure the liberty of the people. The bill of rights was intended to restore the government to its primitive principles. . . .

I am surprised at his proposition of previous amendments, and his assertion that subsequent ones will cause disunion. Shall we not lose our influence and weight in the government to bring about amendments, if we propose them previously? Will not the senators be chosen, and the electors of the President be appointed, and the government brought instantly into action, after the ratification of nine states? In this disunion, when will the effect proposed be produced? But no man here is willing to believe what the honorable gentleman says on this point. I was in hopes we should come to some degree of order. I fear that order is no more. I believe that we should confine ourselves to the particular clause under consideration, and to such other clauses as might be connected with it.

Why have we been told that maxims can alone save nations; that our maxims are our bill of rights; and that the liberty of the press, trial by jury, and religion, are destroyed: Give me leave to say, that the maxims of Virginia are union and justice.

. . . Justice is, and ought to be, our maxim; and must be that of every temperate, moderate, and upright man. I should not say so much on this occasion, were it not that I perceive that the flowers of rhetoric are perverted, in order to make impressions unfavorable and inimical to an impartial and candid decision. What security can arise from a bill of rights? The predilection for it has arisen from a misconception of its principles. It cannot secure the liberties of this country. A bill of rights was used in England to limit the king's prerogative; he could trample on the liberties of the people in every case which was not within the restraint of the bill of rights.

Our situation is radically different from that of the people of England. What have we to do with bills of rights? Six or seven states have none. Massachusetts has declared her bill of rights as no part of her Constitution. Virginia has a bill of rights, but it is no part of her Constitution. By not saying whether it is paramount to the Constitution or not, it has left us in confusion. Is the bill of rights consistent with the Constitution? Why, then, is it not inserted in the Constitution? Does it add any thing to the Constitution? Why is it not in the Constitution? Does it except any thing from the Constitution? Why not put the exceptions in the Constitution? Does it oppose the Constitution? This will produce mischief. The judges will dispute which is paramount. Some will say, the bill of rights is paramount: others will say, that the Constitution, being subsequent in point of time, must be paramount. A bill of rights, therefore, accurately speaking, is quite useless, if no dangerous to a republic.

I had objections to this Constitution. I still have objections to it. . . . The gentleman asks, How comes it to pass that you are now willing to take it? I answer, that I see Virginia in such danger, that, were its defects greater, I would adopt it. These dangers, though not immediately present to our view, yet may not be far distant, if we disunite from the other states. I will join any man in endeavoring to get amendments, after the danger of disunion is removed by a previous adoption.

The honorable gentleman says that the federal spirit leads to disunion. The federal spirit is not superior to human nature, but it cannot be justly charged with having a tendency to disunion. If we were to take the gentleman's discrimination as our guide, the spirit of Virginia would be dictatorial. Virginia dictates to eight states. A single amendment, proposed as the condition of our accession, will operate total disunion.

*　　　*　　　*

[Tuesday, June 10]

Mr. Chairman, I am astonished that the rule of the house to debate regularly has not been observed by gentlemen. Shall we never have order? I must transgress that rule now, not because I think the conduct of the gentleman deserves imitation, but because the honorable gentleman ought to be answered. In that list of facts with which he would touch our affections, he has produced a name (Mr. Jefferson) which will ever be remembered with gratitude by this commonwealth. I hope that his life will be continued, to add, by his future actions, to the brilliancy of his character. Yet I trust that his name was not mentioned to influence any member of this house. Nothwithstanding the celebrity of his character, his name cannot be used as authority against the Constitution. I know not his authority. I have had no letter from him. As far as my information goes, it is only a report circulated through the town, that he wished nine states to adopt, and the others to reject it, in order to get amendments. Which is the ninth state to introduce the government? That illustrious citizen tells you, that he wishes the government to be adopted by nine states, to prevent a schism in the Union. This, sir, is my wish. I will go heart and hand to obtain amendments, but I will never agree to the dissolution of the Union. But unless a ninth state will accede, this must inevitably happen. No doubt he wished Virginia to adopt. I wish not to be bound by any man's opinion; but, admitting the authority which the honorable gentleman has produced to be conclusive, it militates against himself. Is it right to adopt? He says, no; because there is a President. I wish he was eligible after a given number of years.

I wish also some other changes to be made in the Constitution. But am I therefore obliged to run the risk of losing the Union, by proposing amendments previously, when amendments without that risk can be obtained afterwards? Am I to indulge capricious opinions so far as to lose the Union? The friends of the Union will see how far we carry our attachment to it, and will therefore concur with our amendments.

*   *   *

It is also objected that the trial by jury, the writ of habeas corpus, and the liberty of the press, are insecure. But I contend that the habeas corpus is at least on as secure and good a footing as it is in England. In that country, it depends on the will of the legislature. That privilege is secured here by the Constitution, and is only to be suspended in cases of extreme emergency. Is this not a fair footing? After agreeing that the government of England secures liberty, how do we distrust this government? Why distrust ourselves? The liberty of the press is supposed to be in danger. If this were the case, it would produce extreme repugnancy in my mind. If it ever will be suppressed in this country, the liberty of the people will not be far from being sacrificed. Where is the danger of it? He says that every power is given to the general government that is not reserved to the states. Pardon me if I say the reverse of the proposition is true. I defy any one to prove the contrary. Every power not given it by this system is left with the states. This being the principle, from what part of the Constitution can the liberty of the press be said to be in danger?

[Here his excellency read the 8th section of the 1st article, containing all the powers given to Congress.]

Go through these powers, examine every one, and tell me if the most exalted genius can prove that the liberty of the press is in danger. The trial by jury is supposed to be in danger also. It is secured in criminal cases, but supposed to be taken away in civil cases. It is not relinquished by the Constitution; it is only not provided for. Look at the interest of Congress to suppress it. Can it be in any manner advantageous for them to suppress it? In equitable cases, it ought not to prevail, nor with respect to admiralty causes; because there will be an undue leaning against those characters, of whose business courts of admiralty will have cognizance. I will rest myself secure under this reflection—that it is impossible for the most suspicious or malignant mind to show that it is the interest of Congress to infringe on this trial by jury.

Freedom of religion is said to be in danger. I will candidly say, I once thought that it was, and felt great repugnance to the Constitution for that reason. I am willing to acknowledge my apprehensions removed; and I will inform you by what process of reasoning I did remove them. The Constitution provides that "the senators and representatives before mentioned, and the members of the several state legislatures, and all executive and judicial officers, both of the United States and of the several states, shall be bound, by oath or affirmation, to support this Constitution; but no religious test shall ever be required as a qualification to any office or public trust under the United States." It has been said that, if the exclusion of the religious test were an exception from the general power of Congress, the power over religion would remain. I inform those who are of this opinion, that no power is given expressly to Congress over religion. The senators and representatives, members of the state legislatures, and executive and judicial officers, are bound, by oath or affirmation, to support this Constitution. This only binds them to support it in the exercise of the powers constitutionally given it. The exclusion of religious tests is an exception from this general provision, with respect to oaths or affirmations. Although officers, &c., are to swear that they will support this Constitution, yet they are not bound to support one mode of worship, or to adhere to one particular sect. It puts all sects on the same footing. A man of abilities and character, of any sect whatever, may be admitted to any office or public trust under the United States. I am a friend to a variety of sects, because they keep one another in order. How many different sects are we composed of throughout the United States! How many different sects will be in Congress! We cannot enumerate the sects that may be in Congress! And there are now so many in the United States, that they will prevent the establishment of any one sect, in prejudice to the rest, and will forever oppose all attempts to infringe religious liberty. If such an attempt be made, will not the alarm be sounded throught America? If Congress should be as wicked as we are foretold they will be, they would not run the risk of exciting the resentment of all, or most, of the religious sects in America.

The judiciary is drawn up in terror. Here I have an objection of a different nature. I object to the appellate jurisdiction as the greatest evil in it. But I look at the Union—the object which guides me. When I look at the Union, objects of less consideration vanish, and I hope that the inconvenience will be redressed, and that Congress will prohibit the appeal with respect to matters of fact. When it respects only matters of law, no danger can possibly arise from it. Can Congress have any interest in continuing appeals of fact? If Pennsylvania has an interest in continuing it, will not Georgia, North Carolina, South Carolina, Virginia, New York, and the Eastern States, have an interest in discontinuing it? What advantage will its continuance be to Maryland, New Jersey, or Delaware? Is there not unanimity against it in Congress almost? Kentucky will be equally opposed to it. Thus, sir, all these will be opposed to one state. If Congress wish to aggrandize themselves by oppressing the people, the judiciary must first be corrupted! No man says any thing against them; they are more independent than in England.

٭   ٭   ٭

Mr. John Marshall: Mr. Chairman, I conceive that the object of the discussion now before us is, whether democracy or despotism be most eligible. I am sure that those who framed the system submitted to our investigation, and those who now support it, intend the establishment and security of the former. The supporters of the Constitution claim the title of being firm friends of the liberty and the rights of mankind. They say that they consider it as the best means of protecting liberty. We, sir, idolize democracy. Those who oppose it have bestowed eulogiums on monarchy. We prefer this system to any monarchy, because we are convinced that it has a greater tendency to secure our liberty and promote our happiness. We admire it, because we think it a well-regulated democracy. It is recommended to the good people of this country: they are, through us, to declare whether it be such a plan of government as will establish and secure their freedom.

Permit me to attend to what the honorable gentleman (Mr. Henry) has said. He has expatiated on the necessity of a due attention to certain maxims—to certain fundamental principles, from which a free people ought never to depart. I concur with him in the propriety of the observance of such maxims. They are necessary in any government, but more essential to a democracy than to any other. What are the favorite maxims of democracy? A strict observance of justice and public faith, and a steady adherence to virtue. These, sir, are the principles of a good government. No mischief, no misfortune, ought to deter us from a strict observance of justice and public faith. Would to Heaven that these principles had been observed under the present government! Had this been the case, the friends of liberty would not be so willing now to part with it. Can we boast that our government is founded on these maxims? Can we pretend to the enjoyment of political freedom or security, when we are told that a man has been, by an act of Assembly, struck out of existence without a trial by jury, without examination, without being confronted with his accusers and witnesses, without the benefits of the law of the land? Where is our safety, when we are told that this act was justifiable because the person was not a Socrates? What has become of the worthy member's maxims? Is this one of them? Shall it be a maxim that a man shall be deprived of his life without the benefit of law? Shall such a deprivation of life be justified by answering, that the man's life was not taken *secundum artem* because he was a bad man? Shall it be a maxim that government ought not to be empowered to protect virtue?

*   *   *

He then stated the necessity and probability of obtaining amendments. This we ought to postpone until we come to that clause, and make up our minds whether there be any thing unsafe in this system. He conceived it impossible to obtain amendments after adopting it. If he was right, does not his own argument prove that, in his own conception, previous amendments cannot be had? for, sir, if subsequent amendments cannot be obtained, shall we get amendments before we ratify? The reasons against the latter do not apply against the former. There are in this state, and in every state in the Union, many who are decided enemies of the Union. Reflect on the probable conduct of such men. What will they do? They will bring amendments which are local in their nature, and which they know will not be accepted. What security have we that other states will not do the same? We are told that many in the states were violently opposed to it. They are more mindful of local interests. They will never propose such amendments as they think would be obtained. Disunion will be their object. This will be attained by the proposal of unreasonable amendments. This, sir, though a strong cause, is not the only one that will militate against previous amendments. Look at the comparative temper of this country now, and when the late federal Convention met. We had no idea then of any particular system. The formation of the most perfect plan was our object and wish. It was imagined that the states would accede to, and be pleased with, the proposition that would be made them. Consider the violence of opinions, the prejudices and animosities which have been since imbibed. Will not these operate greatly against mutual concessions, or a friendly concurrence?

*   *   *

Mr. Harrison then addressed the chair, but spoke so low that he could not be distinctly heard. He observed, that the accusation of the General Assembly, with respect to Josiah Phillips, was very unjust; that he was a man who, by the laws of nations, was entitled to no privilege of trial, &c.; that the Assembly had uniformly been lenient and moderate in their measures; and that, as the debates of this Convention would probably be published, he thought it very unwarrantable to utter expressions here which might induce the world to believe that the Assembly of Virginia had committed murder. He added some observations on the plan of government; that it certainly would operate an infringement of the rights and liberties of the people; that he was amazed that gentlemen should attempt to misrepresent facts to persuade the Convention to adopt such a system; and that he trusted they would not ratify it as it then stood.

Mr. George Nicholas, in reply to Mr. Harrison, observed, that the turpitude of a man's character was not a sufficient reason to deprive him of his life without a trial; that such a doctrine as that was a subversion of every shadow of freedom; that a fair trial was necessary to determine whether accusations against men's characters were well-founded or not; and that no person would be safe, were it once adopted as a maxim, that a man might be condemned without a trial. Mr. Nicholas then proceeded: Although we have sat eight days, so little has been done, that we have hardly begun to discuss the question regularly. The rule of the house to proceed clause by clause has been violated. Instead of doing this, gentlemen alarm us by declamations without reason or argument—by bold assertions that we are going to sacrifice our liberties. It is a fact known to many members within my hearing, that several members have tried their interest without doors to induce others to oppose this system. Every local interest that could affect their minds has been operated upon.

Can it be supposed that gentlemen elected, for their ability and integrity, to represent the people of Virginia in this Convention, to determine on this important question, whether or not we shall be connected with the other states in the Union—can it be thought, I say, that gentlemen in a situation like this will be influenced by motives like these? An answer which has been given is, that, if this Constitution be adopted, the western countries will be lost. It is better that a few countries should be lost, than all America. But, sir, no such consequence can follow from its adoption. They will be much more secure than they are at present. This Constitution, sir, will secure the equal liberty and happiness of all. It will do immortal honor to the gentlemen who formed it. I shall show the inconsistency of the gentleman who entertained us so long, (Mr. Henry.) He insisted that subsequent amendments would go to a dissolution of the Union; that Massachusetts was opposed to it in its present state. Massachusetts has absolutely ratified it, and has gone further, and said that such and such amendments shall be proposed by their representatives.

But such was the attachment of that respectable state to the Union, that, even at that early period, she ratified it unconditionally, and depended on the probability of obtaining amendments hereafter. Can this be a dissolution of the Union? Does this indicate an aversion to the Union on the part of that state? or can an imitation of her conduct injure us? He tells us that our present government is strong. How can that government be strong which depends on humble supplications for its support? Does a government which is dependent for its existence on others, and which is unable to afford protection to the people, deserve to be continued? But the honorable gentleman has no objections to see little storms in republics; they may be useful in the political as well as in the natural world. Every thing the great Creator has ordained in the natural world is founded on consummate wisdom: but let him tell us what advantages convulsions, dissensions, and bloodshed, will produce in the political world. Can disunion be the means of securing the happiness of the people in this political hemisphere? The worthy member has enlarged on our bill of rights.

Let us see whether his encomiums on the bill of rights be consistent with his other arguments. Our declaration of rights says that all men are by nature equally free and independent. How comes the gentleman to reconcile himself to a government wherein there are an hereditary monarch and nobility? He objects to this change, although our present federal system is totally without energy. He objects to this system, because he says it will prostrate your bill of rights. Does not the bill of rights tell you that a majority of the community have an indubitable right to alter any government which shall be found inadequate to the security of the public happiness? Does it not say "that no free government, or the blessings of liberty, can be preserved to any people, but by a firm adherence to justice, moderation, temperance, frugality, and virtue, and by frequent recurrence to fundamental principles"? Have not the inadequacy of the present system, and repeated flagrant violations of justice, and the other principles recommended by the bill of rights, been amply proved? As this plan of government will promote our happiness and establish justice, will not its adoption be justified by the very principles of your bill of rights?

* * *

I beg gentlemen seriously to reflect on this important business. They say amendments may be previously obtained, but acknowledged to be difficult. Will you join in an opposition that so directly tends to disunion? Can any member here think of disunion, or a partial confederacy, without horror? Yet both are expressly preferred to union, unless this system be amended previously. But, says the worthy member, why should not previous amendments be obtained? Will they not be agreed to, as the eight adopting states are friends to the union? But what follows? If they are so, they will agree to subsequent amendments. If you recommend alterations after ratifying, the friendship of the adopting states to the union, and the desires of several of them to have amendments, will lead them to gratify every reasonable proposal. By this means you secure the government and union. But if you reject the Constitution, and say you must have alterations as the previous condition of adoption, you sacrifice the union, and all the valuable parts of it.

* * *

But it is objected to for want of a bill of rights. It is a principle universally agreed upon, that all powers not given are retained. Where, by the Constitution, the general government has general powers for any purpose, its powers are absolute. Where it has powers with some exceptions, they are absolute only as to those exceptions. In either case, the people retain what is not conferred on the general government, as it is by their positive grant that it has any of its powers. In England, in all disputes between the king and people, recurrence is had to the enumerated rights of the people, to determine. Are the rights in dispute secured? Are they included in Magna Charta, Bill of Rights, &c.? If not, they are, generally speaking, within the king's prerogative. In disputes between Congress and the people, the reverse of the proposition holds. Is the disputed right enumerated? If not, Congress cannot meddle with it.

Which is the most safe? The people of America know what they have relinquished for certain purposes. They also know that they retain every thing else, and have a right to resume what they have given up, if it be perverted from its intended object. The king's prerogative is general, with certain exceptions. The people are, therefore, less secure than we are. Magna Charta, Bill of Rights, &c., secure their liberty. Our Constitution itself contains an English Bill of Rights. The English Bill of Rights declares that Parliaments shall be held frequently. Our Constitution says that Congress shall sit annually. The English Declaration of Rights provides that no laws shall be suspended. The Constitution provides that no laws shall be suspended, except one, and that in time of rebellion or invasion, which is the writ of habeas corpus. The Declaration of Rights says that there should be no army in time of peace without the consent of Parliament. Here we cannot have an army even in time of war, with the approbation of our representatives, for more than two years.

The liberty of the press is secured. What secures it in England? Is it secured by Magna Charta, the Declaration of Rights, or by any other express provision? It is not. They have no express security for the liberty of the press. They have a reliance on Parliament for its protection and security. In the time of King William, there passed an act for licensing the press. That was repealed. Since that time, it has been looked upon as safe. The people have depended on their representatives. They will not consent to pass an act to infringe it, because such an act would irritate the nation. It is equally secure with us. As to the trial by jury, consider in what situation it is by the state Constitution. It is not on a better footing. It is by implication under the control of the legislature, because it has left particular cases to be decided by the legislature. Here it is secured in criminal cases, and left to the legislatures in civil cases. One instance will prove the evil tendency of fixing it in the Constitution. It will extend to all cases. Causes in chancery, which, strictly speaking, never are, nor can be, well tried by a jury, would then be tried by that mode, and could not be altered, though found to be inconvenient.

*   *   *

[Wednesday, June 11]

Mr. Mason: . . . My honorable colleague in the late Convention [Gov. Randolph] seems to raise phantoms, and to show a singular skill in exorcisms, to terrify and compel us to take the new government, with all its sins and dangers. I know that he once saw as great danger in it as I do. What has happened since to alter his opinion? If any thing, I know it not. But the Virginia legislature has occasioned it, by postponing the matter. The Convention had met in June, instead of March or April. The liberty or misery of millions yet unborn are deeply concerned in our decision. When this is the case, I cannot imagine that the short period between the last of September and first of June ought to make any difference. The union between England and Scotland has been strongly instanced by the honorable gentleman to prove the necessity of our acceding to this new government. He must know that the act of union secured the rights of the Scotch nation. The rights and privileges of the people of Scotland are expressly secured. We wish only our rights to be secured. We must have such amendments as will secure the liberties and happiness of the people on a plain, simple construction, not on a doubtful ground. We wish to give the government sufficient energy, on real republican principles; but we wish to withhold such powers as are not absolutely necessary in themselves, but are extremely dangerous. We wish to shut the door against corruption in that place where it is most dangerous—to secure against the corruption of our own representatives. We ask such amendments as will point out what powers are reserved to the state governments, and clearly discriminate between them and those which are given to the general government, so as to prevent future disputes and clashing of interests. Grant us amendments like these, and we will cheerfully, with our hands and hearts, unite with those who advocate it, and we will do every thing we can to support and carry it into execution. But in its present form we never can accede to it. Our duty to God and to our posterity forbids it. We acknowledge the defects of the Confederation, and the necessity of a reform. We ardently wish for a union with our sister states, on terms of security. This I am bold to declare is the desire of most of the people. On these terms we will most cheerfully join with the warmest friends of this Constitution. On another occasion I shall point out the great dangers of this Constitution, and the amendments which are necessary. I will likewise endeavor to show that amendments after ratification are delusive and fallacious—perhaps utterly impracticable.

*   *   *

[Thursday, June 12]

Mr. Edmund Pendleton: . . . Permit me to deliver a few sentiments on the great and important subject of previous and subsequent amendments. When I sat down to read that paper, I did not read it with an expectation that it was perfect, and that no man would object to it. I had learned, sir, that an expectation of such perfection in any institute devised by man, was as vain as the search for the philosopher's stone. I discovered objections—I thought I saw there some sown seeds of disunion—not in the immediate operation of the government, but which might happen in some future time. I wish amendments to remove these. But these remote possible errors may be eradicated by the amendatory clause in the Constitution. I see no danger in making the experiment, since the system itself points out an easy mode of removing any errors which shall have been experienced. In this view, then, I think we may safely trust in the government. With respect to the eight states who have already acceded to it, do gentlemen believe that, should we propose amendments as the *sine qua non* of our adoption, they would listen to our proposals? I conceive, sir, that they would not retract. They would tell us—No, gentlemen, we cannot accept of your conditions. You put yourselves upon the ground of opposition. Your amendments are dictated by local considerations. We, in our adoption, have been influenced by considerations of general utility to the Union. We cannot abandon principles, like these, to gratify you. Thus, sir, by previous amendments, we present a hostile countenance. If, on the contrary, we imitate the conduct of those states, our language will be conciliatory and friendly. Gentlemen, we put ourselves on the same ground that you are on. We are not actuated by local considerations, but by such as affect the people of America in general. This conduct will give our amendments full weight.

I was surprised when I heard introduced the opinion of a gentleman (Mr. Jefferson) whom I highly respect. I know the great abilities of that gentleman. Providence has, for the good of mankind, accompanied those extensive abilities with a disposition to make use of them for the good of his fellow-beings; and I wish, with all my heart, that he was here to assist us on this interesting occasion. As to his letter, impressed as I am with the force of his authority, I think it was improper to introduce it on this occasion. The opinion of a private individual, however enlightened, ought not to influence our decision. But, admitting that this opinion ought to be conclusive with us, it strikes me in a different manner from the honorable gentleman. I have seen the letter in which this gentleman has written his opinion upon this subject. It appears that he is possessed of that Constitution, and has in his mind the idea of amending it—he has in his mind the very question, of subsequent or previous amendments, which is now under consideration. His sentiments on this subject are as follows: "I wish, with all my soul, that the nine first conventions may accept the new Constitution, because it will secure to us the good it contains, which I think great and important. I wish the four latest, whichever they be, may refuse to accede to it till amendments are secured." He then enumerates the amendments which he wishes to be secured, and adds, "We must take care, however, that neither this nor any other objection to the form, produce a schism in our Union. That would be an incurable evil; because friends falling out never cordially reunite." Are these sentiments in favor of those who wish to prevent its adoption by previous amendments? He wishes the first nine states to adopt it. What are his reasons? Because he thinks it will secure to us the good it contains, which he thinks great and important; and he wishes the other four may refuse it, because he thinks it may tend to obtain necessary amendments. But he would not wish that a schism should take place in the Union on any consideration. If, then, we are to be influenced by his opinion at all, we shall ratify it, and secure thereby the good it contains. . . .

* * *

Mr. Henry: Mr. Chairman, once more I find it necessary to trespass on your patience. An honorable gentleman, several days ago, observed, that the great object of this government was justice. We were told before, that the greater consideration was union. However, the consideration of justice seems to have been what influenced his mind when he made strictures on the proceedings of the Virginia Assembly. I thought the reasons of that transaction had been sufficiently explained.

It is exceedingly painful to me to be objecting; but I must make a few observations. I shall not again review the catalogue of dangers which the honorable gentleman entertained us with. They appear to me absolutely imaginary. They have, in my conception, been proved to be such.

* * *

The honorable gentleman has endeavored to explain the opinion of Mr. Jefferson, our common friend, into an advice to adopt this new government. What are his sentiments? He wishes nine states to adopt, and that four states may be found somewhere to reject it. Now, sir, I say, if we pursue his advice, what are we to do? To prefer form to substance? For, give me leave to ask, what is the substantial part of his counsel? It is, sir, that four states should reject. They tell us that, from the most authentic accounts, New Hampshire will adopt it. When I denied this, gentlemen said they were absolutely certain of it. Where, then, will four states be found to reject, if we adopt it? If we do, the counsel of this enlightened and worthy countryman of ours will be thrown away; and for what? He wishes to secure amendments and a bill of rights, if I am not mistaken. I speak from the best information, and if wrong, I beg to be put right. His amendments go to that despised thing, called a bill of rights, and all the rights which are dear to human nature—trial by jury, the liberty of religion and the press, &c. Do not gentlemen see that, if we adopt, under the idea of following Mr. Jefferson's opinion, we amuse ourselves with the shadow, while the substance is given away? If Virginia be for adoption, what states will be left, of sufficient respectability and importance to secure amendments by their rejection? As to North Carolina, it is a poor, despised place. Its dissent will not have influence to introduce any amendments. Where is the American spirit of liberty? Where will you find attachment to the rights of mankind, when Massachusetts, the great northern state, Pennsylvania, the great middle state, and Virginia, the great southern state, shall have adopted this government?

Where will you find magnanimity enough to reject it? Should the remaining states have this magnanimity, they will not have sufficient weight to have the government altered. This state has weight and importance. Her example will have powerful influence—her rejection will procure amendments. Shall we, by our adoption, hazard the loss of amendments? Shall we forsake that importance and respectability which our station in America commands, in hopes that relief will come from an obscure part of the Union? I hope my countrymen will spurn at the idea.

The necessity of amendments is universally admitted. It is a word which is reechoed from every part of the continent. A majority of those who hear me think amendments are necessary. Policy tells us they are necessary. Reason, self-preservation, and every idea of propriety, powerfully urge us to secure the dearest rights of human nature. Shall we, in direct violation of these principles, rest this security upon the uncertainty of its being obtained by a few states, more weak and less respectable than ourselves, and whose virtue and magnanimity may be overborne by the example of so many adopting states? Poor Rhode Island, and North Carolina, and even New York, surrounded with federal walls on every side, may not be magnanimous enough to reject; and if they do reject it, they will have but little influence to obtain amendments. I ask, if amendments be necessary, from whence can they be so properly proposed as from this state? The example of Virginia is a powerful thing, particularly with respect to North Carolina, whose supplies must come through Virginia. Every possible opportunity of procuring amendments is gone, our power and political salvation are gone, if we ratify unconditionally.

*   *   *

Mr. Madison: . . . The honorable member has introduced the subject of religion. Religion is not guarded; there is no bill of rights declaring that religion should be secure. Is a bill of rights a security for religion? Would the bill of rights, in this state, exempt the people from paying for the support of one particular sect, if such sect were exclusively established by law? If there were a majority of one sect, a bill of rights would be a poor protection for liberty. Happily for the states, they enjoy the utmost freedom of religion. This freedom arises from that multiplicity of sects which pervades America, and which is the best and only security for religious liberty in any society; for where there is such a variety of sects, there cannot be a majority of any one sect to oppress and persecute the rest. Fortunately for this commonwealth, a majority of the people are decidedly against any exclusive establishment. I believe it to be so in the other states. There is not a shadow of right in the general government to intermeddle with religion. Its least interference with it would be a most flagrant usurpation. I can appeal to my uniform conduct on this subject, that I have warmly supported religious freedom. It is better that this security should be depended upon from the general legislature, than from one particular state. A particular state might concur in one religious project. But the United States abound in such a variety of sects, that it is a strong security against religious persecution; and it is sufficient to authorize a conclusion, that no one sect will ever be able to outnumber or depress the rest.

* * *

[Monday, June 14]

Mr. George Mason still thought that there ought to be some express declaration in the Constitution, asserting that rights not given to the general government were retained by the states. He apprehended that, unless this was done, many valuable and important rights would be concluded to be given up by implication. All governments were drawn from the people, though many were perverted to their oppression. The government of Virginia, he remarked, was drawn from the people; yet there were certain great and important rights, which the people, by their bill of rights, declared to be paramount to the power of the legislature. He asked, Why should it not be so in this Constitution? Was it because we were more substantially represented in it than in the state government? If, in the state government, where the people were substantially and fully represented, it was necessary that the great rights of human nature should be secure from the encroachments of the legislature, he asked if it was not more necessary in this government, where they were but inadequately represented? He declared that artful sophistry and evasions could not satisfy him. He could see no clear distinction between rights relinquished by a positive grant, and lost by implication. Unless there were a bill of rights, implication might swallow up all our rights.

Mr. Henry: Mr. Chairman, the necessity of a bill of rights appears to me to be greater in this government than ever it was in any government before. I have observed already, that the sense of the European nations, and particularly Great Britain, is against the construction of rights being retained which are not expressly relinquished. I repeat, that all nations have adopted this construction—that all rights not expressly and unequivocally reserved to the people are impliedly and incidentally relinquished to rulers, as necessarily inseparable from the delegated powers. It is so in Great Britain; for every possible right, which is not reserved to the people by some express provision or compact, is within the king's prerogative. It is so in that country which is said to be in such full possession of freedom. It is so in Spain, Germany, and other parts of the world. Let us consider the sentiments which have been entertained by the people of America on this subject. At the revolution, it must be admitted that it was their sense to set down those great rights which ought, in all countries, to be held inviolable and sacred. Virginia did so, we all remember. She made a compact to reserve, expressly, certain rights.

When fortified with full, adequate, and abundant representation, was she satisfied with that representation? No. She most cautiously and guardedly reserved and secured those invaluable, inestimable. rights and privileges, which no people, inspired with the least glow of patriotic liberty, ever did, or ever can, abandon. She is called upon now to abandon them, and dissolve that compact which secured them to her. She is called upon to accede to another compact, which most infallibly supersedes and annihilates her present one. Will she do it? This is the question. If you intend to reserve your unalienable rights, you must have the most express stipulation; for, if implication be allowed, you are ousted of those rights. If the people do not think it necessary to reserve them, they will be supposed to be given up. How were the congressional rights defined when the people of America united by a confederacy to defend their liberties and rights against the tyrannical attempts of Great Britain? The states were not then contented with implied reservation. No, Mr. Chairman. It was expressly declared in our Confederation that every right was retained by the states, respectively, which was not given up to the government of the United States. But there is no such thing here. You, therefore, by a natural and unavoidable implication, give up your rights to the general government.

Your own example furnishes an argument against it. If you give up these powers, without a bill of rights, you will exhibit the most absurd thing to mankind that ever the world saw—a government that has abandoned all its powers—the powers of direct taxation, the sword, and the purse You have disposed of them to Congress, without a bill of rights—without check, limitation, or control. And still you have checks and guards; still you keep barriers—pointed where? Pointed against your weakened, prostrated, enervated state government! You have a bill of rights to defend you against the state government, which is bereaved of all power, and yet you have none against Congress, though in full and exclusive possession of all power! You arm yourselves against the weak and defenceless, and expose yourselves naked to the armed and powerful. Is not this a conduct of unexampled absurdity? What barriers have you to oppose to this most strong, energetic government? To that government you have nothing to oppose. All your defence is given up. This is a real, actual defect. It must strike the mind of every gentleman. When our government was first instituted in Virginia, we declared the common law of England to be in force.

That system of law which has been admired, and has protected us and our ancestors, is excluded by that system. Added to this, we adopted a bill of rights. By this Constitution, some of the best barriers of human rights are thrown away. Is there not an additional reason to have a bill of rights? By the ancient common law, the trial of all facts is decided by a jury of impartial men from the immediate vicinage This paper speaks of different juries from the common law in criminal cases; and in civil controversies excludes trial by jury altogether. There is, therefore, more occasion for the supplementary check of a bill of rights now than then. Congress, from their general powers, may fully go into business of human legislation. They may legislate, in criminal cases, from treason to the lowest offence—petty larceny. They may define crimes and prescribe punishments. In the definition of crimes, I trust they will be directed by what wise representatives ought to be governed by. But when we come to punishments, no latitude ought to be left, nor dependence put on the virtue of representatives. What says our bill of rights?—"that excessive bail ought not to be required, nor excessive fines imposed, nor cruel and unusual punishments inflicted." Are you not, therefore, now calling on those gentlemen who are to compose Congress, to prescribe trials and define punishments without this control? Will they find sentiments there similar to this bill of rights? You let them loose; you do more—you depart from the genius of your country. That paper tells you that the trial of crimes shall be by jury, and held in the state where the crime shall have been committed. Under this extensive provision, they may proceed in a manner extremely dangerous to liberty: a person accused may be carried from one extremity of the state to another, and be tried, not by an impartial jury of the vicinage, acquainted with his character and the circumstances of the fact, but by a jury unacquainted with both, and who may be biased against him. Is not this sufficient to alarm men? How different is this from the immemorial practice of your British ancestors, and your own! I need not tell you that, by the common law, a number of hundredors were required on a jury, and that afterwards it was sufficient if the jurors came from the same county. With less than this the people of England have never been satisfied. That paper ought to have declared the common law in force.

In this business of legislation, your members of Congress will loose the restriction of not imposing excessive fines, demanding excessive bail, and inflicting cruel and unusual punishments. These are prohibited by your declaration of rights. What has distinguished our ancestors?—That they would not admit of tortures, or cruel and barbarous punishment. But Congress may introduce the practice of the civil law, in preference to that of the common law. They may introduce the practice of France, Spain, and Germany—of torturing, to extort a confession of the crime. They will say that they might as well draw examples from those countries as from Great Britain, and they will tell you that there is such a necessity of strengthening the arm of government, that they must have a criminal equity, and extort confession by torture, in order to punish with still more relentless severity. We are then lost and undone. And can any man think it troublesome, when we can, by a small interference, prevent our rights from being lost? If you will, like the Virginian government, give them knowledge of the extent of the rights retained by the people, and the powers of themselves, they will, if they be honest men, thank you for it. Will they not wish to go on sure grounds? But if you leave them otherwise, they will not know how to proceed; and, being in a state of uncertainty, they will assume rather than give up powers by implication.

A bill of rights may be summed up in a few words. What do they tell us?—That our rights are reserved. Why not say so? Is it because it will consume too much paper? Gentlemen's reasoning against a bill of rights does not satisfy me. Without saying which has the right side, it remains doubtful. A bill of rights is a favorite thing with the Virginians and the people of the other states likewise. It may be their prejudice, but the government ought to suit their geniuses; otherwise, its operation will be unhappy. A bill of rights, even if its necessity be doubtful, will exclude the possibility of dispute; and, with great submission, I think the best way is to have no dispute. In the present Constitution, they are restrained from issuing general warrants to search suspected places, or seize persons not named, without evidence of the commission of a fact, &c. There was certainly some celestial influence governing those who deliberated on that Constitution; for they have, with the most cautious and enlightened circumspection, guarded those indefeasible rights which ought ever to be held sacred! The officers of Congress may come upon you now, fortified with all the terrors of paramount federal authority. Excisemen may come in multitudes; for the limitation of their numbers no man knows. They may, unless the general government be restrained by a bill of rights, or some similar restriction, go into your cellars and rooms, and search, ransack, and measure, every thing you eat, drink, and wear. They ought to be restrained within proper bounds. With respect to the freedom of the press, I need say nothing; for it is hoped that the gentlemen who shall compose Congress will take care to infringe as little as possible the rights of human nature. This will result from their integrity. They should, from prudence, abstain from violating the rights of their constituents. They are not, however, expressly restrained. But whether they will intermeddle with that palladium of our liberties or not, I leave you to determine.

Mr. Grayson thought it questionable whether rights not given up were reserved. A majority of the states, he observed, had expressly reserved certain important rights by bills of rights, and that in the Confederation there was a clause declaring expressly that every power and right not given up was retained by the states. It was the general sense of America that such a clause was necessary; otherwise, why did they introduce a clause which was totally unnecessary? It had been insisted, he said, in many parts of America, that a bill of rights was only necessary between a prince and people, and not in such a government as this, which was a compact between the people themselves. This did not satisfy his mind; for so extensive was the power of legislation, in his estimation, that he doubted whether, when it was once given up, any thing was retained. He further remarked, that there were some negative clauses in the Constitution, which refuted the doctrine contended for by the other side. For instance; the 2d clause of the 9th section of the 1st article provided that "the privilege of the writ of habeas corpus shall not be suspended, unless when, in cases of rebellion or invasion, the public safety may require it." And, by the last clause of the same section, "no title of nobility shall be granted by the United States." Now, if these restrictions had not been here inserted, he asked whether Congress would not most clearly have had a right to suspend that great and valuable right, and to grant titles of nobility. When, in addition to these considerations, he saw they had an indefinite power to provide for the general welfare, he thought there were great reasons to apprehend great dangers. He thought, therefore, that there ought to be a bill of rights.

Mr. George Nicholas, in answer to the two gentlemen last up, observed that, though there was a declaration of rights in the government of Virginia, it was no conclusive reason that there should be one in this Constitution, for, if it was unnecessary in the former, its omission in the latter could be no defect. They ought, therefore, to prove that it was essentially necessary to be inserted in the Constitution of Virginia. There were five or six states in the Union which had no bill of rights, separately and distinctly as such; but they annexed the substance of a bill of rights to their respective constitutions. These states, he further observed, were as free as this state, and their liberties as secure as ours. If so, gentlemen's arguments from the precedent were not good. In Virginia, all powers were given to the government without any exception. It was different in the general government, to which certain special powers were delegated for certain purposes. He asked which was the more safe. Was it safer to grant general powers than certain limited powers? This much as to the theory, continued he. What is the practice of this invaluable government? Have your citizens been bound by it? They have not, sir. You have violated that maxim, "that no man shall be condemned without a fair trial." That man who was killed, not *secundum artem,* was deprived of his life without the benefit of law, and in express violation of this declaration of rights, which they confide in so much. But, sir, this bill of rights was no security. It is but a paper check. It has been violated in many other instances. Therefore, from theory and practice, it may be concluded that this government, with special powers, without any express exceptions, is better than a government with general powers and special exceptions. But the practice of England is against us. The rights there reserved to the people are to limit and check the king's prerogative. It is easier to enumerate the exceptions to his prerogative, than to mention all the cases to which it extends. Besides, these reservations, being only formed in acts of the legislature, may be altered by the representatives of the people when they think proper. No comparison can be made of this with the other governments he mentioned. There is no stipulation between the king and people. The former is possessed of absolute, unlimited authority.

But, sir, this Constitution is defective because the common law is not declared to be in force! What would have been the consequence if it had? It would be immutable. But now it can be changed or modified as the legislative body may find necessary for the community. But the common law is not excluded. There is nothing in that paper to warrant the assertion. As to the exclusion of a jury from the vicinage, he has mistaken the fact. The legislature may direct a jury to come from the vicinage. But the gentleman says that, by this Constitution, they have power to make laws to define crimes and prescribe punishments; and that, consequently, we are not free from torture. Treason against the United States is defined in the Constitution, and the forfeiture limited to the life of the person attainted. Congress have power to define and punish piracies and felonies committed on the high seas, and offences against the laws of nations; but they cannot define or prescribe the punishment of any other crime whatever, without violating the Constitution. If we had no security against torture but our declaration of rights, we might be tortured to-morrow; for it has been repeatedly infringed and disregarded. A bill of rights is only an acknowledgment of the preëxisting claim to rights in the people. They belong to us as much as if they had been inserted in the Constitution. But it is said that, if it be doubtful, the possibility of dispute ought to be precluded. Admitting it was proper for the Convention to have inserted a bill of rights, it is not proper here to propose it as the condition of our accession to the Union. Would you reject this government for its omission, dissolve the Union, and bring miseries on yourselves and posterity? I hope the gentleman does not oppose it on this ground solely. Is there another reason? He said that it is not only the general wish of this state, but all the states, to have a bill of rights. If it be so, where is the difficulty of having this done by way of subsequent amendment? We shall find the other states willing to accord with their own favorite wish. The gentleman last up says that the power of legislation includes every thing. A general power of legislation does. But this is a special power of legislation. Therefore, it does not contain that plenitude of power which he imagines. They cannot legislate in any case but those particularly enumerated. No gentleman, who is a friend to the government, ought to withhold his assent from it for this reason.

Mr. George Mason replied that the worthy gentleman was mistaken in his assertion that the bill of rights did not prohibit torture; for that one clause expressly provided that no man can give evidence against himself; and that the worthy gentleman must know that, in those countries where torture is used, evidence was extorted from the criminal himself. Another clause of the bill of rights provided that no cruel and unusual punishments shall be inflicted; therefore, torture was included in the prohibition.

Mr. Nicholas acknowledged the bill of rights to contain that prohibition, and that the gentleman was right with respect to the practice of extorting confession from the criminal in those countries where torture is used; but still he saw no security arising from the bill of rights as separate from the Constitution, for that it had been frequently violated with impunity.

*   *   *

[Tuesday, June 15]

Mr. Henry: Mr. Chairman, we have now come to the 9th section, and I consider myself at liberty to take a short view of the whole. I wish to do it very briefly. Give me leave to remark that there is a bill of rights in that government.

There are express restrictions, which are in the shape of a bill of rights; but they bear the name of the 9th section. The design of the negative expressions in this section is to prescribe limits beyond which the powers of Congress shall not go. These are the sole bounds intended by the American government. Whereabouts do we stand with respect to a bill of rights? Examine it, and compare it to the idea manifested by the Virginian bill of rights, or that of the other states. The restraints in this congressional bill of rights are so feeble and few, that it would have been infinitely better to have said nothing about it. The fair implication is, that they can do every thing they are not forbidden to do. What will be the result if Congress, in the course of their legislation, should do a thing not restrained by this 9th section? It will fall as an incidental power to Congress, not being prohibited expressly in the Constitution. The first prohibition is, that the privilege of the writ of habeas corpus shall not be suspended but when, in case of rebellion or invasion, the public safety may require it. It results clearly that, if it had not said so, they could suspend it in all cases whatsoever. It reverses the position of the friends of this Constitution, that every thing is retained which is not given up; for, instead of this, every thing is given up which is not expressly reserved. It does not speak affirmatively, and say that it shall be suspended in those cases; but that it shall not be suspended but in certain cases; going on a supposition that every thing which is not negatived shall remain with Congress. If the power remains with the people, how can Congress supply the want of an affirmative grant? They cannot do it but by implication, which destroys their doctrine. The Virginia bill of rights interdicts the relinquishment of the sword and purse without control. That bill of rights secures the great and principal rights of mankind. But this bill of rights extends to but very few cases, and is destructive of the doctrine advanced by the friends of that paper.

If ex post facto laws had not been interdicted, they might also have been extended by implication at pleasure. Let us consider whether this restriction be founded in wisdom or good policy. If no ex post facto laws be made, what is to become of the old Continental paper dollars? Will not this country be forced to pay in gold and silver, shilling for shilling? Gentlemen may think that this does not deserve an answer. But it is an all-important question, because the property of this country is not commensurate to the enormous demand. Our own government triumphs, with infinite superiority, when put in contrast with that paper. The want of a bill of rights will render all their laws, however oppressive, constitutional.

If the government of Virginia passes a law in contradiction to our bill of rights, it is nugatory. By that paper the national wealth is to be disposed of under the veil of secrecy, for the publication from time to time will amount to nothing, and they may conceal what they may think requires secrecy. How different it is in your own government! Have not the people seen the journals of our legislature every day during every session? Is not the lobby full of people every day? Yet gentlemen say that the publication from time to time is a security unknown in our state government! Such a regulation would be nugatory and vain, or at least needless, as the people see the journals of our legislature, and hear their debates, every day. If this be not more secure than what is in that paper, I will give up that I have totally misconceived the principles of the government. You are told that your rights are secured in this new government. They are guarded in no other part but this 9th section. The few restrictions in that section are your only safeguards. They may control your actions, and your very words, without being repugnant to that paper. The existence of your dearest privileges will depend on the consent of Congress, for they are not within the restrictions of the 9th section.

If gentlemen think that securing the slave trade is a capital object; that the privilege of the habeas corpus is sufficiently secured; that the exclusion of ex post facto laws will produce no inconvenience; that the publication from time to time will secure their property; in one word, that this section alone will sufficiently secure their liberties,—I have spoken in vain. Every word of mine, and of my worthy coadjutor, is lost. I trust that gentlemen, on this occasion, will see the great objects of religion, liberty of the press, trial by jury, interdiction of cruel punishments, and every other sacred right, secured, before they agree to that paper. These most important human rights are not protected by that section, which is the only safeguard in the Constitution. My mind will not be quieted till I see something substantial come forth in the shape of a bill of rights.

*   *   *

Gov. Randolph: . . . On the subject of a bill of rights, the want of which has been complained of, I will observe that it has been sanctified by such reverend authority, that I feel some difficulty in going against it. I shall not, however, be deterred from giving my opinion on this occasion, let the consequence be what it may. At the beginning of the war, we had no certain bill of rights; for our charter cannot be considered as a bill of rights; it is nothing more than an investiture, in the hands of the Virginia citizens, of those rights which belonged to British subjects. When the British thought proper to infringe our rights, was it not necessary to mention, in our Constitution, those rights which ought to be paramount to the power of the legislature? Why is the bill of rights distinct from the Constitution? I consider bills of rights in this view—that the government should use them, when there is a departure from its fundamental principles, in order to restore them.

This is the true sense of a bill of rights. If it be consistent with the Constitution, or contain additional rights, why not put it in the Constitution? If it be repugnant to the Constitution, here will be a perpetual scene of warfare between them. The honorable gentleman has praised the bill of rights of Virginia, and called it his guardian angel, and vilified this Constitution for not having it. Give me leave to make a distinction between the representatives of the people of a particular country, who are appointed as the ordinary legislature, having no limitation to their powers, and another body arising from a compact, and with certain delineated powers. Were a bill of rights necessary in the former, it would not be in the latter; for the best security that can be in the latter is the express enumeration of its powers. But let me ask the gentleman where his favorite rights are violated. They are not violated by the 10th section, which contains restrictions on the states. Are they violated by the enumerated powers? [Here his excellency read from the 8th to the 12th article of the bill of rights.] Is there not provision made, in this Constitution, for the trial by jury in criminal cases? Does not the 3d article provide that the trial of all crimes shall be by jury, and held where the said crimes shall have been committed? Does it not follow that the cause and nature of the accusation must be produced?— because, otherwise, they cannot proceed on the cause. Every one knows that the witnesses must be brought before the jury, or else the prisoner will be discharged. Calling of evidence in his favor is coincident to his trial. There is no suspicion that less than twelve jurors will be thought sufficient. The only defect is, that there is no speedy trial. Consider how this could have been amended. We have heard complaints against it because it is supposed the jury is to come from the state at large. It will be in their power to have juries from the vicinage. And would not the complaints have been louder if they had appointed a federal court to be had in every county in the state? Criminals are brought, in this state, from every part of the country to the general court, and jurors from the vicinage are summoned to the trials. There can be no reason to prevent the general government from adopting a similar regulation.

As to the exclusion of excessive bail and fines, and cruel and unusual punishments, this would follow of itself, without a bill of rights. Observations have been made about watchfulness over those in power which deserve our attention. There must be a combination; we must presume corruption in the House of Representatives, Senate, and President, before we can suppose that excessive fines can be imposed or cruel punishments inflicted. Their number is the highest security. Numbers are the highest security in our own Constitution, which has attracted so many eulogiums from the gentlemen. Here we have launched into a sea of suspicions. How shall we check power? By their numbers. Before these cruel punishments can be inflicted, laws must be passed, and judges must judge contrary to justice. This would excite universal discontent and detestation of the members of the government. They might involve their friends in the calamities resulting from it, and could be removed from office. I never desire a greater security than this, which I believe to be absolutely sufficient.

That general warrants are grievous and oppressive, and ought not to be granted, I fully admit. I heartily concur in expressing my detestation of them. But we have sufficient security here also. We do not rely on the integrity of any one particular person or body, but on the number and different orders of the members of the government—some of them having necessarily the same feelings with ourselves. Can it be believed that the federal judiciary would not be independent enough to prevent such oppressive practices? If they will not do justice to persons injured, may they not go to our own state judiciaries, and obtain it?

Gentlemen have been misled, to a certain degree, by a general declaration that the trial by jury was gone. We see that, in the most valuable cases, it is reserved. Is it abolished in civil cases? Let him put his finger on the part where it is abolished. The Constitution is silent on it. What expression would you wish the Constitution to use, to establish it? Remember we were not making a constitution for Virginia alone, or we might have taken Virginia for our directory. But we were forming a constitution for thirteen states. The trial by jury is different in different states. In some states it is excluded in cases in which it is admitted in others. In admiralty causes it is not used. Would you have a jury to determine the case of a capture? The Virginia legislature thought proper to make an exception of that case. These depend on the law of nations, and no twelve men that could be picked up could be equal to the decision of such a matter.

Then, sir, the freedom of the press is said to be insecure. God forbid that I should give my voice against the freedom of the press. But I ask, (and with confidence that it cannot be answered,) Where is the page where it is restrained? If there had been any regulation about it, leaving it insecure, then there might have been reason for clamors. But this is not the case. If it be, I again ask for the particular clause which gives liberty to destroy the freedom of the press.

He has added religion to the objects endangered, in his conception. Is there any power given over it? Let it be pointed out. Will he not be contented with the answer that has been frequently given to that objection? The variety of sects which abounds in the United States is the best security for the freedom of religion. No part of the Constitution, even if strictly construed, will justify a conclusion that the general government can take away or impair the freedom of religion.

The gentleman asks, with triumph, Shall we be deprived of these valuable rights? Had there been an exception, or an express infringement of those rights, he might object; but I conceive every fair reasoner will agree that there is no just cause to suspect that they will be violated.

But he objects that the common law is not established by the Constitution. The wisdom of the Convention is displayed by its omission, because the common law ought not to be immutably fixed. Is it established in our own Constitution, or the bill of rights, which has been resounded through the house? It is established only by an act of the legislature, and can therefore be changed as circumstances may require it. Let the honorable gentleman consider what would be the destructive consequences of its establishment in the Constitution. Even in England, where the firmest opposition has been made to encroachments upon it, it has been frequently changed. What would have been our dilemma if it had been established? Virginia has declared that children shall have equal portions of the real estate of their intestate parents, and it is consistent with the principles of a republican government.

The immutable establishment of the common law would have been repugnant to that regulation. It would, in many respects, be destructive to republican principles, and productive of great inconveniences. I might indulge myself by showing many parts of the common law which would have this effect. I hope I shall not be thought to speak ludicrously, when I say the writ of burning heretics would have been revived by it. It would tend to throw real property into few hands, and prevent the introduction of many salutary regulations. Thus, were the common law adopted in that system, it would destroy the principles of republican government. But this is not excluded. It may be established by an act of legislature. Its defective parts may be altered, and it may be changed and modified as the convenience of the public may require it.

I said, when I opened my observations, that I thought the friends of the Constitution were mistaken when they supposed the powers granted by the last clause of the 8th section to be merely incidental; and that its enemies were equally mistaken when they put such an extravagant construction upon it.

My objection is, that the clause is ambiguous, and that that ambiguity may injure the states. My fear is, that it will, by gradual accessions, gather to a dangerous length. This is my apprehension, and I disdain to disown it. I will praise it where it deserves it, and censure it where it appears defective. But, sir, are we to reject it, because it is ambiguous in some particular instances? I cast my eyes to the actual situation of America. I see the dreadful tempest, to which the present calm is a prelude, if disunion takes place. I see the anarchy which must happen if no energetic government be established. In this situation, I would take the Constitution, were it more objectionable than it is; for, if anarchy and confusion follow disunion, an enterprising man may enter into the American throne. I conceive there is no danger. The representatives are chosen by and from among the people. They will have a fellow-feeling for the farmers and planters. The twenty-six senators, representatives of the states, will not be those desperadoes and horrid adventurers which they are represented to be. The state legislatures, I trust, will not forget the duty they owe to their country so far as to choose such men to manage their federal interests. I trust that the members of Congress themselves will explain the ambiguous parts; and if not, the states can combine in order to insist on amending the ambiguities. I would depend on the present actual feeling of the people of America, to introduce any amendment which may be necessary. I repeat it again, though I do not reverence the Constitution, that its adoption is necessary to avoid the storm which is hanging over America, and that no greater curse can befall her than the dissolution of the political connection between the states. Whether we shall propose previous or subsequent amendments, is now the only dispute. It is supererogation to repeat again the arguments in support of each; but I ask gentlemen whether, as eight states have adopted it, it be not safer to adopt it, and rely on the probability of obtaining amendments, than, by a rejection, to hazard a breach of the Union?

*   *   *

[Friday, June 20]

Mr. Henry: . . . The honorable gentleman has told us that our representatives will mend every defect. I do not know how often we have recurred to that source, but I can find no consolation in it. Who are they? Ourselves. What is their duty? To alter the spirit of the Constitution—to new model it? Is that their duty, or ours? It is our duty to rest our rights on a certain foundation, and not trust to future contingencies.

We are told of certain difficulties. I acknowledge it is difficult to form a constitution. But I have seen difficulties conquered which were as unconquerable as this. We are told that trial by jury is difficult to be had in certain cases. Do we not know the meaning of the term? We are also told it is a technical term. I see one thing in this Constitution; I made the observation before, and I am still of the same opinion, that every thing with respect to privileges is so involved in darkness, it makes me suspicious—not of those gentlemen who formed it, but of its operations in its present form. Could not precise terms have been used? You find, by the observations of the gentleman last up, that, when there is a plenitude of power, there is no difficulty; but when you come to a plain thing, understood by all America, there are contradictions, ambiguities, difficulties, and what not. Trial by jury is attended, it seems, with insuperable difficulties, and therefore omitted altogether in civil cases. But an idea is held out that it is secured in criminal cases. I had rather it had been left out altogether than have it so vaguely and equivocally provided for. Poor people do not understand technical terms. Their rights ought to be secured in language of which they know the meaning. As they do not know the meaning of such terms, they may be injured with impunity. If they dare oppose the hands of tyrannical power, you will see what has been practised elsewhere. They may be tried by the most partial powers, by their most implacable enemies, and be sentenced and put to death, with all the forms of a fair trial. I would rather be left to the judges. An abandoned juror would not dread the loss of character like a judge. From these, and a thousand other considerations, I would rather the trial by jury were struck out altogether. There is no right of challenging partial jurors. There is no common law of America, (as has been said,) nor constitution, but that on your table. If there be neither common law nor constitution, there can be no right to challenge partial jurors. Yet the right is as valuable as the trial by jury itself.

*   *   *

To hear gentlemen of such penetration make use of such arguments, to persuade us to part with that trial by jury, is very astonishing. We are told that we are to part with that trial by jury which our ancestors secured their lives and property with, and we are to build castles in the air, and substitute visionary modes of decision for that noble palladium. I hope we shall never be induced, by such arguments, to part with that excellent mode of trial. No appeal can now be made as to fact in common-law suits. The unanimous verdict of twelve impartial men cannot be reversed. I shall take the liberty of reading to the committee the sentiments of the learned Judge Blackstone, so often quoted, on the subject.

[Here Mr. Henry read the eulogium of that writer on this trial. *Blackstone's Commentaries*, iii. 319.]

The opinion of this learned writer is more forcible and cogent than any thing I could say. Notwithstanding the transcendent excellency of this trial, its essentiality to the preservation of liberty, and the extreme danger of substituting any other mode, yet we are now about to alienate it.

But on this occasion, as on all others, we are admonished to rely on the wisdom and virtue of our rulers. We are told that the members from Georgia, New Hampshire, &c., will not dare to infringe this privilege; that, as it would excite the indignation of the people, they would not attempt it: that is, the enormity of the offence is urged as a security against its commission. It is so abominable that Congress will not exercise it. Shall we listen to arguments like these, when trial by jury is about to be relinquished? I beseech you to consider before you decide. I ask you, What is the value of that privilege? When Congress, in all the plenitude of their arrogance, magnificence, and power, can take it from you, will you be satisfied? Are we to go so far as to concede every thing to the virtue of Congress? Throw yourselves at once on their mercy; be no longer free than their virtue will predominate: if this will satisfy republican minds, there is an end of every thing. I disdain to hold any thing of any man. We ought to cherish that disdain America viewed with indignation the idea of holding her rights of England. The Parliament gave you the most solemn assurances that they would not exercise this power. Were you satisfied with their promises? No. Did you trust any man on earth? No. You answered that you disdained to hold your innate, indefeasible rights of any one. Now, you are called upon to give an exorbitant and most alarming power. The genius of my countrymen is the same now that it was then. They have the same feelings. They are equally martial and bold. Will not their answer therefore be the same? I hope that gentlemen will, on a fair investigation, be candid, and not on every occasion recur to the virtue of our representatives.

When deliberating on the relinquishment of the sword and purse, we have a right to some other reason than the possible virtue of our rulers. We are informed that the strength and energy of the government call for the surrender of this right. Are we to make our country strong by giving up our privileges? I tell you that, if you judge from reason, or the experience of other nations, you will find that your country will be great and respectable according as you will preserve this great privilege. It is prostrated by that paper. Juries from the vicinage being not secured, this right is in reality sacrificed. All is gone. And why? Because a rebellion may arise. Resistance will come from certain countries, and juries will come from the same countries.

I trust the honorable gentleman, on a better recollection, will be sorry for this observation. Why do we love this trial by jury? Because it prevents the hand of oppression from cutting you off. They may call any thing rebellion, and deprive you of a fair trial by an impartial jury of your neighbors. Has not your mother country magnanimously preserved this noble privilege upwards of a thousand years? Did she relinquish a jury of the vicinage because there was a possibility of resistance to oppression? She has been magnanimous enough to resist every attempt to take away this privilege. She has had magnanimity enough to rebel when her rights were infringed. That country had juries of hundredors for many generations. And shall Americans give up that which nothing could induce the English people to relinquish? The idea is abhorrent to my mind. There was a time when we should have spurned at it. This gives me comfort—that, as long as I have existence, my neighbors will protect me. Old as I am, it is probable I may yet have the appellation of rebel. I trust that I shall see congressional oppression crushed in embryo. As this government stands, I despise and abhor it. Gentlemen demand it, though it takes away the trial by jury in civil cases, and does worse than take it away in criminal cases. It is gone unless you preserve it now. I beg pardon for speaking so long. Many more observations will present themselves to the minds of gentlemen when they analyze this part. We find enough, from what has been said, to come to this conclusion—that it was not intended to have jury trials at all; because, difficult as it was, the name was known, and it might have been inserted. Seeing that appeals are given, in matters of fact, to the Supreme Court, we are led to believe that you must carry your witnesses an immense distance to the seat of government, or decide appeals according to the Roman law. I shall add no more, but that I hope that gentlemen will recollect what they are about to do, and consider that they are going to give up this last and best privilege.

Mr. Pendleton: Mr. Chairman, before I enter upon the objections made to this part, I will observe that I should suppose, if there were any person in this audience who had not read this Constitution, or who had not heard what has been said, and should have been told that the trial by jury was intended to be taken away, he would be surprised to find, on examination, that there was no exclusion of it in civil cases, and that it was expressly provided for in criminal cases. I never could see such intention, or any tendency towards it. I have not heard any arguments of that kind used in favor of the Constitution. If there were any words in it which said that trial by jury should not be used, it would be dangerous. I find it secured in criminal cases, and that the trial is to be had in the state where the crime shall have been committed. It is strongly insisted that the privilege of challenging, or excepting to the jury, is not secured. When the Constitution says that the trial shall be by jury, does it not say that every incident will go along with it? I think the honorable gentleman was mistaken yesterday in his reasoning on the propriety of a jury from the vicinage.

He supposed that a jury from the neighborhood is had from this view— that they should be acquainted with the personal character of the person accused. I thought it was with another view—that the jury should have some personal knowledge of the fact, and acquaintance with the witnesses, who will come from the neighborhood. How is it understood in this state? Suppose a man, who lives in Winchester, commits a crime at Norfolk; the jury to try him must come, not from Winchester, but from the neighborhood of Norfolk. Trial by jury is secured by this system in criminal cases, as are all the incidental circumstances relative to it.

*　　　*　　　*

Mr. Marshall: . . . The exclusion of trial by jury, in this case, he urged to prostrate our rights. Does the word court only mean the judges? Does not the determination of a jury necessarily lead to the judgment of the court? Is there any thing here which gives the judges exclusive jurisdiction of matters of fact? What is the object of a jury trial? To inform the court of the facts. When a court has cognizance of facts does it not follow that they can make inquiry by a jury? It is impossible to be otherwise. I hope that in this country, where impartiality is so much admired, the laws will direct facts to be ascertained by a jury. But, says the honorable gentleman, the juries in the ten miles square will be mere tools of parties, with which he would not trust his person or property; which, he says, he would rather leave to the court. Because the government may have a district of ten miles square, will no man stay there but the tools and officers of the government? Will nobody else be found there? Is it so in any other part of the world, where a government has legislative power? Are there none but officers, and tools of the government of Virginia, in Richmond? Will there not be independent merchants, and respectable gentlemen of fortune, within the ten miles square? Will there not be worthy farmers and mechanics? Will not a good jury be found there, as well as any where else? Will the officers of the government become improper to be on a jury? What is it to the government whether this man or that man succeeds? It is all one thing. Does the Constitution say that juries shall consist of officers, or that the Supreme Court shall be held in the ten miles square? It was acknowledged, by the honorable member, that it was secure in England. What makes it secure there? Is it their constitution? What part of their constitution is there that the Parliament cannot change? As the preservation of this right is in the hands of Parliament, and it has ever been held sacred by them, will the government of America be less honest than that of Great Britain? Here a restriction is to be found. The jury is not to be brought out of the state. There is no such restriction in that government; for the laws of Parliament decide every thing respecting it. Yet gentlemen tell us that there is safety there, and nothing here but danger. It seems to me that the laws of the United States will generally secure trials by a jury of the vicinage, or in such manner as will be most safe and convenient for the people.

But it seems that the right of challenging the jurors is not secured in this Constitution. Is this done by our own Constitution, or by any provision of the English government? Is it done by their Magna Charta, or bill of rights? This privilege is founded on their laws. If so, why should it be objected to the American Constitution, that it is not inserted in it? If we are secure in Virginia without mentioning it in our Constitution, why should not this security be found in the federal court?

*   *   *

We are satisfied with the provision made in this country on the subject of trial by jury. Does our Constitution direct trials to be by jury? It is required in our bill of rights, which is not a part of the Constitution. Does any security arise from hence? Have you a jury when a judgment is obtained on a replevin bond, or by default? Have you a jury when a motion is made for the commonwealth against an individual; or when a motion is made by one joint obligor against another, to recover sums paid as security? Our courts decide in all these cases, without the intervention of a jury; yet they are all civil cases. The bill of rights is merely recommendatory. Were it otherwise, the consequence would be that many laws which are found convenient would be unconstitutional. What does the government before you say? Does it exclude the legislature from giving a trial by jury in civil cases? If it does not forbid its exclusion, it is on the same footing on which your state government stands now. The legislature of Virginia does not give a trial by jury where it is not necessary, but gives it wherever it is thought expedient. The federal legislature will do so too, as it is formed on the same principles.

*   *   *

[Monday, June 23]

Mr. Henry: . . . He observed, that, as Congress had a right to organize the federal judiciary, they might or might not have recourse to a jury, as they pleased. He left it to the candor of the honorable gentleman to say whether those persons who were at the expense of taking witnesses to Philadelphia, or wherever the federal judiciary may sit, could be certain whether they were to be heard before a jury or not. An honorable gentleman (Mr. Marshall) the other day observed, that he conceived the trial by jury better secured under the plan on the table than in the British government, or even in our bill of rights. I have the highest veneration and respect for the honorable gentleman, and I have experienced his candor on all occasions; but, Mr. Chairman, in this instance, he is so materially mistaken that I cannot but observe, he is much in error. I beg the clerk to read that part of the Constitution which relates to trial by jury. [The clerk then read the 8th article of the bill of rights.]

Mr. Marshall rose to explain what he had before said on this subject: he informed the committee that the honorable gentleman (Mr. Henry) must have misunderstood him. He said that he conceived the trial by jury was as well secured, and not better secured, in the proposed new Constitution as in our bill of rights. [The clerk then read the 11th article of the bill of rights.]

Mr. Henry: Mr. Chairman: the gentleman's candor, sir, as I informed you before, I have the highest opinion of, and am happy to find he has so far explained what he meant; but, sir, has he mended the matter? Is not the ancient trial by jury preserved in the Virginia bill of rights? and is that the case in the new plan? No, sir; they can do it if they please. Will gentlemen tell me the trial by a jury of the vicinage where the party resides is preserved? True, sir, there is to be a trial by the jury in the state where the fact was committed; but, sir, this state, for instance, is so large that your juries may be collected five hundred miles from where the party resides—no neighbors who are acquainted with their characters, their good or bad conduct in life, to judge of the unfortunate man who may be thus exposed to the rigor of that government. Compare this security, then, sir, in our bill of rights with that in the new plan of government; and in the first you have it, and in the other, in my opinion, not at all. But, sir, in what situation will our citizens be, who have made large contracts under our present government? They will be called to a federal court, and tried under the retrospective laws; for it is evident, to me at least, that the federal court must look back, and give better remedies, to compel individuals to fulfil them.

The whole history of human nature cannot produce a government like that before you. The manner in which the judiciary and other branches of the government are formed, seems to me calculated to lay prostrate the states, and the liberties of the people. But, sir, another circumstance ought totally to reject that plan, in my opinion; which is, that it cannot be understood, in many parts, even by the supporters of it. A constitution, sir, ought to be, like a beacon, held up to the public eye, so as to be understood be every man. Some gentlemen have observed that the word jury implies a jury of the vicinage. There are so many inconsistencies in this, that, for my part, I cannot understand it. By the bill of rights of England, a subject has a right to a trial by his peers. What is meant by his peers? Those who reside near him, his neighbors, and who are well acquainted with his character and situation in life. Is this secured in the proposed plan before you? No, sir. . .

*   *   *

[Tuesday, June 24]

Mr. Wythe arose, and addressed the chairman; but he spoke so very low that his speech could not be fully comprehended. He took a cursory view of the situation of the United States previous to the late war, their resistance to the oppression of Great Britain, and the glorious conclusion and issue of that arduous conflict. To perpetuate the blessings of freedom, happiness, and independence, he demonstrated the necessity of a firm, indissoluble union of the states. He expatiated on the defects and inadequacy of the Confederation, and the consequent misfortunes suffered by the people. He pointed out the impossibility of securing liberty without society, the impracticability of acting personally, and the inevitable necessity of delegating power to agents. He then recurred to the system under consideration. He admitted its imperfection, and the propriety of some amendments. But the excellency of many parts of it could not be denied by its warmest opponents. He thought that experience was the best guide, and could alone develop its consequences. Most of the improvements that had been made in the science of government, and other sciences, were the result of experience. He referred it to the advocates for amendments, whether, if they were indulged with any alterations they pleased, there might not still be a necessity of alteration.

He then proceeded to the consideration of the question of previous or subsequent amendments. The critical situation of America, the extreme danger of dissolving the Union, rendered it necessary to adopt the latter alternative. He saw no danger from this. It appeared to him, most clearly, that any amendments which might be thought necessary would be easily obtained after ratification, in the manner proposed by the Constitution, as amendments were desired by all the states, and had already been proposed by the several states. He then proposed that the committee should ratify the Constitution, and that whatsoever amendments might be deemed necessary should be recommended to the consideration of the Congress which should first assemble under the Constitution, to be acted upon according to the mode prescribed therein.

> [The resolution of ratification proposed by Mr. Wythe was then read by the clerk; which see hereafter in the report of the committee to the Convention.]

Mr. Henry, after observing that the proposal of ratification was premature, and that the importance of the subject required the most mature deliberation, proceeded thus:

The honorable member must forgive me for declaring my dissent from it; because, if I understand it rightly, it admits that the new system is defective, and most capitally; for, immediately after the proposed ratification, there comes a declaration that the paper before you is not intended to violate any of these three great rights—the liberty of religion, liberty of the press, and the trial by jury. What is the inference when you enumerate the rights which you are to enjoy? That those not enumerated are relinquished. There are only three things to be retained—religion, freedom of the press, and jury trial. Will not the ratification carry every thing, without excepting these three things? Will not all the world pronounce that we intended to give up all the rest? Every thing it speaks of, by way of rights, is comprised in these things. Your subsequent amendments only go to these three amendments.

I feel myself distressed, because the necessity of securing our personal rights seems not to have pervaded the minds of men; for many other valuable things are omitted: for instance, general warrants, by which an officer may search suspected places, without evidence of the commission of a fact, or seize any person without evidence of his crime, ought to be prohibited. As these are admitted, any man may be seized, any property may be taken, in the most arbitrary manner, without any evidence or reason. Every thing the most sacred may be searched and ransacked by the strong hand of power. We have infinitely more reason to dread general warrants here than they have in England, because there, if a person be confined, liberty may be quickly obtained by the writ of habeas corpus. But here a man living many hundred miles from the judges may get in prison before he can get that writ.

Another most fatal omission is with respect to standing armies. In our bill of rights of Virginia, they are said to be dangerous to liberty, and it tells you that the proper defence of a free state consists in militia; and so I might go on to ten or eleven things of immense consequence secured in your bill of rights, concerning which that proposal is silent. Is that the language of the bill of rights in England? Is it the language of the American bill of rights, that these three rights, and these only, are valuable? Is it the language of men going into a new government? Is it not necessary to speak of those things before you go into a compact? How do these three things stand? As one of the parties, we declare we do not mean to give them up. This is very dictatorial—much more so than the conduct which proposes alterations as the condition of adoption. In a compact there are two parties—one excepting, and another proposing. As a party, we propose that we shall secure these three things; and before we have the assent of the other contracting party, we go into the compact, and leave these things at their mercy.

What will be the consequence? Suppose the other states shall call this dictatorial. They will say, Virginia has gone into the government, and carried with her certain propositions, which, she says, ought to be concurred in by the other states. They will declare that she has no right to dictate to other states the conditions on which they shall come into the Union. According to the honorable member's proposal, the ratification will cease to be obligatory unless they accede to these amendments. We have ratified it. You have committed a violation, will they say. They have not violated it. We say, we will go out of it. You are then reduced to a sad dilemma—to give up these three rights, or leave the government. This is worse than our present Confederation, to which we have hitherto adhered honestly and faithfully. We shall be told we have violated it, because we have left it for the infringement and violation of conditions which they never agreed to be a part of the ratification. The ratification will be complete. The proposal is made by the party. We, as the other, accede to it, and propose the security of these three great rights; for it is only a proposal. In order to secure them, you are left in that state of fatal hostility which I shall as much deplore as the honorable gentleman. I exhort gentlemen to think seriously before they ratify this Constitution, and persuade themselves that they will succeed in making a feeble effort to get amendments after adoption.

With respect to that part of the proposal which says that every power not granted remains with the people, it must be previous to adoption, or it will involve this country in inevitable destruction. To talk of it as a thing subsequent, not as one of your unalienable rights, is leaving it to the casual opinion of the Congress who shall take up the consideration of that matter. They will not reason with you about the effect of this Constitution. They will not take the opinion of this committee concerning its operation. They will construe it as they please. If you place it subsequently, let me ask the consequences. Among ten thousand implied powers which they may assume, they may, if we be engaged in war, liberate every one of your slaves if they please. And this must and will be done by men, a majority of whom have not a common interest with you. They will, therefore, have no feeling of your interests. It has been repeatedly said here, that the great object of a national government was national defence. That power which is said to be intended for security and safety may be rendered detestable and oppressive. If they give power to the general government to provide for the general defence, the means must be commensurate to the end. All the means in the possession of the people must be given to the government which is intrusted with the public defence. In this state there are two hundred and thirty-six thousand blacks, and there are many in several other states. But there are few or none in the Northern States; and yet, if the Northern States shall be of opinion that our slaves are numberless, they may call forth every national resource. May Congress not say, that every black man must fight? Did we not see a little of this last war? We were not so hard pushed as to make emancipation general; but acts of Assembly passed that every slave who would go to the army should be free. Another thing will contribute to bring this event about. Slavery is detested. We feel its fatal effects—we deplore it with all the pity of humanity. Let all these considerations, at some future period, press with full force on the minds of Congress. Let that urbanity, which I trust will distinguish America, and the necessity of national defence,—let all these things operate on their minds; they will search that paper, and see if they have power of manumission. And have they not, sir? Have they not power to provide for the general defence and welfare? May they not think that these call for the abolition of slavery? May they not pronounce all slaves free, and will they not be warranted by that power? This is no ambiguous implication or logical deduction. The paper speaks to the point: they have the power in clear, unequivocal terms, and will clearly and certainly exercise it. As much as I deplore slavery, I see that prudence forbids its abolition. I deny that the general government ought to set them free, because a decided majority of the states have not the ties of sympathy and fellow-feeling for those whose interest would be affected by their emancipation. The majority of Congress is to the north, and the slaves are to the south.

In this situation, I see a great deal of the property of the people of Virginia in jeopardy, and their peace and tranquillity gone. I repeat it again, that it would rejoice my very soul that every one of my fellow-beings was emancipated. As we ought with gratitude to admire that decree of Heaven which has numbered us among the free, we ought to lament and deplore the necessity of holding our fellowmen in bondage. But is it practicable, by any human means, to liberate them without producing the most dreadful and ruinous consequences? We ought to possess them in the manner we inherited them from our ancestors, as their manumission is incompatible with the felicity of our country. But we ought to soften, as much as possible, the rigor of their unhappy fate. I know that, in a variety of particular instances, the legislature, listening to complaints, have admitted their emancipation. Let me not dwell on this subject. I will only add that this, as well as every other property of the people of Virginia, is in jeopardy, and put in the hands of those who have no similarity of situation with us. This is a local matter, and I can see no propriety in subjecting it to Congress.

With respect to subsequent amendments, proposed by the worthy member, I am distressed when I hear the expression. It is a new one altogether, and such a one as stands against every idea of fortitude and manliness in the states, or any one else. Evils admitted in order to be removed subsequently, and tyranny submitted to in order to be excluded by a subsequent alteration, are things totally new to me. But I am sure the gentleman meant nothing but to amuse the committee. I know his candor. His proposal is an idea dreadful to me. I ask, does experience warrant such a thing from the beginning of the world to this day? Do you enter into a compact first, and afterwards settle the terms of the government? It is admitted by every one that this is a compact.

Although the Confederation be lost, it is a compact, constitution, or something of that nature. I confess I never heard of such an idea before. It is most abhorrent to my mind. You endanger the tranquillity of your country, you stab its repose, if you accept this government unaltered. How are you to allay animosities?—for such there are, great and fatal.

He flatters me, and tells me that I could influence the people, and reconcile them to it. Sir, their sentiments are as firm and steady as they are patriotic. Were I to ask them to apostatize from their native religion, they would despise me. They are not to be shaken in their opinions with respect to the propriety of preserving their rights. You never can persuade them that it is necessary to relinquish them. Were I to attempt to persuade them to abandon their patriotic sentiments, I should look on myself as the most infamous of men.

I believe it to be a fact that the great body of yeomanry are in decided opposition to it. I may say with confidence that, for nineteen counties adjacent to each other, nine tenths of the people are conscientiously opposed to it. I may be mistaken, but I give you it as my opinion; and my opinion is founded on personal knowledge, in some measure, and other good authority. I have not hunted popularity by declaiming to injure this government. Though public fame might say so, it was not owing to me that this flame of opposition has been kindled and spread. These men never will part with their political opinions. If they should see their political happiness secured to the latest posterity, then, indeed, they may agree to it. Subsequent amendments will not do for men of this cast. Do you consult the Union in proposing them? You may amuse them as long as you please, but they will never like it. You have not solid reality—the hearts and hands of the men who are to be governed.

Have gentlemen no respect to the actual dispositions of the people in the adopting states? Look at Pennsylvania and Massachusetts. These two great states have raised as great objections to that government as we do. There was a majority of only nineteen in Massachusetts. We are told that only ten thousand were represented in Pennsylvania, although seventy thousand had a right to be represented. Is not this a serious thing? Is it not worth while to turn your eyes, for a moment, from subsequent amendments to the situation of your country? Can you have a lasting union in these circumstances? It will be in vain to expect it. But if you agree to previous amendments, you shall have union, firm and solid.

I cannot conculde without saying that I shall have nothing to do with it, if subsequent amendments be determined upon. Oppressions will be carried on as radically by the majority when adjustments and accommodations will be held up. I say, I conceive it my duty, if this government is adopted before it is amended, to go home. I shall act as I think my duty requires. Every other gentleman will do the same. Previous amendments, in my opinion, are necessary to procure peace and tranquillity. I fear, if they be not agreed to, every movement and operation of government will cease; and how long that baneful thing, civil discord, will stay from this country, God only knows.

When men are free from restraint, how long will you suspend their fury? The interval between this and bloodshed is but a moment. The licentious and wicked of the community will seize with avidity every thing you hold. In this unhappy situation, what is to be done? It surpasses my stock of wisdom. If you will, in the language of freemen, stipulate that there are rights which no man under heaven can take from you, you shall have me going along with you; not otherwise.

> [Here Mr. Henry informed the committee that he had a resolution prepared, to refer a declaration of rights, with certain amendments to the most exceptionable parts of the Constitution, to the other states in the confederacy, for their consideration, previous to its ratification. The clerk then read the resolution, the declaration of rights, and amendments which were nearly the same as those ultimately proposed by the Convention; which see at the conclusion.]

Mr. Henry then resumed the subject. I have thus candidly submitted to you, Mr. Chairman, and this committee, what occurred to me as proper amendments to the Constitution, and a declaration of rights containing those fundamental, unalienable privileges, which I conceive to be essential to liberty and happiness. I believe that, on a review of these amendments, it will still be found that the arm of power will be sufficiently strong for national purposes, when these restrictions shall be a part of the government. I believe no gentleman who opposes me in sentiments will be able to discover that any one feature of a strong government is altered; and at the same time your unalienable rights are secured by them. The government unaltered may be terrible to America, but can never be loved till it be amended. You find all the resources of the continent may be drawn to a point. In danger, the President may concentre to a point every effort of the continent. If the government be constructed to satisfy the people, and remove their apprehensions, the wealth and the strength of the continent will go where public utility shall direct. This government, with these restrictions, will be a strong government, united with the privileges of the people. In my weak judgment, a government is strong when it applies to the most important end of all governments—the rights and privileges of the people. In the honorable member's proposal, jury trial, the press and religion, and other essential rights, are not to be given up. Other essential rights—what are they? The world will say that you intended to give them up. When you go into an enumeration of your rights, and stop that enumeration, the inevitable conclusion is, that what is omitted is intended to be surrendered.

Anxious as I am to be as little troublesome as possible, I cannot leave this part of the subject without adverting to one remark of the honorable gentleman. He says that, rather than bring the Union into danger, he will adopt it with its imperfections. A great deal is said about disunion, and consequent dangers. I have no claim to a greater share of fortitude than others; but I can see no kind of danger. I form my judgment on a single fact alone—that we are at peace with all the world; nor is there any apparent cause of a rupture with any nation in the world. Is it among the American states that the cause of disunion is to be feared? Are not the states using all their efforts for the promotion of union? New England sacrifices local prejudices for the purposes of union. We hear the necessity of the union, and predilection for the union, reechoed from all parts of the continent; and all at once disunion is to follow! If gentlemen dread disunion, the very thing they advocate will inevitably produce it. A previous ratification will raise insurmountable obstacles to union. New York is an insurmountable obstacle to it, and North Carolina also. They will never accede to it, till it be amended. A great part of Virginia is opposed most decidedly to it as it stands. This very spirit, which will govern us in these three states, will find a kindred spirit in the adopting states. Give me leave to say that it is very problematical if the adopting states can stand on their own legs. I hear only on one side, but as far as my information goes, there are heartburnings and animosities among them. Will these animosities be cured by subsequent amendments?

*   *   *

Gov. Randolph: . . . The honorable gentleman says there is no restraint on the power of issuing general warrants. If I be tedious in asking where is that power, you will ascribe it to him who has put me to the necessity of asking. They have no such power given them: if they have, where is it?

Again he recurs to standing armies, and asks if Congress cannot raise such. Look at the bill of rights provided by the honorable gentleman himself, and tell me if there be no great security by admitting it when necessary. It says that standing armies should be avoided in time of peace. It does not absolutely prohibit them. Is there any clause in it, or in the Confederation, which prevents Congress from raising an army? No: it is left to the discretion of Congress. It ought to be in the power of Congress to raise armies, as the existence of society might, at some future period, depend upon it. But it should be recommended to them to use the power only when necessary. I humbly conceive that you have as great security as you could desire from that clause in the Constitution which directs that money for supporting armies will be voted for every two years—as, by this means, the representatives who will have appropriated money unnecessarily, or imprudently, to that purpose, may be removed, and a new regulation made. Review the practice of the favorite nation of the honorable gentleman. In their bill of rights there is no prohibition of a standing army, but only that it ought not to be maintained without the consent of the legislature. Can it be done here without the consent of the democratic branch? Their consent is necessary to every bill, and money bills can originate with them only. Can an army, then, be raised or supported without their approbation?

[His excellency then went over all the articles of Mr. Henry's proposed declaration of rights, and endeavored to prove that the rights intended to be thereby secured were either provided for in the Constitution itself, or could not be infringed by the general government, as being unwarranted by any of the powers which were delegated therein; for that it was in vain to provide against the exercise of a power which did not exist.]

He then proceeded to examine the nature of some of the amendments proposed by the honorable gentleman. As to the reservation of rights not expressly given away he repeated what he had before observed of the 2d article of the Confederation, that it was interpreted to prohibit Congress from granting passports, although such a power was necessarily incident to that of making war. Did not this, says he show the vanity of all the federal authority? Gentlemen have displayed great wisdom in the use they make of the experience of the defects in the old Confederation. When we see the defect of that article, are we to repeat it? Are those gentlemen zealous friends to the Union, who profess to be so here, and yet insist on a repetition of measures which have been found destructive to it? I believe their professions, but they must pardon me when I say their arguments are not true.

[His excellency then read the 2d amendment proposed, respecting the number of representatives.]

What better security have you under these words than under the clause in the paper before you? This puts it in the power of your representatives to continue the number of it in that paper. They may always find a pretext to justify their regulations concerning it. They may continue the number at two hundred, when an augmentation would be necessary.

As to the amendment respecting direct taxation, the subject has been so fully handled, and is so extensive in its nature, that it is needless to say any thing of it.

The 4th amendment goes on the wide field of indiscriminate suspicion that every one grasps after offices, and that Congress will create them unnecessarily. Perhaps it will exclude the most proper from offices of great importance to the community.

[Here he read the 5th amendment.]—I beg the honorable gentleman to tell me on what subject Congress will exercise this power improperly. If there be any treachery in their view, the words in this amendment are broad enough to allow it. It is as good a security in this Constitution, as human ingenuity can devise; for if they intend any treachery, they will not let you see it.

[Here he read the 7th and 8th amendments.]—I have never hesitated to acknowledge that I wished the regulation of commerce had been put in the hands of a greater body than it is in the sense of the Constitution. But I appeal to my colleagues in the federal Convention, whether this was not a sine qua non of the Union. Of all the amendments, this is the most destructive, which requires the consent of three fourths of both houses to treaties ceding or restraining territorial rights. This is priding in the Virginia sovereignty, in opposition to the majority. This suspected Congress, these corrupt sixty-five and corrupt twenty-six, are brought so low they cannot be trusted, lest they should have it in their power to lop off part of Virginia—cede it, so as that it should become a colony to some foreign state. There is no power in the Constitution to cede any part of the territories of the United States. The whole number of Congress, being unanimous, have no power to suspend or cede territorial rights. But this amendment admits, in the fullest latitude, that Congress have a right to dismember the empire.

His amendment respecting the militia is unnecessary. The same powers rest in the states by the Constitution. Gentlemen were repeatedly called upon to show where the power of the states over the militia was taken away, but they could not point it out.

[He read the 12th amendment.]—Will this be a melioration of the Constitution? I wish to know what is meant by the words police and good government! These words may lead to complete tyranny in Congress. Perhaps some gentlemen think that these words relate to particular objects, and that they will diminish and confine their power. They are most extensive in their significations, and will stretch and dilate it, and all the imaginary horrors of the honorable gentleman will be included in this amendment.

[He read the 13th amendment.]—I was of this opinion myself; but I informed you before why I changed it.

[He read the 14th amendment.]—If I were to propose an amendment on this subject, it would be to limit the word arising. I would not discard it altogether, but define its extent. The jurisdiction of the judiciary in cases arising under the system, I should wish to be defined, so as to prevent its being extended unnecessarily: I would restrain the appellate cognizance as to fact, and prevent oppressive and vexatious appeals.

[He read the 15th amendment.]—The right of challenging and excepting, I hope, has clearly appeared to the committee to be a necessary appendage of the trial by jury itself.

Permit me now to make a few remarks on the proposal of these amendments, previous to our ratification. The first objection arises from the paper itself. Can you conceive, or does any man believe, that there are twelve, or even nine, states in the whole Union, that would subscribe to this paper?—a paper fraught with, perhaps, more defects than the Constitution itself. What are we about to do? To make this the condition of our coming into this government? I hope gentlemen will never agree to this. If we declare that these amendments, and a bill of rights containing twenty articles, must be incorporated into the Constitution before we assent to it, I ask you whether you may not bid a long farewell to the Union? It will produce that deplorable thing—the dissolution of the Union—which no man yet has dared openly to advocate. No, say the gentlemen, because Maryland kept off three years from the confederacy, and no injury happened. This very argument carries its own refutation with it. The war kept us together, in spite of the discordance of the states. There is no war now. All the nations of Europe have their eyes fixed on America, and some of them perhaps cast wistful looks at you. Their gold may be tried, to sow disunion among us. The same bondage which kept us before together, does not now exist. Let gentlemen seriously ponder the calamitious consequences of dissolving the Union in our present situation. I appeal to the great Searcher of hearts, on this occasion, that we behold the greatest danger that ever happened hanging over us; for previous amendments are but another name for rejection. They will throw Virginia out of the Union, and cause heartaches to many of those gentlemen who may vote for them. But let us consider things calmly. Reflect on the facility of obtaining amendments if you adopt, and weigh the danger if you do not. Recollect that many other states have adopted it, who wish for many amendments. I ask you if it be not better to adopt, and run the chance of amending it hereafter, than run the risk of endangering the Union. The Confederation is gone; it has no authority. If, in this situation, we reject the Constitution, the Union will be dissolved, the dogs of war will break loose, and anarchy and discord will complete the ruin of this country. Previous adoption will prevent these deplorable mischiefs. The union of sentiments with us in the adopting states will render subsequent amendments easy. I therefore rest my happiness with perfect confidence on this subject.

*   *   *

Mr. Madison: . . . It is a most awful thing that depends on our decision— no less than whether the thirteen states shall unite freely, peaceably, and unanimously, for security of their common happiness and liberty, or whether every thing is to be put in confusion and disorder. Are we to embark in this dangerous enterprise, uniting various opinions to contrary interests, with the vain hope of coming to an amicable concurrence?

It is worthy of our consideration that those who prepared the paper on the table found difficulties not to be described in its formation: mutual deference and concession were absolutely necessary. Had they been inflexibly tenacious of their individual opinions, they would never have concurred. Under what circumstances was it formed? When no party was formed, or particular proposition made, and men's minds were calm and dispassionate. Yet, under these circumstances, it was difficult, extremely difficult, to agree to any general system.

Suppose eight states only should ratify, and Virginia should propose certain alterations, as the previous condition of her accession. If they should be disposed to accede to her proposition, which is the most favorable conclusion, the difficulty attending it will be immense. Every state which has decided it, must take up the subject again. They must not only have the mortification of acknowledging that they had done wrong, but the difficulty of having a reconsideration of it among the people, and appointing new conventions to deliberate upon it. They must attend to all the amendments, which may be dictated by as great a diversity of political opinions as there are local attachments. When brought together in one assembly, they must go through, and accede to, every one of the amendments. The gentlemen who, within this house, have thought proper to propose previous amendments, have brought no less than forty amendments, a bill of rights which contains twenty amendments, and twenty other alterations, some of which are improper and inadmissible. Will not every state think herself equally entitled to propose as many amendments? And suppose them to be contradictory! I leave it to this Convention whether it be probable that they can agree, or agree to any thing but the plan on the table; or whether greater difficulties will not be encountered than were experienced in the progress of the formation of the Constitution.

I have said that there was a great contrariety of opinions among the gentlemen in the opposition. It has been heard in every stage of their opposition. I can see, from their amendments, that very great sacrifices have been made by some of them. Some gentlemen think that it contains too much state influence; others, that it is a complete consolidation; and a variety of other things. Some of them think that the equality in the Senate is not a defect; others, that it is the bane of all good government. I might, if there were time, show a variety of other cases where their opinions are contradictory. If there be this contrariety of opinions in this house, what contrariety may not be expected, when we take into view thirteen conventions equally or more numerous! Besides, it is notorious, from the debates which have been published, that there is no sort of uniformity in the grounds of the opposition.

The state of New York has been adduced. Many in that state are opposed to it from local views. The two who opposed it in the general Convention from that state are in the state Convention. Every step of this system was opposed by those two gentlemen. They were unwilling to part with the old Confederation. Can it be presumed, then, sir, that gentlemen in this state, who admit the necessity of changing, should ever be able to unite in sentiments with those who are totally averse to any change?

I have revolved this question in my mind with as much serious attention, and called to my aid as much information, as I could, yet I can see no reason for the apprehensions of gentlemen; but I think that the most happy effects for this country would result from adoption, and if Virginia will agree to ratify this system, I shall look upon it as one of the most fortunate events that ever happened for human nature. I cannot, therefore, without the most excruciating apprehensions, see a possibility of losing its blessings. It gives me infinite pain to reflect that all the earnest endeavors of the warmest friends of their country to introduce a system promotive of our happiness, may be blasted by a rejection, for which I think, with my honorable friend, that previous amendments are but another name. The gentlemen in opposition seem to insist on those amendments, as if they were all necessary for the liberty and happiness of the people. Were I to hazard an opinion on the subject, I would declare it infinitely more safe, in its present form, than it would be after introducing into it that long train of alterations which they call amendments.

With respect to the proposition of the honorable gentleman to my left, (Mr. Wythe,) gentlemen apprehend that, by enumerating three rights, it implied there were no more. The observations made by a gentleman lately up, on that subject, correspond precisely with my opinion. That resolution declares that the powers granted by the proposed Constitution are the gift of the people, and may be resumed by them when perverted to their oppression, and every power not granted thereby remains with the people, and at their will. It adds, likewise, that no right, of any denomination, can be cancelled, abridged, restrained, or modified, by the general government, or any of its officers, except in those instances in which power is given by the Constitution for these purposes. There cannot be a more positive and unequivocal declaration of the principle of the adoption—that every thing not granted is reserved. This is obviously and self-evidently the case, without the declaration. Can the general government exercise any power not delegated? If an enumeration be made of our rights, will it not be implied that every thing omitted is given to the general government? Has not the honorable gentleman himself admitted that an imperfect enumeration is dangerous? Does the Constitution say that they shall not alter the law of descents, or do those things which would subvert the whole system of the state laws? If it did, what was not excepted would be granted. Does it follow, from the omission of such restrictions, that they can exercise powers not delegated? The reverse of the proposition holds. The delegation alone warrants the exercise of any power.

With respect to the amendments proposed by the honorable gentleman, it ought to be considered how far they are good. As far as they are palpably and insuperably objectionable, they ought to be opposed. One amendment he proposes is, that any army which shall be necessary shall be raised by the consent of two thirds of the states. I most devoutly wish that there may never be an occasion for having a single regiment. There can be no harm in declaring that standing armies, in time of peace, are dangerous to liberty, and ought to be avoided, as far as it may be consistent with the protection of the community. But when we come to say that the national security shall depend, not on a majority of the people of America, but that it may be frustrated by less than one third of the people of America, I ask if this be a safe or proper mode. What parts of the United States are most likely to stand in need of this protection? The weak parts, which are the Southern States. Will it be safe to leave the United States at the mercy of one third of the states—a number which may comprise a very small proportion of the American people? They may all be in that part of America which is least exposed to danger. As far as a remote situation from danger would render exertions for public defence less active, so far the Southern States would be endangered.

The regulation of commerce, he further proposed, should depend on two thirds of both houses. I wish I could recollect the history of this matter; but I cannot call it to mind with sufficient exactness. But I well recollect the reasoning of some gentlemen on that subject. It was said, and I believe with truth, that every part of America does not stand in equal need of security. It was observed that the Northern States were most competent to their own safety. Was it reasonable, asked they, that they should bind themselves to the defence of the Southern States, and still be left at the mercy of the minority for commercial advantages? Should it be in the power of the minority to deprive them of this and other advantages, when they were bound to defend the whole Union, it might be a disadvantage for them to confederate.

These were his arguments. This policy of guarding against political inconveniences, by enabling a small part of the community to oppose the government, and subjecting the majority to a small minority, is fallacious. In some cases it may be good; in others it may be fatal. In all cases, it puts it in the power of the minority to decide a question which concerns the majority.

I was struck with surprise when I heard him express himself alarmed with respect to the emancipation of slaves. Let me ask, if they should even attempt it, if it will not be a usurpation of power. There is no power to warrant it, in that paper. If there be, I know it not. But why should it be done? Says the honorable gentleman, for the general welfare: it will infuse strength into our system. Can any member of this committee suppose that it will increase our strength? Can any one believe that the American councils will come into a measure which will strip them of their property, and discourage and alienate the affections of five thirteenths of the Union? Why was nothing of this sort aimed at before? I believe such an idea never entered into any American breast, nor do I believe it ever will enter into the heads of those gentlemen who substitute unsupported suspicions for reasons.

I am persuaded that the gentlemen who contend for previous amendments are not aware of the dangers which must result. Virginia, after having made opposition, will be obliged to recede from it. Might not the nine states say, with a great deal of propriety, "It is not proper, decent, or right, in you, to demand that we should reverse what we have done. Do as we have done; place confidence in us, as we have done in one another; and then we shall freely, fairly, and dispassionately consider and investigate your propositions, and endeavor to gratify your wishes. But if you do not do this, it is more reasonable that you should yield to us than we to you. You cannot exist without us; you must be a member of the Union.

The case of Maryland, instanced by the gentleman, does not hold. She would not agree to confederate, because the other states would not assent to her claims of the western lands. Was she gratified? No; she put herself like the rest. Nor has she since been gratified. The lands are in the common stock of the Union.

As far as his amendments are not objectionable, or unsafe, so far they may be subsequently recommended—not because they are necessary, but because they can produce no possible danger, and may gratify some gentlemen's wishes. But I never can consent to his previous amendments, because they are pregnant with dreadful dangers.

Mr. Henry: . . . The honorable gentleman last up agrees that there are defects, and by and by, he says there is no defect. Does not this amount to a declaration that subsequent amendments are not necessary? His arguments, great as the gentleman's abilities are, tend to prove that amendments cannot be obtained after adoption. Speaking of forty amendments, he calculated that it was something like impracticability to obtain them. I appeal, there-fore, to the candor of the honorable gentleman, and this committee, whether amendments be not absolutely unattainable, if we adopt; for he has told us that, if the other states will do like this, they cannot be previously obtained. Will the gentleman bring this home to himself? This is a piece of information which I expected. The worthy member who proposed to ratify has also proposed that what amendments may be deemed necessary should be recom-mended to Congress, and that a committee should be appointed to consider what amendments were necessary. But what does it all come to at last? That it is a vain project, and that it is indecent and improper. I will not argue unfairly, but I will ask him if amendments are not unattainable. Will gentlemen, then, lay their hands on their hearts, and say that they can adopt it in this shape? When we demand this security of our privileges, the language of Virginia is not that of respect! Give me leave to deny. She only asks amendments previous to her adoption of the Constitution.

Was the honorable gentleman accurate, when he said that they could exist better without us than we could without them? I will make no comparison. But I will say that the states which have adopted will not make a respectable appearance without us. Would he advise them to refuse us admission when we profess ourselves friends to the Union, and only solicit them to secure our rights? We do not reject a connection with them. We only declare that we will adopt it, if they will but consent to the security of rights essential to the general happiness.

He told you to confine yourselves to amendments which were indisputably true, as applying to several parts of the system proposed. Did you hear any thing like the admission of the want of such amendments from any one else? I will not insist on any that does not stand on the broad basis of human rights. He says there are forty. I say there is but one half the number, for the bill of rights is but one amendment.

He tells you of the important blessings which he imagines will result to us and mankind in general from the adoption of this system. I see the awful immensity of the dangers with which it is pregnant. I see it. I feel it. I see beings of a higher order anxious concerning our decision. When I see beyond the horizon that bounds human eyes, and look at the final consummation of all human things, and see those intelligent beings which inhabit the ethereal mansions reviewing the political decisions and revolutions which, in the progress of time, will happen in America, and the consequent happiness or misery of mankind, I am led to believe that much of the account, on one side or the other, will depend on what we now decide. Our own happiness alone is not affected by the event. All nations are interested in the determination. We have it in our power to secure the happiness of one half of the human race. Its adoption may involve the misery of the other hemisphere.

[Here a violent storm arose, which put the house in such disorder, that Mr. Henry was obliged to conclude.]

*   *   *

[Wednesday, June 25]

Mr. Nicholas: Mr. Chairman, I do not mean to enter into any further debate. The friends of the Constitution wish to take up no more time, the matter being now fully discussed. They are convinced that further time will answer no end but to serve the cause of those who wish to destroy the Constitution. We wish it to be ratified, and such amendments as may be thought necessary to be subsequently considered by a committee, in order to be recommended to Congress, to be acted upon according to the amendatory mode presented in itself. Gentlemen in the opposition have said that the friends of the Constitution would depart after the adoption, without entering into any consideration of subsequent amendments. I wish to know their authority. I wish for subsequent amendments as a friend to the Constitution; I trust its other friends wish so too; and I believe no gentleman has any intention of departing. The amendments contained in this paper are those we wish; but we shall agree to any others which will not destroy the spirit of the Constitution, or that will better secure liberty.

He then moved that the clerk should read the resolution proposed by Mr. Wythe, in order that the question might be put upon it; which being done, Mr. Tyler moved to read the amendments and bill of rights proposed by Mr. Henry, for the same purpose.

Mr. Harrison: Mr. Chairman, the little states refused to come into the Union without extravagant concessions. It will be the same case on every other occasion. Can it be supposed that the little states, whose interest and importance are greatly advanced by the Constitution as it now stands, will ever agree to any alteration which must infallibly diminish their political influence? On this occasion, let us behave with that fortitude which animated us in our resistance to Great Britain.

The situation and disposition of the states render subsequent amendments dangerous and impolitic, and previous amendments eligible.

New Hampshire does not approve of the Constitution as it stands.

They have refused it so. In Massachusetts, we are told that there was a decided majority in their Convention who opposed the Constitution as it stood, and were in favor of previous amendments, but were afterwards, by the address and artifice of the federalists, prevailed upon to ratify it.

Rhode Island is not worthy the attention of this house. She is of no weight or importance to influence any general subject of consequence.

Connecticut adopted it, without proposing amendments.

New York, we have every reason to believe, will reject the Constitution, unless amendments be obtained. Hence it clearly appears that there are three states which wish for amendments.

Jersey, Pennsylvania, and Delaware, have adopted it unconditionally.

In Maryland, there is a considerable number who wish amendments to be had.

Virginia is divided, let this question be determined which way it will. One half of the people, at least, wish amendments to be obtained.

North Carolina is decidedly against it. South Carolina has proposed amendments.

Under this representation, it appears that there are seven states who wish to get amendments. Can it be doubted, if the seven states insert amendments as the condition of their accession, that they would be agreed to? Let us not, then, be persuaded into an opinion that the Union will be dissolved if we should reject it. I have no such idea.

As far as I am acquainted with history, there never existed a constitution where the liberty of the people was established in this way. States have risen by gradual steps: let us follow their example. The line which we ought to pursue is equally bounded. How comes that paper on your table to be now here discussed? The state of Virginia, finding the power of the Confederation insufficient for the happiness of the people, invited the other states to call a convention, in order that the powers of Congress might be enlarged. I was not in the Assembly then; and if I had been, I have no vanity to suppose I could have decided more cautiously. They were bound to do what we ought to do now. I have no idea of danger to the Union. A vast majority, from every calculation, are invincibly attached to it. I see an earnest desire in gentlemen to bring this country to be great and powerful. Considering the very late period when this country was first settled, and the present state of population and wealth, this is impossible now. The attempt will bring ruin and destruction upon us. These things must not be forced. They must come of course, like the course of rivers, gently going on. As to the inconveniences, to me, from adoption, they are none at all. I am not prejudiced against New England, or any part. They are held up to us as a people from whom protection will come. Will any protection come from thence for many years? When we were invaded, did any gentleman from the Northern States come to relieve us? No, sir, we were left to be buffeted. General Washington, in the greatness of his soul, came with the French auxiliaries, and relieved us opportunely. Were it not for this, we should have been ruined. I call Heaven to witness that I am a friend to the Union. But I conceive the measure of adoption to be unwarrantable, precipitate, and dangerously impolitic. Should we rush into sudden perdition, I should resist with the fortitude of a man. As to the amendments proposed by gentlemen, I do not object to them: they are inherently good. But they are put in the wrong place—subsequent instead of previous. [Mr. Harrison added other observations, which could not be heard.]

Mr. Madison: Mr. Chairman, I should not have risen at all, were it not for what the honorable gentleman said. If there be any suspicions that, if the ratification be made, the friends of the system will withdraw their concurrence, and much more, their persons, it shall never be with my approbation. Permit me to remark that, if he has given us a true state of the disposition of the several members of the Union, there is no doubt they will agree to the same amendments after adoption. If we propose the conditional amendments, I entreat gentlemen to consider the distance to which they throw the ultimate settlement, and the extreme risk of perpetual disunion. They cannot but see how easy it will be to obtain subsequent amendments. They can be proposed when the legislatures of two thirds of the states shall make application for that purpose; and the legislatures of three fourths of the states, or conventions in the same, can fix the amendments so proposed. If there be an equal zeal in every state, can there be a doubt that they will concur in reasonable amendments? If, on the other hand, we call on the states to rescind what they have done, and confess that they have done wrong, and to consider the subject again, it will produce such unnecessary delays, and is pregnant with such infinite dangers, that I cannot contemplate it without horror. There are uncertainty and confusion on the one hand, and order, tranquillity, and certainty, on the other. Let us not hesitate to elect the latter alternative. Let us join with cordiality in those alterations we think proper. There is no friend to the Constitution but who will concur in that mode.

Mr. Monroe, after an exordium which could not be heard, remarking that the question now before the committee was, whether previous or subsequent amendments were the most prudent, strongly supported the former. He could not conceive that a conditional ratification would, in the most remote degree, endanger the Union; for that it was as clearly the interest of the adopting states to be united with Virginia, as it could be her interest to be in union with them. He demanded if they would arm the states against one another, and make themselves enemies of those who were respectable and powerful from their situation and numbers. He had no doubt that they would, in preference to such a desperate and violent measure, come forward and make a proposition to the other states, so far as it would be consistent with the general interest. Adopt it now, unconditionally, says he, and it will never be amended, not even when experience shall have proved its defects. An alteration will be a diminution of their power, and there will be great exertions made to prevent it. I have no dread that they will immediately infringe the dearest rights of the people, but that the operation of the government will be oppressive in process of time. Shall we not pursue the dictates of common sense, and the example of all free and wise nations, and insist on amendments with manly fortitude?

*   *   *

Mr. Henry: Mr. Chairman, when we were told of the difficulty of obtaining previous amendments, I contended that they might be as easily obtained as subsequent amendments. We are told that nine states have adopted it. If so, when the government gets in motion, have they not a right to consider our amendments as well as if we adopted first? If we remonstrate, may they not consider and admit our amendments? But now, sir, when we have been favored with a view of their subsequent amendments, I am confirmed in what I apprehended; and that is, subsequent amendments will make our condition worse; for they are placed in such a point of view as will make this Convention ridiculous. I speak in plain, direct language. It is extorted from me. If this Convention will say, that the very right by which amendments are desired is not secured, then I say our rights are not secured. As we have the right of desiring amendments, why not exercise it? But gentlemen deny this right. It follows, of course, that, if this right be not secured, our other rights are not. The proposition of subsequent amendments is only to lull our apprehensions. We speak the language of contradiction and inconsistency, to say that rights are secured, and then say that they are not. Is not this placing this Convention in a contemptible light? Will not this produce contempt of us in Congress, and every other part of the world? Will gentlemen tell me that they are in earnest about these amendments?

I am convinced they mean nothing serious. What are the rights which they do not propose to secure—which they reject?—for I contend there are many essential and vital rights which are omitted. One is the power of direct taxation. Gentlemen will not even give this invaluable right a place among their subsequent amendments. And do gentlemen mean seriously that they will oppose us on this ground on the floor of Congress? If Virginia thinks it one of her dearest rights, she need not expect to have it amended. No, sir; it will be opposed. Taxes and excises are to be laid on us. The people are to be oppressed, and the state legislature prostrated. Very material amendments are omitted. With respect to your militia, we only request that, if Congress should refuse to find arms for them, this country may lay out their own money to purchase them. But what do the gentlemen on the other side say? As much as that they will oppose you in this point also; for, if my recollection has not failed me, they have discarded this also. And shall we be deprived of this privilege? We propose to have it, in case there shall be a necessity to claim it. And is this claim incompatible with the safety of this country—with the grandeur and strength of the United States? If gentlemen find peace and rest on their minds, when the relinquishment of our rights is declared to be necessary for the aggrandizement of the government, they are more contented than I am.

Another thing which they have not mentioned, is the power of treaties. Two thirds of the senators present can make treaties; and they are, when made, to be the supreme law of the land, and are to be paramount to the state constitutions. We wish to guard against the temporary suspension of our great national rights. We wish some qualification of this dangerous power. We wish to modify it. One amendment which has been wished for, in this respect, is, that no treaty should be made without the consent of a considerable majority of both houses. I might go on and enumerate many other great rights entirely neglected by their subsequent amendments; but I shall pass over them in silence. I am astonished at what my worthy friend (Mr. Innes) said—that we have no right of proposing previous amendments. That honorable gentleman is endowed with great eloquence—eloquence splendid, magnificent, and sufficient to shake the human mind! He has brought the whole force of America against this state. He has also strongly represented our comparative weakness, with respect to the powers of Europe. But when I review the actual state of things, I see that dangers from thence are merely ideal. His reasoning has no effect on me. He cannot shake my political faith. He admits our power over subsequent amendments, though not over previous amendments. Where is the distinction between them? If we have a right to depart from the letter of our commission in one instance, we have in the other; for subsequent amendments have no higher authority than previous. We shall be absolutely certain of escaping danger in the one case, but not in the other. I think the apprehension expressed by another honorable gentleman has no good foundation. He apprehended civil discord if we did not adopt. I am willing to concede that he loves his country. I will, for the sake of argument, allow that I am one of the meanest of those who love their country. But what does this amount to? The great and direct end of government is liberty. Secure our liberty and privileges, and the end of government is answered. If this be not effectually done, government is an evil. What amendments does he propose which secure our liberty? I ask pardon if I make a mistake, but it seems to me that his proposed subsequent amendments do not secure one single right. They say that your rights are secured in the paper on the table, so that these subsequent amendments are a mere supererogation. They are not necessary, because the objects intended to be secured by them are secured already. What is to become of the trial by jury? Had its security been made a part of the Constitution, it would have been sufficiently guarded. But as it is, in that proposition it is by no means explicitly secured. Is it not trifling to admit the necessity of securing it, and not do it in a positive, unequivocal manner? I wish I could place it in any other view than a trifling one. It is only intended to attack every project of introducing amendments. If they are serious why do they not join us, and ask, in a manly, firm, and resolute manner, for these amendments? Their view is to defeat every attempt to amend. When they speak of their subsequent recommendations, they tell you that amendments must be got, and the next moment they say they are unnecessary!

I beg pardon of this house for having taken up more time than came to my share, and I thank them for the patience and polite attention with which I have been heard. If I shall be in the minority, I shall have those painful sensations which arise from a conviction of being overpowered in a good cause. Yet I will be a peaceable citizen. My head, my hand, and my heart, shall be at liberty to retrieve the loss of liberty, and remove the defects of that system in a constitutional way. I wish not to go to violence, but will wait with hopes that the spirit which predominated in the revolution is not yet gone, nor the cause of those who are attached to the revolution yet lost. I shall therefore patiently wait in expectation of seeing that government changed, so as to be compatible with the safety, liberty, and happiness, of the people.

Gov. Randolph: Mr. Chairman, one parting word I humbly supplicate.

The suffrage which I shall give in favor of the Constitution will be ascribed, by malice, to motives unknown to my breast. But, although for every other act of my life I shall seek refuge in the mercy of God, for this I request his justice only. Lest, however, some future annalist should, in the spirit of party vengeance, deign to mention my name, let him recite these truths—that I went to the federal Convention with the strongest affection for the Union; that I acted there in full conformity with this affection; that I refused to subscribe, because I had, as I still have, objections to the Constitution, and wished a free inquiry into its merits; and that the accession of eight states reduced our deliberations to the single question of Union or no Union.

*   *   *

Mr. President now resumed the chair, and Mr. Matthews reported, that the committee had, according to order, again had the proposed Constitution under their consideration, and had gone through the same, and come to several resolutions thereupon, which he read in his place, and afterwards delivered in at the clerk's table, where the same were again read, and are as followeth:

Whereas the powers granted under the proposed Constitution are the gift of the people, and every power not granted thereby remains with them, and at their will,—no right, therefore, of any denomination, can be cancelled, abridged, restrained, or modified, by the Congress, by the Senate or House of Representatives, acting in any capacity, by the President, or any department or officer of the United States, except in those instances in which power is given by the Constitution for those purposes; and, among other essential rights, liberty of conscience and of the press cannot be cancelled, abridged, restrained, or modified, by any authority of the United States.

And whereas any imperfections, which may exist in the said Constitution, ought rather to be examined in the mode prescribed therein for obtaining amendments, than by a delay, with a hope of obtaining previous amendments, to bring the Union into danger,

Resolved, That it is the opinion of this committee, that the said Constitution be ratified. But in order to relieve the apprehensions of those who may be solicitous for amendments,

Resolved, That it is the opinion of this committee, that whatsoever amendments may be deemed necessary, be recommended to the consideration of the Congress which shall first assemble under the said Constitution, to be acted upon according to the mode prescribed in the 5th article thereof.

The 1st resolution being read a second time, a motion was made, and the question being put, to amend the same by substituting, in lieu of the said resolution and its preamble, the following resolution,

Resolved, That, previous to the ratification of the new Constitution of government recommended by the late federal Convention, a declaration of rights, asserting, and securing from encroachment, the great principles of civil and religious liberty, and the unalienable rights of the people, together with amendments to the most exceptionable parts of the said Constitution of government, ought to be referred by this Convention to the other states in the American confederacy for their consideration,

It passed in the negative—ayes, 80; noes, 88.

On motion of Mr. Patrick Henry, seconded by Mr. Theodorick Bland the ayes and noes, on the said question, were taken, as follows: —

Ayes

Edmund Custis,
John Pride,
Edmund Booker,
William Cabell,
Samuel Jordan Cabell,
John Trigg,
Charles Clay,
H. Lee of Bourbon,
John Jones,
Binns Jones,
Charles Patteson,
David Bell,
Robert Alexander,
Edmund Winston,
Thomas Read,

Benjamin Harrison,
John Tyler,
David Patteson,
Stephen Pankey,
Joseph Michaux,
Thomas H. Drew,
French Strother,
Joel Early,
Joseph Jones,
William Watkins,
Meriwether Smith,
James Upshaw,
John Fowler,
Samuel Richardson,
Joseph Haden,

John Early,
Thomas Arthurs,
John Guerrant,
William Sampson,
Isaac Coles,
George Carrington,
Parker Goodall,
J. Carter Littlepage,
Thomas Cooper,
John Marr,
Thomas Roane,
Holt Richeson,
Benjamin Temple,
S. Thompson Mason,
William White,
Jonathan Patteson,
Christopher Robertson,
John Logan,
Henry Pawling,
John Miller,
Green Clay,
Samuel Hopkins,
Richard Kennon,
Thomas Allen,
Alexander Robertson,

John Evans,
Walter Crocket,
Abraham Trigg,
Matthew Walton,
John Steele,
Robert Williams,
J. Wilson, of Pittsylvania,
Thomas Turpin,
Patrick Henry,
Robert Lawson,
Edmund Ruffin,
Theodorick Bland,
William Grayson,
Cuthbert Bullitt,
Thomas Carter,
Henry Dickenson,
James Monroe,
John Dawson,
George Mason,
Andrew Buchanan,
John Powell Briggs
Thomas Edmunds,
Richard Carey,
Samuel Edminson,
James Montgomery.

Noes

E. Pendleton, President,
George Parker,
George Nicholas,
Wilson Nicholas,
Zachariah Johnson,
Archibald Stuart,
William Dark,
Adam Stephen,
Martin M'Ferran,
William Fleming,
James Taylor, of Caroline,
Paul Carrington,
Miles King,
Worlich Westwood,
David Stuart,
Charles Simms,
Humphrey Marshall,

Martin Pickett,
Humphrey Brooke,
J. Sherman Woodcock,
Alexander White,
Warner Lewis,
Thomas Smith,
George Clendinen,
John Stewart,
William Mason,
Daniel Fisher,
Andrew Woodrow,
Ralph Humphreys,
George Jackson,
John Prunty,
Isaac Vanmeter,
Abel Seymour,
Governor Randolph,

John Marshall,
Nathaniel Burwell,
Robert Andrews,
James Johnson,
Robert Breckenridge,
Rice Bullock,
William Fleet,
Burdet Ashton,
William Thornton,
J. Gordon, of Lancaster,
Henry Towles,
Levin Powell,
Wm. Overton Callis,
Ralph Wormley, Jr.,
Francis Corbin,
William M'Clerry,
Willis Riddick,
Solomon Shepherd,
William Clayton,
Burwell Bassett,
James Webb,
James Taylor, of Norfolk,
John Stringer,
Littleton Eyre,
Walter Jones,
Thomas Gaskins,
Archibald Woods,

Ebenezer Zane,
James Madison,
J. Gordon, of Orange,
William Ronald,
Anthony Walke,
Thomas Walke,
Benjamin Wilson,
J. Wilson, of Randolph,
Walker Tomlin,
William Peachy,
William M'Kee,
Andrew Moore,
Thomas Lewis,
Gabriel Jones,
Jacob Rinker,
John Williams,
Benjamin Blunt,
Samuel Kello,
John Hartwell Cocke,
John Allen,
Cole Digges,
H. Lee, of Westmoreland,
Bushrod Washington,
John Blair,
George Wythe,
James Innes,
Thomas Matthews.

And then, the main question being put that the Convention do agree with the committee in the said 1st resolution, it was resolved in the affirmative—ayes, 89; noes, 79.

On the motion of Mr. George Mason, seconded by Mr. Patrick Henry, the ayes and noes, on the said main question, were taken, as follows—

Ayes

E. Pendleton, President,
George Parker,
George Nicholas,
Wilson Nicholas,
Zachariah Johnson,
Archibald Stuart,
William Dark,
Adam Stephen,
Martin M'Ferran,
William Fleming,

James Taylor, of Caroline,
Paul Carrington,
David Patteson,
Miles King,
Worlich Westwood,
David Stuart,
Charles Simms,
Humphrey Marshall,
Martin Pickett,
Humphrey Brooke,

John S. Woodcock,
Alexander White,
Warner Lewis,
Thomas Smith,
George Clendinen,
John Stewart,
William Mason,
Daniel Fisher,
Andrew Woodrow,
Ralph Humphreys,
George Jackson,
John Prunty,
Isaac Vanmeter,
Abel Seymour,
Governor Randolph,
John Marshall,
Nathaniel Burwell,
Robert Andrews,
James Johnson,
Robert Breckenridge,
Rice Bullock,
William Fleet,
Burdet Ashton,
William Thornton,
J. Gordon, of Lancaster,
Henry Towles,
Levin Powell,
W. Overton Callis,
Ralph Wormley, Jun.,
Francis Corbin,
William M'Clerry,
Willis Riddick,
Solomon Shepherd,
William Clayton,
Burwell Bassett,

James Webb,
J. Taylor, of Norfolk,
John Stringer,
Littleton Eyre,
Walter Jones,
Thomas Gaskins,
Archibald Woods,
Ebenezer Zane,
James Madison,
James Gordon, of Orange,
William Ronald,
Anthony Walke,
Thomas Walke,
Benjamin Wilson,
J. Wilson, of Randolph,
Walker Tomlin,
William Peachy,
William M'Kee,
Andrew Moore,
Thomas Lewis,
Gabriel Jones,
Jacob Rinker,
John Williams,
Benjamin Blunt,
Samuel Kello,
John Hartwell Cocke,
John Allen,
Cole Digges,
H. Lee, of Westmoreland,
Bushred Washington,
John Blair,
George Wythe,
James Innes,
Thomas Matthews.

Noes

Edmund Custis,
John Pride,
Edmund Brooker,
William Cabell,
Samuel Jordan Cabell,
John Trigg,
Charles Clay,
Henry Lee, of Bourbon,

John Jones,
Binns Jones,
Charles Patteson,
David Bell,
Robert Alexander,
Edmund Winston,
Thomas Read,
John Tyler,

Stephen Pankey,
Joshua Michaux,
Thomas H. Drew,
French Strother,
Joel Early,
Joseph Jones,
William Walkins,
Meriwether Smith,
James Upshaw,
John Fowler,
Samuel Richardson,
Joseph Haden,
John Early,
Thomas Arthurs,
John Guerrant,
William Sampson,
Isaac Coles,
George Carrington,
Parker Goodall,
John Carter Littlepage,
Thomas Cooper,
John Marr,
Thomas Roane,
Holt Richeson,
Benjamin Temple,
Stephens T. Mason,
William White,
Jonathan Patteson,
Christopher Robertson,
John Logan,
Henry Pawling,

John Miller,
Green Clay,
Samuel Hopkins,
Richard Kennon,
Thomas Allen,
Alexander Robertson,
John Evans,
Walter Crocket,
Abraham Trigg,
Matthew Walton,
John Steele,
Robert Williams,
J. Wilson, of Pittsylvania,
Thomas Turpin,
Patrick Henry,
Robert Lawson,
Edmund Ruffin,
Theodorick Bland,
William Grayson,
Cuthbert Bullitt,
Thomas Carter,
Henry Dickenson,
James Monroe,
John Dawson,
George Mason,
Andrew Buchanan,
John Howell Briggs,
Thomas Edmunds,
Richard Cary,
Samuel Edminson,
James Montgomery.

The 2d resolution being then read a second time, a motion was made, and, the question being put to amend the same by striking out the preamble thereto, it was resolved in the affirmative,

And then, the main question being put, that the Convention do agree with the committee in the 2d resolution so amended, it was resolved in the affirmative.

On motion. Ordered, That a committee be appointed to prepare and report a form of ratification pursuant to the first resolution; and that Governor Randolph, Mr. Nicholas, Mr. Madison, Mr. Marshall, and Mr. Corbin, compose the said committee.

On motion, Ordered, That a committee be appointed to prepare and report such amendments as by them shall be deemed necessary, to be recommended, pursuant to the second resolution; and that the Hon. George

Wythe, Mr. Harrison, Mr. Matthews, Mr. Henry, Governor Randolph, Mr. George Mason, Mr. Nicholas, Mr. Grayson, Mr. Madison, Mr. Tyler, Mr. John Marshall, Mr. Monroe, Mr. Ronald, Mr. Bland, Mr. Meriwether Smith, Mr. Paul Carrington, Mr. Innes, Mr. Hopkins, Mr. John Blair, and Mr. Simms, compose the said committee.

His excellency, Governor Randolph, reported, from the committee appointed, according to order, a form of ratification, which was read and agreed to by the Convention, in the words following: Virginia, to wit:

We, the delegates of the people of Virginia, duly elected in pursuance of a recommendation from the General Assembly, and now met in Convention, having fully and freely investigated and discussed the proceedings of the federal Convention, and being prepared, as well as the most mature deliberation hath enabled us, to decide thereon, Do, in the name and in behalf of the people of Virginia, declare and make known, that the powers granted under the Constitution, being derived from the people of the United States, be resumed by them whensoever the same shall be perverted to their injury or oppression, and that every power, not granted thereby, remains with them, and at their will; that, therefore, no right, of any denomination, can be cancelled, abridged, restrained, or modified, by the Congress, by the Senate or House of Representatives, acting in any capacity, by the President, or any department or officer of the United States, except in those instances in which power is given by the Constitution for those purposes; and that, among other essential rights, the liberty of conscience and of the press cannot be cancelled, abridged, restrained, or modified, by any authority of the United States.

With these impressions, with a solemn appeal to the Searcher of hearts for the purity of our intentions, and under the conviction that whatsoever imperfections may exist in the Constitution ought rather to be examined in the mode prescribed therein, than to bring the Union into danger by delay, with a hope of obtaining amendments previous to the ratification,

We, the said delegates, in the name and behalf of the people of Virginia, do, by these presents, assent to and ratify the Constitution, recommended on the seventeenth day of September, one thousand seven hundred and eighty-seven, by the federal Convention, for the government of the United States; hereby announcing to all those whom it may concern, that the said Constitution is binding upon the said people, according to an authentic copy hereto annexed, in the words following.

[Thursday, June 26]

An engrossed form of the ratification agreed to yesterday, containing the proposed Constitution of government, as recommended by the federal Convention on the seventeenth day of September, one thousand seven hundred and eighty-seven, being prepared by the secretary, was read and signed by the president, in behalf of the Convention.

On motion, Ordered, That the said ratification be transmitted by the president, in the name of this Convention, to the United States in Congress assembled.

On motion, Ordered, That there be allowed to the president of this Convention, for his services, the sum of forty shillings per day, including his daily pay as a member; to the secretary, the sum of forty pounds; to the chaplain, the sum of thirty-two pounds; to the serjeant, the sum of twenty-four pounds; to the clerk of the committee of privileges, the sum of twenty pounds; and to each of the door-keepers, the sum of fifteen pounds, for their respective services.

[Friday, June 27]

Another engrossed form of the ratification, agreed to on Wednesday last, containing the proposed Constitution of government, as recommended by the federal Convention on the seventeenth day of September, one thousand seven hundred and eighty-seven, being prepared by the secretary, was read and signed by the president, in behalf of the Convention.

On motion, Ordered, That the said ratification be deposited by the secretary of this Convention in the archives of the General Assembly of this state.

Mr. Wythe reported, from the committee appointed, such amendments to the proposed Constitution of government for the United States as were by them deemed necessary to be recommended to the consideration of the Congress which shall first assemble under the said Constitution, to be acted upon according to the mode prescribed in the 5th article thereof; and he read the same in his place, and afterwards delivered them in at the clerk's table, where the same were again read, and are as follows:

That there be a declaration or bill of rights asserting, and securing from encroachment, the essential and unalienable rights of the people, in some such manner as the following:

1st. That there are certain natural rights, of which men, when they form a social compact, cannot deprive or divest their posterity; among which are the enjoyment of life and liberty, with the means of acquiring, possessing, and protecting property, and pursuing and obtaining happiness and safety.

2d. That all power is naturally invested in, and consequently derived from, the people; that magistrates therefore are their trustees and agents, at all times amenable to them.

3d. That government ought to be instituted for the common benefit, protection, and security of the people; and that the doctrine of non-resistance against arbitrary power and oppression is absurd, slavish, and destructive to the good and happiness of mankind.

4th. That no man or set of men are entitled to separate or exclusive public emoluments or privileges from the community, but in consideration of public services, which not being descendible, neither ought the offices of magistrate, legislator, or judge, or any other public office, to be hereditary.

5th. That the legislative, executive, and judicial powers of government should be separate and distinct; and, that the members of the two first may be restrained from oppression by feeling and participating the public burdens, they should, at fixed periods, be reduced to a private station, return into the mass of the people, and the vacancies be supplied by certain and regular elections, in which all or any part of the former members to be eligible or ineligible, as the rules of the Constitution of government, and the laws, shall direct.

6th. That the elections of representatives in the legislature ought to be free and frequent, and all men having sufficient evidence of permanent common interest with, and attachment to, the community, ought to have the right of suffrage; and no aid, charge, tax, or fee, can be set, rated, or levied, upon the people without their own consent, or that of their representatives, so elected; nor can they be bound by any law to which they have not, in like manner, assented, for the public good.

7th. That all power of suspending laws, or the execution of laws, by any authority, without the consent of the representatives of the people in the legislature, is injurious to their rights, and ought not to be exercised.

8th. That, in all criminal and capital prosecutions, a man hath a right to demand the cause and nature of his accusation, to be confronted with the accusers and witnesses, to call for evidence, and be allowed counsel in his favor, and to a fair and speedy trial by an impartial jury of his vicinage, without whose unanimous consent he cannot be found guilty, (except in the government of the land and naval forces;) nor can he be compelled to give evidence against himself.

9th. That no freeman ought to be taken, imprisoned, or disseized of his freehold, liberties, privileges, or franchises, or outlawed, or exiled, or in any manner destroyed, or deprived of his life, liberty, or property, but by the law of the land.

10th. That every freeman restrained of his liberty is entitled to a remedy, to inquire into the lawfulness thereof, and to remove the same, if unlawful, and that such remedy ought not to be denied nor delayed.

11th. That, in controversies respecting property, and in suits between man and man, the ancient trial by jury is one of the greatest securities to the rights of the people, and to remain sacred and inviolable.

12th. That every freeman ought to find a certain remedy, by recourse to the laws, for all injuries and wrongs he may receive in his person, property, or character. He ought to obtain right and justice freely, without sale, completely and without denial, promptly and without delay, and that all establishments or regulations contravening these rights are oppressive and unjust.

13th. That excessive bail ought not to be required, nor excessive fines imposed, nor cruel and unusual punishments inflicted.

14th. That every freeman has a right to be secure from all unreasonable searches and seizures of his person, his papers, and property; all warrants, therefore, to search suspected places, or seize any freeman, his papers, or property, without information on oath (or affirmation of a person religiously scrupulous of taking an oath) of legal and sufficient cause, are grievous and oppressive; and all general warrants to search suspected places, or to apprehend any suspected person, without specially naming or describing the place or person, are dangerous, and ought not to be granted.

15th. That the people have a right peaceably to assemble together to consult for the common good, or to instruct their representatives; and that every freeman has a right to petition or apply to the legislature for redress of grievances.

16th. That the people have a right to freedom of speech, and of writing and publishing their sentiments; that the freedom of the press is one of the greatest bulwarks of liberty, and ought not to be violated.

17th. That the people have a right to keep and bear arms; that a well-regulated militia, composed of the body of the people trained to arms, is the proper, natural, and safe defence of a free state; that standing armies, in time of peace, are dangerous to liberty, and therefore ought to be avoided, as far as the circumstances and protection of the community will admit; and that, in all cases, the military should be under strict subordination to, and governed by, the civil power.

18th. That no soldier in time of peace ought to be quartered in any house without the consent of the owner, and in time of war in such manner only as the law directs.

19th. That any person religiously scrupulous of bearing arms ought to be exempted, upon payment of an equivalent to employ another to bear arms in his stead.

20th. That religion, or the duty which we owe to our Creator, and the manner of discharging it, can be directed only by reason and conviction, not by force or violence; and therefore all men have an equal, natural, and unalienable right to the free exercise of religion, according to the dictates of conscience, and that no particular religious sect or society ought to be favored or established, by law, in preference to others.

Amendments to the Constitution

1st. That each state in the Union shall respectively retain every power, jurisdiction, and right, which is not by this Constitution delegated to the Congress of the United States, or to the departments of the federal government.

2d. That there shall be one representative for every thirty thousand according to the enumeration or census mentioned in the Constitution until the whole number of representatives amounts to two hundred; after which, that number shall be continued or increased, as Congress shall direct, upon the principles fixed in the Constitution, by apportioning the representatives of each state to some greater number of people, from time to time, as population increases.

3d. When the Congress shall lay direct taxes or excises, they shall immediately inform the executive power of each state, of the quota of such state, according to the census herein directed, which is proposed to be thereby raised; and if the legislature of any state shall pass a law which shall be effectual for raising such quota at the time required by Congress, the taxes and excises laid by Congress shall not be collected in such state.

4th. That the members of the Senate and House of Representatives shall be ineligible to, and incapable of holding, any civil office under the authority of the United States, during the time for which they shall respectively be elected.

5th. That the journals of the proceedings of the Senate and House of Representatives shall be published at least once in every year, except such parts thereof, relating to treaties, alliances, or military operations, as, in their judgment, require secrecy.

6th. That a regular statement and account of the receipts and expenditures of public money shall be published at least once a year.

7th. That no commercial treaty shall be ratified without the concurrence of two thirds of the whole number of the members of the Senate; and no treaty ceding, contracting, restraining, or suspending, the territorial rights or claims of the United States, or any of them, or their, or any of their rights or claims to fishing in the American seas, or navigating the American rivers, shall be made, but in cases of the most urgent and extreme necessity; nor shall any such treaty be ratified without the concurrence of three fourths of the whole number of the members of both houses respectively.

8th. That no navigation law, or law regulating commerce, shall be passed without the consent of two thirds of the members present, in both houses.

9th. That no standing army, or regular troops, shall be raised, or kept up, in time of peace, without the consent of two thirds of the members present, in both houses.

10th. That no soldier shall be enlisted for any longer term than four years, except in time of war, and then for no longer term than the continuance of the war.

11th. That each state respectively shall have the power to provide for organizing, arming, and disciplining its own militia, whensoever Congress shall omit or neglect to provide for the same. That the militia shall not be subject to martial law, except when in actual service, in time of war, invasion, or rebellion; and when not in actual service of the United States, shall be subject only to such fines, penalties, and punishments, as shall be directed or inflicted by the laws of its own state.

12th. That the exclusive power of legislation given to Congress over the federal town and its adjacent district, and other places, purchased or to be purchased by Congress of any of the states, shall extend only to such regulations as respect the police and good government thereof.

13th. That no person shall be capable of being President of the United States for more than eight years in any term of sixteen years.

14th. That the judicial power of the United States shall be vested in one Supreme Court, and in such courts of admiralty as Congress may from time to time ordain and establish in any of the different states. The judicial power shall extend to all cases in law and equity arising under treaties made, or which shall be made, under the authority of the United States; to all cases affecting ambassadors, other foreign ministers, and consuls; to all cases of admiralty and maritime jurisdiction; to controversies to which the United States shall be a party; to controversies between two or more states, and between parties claiming lands under the grants of different states. In all cases affecting ambassadors, other foreign ministers, and consuls, and those in which a state shall be a party, the Supreme Court shall have original jurisdiction; in all other cases before mentioned, the Supreme Court shall have appellate jurisdiction, as to matters of law only, except in cases of equity, and of admiralty, and maritime jurisdiction, in which the Supreme Court shall have appellate jurisdiction both as to law and fact, with such exceptions and under such regulations as the Congress shall make; but the judicial power of the United States shall extend to no case where the cause of action shall have originated before the ratification of the Constitution, except in disputes between states about their territory, disputes between persons claiming lands under the grants of different states, and suits for debts due to the United States.

15th. That, in criminal prosecutions, no man shall be restrained in the exercise of the usual and accustomed right of challenging or excepting to the jury.

16th. That Congress shall not alter, modify, or interfere in the times, places, or manner of holding elections for senators and representatives, or either of them, except when the legislature of any state shall neglect, refuse, or be disabled, by invasion or rebellion, to prescribe the same.

17th. That those clauses which declare that Congress shall not exercise certain powers, be not interpreted, in any manner whatsoever, to extend the powers of Congress; but that they be construed either as making exceptions to the specified powers where this shall be the case, or otherwise, as inserted merely for greater caution.

18th. That the laws ascertaining the compensation of senators and representatives for their services, be postponed, in their operation, until after the election of representatives immediately succeeding the passing thereof; that excepted which shall first be passed on the subject.

19th. That some tribunal other than the Senate be provided for trying impeachments of senators.

20th. That the salary of a judge shall not be increased or diminished during his continuance in office, otherwise than by general regulations of salary, which may take place on a revision of the subject at stated periods of not less than seven years, to commence from the time such salaries shall be first ascertained by Congress.

*   *   *

And the Convention do, in the name and behalf of the people of this commonwealth, enjoin it upon their representatives in Congress to exert all their influence, and use all reasonable and legal methods, to obtain a ratification of the foregoing alterations and provisions, in the manner provided by the 5th article of the said Constitution; and, in all congressional laws to be passed in the mean time, to conform to the spirit of these amendments, as far as the said Constitution will admit.

And so much of the said amendments as is contained in the first twenty articles, constituting the bill of rights, being read again, Resolved, That this Convention doth concur therein.

The other amendments to the said proposed Constitution, contained in twenty-one articles, being then again read, a motion was made, and the question being put,—to amend the same by striking out the third article, containing these words,

"When Congress shall lay direct taxes or excises, they shall immediately inform the executive power of each state of the quota of such state, according to the census herein directed, which is proposed to be thereby raised; and if the legislature of any state shall pass a law which shall be effectual for raising such quota at the time required by Congress, the taxes and excises laid by Congress shall not be collected in such state,"

It passed in the negative—ayes, 65; noes, 85.

*   *   *

And then, the main question being put, that this Convention doth concur with the committee in the said amendments,

It was resolved in the affirmative.

On motion, Ordered, That the foregoing amendments be fairly engrossed upon parchment, signed by the president of this Convention, and by him transmitted, together with the ratification of the federal Constitution, to the United States in Congress assembled.

On motion, Ordered, That a fair, engrossed copy of the ratification of the federal Constitution, with the subsequent amendments this day agreed to, signed by the president, and attested by the secretary of this Convention, be transmitted by the president, in the name of the Convention, to the executive or legislature of each state in the Union.

Ordered, That the secretary do cause the journal of the proceedings of this Convention to be fairly entered into a well-bound book, and, after being signed by the president, and attested by the secretary, that he deposit the same in the archives of the privy council, or council of state.

On motion, Ordered, That the printer to this Convention do strike, forthwith, fifty copies of the ratification and subsequent amendments of the federal Constitution, for the use of each county in the commonwealth.

On motion, Ordered, That the public auditor be requested to adjust the accounts of the printer to the Convention for his services, and of the workmen who made some temporary repairs and alterations in the new academy, for the accommodation of the Convention, and to grant his warrant on the treasurer for the sum due the respective claimants.

On motion, Resolved, unanimously, That the thanks of the Convention be presented to the president, for his able, upright, and impartial discharge of the duties of that office.

Whereupon the president made his acknowledgment to the Convention for so distinguished a mark of its approbation.

And then the Convention adjourned, *"sine die."*

Signed, Edmund Pendleton, President
Attest, John Beckley, Secretary

Madison to Jefferson, 1788*

Apr. 22, 1788

Dear Sir,

Being just acquainted by letter from President Griffin that Mr. Paradise is in N. York and proposes to sail on the first packet for France I drop you a few lines which will go by that conveyance if they arrive at N. York in time; which however I do not much expect.

The proposed Constitution still engrosses the public attention. The elections for the Convention here are but just over and promulged. From the returns (excepting those from Kentucky which are not yet known,) it seems probable, though not absolutely certain that a majority of the members elect are friends to the Constitution. The superiority of abilities at least seems to lie on that side. The characters of most note which occur to me, are marshalled thus. For the Constitution, Pendleton, Wythe, Blair, Innes, Marshal, Docr. W. Jones, G. Nicholas, Wilson Nicholas, Gabl. Jones, Thos. Lewis, F. Corbin, Ralph Wormley Jr., White of Frederick, Genl. Gates, Genl. A. Stephens, Archd. Stuart, Zachy. Johnson, Docr. Stuart Parson Andrews, H. Lee Jr., Bushrod Washington, considered as a young gentleman of talents: Agst. the Constitution, Mr. Henry, Mason, Harrison, Grayson, Tyler, M. Smith, W. Ronald, Lawson, Bland, Wm. Cabell, Dawson.

The Writings of James Madison, Vol. 5, pp. 120–23.

The Governor is so temperate in his opposition and goes so far with the friends of the Constitution that he cannot properly be classed with its enemies. Monroe is considered by some as an enemy; but I believe him to be a friend though a cool one. There are other individuals of weight whose opinions are unknown to me. R. H. Lee is not elected. His brother, F. L. Lee is a warm friend to the Constitution, as I am told, but also is not elected. So are Jno. & Man Page.

The adversaries take very different grounds of opposition. Some are opposed to the substance of the plan; others, to particular modifications only. Mr. H——y is supposed to aim at disunion. Col. M——n is growing every day more bitter, and outrageous in his efforts to carry his point; and will probably in the end be thrown by the violence of his passions into the politics of Mr. H——y. The preliminary question will be whether previous alterations shall be insisted on or not? Should this be carried in the affirmative, either a conditional ratification, or a proposal for a new Convention will ensue. In either event, I think the Constitution and the Union will be both endangered. It is not to be expected that the States which have ratified will reconsider their determinations, and submit to the alterations prescribed by Virga.. And if a second Convention should be formed, it is as little to be expected that the same spirit of compromise will prevail in it as produced an amicable result to the first. It will be easy also for those who have latent views of disunion, to carry them on under the mask of contending for alterations popular in some but inadmissible in other parts of the U. States.

The real sense of the people of this State cannot be easily ascertained. They are certainly attached and with warmth to a continuance of the Union; and I believe a large majority of the most intelligent and independent, are equally so to the plan under consideration. On a geographical view of them, almost all the Counties in the N. Neck have elected federal Deputies. The Counties on the South side of James River have pretty generally elected adversaries to the Constitution. The intermediate district is much chequered in this respect. The Counties between the blue ridge & the Alleghany have chosen friends to the Constitution without a single exception. Those Westward of the latter have as I am informed, generally though not universally pursued the same rule. Kentucky it is supposed will be divided.

Having been in Virga. but a few weeks, I can give you little account of other matters, and none of your private affairs or connections, particularly of your two nephews. The Winter here as everywhere else in the U. S., was very severe, which, added to short crops of corn, threatened a great scarcity & a high price. It is found however that neither of these evils has taken place. Corn may be purchased for 2 dollars, and even 10s. per barrel. Tobacco is as low at Fredg. as 18s. Per Ct., and not higher at Richmond than 22 or 23s. There is at present a very promising spring especially in the article of fruit. The night before last was so cold as to produce an alarm for the vegetation of all sorts; but it does not appear that anything less vulnerable than young cucumbers had been injured.

I shall ask the favor of Mr. Griffin to send you by Mr. Paradise, or if he should be gone by some other hand, the Debates of the Conventions in Penna. & Massachusetts, and any other publications worth your reading. I am Dear Sir your Affect friend & Servt.

Madison to Alexander Hamilton, 1788*

June 22, 1788

Dear Sir,

The Judiciary Department has been on the anvil for several days; and I presume will still be a further subject of disquisition. The attacks on it have apparently made less impression than was feared. But they may be secretly felt by particular interests that would not make the acknowledgement, and wd. chuse to ground their vote agst. the Constitution on other motives. In the course of this week we hope for a close of the business in some form or other. The opponents will probably bring forward a bill of rights with sundry other amendments as conditions of ratification. Should those fail or be despaired of, an adjournment will I think be attempted. And in case of disappointment here also, some predict a secession. I do not myself concur in the last apprehension; though I have thought it prudent to withold, by a studied fairness in every step on the side of the Constitution, every pretext for rash experiments. The plan meditated by the friends (of) the Constitution is to preface the ratification with some plain & general truths that can not affect the validity of the act; & to subjoin a recommendation which may hold up amendments as objects to be pursued in the constitutional mode. These expedients are rendered prudent by the nice balance of numbers, and the scruples entertained by some who are in general well affected. Whether they will secure us a majority, I dare not positively to declare. Our calculations promise us success by 3 or 4; or possibly 5 or 6 votes. But were there no possibility of mistaking the opinions of some, in reviewing those of so many, the smallness of the majority suggests the danger from ordinary casualties which may vary the result. It unluckily happens that our legislature which meets at this place tomorrow, consists of a considerable majority of antifederal members. This is another circumstance that ought to check our confidence. As individuals they may have some influence, and as coming immediately from the people at large they can give any colour they please to the popular sentiments at this moment, and may in that mode throw a bias on the representatives of the people in Convention. Yrs. affecty.

*H. C. Syrett, ed., *The Papers of Alexander Hamilton* (1962), Vol. 5, p. 61.

Madison to Washington, 1788*

June 27, 1788

Dear Sir,

The Convention came to a final adjournment today. The inclosed is a copy of their Act of ratification with the yeas & nays. A variety of amendments have been since recommended; several of them highly objectionable, but which could not be parried. The Minority are to sign an address this evening which is announced to be of a peace-making complexion. Having not seen it I can give no opinion of my own. I wish it may not have a further object. Mr. H——y declared previous to the final question that altho' he should submit as a quiet citizen, he should seize the first moment that offered for shaking off the yoke in a Constitutional way. I suspect the plan will be to engage 2/3 of the Legislatures in the task of undoing the work; or to get a Congress appointed in the first instance that will commit suicide on their own Authority.

Yrs. most affecty. & respectfy.

Madison to Hamilton, 1788†

June 27, 1788

My dear Sir,

This day put an end to the existence of our Convention. The inclosed is a copy of the Act of Ratification. It has been followed by a number of recomendatory alterations; many of them highly objectionable. One of the most so is an article prohibiting direct taxes where effectual laws shall be passed by the States for the purpose. It was impossible to prevent this error. The minority will sign an address to the people. The genius of it is unknown to me. It is announced as an exhortation to acquiescence in the result of the Convention. Notwithstanding the fair professions made by some, I am so uncharitable as to suspect that the ill-will to the Constitution will produce every peaceable effort to disgrace & destroy it. Mr. H——y declared previous to the final question that although he should submit as a quiet citizen, he should wait with impatience for the favorable moment of regaining in a constitutional way, the lost liberties of his country. My conjecture is that exertions will be made to engage 2/3 ds of the Legislatures in the task of regularly undermining the government. This hint may not be unworthy of your attention.

Yrs. affecly.

*The Writings of James Madison, Vol. 5, p. 234.

†The Papers of Alexander Hamilton, Vol. 5, p. 91.

Madison to Jefferson, 1788*

July 24, 1788

Dear Sir,

Your two last unacknowledged favors were of Decr. 20 and Feby. 6. They were received in Virginia, and no opportunity till the present precarious one by the way of Holland, has enabled me to thank you for them.

I returned here about ten days ago from Richmond which I left a day or two after the dissolution of the Convention. The final question on the new Government was put on the 25th of June. It was twofold: 1. whether previous amendments should be made a condition of ratification. 2. directly on the Constitution in the form it bore. On the first the decision was in the negative, 88 being no, 80 only ay. On the second & definitive question, the ratification was affirmed by 89 ays agst. 79 noes. A number of alterations were then recommended to be considered in the mode pointed out in the Constitution itself. The meeting was remarkably full; Two members only being absent and those known to be on the opposite sides of the question. The debates also were conducted on the whole with a very laudable moderation and decorum, and continued untill both sides declared themselves ready for the question. And it may be safely concluded that no irregular opposition to the System will follow in that State, at least with the countenance of the leaders on that side. What local eruptions may be occasioned by ill-timed or rigorous executions of the Treaty of peace against British debtors, I will not pretend to say. But altho. the leaders, particularly H——y & M—s—n, will give no countenance to popular violences it is not to be inferred that they are reconciled to the event, or will give it a positive support. On the contrary both of them declared they could not go that length, and an attempt was made under their auspices to induce the minority to sign an address to the people which, if it had not been defeated by the general moderation of the party would probably have done mischief.

Among a variety of expedients employed by the opponents to gain proselytes, Mr. Henry first, and after him Colo. Mason, introduced the opinions expressed in a letter from a correspondent (Master Donald or Skipwith, I believe) and endeavored to turn the influence of your name even against parts of which I knew you approved. In this situation I thought it due to truth, as well as that it would be most agreeable to yourself, and accordingly took the liberty to state some of your opinions on the favorable side. I am informed that copies or extracts of a letter from you were handed about at the Maryld. Convention, with a like view of impeding the ratification.

N. Hampshire ratified the Constitution on the 20th Ult; and made the ninth State. The votes stood 57 for and 46 agst. the measure. S. Carolina had previously ratified by a very great majority. The Convention of N. Carolina

*The Writings of James Madison, Vol. 5, pp. 240–43.

is now sitting. At one moment the sense of that State was considered as strongly opposed to the system. It is now said that the time has been for some time turning, which with the example of other States and particularly of Virginia prognosticates a ratification there also. The Convention of New York has been in Session ever since the 17th Ult:, without having yet arrived at any final vote. Two thirds of the members assembled with a determination to reject the Constitution, and are still opposed to it in their hearts. The local situation of N. York, the number of ratifying States and the hope of retaining the federal Government in this City afford however powerful arguments to such men as Jay, Hamilton, the Chancellor, Duane and several others; and it is not improbable that some form of ratification will yet be devised, by which the dislike of the opposition may be gratified, and the State, notwithstanding, made a member of the new Union.

At Fredericksburg on my way hither I found the box with Cork Acorns Sulla & peas addressed to me. I immediately had it forwarded to Orange from whence the contents will be disposed of according to your order. I fear the advanced season will defeat the experiments. The few seeds taken out here by the President at my request & sown in his garden have not come up. I left directions in Virginia for obtaining acorns of the Willow Oak this fall, which shall be sent you as soon as possible. Col. Carrington tells me your request as to the Philosophical Transactions was complied with in part only, the 1st. volume being not to be had. I have enquired of a Delegate here from Rhode Island for further information concerning W. S. Brown, but can learn nothing precise. I shall continue my enquiries, and let you know hereafter the result.

July 26.—We just hear that the Convention of this State have determined by a small majority to exclude from the ratification anything involving a condition & to content themselves with recommending the alterations wished for.

As this will go by way of Holland I consider its reaching you as extremely uncertain. I forbear therefore to enter further into our public affairs at this time. If the packets should not be discontinued, which is surmised by some, I shall soon have an opportunity of writing again. In the mean time I remain with the sincerest affection

Your Friend & Servt.

P.S. Crops in Virginia of all sorts were very promising when I left the State. This was the case also generally throught. the States I passed thro', with local exceptions produced in the wheat fields by a destructive insect which goes under the name of the Hessian fly. It made its first appearance several years ago on Long Island, from which it has spread over half this State and a great part of New Jersey, and seems to be making an annual progress in every direction.

NEW YORK RATIFYING CONVENTION, 1788

Commentary

After the action of the Virginia Convention the scene shifted to New York, the next state to act on ratification. Here, too, the Ratifying Convention was closely divided (if not weighted substantially toward the Antifederalists, as the Hamilton letter [*infra* p. 920) shows, and there were leading men of the day on both sides of the debate: John Jay, Alexander Hamilton, and Chancellor Robert Livingston for the Federalists, and Governor George Clinton, Melancton Smith, and John Lansing for the Antifederalists. Hamilton particularly was effective in the debate, and some of his speeches deserve comparison with his essays in *The Federalist* or indeed with any papers on political science ever written.

The New York Convention assembled on June 17, 1788. From then until July 2, the delegates debated the substantive provisions of the Constitution, especially those relating to the powers and composition of Congress, with emphasis on the power of taxation. So far as we can tell from the report of the debates there was no specific reference to protection of individual liberties or the need for a Bill of Rights before July 2. Hamilton did, however, deal with the subject by implication, stating that the Constitution provided for both of the objects sought "in forming systems of government—*safety* for the people, and *energy* in the administration." The checks and balances contained in the Constitution furnished ample security for the liberties of the people: "give a perfect proportion and balance to its parts, and the powers you give it will never affect your security." Chancellor Livingston also touched upon the matter indirectly, saying that the opposition "wish for checks against what can do no harm. They contend for a phantom." The Constitution itself rejected the notion "that the powers of Congress would be dangerous."

Finally, on July 2, Antifederalist Thomas Tredwell rose and delivered a long attack upon the Constitution's failure to provide specific protections for personal liberties. He emphasized the failure to provide express guarantees for freedom of the press, trial by jury, and the other basic rights of the people: "in forming the Constitution, we have run into the same error which the lawyers and Pharisees of old were charged with, that is, while we have secured the tithes of mint, anise, and cumin, we have neglected the weightier matters of the law." In the Constitution, "we find no security for the rights of individuals. . . . ; here is no bill of rights, no proper restriction of power." Government may be likened to a mad horse which may run away with the rider. "Would he not, therefore, justly be deemed a mad man, and deserve to have his neck broken, who should trust himself on this horse without any bridle at all?"

Unfortunately, the detailed report of the New York debates, from which our extracts are taken (which is from the shorthand record made by Francis Childs, the editor of a New York newspaper) becomes very skimpy for the latter part of the Convention, confining itself to a brief account of the motions introduced after Tredwell's speech. Notes were, however, kept by Gilbert Livingston, and they give us the most complete record we have of the Convention between July 14 and final adjournment. The Livingston Notes (*infra* p. 881) have not heretofore been published. They start, on July 14, in the midst of a debate on conditional versus recommendatory ratification. They enable us to follow the debates on that core issue, as well as the adoption of the Bill of Rights introduced by John Lansing.

After the Tredwell speech, the Convention (sitting in Committee of the Whole) dealt with a series of Antifederalist amendments to the body of the Constitution (two of which bear upon personal liberties, since they relate to the Habeas Corpus and Ex Post Facto Clauses). Then, on July 7, the Bill of Rights issue came to the fore, as "Mr. Lansing then read, and presented . . . a Bill of Rights to be prefixed to the Constitution." From Hamilton's letter to Madison (*infra* p. 921) we can see that the Federalists were not certain whether their opponents would insist upon conditional amendments; but that the Federalists themselves were willing to concede the need for recommendatory amendments.

From a contemporary newspaper (*infra* p. 878) we learn that the Federalists agreed to join with their opponents on an unofficial committee to consider Lansing's amendments, and "endeavor to make such an accommodation, and to arrange the amendments as to bring the business to a quick and friendly decision." The newspaper account (*infra* p. 878) indicates that the committee proceedings did not go smoothly. But an important step toward accommodation had been taken. Then, on July 11, Jay made a motion to ratify and then recommend "whatever amendments may be deemed useful or expedient." Hamilton delivered a powerful speech the next day (of which we have the newspaper account, [*infra* p. 879])supporting the Jay motion and attacking the notion that the Convention could ratify on condition.

Despite the Hamilton argument, Smith moved for the opposition on July 14 or 15 (there is some dispute on the date despite the fact that the report [*infra* p. 874] states that it was July 15) that ratification should be conditional only; the main condition imposed was the calling of a Second Constitutional Convention "for proposing amendments to the said Constitution."

On July 14, Hamilton delivered a second speech attacking the concept of conditional ratification, as well as questioning the power of Congress to call a Second Convention to add amendments. The day following, Hamilton expressly stated the Federalist willingness to recommend amendments along with ratification. The amendments he read are available in his own handwriting (*infra* p. 880). Though far from the Bill of Rights introduced by Lansing, they did represent a Federalist concession, which might lead to

Antifederalist concessions. The big question was now that stated by Jay: "Cannot we endeavour further to accommodate?" Ultimately, the accommodation called for took place with the adoption of the substance of the Lansing proposals, but only as recommendatory amendments.

In another speech on July 15, Hamilton attempted further to conciliate Lansing, but the latter went ahead on July 19 and moved a conditional ratification, with a Bill of Rights prefixed. At this point the Federalists were hard pressed, a delaying motion by them for adjournment having been defeated decisively. Hamilton's letter to Madison (*infra* p. 923) shows that the Federalists were willing even to accept ratification with "a right to recede in case our amendments have not been decided upon . . . within a certain number of years." In the meantime, the debate continued on the details of Lansing's proposed Bill of Rights, with the Federalists led by Hamilton indicating their willingness to accept virtually all the Lansing amendments, provided they were not made conditional. It is of interest that Hamilton was able on July 19 to secure elimination of the word "expressly" in the provision dealing with the reserved powers of the states (anticipating the Hamilton approach to implied powers stated in his famous 1791 opinion on the constitutionality of the United States Bank).

On July 22, Hamilton was able to write Madison that there was a great diversity in the views of the Antifederalists. "Upon the whole however our fears diminish." His feeling on the matter was vindicated on July 23, when a split in the Antifederalist ranks became apparent. The Convention then took up Lansing's motion that ratification be conditional upon prior adoption of his Bill of Rights and other amendments. Melancton Smith (the Antifederalist leader who had made the original motion for conditional ratification) now moved that the Lansing motion be expunged and a substitute accepted providing that ratification be "in confidence" that the amendments would be adopted. This motion carried, as did a further motion to the same effect by Samuel Jones.

The adoption of the Smith and Jones resolutions meant that New York would ratify without conditions, though it would recommend amendments. The Jones motion was carried only by a vote of 31 to 29 (without Antifederalist votes, especially that of Smith, it could scarcely have prevailed). The Antifederalist split continued on July 26, when "the bill of rights, and form of ratification, with the amendments," were voted on. The affirmative prevailed by only 30 to 27.

The Antifederalist split needed to accomplish unconditional ratification was secured by two principal concessions. The first was the acceptance of Lansing's Bill of Rights as a prefix to the instrument of ratification, as well as a list of proposed amendments to the body of the Constitution. Ratification was declared "in confidence" that the proposals would "receive an early and mature consideration." The second concession was an agreement to send a circular letter to the other states urging the calling of a Second Convention to deal with the amendments proposed by the different states. The circular letter was strongly attacked by the Federalists. With Madison in his letter to Washington, they felt that it "has a most pestilent tendency" and would undermine the Constitution. Fortunately, the danger did not materialize; a Second Convention was never called. The Constitution could go into effect with the unconditional ratifications of the states already discussed—which were not weakened (legally speaking) by the fact that five ratifications were accompanied by recommendatory amendments.

As already indicated, the New York ratification was accompanied by a proposed Bill of Rights and other amendments based upon a draft by John Lansing. The New York proposals are even longer than those of Virginia. The proposed New York Bill of Rights contains 25 unnumbered articles and there are 32 other proposed amendments. The provisions included are a numerous and motley lot, covering, as they do, both provisions of fundamental importance and some which could serve only to clutter up the Constitution. It is usually said that the New York proposals added little, if anything, to the development of the federal Bill of Rights. George Mason, in a contemporary letter declared his belief that the New York amendments were modelled upon those he had helped draft in the Virginia Convention. It is, however, plain that the close struggle in New York and that state's strong recommendation (so close to being made conditional) of a Bill of Rights brought great added pressure upon the first Congress under the Constitution. Unless it quickly proposed amendments to meet the popular desire, the New York call for a Second Convention might well be given effect.

The substance of the New York-proposed Bill of Rights is, it must be conceded, similar to that recommended by Virginia, even with regard to the language used in many of the provisions (though the New York proposal contains a prohibition against double jeopardy absent from the Virginia one and was the first official state proposal for such a prohibition; New York also follows Massachusetts in guaranteeing the right to an indictment).

The differences just referred to are matters of detail. There is, however, another difference between the New York-proposed Bill of Rights and all the other state-proposed amendments, one which is so significant that it is surprising that other commentators have overlooked it. The difference referred to was in the New York version of section 39 of Magna Carta (*supra* p. 12): "That no Person ought to be taken imprisoned or disseised of his freehold, or to be exiled or deprived of his Privileges, Franchises, Life, Liberty or Property but by *due process of Law.*" (Emphasis added).

As early as 1354, it is true, a confirmation of Magna Carta by Edward III replaced section 39's "law of the land" with "due Process of The Law," and Coke's classic commentary on Magna Carta considered the two phrases as equivalent. Prior American fundamental laws (starting with the Massachusetts Body of Liberties, 1641, [*supra* p. 69]) also customarily contained different versions of section 39 of Magna Carta. But the New York proposed

Bill of Rights was, so far as can be determined the first American constitutional provision to use the term "due process of Law" in its restatement of section 39, though a 1692 Massachusetts statute did provide for protection of person and property by due process, and the New York Charter of Libertyes, 1683, had used the term "due Course of Law" (*supra* p. 162).

The New York change in language was not a mere matter of style. On the contrary, it constituted a constitutional quantum leap forward. Without it, there might well not have been any Due Process Clause in the Fifth Amendment. (Madison had the New York draft before him, as well as the other state recommendations, when he wrote his draft of what became the Fifth Amendment.) Had the Fifth Amendment followed the Virginia "Law of the Land" rather than the New York "due process" phraseology, the Constitution would have been without its most significant provision—the Due Process Clause. Bearing in mind the extent to which the due process concept, in both the Fifth and Fourteenth Amendments, has served as the basis for the constitutional protection of the rights of Americans, it can scarcely be doubted that a Constitution shorn of the Due Process Clause would have been far less effective in securing such protection.

This is not mere theory. The Constitution of India uses the term "procedure established by law" in place of "due process" and the Supreme Court of that country has interpreted that term to include a law enacted by the Indian Parliament. (Gopalan *v.* State of Madras, [1950] S. C. R. 88.) Hence, property taken by a statute is taken "by law" as the term is used in the Indian Constitution. Similar "Law of the Land" terminology in the federal Constitution would, in all probability, have been interpreted the same way.

We are not certain who wrote the Due Process Clause into the New York-proposed Bill of Rights. Since it appears in the draft introduced by John Lansing, we can assume it was Lansing himself who made this fundamental contribution to our constitutional development. So far as we know, the New York Convention accepted the due process provision in Lansing's draft without debate.

On January 26, 1787, the New York Legislature had passed "An Act concerning the rights of the citizens of this State." That statute contained a provision that no one should be deprived of any right, but by "due process of law." Lansing undoubtedly took his draft Due Process Clause from this 1787 statute (though we do not know who was responsible for the clause there). From Hamilton's Assembly speech of February 6, 1787 (*infra* p. 919), we can see that the draftsman of the 1787 statute did not use the term "due process" in anything like the broad meaning it has since acquired in our constitutional law. Instead, the term was intended as "applicable to the process and proceedings of the courts of justice; they can never be referred to an act of legislature."

Without question, Lansing (and later Madison in drafting what became the Fifth Amendment) used "due process" in the same narrow connotation.

Yet this scarcely affects the crucial significance of what they did. The term "due process" could expand to meet even legislative power; the same was scarcely true of the "Law of the Land" phraseology which would have been used in the Fifth Amendment had Lansing and Madison not employed the "due process" language.

New York Ratifying Convention, 1788*

Debates

[Wednesday, June 25]

Mr. Hamilton: . . . There are two objects in forming systems of government—safety for the people, and energy in the administration. When these objects are united, the certain tendency of the system will be to the public welfare. If the latter object be neglected, the people's security will be as certainly sacrificed as by disregarding the former. Good constitutions are formed upon a comparison of the liberty of the individual with the strength of government: if the tone of either be too high, the other will be weakened too much. It is the happiest possible mode of conciliating these objects, to institute one branch peculiarly endowed with sensibility, another with knowledge and firmness. Through the opposition and mutual control of these bodies, the government will reach, in its operations, the perfect balance between liberty and power. The arguments of the gentlemen chiefly apply to the former branch—the House of Representatives. If they will calmly consider the different nature of the two branches, they will see that the reasoning which justly applies to the representative house, will go to destroy the essential qualities of the Senate. If the former is calculated perfectly upon the principles of caution, why should you impose the same principles upon the latter, which is designed for a different operation? Gentlemen, while they discover a laudable anxiety for the safety of the people, do not attend to the important distinction I have drawn. We have it constantly held up to us, that, as it is our chief duty to guard against tyranny, it is our policy to form all the branches of government for this purpose.

*   *   *

After all our doubts, our suspicions, and speculations, on the subject of government, we must return at last to this important truth—that, when we have formed a constitution upon free principles, when we have given a proper balance to the different branches of administration, and fixed representation upon pure and equal principles, we may, with safety, furnish it

The Debates in the Several State Conventions on the Adoption of the Constitution, Vol. 2, pp. 316–414.

with all the powers necessary to answer, in the most ample manner, the purposes of government. The great desiderata are, free representation and mutual checks. When these are obtained, all our apprehensions of the extent of power are unjust and imaginary. What, then, is the structure of this Constitution? One branch of the legislature is to be elected by the people—by the same people who choose your state representatives. Its members are to hold their offices two years, and then return to their constituents. Here, sir, the people govern; here they act by their immediate representatives. You have also a Senate, constituted by your state legislatures, by men in whom you place the highest confidence, and forming another representative branch. Then, again, you have an executive magistrate, created by a form of election which merits universal admiration. In the form of this government, and in the mode of legislation, you find all the checks which the greatest politicians and the best writers have ever conceived. What more can reasonable men desire? Is there any one branch in which the whole legislative and executive powers are lodged? No. The legislative authority is lodged in three distinct branches, properly balanced; the executive is divided between two branches; and the judicial is still reserved for an independent body, who hold their office during good behavior. This organization is so complex, so skilfully contrived, that it is next to impossible that an impolitic or wicked measure should pass the scrutiny with success. Now, what do gentlemen mean by coming forward and declaiming against this government? Why do they say we ought to limit its power, to disable it, and to destroy its capacity of blessing the people? Has philosophy suggested, has experience taught, that such a government ought not to be trusted with every thing necessary for the good of society? Sir, when you have divided and nicely balanced the departments of government; when you have strongly connected the virtue of your rulers with their interest; when, in short, you have rendered your system as perfect as human forms can be—you must place confidence; you must give power.

We have heard a great deal of the sword and the purse. It is said our liberties are in danger, if both are possessed by Congress. Let us see what is the true meaning of this maxim, which has been so much used, and so little understood. It is, that you shall not place these powers either in the legislative or executive, singly; neither one nor the other shall have both, because this would destroy that division of powers on which political liberty is founded, and would furnish one body with all the means of tyranny. But where the purse is lodged in one branch, and the sword in another, there can be no danger. All governments have possessed these powers: they would be monsters without them, and incapable of exertion. What is your state government? Does not your legislature command what money it pleases? Does not your executive execute the laws without restraint? These distinctions between the purse and the sword have no application to the system, but only to its separate branches. Sir, when we reason about the great interests of a free people, it is high time that we dismiss our prejudices, and banish declamation. In order to induce us to consider the powers given by this Constitution as dangerous, in order to render plausible an attempt to take away the life and spirit of the most important power in government, the gentleman complains that we shall not have a true and safe representation. I asked him what a safe representation was; and he has given no satisfactory answer. The Assembly of New York has been mentioned as a proper standard; but if we apply this standard to the general government, our Congress will become a mere mob, exposed to every irregular impulse, and subject to every breeze of faction. Can such a system afford security? Can you have confidence in such a body? The idea of taking the ratio of representation, in a small society, for the ratio of a great one, is a fallacy which ought to be exposed. It is impossible to ascertain to what point our representation will increase; it may vary from one, to two, three, or four hundred: it depends upon the progress of population. Suppose it to rest at two hundred; is not this number sufficient to secure it against corruption? Human nature must be a much more weak and despicable thing than I apprehend it to be, if two hundred of our fellow-citizens can be corrupted in two years. But suppose they are corrupted; can they, in two years, accomplish their designs? Can they form a combination, and even lay a foundation for a system of tyranny, in so short a period? It is far from my intention to wound the feelings of any gentleman; but I must, in this most interesting discussion, speak of things as they are, and hold up opinions in the light in which they ought to appear; and I maintain that all that has been said of corruption, of the purse and the sword, and of the danger of giving powers, is not supported by principles or fact; that it is mere verbiage and idle declamation. The true principle of government is this—make the system complete in its structure, give a perfect proportion and balance to its parts, and the powers you give it will never affect your security. The question, then, of the division of powers between the general and state governments, is a question of convenience: it becomes a prudential inquiry, what powers are proper to be reserved to the latter; and this immediately involves another inquiry into the proper objects of the two governments. This is the criterion by which we shall determine the just distribution of powers.

*   *   *

[Monday, June 20]

The Chancellor [R. R. Livingston]: . . . Much has been said, sir, about the sword and the purse. These words convey very confused ideas on the gentleman's application of them. . . . Let us see how this matter stands. The states of Pennsylvania and New York form two distinct governments; but New York, Pennsylvania, and the general government, together form one government. The United States and New York make another government;

the United States and Connecticut another, and so on. To the gentleman's optics these things may be clear; but to me they are utter darkness. We have thirteen distinct governments, and yet they are not thirteen governments but one government. It requires the ingenuity of St. Athanasius to understand this political mystery. Were the gentleman a minister of the gospel, I might have faith; but I confess my reason is much too weak for it. Sir, we are attempting to build one government out of thirteen; preserving, however, the states, as parts of the system, for local purposes, and to give it support and beauty. The truth is, the states, and the United States, have distinct objects. They are both supreme. As to national objects, the latter is supreme; as to internal and domestic objects, the former. I can easily conceive of two joint tenures, and of joint jurisdictions without control. If I wanted an example, I might instance the mine, Mr. Chairman, in which you and others have a joint property and concurrent jurisdiction. But why should the states hold the purse? How are they to use it? They have not to pay the civil list, to maintain the army or navy. What will they do with it? What is the sword, which the gentlemen talk of? How is Congress to defend us without a sword? You will also keep that. How shall it be handled? Shall we all take hold of it? I never knew, till now, the design of a curious image I have seen at the head of one of our newspapers. I am now convinced that the idea was prophetic in the printer. It was a figure of thirteen hands, in an awkward position, grasping a perpendicular sword. As the arms which supported it were on every side, I could see no way of moving it, but by drawing it through, with the hazard of dangerously cutting the fingers. For my own part, I should be for crying, "hands off!" But this sword of the gentlemen's is a visionary sword—a mere empty pageant; and yet they would never trust it out of the state scabbard, lest it should wound somebody. They wish for checks against what can do no harm. They contend for a phantom. Gentlemen should consider their arguments before they come here. Sir, our reasoning on this ground is conclusive. If it be necessary to trust our defence to the Union, it is necessary that we should trust it with the sword to defend us, and the purse to give the sword effect. I have heard not a shadow of an argument to shake the truth of this. But the gentlemen will talk—it is expected. It is necessary that they should support, in this house, the opinions they have propagated out of doors, but which perhaps they had themselves too hastily formed.

*   *   *

[Wednesday, July 2]

The Chancellor said, he was very unfortunate in provoking so many able antagonists. They had given a turn to his arguments and expressions which he did not expect. He was, however, happy that he could say, with Sir John Falstaff, that if he had no wit himself, he had been the occasion of wit in others; and therefore he supposed that the ladies, this day, had been as well entertained as yesterday. He went on to explain what the gentleman had imputed to him as contradictions. He had charged him with saying that a federal government could not exist, and yet that he had contended for one. This was false; he had maintained that a single league of states could not long exist, and had proved it by examples. This was fair reasoning, and he had not said any thing to contradict it. He then went through a review of his arguments, to prove that he had been misrepresented, and that he had been consistent throughout. But, said the chancellor, what most deeply wounds me is, that my worthy kinsman across the table, regardless of our common ancestry, and the tender ties of blood, should join his dagger with the rest, and compel me to exclaim, in the dying words of Caesar, "And thou, too Brutus!" The gentleman alleges, first, that I have treated the holy gospel with disdain. This is a serious charge. I deny it. If I have used a phrase disagreeable to him, I certainly have expressed nothing disrespectful of the Scriptures. . . . Sir, if gentlemen will come forward with absurd arguments, imagine erroneous premises, and draw false conclusions, shall they not be exposed? and if their contradictions render them ridiculous, is it my fault? Are not the absurdities of public speakers ridiculed in all countries? Why not expose false reasoning? Why not pluck from Sophistry the delusive veil by which she imposes on the people? If I am guilty of absurdities, let them be detected and displayed. If the fool's cap fits me, clap it on: I will wear it, and all shall laugh. Sir, the very day after I made my first speech to this committee, I was attacked with great severity, and with unusual weapons. A dreadful and terrible beast, with great iron claws and ghastly look, was made to grin horribly in my face. I appeal to this committee, sir, whether gentlemen have not said plainly, that the powers of Congress would be dangerous, and yet impracticable. If they will speak such nonsense, they must be exposed. Their other arguments are equally ridiculous; they reason in confusion. They form a government, to consist of thirteen governments, one controls thirteen, and thirteen control one. With regard to the sword and the purse, I could have no conception of Congress keeping a sword, and the states using it; of Congress using a purse, and the states keeping it; of Congress having power, and the states exercising it. I could not reconcile these things to my reason. Sir, when any argument, on such a subject as this, strikes me as being absurd and ridiculous, I cannot conceal my emotions; I think it my duty to expose it boldly; and I shall continue to do this, without any apprehensions from those virulent attacks which have been aimed at me from every quarter.

Mr. Tredwell. Sir, little accustomed to speak in public, and always inclined, in such an assembly as this, to be a hearer rather than a speaker, on a less important occasion than the present I should have contented myself with a silent vote; but when I consider the nature of this dispute that it is a contest, not between little states and great states (as we have been told,) between little folks and great folks, between patriotism and ambition, between freedom and power; not so much between the navigating and non-navigating states, as between navigating and non-navigating individuals, (for not one of the amendments we contend for has the least reference to the clashing interests of states;) when I consider, likewise, that a people jealous of their liberties, and strongly attached to freedom, have reposed so entire a confidence in this assembly, that upon our determination depends their future enjoyment of those invaluable rights and privileges, which they have so lately and so gallantly defended at every risk and expense, both of life and property,—it appears to me so interesting and important, that I cannot be totally silent on the occasion, lest lisping babes should be taught to curse my name, as a betrayer of their freedom and happiness.

The gentleman who first opened this debate did (with an emphasis which I believe convinced every one present of the propriety of the advice) urge the necessity of proceeding, in our deliberations on this important subject, cooly and dispassionately. With how much candor this advice was given, appears from the subsequent parts of a long speech, and from several subsequent speeches almost totally addressed to our fears. The people of New Jersey and Connecticut are so exceedingly exasperated against us, that, totally regardless of their own preservation, they will take the two rivers of Connecticut and Delaware by their extremities, and, by dragging them over our country, will, by a sweeping deluge, wash us all into the Hudson, leaving neither house nor inhabitant behind them. But if this event should not happen, doubtless the Vermontese, with the British and tories, our natural enemies, would, by bringing down upon us the great Lake Ontario, sweep hills and mountains, houses and inhabitants, in one deluge, into the Atlantic. These, indeed, would be terrible calamities; but terrible as they are, they are not to be compared with the horrors and desolation of tyranny. The arbitrary courts of Philip in the Netherlands, in which life and property were daily confiscated without a jury, occasioned as much misery and a more rapid depopulation of the province, before the people took up arms in their own defence, than all the armies of that haughty monarch were able to effect afterwards; and it is doubtful in my mind, whether governments, by abusing their powers, have not occasioned as much misery and distress, and nearly as great devastations of the human species, as all the wars which have happened since Milton's battle of the angels to the present day. The end or design of government is, or ought to be, the safety, peace, and welfare of the governed. Unwise, therefore, and absurd in the highest degree, would be the conduct of that people, who, in forming a government, should give to their rulers power to destroy them and their property, and thereby defeat the very purpose of their institutions; or, in other words, should give unlimited power to their rulers, and not retain in their own hands the means of their own preservation. The first governments in the world were parental, the powers of which were restrained by the laws of nature; and doubtless the early succeeding governments were formed on the same plan, which, we may suppose, answered tolerably well in the first ages of the world, while the moral sense was strong, and the laws of nature well understood, there being then no lawyers to explain them away. But in after times, when kings became great, and courts crowded, it was discovered that governments should have a right to tyrannize, and a power to oppress; and at the present day, when the *juris periti* are become so skilful in their profession, and quibbling is reduced to a science, it is become extremely difficult to form a constitution which will secure liberty and happiness to the people, or laws under which property is safe. Hence, in modern times, the design of the people, in forming an original constitution of government, is not so much to give powers to their rulers, as to guard against the abuse of them; but, in a federal one, it is different.

Sir, I introduce these observations to combat certain principles which have been daily and confidently advanced by the favorers of the present Constitution, and which appear to me totally indefensible. The first and grand leading, or rather misleading, principle in this debate, and on which the advocates for this system of unrestricted powers must chiefly depend for its support, is that, in forming a constitution, whatever powers are not expressly granted or given the government, are reserved to the people, or that rulers cannot exercise any powers but those expressly given to them by the Constitution. Let me ask the gentlemen who advanced this principle, whether the commission of a Roman dictator, which was in these few words—to take care that the state received no harm—does not come up fully to their ideas of an energetic government; or whether an invitation from the people to one or more to come and rule over them, would not clothe the rulers with sufficient powers. If so, the principle they advance is a false one. Besides, the absurdity of this principle will evidently appear, when we consider the great variety of objects to which the powers of the government must necessarily extend, and that an express enumeration of them all would probably fill as many volumes as Pool's Synopsis of the Critics. But we may reason with sufficient certainty on the subject, from the sense of all the public bodies in the United States, who had occasion to form new constitutions. They have uniformly acted upon a direct and contrary principle, not only in forming the state constitutions and the old Confederation, but also in forming this very Constitution, for we do not find in every state constitution express resolutions made in favor of the people; and it is clear that the late Convention at Philadelphia, whatever might have been the sentiments of some of its members, did not adopt the principle, for they have made certain reservations and restrictions, which, upon that principle, would have been totally useless and unnecessary; and can it be supposed that that wise body, whose only apology for the great ambiguity of many parts of that performance, and the total omission of some things which many esteem essential to the security of liberty, was a great desire of brevity, should so far sacrifice that great and important object, as to insert a number of provisions which they esteemed totally useless? Why is it said that the privilege of the writ of habeas corpus shall not be suspended, unless, in cases of rebellion or invasion, the public safety may require it? What clause in the Constitution, except this very clause itself, gives the general government a power to deprive us of that great privilege, so sacredly secured to us by our state constitutions? Why is it provided that no bill of attainder shall be passed, or that no title of nobility shall be granted? Are there any clauses in the Constitution extending the powers of the general government to these objects? Some gentlemen say that these, though not necessary, were inserted for greater caution. I could have wished, sir, that a greater caution had been used to secure to us the freedom of election, a sufficient and responsible representation, the freedom of the press, and the trial by jury both in civil and criminal cases.

These, sir, are the rocks on which the Constitution should have rested; no other foundation can any man lay, which will secure the sacred temple of freedom against the power of the great, the undermining arts of ambition, and the blasts of profane scoffers—for such there will be in every age—who will tell us that all religion is in vain; that is, that our political creeds, which have been handed down to us by our forefathers as sacredly as our Bibles, and for which more of them have suffered martyrdom than for the creed of the apostles, are all nonsense; who will tell us that paper constitutions are mere paper, and that parchment is but parchment, that jealousy of our rulers is a sin, &c. I could have wished also that sufficient caution had been used to secure to us our religious liberties, and to have prevented the general government from tyrannizing over our consciences by a religious establishment—a tyranny of all others most dreadful, and which will assuredly be exercised whenever it shall be thought necessary for the promotion and support of their political measures. It is ardently to be wished, sir, that these and other invaluable rights of freemen had been as cautiously secured as some of the paltry local interests of some of the individual states. But it appears to me, that, in forming this Constitution, we have run into the same error which the lawyers and Pharisees of old were charged with; that is, while we have secured the tithes of mint, anise, and cumin, we have neglected the weightier matters of the law, judgment, mercy, and faith. Have we not neglected to secure to ourselves the weighty matters of judgment or justice, by empowering the general government to establish one supreme, and as many inferior, courts as they please, whose proceedings they have a right to fix and regulate as they shall think fit, so that we are ignorant whether they shall be according to the common, civil, the Jewish, or Turkish law? What better provisions have we made for mercy, when a man, for ignorantly passing a counterfeit continental note, or bill of credit, is liable to be dragged to a distant county, two or three hundred miles from home, deprived of the support and assistance of friends, to be tried by a strange jury, ignorant of his character, ignorant of the character of the witnesses, unable to contradict any false testimony brought against him by their own knowledge of facts, and with whom the prisoner being unacquainted, he must be deprived totally of the benefit of his challenge? and besides all that, he may be exposed to lose his life, merely for want of property to carry his witnesses to such a distance; and after all this solemn farce and mockery of a trial by jury, if they should acquit him, it will require more ingenuity than I am master of, to show that he does not hold his life at the will and pleasure of the Supreme Court, to which an appeal lies, and consequently depend on the tender mercies, perhaps, of the wicked, (for judges may be wicked;) and what those tender mercies are, I need not tell you. You may read them in the history of the Star Chamber Court in England, and in the courts of Philip, and in your Bible.

This brings me to the third and last weighty matter mentioned in the text—to wit, faith. The word faith may, with great propriety, be applied to the articles of our political creed, which, it is absolutely necessary, should be kept pure and uncorrupted, if we mean to preserve the liberties of our country and the inestimable blessings of a free government. And, sir, I cannot but be seriously alarmed on this head, as has frequently been the case during the present discussion,—gentlemen of the first rank and abilities openly opposing some of the most essential principles of freedom, and endeavoring, by the most ingenious sophistry, and the still more powerful weapons of ridicule, to shake or corrupt our faith therein. Have we not been told that, if government is but properly organized, and the powers were suitably distributed among the several members, it is unnecessary to provide any other security against the abuse of its power? that power thus distributed needs no restriction? Is this a whig principle? Does not every constitution on the continent contradict this position? Why are we told that all restrictions of power are found to be inconvenient? that we ought to put unlimited confidence in our rulers? that it is not our duty to be jealous of men in power? Have we not had an idea thrown out of establishing an aristocracy in our own country,—a government than which none is more dreadful and oppressive?

What the design of the preacher on this occasion is, I will not attempt to determine; far be it from me to judge men's hearts: but thus much I can say, from the best authority, they are deceitful above all things, and desperately wicked. But whatever be the design of the preachers, the tendency of their doctrines is clear; they tend to corrupt our political faith, to take us off our guard, and lull to sleep that jealousy which, we are told by all writers,—and it is proved by all experience,—is essentially necessary for the preservation of freedom. But notwithstanding the strongest assertions that there are no wolves in our country, if we see their footsteps in every public path, we should be very credulous and unwise to trust our flocks abroad, and to believe that those who advised us to do it were very anxious for their preservation.

In this Constitution, sir, we have departed widely from the principles and political faith of '76, when the spirit of liberty ran high, and danger put a curb on ambition. Here we find no security for the rights of individuals, no security for the existence of our state governments; here is no bill of rights, no proper restriction of power; our lives, our property, and our consciences, are left wholly at the mercy of the legislature, and the powers of the judiciary may be extended to any degree short of almighty. Sir, in this Constitution we have not only neglected,—we have done worse,—we have openly violated, our faith,—that is, our public faith.

The seventh article, which is in these words, "The ratifications of the Conventions of nine states shall be sufficient for the establishment of this Constitution between the states so ratifying the same," is so flagrant a violation of the public faith of these states, so solemnly pledged to each other in consolidation as the government of this state, in which legislative powers, to a certain extent, are exercised by the several towns and corporations. The sole difference between a state government under this Constitution, and a corporation under a state government, is, that a state being more extensive than a town, its powers are likewise proportionably extended, but neither of them enjoys the least share of sovereignty; for, let me ask, what is a state government? What sovereignty, what power is left to it, when the control of every source of revenue, and the total command of the militia, are given to the general government? That power which can command both the property and the persons of the community, is the sovereign, and the sole sovereign. The idea of two distinct sovereigns in the same country, separately possessed of sovereign and supreme power, in the same matters at the same time, is as supreme an absurdity, as that two distinct separate circles can be bounded exactly by the same circumference. This, sir, is demonstration; and from it I draw one corollary, which, I think, clearly follows, although it is in favor of the Constitution, to wit—that at least that clause in which Congress guaranties to the several states a republican form of government, speaks honestly; that is, that no more is intended by it than is expressed; and I think it is clear that, whilst the mere form is secured, the substance—to wit, the whole power and sovereignty of our state governments, and with them the liberties of the country—is swallowed up by the general government; for it is well worth observing, that, while our state governments are held up to us as the great and sufficient security of our rights and privileges, it is carefully provided that they shall be disarmed of all power, and made totally dependent on the bounty of Congress for their support, and consequently for their existence,— so that we have scarce a single right secured under either.

Is this, sir, a government for freemen? Are we thus to be duped out of our liberties? I hope, sir, our affairs have not yet arrived to that long-wished-for pitch of confusion, that we are under the necessity of accepting such a system of government as this.

I cannot, sir, express my feelings on a late occasion, when I consider with what unspeakable indignation the spirit of a Montgomery, a Herkimer, a Paris, &c., must have fired at the insults offered to their memories on this floor, and that not by a stranger, but by a brother, when their names, which will ever be dear to freemen, were profanely called upon as an inducement for us to surrender up those rights and privileges, in the defence of which they so gallantly fought, and so gloriously died. We are called upon at this time (I think it is an early day) to make an unconditional surrender of those rights which ought to be dearer to us than our lives.

But I hope, sir, that the memory of these patriot heroes will teach us a duty on this occasion. If we follow their example, we are sure not to err. We ought, sir, to consider—and it is a most solemn consideration—that we may now give away, by a vote, what it may cost the dying groans of thousands to recover; that we may now surrender, with a little ink, what it may cost seas of blood to regain; the dagger of Ambition is now pointed at the fair bosom of Liberty, and, to deepen and complete the tragedy, we, her sons, are called upon to give the fatal thrust. Shall we not recoil at such a deed, and all cry out with one voice, "Hands off!" What distraction has seized us? Is she not our mother, and if the frenzy of any should persist in the parricidal attempt, shall we not instantly interpose, and receive the fatal point into our own bosom? A moment's hesitation would ever prove us to be bastards, not sons. The liberties of the country are a deposit, a trust, in the hands of individuals; they are an entailed estate, which the possessors have no right to dispose of; they belong to our children, and to them we are bound to transmit them as a representative body. The trust becomes tenfold more sacred in our hands, especially as it was committed to us with the fullest confidence in our sentiments, integrity, and firmness. If we should betray that trust on this occasion, I fear (think there is reason to fear) that it will teach a lesson dangerous to liberty—to wit, that no confidence is to be placed in men.

But why, sir, must we be guilty of this breach of trust? Why surrender up the dear-bought liberties of our country? Because we are told, in very positive terms, that nothing short of this will satisfy, or can be accepted by, our future rulers? Is it possible that we can be at a loss for an answer to such declarations as these? Can we not, ought we not to speak like freemen on this occasion, (this perhaps may be the last time when we shall dare to do it,) and declare, in as positive terms, that we cannot, we will not, give up our liberties; that, if we cannot be admitted into the Union as freemen, we will not come in as slaves? This I fully believe to be the language of my constituents; this is the language of my conscience; and, though I may not dare longer to make it the language of my tongue, yet I trust it will ever be the language of my heart. If we act with coolness, firmness, and decision, on this occasion, I have the fullest confidence that the God who has so lately delivered us out of the paw of the lion and the bear, will also deliver us from this Goliath, this uncircumcised Philistine. This government is founded in sin, and reared up in iniquity; the foundations are laid in a most sinful breach of public trust, and the top-stone is a most iniquitous breach of public faith; and I fear, if it goes into operation, we shall be justly punished with the total extinction of our civil liberties. We are invited, in this instance, to become partakers in other men's sins; if we do, we must likewise be content to take our share in the punishment.

We are told, sir, that a government is like a mad horse, which, notwithstanding all the curb you can put upon him, will sometimes run away with his rider. The idea is undoubtedly a just one. Would he not, therefore, justly be deemed a mad man, and deserve to have his neck broken, who should trust himself on this horse without any bridle at all? We are threatened, sir, if we do not come into the Union, with the resentment of our neighboring states. I do not apprehend we have much to fear from this quarter, for our neighbors must have the good sense to discover that not one of our objections is founded on motives of particular state interest. They must see likewise, from the debates, that every selfish idea that has been thrown out has come from those who very improperly call themselves the federal side of the house. A union with our sister states I as ardently desire as any man, and that upon the most generous principles; but a union under such a system as this, I think, is not a desirable thing. The design of a union is safety, but a union upon the proposed plan is certain destruction to liberty. In one sense, indeed, it may bring us to a state of safety, for it may reduce us to such a condition that we may be very sure that nothing worse can happen to us, and consequently we shall have nothing to fear.

This, sir, is a dreadful kind of safety; but I confess it is the only kind of safety I can see in this union. There are no advantages that can possibly arise from a union which can compensate for the loss of freedom, nor can any evils be apprehended from a disunion which are as much to be dreaded as tyranny.

The committee then proceeded through sections 8, 9, and 10, of this article, and the whole of the next, with little or no debate. As the secretary read the paragraphs, amendments were moved, in the order and form hereafter recited.

To the paragraph respecting the borrowing of money, Mr. Lansing proposed the following amendment:

> Provided, That no money be borrowed on the credit of the United States, without the assent of two thirds of the members of both houses present.

To the clause respecting the establishment of post-offices, &c., Mr. Jones moved the following amendment:

> Resolved, as the opinion of the committee, that the power of Congress to establish post-offices and post-roads is not to be construed to extend to the laying out, making, altering, or repairing highways, in any state, without the consent of the legislature of such state.

To the clause respecting the raising and supporting armies, Mr. Lansing proposed the following:

Provided, That no standing army, or regular troops, shall be raised, or kept up, in time of peace, without the consent of two thirds of the members of both houses present.

Respecting the organization and arming the militia, &c.,

Provided, That the militia of any state shall not be marched out of such state without the consent of the executive thereof, nor be continued in service out of the state, without the consent of the legislature thereof, for a longer term than six weeks; and provided, that the power to organize, arm, and discipline the militia, shall not be construed to extend farther than to prescribe the mode of arming and disciplining the same.

Moved by Mr. Smith

Respecting the power to make all laws necessary for the carrying the Constitution into execution,

Providing, That no power shall be exercised by Congress, but such as is expressly given by this Constitution; and all others, not expressly given, shall be reserved to the respective states, to be by them exercised.

Moved by Mr. Lansing

To the clause respecting the power of regulating commerce,

Resolved, as the opinion of this committee, that nothing in the said Constitution contained shall be construed to authorize Congress to grand monopolies, or erect any company with exclusive advantages of commerce.

Moved by Mr. M. Smith

Relative to the right of declaring war,

Resolved, as the opinion of this committee, that the Congress ought not to have the power or right to declare war, without the concurrence of two thirds of the members of each house.

Moved by Mr. Tredwell

Sec. 9. Respecting the privilege of habeas corpus,

Provided, That, whenever the privilege of habeas corpus shall be suspended, such suspension shall in no case exceed the term of six months, or until the next meeting of the Congress.

Moved by Mr. Lansing

Respecting ex post facto laws,

Provided, That the meaning of ex post facto laws shall not be construed to prevent calling public defaulters to account, but shall extend only to crimes.

Moved by Mr. Tredwell

Respecting the ratio in which taxes shall be laid,

> Resolved, as the opinion of this committee, that no capitation tax ought ever to be laid.

Moved by Mr. Tredwell

Clause relative to the publication of the receipts and expenditures,

> Provided, That the words from time to time shall be so construed, as that the receipts and expenditures of public money shall be published at least once in every year, and be transmitted to the executives of the several states, to be laid before the legislatures thereof.

Moved by Mr. Tredwell

Clause relating to the granting titles of nobility,

> Resolved, as the opinion of this committee, that the Congress shall at no time consent that any person, holding any office of profit or trust in or under the United States, shall accept of any title of nobility from any king, prince, or foreign state.

Moved by Mr. M. Smith

[Friday, July 4]

Committee proceeded to article 2.
Sec. 1. Clause respecting the office of President,

> Resolved, as the opinion of this committee, that the President of the United States should hold his office during the term of seven years, and that he should not be eligible a second time.

Moved by Mr. Smith

Sec. 2. Clause 1, respecting the powers of the President,

> Resolved, as the opinion of this committee, that the President of the United States should never command the army, militia, or navy of the United States, in person, without the consent of the Congress; and that he should not have the power to grant pardons for treason, without the consent of the Congress; but that, in cases where persons are convicted of treason, he should have authority to grant reprieves, until their cases can be laid before the Congress.

Moved by Mr. G. Livingston

[Saturday, July 5]

Sec. 2. Clause 2. Amendment moved by Mr. M. Smith:

> Resolved, as the opinion of this committee, that the Congress should appoint, in such manner as they may think proper, a council to advise the President in the appointment of officers; that the said council should continue in office for four years; that they should keep a record of their

proceedings, and sign the same, and always be responsible for their advice, and impeachable for malconduct in office; that the counsellors should have a reasonable allowance for their services, fixed by a standing law; and that no man should be elected a counsellor who shall not have attained to the age of thirty-five years, and who is not either a natural-born citizen, or has not become a citizen before the 4th day of July, 1776.

Clause 3. Motion by Mr. M. Smith:

> Provided, That all commissions, writs, and processes, shall run in the name of the people of the United States, and be tested in the name of the President of the United States, or the person holding his place for the time being, or the first judge of the court out of which the same shall issue.

The committee then took up the 3d article.

Mr. Jones proposed the following amendments, which he explained in a speech of some length, and was followed by Mr. Smith; but no debate ensued:

Resolved, as the opinion of this committee, that nothing in the Constitution now under consideration contained shall be construed so as to authorize the Congress to constitute, ordain, or establish, any tribunals, or inferior courts, with any other than appellate jurisdiction, except such as may be necessary for trial of causes of admiralty and maritime jurisdiction, and for the trial or piracies and felonies committed on the high seas; and in all other cases to which the judicial power of the United States extends, and in which the Supreme Court of the United States has no original jurisdiction, the cause shall be heard, tried, and determined in some of the state courts, with the right of appeal to the Supreme Court of the United States, or other proper tribunal, to be established for the purpose by the Congress, with such exceptions, and under such regulations, as the Congress shall make.

As the secretary went on with this article, Mr. Jones submitted the following amendments:

Res. 1. Resolved, as the opinion of this committee, that all appeals from any courts in this state, proceeding according to the course of the common law, are to be by writ of error, and not otherwise.

Res. 2. Resolved, as the opinion of this committee, that no judge of the Supreme Court of the United States shall, during his continuance in office, hold any other office under the United States, or any of them.

Res. 3. Resolved, as the opinion of this committee, that the judicial power of the United States, as to controversies between citizens of the same state, claiming lands under grants of different states, extends only to controversies relating to such lands as shall be claimed by two or more persons, under grants of different states.

Res. 4. Resolved, as the opinion of this committee, that nothing in the Constitution now under consideration contained, is to be construed to authorize any suit to be brought against any state, in any manner whatever."

Res. 5. Resolved, as the opinion of this committee, that the judicial power of the United States, in cases in which a state shall be a party, is not to be construed to extend to criminal prosecutions.

Res. 6. Resolved, as the opinion of this committee, that the judicial power of the United States, as to controversies between citizens of different states, is not to be construed to extend to any controversy relating to any real estate not claimed under grants of different states.

Res. 7. Resolved, as the opinion of this committee, that the judicial power of the United States, as to controversies between citizens of the same state, claiming lands under grants of different states, extends only to controversies relating to such lands as shall be claimed by two or more persons, under grants of different states.

Res. 8. Resolved, as the opinion of this committee, that the person aggrieved by any judgment, sentence, or decree of the Supreme Court of the United States, with such exceptions, and under such regulations, as the Congress shall make concerning the same, ought, upon application, to have commission, to be issued by the President of the United States, to such learned men as he shall nominate, and by and with the advice and consent of the Senate, appoint, not less than seven, authorizing such commissioners, or any seven or more of them, to correct the errors in such judgment, or to review such sentence and decree, as the case may be, and to do justice to the parties in the premises.

Res. 9. Resolved, as the opinion of this committee, that the jurisdiction of the Supreme Court of the United States, or of any other court to be instituted by the Congress, ought not, in any case, to be increased, enlarged, or extended, by any fiction, collusion, or mere suggestion.

[Monday, July 7]

The secretary continued reading the 4th and 5th articles without interruption. To the 2d clause of article 6th, Mr. Lansing proposed the following amendments:

> Resolved, as the opinion of this committee, that no treaty ought to operate so as to alter the constitution of any state; nor ought any commercial treaty to operate so as to abrogate any law of the United States.

To the 3d clause of article 6th, Mr. M. Smith moved the following addition:

> Resolved, as the opinion of this committee, that all the officers of the United States ought to be bound, by oath or affirmation, not to infringe the constitutions or rights of the respective states.

After the Constitution had been gone through, Mr. M. Smith moved for the following amendment to clause 17, of sec. 8, art. 1:

Resolved, as the opinion of this committee, that the right of the Congress to exercise exclusive legislation over such district, not exceeding ten miles square, as may, by cession of particular states, and the acceptance of Congress, become the seat of the government of the United States, shall not be so exercised as to exempt the inhabitants of such district from paying the same taxes, duties, imposts, and excises, as shall be imposed on the other inhabitants of the state where such district may be, nor shall it be so exercised as to prevent the laws of the state, and all process under those laws, from extending to such district, in all cases of crimes committed without the district, or in cases of contracts made between persons residing within such district and persons residing without it. Nor shall it be so exercised, as to authorize any inhabitant of the said district to bring any suit in any court, which may be established by the Congress within the same, against any citizen or person not an inhabitant of the said district. And it is understood that the stipulations in this Constitution, respecting all essential rights, shall extend as well to this district as to the United States in general. Resolved, further, as the opinion of this committee, that the right of exclusive legislation, with respect to such places as may be purchased for the erection of forts, magazines, arsenals, and dock-yards, and other needful buildings, shall not be construed to authorize the Congress to make any law to prevent the laws of the states in which they may lie, from extending to such places in all civil and criminal matters, except as to such persons as shall be in the service of the United States, nor to them with respect to crimes committed without such places.

Mr. Lansing then read, and presented to the committee, a bill of rights to be prefixed to the Constitution.

[Tuesday, July 8]

Convention met, and adjourned without doing business.

[Wednesday, July 9]

Convention met, and adjourned.

[Thursday, July 10]

Mr. Lansing submitted a plan of amendments, on a new arrangement, and with material alterations. They are divided into three—1st, explanatory; 2d, conditional; 3d, recommendatory.

[Friday, July 11]

Mr. Jay moved the following resolutions:

Resolved, as the opinion of this committee, that the Constitution under consideration ought to be ratified by this Convention.

Resolved, further, as the opinion of this committee, that such parts of the said Constitution as may be thought doubtful ought to be explained and that whatever amendment may be deemed useful, or expedient, ought to be recommended.

Mr. Jay was supported by Mr. Chancellor Livingston and Mr. Chief Justice Morris, and opposed by Mr. Melancton Smith. The debates on this motion continued till Tuesday, the 15th of July; when Mr. Smith moved, as an amendment, to add to the first resolution proposed by Mr. Jay, so that the same, when amended, should read as follows:

> Resolved, as the opinion of this committee, that the Constitution under consideration ought to be ratified by this Convention: upon condition, nevertheless, That until a convention shall be called and convened for proposing amendments to the said Constitution, the militia of this state will not be continued in service out of this state for a longer term than six weeks, without the consent of the legislature thereof: That the Congress will not make or alter any regulation in this state respecting the times, places, and manner of holding elections for senators or representatives unless the legislature of this state should neglect or refuse to make laws or regulations for the purpose, or from any circumstance be incapable of making the same; and that, in those cases, such power will only be exercised until the legislature of this state shall make provision in the premises: That no excise will be imposed on any article of the growth, production, or manufacture of the United States, or any of them, within this state, ardent spirits excepted: And that Congress shall not lay direct taxes within this state, but when the moneys arising from the impost and excise shall be insufficient for the public exigencies; nor then, until Congress shall first have made a requisition upon this state, to assess, levy, and pay the amount of such requisition, made agreeably to the census fixed in the said Constitution, in such way and manner as the legislature of this state judge best; but in such case, if the state shall neglect or refuse to pay its proportion pursuant to such requisition, then the Congress may assess and levy this state's proportion, together with interest at the rate of six per centum, per annum, from the time at which the same was required to be paid.

[Wednesday, July 16]

The Honorable Judge Hobart brought forward a motion for adjournment. On this motion large debates took place, in which Mr. Hobart, Mr. Duane, Mr. Lansing, Mr. Jay, the Chancellor, Mr. Hamilton, and Mr. Bay, were engaged. The motion was rejected.

Mr. Duane then brought forward a plan of ratification, with certain explanations, and with a list of amendments to be recommended. This was rejected.

Mr. Smith's proposition was then resumed, and debated till

[Saturday, July 19]

When Mr. Lansing moved to postpone the several propositions before the house, in order to take into consideration a draft of a conditional ratification, with a bill of rights prefixed, and amendments subjoined. Debates arose on the motion, and it was carried. The committee then proceeded to consider separately the amendments proposed in this plan of ratification.

[Wednesday, July 23]

Mr. Jones moved, that the words on condition, in the form of the ratification, should be obliterated, and that the words in full confidence should be substituted—which was carried.

For the Affirmative

Mr. Jay,	Mr. J. Smith,	Mr. P. Livingston,
Mr. R. Morris,	Mr. Jones,	Mr. Hatfield,
Mr. Hobart,	Mr. Schenck,	Mr. Van Cortland,
Mr. Hamilton,	Mr. Lawrence,	Mr. Crane,
Mr. Robt. R. Livingston,	Mr. Carman,	Mr. Sarls,
Mr. Roosevelt,	Mr. Lefferts,	Mr. Platt,
Mr. Duane,	Mr. Vandervoort,	Mr. M. Smith,
Mr. Harrison,	Mr. Bancker,	Mr. Gilbert Livingston
Mr. Low,	Mr. Ryerss,	Mr. DeWitt,
Mr. Scudder,	Mr. L. Morris,	Mr. Williams.
Mr. Havens,		

For the Negative

Mr. R. Yates,	Mr. Wynkoop,	Mr. Winn,
Mr. Lansing,	Mr. Haring,	Mr. Veeder,
Mr. I. Thompson,	Mr. Woodhull,	Mr. Staring,
Mr. Ten Eyck,	Mr. Wisner,	Mr. Parker,
Mr. Tredwell,	Mr. Wood,	Mr. Baker,
Mr. PRESIDENT,	Mr. Swartwout,	Mr. Hopkins,
Mr. Cantine,	Mr. Akins,	Mr. Van Ness,
Mr. Schoonmaker,	Mr. Harper,	Mr. Bay,
Mr. Clark,	Mr. C. Yates,	Mr. Adgate.
Mr. J. Clinton,	Mr. Frey,	

The committee continued the consideration of the amendments till Thursday; when Mr. Lansing moved to adopt a resolution, that there should be reserved to the state of New York a right to withdraw herself from the Union after a certain number of years, unless the amendments proposed should previously be submitted to a general convention.

This motion was negatived.

The committee proceeded in the consideration of the amendments till

[Friday, July 25]

When, the whole being gone through and amended, the question was put, whether the committee did agree to the same, which was carried in the affirmative.

The committee then rose, and reported.

The report of the committee being considered, the President put the question, whether the Convention did agree to the said report, which was carried in the affirmative.

The Convention then resolved, unanimously, that a circular letter be prepared to be laid before the different legislatures of the United States, recommending a general Convention.

[Saturday, July 26]

The Convention having met, the bill of rights, and form of the ratification of the Constitution, with the amendments, were read, when the question being put, whether the same should pass, as agreed to and ratified by the Convention, it was carried in the affirmative, as follows:

For the Affirmative

Mr. Jay,	Mr. J. Smith,	Mr. P. Livingston,
Mr. Hobart,	Mr. Jones,	Mr. Hatfield,
Mr. Hamilton,	Mr. Schenck,	Mr. Van Cortland,
Mr. Robt. R. Livingston,	Mr. Lawrence,	Mr. Crane,
Mr. Roosevelt,	Mr. Carman,	Mr. Sarls,
Mr. Duane,	Mr. Lefferts,	Mr. Woodhull,
Mr. Harrison,	Mr. Vandervoort,	Mr. Platt,
Mr. Low,	Mr. Bancker,	Mr. M. Smith,
Mr. Scudder,	Mr. Ryerss,	Mr. G. Livingston,
Mr. Havens,	Mr. L. Morris,	Mr. DeWitt.

For the Negative

Mr. R. Yates,	Mr. Wynkoop,	Mr. Veeder,
Mr. Lansing,	Mr. Haring,	Mr. Staring,
Mr. Outhoudt,	Mr. Wisner,	Mr. Parker,
Mr. J. Thompson,	Mr. Wood,	Mr. Williams,
Mr. Tredwell,	Mr. Swartwout,	Mr. Baker,
Mr. Cantine,	Mr. Akins,	Mr. Hopkins,
Mr. Schoonmaker,	Mr. Harper,	Mr. Van Ness,
Mr. Clark,	Mr. Frey,	Mr. Bay,
Mr. J. Clinton,	Mr. Winn,	Mr. Adgate.

Convention adjourned without day.

The Circular Letter from the Convention of the State of New York to the governors of the several states in the Union

July 28, 1788

Sir:

We, the members of the Convention of this state, have deliberately and maturely considered the Constitution proposed for the United States. Several articles in it appear so exceptionable to a majority of us, that nothing but the fullest confidence of obtaining a revision of them by a general convention, and an invincible reluctance to separating from our sister states, could have prevailed upon a sufficient number to ratify it, without stipulating for previous amendments. We all unite in opinion, that such a revision will be necessary to recommend it to the approbation and support of a numerous body of our constituents.

We observe that amendments have been proposed, and are anxiously desired, by several of the states, as well as by this; and we think it of great importance that effectual measures be immediately taken for calling a convention, to meet at a period not far remote; for we are convinced that the apprehensions and discontents, which those articles occasion, cannot be removed or allayed, unless an act to provide for it be among the first that shall be passed by the new Congress.

As it is essential that an application for the purpose should be made to them by two thirds of the states, we earnestly exhort and request the legislature of your state to take the earliest opportunity of making it. We are persuaded that a similar one will be made by our legislature, at their next session; and we ardently wish and desire that the other states may concur in adopting and promoting the measure.

It cannot be necessary to observe, that no government, however constructed, can operate well, unless it possesses the confidence and goodwill of the body of the people; and as we desire nothing more than that the amendments proposed by this or other states be submitted to the consideration and decision of a general convention, we flatter ourselves that motives of mutual affection and conciliation will conspire with the obvious dictates of sound policy to induce even such of the states as may be content with every article in the Constitution to gratify the reasonable desires of that numerous class of American citizens who are anxious to obtain amendments of some of them.

Our amendments will manifest that none of them originated in local views, as they are such as, if acceded to, must equally affect every state in the Union. Our attachment to our sister states, and the confidence we repose in them, cannot be more forcibly demonstrated than by acceding to a government which many of us think very imperfect, and devolving the power of determining whether that government shall be rendered perpetual in its present form, or altered agreeably to our wishes, and a minority of the states with whom we unite.

We request the favor of your excellency to lay this letter before the legislature of your state; and we are persuaded that your regard for our national harmony and good government will induce you to promote a measure which we are unanimous in thinking very conducive to those interesting objects.

We have the honor to be, with the highest respect, your excellency's most obedient servants.

By the unanimous order of the Convention,

George Clinton,
President

New York Ratifying Convention, 1788*

Debates

Newspaper and Manuscript Account

After the amendments [introduced by Lansing, *supra* p. 873] were read [on July 10] it was proposed by Mr. Lansing, that the Convention should adjourn, and that a committee of both parties should be informally appointed, who should endeavor to make such an accommodation, and to arrange the amendments as to bring the business to a quick and friendly decision; accordingly the Convention adjourned.

Mr [John] Jay, the Mayor of New-York [James Duane], the Chief Justice [Richard Morris] Judge [John Sloss] Hobart, Judge [Gozen] Ryerss, Judge [Peter] Lefferts and Mr. [Richard] Hatfield, on the part of the Federalists; and Judge [Robert] Yates, Mr. [John] Lansing, Mr. M[elancton] Smith, Mr. [Thomas] Tredwell, Mr [John] Haring, Mr. [Samuel] Jones and Mr. G[ilbert] Livingston, on the part of the Antifederalists, were the Committee appointed in consequence of Mr. Lansing's motion. (*The Daily Advertiser,* July 15, 1788.)

[July 12]

On Saturday morning, Mr. Jay opened the business by representing the unfairness of the proceedings in the informal Committee. He complained that when met for mutual discussion, they had been insulted by a complete set of propositions presented in a dictatorial manner for their passive acquiescence. He was soon followed by Mr. Hamilton, who in a most argumentative and impassioned address, demonstrated that the propositions before the Committee, would be a total rejection of the Constitution. He opened with a beautiful exordium, in which he described in a delicate but most affecting manner the various ungenerous attempts to prejudice the minds of the Convention against him. He had been represented as "an ambitious man, a man unattached to the interests and insensible to the feelings of the people; and even his supposed talents had been wrested to his dishonor, and produced as a charge against his integrity and virtue. He called on the world to point out an instance in which he had ever deviated from the line of public or private duty. The pathetic appeal fixed the silent sympathetic gaze of the spectators, and made them all his own.

He then proceeded to refute the fallacious reasonings of opposition—and to describe the nature and tendency of a provisional adoption. He proved, in the first place, from the series of papers on which the authority of the present Convention was founded, that it had no possible decisive power, but to adopt

The Papers of Alexander Hamilton, Vol. 5, pp. 156–70.

or reject absolutely: that it had indeed a power to recommend, because this was a natural right of every freeman; but it had none to dictate to or embarrass the union by any restrictions or conditions whatever: that the Committee was not a body commissioned to tender stipulations or form a compact, but to dissent from or agree to a plan of government, which could be altered either in its form or exercise only by an authority equal in all respects, to the one which gave it existence. Having made this point clear, he went on to shew that the future Congress would have no authority to receive us into the union on such terms: that this conditional adoption included evidently a disagreement to and rejection of a part of the Constitution: that Congress, which would hold all the powers it possessed under the Constitution as a simple plan, must consider such a partial rejection in the light of a total one.

That a declaration by any legislature that such and such constitutional powers should not be exercised was in its own nature a nugatory one: that these provisions, making no part of the Constitution, and when accepted by Congress, having, even if consistent with the Constitution, no other than a legal force, would be subject to immediate repeal; that it was indispensibly necessary to good government that the discretion of the legislature should be uncontrolable, except by the Constitution: But by the proposed measure, the discretion of Congress would be limited and controled by a provision not only foreign from, but totally inconsistent with the Constitution; a provision coming from a part of the union without the consent of the other parts; a provision most preposterously calculated to give law to all the sister states. He adduced other arguments to prove that restraining the exercise of a power, or exercising it in a mode different from that pointed out in the form of government, was utterly anti-constitutional, especially when the restraint was only to respect a part of the community.

Mr. Hamilton then urged many forcible reasons to prove that even if it were consistent with the Constitution to accept us on these terms, it was entirely improbable that the other states would submit to it. Their interests and their pride would be opposed to it. Their pride, because the very proposal is an insult; and the animosity of some states, embittered as it is by what they deemed a kind of commercial tyranny, and a system of selfish, partial politics, would receive most pungent gratification from a diminution of our fortune and our power. Their interests would be opposed, because the misfortunes of one powerful state commonly contribute to the prosperity of its neighbors.

Mr. Hamilton, after recapitulating his arguments in a concise and cogent manner, entreated the Convention in a pathetic strain to make a solemn pause, and weigh well what they were about to do, before they decided on a subject so infinitely important. The orator then closed his address, and received from every unprejudiced spectator the murmur of admiration and applause. [*The Daily Advertiser,* July 16, 1788.]

[July 15]

Mr. Hamilton produced the form of a Ratificatn—and also a number of Amendments which he read—& Pledged the Gent of New York to endeavour to obtain them.

Mr. Lansing: Let us take the Question whether we will adopt the Constitution Conditionally or absolutely.

Many of these Ideas are valuable and ought to be introduced into the Amendments.

Mr. Jay: We are endeavouring to agree. Gent See we have brot forth valuable Amendmts. Cannot the Conditional Amendments be paired down so that we may agree? We honestly think Congress must reject such an adoption. Cannot we endeavour further to Accommodate? The Gentlemen have advanced for Accommodation. We have now advanced for Accommodation.

Mr. Harper: We are now where we were 3 or 4 days ago. If the Gent move these as amendmts. we may proceed. If they withdraw their former motion we may proceed. We delay Time without new Light.

Mr. G. Livingston: I explain my conduct of yesterday. It was improper to Submit to Congress to do what they had no power to do. It is now amended agreeable to the 5th. article and my objection removed.

Mr. Hamilton: I ask that Gent if his constituents gave him a Right of Judging can he surrender that right of Judging.

Amendments Proposed by Hamilton

I. That there shall be one representative for every thirty thousand according to the enumeration or census mentioned in the constitution until the whole number of representatives amounts to two hundred; after which that number shall be continued or increased, but not diminished, as Congress shall direct, and according to such ratio as Congress shall fix, in conformity to the rule prescribed for the apportionment of representatives and direct taxes.

II. That the Court for the trial of impeachments shall consist of the Senate, the Judges of the Supreme court of the United States and the first or senior judge for the time being of the highest court of general and ordinary common law jurisdiction in each state. That Congress shall by standing laws designate the Courts in the respective states answering this description; and in states having no courts exactly answering this description shall designate some other court, preferring such if any there be, whose judge or judges may hold their places during good behaviour; provided that not more than one judge shall come from one state. That Congress be authorised to pass laws for compensating the said judges and for compelling their attendance; and that a majority at least of the said judges shall be requisite to constituting the said Court. That no person impeached shall sit as a member thereof. That each member shall previous to the entering upon any trial take an oath or affirmation honestly and impartially to hear and determine the cause: and that   of the members present shall be necessary to a conviction.

III. That the authority given to the Executives of the states to fill the vacancies of senators be abolished, and that such vacancies be filled by the respective legislatures.

IV. That the compensation for the senators and representatives be ascertained by standing laws; and that no alteration of the existing rate of compensation shall operate for the benefit of the representatives until after a subsequent election shall have been had.

V. That no appropriation of money in time of peace for the support of an army, shall be by less than two thirds of the representatives and senators present.

VI. That the Executive shall not take the actual command in the field of an army, without the previous desire of Congress.

VII. That each state shall have to provide for organising arming and disciplining its militia, when no provision for that purpose shall have been made by Congress and until such provision shall have been made; and that the militia shall never be subjected to martial law but in time of war rebellion or insurrection.

VIII. That the journals of Congress shall be published at least once a year with the exception of such parts relating to treaties or military operations as in the judgment of either house shall require secrecy.

IX. That the Judicial power of the United States shall extend to no controversy respecting land unless it relate to claims of territory or jurisdiction between states or to claims of land, between individuals or between states and individuals, under the grants of different states.

X. That no judge of the Supreme Court shall hold any other office under the United States or any of them.

XI. That when the number of persons in the district or territory to be laid out for the seat of the government of the United States, shall according to the rule for the apportionment of representatives and direct taxes amount to   such district shall cease to be parcel of the state granting the same and provision shall be made by Congress for their having a distinct representation in that body.

XII. That the representatives Senators, President, Vice President and judges of the United States shall each take an oath or affirmation not to infringe or violate the Constitutions of the respective states.

XIII. That no capitation tax shall ever be laid by Congress.

*Debates**

[Monday, July 14]

Smith—it is an excellent example—we here offer to cut the wood & bring it home to his door till the condition is complied with.

*Gilbert Livingston Papers. Reproduced with permission of NYPL.

Jay—he must reserve the absolute right—& not be oblidged to ask what trees to cut.

Smith—the Atty gives an Absolute conveyance & will give & cut & bring all he wants—till the matter can be referred.

Jay—insists he must have an absolute right & not a Modified privaledge.

Harrison—wishes not to be too hasty on this importt. matter—would have been happy if this was such a ratification as the Congs could accept—would have been foremost in voting for it—powers in Congss & state Legislatures are a deposit of trust in their hand for the public good—such the powers of the constitution therefore cannot acceed to this proposition the powers of taxation, & Militia great & important—is sd these powers will not want to be exercised—yet they may be in case of rebellion &ct & other cases which may happen & if this can possibly exist, we ought not towish that congress should give them use—it ought not to be in the power of Congs to increase or abridge their powers, it is dangerous—it is said Govt may suspend their powers—this contrary to the Law Maxim—because if they suspend for one hour they may for 7 years & so on increase or suspend their powers at will Suppose the county of S was exempted for 2 years on good consn Yet if a great flow of Wealth should come in—would not this change of circumstances make it wise & right to alter the law.

with respect to our own power—we can only reject—or adopt—what evidence of the sence of their constituants—we can only look to the resolution—asks to produce powers varying from the recommendn

the circumstances we are in deserve considn—we have been told it has been adopted from expedience not because it was good—the severl states which have adoptd it, have by their condt sd it is safe—& for the interest of the states to adopt it—does not say it is perfect—yet when coolly discussed it is such that wise men would approve of.

few lessons to be had from other states.

if wise men have made it we ought to think so too.

Gent say we will adopt it—yet annex conds.

does not believe they mean it shall operate condy.—but only to have it consd.

thinks he can shew we have as good chance by recomn as by Condn—if a Majority want the amends we are sure of getting them—suppose there is not a majority for them—the Convn may be assd yet the amends will not be made—importt not to risk a loss of the Union—extreme dangerous toinduce congs to violate the constitun—the vague wishes of their constituents not sufft Authy to make conds & run risks—&t—the only thing which remains is the suspensions for a certain time—Smith has sd it is not probable these powers will soon be used—why then take a risk—to gain nothing—prudence will dictate to leave out the conditions & unite in recommendations

Harper have spent much time in debating about a thing which does not exist cannot exist—have spent three days doing nothing but talk—wishes the proposition may be taken up—and the question put.

Ham[ilton]—wishes the questn may not be put—as it will now be a decision of the comparitive view betwn the two propositions—true it has been largely discussed—on Saturday said he supposed it would amount to a rejection—yet would suggest some Ideas.

recappitulates the args of Saturday—is willing to agree that the constitution was Advisory—it has now become obligatory by the will of the people, especially by the states which have adopted—what is advised—by the instrument—would the people in the difft states—which have agreed—would admit of conditions—a condition on the one part requires a power on the other part to consent—suppose 9 had not agreed to adopt—no power could assent—therefore the Legislature could not mean we should make conds—if all the states had made condns they never could have been organized reflect on this & see wheather it is not conclusive—no questn could ever have been taken on it—in the concurrent resolution of this state—it is referred to have the papers submitted.

if it is stated as the Gent wishes—it must refer to adopt or reject.

These acts are an evidence of the thing intended—& nothing else can determine—the people did vary—& believe the Northern countys did wish amendts but can we be bound by this—in N Y. they knew a Consn was to be submitted—but not to be altered for this we are not met—only to consider from the Acts—we have no binding power beyond these—we may recommend—New terms do not amount to an adoption—Congs cannot abridge their powers—nor extend. A Legislative authority—cannot put it out of their power to alniate [alienate] their power—or suspend their Judgt.

Gent have taken latitude, in stating cases—the Legislative power must be exer[c]ised uniformly tho particular cases may happen as to particular cases—for exemptions.

The Legislature to produce the public good may pledge funds—to borrow money—and lay aside genl powers in this instance.

Gent state the questn wrong, that congs only lay aside the power for a time—but to do this congs must lay aside their powers and conclude to submit this right of Judging—it is not teneble to admit this right—Congs have no authority to propose a Convention—but must wait for nine states to make the proposition to them.

this will lead every man who wishes an adoption into a snare—tho' they donot intend it—congs cannot adopt it.

if these arguments are not sufficient to convince—must abandon the maxim, "that there is force in truth."

wishes Gent would not call for the questn but retire & consider.

No pride of opinion ought to weigh—Genl Good ought to influence—would not for the world loose this glorious oppurtunity of establishing a free government—would not wish to put it to the risk of Arms—must be cautious to listen to Jealousy—Liberty is put to the hazard.

Lansing—we have supposed that it would come to this—we could not suppose a conviction could not be brought.

Jay—suggests—the latter questn postpones the former—both propositions mean an adoption.

Smith—agrees—in sentiment.

Adgate—the gentn & arguments repeated—Congs have exceeded their powers.

G[ilbert] L[ivingston]—thinks there is weight in some arguments wishes to have the matter postponed till tomorrow.

Ham[ilton]—propositions from Congress to the people, they give it force.

Harper—we cant go forward, till this Quest is put.

Duane—why ought this quesn to be called to day of the greatest consequence.

Govr [Governor Clinton]—does not rise to hurry business—to aleviate impressions, which might have been given—the last questn only postpones the general questn.

Wills [Williams]—wishes that the comee may rise and report.

Lansing—was informed that a proposition was to be brought forward this day—wishes to have it now, to consider of it.

Comee rose—Adjd

[Tuesday, July 15]

Smith—the Motion to be made was to substitute his for Mr Jays—now moves to add his as an Amendt.

Bay—wishes to have the questn taken on the Motn without altering.

Lansing—would substitute a new one by way of an Amendt in substance the same as Smith's.

Harper—agrees.

Govr [Governor Clinton]—wishes to have it done—with the sence of the house.

Amendment read.

Ham[ilton]—they were ready to go as far as they thought safe, in recommendatory & explanitory Amends—& secure the Constitun & that Many of the Amends we have proposed—they suppose wrong—yet they will bring forward Amends & will be pledged for to obtain those which they bring forward—as far as they can.

Reads a form of Adoption.

Reads a list of Amends—which they think would be of real service.

Wish to give the Govt a safe constructn & that they should have strong power.

Wishes to move these propositions as an amendt that in some manner they may be jointly considered with those before the committee.

for those as mentioned in these propositions the Members of N Y would pledge themselves to endeavor for their adoption.

Lansing—wishes the gent who read the propositions would bring make a formal motion to bring them before the house—does not wish to reject them entirely—as there are many good Ideas in them—but wishes the questn to be taken wheather the convention will adopt the constitution without conditional amends.

Jay—it must be evident from the props that they wish to accommodate—& pledge themselves to endeavor an amendt—does not this weigh—tounite all our force—is it not certain that the conds will render our admittance into the Union uncertain—all has been said, that can be—that the conds will amount to a rejection—declare that they think it will destroy the constitution —shall we not accommodate—each appear to have a disposition to advance—had we not better wait, and endeavor to meet.

Harper—we do not advance one step—here are propositions mentioned, but nothing regularly before the committee till there is a Motion on them—we cannot notice them.

Lansing—wishes to have something decidedly may bring these matters before the house—they now stand on the same ground they did—& have not made any real advances.

Harper—cannot go on till the questn is taken.

Ham[ilton]—hopes the questn will not be pressed—as the amends expressly contemplate a condition—hopes time will be taken to consider of the new propositions—and not pass the rubicon but by hastily taking this questn—which must be binding finally.

Harper—we cannot advance without taking the questn unless the propositions are brought in by a motion.

Duane—the Gent is right as to order.

Govr [Governor Clinton]—the propositions are the same—substantially the same as the first Motion of Mr Jay—no new motion can bring it regularly before us.

Jay—When we consider that the Amends are in conformity to the Motion on the table—they are proper.

Govr [Governor Clinton]—sorry the Gent does not understand him a Motion containing three propositions.

Lansing—must be reduced to the point we set off from—wishes not to take the questn in the present form—but wants to have the Genl questn on conditions taken.

GL

Ham

G[ilbert] Livingston] old Compact.

Chan[cellor Livingston]—does not think the Old confedn binding that all the parties to it have broke it—therefore its force null—Gent say no compact can be binding—a true rule is—if one party break the compact the other must compell an obedience—compares the compact with great Brittn all have violated—therefore gone—Gent to the proposition—does not reflect—wheather congress have a right to receive us—says they have no right—we have no right toexpect they will receive us—Gent shakes his head—he will not go with his party if he consents to this—at least doubtful wheather congress will take us in—then wholly a questn of policy.

states the reasons he mentioned the other day.

Smith

Chan—the gent is perfectly welcome—to use such arguments as he pleases—if he thinks the propositions are nothing—the gent shows as little sence in so violently opposing nothing as we do in bringing them forward on compacts.

Congress have no right to receive—combats this.

if Congress by admg us to abrogate their power then he admits they cannot do it—but holds they may suspend—which is all we ask.

doubtful—if congs would refuse to accept us when it was doubtful—would suffer any distress, before he would submit to such a govt.

Congress setting in this state, ought not to be put in competition with Liberty

Wishes to retain congress here, if we could, but it is a very uncertain event.

came forward manfully—with old propositions.

Lansing—Calls the attention of the committee to the point—is willing to hear all that can be said—but wants to have the questn.

Chan[cellor Livingston]—combats the Idea, that he called us childn he only combats the arguments—not the Gent of the committee.

Men beget children—children do not

Ham[ilton]—extreemly sorry Lan[sing] cannot see the matter as he does— has this consolation, that they have done all they could to conciliate— heartily wishes the matter may be postponed till tomorrow.

Gent have mentd the breach of the Confedn—considers the clause of amendt in it only going to the mode of Govt

people may alter their Govt

Motn that the committee rise.

Harpr [Harper]—we must take the questn before we can go on—yet does not wish to hurry

Wills [Williams]—the great point—will congress—admit us in this way— thinks they will A Union is necessy & congress will be unwillg to reject the state.—a great division throut the states difficult to say where the ballance lies.

Congs will wish to have our impost & assistant.

what do the Gent ask? one day more—let us give it.

Adjournment—does not wish it.

Lansing—if any Gent opposed to us—wish a day—we is willing to give it—but if it is requested, for us to consider does not wish it.

Carman—wishes time to consider.

Smith—if the arguments of the gent are true we must alter our propositions—his object is to have the constitution again considered by a convention—to secure this is our only object.

questn—to adjourn—add

[Wednesday, July 16]

Hobart—wishes a pause for a time to consider of the highest consequence—on one hand a part of the state insist on an unconditional adoption—on the other a conditional one we had better adjourn—& give time for the people to consider—have we not reason to apprehend dreadful consequences if this question is taken this day—the Comercial people may devise a mode to meet their Northern brethern—while there is a ray of hope—we ought not to loose sight of it—moves for an adjournment—seconded by Mr. Duane—and urges the propriety of it—as Mayor, the political father of a great City—has motives peculiar to himself—to wish for peace.

Motion read by the secretary.

Lansing—opposes the motion—two reasons urged one to consult with our constituents—that we might the better determine—much has been said on the subject of the proposition before the committee of this house—condl—amends—no conviction has been produced by all that has been said—if we adjourn—the country will be in a flame—& when we return we shall not be able to deliberate as coolly as we now do.

Harper—wishes a call of the members in town.

Tredwell—objects to it as an argumentative motion—it comes from the wrong side of the house—if the Gent. will say that their sentiments are changed—he will consent.

Chanr. [Chancellor Livingston]—it is not for our sentiments but for our constituents—Gent. have said that they wish to meet us on middle ground—this supposes a change of sentiment in our constituents—argumentative no objection—the rules say nothing about it—Lansing observd that heat will be kept up—thinks not—they will be pleased by this appeal—the Convenn. are convinced a convenn. cannot be obtd. in the mode proposed—will not both sides of the house publish our sentiments which will tend to increase the heat—thinks the heats by this means will be allayed are the Gent. fully impressed that no other Mode can be adopted preferable to the one before us—we do want to consult our friends.

Jay—mentn. a few reasons—Lansg. supposes it would increase heats—some weight at first sight—this will depend on the temper with which we go home—if we go with an intention to investigate it will have a different effect—the southern wish an adoption unlimited—the North wish conditions—if we go home and carry the proper information from both quarters—and give them a state of the business before us—with the general reason for and against conditional amendments.

Jay—equally impressed with a desire of peace—but thinks it would have a different effect—will the people from the north stop here—they will ask us our opinions—we must tell them—we are not safe—if we go off the ground we stand on—gent. from the southward will not tell their consts. that it is their opinion they ought to adopt with conds. we must tell our constits. our sentiments—News papers would teem with different sentiments—ferment will continue till the final question is taken—the sooner it is taken the better—we have been in as perilous times as the present & have got safe thro'.

Lansing—still of the same opinion—Jay has stated a process of language us & our conss. before we can talk so—we must have a change of sentiments ourselves till that is done—we have nothing to ask from our consts.—we have gone a considerable length to meet the gent.—they have remained on the ground they first took—has determined on the main question on Mature deliberation.

Duane—with great concern he sees that a gent. that has great influence takes this questn. in the point of light he does—can the gent. know it must be conjecture—a mere chance is an object sufficient—to induce us to try—Gent. say they have condescended—made advances—to accommodate—to my mind a conditional amendment is a rejection—then where is the spirit of accommodation—Memrs. of congress are to be sworn—they cannot in my opn. admit us without committg. perjury—if we go home & try to reconcile it will have a good effect—but if we try to inflame—it will have the contrary—reprobates the Idea of mentioning the worst of consequences on this occasion—the idea of war blood &ct.—probable bad consequences to determine hastily—even this makes it wise.

Harper—1t. is there any Gent. here which can say there is a possibility that our consts. have changed their minds—the probability is they have not—the professional man will not change—then it is we that must change.

Duane—thinks it is probable they will conciliate.

Bay—the Gent. Duane has painted sad scene himself—he faults me for braving danger—cool reason ought to regulate us, not passion in the begining of the war we relied on providence—so we do now.

Lansing—rises to ansr. Duane he says we oppose conjectures to conjectures—the subjt. has been exhausted—is not convind. he is wrong came here to express the sentiments of his conss. yet ought to be open to conviction.

Chan[cellor Livingston]—observes on the pictures of horror—& that Bay supposes they were held up for bad designs—not so, in the war we did consider—and determine—it is wise to chuse the least of two evils—the Gent. himself acceeds to this in his own Mode—for if a conventn. do not mend the Consn. then we must according to the Gents own propositions accept it—Lansg. has observd. that they have approached us—not so—no middle ground—only a right and a wrong—his principle, we have only a right to accept or reject—how can we do what would amount to a rejection—

the Gent. has given the strongest reason for an adjount. for he says he is not satisfied with the mode of adoptn. therefore he ought to consider & Consult.

Lawrence—advantages & disadvantages help up—wishes to be indulged with time.

Jay—wishes to give time—Gent. on the other side would run any risk—risk to be recd. into the Union—this a serious risk indeed would it not be prudent to let their constituents consult, whether they will be willing with us to run this risk.

Tredl. [Tredwell] thinks this Motion an affront to the house without giving evidences of a change of sentiment—we know the mind our constituents—they will not accept without amendt. ·

Hubb [Hobart?]—wishes to exculpate himself from the imputation of affront.

Lansing—thinks it was not intendd. as an afront however it operates to postpone the old questn.—consents it should go off.

Ham[ilton]—Gent. supposes he meant that the questn. should be finally taken this day—did not mean to proclude himself from offering any other matter.

Duane—remarks on Mr. Lansg. Tredwell's obsn. of afront— is it an afront to wish time to consult—can he ansr. for every member of this house—wished Gent. would not wish to irritate—the Gents. observatn. indecent & tend to irritate—has never before observd. any want of temper in that Gent.—every Gent. has a right to time.

Tred[well]—does not mean to be warm—but still thinks it an affront—this Motn. ought to come from our side of the house—as the reasons mentd. in the resolution—hold up the Idea of change of sentiment in our side of the house—which does not apr.

Duane—the Gent. treats this house like Armies—he speaks of his constituents these—are my brethren—my fellow citizens—whom I love—confident the line of conduct the Gent. has taken will have a bad effect.

Lansg—wished to have the General questn.—yesterday it was put off—now on another questn.—one day more is requested—it might thus go on for 6 months—Duane reprobates Tredl. for his expressn.—yet themselves have help up a southern & northern interest—which was improper.

Jay—Mentd. this to shew the propriety of considering the Matter at home—reprobates Tredwell's observation—yet pities him—he is almost consumed.

Wills. [Williams]—wishes to adjourn till four o Clock.

Platt—wishes to adjn. till the usual time.

Wills. [Williams]—consents.

Duane—with great concern he sees that a gent. that has great influence takes this questn. in the point of light he does—can the Gent. know, it must be conjecture—a mere chance is an object sufficient—to induce me to try—Gent. say they have condescended—made advances—to accommodate—

to my mind a conditional amendment is a rejection—then where is the spirit of acco

Adgate—wishes to adjn. till four o Clock.

Adjd. till 10 o Clock to morrow.

[Thursday, July 17]

Convention met

took up the order of the day.

Motion for adjournment

Tredl. [Tredwell]—Moved to have the preamble or argumentative part of the Motion struck out.

Harpr.—secondd.—it would be improper to have the preamble on the minutes.

Duane—wishes it to stand.

Lansing—content it should stand—but it will be supposed that the whole reasons for an adjournment are expressed in the preamble.

Ham[ilton]—the question will be first taken on the Resolve—thus if the convenn. do not chuse the preamble will be struck out.

Jones—wishes the preamble withdrawn.

Jay—no difficulty—first take the vote &ct. as Ham[ilton].

Jones—will not the preamble come on the Minutes.

Jay—cannot be before us till after the questn.

Tredl. [Tredwell]—Movd. to have the preamble struck out.

Jay—out of order—questn. must be first taken on the Resolution.

Tredl. [Tredwell]—withdraws his Motion.

Motion for adjt. read.

Questn. on the Adjt. called for.

Ham[ilton]—scarce any new reasons to be offered they are short—& must have the force it may do good.—cannot do evil—while men hope, they never become enraged—both practice hope to succeed, therefore will not heat.

things have changed—since we came here—therefore decent we should consult our constituents.

good may come—& no evil can come.

takes notice of an observn. by a Gent.—we are to take no notice of consequences—& compare it to our spirit in 76.

is this a just comparison—or a just state of facts.

Brittn. 3,000 Miles off—we had no share in the representation—they claimd. absolute powr. over us—is this the case here? by no means—A Majority of the patriots of America think it sufft. there may be some things in it we would wish Altered—this therefore not paralel.

this Govt. built on all the principles of free govt. representation &ct.—therefore the comparison not just—Difference of Opinion respecting the supposed

Gent. look at it only to find out the defects and not to discover its securities—& beauties—terms—on this that Gent. say the state Govts. will be destroyed—he says they are necessary, & that they will be preserved.

supposes that if the adopn. takes place as proposed we are out of the Union—some may think we may then enjoy our impost &ct.—but lays it down—the Union will not permit us to remain so—because their interest & safety will not permit it—it would divide the whole—we could not subsist without an Alliance with Brittain—this not probable—this state of importance—if so Gent. will say Congr. will do every thing to take us in—will answer this presently.

Lansing—rises to order—these observations out of order—have been heretofore mentioned the question before the house now is solely on the Mo. for adjt.

Ham[ilton] & Chan[cellor Livingston]—proper to consider the Merits of the original subject.

Harpr. [Harper]—certainly out of order.

Lansing—wishes the questn. on order.

Jay—thinks the Gent. is in order—he thinks we should adjn. & wants to give his reasons—the state is this—a mode of adoption is on the table—we think it would be injurious & therefore wish an adjt.

he lays down reasons which become premisses from which we draw conclusions.

Admits we all wish to be in the Union.

Smith & Jones—go on.

Ham[ilton]—gave reasons why we would be out of the Union.

Amends. have been proposed—with a desire to consiliate and appease—therefore not adoptd. an expedience—but the amends. proposed for expedience.

in Massachusetts—now a fedl. representation.

Connecticut—an election—Antis. left out.

N. Ham. adopted—after an adt.

Pensylvania—2/3ds. adopted—parties are now united.

Virginia—a considerable opposition—reads a letter from a Gent. there, that an address from the Anti's was rejected.

Now what have we to hope for from other states—assistance against what? Will they assist us to oppose themselves—can we compare our strength against the whole—they will have the powers of Govt. & the wealth of the whole country against us—the seaports all for them—is there hope of prevailg. in so unequal a contest—whence are we to derive means of assistance —foreign powers?—Whom—France or great Brittn.—France is the Ally of United States.

Great Brittain? what object could she have has totally given up her claim to this country—will she take the weaker by the hand to oppose the stronger— who would wish again to come under her dominion—but she never will—because no interest   this not all—we are divided among our selves—the southern district warmly attached to this Govt.—this a fact—and a sentimt. which will increase—the Census will give the Northern a superiority—deeply impressed with the bad consequences.

is it in the power of the Northern to compel the southern—impracticable—they will be aided & protected by the Union hopes—the election of separation will never be made—it will take place if we reject the Constn.

What will be the situatn. of the rest of the state—even if they can exist—they must support their whole govt.—pay taxes—& must defend themselves &t.—it is said this will not happen—if they are brought to the alternative—to adopt reject the Constitution—or seperate from the rest of the state—they undoubtedly will sept. will congress—overcome the obsticles to receive us—they will not—they are jealous of us—and view us as a selfish sister—our neighbours nearest especially.

the constitutn. the oath in it—are against us.

their interest in having us with them will be diminished—by consg. that they can have our port—the chief source of wealth—this our disunion—weakens the force of the state.

pause, & suppose the Minorities in the other states would go with us—to resist—is this desireable—to have the country divided into two Marshal bands—who will comd.—in this case at any rate, adieu to liberty.

A despotism will follow.

can any man wish to run this risk—the cause of Republicanism—should induce us to avoid this—in our late revolution we endeavd. to revive this kind of Govt. & trust to Joint councils.

distinguished patriots on both sides—tho Most for the Govt—Hancock acquiesses tho' in a situation that might tempt him to oppose it.

Adams—he first conceived the bold Idea of independence—he is for it.

Govr. Livingston, born a republican—he for it.

Dickenson—Franklin—this old grey headed patriot looking into the grave approves it.

Genl. Washington—came forward—disinterested hazarded all without reward—all parties—Whigs & Tories admired & put confidence in him—at the close of the war—at the head of a discontented Army—did he take advantage of the situation of the army or country No— he provd. himself a patriot—this man—came forward again—and hazarded his harvest of Glory—in this case he saw the work he had been engaged in was but half finished—he came forward and, approved this Consn.—is it in human nature to suppose that these good men should loose their virtue and acquiess in a Govt. that is substancially defective to the liberties of their country.

departed heroes.

Our sister states invite us—they have been as jealous of their Liberty as we—More safety in joining with us, than to neglect our invitation—all mankind—Heaven patronised us—it now invites us—is it not wonderful, that 10 states should adopt it.

let us take care not to oppose the whole country—if on the verge of eternity would exhort us to union.

Lansing—shall call the attention of the house to the point—a part of the house wish the adoptn. of a mode—in which the adopn. of congss. will be risked.

Wills. [Williams]—the questn. is wheather we shall adjourn or not—wished a middle line—cannot vote for a rejection—& cannot vote for an unconditional adopn.—wishes some mode may be thot of.

Smith—was not present—& heard the whole of what has been said—the questn. at present is for an adjournt.—still wishes something may be brought forward to conciliate.

Hobart—Made this Motion—purely to put off the questn. before the house—but wishes some thing may be proposed—to conciliate.

Question put

for an adjournment—22

against it—40

Motn. to go into the committee of the whole.

In Committee

Jays. Motn. read.

Smiths Motn. read.

Jones—Wishes both may be taken back, as it is not proper to ingraft one on the other—especially as the questn. on one would forestall himself.

Lansing—1t. a proposition was submitted to adopt conditionally—the 1t. A Motion was made for an absolute rejection or adoption the other Movd. as an amendt.—the questn. for a Condl. amendt. must be taken before we can proceed.

Duane—states the situation of the business before the Comee.

Lansing—this questn. must be taken, to determine on Conds. first or last—best first.

Jones—improper to take a questn. which will give a compleetn. to the whole business—before we have gone thro' the matter which we do not agree in.

Lansing—no amoment in what manner it is brought in—but the questn. that will give a compleetn. must be taken.

Jay—taking this single question—will involve 30 propositions in it.

Lansing—shows how this questn. will give a compleetn. to the business—reads the different propositions we ought not to be actuated by improper motives.

Jones—hopes we are all thus actuated—Never saw any good from inverting the order of things—why should we take a questn. on the conditional amendts. which may foreclose us.

Smith—disputing about nothing—first a motion from the Gent. from N.Y. himself movd. an amendt.—the Gent. from N.Y. have brought another—we must go properly thro' them—wishes to submit something—but does not how to bring them in—thinks it best to withdraw the whole.

Lansing—will consent that a questn. should be taken—which proposition should be the basis.

Duane—Moves that Smiths propn. be postponed and his taken up.

Jay—explains.

Smith—now a questn. before the house wheather we set aside his Motion.

Harper—explains.

Duane—explains.

Harper—Do. Do.

Jones—believes that we yet do not understand explains.

Govr. [Governor Clinton]—all out of order—wishes to preserve it explains.

Duane—the Chair will correct the matter, and state the facts.

Hamn. [Hamilton]—Gent. forgets facts—explains.

Govr. [Governor Clinton] willing to take the questn. either way.

Harper—again explains (itterum que)—second Motion cannot be taken till the first is withdrawn.

Smith—business simple—the questn. which shall be the basis—of consideration.

Jones—really does not understand it so—explains.

both propositions read.

Questn. for postponeing Smiths Motion.

division taken.

for the question—20

against it—41

Smith—when he laid the proposition before the committee he really did believe—congress would receive us on the adoption proposd. yet at present considers it very doubtful. Our Objects were—to propose a mode which would bring us into the Union—next to have our objections considered by a convention he did suppose then, that congress had power to call a convention—now finds he was mistaken—next object—to secure the Amendt.

keeping this object in view—if we can be admitted—& yet have a reconsideration—

Objectn. that congress cannot relinquish any part of their power—then it would be wise to relinquish our plan—and adopt one. I shall have the honor to propose—which I think will avoid the objections on both sides.

May be left alone—yet duty oblidges him to bring them—& risk them.

brings forward his propositions—reads it—perhaps other reasons may be added &c.

Whenever the amendments are considered—the Govt. is to take effect—in this case we withdraw—if in a certain time they are not submitted.

Moves to postpone the motion before the house & take up the propositions committee rose & reported
Adjournd.

[Friday, July 18]

Convention met
in Committee
Proposition of Yesterday by Mr. Smith read.

Platt—when he seconded the Motn. of Mr. Smith he supposed it obviated the objections which were brought against the first—Motion that the committee rise.

Hopkins—objects, without something is said on the propositions to illucidate.

Platt—mentions his reasons as above—thinks the gent. opposed to us may wish to take More time.

Harper—sees no reason why the commee. should rise—Moves as an amendt.—that the question on the two propositions be taken.

Lansing—dont see the advantage proposed by the commees. risg.—the propposition don't meet with his approbn.—the govt. if in Opperation for four years cannot be again dissolved.

Wills. [Williams]—does not approve of the proposition of yesterday—but doubts wheather we shall be recd. by congress—the eyes of the whole country are on us let us take every step.

Jay—considers the last proposition less evil than the former—& shall vote for making it the basis—to proceed on.

Committee rose—Adjd.

[Saturday, July 19]

Met—in Committee.

Lansing—now 3 proposis. before the committee best resort to his system to resort to take one of the propns. as a basis—& go thro' it by clauses—Movs. to take up the first.

Smith—supposes that this may be done by consent—as we go thro' Amends. may be proposed—to any or all the different articles.

Harper—it must be by Motion or it cannot come on the minutes.

Govr. [Governor Clinton]—thinks this is the proposition of Mr. Smith himself when he moved it—Gent. are not bound—to the whole—but may object to any part.

Lansings Motion read—question.

Govr. [Governor Clinton]—explains.

Judge Morris explains order.

Jones—explains.

on the question that all the propositions before the comee. be postponed—and to take up the first proposition of Smith as the basis

for the Motion—41

against it—18

Govr. [Governor Clinton]—Movs. that we proceed to read the propositions by paragraphs.

Secretary read the first clause.

agreed—to leave the formal part & proceed to the articles.

1—Articles of the Bill of rights read.

Jay, why not insert all the unallianible rights & these three selected.

Harper—if the Gent. wants any added—wishes he would suggest them.

Jay—if there was any necessity to mention them or have a Bill or [sic] rights at all—he would do it.

Lansing—if the line was to be drawn between the Jurisdictions of the state & Genl. Govt. so that the power of the Genl. Govt. shall not extend to individuals this may be proper.

Jay—Govt. must have power to restrain—as the clause stands it is so inaccurate, he cannot vote for it—if the committee will agree to amend it he will agree.

the question put on the sentiment, or principle of the first article—Unanimous.

Jones—wishes the whole of the bill of rights should be committed to select comee.

2 Article read—agreed.

3 Do.

Jay—you cannot make a right—you can only declare what a right is.

Govr. [Governor Clinton] it is a political right.

Smith—the source is—this is a right which we all enjoy ~~this right~~ before this New Govt. should be adopted.

Tredwell—we insert it before here because, we cannot find it in the new constn.

Ham[ilton]—the spirit of the 2d. clause he agrees with—& will agree in—the Jury of the vicinage in some cases cannot be good—however will not insist on it—a Jury—is security sufficient—without saying of the Country—Moves to strike out "of the country."

Govr. [Governor Clinton]—wishes it should stand.

Jones—Do.—who shall designate whence the Jury should be called—the prosecutor may lay his venue where he pleases.

Ham[ilton]—this could be done by the Legislature—in Engd. this has been done—as in the rebellion in Scotland.

questn. on the 3d. article [rights of criminal defendants]—agreed.

4th—article [due process] read—agreed.

5—Do.—[double jeopardy]—Do.

6—Do.—[speedy trial]—Do.

7—Do.—[jury in civil cases]—

Ham[ilton]—this article he thinks includes more than Gent. intend—in the Admiralty—& Chancery there is no Jury—"to remain" may be intended to qu[a]llify this—in some states—the trial by Jury in both the Courts above mentd. are in use.

On treaties & Laws of Nations—the supreme Judicial ought to be the last resort.

difficultied [sic] to remedy this—so as to agree to it—& not clash with other states.

Yates—the object, to secure the trial by Jury in all cases where they heretofore were of use—this ought to be held inviolate—and was intended to provide agt. the Genl. Govt. taking this right away.

Jay—the word "accustomed" will not take the objectn. away—because in admiralty cases an appeal should lay—where the whole matter should go up.

Ham[ilton]—Comn. Law—will not do in Connecticut—neither accustomed.

Govr. [Governor Clinton]—we wish to get the Idea.

Jones—we can get over the difficulty & yet retain an Idea—if we say—according to the com. Law will do—The Court of Exchequer in Engd.—proceed in both with, in some cases—in other without a Jury—In Jersey & Connecticut—since the revolution, have directed the Court of Admiralty must be by Jury.

Lansing—we only want the sentiment.

Smith—the committee will word it.

7th article as amended—agreed to.

8—Bail—or unusual excessive punisht.—agreed.

9—every freeman secure agt. Genl. Warrants—agreed.

10—rights of the people to consult and petition—agreed.

11—the freedom of the press—agreed.

12—Militia—according to ancient Usage.

Ham[ilton]—opposed to the leading idea of this clause—it tends to render the Militia of no service—in swisd. & england—there must be select corps—the whole people can never be fully trained if we agree to this, you oblidge the govt. to have a standing army.

does not depend on regulations on paper for safety—but on the Genius of our country—was mistaken as to the clause.

objects only to the words "past usages."

Govr [Governor Clinton]—the object is to keep the Militia well armed, the Comee will word it.

Jones—will mention one difficulty "past usages" are indeffinate—as there have been in our state many alterations.

12—Art—agreed.

13—standing armies—agreed.

14—quartering soldiers—agreed.

15—exemption of Quakers.

Jay—if it means Quakers—is content—but if it will comprehend every person who in time of War will declare they are con[sc]ientious about it—he will not.

Smith—this must be defined by the law—as there are more sects than one which are scrupulous.

Jones—it may opperate ill—those who are scrupulous to bear arms—object to pay the fine.

Ham[ilton]—is willing those who are now scrupulous may be exempted—but does not wish to encourage this idea.

the sence of the committee on this clause taken—to be transposed—agreed.

16—liberty of conscience—agreed.

Smith—Movd to accept the Virginia amendt to take this up in the Committee.

explanitory amendt

1—Elections.

Ham[ilton]—an explanitory clause ought to explain, not to affix a new Idea.—the dividing the state into districts is explanitory but the quallifying part is not.

Jay—wishes it to go farther—if recommendatory & would have a freeholder elected.

Smith—consents to divide the proposition.

Ham[ilton]—consents.

Tredwell—if it is not good—they will do no hurt all the explanitory amends ought to be recommendatory.

Smith—wishes to adopt the Article as mentioned in the propositions introduced by Mr Jay.

questn on the clause on the emended clause—agreed.

2d—No power to be exercised—but what is expressly given.

Ham[ilton]—combats the propriety of the word "expressly"—congress one to regulate trade—now they must do a thousand things not expressly given—Virginia say not given

Harper—the Committee may correct this.

Yates—agrees—that in grantg genl powers —the powers to execute are implied.

questn on the paragraph—agreed.

3d Habs Corpus—ex post facto laws—agreed.

4—appeals—by writt of error—agreed.

Ham—would not object to the Idea—recommends their Amendt.

5—extention of the Judicial power—with respect to lands—agreed.

6—no suit to be brought against the state—agreed.

7—inumeral prosecutions—agreed.

8—farthe[r] explination.

Ham[ilton]—this cannot be by way of explanation—by may be by recommendation.

question—agreed—may be by way of a recommendatory amendment—questn agreed.

9—no Monopilies or companys.

Ham[ilton]—this not an explanitory amendt—may be recommendatory—which he would wish.

in regulating commerce—this power seems to be incident—thinks that it may be possible that it will be useful—therefore thinks it ought to be left out.

Jones—it cannot be an explanation.

Lansing—Congress have no power about the business except a regulation of commerce.

Ham[ilton]—agrees—here the difficulty already occurs respecting the word "expressly" moves to transfer it to the list of recommendatory amends.

Govr [Governor Clinton]—best to let it stand, at present—determining respecting the word "expressly" would fix his mind—questn on the Motion—for transferring Carried—for transferring.

10—No treaty to alter the Constin of any state—agreed.

11—Jurisdictn of the Courts not to be extended by sections &ct agreed.

12—powers of congress—not to be extended by implication—agreed.

Govr [Governor Clinton]—the comee now thro' the explanitory amends wishes a Comee should be apointed to take these matters and others not considd.

Ham[ilton]—wishes rather to consider of the amendts in the abstract—& leave the classing of them to an after consideration.

Comee rose.

Jones—it will be impossible for the comittee to arange before Monday.

an informal committee appointed.

Harrison, Duane—Yates, Smith.

Adjourned till 11 o Clock—Monday

[Monday, July 21]

I was sick—did not attend—the house went thro several amends

on the Excise—Affirmative	38
on the Excise—Negative	16
direct taxes	Do Do

standing Armies—not to be kept up without consent of 2/3ds—Mr Ham[ilton] moved an amendt to substitute—no appropriations of Money in of Army—agt his amendt 38—for it 14.

the questn on the original amendt—carried.

Representation—200—agreed.

Recall of senators—carried 36—vs—18

Senator not to hold another office—carried 35-vs 19.

Money borrowed—2/3ds necessary—carried.

Adjourned.

[Tuesday, July 22]

in Committee.

on the clause respecting a Nobility—amended on Hams Motion—that no person shall accept &ct—unanimous—agreed.

that the president shall not be elected a 3d time.

Hammilton objects because—there is no security in it—the people are excluded from chusing perhaps your best man.

Smith should rather have him elected for 8ys & not eligible again—Movd for it—Jay seconded his Motn.

Ham[ilton]—apposes—a temptation for an avaritious man—to plunder—& make the best of his time—has not the motive to please.

Smith much may be said on both sides—as the consn stands his appointment will amount to an appointment for life—no system can be hit on which will not have objections to it—in this case he will be obliged to steal from the people what in the other case he must wrest by violence.

Ham[ilton] does not see the danger—in Connecticut—it has never decended from Father to son.—safety in the mode of election.

Govr [Governor Clinton]—thinks it puts it too much out of the object of the prest to make not again eligible.

Jay—the amendt does not leave him sufficiently independent.

Wills [Williams]—wished to have it 8 Years in 12.

Ham[ilton]—Check in the constn agt mal adn as the senate must appoint on his Nomination his bad system would be discovered.

Jay—will not press—hardly knows how to chose difficulties on every hand—a Govt as it was called opperated in this state 20 Years ago—the Legislature & Govr playd into each others hands—it may be so again.—as it stands—the president is under eternal temptation to do wrong—senate a check what kind of a check?—to do wrong—& to do right—as it serves their interest.

Ham[ilton]—so long as we are pursuing republican Govts we must submit to these risks a long chain & complication of influence necessy to do mischief—senate—assy—& people—elections—&c.

in this business you have as much security as any system can produce under a Republican Govt.

Lawrence opposes Wills—Motn—thinks it liable to the objects to the clause.

questn on William's motion—lost.

questn on Smith's motion—lost.

quest on the amendt

that no person shall be eligible as prest a third time—carried for the amendt

Amendt that the president shall never command the army or navy in person without the consent of congress.

Smith—wishes to adopt the amendt proposed by the Gent from N.Y., that the executive shall ~~never~~ not in person take the actual command of the army ~~or navy~~ in the field without the previous desire of ~~the legislature~~ congress.

agreed to unanimously.

~~shall~~ may not have power to at his discretion to grant pardon treason by only reference &t till the case be laid before congress.

agreed—unanimously.

that congress apoint, a council of appointment impeachable &ct.

Ham[ilton]—among other reasons agt it mentions the probability of having the appointments better thro' the states, as the senators represent all the states.

for the amendt—10

against it—46

all process in the name of the people &ct

agreed unanimously.

No judge of the supm Court shall hold any other office &ct agreed—Unanimously.

all officers of the United States—to take an oath ~~to preserve~~ not to infringe the constitutions & rights of the respective states—~~agreed unani~~mously.

Congress shall not declare without the concurrence of 2/3ds present—~~agreed unan~~

Chan[cellor Livingston]—a false principle—in Govt that a Minority should ever govern—especially in our states.

On the question of the amendment

for it—32

against it—25

Right of congress &ct over the 10 Miles square &ct. explanitory.

Ham[ilton] moves to substitute the amendt proposed to this clause by the Gent from N.Y.

Lansing—1 reason assd why congress should have exclusive jurisdn is because no 1 state should have an influence when they sit—by the last amendt they that is the 10 mile inhabitants are to be represented in congress &ct

on division-for substituting the last amendt 18

against it 39

questn on the amendt—carried

Forts—Magazines—Dock Yards &ct may not be Cities of refuge.

agreed—Unanimously.

that an account of expenditures—shall and in every year be submitted &ct.

Ham[ilton]—improper in a war, or in the eve of a war to publish a state of accounts &ct to all the world.

on questn—lost—GL voted for it.

Congress shall not establish any inferior Court &ct.

Ham[ilton]—this will increase appeals—but does not much oppose.

Jones—this will seldom happen & cannot last.

Ham[ilton]—it may opperate to the prejudice of the poor.

On the Question—for it—37

against it—16

that persons aggrieved in Supm Court—court of Errors constituted—by special commission.

Ham[ilton] Chan[cellor Livingston]—objects because the Court apd by Legislature. these Judges or commissioners may be under the same influence as the Legislature themselves—therefore to be avoided.

Ham[ilton]—of the same opinion.

Jones—Wishes security under these Courts—sees great inconveniencey in having a Court totally independent—wishes some mode to remedy the evil.

Ham[ilton]—there Must be a Court—in the last resort—why not safely placed in the supm Court—rather than in an advanticious Court—or in the senate.

Chan[cellor Livingston]—the Ionic Council—& supm Court in Germany—have both Original—and appellate Jurisdictn

Jones—this Mode now proposed has been long in use in Engd & is used to this day—without complaint.

Ham[ilton]—if it goes to the causes in which the supm Ct have original Jurisdn should not so strongly oppose it but if it goes to those causes which are brot before them on appeal—strongly dissents.

Bay—if it is intended—only to contemplate causes in which the supm Court have Origl Jurisdn it ought to go so forward.

so altered—on the question—on the Clause.

as altered—agreed.

Habeas Corpus—agreed.

Power of Congress over the Militia &t—Organising &ct.

Ham[ilton]—wishes to know what objectn gent have to Congss organizing the Militia.

On the questn

agreed to strike out the clause withdraw the amendment at present.

Ham[ilton]—Moves an amendt that a court for trial of impeachments be constituted, prout.

thinks this amendt will obviate many of the objections against the senate.

On the question—agreed.

that the vacancies in senate be filled by the state Legislats—agreed.

that Laws for altering Wages of senate & Assemy shall not profit those who make the Law—agreed.

that Journals of Congss shall be published one a year—agreed.

Judiciary—with respect to the extention of its Jurisdiction &ct—agreed.

Wills [Williams]—Moovs that no cappitation tax be ever laid by congress—agreed unanimously.

clause to divide for choosing a Citizen for one [*sic*] the representatives &ct President &ct be a substancial freeholder &ct

Lansing—wishes the clause to lay over till tomorrow.

Jay—no objections.

Chan[cellor Livingston]—dont see the utility in confining the choice of delegates to the particular district—is abridging the rights of election.

Smith—it is necessy that a knowledge of the different parts.

Questn that repreta[ti]ves live in the district.—agreed.

adjourned.

[Wednesday, July 23]

met—in Comee

the informal Comee reported—the Comee went into the report of the amends by paragraph.

an Introduction to an adoption was read—agreed to.

Lansing, introduces Smiths first plan—as a basis to proceed on Smiths 2d plan being withdrawn.

Ham[ilton]—thinks we ought to proceed on the report & if any Gent wishes to introduce an amendt he has a right to do it.

Lansing—we have been on the proposition—of Smith

Smith—does not suppose this introduction was intended to exclude any thing that might be proposed.

Duane—thinks we ought to proceed on the report.

Yates—was one of the informal comee—after going thro' the amends—drafted a plan of Ratification—not with an intention to alter the Mode of proceedings before the committee.

Govr [Governor Clinton]—inquire what was the business of the Informal committee—the adoption or form of it, was not committed to them—therefore must not be bound by it.

Lansing Movd to take up Smiths et Motn as the Basic

Morris—if the report must be recd & entered in the Munutes—the whole must be gone thro.

Jones—the report of an informal committee never comes on the minutes.

questn wheather the sd lt Mon of Smith be taken up—agreed.

Smith Movd an amendt to the introduction.

question put—for the motion—40

against it—19

a debate wheather the conditions in the first place be seperated from the questn

Yates—wishes to have the questn on the condition first taken.

Jones—Moves to have the words "that the people of the state are bound by it."

Harper—there may be persons who now would vote for this questn hereafter may vote against the constitution unless under such restrictions as he chuses.

Jones Moves that upon Condition be struck out & in full confidence inserted.

Smith gave Reasons—why he will vote for the amendment.

Govr [Governor Clinton]—does not rise to give sentiment on this questn because Gent may connect his character as Govr & representative.

Harper—dont understand the reasoning—some say congress can accept us if the[y] will—if it depends on their will—& they will not—would not chuse to submit to their will.

Jay—rises to explain—is convinced that congress can.

Smith—Justifies what he said.

Platt—it has become fashionable for Gent to give reasons for his actions—has made up his Mind & shall pursue what he thinks will ultimately tend to the happiness of the people in this case shall vote for amendment.

On the question for the amendment

for it—31

against it—29

Adjourned till tomorrow.

[Thursday, July 24]

met in Committee.

the paragraph last under consideration—that is the ratification as amended—also the Amendt respecting the Militia.

for the Clause & amendt—32

against—22

the amendment respecting elections read—agreed unanimously.

Jay—Most ardently wishes & hopes the business might be so carried thro'—it is no more a paper—but it is a government—let us be Unanimous in pursuing the Object—to get a convention—to reconsider the constitution thinks Gent are at liberty to consider the circumstances that we are in—he himself wishes some amendments as well as others—wishes we may go hand in hand to obtain them.

the Amendment respecting excise read—agreed—unanimously.

Requisition clause—read—agreed—unanimy.

Lansing—a gent from Dutchess promised to being forward a Motion for an adoption—with right to withdraw in   years if the Amends are not submitted to a convention in the mode prescribed &t—as he has not done it—Lansing Moves it.

Jay—feels great regret in this case was in hope to have gone in unity.—this is giving with one hand and taking back with the other—two clauses contradictory one comes in—the other provides to come out—will we at 4 years end—be easier to be out than now—can we get this condn without the Coopperation of our sister states they are important as we—as jealous as we.

is their not if we join C the most important states are for a convention—nothing can possible prevent a convention it displays distrust—& is a condition a reservation—will not the 10 states say we have come in without reservation—why should N.Y.—it will remove congress—consequences among ourselves—one side will be pleased—because they have carried all their amendments—the other because we have adopted such measures as will bring us into the union—all pleased because we have the highest possible prospect of a convention for amendments—we are now one people all pledged for amends.

we on opposite sides—have formerly agreed. Many I see here have formerly been with me in forming another constitution.

Lansing—this Morning voted, on a presumpn that this Motn would be carried wishes peace &t but does not expect it. till the convention does set—if their is so strong an Interest to bring about a Convenn our reservation will not affect our union. All we stipulate is a reconsideration.

present Congress cannot anticipate—if doubtful congress will remove—thinks they have no business with it—but if they should their removal—is not of so much importance as our Liberties.

Ham[ilton]—Was in hopes this Morning of Unanimity when this Motion was first mentioned thot more favourably of it than the other one—but since thinks otherwise—has taken advice with men of character—they think it will not do proposed to read a Letter—reads it—supposes this adoption—unconditional—and would viciate the business &t.

himself wrote favourably for it.

the terms of the constitution import a perpetual compact between the different states this certainly is not.

treaties and engagements with foreign Nations—are perpetual—this cannot be under this adoption—the oath to be taken—stands in the way.

states & men are averse to inequality—they fully bound—& we partially.

should we risk so much—on so little—Motives of expediency too much relied on.

if they do not accept us—will they not sooner have a new convenn than accept us so is it worth the jeopardy by which it must be obtained—is it not of importance that we Join—unanimously to procure a convention? the obsern of Lansg does not meet the obje as they will contemplate wheather this is a ratificn if they have any doubt, they will apt Congs to meet on certain federal Ground—Interest of some states against us—if they are driven away by us the people will be dissatisfied &t.

We have done every thing which possibly can insure our wish—this we shall loose by a second state convention—we shall not be represented in Congress—& this for no real end.

Moves to have the question postponed & that a circular letter be wrote.

Tredl [Tredwell]—we will remove the arguments of the Gent—perpetual means—as long as from the time the confederation was formed till next feby—the other—federal Ground—this is not to be found in America unless Rhode Isld unless you go to Switzerland &c

Jay—wishes Gent would seriously consider—not out [of] humor—yet distressed—high hopes before—now distressed—by this thread to be decided—they will go with Gent on this principle, that the consn is adopted
had once higher hopes of it than he now has   it was tried in Virginia—believe in his conscience it would keep us out of the union.

We cannot remain out of the Union.

unpleasant to have another convention do the work we are here come to do—wishes to postpone till tomorrow.

Ham[ilton]—withdraws his Motion—to let the question come on.

Adgate—wishes not to postpone—gent think Much of Unanimity—but this only means that we should totally adopt—they ought to think of the parts of the state, that are opposed to the Consn—they ought to give up something too.

Jay   Gent right—but what ought we to do should we keep out of the Union?—no he does not wish this—we think this would do it—we come in with them in every thing but a rejection—& that they themselves do not want.

Adgate—this business has been affected by degrees this has heretofore been conceived—to have been a Mode that would bring us in Gent now say we cannot—but if we May does not doubt we shall—they must violate the old Confedn.

Ham[ilton]—Adge intimates that they have come down to our Ideas—this is not so—yet we are willing to go as far as we can and be received—the Gent will see that we have made an effort to try to come to this—have taken advice—who are of the same opinion which we now hold—has had a great inclination to meet the house on this ground—but is now fully of opinion it will not do.

Lansing—the   states the matter as an impression of the Moment—or as an opinion.

Wynkoop. Many arguments have been thrown out—that we should forget from whence we came—2/3 were agt an uncondl adopn have been cooled down—now we wish an adoptn and a convenn to amend—the people different opinions about it like it others dislike—for whom are we to act, for ourselves or constituents—they will not be satisfied—what can we say—do we not show that we are not selfish—they are to help reconsider—we do not want to remain disunited Who are Congress—they are from the different states—the greater part from states who are discontented—but here we are brought down from one point to another till we are brought to an unconditional adoption.

cannot see why Gent are so urgent for—we were not sent to consider any thing respecting the removal of congress—we are not to sacrifice the liberty of the people—dont think the people of the united states so haughty, as to refuse us—does not wish confusion—how can we answer to give up the liberty of the people.

Tredl—Would observe on the Bill of rights—which if it was properly secured—would alter his opinion on the present question.

On the question on Mr Lansings Motion

for it——

against it——

Judge Morris—the question is wheather it will bring us in that Union or not—treaties must be perpetual for those purposes we are not in the Union.

Adgate—Whould answer that Gent with respect to the treaties now in force—13 states made them—now possibly only 11—when that Union is broke—what is to become of the treatie with Great Brittn—and the fortresses they hold on our frontier.

Chanr [Chancellor Livingston]—the Gents argument fails unless it serves to shew that we ought to come in—What is the object of the Motion—to procure a convention? will it be possible for us to receed at the end of the term? no—then what effects will it have—will not the people out doors say you had better stay out—than pretend to do a thing which is impossible for us to do—no good effects can possibly flow—we are not satisfied with it—& why will our constituents be.

if he could believe the liberties of the Country were in danger—he would not advocate it—Moves the Committee to rise.

Lansg [Lansing]—When we brought this Mon forward he did not think this proposition as good as the first—yet if the constn is not reconsidered we can resist without being rebels—it will give some security—has never declared that he thot that this would be distructive of liberty.

Ham[ilton]—Adgate has mentioned an important Idea.

What will be the effect of the treatie with great Brittn—if they all unite it will stand   if we do not—those who do not come in will perhaps be excluded—this a very important concern.

Acquiescence of a time is a waver of a right—when the Liberties of the country are in danger—shall not wait for law constructions.

Lansing—merely me[a]nt to state that it would become their interest as well as ours.

Chan[cellor Livingston]—why will this Measure induce a convention More than the other—Your Circular Letter will do it does not wish to have a right to take up arms when ever this Govt becomes unfriendly to liberty every state has a right to draw the sword—let Gent ask themselves—wheather it is worthy of them.

Adge [Adgate]—in regard to the treatie with G. B. it would not opperate with a part—if there was a sepperation—the framers of the Constn have been very negligent of a part—as 9 states may here unite.

Ham[ilton]—the Convn knew that every state would have an opportunity to agree—or not agree with respect to the treatie—it is too late now as 10 states have adopted it.

Jay—wishes something may take place to bring us together—some express reservation of state rights—which would satisfy us all.

Govr [Governor Clinton]—the only thing which would make him solicitous, is that many Gent heretofore voted under an impression that this questn would be put.

Tred[well]—thinks the constn formed to enslave.

Lawrence—wishes the committee to rise.

Lansing—wishes to have the question.

Jay—has no particular plan—wishes to do any thing possible—would wish to meet some Gent who wanted to have the Bill of rights better guarded—Men ought not to be influenced by a threat—if they act properly—they will not.

Govr [Governor Clinton]—if the gent can convince him that there is a threat in it, he will give it up.—if we rejected the constitun our sister states could not find fault with us—here we go further, we adopt—& only ask a reconsideratn   does not rise to

Jay—takes the Gent on his own ground—let us ask them—but not put it in before we ask them.

Govr [Governor Clinton]—no threat for the reasons before mend—there is a difference whether we adopt or ask an Reconsideration.

Jay—5 other states want amends as well as we—they will trust us—but we will not trust them—this looks like a threat.

this questn reduces it to this point—will—ought they to receive us, on terms which none of the other states have thought of, & is it right in us to ask it—don't they love liberty &ct as well as we.

Govr [Governor Clinton]—rises not to shew he does not wish to press the question.

Duane—the questn is not wheather congress will not—it is his opinion congress cannot   the terms proposed alters the thing—therefore they cannot—thinks they would incline to to [sic] do it—if it was in their power if we agree to this proposition we go away and leave the constn unratified.

committee rose—adjd till tomorrow.

[Friday, July 25]

met in Committee.

proposition of yesterday read.

Jay rises—not to debate—yesterday gave the fullest assurances that they meant to go hand in hand with us—& produced draft [of] a Letter intended to be sent to the several states.

Platt—for duties he owes himself, wishes to expn when this proposition was brought forward it was supposed—it would bring us into the Union—What was the object?—to come into the Union—fears this proposn will not.

Smith—this proposn was submitted by him as a Middle Ground—& hoped both sides of the house would be pleased with it—but finding that neither will be pleased—and that the plan itself will not ansr the end proposed as to the constitution—or the house as it would make the breach worse—must be against it.

G[ilbert] L[ivingston]—said he was formerly for it but now has a doubt on act of Congss makeing treaties which must endure perpetually & thinks congss cannot make a treaty for a longer time than they stand for, which doubt he wished to have removed by any Gent.

no person spoke before the questn

On the question for adopting the amendment

for it—28

against it—31

Tredwell Movd to have the introduction of the bill of rights altered.

Jones—thinks it stands better as it is.

Tredl [Tredwell]—As it stands—not a single right remains.

Duane—better as it stands.

Lawrence—wishes to have the expressions as strong as possible.

Govr [Governor Clinton]—was content before—as it stood—but now from what Duane has said—he has doubts.

Harper—never expected to hear passive obedience preached in an Assembly of Americans—we will preserve our rights if we can, if we cannot, & must surrender at discretion we must abide the consequences.

Smith—as it stands—it perfectly secures you as much—as any other words possibly can.

Lawrence—a great difference between the words reservation & Confidence.

Smith—still thinks it as secure in the one case as the other—the word ~~confidence~~ reservation.

Govr [Governor Clinton]—wants to know if the rights are really secured or not—this he will insist on—not to depend on an illusion.

Smith—what security can any one, have respecting any right—but the confidence you put in the government which is to exercise the power.

Govr [Governor ~~Livingston~~ Clinton]—Smiths reasoning proves too much if it proves any thing—if the confidence we had in govt was to be our only safety—why have we sat here so long—let us have these rights clearly expressed.

Smith—did not by any means intend what the Honl Govr supposed.

Jay—not very anitious—is willing to have it expressed as strongly as possible—even expressly reserving all the rights not granted in the constitution.

on the question for reconsideration on Mr Tredwells motion.

for it—37

against it—27

on the motion.

Jones—Wishes to know what greater security we have under one word, than another word.

Tredwell—the difference between words—is greater in one case than the other.

Lansing movd an amendment—prout.

Harper—dont like it as well, as it stood—yet we seem to be so fluctuating— as that we must vote for it.

Tredl [Tredwell]—cant vote for it—& yet dont like to vote for it wishes to have it altered.

Smith—2 things may be consistant—and yet not have all the things expressed in both.

the question on Lansings Motion—put—and carried unanimously.

The Ratification read—with the amends

The question put, on the form of the ratification.

for it—31

against it—28

committee rose—and reported the form of the ratification agreed on in committee.

President in the Chair.

On the question wheather the convention agree to the report of the committee

for—30

against it—25

Ordered the report ~~to~~ be engrossed.

Motion that a commee be appointed to ~~take into considn~~ prepare a circular Letter &t

Agreed unanimously.

$$\left.\begin{array}{l}\text{Mr Jay} \\ \text{Mr Lansing} \\ \text{Mr Smith}\end{array}\right\} \text{Committee}$$

Convention adjourned till 5 oClock this afternoon.
Met—in Comee
went thro the amendments.
Adjourned till 9 oClock tomorrow mo[rni]g

[Saturday, July 26]

Committee met.

Mr Jay from the ~~unformed~~ Committee to draft a Letter to the different states— reported the same—agreed with the report.

Ordered—12 Coppies of the ~~report~~ Letter be engrossed.

Ordered that the engrossed ratification be ~~engrossed~~ read—previous to the final question—the same was read.

G L

Wisner—wishes to be indulged—yesterday voted for the constn wished
to give it one day longer—came here deterd to reject it—but we have gone from one step to another—has viewd it—thoroughly—cannot vote for it—yet if [it] is carried will aid it all he can.

On the final question—on the engrossed ratification it was carried in the Affirmative
   for it—30
   against it—27

New York Proposed Amendments, 1788*

We the Delegates of the People of the State of New York, duly elected and Met in Convention, having maturely considered the Constitution for the United States of America, agreed to on the seventeenth day of September, in the year One thousand Seven hundred and Eighty seven, by the Convention then assembled at Philadelphia in the Common-wealth of Pennsylvania (a Copy whereof precedes these presents) and having also seriously and deliberately considered the present situation of the United States, Do declare and make known.

That all Power is originally vested in and consequently derived from the People, and that Government is instituted by them for their common Interest Protection and Security.

That the enjoyment of Life, Liberty and the pursuit of Happiness are essential rights which every Government ought to respect and preserve.

That the Powers of Government may be reassumed by the People, whensoever it shall become necessary to their Happiness; that every Power, Jurisdiction and right, which is not by the said Constitution clearly delegated to the Congress of the United States, or the departments of the Government

*Documentary History of the Constitution of the United States, Vol. 2, pp. 190–203.

thereof, remains to the People of the several States, or to their respective State Governments to whom they may have granted the same; And that those Clauses in the said Constitution, which declare, that Congress shall not have or exercise certain Powers, do not imply that Congress is entitled to any Powers not given by the said Constitution; but such Clauses are to be construed either as exceptions to certain specified Powers, or as inserted merely for greater Caution.

That the People have an equal, natural and unalienable right, freely and peaceably to Exercise their Religion according to the dictates of Conscience, and that no Religious Sect or Society ought to be favoured or established by Law in preference of others.

That the People have a right to keep and bear Arms; that a well regulated Militia, including the body of the People capable of bearing Arms, is the proper, natural and safe defence of a free State;

That the Militia should not be subject to Martial Law except in time of War, Rebellion or Insurrection.

That standing Armies in time of Peace are dangerous to Liberty, and ought not to be kept up, except in Cases of necessity; and that at all times, the Military should be under strict Subordination to the civil Power.

That in time of Peace no Soldier ought to be quartered in any House without the consent of the Owner, and in time of War only by the Civil Magistrate in such manner as the Laws may direct.

That no Person ought to be taken imprisoned or disseised of his freehold, or be exiled or deprived of his Privileges, Franchises, Life, Liberty or Property but by due process of Law.

That no Person ought to be put twice in Jeopardy of Life or Limb for one and the same Offence, nor, unless in case of impeachment, be punished more than once for the same Offence.

That every Person restrained of his Liberty is entitled to an enquiry into the lawfulness of such restraint, and to a removal thereof if unlawful, and that such enquiry and removal ought not to be denied or delayed, except when on account of Public Danger the Congress shall suspend the privilege of the Writ of Habeas Corpus.

That excessive Bail ought not to be required; nor excessive Fines imposed; nor Cruel or unusual Punishments inflicted.

That (except in the Government of the Land and Naval Forces, and of the Militia when in actual Service, and in cases of Impeachment) a Presentment or Indictment by a Grand Jury ought to be observed as a necessary preliminary to the trial of all Crimes cognizable by the Judiciary of the United States, and such Trial should be speedy, public, and by an impartial Jury of the County where the Crime was committed; and that no person can be found Guilty without the unanimous consent of such Jury. But in cases of Crimes not committed within any County of any of the United States, and in Cases of Crimes committed within any County in which a general Insurrection may prevail, or which may be in the possession of a foreign Enemy, the enquiry and trial may be in such County as the Congress shall by Law direct; which County in the two Cases last mentioned should be as near as conveniently may be to that County in which the Crime may have been committed. And that in all Criminal Prosecutions, the Accused ought to be informed of the cause and nature of his Accusation, to be confronted with his accusers and the Witnesses against him, to have the means of producing his Witnesses, and the assistance of Council for his defense, and should not be compelled to give Evidence against himself.

That the trial by Jury in the extent that it obtains by the Common Law of England is one of the greatest securities to the rights of a free People, and ought to remain inviolate.

That every Freeman has a right to be secure from all unreasonable searches and seizures of his person his papers or his property, and therefore, that all Warrants to search suspected places or seize any Freeman his papers or property, without information upon Oath or Affirmation of sufficient cause, are grievous and oppressive; and that all general Warrants (or such in which the place or person suspected are not particularly designated) are dangerous and ought not to be granted.

That the People have a right peaceably to assemble together to consult for their common good, or to instruct their Representatives; and that every person has a right to Petition or apply to the Legislature for redress of Grievances. That the Freedom of the Press ought not to be violated or restrained.

That there should be once in four years an Election of the President and Vice President, so that no Officer who may be appointed by the Congress to act as President in case of the removal, death, resignation or inability of the President and Vice President can in any case continue to act beyond the termination of the period for which the last President and Vice President were elected.

That nothing contained in the said Constitution is to be construed to prevent the Legislature of any State from passing Laws at its discretion from time to time to divide such State into convenient Districts, and to apportion its Representatives to and amongst such Districts.

That the Prohibition contained in the said Constitution against *ex post facto* Laws, extends only to Laws concerning Crimes.

That all Appeals in Causes determineable according to the course of the common Law, ought to be by Writ of Error and not otherwise.

That the Judicial Power of the United States in cases in which a State may be a party, does not extend to criminal Prosecutions, or to authorize any Suit by any Person against a State.

That the Judicial Power of the United States as to Controversies between Citizens of the same State claiming Lands under Grants of different States is not to be construed to extend to any other Controversies between them except those which relate to such Lands so claimed under Grants of different States.

That the Jurisdiction of the Supreme Court of the United States, or of any other Court to be instituted by the Congress, is not in any case to be encreased enlarged or extended by any Fiction Collusion or mere suggestion;—And That no Treaty is to be construed so to operate as to alter the Constitution of any State.

Under these impressions and declaring that the rights aforesaid cannot be abridged or violated, and that the Explanations aforesaid are consistent with the said Constitution, And in confidence that the Amendments which shall have been proposed to the said Constitution will receive an early and mature Consideration: We the said Delegates, in the Name and in the behalf of the People of the State of New York Do by these presents Assent to and Ratify the said Constitution. In full Confidence nevertheless that until a Convention shall be called and convened for proposing Amendments to the said Constitution, the Militia of this State will not be continued in Service out of this State for a longer term than six weeks without the Consent of the Legislature thereof;—that the Congress will not make or alter any Regulation in this State respecting the times places and manner of holding Elections for Senators or Representatives unless the Legislature of this State shall neglect or refuse to make Laws or regulations for the purpose, or from any circumstance be incapable of making the same, and that in those cases such power will only be exercised until the Legislature of this State shall make provision in the Premises;—that no Excise will be imposed on any Article of the Growth production or Manufacture of the United States, or any of them within this State, Ardent Spirits excepted; And that the Congress will not lay direct Taxes within this State, but when the Monies arising from the Impost and Excise shall be insufficient for the public Exigencies, nor then, until Congress shall first have made a Requisition upon this State to assess levy and pay the Amount of such Requisition made agreably to the Census fixed in the said Constitution in such way and manner as the Legislature of this State shall judge best, but that in such case, if the State shall neglect or refuse to pay its proportion pursuant to such Requisition, then the Congress may assess and levy this States proportion together with Interest at the Rate of six per Centum per Annum from the time at which the same was required to be paid.

Done in Convention at Poughkeepsie in the County of Dutchess in the State of New York the twenty sixth day of July in the year of our Lord One thousand Seven hundred and Eighty eight.

By Order of the Convention
Geo: Clinton, President
Attested
John McKesson ⎱ *Secretaries*
Abm. B. Bancker ⎰

And the Convention do in the Name and Behalf of the People of the State of New York enjoin it upon their Representatives in the Congress, to Exert all their Influence, and use all reasonable means to Obtain a Ratification of the following Amendments to the said Constitution in the manner prescribed therein; and in all Laws to be passed by the Congress in the meantime to conform to the spirit of the said Amendments as far as the Constitution will admit.

That there shall be one Representative for every thirty thousand Inhabitants, according to the enumeration or Census mentioned in the Constitution, until the whole number of Representatives amounts to two hundred; after which that number shall be continued or encreased but not diminished, as Congress shall direct, and according to such ratio as the Congress shall fix, in conformity to the rule prescribed for the Apportionment of Representatives and direct Taxes.

That the Congress do not impose any Excise on any Article (except Ardent Spirits) of the Growth Production or Manufacture of the United States, or any of them.

That Congress do not lay direct Taxes but when the Monies arising from the Impost and Excise shall be insufficient for the Public Exigencies, nor then until Congress shall first have made a Requisition upon the States to assess levy and pay their respective proportions of such Requisition, agreably to the Census fixed in the said Constitution, in such way and manner as the Legislatures of the respective States shall judge best; and in such Case, if any State shall neglect or refuse to pay its proportion pursuant to such Requisition, then Congress may assess and levy such States proportion, together with Interest at the rate of six per Centum per Annum, from the time of Payment prescribed in such Requisition.

That the Congress shall not make or alter any Regulation in any State respecting the times places and manner of holding Elections for Senators or Representatives, unless the Legislature of such State shall neglect or refuse to make Laws or Regulations for the purpose, or from any circumstance be incapable of making the same; and then only until the Legislature of such State shall make provision in the premises; provided that Congress may prescribe the time for the Election of Representatives.

That no Persons except natural born Citizens, or such as were Citizens on or before the fourth day of July one thousand seven hundred and seventy six, or such as held Commissions under the United States during the War, and have at any time since the fourth day of July one thousand seven hundred and seventy six become Citizens of one or other of the United States, and who shall be Freeholders, shall be eligible to the Places of President, Vice President, or Members of either House of the Congress of the United States.

That the Congress do not grant Monopolies or erect any Company with exclusive Advantages of Commerce.

That no standing Army or regular Troops shall be raised or kept up in time of peace, without the consent of two-thirds of the Senators and Representatives present, in each House.

That no Money be borrowed on the Credit of the United States without the Assent of two-thirds of the Senators and Representatives present in each House.

That the Congress shall not declare War without the concurrence of two-thirds of the Senators and Representatives present in each House.

That the Privilege of the Habeas Corpus shall not by any Law be suspended for a longer term than six Months, or until twenty days after the Meeting of the Congress next following the passing of the Act for such suspension.

That the Right of the Congress to exercise exclusive Legislation over such District, not exceeding ten Miles square, as may by cession of a particular State, and the acceptance of Congress, become the Seat of the Government of the United States, shall not be so exercised, as to exempt the Inhabitants of such District from paying the like Taxes Imposts Duties and Excises, as shall be imposed on the other Inhabitants of the State in which such District may be; and that no person shall be privileged within the said District from Arrest for Crimes committed, or Debts contracted out of the said District.

That the Right of exclusive Legislation with respect to such places as may be purchased for the Erection of Forts, Magazines, Arsenals, Dockyards and other needful Buildings, shall not authorize the Congress to make any Law to prevent the Laws of the States respectively in which they may be, from extending to such places in all civil and Criminal Matters except as to such Persons as shall be in the Service of the United States; nor to them with respect to Crimes committed without such Places.

That the Compensation for the Senators and Representatives be ascertained by standing Laws; and that no alteration of the existing rate of Compensation shall operate for the Benefit of the Representatives, until after a subsequent Election shall have been had.

That the Journals of the Congress shall be published at least once a year, with the exception of such parts relating to Treaties or Military operations, as in the Judgment of either House shall require Secrecy; and that both Houses of Congress shall always keep their Doors open during their Sessions, unless the Business may in their Opinion requires Secrecy. That the yeas & nays shall be entered on the Journals whenever two Members in either House may require it.

That no Capitation Tax shall ever be laid by the Congress.

That no person be eligible as a Senator for more than six years in any term of twelve years; and that the Legislatures of the respective States may recal their Senators or either of them, and ["to" stricken out] elect others in their stead, to serve the remainder of the time for which the Senators so recalled were appointed.

That no Senator or Representative shall during the time for which he was elected be appointed to any Office under the Authority of the United States.

That the Authority given to the Executives of the States to fill the vacancies of Senators be abolished, and that such vacancies be filled by the respective Legislatures.

That the Power of Congress to pass uniform Laws concerning Bankruptcy shall only extend to Merchants and other Traders; and that the States respectively may pass Laws for the relief of other Insolvent Debtors.

That no Person shall be eligible to the Office of President of the United States a third time.

That the Executive shall not grant Pardons for Treason, unless with the Consent of the Congress; but may at his discretion grant Reprieves to persons convicted of Treason, until their Cases, can be laid before the Congress.

That the President or person exercising his Powers for the time being, shall not command an Army in the Field in person, without the previous desire of the Congress.

That all Letters Patent, Commissions, Pardons, Writs and Process of the United States, shall run in the Name of the People of the United States, and be tested in the Name of the President of the United States, or the person exercising his powers for the time being, or the first Judge of the Court out of which the same issue, as the case may be.

That the Congress shall not constitute ordain or establish any Tribunals or Inferior Courts, with any other than Appelate Jurisdiction, except such as may be necessary for the Tryal of Causes of Admiralty and Maritime Jurisdiction, and for the Trial of Piracies and Felonies committed on the High Seas; and in all other Cases to which the Judicial Power of the United States extends, and in which the Supreme Court of the United States has not original Jurisdiction, the Causes shall be heard tried, and determined in some one of the State Courts, with the right of Appeal to the Supreme Court of the United States, or other proper Tribunal to be established for that purpose by the Congress, with such exceptions, and under such regulations as the Congress shall make.

That the Court for the Trial of Impeachments shall consist of the Senate, the Judges of the Supreme Court of the United States, and the first or Senior Judge for the time being, of the highest Court of general and ordinary common Law Jurisdiction in each State;—that the Congress shall by standing Laws designate the Courts in the respective States answering this Description, and in States having no Courts exactly answering this Description, shall designate some other Court, preferring such if any there be, whose Judge or Judges may hold their places during good Behaviour—Provided that no more than one Judge, other than Judges of the Supreme Court of the United States, shall come from one State—That the Congress be authorized to pass Laws for compensating the said Judges for such Services and for compelling their Attendance—and that a Majority at least of the said Judges shall be requisite to constitute the said Court—that no person impeached shall sit as a Member thereof. That each Member shall previous to the entering upon any Trial take an Oath or Affirmation, honestly and impartially to hear and determine the Cause—and that a Majority of the Members present shall be necessary to a Conviction.

That persons aggrieved by any Judgment, Sentence or Decree of the Supreme Court of the United States in any Cause in which that Court has original Jurisdiction, with such exceptions and under such Regulations as the Congress shall make concerning the same, shall upon application, have a Commission to be issued by the President of the United States, to such Men learned in the Law as he shall nominate, and by and with the Advice and consent of the Senate appoint, not less than seven, authorizing such Commissioners, or any seven or more of them, to correct the Errors in such Judgment or to review such Sentence and Decree, as the case may be, and to do Justice to the parties in the Premises.

That no Judge of the Supreme Court of the United States shall hold any other Office under the United States, or any of them.

That the Judicial Power of the United States shall extend to no Controversies respecting Land, unless it relate to Claims of Territory or Jurisdiction between States, or to Claims of Land between Individuals, or between States and Individuals under the Grants of different States.

That the Militia of any State shall not be compelled to serve without the limits of the State for a longer term than six weeks, without the Consent of the Legislature thereof.

That the words without the Consent of the Congress in the seventh Clause of the ninth Section of the first Article of the Constitution, be expunged.

That the Senators and Representatives and all Executive and Judicial Officers of the United States shall be bound by Oath or Affirmation not to infringe or violate the Constitutions or Rights of the respective States.

That the Legislatures of the respective States may make Provision by Law, that the Electors of the Election Districts to be by them appointed shall chuse a Citizen of the United States who shall have been an Inhabitant of such District for the Term of one year immediately preceeding the time of his Election, for one of the Representatives of such State.

Done in Convention at Poughkeepsie in the County of Dutchess in the State of New York the twenty sixth day of July in the year of our Lord One thousand seven hundred and Eighty eight.

By order of the Convention
Geo: Clinton, President

Attested
  John McKesson } *Secretaries*
  Abm. B. Bancker |

Remarks of Hamilton on an Act for Regulating Elections, 1787*

Feb. 6, 1787

Mr. Hamilton observed that when the discriminating clauses admitted into the bill by that house, were introduced, he was restrained by motives of respect for the sense of a respectable part of the house, from giving it any other opposition, than a simple vote. The limited operation, they would have, made him less anxious about their adoption: but he could not reconcile it to his judgment, or feelings, to observe a like silence on the amendment proposed by the senate. Its operation would be very extensive; it would include almost every man in the city, concerned in navigation during the war.

We had in a former debate, travelled largely over the ground of the constitution, as applied to legislative disqualifications; He would not repeat what he had said, but he hoped to be indulged by the house in explaining a sentence in the constitution, which seems not well understood by some gentlemen. In one article of it, it is said no man shall be disfranchised or deprived of any right he enjoys under the constitution, but by the law of the land, or the judgment of his peers. Some gentlemen hold that the law of the land will include an act of the legislature. But Lord Coke, that great luminary of the law, in his comment upon a similar clause, in Magna Charta, interprets the law of the land to mean presentment and indictment, and process of outlawry, as contradistinguished from trial by jury. But if there were any doubt upon the constitution, the bill of rights enacted in this very session removes it. It is there declared that, no man shall be disfranchised or deprived of any right, but by due process of law, or the judgment of his peers. The words "due process" have a precise technical import, and are only applicable to the process and proceedings of the courts of justice; they can never be referred to an act of legislature.

Are we willing then to endure the inconsistency of passing a bill of rights, and committing a direct violation of it in the same session? in short, are we ready to destroy its foundations at the moment they are laid?

Our having done it to a certain degree is to be lamented; but it is no argument for extending it.

*   *   *

Hamilton to Madison, 1788†

June 8, 1788

My Dear Sir,

In my last I think I informed you that the elections had turned out, beyond expectation, favourable to the antifederal party. They have a

---

The Papers of Alexander Hamilton, Vol. 4, pp. 34–36.
†*The Papers of Alexander Hamilton*, Vol. 5, pp. 2–4.

majority of two thirds in the Convention and according to the best estimate I can form of about four sevenths in the community. The views of the leaders in this City are pretty well ascertained to be turned towards a long adjournment say till next spring or Summer. Their incautious ones observe that this will give an opportunity to the state to see how the government works and to act according to circumstances.

My reasonings on the fact are to this effect. The leaders of the party hostile to the constitution are equally hostile to the Union. They are however afraid to reject the constitution at once because that step would bring matters to a crisis between this state and the states which had adopted the Constitution and between the parties in the state. A separation of the Southern district from the other part of the state it is perceived would become the object of the Federalists and of the two neighbouring states. They therefore resolve upon a long adjournment as the safest and most artful course to effect their final purpose. They suppose that when the Government gets into operation it will be obliged to take some steps in respect to revenue &c. which will furnish topics of declamation to its enemies in the several states and will strengthen the minorities. If any considerable discontent should show itself they will stand ready to head the opposition. If on the contrary the thing should go on smoothly and the sentiments of our own people should change they can then elect to come into the Union. They at all events take the chances of time and the chapter of accidents.

How far their friends in the Country will go with them I am not able to say, but as they have always been found very obsequious we have little reason to calculate upon an uncompliant temper in the present instance.

For my own part the more I can penetrate the views of the Antifederal party in this state, the more I dread the consequences of the non adoption of the Constitution by any of the other states, the more I fear an eventual disunion and civil war. God grant that Virginia may accede. Her example will have a vast influence on our politics. New Hampshire, all accounts give us to expect, will be an assenting state.

The number of the volumes of the Federalist which you desired have been forwarded as well the se[c]ond as first, to the care of Governor Randolph. It was impossible to correct a certain error.

In a former letter I requested you to communicate to me by express the event of any decisive question in favour of the constitution authorising changes of horses &c with an assurance to the person sent that he will be liberally paid for his diligence.

Hamilton to Madison, 1788*

June 25, 1788

My Dear Sir,

I am very sorry to find by your letter of the 13th that your prospects are so critical. Our chance of success here is infinitely slender, and none at all if

*The Papers of Alexander Hamilton, Vol. 5, p. 80.

you go wrong. The leaders of the Antifederalists finding their part seems somewhat squeamish about rejection, are obliged at present to recur to the project of conditional amendments. We are going on very deliberately in the discussion and hitherto not without effect.

Communicate this to our friend G. Morris, to whom I have not time to write. And add, if you please, that his friend would certainly be exposed to a suit; but may pay in our paper money; the depreciation of which is about seven per Cent. It is possible however that a jury in estimating damages would calculate the sterling money at the current exchange in paper. But this is not probable.

Yrs. Affy

Hamilton to Madison, 1788*

July 8, 1788

My Dear Sir,

I felicitate you sincerely on the event in Virginia; but my satisfaction will be allayed, if I discover too much facility in the business of amendment-making. I fear the system will be wounded in some of its vital parts by too general a concurrence in some very injudicious recommendations. I allude more particularly to the power of taxation. The more I consider requisition in any shape the more I am out of humour with it.

We yesterday passed through the constitution. To day some definitive proposition is to be brought forward; but what we are at a loss to judge. We have good reason to believe that our opponents are not agreed, and this affords some ground of hope. Different things are thought of—Conditions precedent, or previous amendments; Conditions subsequent, or the proposition of amendments upon condition, that if they are not adopted within a limited time, the state shall be at liberty to withdraw from the Union, and lastly recommendatory amendments. In either case constructive declarations will be carried as far as possible. We will go as far as we can in the latter without invalidating the act, and will concur in rational recommendations. The rest for our opponents.

We are informed, There has been a disturbance in the City of Albany on the 4th of July which has occasioned bloodshed. The antifederalists were the aggressors & the Federalists the Victors. Thus stand our accounts at present. We trust however the matter has passed over & tranquility been restored.

Yrs. Affecty

Extract of a Letter from Poughkeepse, Dated July 11, 1788†

When the Convention met on thursday Mr Lansing came forward with the amendments, arranged in three classes—explanatory, conditional and recom-

*The Papers of Alexander Hamilton, Vol. 5, pp. 147–48.

†Documentary History of the Constitution of the United States, Vol. 5, pp. 60–61.

mendatory. The bill of rights is among those that are explanatory. The following are conditional. 1. That there shall be no standing army in time of peace, without the consent of two thirds of Congress: 2. That there shall be no direct taxes, nor excises on american manufactures. 3. That the militia shall not be ordered out of the state, except by the previous consent of the executive thereof; nor then for a longer time than six weeks, without the consent of the state Legislature; & 4thly. That there shall be no interference in the elections, unless when a state shall neglect or refuse to provide for the same.

In reading the amendments, Mr Lansing observed, that they had not only been changed in form, but in substance. One of them has been changed indeed: it is Melancton Smith's first amendment, and about which there was several days debate: the original amendment was for having the house of representatives doubled in the first instance, & that it shou'd increase at the rate of one for every 20,000 till it got to 300. As it now stands, it is that there shall be a representative for every 30,000 till it get to 200; beyond which it may not go.

After the amendments were read, it was proposed by Mr Lansing that the Convention shou'd adjourn, and that a committee of both parties shou'd be informally appointed, who shou'd endeavour to make such an accomodation, and so to arrange the amendments as to bring the business to a quick and friendly decision: accordingly the convention adjourned.

Mr Jay, Mr Duane, the Chief Justice, Judge Hobart, Judge Ryeress Judge Lefferts and Mr Hatfield, on the part of the Federalists; & Judge Yates, Mr Lansing, Mr M. Smith, Mr Tredwell, Mr Haring, Mr Jones and Mr G. Livingstone on the part of the antifederalists, were the committee appointed conformably to Mr Lansings motion.

When the committee met Mr Jay declared that the word conditional shou'd be erased before there cou'd be any discussion on the merits of the amendment: this occasion'd an hours debate, and the antis determing not to give up that point, the committee was dissolved with out effecting any thing. In this committee Mr Jones & Mr Smith discovered dispositions somewhat moderated; but the others were quite violent.

Extract of Another Letter of the Same Date

This morning Mr Jay brought forward the grand question, by a resolution for adopting the constitution; he spoke forcibly and commanded great attention: The Chancellor also spoke with his usual energy and brilliancy. Our worthy Chief Justice was also on his legs. Mr Smith, Mr Lansing, and the Governor spoke against the resolution, and from what fell from them, they seem determin'd to support a conditional adoption: this the Federalists consider as a rejection under another name, and will protest against.

Hamilton to Madison, 1788*

July 19, 1788

I thank you My Dear Sir for yours by the post. Yesterday I communicated to Duer our situation which I presume he will have communicated to you. It remains exactly the same, no further question having been taken. I fear the footing mentioned in my letter to Duer is the best upon which it can be placed; but every thing possible will yet be attempted to bring the party from that stand to an unqualified ratification. Let me know your idea of the possibility of our being received on that plan. You will understand that the only qualification will be the reservation of a right to recede in case our amendments have not been decided upon in one of the modes pointed out in the Constitution within a certain number of years, perhaps five or seven.

If this can in the first instance be admitted as a ratification I do not fear any further consequences. Congress will I presume recommend certain amendments to render the structure of the government more secure. This will satisfy the more considerate and honest opposers of the constitution, and with the aid of time will break up the party.

Yrs. affecy

Madison to Hamilton, 1788†

July 20, 1788

My dear Sir,

Yours of yesterday is this instant come to hand & I have but a few minutes to answer it. I am sorry that your situation obliges you to listen to propositions of the nature you describe. My opinion is that a reservation of a right to withdraw if amendments be not decided on under the form of the Constitution within a certain time, is a conditional ratification, that it does not make N. York a member of the New Union, and consequently that she could not be received on that plan. Compacts must be reciprocal, this principle would not in such a case be preserved. The Constitution requires an adoption in toto, and for ever. It has been so adopted by the other States. An adoption for a limited time would be as defective as an adoption of some of the articles only. In short any condition whatever must viciate the ratification. What the new Congress by virtue of the power to admit new States, may be able & disposed to do in such a case, I do not enquire as I suppose that is not the material point at present. I have not a moment to add more. Know my fervent wishes for your success & happiness.

*The Papers of Alexander Hamilton, Vol. 5, p. 177.
†The Papers of Alexander Hamilton, Vol. 5, p. 184.

This idea of reserving right to withdraw was started at Richmd. & considered as a conditional ratification which was itself considered as worse than a rejection.

Hamilton to Madison, 1788*

July 22, 1788

Dr Sir,

I wrote to you by the last post since which nothing material has turned up here. We are debating on amendments without having decided what is to be done with them. There is so great a diversity in the views of our opponents that it is impossible to predict any thing. Upon the whole however our fears diminish.

Yrs. Affecly

I take the liberty for certain reasons to put the inclosed under cover to you. Be so good as to send it to my office to the care of Mr. De Haert where it will be called for.

Madison to Jefferson, 1788†

Aug. 10, 1788

Dear Sir,

Mr. Warville Brissot has just arrived here, and I seize an opportunity suddenly brought to my knowledge to thank you for your several favors, and particularly for the pedometer. Answers to the letters must be put off for the next opportunity.

My last went off just as a vote was taken in the Convention of this State which foretold the ratification of the new Government. The latter act soon followed and is inclosed. The form of it is remarkable. I inclose also a circular address to the other States on the subject of amendments, from which mischiefs are apprehended. The great danger in the present crisis is that if another Convention should be soon assembled it would terminate in discord, or in alterations of the federal system which would throw back essential powers into the State Legislatures. The delay of a few years will assuage the jealousies which have been artificially created by designing men and will at the same time point out the faults which really call for amendment. At present the public mind is neither sufficiently cool nor sufficiently informed sor so delicate an operation.

* The Papers of Alexander Hamilton, Vol. 5, p. 187.
† The Writings of James Madison, Vol. 5, p. 244.

The Convention of North Carolina met on the 21st Ult: Not a word has yet been heard from its deliberations. Rhode Island has not resumed the subject since it was referred to & rejected by the people in their several Towns.

*   *   *

Madison to Washington, 1788*

Aug. 15, 1788

Dear Sir,

I have been duly favored with yours of the 3d. instant. The length of the interval since my last has proceeded from a daily expectation of being able to communicate the final arrangement for introducing the new Government. The place of meeting has undergone much discussion as you conjectured and still remains to be fixed. Philada. was first named, & negatived by a voice from Delaware. N. York came forward next. Lancaster was opposed to it & failed. Baltimore was next tried and to the surprise of every one had seven votes. It was easy to see that that ground had it been free from objection was not maintainable, accordingly the next day N. York was inserted in the place of it with the aid of the vote of Rhode Island. Rhode Island has refused to give a final vote in the business and has actually retired from Congress. The question will now be resumed between N. York & Philada. It was much to be wished that a fit place for a respectable outset to the Govt. could be found more central than either. The former is inadmissible if any regard is to be had to the Southern or Western Country. It is so with me for another reason, that it tends to stop the final & permanent seat short of the Potowmac certainly, and probably in the State of N. Jersey. I know this to be one of the views of the Advocates for N. York. The only chance the Potowmac has is to get things in such a train that a coalition may take place between the Southern & Eastern States on the subject and still more than the final seat may be undecided for two or three years, within which period the Western & S Western population will enter more into the estimate. Wherever Congress may be, the choice if speedily made will not be sufficiently by that consideration. In this point of view I am of opinion Baltimore would have been unfriendly to the true object. It would have retained Congress but a moment, so many states being North of it, and dissatisfied with it, and would have produced a coalition among those States & a precipitate election of the permanent seat & an intermediate removal to a more northern position.

You will have seen the circular letter from the Convention of this State. It has a most pestilent tendency. If an early General Convention cannot be parried, it is seriously to be feared that the system which has resisted so

*The Writings of James Madison, Vol. 5, pp. 248–50.

many direct attacks may be at last successfully undermined by its enemies. It is now perhaps to be wished that Rho. Island may not accede till this new crisis of danger be over. Some think it would have been better if even N. York had held out till the operation of the Government could have dissipated the fears which artifice had created and the attempts resulting from those fears & artifices. We hear nothing yet from N. Carolina more than comes by way of Petersburg.

With highest respect & attachment
I remain Dr. Sir your affecte. Servt.

Madison to Washington, 1788*

Aug. 24, 1788

Dear Sir,

I was yesterday favored with yours of the 17th, 18th, under the same cover with the papers from Mr. Pleasants. The circular letter from this State is certainly a matter of as much regret as the unanimity with which it passed is matter of surprize. I find it is every where, and particularly in Virginia laid hold of as the signal for united exertions in pursuit of early amendments. In Pennsylva. the antifederal leaders are I understand soon to have a meeting at Harrisburg, in order to concert proper arrangements on the part of that State. I begin now to accede to the opinion, which has been avowed for some time by many, that the circumstances involved in the ratification of New York will prove more injurious than a rejection would have done. The latter wd have rather alarmed the well meaning antifederalists elsewhere, would have had no ill effect on the other party, would have excited the indignation of the neighbouring States, and would have been necessarily followed by a speedy reconsideration of the subject. I am not able to account for the concurrence of the federal part of the Convention in the circular address, on any other principle than the determination to purchase an immediate ratification in any form or at any price, rather than disappoint this City of a chance for the new Congress. This solution is sufficiently justified by the eagerness displayed on this point, and the evident disposition to risk and sacrifice everything to it. Unfortunately the disagreeable question continues to be undecided, and is now in a state more perplexing than ever. By the last vote taken, the whole arrangement was thrown out, and the departure of Rho. Island & the refusal of N. Carolina to participate further in the business, has left eleven States only to take it up anew. In this number there are not seven States for any place, and the disposition to relax as usually

*The Writings of James Madison, Vol. 5, pp. 256–57.

happens, decreases with the progress of the contest. What and when the issue is to be is really more than I can foresee. It is truly mortifying that the outset of the new Government should be immediately preceded by such a display of locality, as portends the continuance of the evil which has dishonored the old and gives countenance to some of the most popular arguments which have been inculcated by the southern antifederalists.

* * *

Washington to Hamilton, 1788*

Aug. 28, 1788

Dear Sir,

I have had the pleasure to receive your letter dated the 13th.—accompanied by one addressed to General Morgan. I will forward the letter to Gener[a]l Morgan by the first conveyance, and add my particular wishes that he would comply with the request contained in it. ·Although I can scarcely imagine how the Watch of a British Officer, killed within their lines, should have fallen into his hands (who was many miles from the scene of action) yet, if it so happened, I flatter myself there will be no reluctance or delay in restoring it to the family.

As the perusal of the political papers under the signature of Publius has afforded me great satisfaction, I shall certainly consider them as claiming a most distinguished place in my library. I have read every performance which has been printed on one side and the other of the great question lately agitated (so far as I have been able to obtain them) and, without an unmeaning compliment I will say that I have seen no other so well calculated (in my judgment) to produce conviction on an unbiassed mind, as the Production of your Triumvirate—when the transient circumstances & fugitive performances which attended this crisis shall have disappeared, that work will merit the notice of Posterity; because in it are candidly discussed the principles of freedom & the topics of government, which will be always interesting to mankind so long as they shall be connected in Civil Society.

The Circular Letter from your Convention, I presume, was the equivalent by wch. you obtained an acquiescence in the proposed Constitution: Nothwithstanding I am not very well satisfied with the tendency of it; yet the Federal affairs have proceeded, with few exceptions, in so good a train, that I hope the political Machine may be put in motion, without much effort or hazard of miscarrying.

* * *

*The Papers of Alexander Hamilton, Vol. 5, pp. 206–7.

Jefferson to Mr. Short, 1788*

Sept. 20, 1788

. . . the Convention of Virginia annexed to their ratification of the new Constitution a copy of the state Declaration of rights, not by way of Condition, but to announce their attachment to them. they added also propositions for specific alterations of the constitution. among these was one for rendering the President incapable of serving more than 8 years in any term of 16. New York has followed the example of Virginia, expressing the substance of her bill of rights (i. e. Virginia's) & proposing amendments; these last differ much from those of Virginia. but they concur as to the President, only proposing that he shall be incapable of being elected more than twice. but I own I should like better than either of these, what Luther Martin tells us was repeatedly voted & adhered to by the federal convention, & only altered about 12. days before their rising when some members had gone off, to wit, that he should be elected for 7. years & incapable for ever after. but New York has taken another step which gives uneasiness. she has written a circular letter to all the legislatures, asking their concurrence in an immediate Convention for making amendments. no news yet from N. Carolina. electors are to be chosen the 1st. Wednesday in January, the President to be elected the 1st. Wednesday in February, the new legislature to meet the 3d. week in March. the place is not yet decided on. Philadelphia was first proposed & had 6½ votes. the half vote was Delaware, one of whose members wanted to take a vote on Wilmington. then Baltimore was proposed & carried, and afterwards rescinded, so that the matter stood open as ever on the 10th. of August: but it was allowed the dispute lay only between N. York & Philadelphia, & rather thought in favor of the last. the R. island delegates had retired from Congress. . . . Congress had referred the decision as to the independance of Kentucké to the new government. Brown ascribes this to the jealousy of the Northern states, who want Vermont to be received at the same time in order to preserve a balance of interests in Congress. he was just setting out for Kentucké, disgusted, yet disposed to persuade to an acquiescence, tho' doubting they would immediately separate from the union. the principal obstacle to this, he thought, would be the Indian war.—the following is a quotation from a letter from Virginia dated July 12. 'P——n, tho' much impaired in health, & in every respect in the decline of life, shewed as much zeal to carry the new constn, as if he had been a young man: perhaps more than he discovered in the commencement of the late revolution in his opposition to Great Britain. W—e acted as chairman to the commee of the whole & of course took but little part in the debate: but was for the adoption relying on subsequent amendments. B—r said nothing, but was for it. the G——r exhibited a curious spectacle to view. having refused to sign the

*Documentary History of the Constitution of the United States, Vol. 5, pp. 68–70.

paper, every body supposed him against it. but he afterwards had written a letter; & having taken a part which might be called rather vehement, than active, he was constantly labouring to shew that his present conduct was consistent with that letter, & that letter with his refusal to sign. M—d——n took the principal share in the debate for it: in which, together with the aid I have already mentioned, he was somewhat assisted by I—nn—s, Lee, M——l, C——n & G. N——s. M—s—n, H——y & Gr——n were the principal supporters of the opposition. the discussion, as might be expected where the parties were so nearly on a balance, was conducted generally with great order, propriety & respect of either party to the other.

*　　*　　*

Madison to Jefferson, 1788*

Sept. 21, 1788

Dear Sir,

Being informed of a circuitous opportunity to France I make use of it to forward the inclosures. By one of them you will find that Congress have been at length brought into the true policy which is demanded by the situation of the Western Country. An additional resolution on the secret journal puts an end to all negociation with Spain, referring the subject of a treaty, after this assertion of right to the Mississippi, to the new government. The communication in my last will have shewn you the crisis of things in that quarter, a crisis however not particularly known to Congress, and will be a key to some of the Kentucky toasts in the Virga Gazette.

The Circular letter from the New York Convention has rekindled an ardor among the opponents of the federal Constitution for an immediate revision of it by another General Convention. You will find in one of the papers inclosed the result of the consultations in Pennsylvania on that subject. Mr. Henry and his friends in Virginia enter with great zeal into the scheme. Governor Randolph also espouses it; but with a wish to prevent if possible danger to the article which extends the power of the Government to internal as well as external taxation. It is observable that the views of the Pennsylva meeting do not rhyme very well with those of the Southern advocates for a Convention; the objects most eagerly pursued by the latter being unnoticed in the Harrisburg proceedings. The effect of the circular letter on other States is less known. I conclude that it will be the same everywhere among those who opposed the Constitution, or contended for a conditional ratification of it. Whether an early Convention will be the result of this united effort, is more than can at this moment be foretold. The measure will certainly be industriously opposed in some parts of the Union, not only by those who

*The Writings of James Madison, Vol. 5, pp. 262–64.

wish for no alterations, but by others who would prefer the other mode provided in the Constitution, as most expedient at present, for introducing those supplemental safeguards to liberty agst which no objections can be raised; and who would moreover approve of a Convention for amending the frame of the Government itself, as soon as time shall have somewhat corrected the feverish state of the public mind, and trial have pointed its attention to the true defects of the systems.

*   *   *

Madison to G. L. Turberville, 1788*

Nov. 2, 1788

Dear Sir,

Your favor of the 20th Ult. not having got into my hands in time to be acknowledged by the last mail, I have now the additional pleasure of acknowledging along with it your favor of the 24, which I recd yesterday.

You wish to know my sentiments on the project of another general Convention as suggested by New York. I shall give them to you with great frankness, though I am aware they may not coincide with those in fashion at Richmond or even with your own. I am not of the number if there be any such, who think the Constitution lately adopted a faultless work. On the contrary there are amendments wch I wished it to have received before it issued from the place in which it was formed. These amendments I still think ought to be made, according to the apparent sense of America and some of them at least, I presume will be made. There are others concerning which doubts are entertained by many, and which have both advocates and opponents on each side of the main question. These I think ought to receive the light of actual experiment, before it would be prudent to admit them into the Constitution. With respect to the first class, the only question is which of the two modes provided be most eligible for the discussion and adoption of them. The objections agst a Convention which give a preference to the other mode in my judgment are the following I. It will add to the difference among the States on the merits, another and an unnecessary difference concerning the mode. There are amendments which in themselves will probably be agreed to by all the States, and pretty certainly by the requisite proportion of them. If they be contended for in the mode of a Convention, there are unquestionably a number of States who will be so averse and apprehensive as to the mode, that they will reject the merits rather than agree to the mode. A Convention therefore does not appear to be the most convenient or probable Channel for getting to the object. 2. A Convention cannot be called

*The Writings of James Madison, Vol. 5, pp. 297–301.

without the unanimous consent of the parties who are to be bound by it, if first principles are to be recurred to; or without the previous application of 2/3 of the State legislatures, if the forms of the Constitution are to be pursued. The difficulties in either of these cases must evidently be much greater than will attend the origination of amendments in Congress, which may be done at the instance of a single State Legislature, or even without a single instruction on the subject. 3. If a General Convention were to take place for the avowed and sole purpose of revising the Constitution, it would naturally consider itself as having a greater latitude than the Congress appointed to administer and support as well as to amend the system; it would consequently give greater agitation to the public mind; an election into it would be courted by the most violent partizans on both sides; it wd probably consist of the most heterogeneous characters; would be the very focus of that flame which has already too much heated men of all parties; would no doubt contain individuals of insidious views, who under the mask of seeking alterations popular in some parts but inadmissible in other parts of the Union might have a dangerous opportunity of sapping the very foundations of the fabric. Under all these circumstances it seems scarcely to be presumable that the deliberations of the body could be conducted in harmony, or terminate in the general good. Having witnessed the difficulties and dangers experienced by the first Convention, which assembled under every propitious circumstance, I should tremble for the result of a Second, meeting in the present temper of America and under all the disadvantages I have mentioned. 4. It is not unworthy of consideration that the prospect of a second Convention would be viewed by all Europe as a dark and threatening Cloud hanging over the Constitution just established, and, perhaps over the Union itself; and wd therefore suspend at least the advantages this great event has promised us on that side. It is a well-known fact that this event has filled that quarter of the Globe with equal wonder and veneration, that its influence is already secretly but powerfully working in favor of liberty in France, and it is fairly to be inferred that the final event there may be materially affected by the prospect of things here. We are not sufficiently sensible of the importance of the example which this Country may give to the world, nor sufficiently attentive to the advantages we may reap from the late reform, if we avoid bringing it into danger. The last loan in Holland and that alone, saved the U. S. from Bankruptcy in Europe; and that loan was obtained from a belief that the Constitution then depending wd be certainly speedily, quietly, and finally established, & by that means put America into a permanent capacity to discharge with honor & punctuality all her engagements.

NORTH CAROLINA CONVENTION, 1788

Commentary

The North Carolina Convention, which met to decide whether that state should ratify the federal Constitution, assembled on July 21, 1788. From the beginning, the Convention was dominated by a large Antifederalist majority. This made matters most difficult for those supporting ratification, who were led by James Iredell, later a Supreme Court Justice. Throughout the debate, the Antifederalists hammered at the Bill of Rights issue, saying that they would "never swallow the Constitution till it is amended." The Federalists sought to answer their arguments, particularly Iredell, who stressed the absence of need for a Bill of Rights, except in a system like the British one, where the legislature possesses undefined powers; "Of what use, therefore, can a bill of rights be in this Constitution, where the people expressly declare how much power they do give, and consequently retain all they do not?"

The Antifederalists remained unconvinced, saying the words spoken by their opponents "have gone in at one ear, and out at the other." Samuel Spencer expressed a widespread view when he declared, "I wish to have a bill of rights, to secure those unalienable rights, . . . though it might not be of any other service, it would at least satisfy the minds of the people."

The Federalists were willing to concede the point in accordance with the Virginia example. But their opponents were unwilling to accept anything less than (to quote their leader, Willie Jones) "amendments to be made previous to adoption by this state." On this issue, the Federalists would not yield, emphasizing that, "In regard to amending before or after the adoption, the difference is very great." They emphasized the danger of proposing amendments and then being "out of the Union till all these be agreed to by the other states." The Federalists knew, however, that they did not have the votes. As Iredell put it, "It is useless to contend any longer against a majority that is irresistible." Nevertheless, Iredell went through the motions of moving that amendments "be proposed subsequent to the ratification on the part of this state, and not previous to it." Six proposed amendments to be recommended were added to the motion (*infra* p. 973). Iredell's motion was overwhelmingly defeated, 184 to 84.

The majority then voted a resolution that a Declaration of Rights and other amendments be adopted "previous to the ratification of the Constitution." A Declaration of Rights and twenty-six proposed amendments accompanied the resolution (*infra* p. 966). Before adjourning, the Convention adopted "by a large majority" a resolution declaring that "this Convention has thought proper neither to ratify nor reject the Constitution." This left North Carolina outside the new constitutional system—a situation that continued until the first Congress itself passed the Bill of Rights as amendments to be submitted to the states for ratification. A new North Carolina Convention then voted ratification of the Constitution, on November 21, 1789.

The Bill of Rights and proposed amendments voted by the North Carolina Convention are not important for their substantive provisions, since (as Willie Jones expressly conceded) "I have, in my proposition, adopted, word for word, the Virginia amendments, with one or two additional ones." The North Carolina proposed Declaration of Rights was a verbatim copy of that recommended by the Virginia Ratifying Convention. The other proposed amendments were also those urged by Virginia, with one copied from Massachusetts (Article 22), and five new provisions (none of which is relevant to the subject of individual rights). The significance of the North Carolina proposals lies in the impetus they gave to the Bill of Rights movement. North Carolina was the one state to refuse to ratify until a Bill of Rights was adopted. To gain her adherence to the new Union (and also that of Rhode Island, which failed to call a Ratifying Convention before 1790), the Federalists knew they would have to propose amendments when the new Congress assembled. Added to the pressure exerted by the recommendatory amendments proposed by Massachusetts, South Carolina, New Hampshire, Virginia, and New York, this gave the Bill of Rights movement a momentum that was virtually irresistible.

North Carolina Convention Debates, 1788*

[Friday, July 25]

Mr. Bloodworth: . . . I hope gentlemen will exercise their own understanding on this occasion, and not let their judgment be led away by these shining characters, for whom, however, I have the highest respect. This Constitution, if adopted in its present mode, must end in the subversion of our liberties. Suppose it takes place in North Carolina; can farmers elect them? No, sir. The elections may be in such a manner that men may be appointed who are not representatives of the people. This may exist, and it ought to be guarded against. As to the place, suppose Congress should order the elections to be held in the most inconvenient place in the most inconvenient district; could every person entitled to vote attend at such a place? Suppose they should order it to be laid off into so many districts, and order the election to be held within each district, yet may not their power over the manner of election enable them to exclude from voting every description of men they please? The democratic branch is so much endangered, that no arguments can be made use of to satisfy my mind to it. The honorable gentleman has amused us with learned discussions, and told us he will condescend to propose

*The Debates in the Several State Conventions on the Adoption of the Constitution, Vol. 4, pp. 55–251.

amendments. I hope the representatives of North Carolina will never swallow the Constitution till it is amended.

Mr. Goudy: Mr. Chairman, the invasion of these states is urged as a reason for this clause. But why did they not mention that it should be only in cases of invasion? But that was not the reason, in my humble opinion. I fear it was a combination against our liberties. I ask, when we give them the purse in one hand, and the sword in another, what power have we left? It will lead to an aristocratical government, and establish tyranny over us. We are freemen, and we ought to have the privileges of such.

Gov. Johnston: Mr. Chairman, I do not impute any impure intentions to the gentlemen who formed this Constitution. I think it unwarrantable in any one to do it. I believe that were there twenty conventions appointed, and as many constitutions formed, we never could get men more able and disinterested than those who formed this; nor a constitution less exceptionable than that which is now before you. I am not apprehensive that this article will be attended with all the fatal consequences which the gentleman conceives. I conceive that Congress can have no other power than the states had. The states, with regard to elections, must be governed by the articles of the Constitution; so must Congress. But I believe the power, as it now stands, is unnecessary. I should be perfectly satisfied with it in the mode recommended by the worthy member on my right hand. Although I should be extremely cautious to adopt any constitution that would endanger the rights and privileges of the people, I have no fear in adopting this Constitution, and then proposing amendments.

*   *   *

Mr. Maclaine: Mr. Chairman, the reverend gentleman from Guilford has made an objection which astonishes me more than any thing I have heard. He seems to be acquainted with the history of England, but he ought to consider whether his historical references apply to this country. He tells us of triennial elections being changed to septennial elections. This is an historical fact we well know, and the occasion on which it happened is equally well known. They talk as loudly of constitutional rights and privileges in England as we do here, but they have no written constitution. They have a common law,—which has been altered from year to year, for a very long period,—Magna Charta, and bill of rights. These they look upon as their constitution. Yet this is such a constitution as it is universally considered Parliament can change. Blackstone, in his admirable Commentaries, tells us that the power of the Parliament is transcendent and absolute, and can do and undo every thing that is not naturally impossible. The act, therefore, to which the reverend gentleman alludes, was not unconstitutional. Has any man said that the legislature can deviate from this Constitution? The legislature is to be guided by the Constitution. They cannot travel beyond its bounds. The reverend gentleman says, that, though the representatives are to be elected for two years, they may pass an act prolonging their appointment for twenty years, or for natural life, without any violation of the Constitution. Is it possible for any common understanding or sense to put this construction upon it? Such an act, sir, would be a palpable violation of the Constitution: were they to attempt it, sir, the country would rise against them. After such an unwarrantable suggestion as this, any objection may be made to this Constitution. It is necessary to give power to the government. I would ask that gentleman who is so much afraid it will destroy our liberties, why he is not as much afraid of our state legislature; for they have much more power than we are now proposing to give this general government. They have an unlimited control over the purse and sword; yet no complaints are made. Why is he not as much afraid that our legislature will call out the militia to destroy our liberties? Will the militia be called out by the general government to enslave the people—to enslave their friends, their families, themselves? The idea of the militia being made use of, as an instrument to destroy our liberties, is almost too absurd to merit a refutation. It cannot be supposed that the representatives of our general government will be worse men than the members of our state government. Will we be such fools as to send our greatest rascals to the general government? We must be both fools as well as villains to do so.

Gov. Johnston: Mr. Chairman, I shall offer some observations on what the gentleman said. A parallel has been drawn between the British Parliament and Congress. The powers of Congress are all circumscribed, defined, and clearly laid down. So far they may go, but no farther. But, sir, what are the powers of the British Parliament? They have no written constitution in Britain. They have certain fundamental principles and legislative acts, securing the liberty of the people; but these may be altered by their representatives, without violating their constitution, in such manner as they may think proper. Their legislature existed long before the science of government was well understood. From very early periods, you find their Parliament in full force. What is their Magna Charta? It is only an act of Parliament. Their Parliament can, at any time, alter the whole or any part of it. In short, it is no more binding on the people than any other act which has passed. The power of the Parliament is, therefore, unbounded. But, sir, can Congress alter the Constitution? They have no such power. They are bound to act by the Constitution. They dare not recede from it. At the moment that the time for which they are elected expires, they may be removed. If they make bad laws, they will be removed; for they will be no longer worthy of confidence. The British Parliament can do every thing they please. Their bill of rights is only an act of Parliament, which may be, at any time, altered or modified, without a violation of the constitution. The people of Great Britain have no constitution to control their legislature. The king, lords, and commons, can do what they please.

Mr. Caldwell observed, that whatever nominal powers the British Parliament might possess, yet they had infringed the liberty of the people in the most flagrant manner, by giving themselves power to continue four years in Parliament longer than they had been elected for—that though they were only chosen for three years by their constituents, yet they passed an act that representatives should for the future, be chosen for seven years—that this Constitution would have a dangerous tendency—that this clause would enable them to prolong their continuance in office as long as they pleased—and that, if a constitution was not agreeable to the people, its operation could not be happy.

Gov. Johnston replied, that the act to which allusion was made by the gentleman was not unconstitutional; but that, if Congress were to pass an act prolonging the terms of elections of senators or representatives, it would be clearly unconstitutional.

Mr. Maclaine observed, that the act of Parliament referred to was passed on urgent necessity, when George I ascended the throne, to prevent the Papists from getting into Parliament; for parties ran so high at that time, that Papists enough might have got in to destroy the act of settlement which excluded the Roman Catholics from the succession to the throne.

*   *   *

[Monday, July 28]

Article 3d, 1st and 2d sections, read.

Mr. Spencer: Mr. Chairman, I have objections to this article. I object to the exclusive jurisdiction of the federal court in all cases of law and equity arising under the Constitution and the laws of the United States, and to the appellate jurisdiction of controversies between the citizens of different states, and a few other instances. To these I object, because I believe they will be oppressive in their operation. I would wish that the federal court should not interfere, or have any thing to do with controversies to the decision of which the state judiciaries might be fully competent, nor with such controversies as must carry the people a great way from home. With respect to the jurisdiction of cases arising under the Constitution, when we reflect on the very extensive objects of the plan of government, the manner in which they may arise, and the multiplicity of laws that may be made with respect to them, the objection against it will appear to be well founded. If we consider nothing but the articles of taxation, duties, and excises, and the laws that might be made with respect to these, the cases will be almost infinite. If we consider that it is in contemplation that a stamp duty shall take place throughout the continent; that all contracts shall be on stamp paper; that no contracts shall be of validity but what would be thus stamped,—these cases will be so many that the consequences would be dreadful. It would be necessary to appoint judges to the federal Supreme Court, and other inferior departments, and such a number of inferior courts in every district and county, with a correspondent number of officers, that it would cost an immense expense without any apparent necessity, which must operate to the distress of the inhabitants. There will be, without any manner of doubt, clashings and animosities between the jurisdiction of the federal courts and of the state courts, so that they will keep the country in hot water. It has been said that the impropriety of this was mentioned by some in the Convention. I cannot see the reasons of giving the federal courts jurisdiction in these cases; but I am sure it will occasion great expense unnecessarily. The state judiciaries will have very little to do. It will be almost useless to keep them up. As all officers are to take an oath to support the general government, it will carry every thing before it. This will produce that consolidation through the United States which is apprehended. I am sure that I do not see that it is possible to avoid it. I can see no power that can keep up the little remains of the power of the states. Our rights are not guarded. There is no declaration of rights, to secure to every member of the society those unalienable rights which ought not to be given up to any government. Such a bill of rights would be a check upon men in power. Instead of such a bill of rights, this Constitution has a clause which may warrant encroachments on the power of the respective state legislatures. I know it is said that what is not given up to the United States will be retained by the individual states. I know it ought to be so, and should be so understood; but, sir, it is not declared to be so. In the Confederation it is expressly declared that all rights and powers, of any kind whatever, of the several states, which are not given up to the United States, are expressly and absolutely retained, to be enjoyed by the states. There ought to be a bill of rights, in order that those in power may not step over the boundary between the powers of government and the rights of the people, which they may do when there is nothing to prevent them. They may do so without a bill of rights; notice will not be readily taken of the encroachments of rulers, and they may go a great length before the people are alarmed. Oppression may therefore take place by degrees; but if there were express terms and bounds laid down, when these were passed by, the people would take notice of them, and oppressions would not be carried on to such a length. I look upon it, therefore, that there ought to be something to confine the power of this government within its proper boundaries. I know that several writers have said that a bill of rights is not necessary in this country; that some states had them not, and that others had. To these I answer, that those states that have them not as bills of rights, strictly so called, have them in the frame of their constitution, which is nearly the same.

There has been a comparison made of our situation with Great Britain. We have no crown, or prerogative of a king, like the British constitution. I take it, that the subject has been misunderstood. In Great Britain, when the king attempts to usurp the rights of the people, the declaration and bill of rights are a guard against him. A bill of rights would be necessary here to guard against our rulers. I wish to have a bill of rights, to secure those unalienable rights, which are called by some respectable writers the *residuum* of human rights, which are never to be given up. At the same time that it would give security to individuals, it would add to the general strength. It might not be so necessary to have a bill of rights in the government of the United States, if such means had not been made use of as endanger a consolidation of all the states; but at any event, it would be proper to have one, because, though it might not be of any other service, it would at least satisfy the minds of the people. It would keep the states from being swallowed up by a consolidated government.

* * *

Mr. Maclaine: . . . The gentleman has wandered out of his way to tell us—what has so often been said out of doors—that there is no declaration of rights; that consequently all our rights are taken away. It would be very extraordinary to have a bill of rights, because the powers of Congress are expressly defined; and the very definition of them is as valid and efficacious a check as a bill of rights could be, without the dangerous implication of a bill of rights. The powers of Congress are limited and enumerated. We say we have given them those powers, but we do not say we have given them more. We retain all those rights which we have not given away to the general government. The gentleman is a professional man. If a gentleman had made his last will and testament, and devised or bequeathed to a particular person the sixth part of his property, or any particular specific legacy, could it be said that that person should have the whole estate? If they can assume powers not enumerated, there was no occasion for enumerating any powers. The gentleman is learned. Without recurring to his learning, he may only appeal to his common sense; it will inform him that, if we had all power before, and give away but a part, we still retain the rest. It is as plain a thing as possibly can be, that Congress can have no power but what we expressly give them. There is an express clause which, however disingenuously it has been perverted from its true meaning, clearly demonstrates that they are confined to those powers which are given them. This clause enables them to "make all laws which shall be necessary and proper for carrying into execution the foregoing powers, and all other powers vested by this Constitution in the government of the United States, or any department or officers thereof." This clause specifies that they shall make laws to carry into execution all the powers vested by this Constitution; consequently, they can make no laws to execute any other power. This clause gives no new power, but declares that those already given are to be executed by proper laws. I hope this will satisfy gentlemen.

Gov. Johnston: Mr. Chairman, the learned member from Anson says that the federal courts have exclusive jurisdiction of all cases in law and equity arising under the Constitution and laws of the United States. The opinion which I have always entertained is, that they will, in these cases, as well as in several others, have concurrent jurisdiction with the state courts, and not exclusive jurisdiction. I see nothing in this Constitution which hinders a man from bringing suit wherever he thinks he can have justice done him. The jurisdiction of these courts is established for some purposes with which the state courts have nothing to do, and the Constitution takes no power from the state courts which they now have. They will have the same business which they have now, and if so, they will have enough to employ their time. We know that the gentlemen who preside in our superior courts have more business than they can determine. Their complicated jurisdiction, and the great extent of country, occasions them a vast deal of business. The addition of the business of the United States would be no manner of advantage to them. It is obvious to every one that there ought to be one Supreme Court for national purposes. But the gentleman says that a bill of rights was necessary. It appears to me, sir, that it would have been the highest absurdity to undertake to define what rights the people of the United States were entitled to; for that would be as much as to say they were entitled to nothing else. A bill of rights may be necessary in a monarchical government, whose powers are undefined. Were we in the situation of a monarchical country? No, sir. Every right could not be enumerated, and the omitted rights would be sacrificed, if security arose from an enumeration. The Congress cannot assume any other powers than those expressly given them, without a palpable violation of the Constitution. Such objections as this, I hope, will have no effect on the minds of any members in this house. When gentlemen object, generally, that it tends to consolidate the states and destroy their state judiciaries, they ought to be explicit, and explain their meaning. They make use of contradictory arguments. The Senate represents the states, and can alone prevent this dreaded consolidation; yet the powers of the Senate are objected to. The rights of the people, in my opinion, cannot be affected by the federal courts. I do not know how inferior courts will be regulated. Some suppose the state courts will have this business. Others have imagined that the continent would be divided into a number of districts, where courts would be held so as to suit the convenience of the people. Whether this or some other mode will be appointed by Congress, I know not; but this I am sure of, that the state judiciaries are not divested of their present judicial cognizance, and that we have every security that our ease and convenience will be consulted. Unless Congress had this power, their laws could not be carried into execution.

Mr. Bloodworth: Mr. Chairman, the worthy gentleman up last has given the information on the subject which I had never heard before. Hearing so many opinions, I did not know which was right. The honorable gentleman has said that the state courts and the courts of the United States would have concurrent jurisdiction. I beg the committee to reflect what would be the consequence of such measures It has ever been considered that the trial by jury was one of the greatest rights of the people. I ask whether, if such causes go into the federal court, the trial by jury is not cut off, and whether there is any security that we shall have justice done us. I ask if there be any security that we shall have juries in civil causes. In criminal cases there are to be juries, but there is no provision made for having civil causes tried by jury. This concurrent jurisdiction is inconsistent with the security of that great right. If it be not, I would wish to hear how it is secured. I have listened with attention to what the learned gentlemen have said, and have endeavored to see whether their arguments had any weight; but I found none in them. Many words have been spoken, and long time taken up; but with me they have gone in at one ear, and out at the other. It would give me much pleasure to hear that the trial by jury was secured.

Mr. J. M'Dowall: Mr. Chairman, the objections to this part of the Constitution have not been answered to my satisfaction yet. We know that the trial by a jury of the vicinage is one of the greatest securities for property. If causes are to be decided at such a great distance, the poor will be oppressed; in land affairs, particularly, the wealthy suitor will prevail. A poor man, who has a just claim on a piece of land, has not substance to stand it. Can it be supposed that any man, of common circumstances, can stand the expense and trouble of going from Georgia to Philadelphia, there to have a suit tried? And can it be justly determined without the benefit of a trial by jury? These are things which have justly alarmed the people. What made the people revolt from Great Britain? The trial by jury, that great safeguard of liberty, was taken away, and a stamp duty was laid upon them. This alarmed them, and led them to fear that greater oppressions would take place. We then resisted. It involved us in a war, and caused us to relinquish a government which made us happy in every thing else. The war was very bloody, but we got our independence. We are now giving away our dear-bought rights. We ought to consider what we are about to do before we determine.

Mr. Spaight: Mr. Chairman, the trial by jury was not forgotten in the Convention; the subject took up a considerable time to investigate it. It was impossible to make any one uniform regulation for all the states, or that would include all cases where it would be necessary. It was impossible, by one expression, to embrace the whole. There are a number of equity and maritime cases, in some of the states, in which jury trials are not used. Had the Convention said that all causes should be tried by a jury, equity and maritime cases would have been included. It was therefore left to the legislature to say in what cases it should be used; and as the trial by jury is in full force in the state courts, we have the fullest security.

Mr. Iredell: Mr. Chairman, I have waited a considerable time, in hopes that some other gentleman would fully discuss this point. I conceive it to be my duty to speak on every subject whereon I think I can throw any light; and it appears to me that some things ought to be said which no gentleman has yet mentioned. The gentleman from New Hanover said that our arguments went in at one ear, and out at the other. This sort of language, on so solemn and important an occasion, gives me pain. [Mr. Bloodworth here declared that he did not mean to convey any disrespectful idea by such an expression; that he did not mean an absolute neglect of their arguments, but that they were not sufficient to convince him; that he should be sorry to give pain to any gentleman; that he had listened, and still would listen, with attention, to what would be said. Mr. Iredell then continued.] I am by no means surprised at the anxiety which is expressed by gentlemen on this subject. Of all the trials that ever were instituted in the world, this, in my opinion, is the best, and that which I hope will continue the longest. If the gentlemen who composed the Convention had designedly omitted it, no man would be more ready to condemn their conduct than myself. But I have been told that the emission of it arose from the difficulty of establishing one uniform, unexceptionable mode; this mode of trial being different, in many particulars, in the several states. Gentlemen will be pleased to consider that there is a material difference between an article fixed in the Constitution, and a regulation by law. An article in the Constitution, however inconvenient it may prove by experience, can only be altered by altering the Constitution itself, which manifestly is a thing that ought not to be done often. When regulated by law, it can easily be occasionally altered so as best to suit the conveniences of the people. Had there been an article in the Constitution taking away that trial, it would justly have excited the public indignation. It is not taken away by the Constitution. Though that does not provide expressly for a trial by jury in civil cases, it does not say that there shall not be such a trial. The reasons of the omission have been mentioned by a member of the late General Convention, (Mr. Spaight.) There are different practices in regard to this trial in different states. In some cases, they have no juries in admiralty and equity cases; in others, they have juries in these cases, as well as in suits at common law. I beg leave to say that, if any gentleman of ability and knowledge of the subject will only endeavor to fix upon any one rule that would be pleasing to all the states under the impression of their present different habits, he will be convinced that it is impracticable. If the practice of any particular state had been adopted, others, probably, whose practice had been different, would have been discontented. This is a consequence that naturally would have ensued, had the provision been made in the Constitution itself. But when the regulation is to be by law,—as that law, when found injudicious, can be easily repealed, a majority may be expected to agree upon some method, since some method or other must be first tried, and there is a greater chance of the favorite method of one state being in time preferred. It is not to be presumed that the Congress would dare to deprive the people of this valuable privilege. Their own interest will operate as an additional guard, as none of them could tell how soon they might have occasion for such a trial themselves. The greatest danger from ambition is in criminal cases. But here they have no option. The trial must be by jury, in the state wherein the offence is committed; and the writ of habeas corpus will in the mean time secure the citizen against arbitrary imprisonment, which has been the principal source of tyranny in all ages.

*   *   *

With regard to a bill of rights, this is a notion originating in England, where no written constitution is to be found, and the authority of their government is derived from the most remote antiquity. Magna Charta itself is no constitution, but a solemn instrument ascertaining certain rights of individuals, by the legislature for the time being; and every article of which the legislature may at any time alter. This and a bill of rights also, the invention of later times, were occasioned by great usurpations of the crown, contrary, as was conceived, to the principles of their government, about which there was a variety of opinions. But neither that instrument, nor any other instrument, ever attempted to abridge the authority of Parliament, which is supposed to be without any limitation whatever. Had their constitution been fixed and certain, a bill of rights would have been useless, for the constitution would have shown plainly the extent of that authority which they were disputing about. Of what use, therefore, can a bill of rights be in this Constitution, where the people expressly declare how much power they do give, and consequently retain all they do not? It is a declaration of particular powers by the people to their representatives, for particular purposes. It may be considered as a great power of attorney, under which no power can be exercised but what is expressly given. Did any man ever hear, before, that at the end of a power of attorney it was said that the attorney should not exercise more power than was there given him? Suppose, for instance, a man had lands in the counties of Anson and Caswell, and he should give another a power of attorney to see his lands in Anson, would the other have any authority to sell the lands in Caswell?—or could he, without absurdity, say, "'Tis true you have not expressly authorized me to sell the lands in Caswell; but as you had lands there, and did not say I should not, I thought I might as well sell those lands as the other." A bill of rights, as I conceive, would not only be incongruous, but dangerous. No man, let his ingenuity be what it will, could enumerate all the individual rights not relinquished by this Constitution. Suppose, therefore, an enumeration of a great many, but an omission of some, and that, long after all traces of our present disputes were at an end, any of the omitted rights should be invaded, and the invasion be complained of; what would be the plausible answer of the government to such a complaint? Would they not naturally say, "We live at a great distance from the time when this Constitution was established. We can judge of it much better by the ideas of it entertained at the time, than by any ideas of our own. The bill of rights, passed at that time, showed that the people did not think every power retained which was not given, else this bill of rights was not only useless, but absurd. But we are not at liberty to charge an absurdity upon our ancestors, who have given such strong proofs of their good sense, as well as their attachment to liberty. So long as the rights enumerated in the bill of rights remain unviolated, you have no reason to complain. This is not one of them." Thus a bill of rights might operate as a snare rather than a protection. If we had formed a general legislature, with undefined powers, a bill of rights would not only have been proper, but necessary; and it would have then operated as an exception to the legislative authority in such particulars. It has this effect in respect to some of the American constitutions, where the powers of legislation are general. But where they are powers of a particular nature, and expressly defined, as in the case of the Constitution before us, I think, for the reasons I have given, a bill of rights is not only unnecessary, but would be absurd and dangerous.

Mr. J. M'Dowall: Mr. Chairman, the learned gentleman made use of several arguments to induce us to believe that the trial by jury, in civil cases, was not in danger, and observed that, in criminal cases, it is provided that the trial is to be in the state where the crime was committed. Suppose a crime is committed at the Mississippi; the man may be tried at Edenton. They ought to be tried by the people of the vicinage; for when the trial is at such an immense distance, the principal privilege attending the trial by jury is taken away; therefore the trial ought to be limited to a district or certain part of the state. It has been said, by the gentleman from Edenton, that our representatives will have virtue and wisdom to regulate all these things. But it would give me much satisfaction, in a matter of this importance, to see it absolutely secured. The depravity of mankind militates against such a degree of confidence. I wish to see every thing fixed.

Gov. Johnston: Mr. Chairman, the observations of the gentleman last up confirm what the other gentleman said. I mean that, as there are dissimilar modes with respect to the trial by jury in different states, there could be no general rule fixed to accommodate all. He says that this clause is defective, because the trial is not to be by a jury of the vicinage. Let us look at the state of Virginia, where, as long as I have known it, the laws have been executed so as to satisfy the inhabitants, and, I believe, as well as in any part of the Union. In that country, juries are summoned every day from the by-standers. We may expect less partiality when the trial is by strangers; and were I to be tried for my property or life, I would rather be tried by disinterested men, who were not biased, than by men who were perhaps intimate friends of my opponent. Our mode is different from theirs; but whether theirs be better than ours or not, is not the question. It would be improper for our delegates to impose our mode upon them, or for theirs to impose their mode upon us. The trial will probably be, in each state, as it has been hitherto used in such state, or otherwise regulated as conveniently as possible for the people. The delegates who are to meet in Congress will, I hope, be men of virtue and wisdom. If not, it will be our own fault. They will have it in their power to make necessary regulations to accommodate the inhabitants of each state. In the Constitution, the general principles only are laid down. It will be the object of the future legislation to Congress to make such laws as will be most convenient for the people. With regard to a bill of rights, so much spoken of, what the gentleman from Edenton has said, I hope, will obviate the objections against the want of it. In a monarchy, all power may be supposed to be vested in the monarch, except what may be reserved by a bill of rights. In England, in every instance where the rights of the people are not declared, the prerogative of the king is supposed to extend. But in this country, we say that what rights we do not give away remain with us.

Mr. Bloodworth: Mr. Chairman, the footing on which the trial by jury is, in the Constitution, does not satisfy me. Perhaps I am mistaken; but if I understand the thing right, the trial by jury is taken away. If the Supreme Federal Court has jurisdiction both as to law and fact, it appears to me to be taken away. The honorable gentleman who was in the Convention told us that the clause, as it now stands, resulted from the difficulty of fixing the mode of trial. I think it was easy to have put it on a secure footing. But, if the genius of the people of the United States is so dissimilar that our liberties cannot be secured, we can never hang long together. Interest is the band of social union; and when this is taken away, the Union itself must dissolve.

Mr. Maclaine: Mr. Chairman, I do not take the interest of the states to be so dissimilar; I take them to be all nearly alike, and inseparably connected. It is impossible to lay down any constitutional rule for the government of all the different states in each particular. But it will be easy for the legislature to make laws to accommodate the people in every part of the Union, as circumstances may arise. Jury trial is not taken away in such cases where it may be found necessary. Although the Supreme Court has cognizance of the appeal, it does not follow but that the trial by jury may be had in the court below, and the testimony transmitted to the Supreme Court, who will then finally determine, on a review of all the circumstances. This is well known to be the practice in some of the states. In our own state, indeed, when a cause is instituted in the county court, and afterwards there is an appeal upon it, a new trial is had in the superior court, as if no trial had been had before. In other countries, however, when a trial is had in an inferior court, and an appeal is taken, no testimony can be given in the court above, but the court determines upon the circumstances appearing upon the record. If I am right, the plain inference is, that there may be a trial in the inferior courts, and that the record, including the testimony, may be sent to the Supreme Court. But if there is a necessity for a jury in the Supreme Court, it will be a very easy matter to empanel a jury at the bar of the Supreme Court, which may save great expense, and be very convenient to the people. It is impossible to make every regulation at once. Congress, who are our own representatives, will undoubtedly make such regulations as will suit the convenience and secure the liberty of the people.

Mr. Iredell declared it as his opinion that there might be juries in the Superior Court as well as in the inferior courts, and that it was in the power of Congress to regulate it so.

[Tuesday, July 29]

Mr. Kennion in the chair.

Mr. Spencer: Mr. Chairman, I hope to be excused for making some observations on what was said yesterday, by gentlemen, in favor of these two clauses. The motion which was made that the committee should rise, precluded me from speaking then. The gentlemen have showed much moderation and candor in conducting this business; but I still think that my observations are well founded, and that some amendments are necessary. The gentleman said, all matters not given up by this form of government were retained by the respective states. I know that it ought to be so; it is the general doctrine, but it is necessary that it should be expressly declared in the Constitution, and not left to mere construction and opinion. I am authorized to say it was heretofore thought necessary. The Confederation says, expressly, that all that was not given up by the United States was retained by the respective states. If such a clause had been inserted in this Constitution, it would have superseded the necessity of a bill of rights. But that not being the case, it was necessary that a bill of rights, or something of that kind, should be a part of the Constitution. It was observed that, as the Constitution is to be a delegation of power from the several states to the United States, a bill of rights was unnecessary. But it will be noticed that this is a different case.

The states do not act in their political capacities, but the government is proposed for individuals. The very caption of the Constitution shows that this is the case. The expression, "We, the people of the United States," shows that this government is intended for individuals; there ought, therefore, to be a bill of rights. I am ready to acknowledge that the Congress ought to have the power of executing its laws. Heretofore, because all the laws of the Confederation were binding on the states in their political capacities, courts had nothing to do with them; but now the thing is entirely different. The laws of Congress will be binding on individuals, and those things which concern individuals will be brought properly before the courts. In the next place, all the officers are to take an oath to carry into execution this general government, and are bound to support every act of the government, of whatever nature it may be. This is a fourth reason for securing the rights of individuals. It was also observed that the federal judiciary and the courts of the states, under the federal authority, would have concurrent jurisdiction with respect to any subject that might arise under the Constitution. I am ready to say that I most heartily wish that, whenever this government takes place, the two jurisdictions and the two governments—that is, the general and the several state governments—may go hand in hand, and that there may be no interference, but that every thing may be rightly conducted. But I will never concede that it is proper to divide the business between the two different courts. I have no doubt that there is wisdom enough in this state to decide the business, without the necessity of federal assistance to do our business. The worthy gentleman from Edenton dwelt a considerable time on the observations on a bill of rights, contending that they were proper only in monarchies, which were founded on different principles from those of our government; and, therefore, though they might be necessary for others, yet they were not necessary for us. I still think that a bill of rights is necessary. This necessity arises from the nature of human societies. When individuals enter into society, they give up some rights to secure the rest. There are certain human rights that ought not to be given up, and which ought in some manner to be secured. With respect to these great essential rights, no latitude ought to be left. They are the most inestimable gifts of the great Creator, and therefore ought not to be destroyed, but ought to be secured. They ought to be secured to individuals in consideration of the other rights which they give up to support society.

The trial by jury has been also spoken of. Every person who is acquainted with the nature of liberty need not be informed of the importance of this trial. Juries are called the bulwarks of our rights and liberty; and no country can ever be enslaved as long as those cases which affect their lives and property are to be decided, in a great measure, by the consent of twelve honest, disinterested men, taken from the respectable body of yeomanry. It is highly improper that any clause which regards the security of the trial by jury should be any way doubtful. In the clause that has been read, it is ascertained that criminal cases are to be tried by jury in the states where they are committed. It has been objected to that clause, that it is not sufficiently explicit. I think that it is not. It was observed that one may be taken to a great distance. One reason of the resistance to the British government was, because they required that we should be carried to the country of Great Britain, to be tried by juries of that country. But we insisted on being tried by juries of the vicinage, in our own country. I think it therefore proper that something explicit should be said with respect to the vicinage.

With regard to that part, that the Supreme Court shall have appellate jurisdiction both as to law and fact, it has been observed that, though the federal court might decide without a jury, yet the court below, which tried it, might have a jury. I ask the gentleman what benefit would be received in the suit by having a jury trial in the court below, when the verdict is set aside in the Supreme Court. It was intended by this clause that the trial by jury should be suppressed in the superior and inferior courts. It has been said, in defence of the omission concerning the trial by jury in civil cases, that one general regulation could not be made; that in several cases the constitution of several states did not require a trial by jury,—for instance, in cases of equity and admiralty,—whereas in others it did, and that, therefore, it was proper to leave this subject at large. I am sure that, for the security of liberty, they ought to have been at the pains of drawing some line. I think that the respectable body who formed the Constitution should have gone so far as to put matters on such a footing as that there should be no danger. They might have provided that all those cases which are now triable by a jury should be tried in each state by a jury, according to the mode usually practised in such state. This would have been easily done, if they had been at the trouble of writing five or six lines. Had it been done, we should have been entitled to say that our rights and liberties were not endangered. If we adopt this clause as it is, I think, notwithstanding what gentlemen have said, that there will be danger. There ought to be some amendments to it, to put this matter on a sure footing. There does not appear to me to be any kind of necessity that the federal court should have jurisdiction in the body of the country. I am ready to give up that, in the cases expressly enumerated, an appellate jurisdiction (except in one or two instances) might be given. I wish them also to have jurisdiction in maritime affairs, and to try offences committed on the high seas. But in the body of a state, the jurisdiction of the courts in that state might extend to carrying into execution the laws of Congress. It must be unnecessary for the federal courts to do it, and would create trouble and expense which might be avoided. In all cases where appeals are proper, I will agree that it is necessary there should be one Supreme Court. Were those things properly regulated, so that the Supreme Court might not be oppressive, I should have no objection to it.

*   *   *

Mr. Maclaine: . . . I hope, sir, that all power is in the people, and not in the state governments. If he will not deny the authority of the people to delegate power to agents, and to devise such a government as a majority of them thinks will promote their happiness, he will withdraw his objection. The people, sir, are the only proper authority to form a government. They, sir, have formed their state governments, and can alter them at pleasure. Their transcendent power is competent to form this or any other government which they think promotive of their happiness. But the gentleman contends that there ought to be a bill of rights, or something of that kind—something declaring expressly, that all power not expressly given to the Constitution ought to be retained by the states, and he produces the Confederation as an authority for its necessity. When the Confederation was made, we were by no means so well acquainted with the principles of government as we are now. We were then jealous of the power of our rulers, and had an idea of the British government when we entertained that jealousy. There is no people on earth so well acquainted with the nature of government as the people of America generally are. We know now that it is agreed upon by most writers, and men of judgment and reflection, that all power is in the people, and immediately derived from them. The gentleman surely must know that, if there be certain rights which never can, nor ought to, be given up, these rights cannot be said to be given away, merely because we have omitted to say that we have not given them up. Can any security arise from declaring that we have a right to what belongs to us? Where is the necessity of such a declaration? If we have this inherent, this unalienable, this indefeasible title to those rights, if they are not given up, are they not retained? If Congress should make a law beyond the powers and the spirit of the Constitution, should we not say to Congress, "You have no authority to make this law. There are limits beyond which you cannot go. You cannot exceed the power prescribed by the Constitution. You are amenable to us for your conduct. This act is unconstitutional. We will disregard it, and punish you for the attempt."

But the gentleman seems to be most tenacious of the judicial power of the states. The honorable gentleman must know, that the doctrine of reservation of power not relinquished, clearly demonstrates that the judicial power of the states is not impaired. He asks, with respect to the trial by jury, "When the cause has gone up to the superior court, and the verdict is set aside, what benefit arises from having had a jury trial in the inferior court?" I would ask the gentleman, "What is the reason, that, on a special verdict or case agreed, the decision is left to the court?" There are a number of cases where juries cannot decide. When a jury finds the fact specially, or when it is agreed upon by the parties, the decision is referred to the court. If the law be against the party, the court decides against him; if the law be for him, the court judges accordingly. He, as well as every gentleman here, must know that, under the Confederation, Congress set aside juries. There was an appeal given to Congress: did Congress determine by a jury? Every party carried his testimony in writing to the judges of appeal, and Congress determined upon it.

The distinction between matters of law and of fact has not been sufficiently understood, or has been intentionally misrepresented. On a demurrer in law, in which the facts are agreed upon by the parties, the law arising thereupon is referred to the court. An inferior court may give an erroneous judgment; an appeal may be had from this court to the Supreme Federal Court, and a right decision had. This is an instance wherein it can have cognizance of matter of law solely. In cases where the existence of facts has been first disputed by one of the parties, and afterwards established as in a special verdict, the consideration of these facts, blended with the law, is left to the court. In such cases, inferior courts may decide contrary to justice and law, and appeals may be had to the Supreme Court. This is an instance wherein it may be said they have jurisdiction both as to law and fact. But where facts only are disputed, and where they are once established by a verdict, the opinion of the judges of the Supreme Court cannot, I conceive, set aside these facts; for I do not think they have the power so to do by this Constitution.

* * *

Mr. Maclaine replied, that the gentleman's objections to the want of a bill of rights had been sufficiently answered; that the federal jurisdiction was well guarded, and that the federal courts had not, in his opinion, cognizance, in any one case, where it could be alone vested in the state judiciaries with propriety or safety. The gentleman, he said, had acknowledged that the laws of the Union could not be executed under the existing government; and yet he objected to the federal judiciary's having cognizance of such laws, though it was the only probable means whereby they could be enforced. The treaty of peace with Great Britain was the supreme law of the land; yet it was disregarded, for want of a federal judiciary. The state judiciaries did not enforce an observance of it. The state courts were highly improper to be intrusted with the execution of the federal laws, as they were bound to judge according to the state laws, which might be repugnant to those of the Union.

Mr. Iredell: Mr. Chairman, I beg leave to make a few observations on some remarks that have been made on this part of the Constitution. The honorable gentleman said that it was very extraordinary that the Convention should not have taken the trouble to make an addition of five or six lines, to secure the trial by jury in civil cases. Sir, if by the addition, not only of five or six lines, but of five or six hundred lines, this invaluable object could have been secured, I should have thought the Convention criminal in omitting it; and instead of meriting the thanks of their country, as I think they do now, they might justly have met with its resentment and indignation. I am persuaded the omission arose from the real difficulty of the case. The gentleman says that a mode might have been provided, whereby the trial by jury might have been secured satisfactorily to all the states. I call on him to show that mode. I know of none; nor do I think it possible for any man to devise one to which some states would not have objected. It is said, indeed, that it might have been provided that it should be as it had been heretofore. Had this been the case, surely it would have been highly incongruous.

The trial by jury is different in different states. It is regulated in one way in the state of North Carolina, and in another way in the state of Virginia. It is established in a different way from either in several other states. Had it, then, been inserted in the Constitution, that the trial by jury should be as it had been heretofore, there would have been an example, for the first time in the world, of a judiciary belonging to the same government being different in different parts of the same country. What would you think of an act of Assembly which should require the trial by jury to be had in one mode in the county of Orange, and in another mode in Granville, and in a manner different from both in Chatham? Such an act of Assembly, so manifestly injudicious, impolitic, and unjust, would be repealed next year.

But what would you say of our Constitution, if it authorized such an absurdity? The mischief, then, could not be removed without altering the Constitution itself. It must be evident, therefore, that the addition contended for would not have answered the purpose. If the method of any particular state had been established, it would have been objected to by others, because, whatever inconveniences it might have been attended with, nothing but a change in the Constitution itself could have removed them; whereas, as it is now, if any mode established by Congress is found inconvenient, it can easily be altered by a single act of legislation. Let any gentleman consider the difficulties in which the Convention was placed. A union was absolutely necessary. Every thing could be agreed upon except the regulation of the trial by jury in civil cases. They were all anxious to establish it on the best footing, but found they could fix upon no permanent rule that was not liable to great objections and difficulties. If they could not agree among themselves, they had still less reason to believe that all the states would have unanimously agreed to any one plan that could be proposed. They, therefore, thought it better to leave all such regulations to the legislature itself, conceiving there could be no real danger, in this case, from a body composed of our own representatives, who could have no temptation to undermine this excellent mode of trial in civil cases, and who would have, indeed, a personal interest, in common with others, in making the administration of justice between man and man secure and easy.

In criminal cases, however, no latitude ought to be allowed. In these the greatest danger from any government subsists, and accordingly it is provided that there shall be a trial by jury, in all such cases, in the state wherein the offence is committed. I thought the objection against the want of a bill of rights had been obviated unanswerably. It appears to me most extraordinary. Shall we give up any thing but what is positively granted by that instrument? It would be the greatest absurdity for any man to pretend that, when a legislature is formed for a particular purpose, it can have any authority but what is so expressly given to it, any more than a man acting under a power of attorney could depart from the authority it conveyed to him, according to an instance which I stated when speaking on the subject before. As for example:—if I had three tracts of land, one in Orange, another in Caswell, and another in Chatham, and I gave a power of attorney to a man to sell the two tracts in Orange and Caswell, and he should attempt to sell my land in Chatham, would any man of common sense suppose he had authority to do so? In like manner, I say, the future Congress can have no right to exercise any power but what is contained in that paper. Negative words, in my opinion, could make the matter no plainer than it was before. The gentleman says that unalienable rights ought not to be given up. Those rights which are unalienable are not alienated. They still remain with the great body of the people. If any right be given up that ought not to be, let it be shown. Say it is a thing which affects your country, and that it ought not to be surrendered: this would be reasonable. But when it is evident that the exercise of any power not given up would be a usurpation, it would be not only useless, but dangerous, to enumerate a number of rights which are not intended to be given up; because it would be implying, in the strongest manner, that every right not included in the exception might be impaired by the government without usurpation; and it would be impossible to enumerate every one. Let any one make what collection or enumeration of rights he pleases, I will immediately mention twenty or thirty more rights not contained in it.

Mr. Bloodworth: Mr. Chairman, I have listened with attention to the gentleman's arguments; but whether it be for want of sufficient attention, or from the grossness of my ideas, I cannot be satisfied with his defence of the omission, with respect to the trial by jury. He says that it would be impossible to fall on any satisfactory mode of regulating the trial by jury, because there are various customs relative to it in the different states. Is this a satisfactory cause for the omission? Why did it not provide that the trial by jury should be preserved in civil cases? It has said that the trial should be by jury in criminal cases; and yet this trial is different in its manner in criminal cases in the different states. If it has been possible to secure it in criminal cases, notwithstanding the diversity concerning it, why has it not been possible to secure it in civil cases? I wish this to be cleared up. By its not being provided for, it is expressly provided against. I still see the necessity of a bill of rights. Gentlemen use contradictory arguments on this subject, if I recollect right. Without the most express restrictions, Congress may trample on your rights. Every possible precaution should be taken when we grant powers. Rulers are always disposed to abuse them. I beg leave to call gentlemen's recollection to what happened under our Confederation. By it, nine states are required to make a treaty; yet seven states said that they could, with propriety, repeal part of the instructions given our secretary for foreign affairs, which prohibited him from making a treaty to give up the Mississippi to Spain, by which repeal the rest of his instructions enabled him to make such treaty. Seven states actually did repeal the prohibitory part of these instructions, and they insisted it was legal and proper. This was in fact a violation of the Confederation. If gentlemen thus put what construction they please upon words, how shall we be redressed, if Congress shall say that all that is not expressed is given up, and they assume a power which is expressly inconsistent with the rights of mankind? Where is the power to pretend to deny its legality? This has occurred to me, and I wish it to be explained.

Mr. Spencer: Mr. Chairman, the gentleman expresses admiration as to what we object with respect to a bill of rights, and insists that what is not given up in the Constitution is retained. He must recollect I said, yesterday, that we could not guard with too much care those essential rights and liberties which ought never to be given up. There is no express negative—no fence against their being trampled upon. They might exceed the proper boundary without being taken notice of. When there is no rule but a vague doctrine, they might make great strides, and get possession of so much power that a general insurrection of the people would be necessary to bring an alteration about. But if a boundary were set up, when the boundary is passed, the people would take notice of it immediately. These are the observations which I made; and I have no doubt that, when he reflects, he will acknowledge the necessity of it. I acknowledge, however, that the doctrine is right; but if that Constitution is not satisfactory to the people, I would have a bill of rights, or something of that kind, to satisfy them.

*   *   *

[Wednesday, July 30]

Mr. J. M'Dowall: Mr. Chairman, I was in hopes that amendments would have been brought forward to the Constitution before the idea of adopting it had been thought of or proposed. From the best information, there is a great proportion of the people in the adopting states averse to it as it stands. I collect my information from respectable authority. I know the necessity of a federal government. I therefore wish this was one in which our liberties and privileges were secured; for I consider the Union as the rock of our political salvation. I am for the strongest federal government. A bill of rights ought to have been inserted to ascertain our most valuable and unalienable rights.

*   *   *

Mr. Willie Jones was against ratifying in the manner proposed. He had attended, he said, with patience to the debates of the speakers on both sides of the question. One party said the Constitution was all perfection. The other party said it wanted a great deal of perfection. For his part, he thought so. He treated the dangers which were held forth in case of non-adoption, as merely ideal and fanciful. After adding other remarks, he moved that the previous question might be put, with an intention, as he said, if that was carried, to introduce a resolution which he had in his hand, and which he was then willing to read if gentlemen thought proper, stipulating for certain amendments to be made previous to the adoption by this state.

Gov. Johnston begged gentlemen to recollect that the proposed amendments could not be laid before the other states unless we adopted and became part of the Union.

Mr. Taylor wished that the previous question might be put, as it would save much time. He feared the motion first made was a manoeuvre or contrivance to impose a constitution on the people which a majority disapproved of.

Mr. Iredell wished the previous should be withdrawn, and that they might debate the first question. The great importance of the subject, and the respectability of the gentleman who made the motion, claimed more deference and attention than to decide it in the very moment it was introduced, by getting rid of it by the previous question. A decision was now presented in a new form by a gentleman of great influence in the house, and gentlemen ought to have time to consider before they voted precipitately upon it.

A desultory conversation now arose. Mr. J. Galloway wished the question to be postponed till to-morrow morning.

Mr. J. M'Dowall was for immediately putting the question. Several gentlemen expatiated on the evident necessity of amendments.

Gov. Johnston declared that he disdained all manoeuvres and contrivance; that an intention of imposing an improper system on the people, contrary to their wishes, was unworthy of any man. He wished the motion to be fairly and fully argued and investigated. He observed that the very motion before them proposed amendments to be made, that they were proposed as they had been in other states. He wished, therefore, that the motion for the previous question should be withdrawn.

Mr. Willie Jones could not withdraw his motion. Gentlemen's arguments, he said, had been listened to attentively, but he believed no person had changed his opinion. It was unnecessary, then, to argue it again. His motion was not conclusive. He only wished to know what ground they stood on—whether they should ratify it unconditionally or not.

Mr. Spencer wished to hear the arguments and reasons for and against the motion. Although he was convinced the house wanted amendments, and that all had nearly determined the question in their own minds, he was for hearing the question argued, and had no objection to the postponement of it till to-morrow.

Mr. Iredell urged the great importance of consideration; that the consequence of the previous question, if carried, would be an exclusion of this state out of the Union. He contended that the house had no right to make a conditional ratification; and, if excluded from the Union, they could not be assured of an easy admission at a future day, though the impossibility of existing out of the Union must be obvious to every thinking man. The gentleman from Halifax had said that his motion would not be conclusive. For his part, he was certain it would be tantamount to immediate decision.

He trusted gentlemen would consider the propriety of debating the first motion at large.

Mr. Person observed, that the previous question would produce no inconvenience. The other party, he said, had all the debating to themselves, and would probably have it again, if they insisted on further argument. He saw no propriety in putting it off till to-morrow, as it was not customary for a committee to adjourn with two questions before them.

Mr. Shepherd declared that, though he had made up his mind, and believed other gentlemen had done so, yet he had no objection to giving gentlemen an opportunity of displaying their abilities, and convincing the rest of their error if they could. He was for putting it off till to-morrow.

Mr. Davie took notice that the gentleman from Granville had frequently used ungenerous insinuations, and had taken much pains out of doors to irritate the minds of his countrymen against the Constitution. He called upon gentlemen to act openly and aboveboard, adding that a contrary conduct, on this occasion, was extremely despicable. He came thither, he said, for the common cause of his country, and he knew no party, but wished the business to be conducted with candor and moderation. The previous question he thought irregular, and that it ought not to be put till the other question was called for; that it was evidently intended to preclude all further debate, and to precipitate the committee upon the resolution which it had been suggested was immediately to follow, which they were not then ready to enter upon; that he had not fully considered the consequences of a conditional ratification, but at present they appeared to him alarmingly dangerous, and perhaps equal to those of an absolute rejection.

Mr. Willie Jones observed, that he had not intended to take the house by surprise; that, though he had his motion ready, and had heard of the motion which was intended for ratification, he waited till that motion should be made, and had afterwards waited for some time, in expectation that the gentleman from Halifax, and the gentleman from Edenton, would both speak to it. He had no objection to adjourning, but his motion would be still before the house.

Here there was a great cry for the question.

Mr. Iredell: [The cry for the question still continuing.] Mr. Chairman, I desire to be heard, notwithstanding the cry of "The question! the question!" Gentlemen have no right to prevent any member from speaking to it, if he thinks fit. [The house subsided into order.] Unimportant as I may be myself, my constituents are as respectable as those of any member in the house. It has, indeed, sir, been my misfortune to be under the necessity of troubling the house much oftener than I wished, owing to a circumstance which I have greatly regretted—that so few gentlemen take a share in our debates, though many are capable of doing so with propriety. I should have spoken to the question at large before, if I had not fully depended on some other gentleman doing it; and therefore I did not prepare myself by taking notes of what was said. However, I beg leave now to make few observations. I think this Constitution safe. I have not heard a single objection which, in my opinion, showed that it was dangerous. Some particular parts have been objected to, and amendments pointed out. Though I think it perfectly safe, yet, with respect to any amendments which do not destroy the substance of the Constitution, but will tend to give greater satisfaction, I should approve of them, because I should prefer that system which would most tend to conciliate all parties. On these principles, I am of opinion that some amendments should be proposed.

The general ground of the objections seems to be, that the power proposed to the general government may be abused. If we give no power but such as may not be abused, we shall give none; for all delegated powers may be abused. There are two extremes equally dangerous to liberty. These are tyranny and anarchy. The medium between these two is the true government to protect the people. In my opinion, this Constitution is well calculated to guard against both these extremes. The possibility of general abuses ought not to be urged, but particular ones pointed out.

*   *   *

We must be contented if powers be as well guarded as the nature of them will permit. In regard to amending before or after the adoption, the difference is very great. I beg leave to state my idea of that difference. I mentioned, one day before, the adoption by ten states. When I did so, it was not to influence any person with respect to the merits of the Constitution, but as a reason for coolness and deliberation. In my opinion, when so great a majority of the American people have adopted it, it is a strong evidence in its favor; for it is not probable that ten states would have agreed to a bad constitution. If we do not adopt, we are no longer in the Union with the other states. We ought to consider seriously before we determine our connection with them. The safety and happiness of this state depend upon it. Without that union, what would have been our condition now? A striking instance will point out this very clearly. At the beginning of the late war with Great Britain, the Parliament thought proper to stop all commercial intercourse with the American provinces. They passed a general prohibitory act, from which New York and North Carolina were at first excepted. Why were they excepted? They had been as active in opposition as the other states; but this was an expedient to divide the Northern from the Middle States, and to break the heart of the Southern. Had New York and North Carolina been weak enough to fall into this snare, we probably should not now have been an independent people. [Mr. Person called to order, and intimated that the gentleman meant to reflect on the opposers of the Constitution, as if they were friendly to the British interest. Mr. Iredell warmly resented the interruption, declaring he was perfectly in order, that it was disorderly to interrupt him; and, in respect to Mr. Person's insinuation as to his intention, he declared, in the most solemn manner, he had no such, being well assured the opposers of the Constitution were equally friendly to the independence of America as its supporters. He then proceeded:]

I say, they endeavored to divide us. North Carolina and New York had too much sense to be taken in by their artifices. Union enabled us then to defeat their endeavors: union will enable us to defeat all the machinations of our enemies hereafter. The friends of their country must lament our present unhappy divisions. Most free countries have lost their liberties by means of dissensions among themselves. They united in war and danger. When peace and apparent security came, they split into factions and parties, and thereby became a prey to foreign invaders. This shows the necessity of union. In urging the danger of disunion so strongly, I beg leave again to say, that I mean not to reflect on any gentleman whatsoever, as if his wishes were directed to so wicked a purpose. I am sure such an insinuation as the gentleman from Granville supposed I intended, would be unjust, as I know some of the warmest opposers of Great Britain are now among the warmest opponents of the proposed Constitution. Such a suggestion never entered my head; and I can say with truth that, warmly as I am attached to this Constitution, and though I am convinced that the salvation of our country depends upon the adoption of it, I would not procure its success by one unworthy action or one ungenerous word. A gentleman has said that we ought to determine in the same manner as if no state had adopted the Constitution. The general principle is right; but we ought to consider our peculiar situation. We cannot exist by ourselves. If we imitate the examples of some respectable states that have proposed amendments subsequent to their ratification, we shall add our weight to have these amendments carried, as our representatives will be in Congress to enforce them. Gentlemen entertain a jealousy of the Eastern States. To withdraw ourselves from the Southern States will be increasing the northern influence. The loss of one state may be attended with particular prejudice. It will be a good while before amendments of any kind can take place; and in the mean time, if we do not adopt, we shall have no share or agency in their transactions, though we may be ultimately bound by them. The first session of Congress will probably be the most important of any for many years. A general code of laws will then be established in execution of every power contained in the Constitution. If we ratify, and propose amendments, our representatives will be there to act in this important business. If we do not, our interest may suffer; nor will the system be afterwards altered merely to accommodate our wishes. Besides that, one house may prevent a measure from taking place, but both must concur in repealing it. I therefore think an adoption proposing subsequent amendments far safer and more desirable than the other mode; nor do I doubt that every amendment, not of a local nature, nor injuring essentially the material power of the Constitution, but principally calculated to guard against misconstruction the real liberties of the people, will be readily obtained.

The previous question, after some desultory conversation, was now put: for it, 183; against it, 84; majority in favor of the motion, 99.

[Thursday, July 31]

Gov. Johnston: Mr. Chairman, it appears to me that, if the motion made yesterday, by the gentleman from Halifax, be adopted, it will not answer the intention of the people. It determines nothing with respect to the Constitution. We were sent here to determine upon it. [Here his excellency read the resolution of the Assembly under which the Convention met.] If we do not decide upon the Constitution, we shall have nothing to report to Congress. We shall be entirely out of the Union, and stand by ourselves. I wish gentlemen would pause a moment before they decide so awful a question. To whom are we to refer these amendments which are to be proposed as the condition of our adoption? The present Congress have nothing to do with them. Their authority extends only to introduce the new government, not to receive any proposition of amendments. Shall we present them to the new Congress? In what manner can that be done? We shall have no representatives to introduce them. We may indeed appoint ambassadors to the United States of America, to represent what scruples North Carolina has in regard to their Constitution. I know no other way. A number of states have proposed amendments to the Constitution, and ratified in the mean time. These will have great weight and influence in Congress, and may prevail in getting material amendments proposed. We shall have no share in voting upon any of these amendments; for, in my humbler opinion, we shall be entirely out of the Union, and can be considered only as a foreign power. It is true, the United States may admit us hereafter. But they may admit us on terms unequal and disadvantageous to us. In the mean time, many of their laws, by which we shall be hereafter bound, may be particularly injurious to the interests of this state, as we shall have no share in their formation. Gentlemen say they will not be influenced by what others have done. I must confess that the example of great and good men, and wise states, has great weight with me.

It is said there is a probability New York will not adopt this Constitution. Perhaps she may not. But it is generally supposed that the principal reason of her opposing it arises from a selfish motive. She has it now in her power to tax indirectly two contiguous states. Connecticut and New Jersey contribute to pay a great part of the taxes of that state, by consuming large quantities of goods, the duties of which are now levied for the benefit of New York only. A similar policy may induce the United States to lay restrictions on us, if we are out of the Union. These considerations ought to have great weight with us. We can derive very little assistance from any thing New York will do on our behalf. Her views are diametrically opposite to ours. That state wants all her imposts for her own exclusive support. It is our interest that all imposts should go into the general treasury. Should Congress receive our commissioners, it will be a considerable time before this business will be decided on. It will be some time after Congress meets before a convention is appointed, and some time will elapse before the convention meets. What they will do, will be transmitted to each of the states, and then a convention, or the legislature, in each state, will have to ratify it ultimately. This will probably take up eighteen months or two years. In the mean time, the national government is going on. Congress will appoint all the great officers, and will proceed to make laws and form regulations for the future government of the United States. This state, during that time, will have no share in their proceedings, or any negative on any business before them. Another inconvenience which will arise is this: we shall be deprived of the benefit of the impost, which, under the new government, is an additional fund; all the states having a common right to it. By being in the Union we should have a right to our proportionate share of all the duties and imposts collected in all the states. But by adopting this resolution, we shall lose the benefit of this, which is an object worthy of attention. Upon the whole, I can see no possible good that will result to this state from following the resolution before us. I have not the vanity to think that any reasons I offer will have any weight. But I came from a respectable county to give my reasons for or against the Constitution. They expect them from me, and to suppress them would be a violation of my duty.

Mr. Willie Jones: Mr. Chairman, the gentleman last up has mentioned the resolution of Congress now lying before us, and the act of Assembly under which we met here, which says that we should deliberate and determine on the Constitution. What is to be inferred from that? Are we to ratify it at all events? Have we not an equal right to reject? We do not determine by neither rejecting nor adopting. It is objected we shall be out of the Union. So I wish to be. We are left at liberty to come in at any time. It is said we shall suffer a great loss for want of a share of the impost. I have no doubt we shall have it when we come in, as much as if we adopted now. I have a resolution in my pocket, which I intend to introduce if this resolution is carried, recommending it to the legislature to lay an impost, for the use of Congress, on goods imported into this state, similar to that which may be laid by Congress on goods imported into the adopting states. This shows the committee what is my intention, and on what footing we are to be. This being the case, I will forfeit my life that we shall come in for a share. It is said that all the offices of Congress will be filled, and we shall have no share in appointing the officers. This is an objection of very little importance. Gentlemen need not be in such haste. If left eighteen months or two years without offices, it is no great cause of alarm. The gentleman further said that we could send no representatives, but must send ambassadors to Congress, as a foreign power. I assert the contrary; and that, whenever a convention of the states is called, North Carolina will be called upon like the rest. I do not know what these gentlemen would desire.

I am very sensible that there is a great majority against the Constitution. If we take the question as they propose they know it would be rejected, and bring on us all the dreadful consequences which they feelingly foretell, but which can never in the least alarm me. I have endeavored to fall in with their opinions, but could not. We have a right, in plain terms, to refuse it if we think proper. I have, in my proposition, adopted, word for word, the Virginia amendments, with one or two additional ones. We run no risk of being excluded from the Union when we think proper to come in. Virginia, our next neighbor, will not oppose our admission. We have a common cause with her. She wishes the same alterations. We are of the greatest importance to her. She will have great weight in Congress; and there is no doubt but she will do every thing she can to bring us into the Union. South Carolina and Georgia are deeply interested in our being admitted. The Creek nation would overturn these two states without our aid. They cannot exist without North Carolina. There is no doubt we shall obtain our amendments, and come into the Union when we please. Massachusetts, New Hampshire, and other states, have proposed amendments. New York will do also, if she ratifies. There will be a majority of the states, and the most respectable, important, and extensive states also, desirous of amendments, and favorable to our admission.

As great names have been mentioned, I beg leave to mention the authority of Mr. Jefferson, whose great abilities and respectability are well known. When the Convention sat in Richmond, in Virginia, Mr. Madison received a letter from him. In that letter he said he wished nine states would adopt it, not because it deserved ratification, but to preserve the Union. But he wished that the other four states would reject it, that there might be a certainty of obtaining amendments. Congress may go on, and take no notice of our amendments; but I am confident they will do nothing of importance till a convention be called. If I recollect rightly, amendments may be ratified either by conventions or the legislatures of the states. In either case, it may take up about eighteen months. For my part, I would rather be eighteen years out of the Union than adopt it in its present defective form.

Gov. Johnston: Mr. Chairman, I wish to clear myself from the imputation of the gentleman last up. If any part of my conduct warrants his aspersion,— if ever I hunted after offices, or sought public favors to promote private interest,—let the instances be pointed out. If I know myself I never did. It is easy for any man to throw out illiberal and ungenerous insinuations. I have no view to offices under this Constitution. My views are much humbler. When I spoke of Congress establishing offices, I meant great offices, the establishment of which might affect the interests of the states; and I added that they would proceed to make laws, deeply affecting us, without any influence of our own. As to the appointment of the officers, it is of no importance to me who is an officer, if he be a good man.

Mr. Jones replied, that in every publication one might see ill motives assigned to the opposers of the Constitution. One reason assigned for their opposition was, that they feared the loss of their influence, and diminution of their importance. He said, that it was fair its opposers should be permitted to retort, and assign a reason equally selfish for the conduct of its friends. Expectation to offices might influence them, as well as the loss of office and influence might bias the others. He intended no allusion to that gentleman, for whom he declared he had the highest respect.

Mr. Spencer rose in support of the motion of the gentleman from Halifax. He premised, that he wished no resolution to be carried without the utmost deliberation and candor. He thought the proposition was couched in such modest terms as could not possibly give offence to the other states; that the amendments it proposed were to be laid before Congress, and would probably be admitted, as they were similar to those which were wished for and proposed by several of the adopting states. He always thought it more proper, and agreeable to prudence, to propose amendments previous, rather than subsequent, to ratification. He said that, if two or more persons entered into a copartnership, and employed a scrivener to draw up the articles of copartnership in a particular form, and, on reading them, they found them to be erroneous,—it would be thought very strange if any of them should say, "Sign it first, and we shall have it altered hereafter." If it should be signed before alteration, it would be considred as an act of indiscretion. As, therefore, it was a principle of prudence, in matters of private property, not to assent to any obligation till its errors were removed, he thought the principle infinitely more necessary to be attended to in a matter which concerned such a number of people, and so many millions yet unborn. Gentlemen said they should be out of the Union. He observed, that they were before confederated with the other states by a solemn compact, which was not to be dissolved without the consent of every state in the Union. North Carolina had not assented to its dissolution. If it was dissolved, it was not their fault, but that of the adopting states. It was a maxim of law that the same solemnities were necessary to destroy, which were necessary to create, a deed or contract. He was of opinion that, if they should be out of the Union by proposing previous amendments, they were as much so now. If the adoption by nine states enabled them to exclude the other four states, he thought North Carolina might then be considered as excluded. But he did not think that doctrine well founded. On the contrary, he thought each state might come into the Union when she thought proper. He confessed it gave him some concern, but he looked on the short exclusion of eighteen months—if it might be called exclusion—as infinitely less dangerous than an unconditional adoption. He expected the amendments would be adopted, and when they were, this state was ready to embrace it. No great inconvenience could result from this. [Mr. Spencer made some other remarks, but spoke too low to be heard.]

Mr. Iredell: Mr. Chairman, in my opinion, this is a very awful moment. On a right decision of this question may possibly depend the peace and happiness of our country for ages. Whatever be the decision of the house on this subject, it ought to be well weighed before it is given. We ought to view our situation in all its consequences, and determine with the utmost caution and deliberation. It has been suggested, not only out of doors, but during the course of the debates, that, if we are out of the Union, it will be the fault of other states, and not ours. It is true that, by the Articles of Confederation, the consent of each state was necessary for any alteration. It is also true that the consent of nine states renders the Constitution binding on them. The unhappy consequences of that unfortunate article in this Confederation produced the necessity of this article in the Constitution. Every body knows that, through the peculiar obstinacy of Rhode Island, many great advantages were lost. Notwithstanding her weakness, she uniformly opposed every regulation for the benefit and honor of the Union at large. The other states were driven to the necessity of providing for their own security and welfare, without waiting for the consent of that little state. The deputies from twelve states unanimously concurred in opinion that the happiness of all America ought not to be sacrificed to the caprice and obstinacy of so inconsiderable a part.

It will often happen, in the course of human affairs, that the policy which is proper on common occasions fails, and that laws which do very well in the regular administration of a government cannot stand when every thing is going into confusion. In such a case, the safety of the community must supersede every other consideration, and every subsisting regulation which interferes with that must be departed from, rather than that the people should be ruined. The Convention, therefore, with a degree of manliness which I admire, dispensed with a unanimous consent for the present change, and at the same time provided a permanent remedy for this evil, not barely by dispensing with the consent of one member in future alterations, but by making the consent of nine sufficient for the whole, if the rest did not agree, considering that the consent of so large a number ought in reason to govern the whole; and the proportion was taken from the old Confederation, which in the most important cases required the consent of nine, and in every thing, except the alteration of the Constitution, made that number sufficient. It has been objected, that the adoption of this government would be improper, because it would interfere with the oath of allegiance to the state. No oath of allegiance requires us to sacrifice the safety of our country. When the British government attempted to establish a tyranny in America, the people did not think their oath of allegiance bound them to submit to it. I had taken that oath several times myself, but had no scruple to oppose their tyrannical measures. The great principle is, The safety of the people is the supreme law. Government was originally instituted for their welfare, and whatever may be its form, this ought to be its object. This is the fundamental principle on which our government is founded. In other countries, they suppose the existence of original compact, and infer that, if the sovereign violates his part of it, the people have a right to resist. If he does not, the government must remain unchanged, unless the sovereign consents to an alteration. In America, our governments have been clearly created by the people themselves. The same authority that created can destroy; and the people may undoubtedly change the government, not because it is ill exercised, but because they conceive another form will be more conducive to their welfare. I have stated the reasons for departing from the rigid article in the Confederation requiring a unanimous consent. We were compelled to do this, or see our country ruined. In the manner of the dispensation, the Convention, however, appear to have acted with great prudence, in copying the example of the Confederation in all other particulars of the greatest moment, by authorizing nine states to bind the whole. It is suggested, indeed, that, though ten states have adopted this new Constitution, yet, as they had no right to dissolve the old Articles of Confederation, these still subsist, and the old Union remains, of which we are a part. The truth of that suggestion may well be doubted, on this ground: when the principles of a constitution are violated, the constitution itself is dissolved, or may be dissolved at the pleasure of the parties to it. Now, according to the Articles of Confederation, Congress had authority to demand money, in a certain proportion, from the respective states, to answer the exigencies of the Union. Whatever requisitions they made for that purpose were constitutionally binding on the states. The states had no discretion except as to the mode of raising the money. Perhaps every state has committed repeated violations of the demands of Congress. I do not believe it was from any dishonorable intention in many of the states; but whatever was the cause, the fact is, such violations were committed. The consequence is that, upon the principle I have mentioned, (and in which I believe all writers agree,) the Articles of Confederation are no longer binding. It is alleged that, by making the consent of nine sufficient to form a government for themselves, the first nine may exclude the other four. This is a very extraordinary allegation. When the new Constitution was proposed, it was proposed to the thirteen states in the Union. It was desired that all should agree, if possible; but if that could not be obtained, they took care that nine states might at least save themselves from destruction. Each, undoubtedly, had a right on the first proposition, because it was proposed to them all. The only doubt can be, whether they had a right afterwards. In my opinion, when any state has once rejected the Constitution, it cannot claim to come in afterwards as a matter of right.

If it does not, in plain terms, reject, but refuses to accede for the present, I think the other states may regard this as an absolute rejection, and refuse to admit us afterwards but at their pleasure, and on what terms they please. Gentlemen wish for amendments. On this subject, though we may differ as to the necessity of amendments, I believe none will deny the propriety of proposing some, if only for the purpose of giving more general satisfaction. The question, then, is, whether it is most prudent for us to come into the Union immediately, and propose amendments, (as has been done in the other states,) or to propose amendments, and be out of the Union till all these be agreed to by the other states. The consequences of either resolution I beg leave to state. By adopting, we shall be in the Union with our sister states, which is the only foundation of our prosperity and safety. We shall avoid the danger of a separation, a danger of which the latent effects are unknown. So far am I convinced of the necessity of the Union, that I would give up many things against my own opinion to obtain it. If we sacrificed it by a rejection of the Constitution, or a refusal to adopt, (which amounts, I think, nearly to the same thing,) the very circumstance of disunion may occasion animosity between us and the inhabitants of the other states, which may be the means of severing us forever.

We shall lose the benefit which must accrue to the other states from the new government. Their trade will flourish; goods will sell cheap; their commodities will rise in value; and their distresses, occasioned by the war, will gradually be removed. Ours, for want of these advantages, will continue. Another very material consequence will result from it: we shall lose our share of the imposts in all the states, which, under this Constitution, is to go into the federal treasury. It is the particular local interest of this state to adopt, on this account, more, perhaps, than that of any other member of the Union. At present, all these imposts go into the respective treasury of each state, and we well know our own are of little consequence, compared to those of the other states in general. The gentleman from Halifax (Mr. Jones) has offered an expedient to prevent the loss of our share of the impost. In my opinion, that expedient will not answer the purpose. The amount of duties on goods imported into this state is very little; and if these resolutions are agreed to, it will be less. I ask any gentleman whether the United States would receive, from the duties of this state, so much as would be our proportion, under the Constitution, of the duties on goods imported in all the states. Our duties would be no manner of compensation for such proportion. What would be the language of Congress on our holding forth such an offer? "If you are willing to enjoy the benefits of the Union, you must be subject to all the laws of it. We will make no partial agreement with you." This would probably be their language. I have no doubt all America would wish North Carolina to be a member of the Union. It is of importance to them. But we ought to consider whether ten states can do longer without one, or one without ten. On a competition, which will give way? The adopting states will say, "Other states had objections as well as you; but rather than separate, they agreed to come into the Union, trusting to the justice of the other states for the adoption of proper amendments afterwards. One most respectable state, Virginia, has pursued this measure, though apparently averse to the system as it now stands. But you have laid down the condition on which alone you will come into the Union. We must accede to your particular propositions, or be disunited from you altogether. Is it fit that North Carolina shall dictate to the whole Union? We may be convinced by your reason, but our conduct will certainly not be altered by your resistance."

I beg leave to say, if Virginia thought it right to adopt and propose amendments, under the circumstances of the Constitution at that time, surely it is much more so for us in our present situation. That state, as was justly observed, is a most powerful and respectable one. Had she held out, it would have been a subject of most serious alarm. But she thought the risk of losing the union altogether too dangerous to be incurred. She did not then know of the ratification of New Hampshire. If she thought it necessary to adopt, when only eight states had ratified, is it not much more necessary for us after the ratification by ten? I do not say that we ought servilely to imitate any example. But I may say, that the examples of wise men and intelligent nations are worthy of respect; and that, in general, we may be much safer in following than in departing from them. In my opinion, as many of the amendments proposed are similar to amendments recommended not only by Virginia, but by other states, there is great probability of their being obtained. All the amendments proposed, undoubtedly, will not be, nor I think ought to be; but such as tend to secure more effectually the liberties of the people against an abuse of the powers granted in all human probability, will; for in such amendments all the states are equally interested. The probability of such amendments being obtained is extremely great; for though three states ratified the Constitution unanimously, there has been a considerable opposition in the other states. In New Hampshire, the majority was small. In Massachusetts, there was a strong opposition. In Connecticut, the opposition was about one third: so it was in Pennsylvania. In Maryland, the minority was small, but very respectable. In Virginia, they had little more than a bare majority. There was a powerful minority in South Carolina. Can any man pretend to say that, thus circumstanced, the states would disapprove of amendments calculated to give satisfaction to the people at large? There is a very great probability, if not an absolute certainty, that amendments will be obtained. The interest of North Carolina would add greatly to the scale in their favor. If we do not accede, we may injure the states who wish for amendments, by withdrawing ourselves from their assistance. We are not, at any event, in a condition to stand alone. God forbid we should be a moment separated from our sister states! If we are, we shall be in great danger of a separation forever. I trust every gentleman will pause before he contributes to so awful an event.

We have been happy in our connection with the other states. Our freedom, independence, every thing dear to us, has been derived from that union we are now going rashly to dissolve. If we are to be separated, let every gentleman well weigh the ground he stands on before he votes for the separation. Let him not have to reproach himself, hereafter, that he voted without due consideration for a measure that proved the destruction of his country.

*   *   *

[Friday, August 1]

Mr. Iredell: Mr. President: I believe, sir, all debate is now at an end. It is useless to contend any longer against a majority that is irresistible. We submit, with the deference that becomes us, to the decision of a majority; but my friends and myself are anxious that something may appear on the Journal to show our sentiments on the subject. I have therefore a resolution in my hand to offer, not with a view of creating any debate, (for I know it will be instantly rejected,) but merely that it may be entered on the Journal, with the yeas and nays taken upon it, in order that our constituents and the world may know what our opinions really were on this important occasion. We prefer this to the exceptionable mode of a protest, which might increase the spirit of party animosity among the people of this country, which is an event we wish to prevent, if possible. I therefore, sir, have the honor of moving—"That the consideration of the report of the committee be postponed in order to take up the consideration of the following resolution."

Mr. Iredell then read the resolution in his place, and afterwards delivered it in at the clerk's table, and his motion was seconded by Mr. John Skinner.

Mr. Joseph M'Dowall, and several other gentlemen, most strongly objected against the propriety of this motion. They thought it improper, unprecedented, and a great contempt of the voice of the majority.

Mr. Iredell replied, that he thought it perfectly regular, and by no means a contempt of the majority. The sole intention of it was to show the opinion of the minority, which could not, in any other manner, be so properly done. They wished to justify themselves to their constituents, and the people at large would judge between the merits of the two propositions. They wished also to avoid, if possible, the disagreeable alternative of a protest. This being the first time he ever had the honor of being a member of a representative body, he did not solely confide in his own judgment, as to the proper manner of bringing his resolution forward, but had consulted a very respectable and experienced member of that house, who recommended this method to him; and he well knew it was conformable to a frequent practice in Congress, as he had observed by their Journals. Each member had an equal right to make a motion, and if seconded, a vote ought to be taken upon it; and he trusted the majority would not be so arbitrary as to prevent them from taking this method to deliver their sentiments to the world.

He was supported by Mr. Maclaine and Mr. Spaight.

Mr. Willie Jones and Mr. Spencer insisted on its being irregular, and said they might protest. Mr. Jones said, there never was an example of the kind before; that such a practice did not prevail in Congress when he was a member of it, and he well knew no such practice had ever prevailed in the Assembly.

Mr. Davie said, he was sorry that gentlemen should not deal fairly and liberally with one another. He declared it was perfectly parliamentary, and the usual practice in Congress. They were in possession of the motion, and could not get rid of it without taking a vote upon it. It was in the nature of a previous question. He declared that nothing hurt his feelings so much as the blind tyranny of a dead majority.

After a warm discussion on this point by several gentlemen on both sides of the house, it was at length intimated to Mr. Iredell, by Mr. Spaight, across the house, that Mr. Lenoir, and some other gentlemen of the majority, wished he would withdraw his motion for the present, on purpose that the resolution of the committee might be first entered on the Journal, which had not been done; and afterwards his motion might be renewed. Mr. Iredell declared he would readily agree to this, if the gentleman who had seconded him would, desiring the house to remember that he only withdrew his motion for that reason, and hoped he should have leave to introduce it afterwards; which seemed to be understood. He accordingly, with the consent of Mr. Skinner, withdrew his motion; and the resolution of the committee of the whole house was then read, and ordered to be entered on the Journal. The resolution was accordingly read and entered, as follows, viz.:

Resolved, That a declaration of rights, asserting and securing from encroachment the great principles of civil and religious liberty, and the unalienable rights of the people, together with amendments to the most ambiguous and exceptionable parts of the said Constitution of government, ought to be laid before Congress, and the convention of the states that shall or may be called for the purpose of amending the said Constitution, for their consideration, previous to the ratification of the Constitution aforesaid on the part of the state of North Carolina.

Declaration of Rights

1. That there are certain natural rights, of which men, when they form a social compact, cannot deprive or divest their posterity, among which are the enjoyment of life and liberty, with the means of acquiring, possessing, and protecting property, and pursuing and obtaining happiness and safety.

2. That all power is naturally vested in, and consequently derived from, the people; that magistrates, therefore, are their trustees and agents, and at all times amenable to them.

3. That government ought to be instituted for the common benefit, protection, and security, of the people; and that the doctrine of non-resistance

against arbitrary power and oppression is absurd, slavish, and destructive to the good and happiness of mankind.

4. That no man or set of men are entitled to exclusive or separate public emoluments or privileges from the community, but in consideration of public services, which not being descendible, neither ought the offices of magistrate, legislator, or judge, or any other public office, to be hereditary.

5. That the legislative, executive, and judiciary powers of government should be separate and distinct, and that the members of the two first may be restrained from oppression by feeling and participating the public burdens: they should, at fixed periods, be reduced to a private station, return into the mass of the people, and the vacancies be supplied by certain and regular elections, in which all or any part of the former members to be eligible or ineligible, as the rules of the constitution of government and the laws shall direct.

6. That elections of representatives in the legislature ought to be free and frequent, and all men having sufficient evidence of permanent common interest with, and attachment to, the community, ought to have the right of suffrage; and no aid, charge, tax, or fee, can be set, rated, or levied, upon the people without their own consent, or that of their representatives so elected; nor can they be bound by any law to which they have not in like manner assented for the public good.

7. That all power of suspending laws, or the execution of laws, by any authority, without the consent of the representatives of the people in the legislature, is injurious to their rights, and ought not to be exercised.

8. That, in all capital and criminal prosecutions, a man hath a right to demand the cause and nature of his accusation, to be confronted with the accusers and witnesses, to call for evidence, and be allowed counsel in his favor, and a fair and speedy trial by an impartial jury of his vicinage, without whose unanimous consent he cannot be found guilty, (except in the government of the land and naval forces;) nor can he be compelled to give evidence against himself.

9. That no freeman ought to be taken, imprisoned, or disseized of his freehold, liberties, privileges, or franchises, or outlawed or exiled, or in any manner destroyed, or deprived of his life, liberty, or property, but by the law of the land.

10. That every freeman, restrained of his liberty, is entitled to a remedy to inquire into the lawfulness thereof, and to remove the same if unlawful; and that such remedy ought not to be denied nor delayed.

11. That, in controversies respecting property, and in suits between man and man, the ancient trial by jury is one of the greatest securities to the rights of the people, and ought to remain sacred and inviolable.

12. That every freeman ought to find a certain remedy, by recourse to the laws, for all injuries and wrongs he may receive in his person, property, or

character; he ought to obtain right and justice freely without sale, completely and without denial, promptly and without delay; and that all establishments or regulations contravening these rights are oppressive and unjust.

13. That excessive bail ought not to be required, nor excessive fines imposed, nor cruel and unusual punishments inflicted.

14. That every freeman has a right to be secure from all unreasonable searches and seizures of his person, his papers and property; all warrants, therefore, to search suspected places, or to apprehend any suspected person, without specially naming or describing the place or person, are dangerous, and ought not to be granted.

15. That the people have a right peaceably to assemble together, to consult for the common good, or to instruct their representatives; and that every freeman has a right to petition or apply to the legislature for redress of grievances.

16. That the people have a right to freedom of speech, and of writing and publishing their sentiments; that freedom of the press is one of the greatest bulwarks of liberty, and ought not to be violated.

17. That the people have a right to keep and bear arms; that a well regulated militia, composed of the body of the people, trained to arms, is the proper, natural, and safe defence of a free state; that standing armies, in time of peace, are dangerous to liberty, and therefore ought to be avoided, as far as the circumstances and protection of the community will admit; and that, in all cases, the military should be under strict subordination to, and governed by, the civil power.

18. That no soldier, in time of peace, ought to be quartered in any house without the consent of the owner, and in time of war, in such manner only as the laws direct.

19. That any person religiously scrupulous of bearing arms ought to be exempted, upon payment of an equivalent to employ another to bear arms in his stead.

20. That religion, or the duty which we owe to our Creator, and the manner of discharging it, can be directed only by reason and conviction, not by force or violence; and therefore all men have an equal, natural, and unalienable right to the free exercise of religion, according to the dictates of conscience, and that no particular religious sect or society ought to be favored or established by law in preference to others.

Amendments to the Constitution

1. That each state in the Union shall respectively retain every power, jurisdiction, and right, which is not by this Constitution delegated to the Congress of the United States, or to the departments of the federal government.

2. That there shall be one representative for every thirty thousand according to the enumeration or census mentioned in the Constitution, until the

whole number of representatives amounts to two hundred; after which that number shall be continued or increased as Congress shall direct, upon the principles fixed in the Constitution, by apportioning the representatives of each state to some greater number of the people, from time to time, as the population increases.

3. When Congress shall lay direct taxes or excises, they shall immediately inform the executive power of each state of the quota of such state, according to the census herein directed, which is proposed to be thereby raised; and if the legislature of any state shall pass any law which shall be effectual for raising such quota at the time required by Congress, the taxes and excises laid by Congress shall not be collected in such state.

4. That the members of the Senate and House of Representatives shall be ineligible to, and incapable of holding, any civil office under the authority of the United States, during the time for which they shall respectively be elected.

5. That the Journals of the proceedings of the Senate and House of Representatives shall be published at least once in every year, except such parts thereof relating to treaties, alliances, or military operations, as in their judgment require secrecy.

6. That a regular statement and account of receipts and expenditures of all public moneys shall be published at least once in every year.

7. That no commercial treaty shall be ratified without the concurrence of two thirds of the whole number of the members of the Senate. And no treaty, ceding, contracting, restraining, or suspending, the territorial rights or claims of the United States, or any of them, or their, or any of their, rights or claims of fishing in the American seas, or navigating the American rivers, shall be made, but in cases of the most urgent and extreme necessity; nor shall any such treaty be ratified without the concurrence of three fourths of the whole number of the members of both houses respectively.

8. That no navigation law, or law regulating commerce, shall be passed without the consent of two thirds of the members present in both houses.

9. That no standing army or regular troops shall be raised or kept up in time of peace, without the consent of two thirds of the members present in both houses.

10. That no soldier shall be enlisted for any longer term than four years, except in time of war, and then for no longer term than the continuance of the war.

11. That each state respectively shall have the power to provide for organizing, arming, and disciplining its own militia, whensoever Congress shall omit or neglect to provide for the same; that the militia shall not be subject to martial law, except when in actual service in time of war, invasion, or rebellion; and when not in the actual service of the United States, shall be subject only to such fines, penalties, and punishments, as shall be directed or inflicted by the laws of its own state.

12. That Congress shall not declare any state to be in rebellion, without the consent of at least two thirds of all the members present in both houses.

13. That the exclusive power of legislation given to Congress over the federal town and its adjacent district, and other places purchased or to be purchased by Congress of any of the states, shall extend only to such regulations as respect the police and good government thereof.

14. That no person shall be capable of being President of the United States for more than eight years in any term of fifteen years.

15. That the judicial power of the United States shall be tested in one Supreme Court, and in such courts of admiralty as Congress may from time to time ordain and establish in any of the different states. The judicial power shall extend to all cases in law and equity arising under treaties made, or which shall be made, under the authority of the United States; to all cases affecting ambassadors, other foreign ministers, and consuls; to all cases of admiralty and maritime jurisdiction; to controversies to which the United States shall be a party; to controversies between two or more states, and between parties claiming lands under the grants of different states. In all cases affecting ambassadors, other foreign ministers, and consuls, and those in which a state shall be a party, the Supreme Court shall have original jurisdiction. In all other cases before mentioned, the Supreme Court shall have appellate jurisdiction as to matters of law only, except in cases of equity, and of admiralty and maritime jurisdiction, in which the Supreme Court shall have appellate jurisdiction both as to law and fact, with such exceptions, and under such regulations, as the Congress shall make: but the judicial power of the United States shall extend to no case where the cause of action shall have originated before the ratification of this Constitution, except in disputes between states about their territory, disputes between persons claiming lands under the grants of different states, and suits for debts due to the United States.

16. That, in criminal prosecutions, no man shall be restrained in the exercise of the usual and accustomed right of challenging or excepting to the jury.

17. That Congress shall not alter, modify, or interfere in, the times, places, or manner, of holding elections for senators and representatives, or either of them, except when the legislature of any state shall neglect, refuse, or be disabled, by invasion or rebellion, to prescribe the same.

18. That those clauses which declare that Congress shall not exercise certain powers be not interpreted in any manner whatsoever to extend the power of Congress; but that they be construed either as making exceptions to the specified powers, where this shall be the case, or otherwise as inserted merely for greater caution.

19. That the laws ascertaining the compensation of senators and representatives for their services, be postponed in their operation until after the

election of representatives immediately succeeding the passing thereof, that excepted which shall first be passed on the subject.

20. That some tribunal other than the Senate be provided for trying impeachments of senators.

21. That the salary of a judge shall not be increased or diminished during his continuance in office, otherwise than by general regulations of salary, which may take place on a revision of the subject at stated periods of not less than seven years, to commence from the time such salaries shall be first ascertained by Congress.

22. That Congress erect no company of merchants with exclusive advantages of commerce.

23. That no treaties which shall be directly opposed to the existing laws of the United States in Congress assembled shall be valid until such laws shall be repealed, or made conformable to such treaty; nor shall any treaty be valid which is contradictory to the Constitution of the United States.

24. That the latter part of the 5th paragraph of the 9th section of the 1st article be altered to read thus: 'Nor shall vessels bound to a particular state be obliged to enter or pay duties in any other; nor, when bound from any one of the states, be obliged to clear in another.'

25. That Congress shall not, directly or indirectly, either by themselves or through the judiciary, interfere with any one of the states in the redemption of paper money already emitted and now in circulation, or in liquidating and discharging the public securities of any one of the states, but each and every state shall have the exclusive right of making such laws and regulations, for the above purposes, as they shall think proper.

26. That Congress shall not introduce foreign troops into the United States without the consent of two thirds of the members present of both houses."

Mr. Spencer then moved that the report of the committee be concurred with, and was seconded by Mr. J. M'Dowall.

Mr. Iredell moved that the consideration of that motion be postponed, in order to take into consideration the following resolution:

[Which resolution was the same he introduced before, and which he afterwards, in substance, moved by way of amendment.]

This gave rise to a very warm altercation on both sides, during which the house was in great confusion. Many gentlemen in the majority (particularly Mr. Willie Jones) strongly contended against the propriety of the motion. Several gentlemen in the minority resented, in strong terms, the arbitrary attempt of the majority (as they termed it) to suppress their sentiments; and Mr. Spaight, in particular, took notice, with great indignation, of the motion made to concur with the committee, when the gentleman from Edenton appeared in some measure to have had the faith of the house that he should have an opportunity to renew his motion, which he had withdrawn at the request of some of the majority themselves. Mr. Whitmill Hill spoke with great warmth, and declared that, in his opinion, if the majority persevered in their tyrannical attempt, the minority should secede.

Mr. Willie Jones still contended that the motion was altogether irregular and improper, and made a motion calculated to show that such a motion, made and seconded under the circumstances in which it had been introduced, was not entitled to be entered on the Journal. His motion, being seconded, was carried by a great majority. The yeas and nays were moved for, and were taking, when Mr. Iredell arose, and said he was sensible of the irregularity he was guilty of, and hoped he should be excused for it, but it arose from his desire of saving the house trouble; that Mr. Jones (he begged pardon for naming him) had proposed an expedient to him, with which he should be perfectly satisfied, if the house approved of it, as it was indifferent to him what was the mode, if his object in substance was obtained. The method proposed was, that the motion for concurrence should be withdrawn, and his resolution should be moved by way of an amendment. If the house, therefore, approved of this method, and the gentlemen who had moved and seconded the motion would agree to withdraw it, he hoped it would be deemed unnecessary to proceed with the yeas and nays.

Mr. Nathan Bryan said, the gentleman treated the majority with contempt. Mr. Iredell declared he had no such intention; but as the yeas and nays were taken on a difference between both sides of the house, which he hoped might be accommodated, he thought he might be excused for the liberty he had taken.

Mr. Spencer and Mr. M'Dowall, after some observations not distinctly heard, accordingly withdrew their motion; and it was agreed that the yeas and nays should not be taken, nor the motion which occasioned them entered on the Journal. Mr. Iredell then moved as follows, viz.:

That the report of the committee be amended, by striking out all the words of the said report except the two first, viz.: "Resolved, That," and that the following words be inserted in their room, viz.: —"this Convention, having fully deliberated on the Constitution proposed for the future government of the United States of America by the Federal Convention lately held, at Philadelphia, on the 17th day of September last, and having taken into their serious and solemn consideration the present critical situation of America, which induces them to be of opinion that, though certain amendments to the said Constitution may be wished for, yet that those amendments should be proposed subsequent to the ratification on the part of this state, and not previous to it: —they do, therefore, on behalf of the state of North Carolina, and the good people thereof, and by virtue of the authority to them delegated, ratify the said Constitution on the part of this state; and they do at the same time recommend that, as early as possible, the following amendments to the said Constitution may be proposed for the consideration and adoption of the several states in the Union, in one of the modes prescribed by the 5th article thereof: "

Amendments

1. Each state in the Union shall respectively retain every power, jurisdiction, and right, which is not by this Constitution delegated to the Congress of the United States, or to the departments of the general government; nor shall the said Congress, nor any department of the said government, exercise any act of authority over any individual in any of the said states, but such as can be justified under some power particularly given in this Constitution; but the said Constitution shall be considered at all times a solemn instrument, defining the extent of their authority and the limits of which they cannot rightfully in any instance exceed.

2. There shall be one representative for every thirty thousand, according to the enumeration or census mentioned in the Constitution, until the whole number of representatives amounts to two hundred; after which, that number shall be continued or increased, as Congress shall direct, upon the principles fixed in the Constitution, by apportioning the representatives of each state to some greater number of people, from time to time, as the population increases.

3. Each state respectively shall have the power to provide for organizing, arming, and disciplining, its own militia, whensoever Congress shall omit or neglect to provide for the same. The militia shall not be subject to martial law, except when in actual service in time of war, invasion, or rebellion; and when they are not in the actual service of the United States, they shall be subject only to such fines, penalties, and punishments, as shall be directed or inflicted by the laws of its own state.

4. The Congress shall not alter, modify, or interfere in the times, places, or manner, of holding elections for senators and representatives, or either of them, except when the legislature of any state shall neglect, refuse, or be disabled by invasion or rebellion, to prescribe the same.

5. The laws ascertaining the compensation of senators and representatives, for their services, shall be postponed in their operation until after the election of representatives immediately succeeding the passing thereof; that excepted which shall first be passed on the subject.

6. Instead of the following words in the 9th section of the 1st article, viz., "Nor shall vessels bound to or from one state be obliged to enter, clear, or pay duties, in another," [the meaning of which is by many deemed not sufficiently explicit,] it is proposed that the following shall be substituted: "No vessel bound to one state shall be obliged to enter or pay duties, to which such vessel may be liable at any port of entry, in any other state than that to which such vessel is bound; nor shall any vessel bound from one state be obliged to clear, or pay duties to which such vessel shall be liable at any port of clearance, in any other state than that from which such vessel is bound."

He was seconded by Mr. John Skinner.

The question was then put, "Will the Convention adopt that amendment or not?" and it was negatived; whereupon Mr. Iredell moved that the yeas and nays should be taken, and he was seconded by Mr. Steele. They were accordingly taken, and were as follows:

Yeas
His excellency, Samuel Johnston, President

Messrs. Ja's Iredell,
Archibald Maclaine,
Nathan Keas,
John G. Blount,
Thomas Alderson,
John Johnson,
Andrew Oliver,
Goodwin Elliston,
Charles M'Dowall,
Richard D. Spaight,
William J. Dawson,
James Porterfield,
Wm. Barry Grove,
George Elliott,
Wallis Styron,
William Shepperd,
　Carteret.
James Philips,
John Humphreys,
Michael Payne,
Charles Johnston,
Stephen Cabarrus,
Edmund Blount,
　Chowan.
Henry Abbot,
Isaac Gregory,
Peter Dauge,
Charles Grandy,
Enoch Sawyer,
George Lucas,
John Willis,
John Cade,
Elias Barnes,
Neil Brown,
James Winchester,
William Stokes,
Thomas Stewart,
Josiah Collins,
Thomas Hines,

Nathaniel Jones,
John Steele,
William R. Davie,
Joseph Reddick,
James Gregory,
Thomas Hunter,
　Gates.
Thomas Wyns,
Abraham Jones,
John Eborne,
James Jasper,
Caleb Forman,
Seth Hovey,
John Sloan,
John Moore,
William Maclaine,
Nathan Mayo,
William Slade,
William M'Kenzie,
Robert Erwin,
John Lane,
Thomas Reading,
Edward Everagain,
Enoch Rolfe,
Devotion Davis,
William Skinner,
Joshua Skinner,
Thomas Hervey,
John Skinner,
Samuel Harrel,
Joseph Leech,
Wm. Bridges,
Wm. Burden,
Edmund Blount,
　Tyrel.
Simeon Spruil,
David Tanner,
Whitmill Hill,
Benjamin Smith,

John Sitgreaves,
Nathaniel Allen,
Thomas Owen,
George Wyns,
David Perkins,

Joseph Ferebee,
Wm. Ferebee,
Wm. Baker,
Abner Neale.

Total: 84

Nays

Messrs. Willie Jones,
Samuel Spencer,
Lewis Lanier,
Thomas Wade,
Daniel Gould,
James Bonner,
Alexius M. Foster,
Lewis Dupree,
Thomas Brown,
James Greenlee,
Joseph M'Dowall,
Robert Miller,
Benjamin Williams,
Richard Nixon,
Thomas Armstrong,
Alex. M'Allister,
Robert Dickens,
George Roberts,
John Womack,
Ambrose Ramsey,
James Anderson,
Jos. Stewart,
Wm. Vestal,
Thomas Evans,
Thomas Hardiman,
Robert Weakly,
Wm. Donnelson,
Wm. Dobins,
Robert Diggs,
Bythel Bell,
Elisha Battle,
Wm. Fort,
Etheld. Gray,
Wm. Lancaster,
Thomas Sherrod,
John Norward,

Sterling Dupree,
Robert Williams,
Richard Moye,
Arthur Forbes,
David Caldwell,
Wm. Goudy,
Daniel Gillespie,
John Anderson,
John Hamilton,
Thomas Person,
Joseph Taylor,
Thornton Yancey,
Howell Lewis, Jun.,
E. Mitchell,
George Moore,
George Ledbetter,
Wm. Porter,
Zebedee Wood,
Edmund Waddell,
James Galloway,
J. Regan,
Joseph Winston,
James Gains,
Charles M'Annelly,
Absalom Bostick,
John Scott,
John Dunkin,
David Dodd,
Curtis Ivey,
Lewis Holmes,
Richard Clinton,
H. Holmes,
Robert Alison,
James Stewart,
John Tipton,
John Macon,

Thomas Christmass,
H. Monfort,
Wm. Taylor,
James Hanley,
Britain Saunders,
Wm. Lenoir,
R. Allen,
John Brown,
Joseph Herndon,
James Fletcher,
Lemuel Burkit,
Wm. Little,
Thomas King,
Nathan Bryan,
John H. Bryan,
Edward Whitty,
Robert Alexander,
James Johnson,
John Cox,
John Carrel,
Cornelius Doud,
Thomas Tyson,
W. Martin,
Thomas Hunter
  Martin.
John Graham,
Wm. Loftin,
Wm. Kindal,
Thomas Ussery,
Thomas Butler,
John Bentford,
James Vaughan,
Robert Peebles,
James Vinson,
Wm. S. Marnes,
Howell Ellin,
Redman Bunn,
John Bonds,
David Pridgen,
Daniel Yates,
Thomas Johnston,
John Spicer,
A. Tatom,
Alex. Mebane,

Wm. Mebane,
Wm. M'Cauley,
Wm. Shepperd,
  Orange.
Jonathan Linley,
Wyatt Hawkins,
James Payne,
John Graves,
John Blair,
Joseph Tipton,
Wm. Bethell,
Abraham Phillips,
John May,
Charles Galloway,
James Boswell,
John M'Allister,
David Looney,
John Sharpe,
Joseph Gaitier,
John A. Campbell,
John P. Williams,
Wm. Marshall,
Charles Robertson,
James Gillespie,
Charles Ward,
Wm. Randal,
Frederick Harget,
Richard M'Kinnie,
John Cains,
Jacob Leonard,
Thomas Carson,
Richard Singleton,
James Whitside,
Caleb Phifer,
Zachlas Wilson,
Joseph Douglass,
Thomas Dougan,
James Kenan,
John Jones,
Egbert Haywood,
Wm. Wootten,
John Branch,
Henry Hill,
Andrew Bass,

Joseph Boon,
Wm. Farmer,
John Bryan,
Edward Williams,
Francis Oliver,
Matthew Brooks,
Grifith Rutherford,
Geo. H. Barringer,
Timo. Bloodworth,
Everet Pearce,
Asahel Rawlins,
James Wilson,
James Roddy,

Samuel Cain,
B Covington,
J. M'Dowall, Jun.,
Durham Hall,
Jas Bloodworth,
Joel Lane,
James Hinton,
Thomas Devane,
James Brandon,
Wm. Dickson,
Burwell Mooring,
Matthew Locke,
Stokely Donelson.

Total: 184

[Saturday, August 2]

The Convention met according to adjournment.

The report of the committee of the whole Convention, according to order, was taken up and read in the same words as on yesterday; when it was moved by Mr. Person, and seconded by Mr. Macon, that the Convention do concur therewith, which was objected to by Mr. A. Maclaine.

The question being put, "Will the Convention concur with the report of the committee of the whole convention, or not?" it was carried in the affirmative; whereupon Mr. Davie moved for the yeas and nays, and was seconded by Mr. Cabarrus. They were accordingly taken; and those who voted yesterday against the amendment, voted for concurring with the report of the committee: those who voted in favor of the amendment, now voted against a concurrence with the report.

On motion of Mr. Willie Jones, and seconded by Mr. James Galloway, the following resolution was adopted by a large majority, viz.:

Whereas this Convention has thought proper neither to ratify nor reject the Constitution proposed for the government of the United States, and as Congress will proceed to act under the said Constitution, ten states having ratified the same, and probably lay an impost on goods imported into the said ratifying states,—

Resolved, That it be recommended to the legislature of this state, that whenever Congress shall pass a law for collecting an impost in the states aforesaid, this state enact a law for collecting a similar impost on goods imported into this state, and appropriate the money arising therefrom to the use of Congress.

*   *   *

John Brown Cutting to Jefferson, 1788*

Oct. 6, 1788

Truth, lovly truth, obliges me to correct the intelligence transmitted in my two last concerning the purport of the proceedings in North Carolina. It is true that the Convention of that State have not ratified the new federal constitution. But it is not true either that they have absolutely abstracted the state from the ["new" stricken out] Union or manifested a disposition to remain detached therefrom. Neither is it fact that the middle course they have attempted to hold has been taken by so large a majority against so small a minority—as I had reason to believe when I last wrote you.

The day before yesterday the New York packet arrived in fifteen days from Halifax. Having recently come in ["arrived" stricken out] from a rural excursion I knew it not when Mr. Gardner's letter was writing at the other end of the town early yesterday morning; I mean the introductory note I gave him to you: And even now I cannot furnish you with any ["direct" stricken out] accounts which proceed directly from North Carolina itself. But I believe you may rely upon the authenticity of the following extract, namely, "State of North Carolina, In Convention Aug 2. 1788." "Resolved, That a declaration of rights, asserting and securing from incroachment the great principles of civil and religious liberty, and the unalienable rights of the people, together with amendments to the most ambiguous and exceptionable parts of the said Constitution of Government, ought to be laid before Congress, or the Convention of the States that shall or may be called for the purpose of amending the said Constitution, for their consideration, previous to the ratification of the Constitution aforesaid, on the part of the state of North Carolina". Yeas 184. Nays 82. By another account from Virginia, dated Aug. 14—and which I credit as genuine from its intrinsic probability, it appears, that on the opening of the Convention, a motion was made for the question to be put immediately, upon the supposition that every member had made up his mind on the subject and therefore an immediate determination wou'd save both expence and debate. This measure it is thought might have been carried, had not one of the principal supporters of the new government in a most animated and excellent speech, proved the extreme indecorum and impropriety of such precepitance in a business so serious and important: whereupon the motion was withdrawn, and the Constitution being discussed clause by clause in a Committee of the whole Convention, the result was conformable to the principle of the above resolution. It seems to have been taken for granted by this body that Congress wou'd soon call a fresh general Convention to consider of the proposed amendments; and likewise that after deliberating hereon their decision wou'd again be submitted to a new Convention in each state; and that the state of North Carolina not having

Documentary History of the Constitution of the United States, Vol. 5, pp. 81–84.

rejected the Constitution absolutely will not be precluded from calling a Convention again to adopt such an ultimatum shou'd they think proper so to do. Previous to their dissolution, two recommendations to the state legislature passed—the one to make the most speedy and effectual provision for the redemption of the paper money now in circulation—the other to lay an impost for the use of Congress, on goods imported into North Carolina, similar to that which shall be laid by the new Congress on goods imported into the adopting states. These two recommendations are to be transmitted with dispatch both to Congress & to the Executives of the several states.

Through the whole of the discussion of these subjects the Convention manifested every disposition to adhere to the Union and promote the general welfare: But many being previously and positively instructed by their constituents, & themselves perceiving or thinking they perceived, objections to the new constitution which their own vote might have a strong tendency to remove, they thought themselves justified in thus postponing the ultimate decision of the important question, until it shou'd be re-considered by the several states, and such amendments made as might be found universally conciliating.

Most of the amendments proposed by the committee were the same that Virginia and other states recommend. Two only being local to North Carolina. And these two (which are not communicated to me) it is said do not militate with the great principles of the federal system.

This supplement to my late letter altho I have sketch'd it in great haste, contains the substance of all that is known here relevant to North Carolina.

P. S. Shou'd Mr. Parker remain in Paris when this scrawl reaches you an early communication of its contents to him will particularly oblige me.

William R. Davie to Madison, 1789*

June 10, 1789

My private acquaintance with you would by no means warrant a correspondence of this kind, but the interest we have in your public character and exertions will sufficiently apologize for the freedom.

You are well acquainted with the political situation of this State, its unhappy attachment to paper money and that wild scepticism which has prevailed in it since the publication of the Constitution. It has been the uniform cant of the enemies of the Government, that Congress would exert all their influence to prevent the calling of a convention, and would never propose an amendment themselves, or consent to an alteration that would in any manner diminish their powers. The people whose fears had been already alarmed, have received this opinion as fact, and become confirmed in their

*Documentary History of the Constitution of the United States, Vol. 5, pp. 176–77.

opposition; your notification however of the 4th of May has dispersed almost
universal pleasure, we hold it up as a refutation of the gloomy prophecies of
the leaders of the opposition, and the honest part of our antifederalists have
publicly expressed great satisfaction on this event. Our Convention meet
again in November, with powers to adopt the Constitution and any amendments, that may be proposed; this renders it extremely important that the
amendments, if any, should be proposed before that time—and although we
may be nominally a foreign State, yet I hope the alterations will come
officially addressed to the people of this country, an attention however trifling
in itself, that will be of importance in the present state of the public mind
here.

That farrago of amendments borrowed from Virginia is by no means to be
considered as the sense of this country; they were proposed amidst the
violence and confusion of party heat, at a critical moment in our Convention,
and adopted by the opposition without one moment's consideration—I have
collected with some attention the objections of the honest and serious—they
are but few and perhaps necessary—they require some explanation rather
than alteration of the power of Congress over elections—an abridgement of
the jurisdiction of the federal Court in a few instances, and some fixed
regulations respecting appeals—they also insist on the trial by jury being
expressly secured to them in all cases—and a constitutional guaruntee for the
free exercise of their religious rights and privileges—the rule of representation is thought to be too much in the power of Congress—and the Constitution is silent with respect to the existing paper money an important and
interesting property. Instead of a Bill of rights attempting to enumerate the
rights of the individual or the State Governments, they seem to prefer some
general negative ["as will" stricken out] confining Congress to the exercise of
the powers particularly granted, with some express negative restriction in
some important cases.—I am extremely anxious to know the progress of this
delicate and interesting business; and if you could find leisure from the duties
of office and the obligations of Friendship to give me some information on
this subject, it might perhaps be of some consequence to this country, and
would in any event be gratefully acknowledged.

⸪   ✳   ✳

PART SEVEN
FEDERAL BILL OF RIGHTS:
LEGISLATIVE HISTORY

FEDERAL BILL OF RIGHTS: LEGISLATIVE HISTORY

Commentary

When the first Congress under the Constitution assembled in April, 1789, it was James Madison who assumed the leadership role in meeting the widespread demand for a Bill of Rights, which had been expressed so strikingly in the recommendatory amendments submitted by five states, as well as the Pennsylvania minority and the Maryland Committee and the conditional amendments voted by the North Carolina Convention. Critics of the notion of amendments had pointed to the volume and diversity of the state proposals, claiming that it would be impossible to find any common ground for action by the amending process among them. It must be conceded that there was a basis in such criticism; Judge Dumbauld has calculated that 210 different amendments were proposed by the eight states concerned, and, with duplications omitted, these included nearly 100 different substantive provisions.

The picture was not, however, as hopeless as it seemed, so far as drawing up a workable Bill of Rights from the plethora of state-recommended amendments was concerned. That was true because the state proposals reflected the consensus that had developed among Americans with regard to the fundamental rights that ought to be protected by any Bill of Rights worthy of the name. All eight of the states which proposed amendments (either officially or otherwise) recommended a provision like that ultimately included in the Tenth Amendment, reserving to the states powers not delegated to the Federal Government. Seven states recommended a guarantee of jury trial in civil cases. Six urged protection for religious freedom. Five sought guarantees of freedom of the press (with three adding freedom of speech as well), the right to bear arms, trial by jury of the vicinage, and prohibitions against quartering of troops, and unreasonable searches and seizures. Four states asked for protection of the right to "the law of the land" or due process, speedy public trial, assembly and petition, and against escessive bail and fines and cruel and unusual punishments. (See Table [*infra* p. 1167]). As Judge Dumbauld tells us, of 22 amendments which were supported by four or more states, 14 were incorporated by Madison in his recommendations to Congress.

As Jefferson points out in his letter to John Paul Jones (*infra* p. 1003) "even the friends of the Constitution are becoming sensible of the expediency" of a Bill of Rights, "were it only to conciliate the opposition." (See also the Washington letters [*infra* pp. 984, 986, 989].) Madison himself may (*supra* p. 614) originally have been lukewarm toward the addition of a Bill of Rights to the Constitution. As time went on, however, he was induced, both

983

by Jefferson and political realities, to modify his attitude (*supra* p. 593). The ratification struggle showed him the need to concede amendments to provide "every desirable safeguard for popular rights," in order to reconcile at least the more moderate Antifederalists to the new governmental system. This would separate "the well-meaning from the designing opponents, fix on the latter their true character, and give to the Government their due popularity and stability" (*infra* p. 994).

In addition, Madison had come out in favor of amendments as part of his closely contested campaign for election to Congress (the Antifederalists had put up James Monroe as a strong opponent and, as Madison's letter to Washington [*infra* p. 998] shows, had tried to brand Madison as an antiamendment candidate). Madison stated flatly, in a letter to George Eve, a campaign worker, "it is my sincere opinion that the Constitution ought to be revised, and that the first Congress meeting under it, ought to prepare and recommend to the States for ratification, the most satisfactory provisions for all essential rights, particularly the rights of Conscience in the fullest latitude, the Freedom of the press, trials by jury, security against general warrants, etc." (*infra* p. 997).

After his election to the first Congress, Madison acted to make good on his campaign promise, by pressing the amendment issue. The materials that follow trace the legislative history of the Bill of Rights in the first Congress from the May 4 statement by Madison of his intent to introduce the amendments that became the Bill of Rights. We are able to follow the proceedings in the House of Representatives both through the report of the debates in the House contained in the *Annals of Congress*—compiled from newspaper accounts and Lloyd's *Congressional Register*—and the *Journal* of the House. It is far from the verbatim transcript contained in the modern *Congressional Record*, though it does give us an adequate picture of what occurred on the floor of the House. For the Senate the situation is much less satisfactory, for its debates were not reported at that time. Other pertinent noncongressional materials are also included.

Washington to John Armstrong, 1788*

Apr. 25, 1788

Dear Sir,

From some cause or other, which I do not know, your favor of the 20th of February did not reach me till very lately. This must apologize for its not being sooner acknowledged. Although Colonel Blaine forgot to call upon me for a letter before he left Philadelphia, yet I wrote a few lines to you previous to my departure from that place; whether they ever got to your hands, you best know.

*W. C. Ford, ed., *The Writings of George Washington* (1891), Vol. 11, pp. 249–53.

I well remember the observation you made in your letter to me of last year, "that my domestic retirement must suffer an interruption." This took place, notwithstanding it was utterly repugnant to my feelings, my interests, and my wishes. I sacrificed every private consideraton, and personal enjoyment, to the earnest and pressing solicitations of those, who saw and knew the alarming situation of our public concerns, and had no other end in view but to promote the interests of their country; conceiving, that under those circumstances, and at so critical a moment, an absolute refusal to act might on my part be construed as a total disregard of my country, if imputed to no worse motives. Although you say the same motives induce you to think, that another tour of duty of this kind will fall to my lot, I cannot but hope, that you will be disappointed; for I am so wedded to a state of retirement, and find the occupations of a rural life so congenial with my feelings, that to be drawn into public at my advanced age would be a sacrifice, that would admit of no compensation.

Your remarks on the impressions, which will be made on the manners and sentiments of the people by the example of those, who are first called to act under the proposed government, are very just; and I have no doubt but, if the proposed constitution obtains those persons who are chosen to administer it will have wisdom enought to discern the influence, which their example as rulers and legislators may have on the body of the people, and will have virtue enough to pursue that line of conduct, which will most conduce to the happiness of their country. As the first transactions of a nation, like those of an individual upon his first entrance into life, make the deepest impression, and are to form the leading traits in his character, they will undoubtedly pursue those measures, which will best tend to the restoration of public and private faith, and of consequence promote our national respectability and individual welfare.

That the proposed constitution will admit of amendments is acknowledged by its warmest advocates; but to make such amendments as may be proposed by the several States the condition of its adoption would, in my opinion, amount to a complete rejection of it; for, upon examination of the objections, which are made by the opponents in different States, and the amendments, which have been proposed, it will be found, that what would be a favorite object with one State, is the very thing which is strenuously opposed by another. The truth is, men are too apt to be swayed by local prejudices, and those, who are so fond of amendments, which have the particular interest of their own States in view, cannot extend their ideas to the general welfare of the Union. They do not consider, that, for every sacrifice which they make, they receive an ample compensation by the sacrifices, which are made by other States for their benefit; and that those very things, which they give up, operate to their advantage through the medium of the great interest.

In addition to these considerations it should be remembered, that a constitutional door is opened for such amendments, as shall be thought necessary by nine States. When I reflect upon these circumstances, I am surprised to find, that any person, who is acquainted with the critical state of our public affairs, and knows the variety of views, interests, feelings, and prejudices, which must be consulted in framing a general government for these States, and how little propositions in themselves so opposite to each other will tend to promote that desirable end, can wish to make amendments the ultimatum for adopting the offered system.

I am very glad to find, that the opposition in your State, however formidable it has been represented, is generally speaking composed of such characters, as cannot have an extensive influence. Their strength, as well as that of those in the same class in other States, seems to lie in misrepresentation, and a desire to inflame the passions and to alarm the fears by noisy declamation, rather than to convince the understanding by sound arguments or fair and impartial statements. Baffled in their attacks upon the constitution, they have attempted to vilify and debase the characters, who formed it; but even here I trust they will not succeed. Upon the whole, I doubt whether the opposition to the constitution will not ultimately be productive of more good than evil. It has called forth in its defence abilities which would not perhaps have been otherwise expected that have thrown new light upon the science of government. It has given the rights of man a full and fair discussion, and explained them in so clear and forcible a manner, as cannot fail to make a lasting impression upon those, who read the best publications on the subject, and particularly the pieces under the signature of Publius. There will be a greater weight of abilities opposed to the system in the convention of this State, than there has been in any other; but, notwithstanding the unwearied pains which have been taken, and the vigorous efforts which will be made in the convention to prevent its adoption, I have not the smallest doubt but it will obtain here.

*   *   *

Washington to the Marquis de Lafayette, 1788*

*   *   *

Apr. 28, 1788

I notice with pleasure the additional immunities and facilities in trade, which France has granted by the late royal arret to the United States. I flatter myself it will have the desired effect in some measure of augmenting the commercial intercourse. From the productions and wants of the two countries, their trade with each other is certainly capable of great amelioration to be actuated by a spirit of unwise policy. For so surely as ever we shall have an efficient government established, so surely will that government impose retaliating restrictions, to a certain degree, upon the trade of Britain. At present, or under our existing form of confederation, it would be idle to think of making commercial regulations on our part. One State passes a prohibitory law respecting some article, another State opens wide the avenue for its admission. One Assembly makes a system, another Assembly unmakes it. Virginia, in the very last session of her legislature, was about to have passed some of the most extravagant and preposterous edicts on the subject of trade, that ever stained the leaves of a legislative code. It is in vain to hope for a remedy of these, and innumerable other evils, until a general government shall be adopted.

The conventions of six States only have as yet accepted the new constitution. No one has rejected it. It is believed that the convention of Maryland, which is now in session, and that of South Carolina, which is to assemble on the 12th of May, will certainly adopt it. It is also since the elections of members of the convention have taken place in this State, more generally believed, that it will be adopted here, than it was before those elections were made. There will, however, be powerful and eloquent speeches on both sides of the question in the Virginia convention; but as Pendleton, Wythe, Blair, Madison, Jones, Nicholas, Innes, and many other of our first characters, will be advocates for its adoption, you may suppose the weight of abilities will rest on that side. Henry and Mason are its great adversaries. The governor, if he approves it at all, will do it feebly.

On the general merits of this proposed constitution, I wrote to you some time ago my sentiments pretty freely. That letter had not been received by you, when you addressed to me the last of yours, which has come to my hands. I had never supposed that perfection could be the result of accommodation and mutual concession. The opinion of Mr. Jefferson and yourself is certainly a wise one, that the constitution ought by all means to be accepted by nine States before any attempt should be made to procure amendments; for, if that acceptance shall not previously take place, men's minds will be so much agitated and soured, that the danger will be greater than ever of our becoming a disunited people. Whereas, on the other hand, with prudence in temper and a spirit of moderation, every essential alteration may in the process of time be expected.

You will doubtless have seen, that it was owing to this conciliatory and patriotic principle, that the convention of Massachusetts adopted the constitution in toto, but recommended a number of specific alterations, and quieting explanations as an early, serious, and unremitting subject of attention. Now, although it is not to be expected, that every individual in society will or can be brought to agree upon what is exactly the best form of government, yet there are many things in the constitution, which only need to be explained, in order to prove equally satisfactory to all parties. For example, there was not a member of the convention, I believe, who had the least objection to what is contended for by the advocates for a Bill of Rights and

Trial by Jury. The first, where the people evidently retained every thing, which they did not in the express terms give up, was considered nugatory, as you will find to have been more fully explained by Mr. Wilson and others; and, as to the second, it was only the difficulty of establishing a mode, which should not interfere with the fixed modes of any of the States, that induced the convention to leave it as a matter of future adjustment.

There are other points in which opinions would be more likely to vary. As for instance, on the ineligibility of the same person for president, after he should have served a certain course of years. Guarded so effectually as the proposed constitution is, in respect to the prevention of bribery and undue influence in the choice of president, I confess I differ widely myself from Mr. Jefferson and you, as to the necessity or expediency of rotation in that appointment. The matter was fairly discussed in the convention, and to my full conviction, though I cannot have time or room to sum up the argument in this letter. There cannot in my judgment be the least danger, that the president will by any practicable intrigue ever be able to continue himself one moment in office, much less perpetuate himself in it, but in the last stage of corrupted morals and political depravity; and even then, there is as much danger that any other species of domination would prevail. Though, when a people shall have become incapable of governing themselves, and fit for a master, it is of little consequence from what quarter he comes. Under an extended view of this part of the subject, I can see no propriety in precluding ourselves from the services of any man, who on some great emergency shall be deemed universally most capable of serving the public.

In answer to the observations you make on the probability of my election to the presidency, knowing me as you do, I need only say, that it has no enticing charms and no fascinating allurements for me. However, it might not be decent for me to say I would refuse to accept, or even to speak much about an appointment, which may never take place; for, in so doing, one might possibly incure the application of the moral resulting from that fable, in which the fox is represented as inveighing against the sourness of the grapes, because he could not reach them. All that it will be necessary to add, my dear Marquis, in order to show my decided predilections is, that, (at my time of life and under my circumstances,) the increasing infirmities of nature and the growing live of retirement do not permit me to entertain a wish beyond that of living and dying an honest man on my own farm. Let those follow the pursuits of ambition and fame, who have a keener relish for them, or who may have more years in store for the enjoyment.

Mrs. Washington, while she requests that her best compliments may be presented to you, joins with me in soliciting that the same friendly and affectionate memorial of our constant remembrance and good wishes may be made acceptable to Madame de Lafayette and the little ones. I am, &c.

P. S. May 1st. Since writing the foregoing letter, I have received authentic accounts that the Convention of Maryland has ratified the new Constitution by a majority of 63 to 11.

Washington to Jefferson, 1788*

Aug. 31, 1788

Sir,

I was very much gratified a little time ago by the receipt of your letter dated the 2d of May. You have my best thanks for the political information contained in it, as well as for the satisfactory account of the canal of Languedoc. It gives me great pleasure to be made acquainted with the particulars of that stupendous work, though I do not expect to derive any but speculative advantages from it.

When America will be able to embark in projects of such pecuniary extent, I know not; probably not for very many years to come; but it will be a good example, and not without its use, if we can carry our present undertakings happily into effect. Of this we have now the fairest prospect. Notwithstanding the real scarcity of money, and the difficulty of collecting it, the laborers employed by the Potomac Company have made very great progress in removing the obstructions at the Shenandoah, Seneca, and Great Falls; insomuch that, if this summer had not proved unusually rainy, and if we could have had a favorable autumn, the navigation might have been sufficiently opened (though not completed) for boats to have passed from Fort Cumberland to within nine miles of a shipping port, by the first of January next. There remains now no doubt of the practicability of the plan, or that, upon the ulterior operations being performed, this will become the great avenue into the western country; a country which is now settling in an extraordinarily rapid manner, under uncommonly favorable circumstances, and which promises to afford a capacious asylum for the poor and persecuted of the earth.

I do not pretend to judge how far the flames of war, which are kindled in the north of Europe, may be scattered, or how soon they will be extinguished. The European politics have taken so strange a turn, and the nations formerly allied have become so curiously severed, that there are fewer sure premises for calculation, than are usually afforded even on the precarious and doubtful subject. But it appears probable to me, that peace will either take place this year, or hostility be greatly extended in the course of the next. The want of a hearty cooperation between the two imperial powers against the Porte, or the failure of success from any other cause, may accelerate the first contingency. The irritable state, into which several of the other potentates seem to have been drawn, may open the way to the second. Hitherto the event of the contest has proved different from the general expectation. If in our speculations we might count upon discipline, system, and resources, and certainly these are the articles which generally give decisive advantages in war, I had thought full surely the Turks must at least have been driven out of Europe.

*The Writings of George Washington, Vol. 11, pp. 317–23.

Is it not unaccountable, that the Russians and Germans combined are not able to effect so much as the former did alone in the late war? But perhaps these things are all for the best, and may afford room for pacification. I am glad our Commodore Paul Jones has got employment, and heartily wish him success. His new situation may possibly render his talents and services more useful to us at some future day. I was unapprized of the circumstances, which you mention, that Congress had once in contemplation to give him promotion. They will doubtless judge now how far it may be expedient.

By what we can learn from the late foreign gazettes, affairs seem to have come nearly to a crisis in France, and I hope they are beginning to meliorate. Should the contest between the King and the parliaments result in a well-constituted national assembly, it must ultimately be a happy event for the kingdom. But I fear that kingdom will not recover its reputation and influence with the Dutch for a long time to come. Combinations appear also to be forming in other quarters. It is reported by the last European accounts, that England has actually entered into a treaty with Russia, and that the French ambassador at the court of London has asked to be informed of its tenor. In whatever manner the nations of Europe shall endeavor to keep up their prowess in war, and their balance of power in peace, it will be obviously our policy to cultivate tranquillity at home and abroad; and to extend our agriculture and commerce as far as possible.

I am much obliged by the information you gave respecting the credit of different nations among the Dutch money-holders, and fully accord with you with regard to the manner in which our own ought to be used. I am strongly impressed with the expediency of establishing our national faith beyond imputation, and of having recourse to loans only on critical occasions. Your proposal for transferring the whole foreign debt to Holland is highly worthy of consideration. I feel mortified, that there should have been any just ground for the clamor of the foreign officers, who served with us; but, after having received a quarter of their whole debt in specie, and their interest in the same for some time, they have infinitely less reason for complaint than our native officers, of whom the suffering and neglect have been only equalled by their patience and patriotism. A great proportion of the officers and soldiers of the American army have been compelled by indigence to part with their securities for one eighth of the nominal value; yet their conduct is very different from what you represented that of the French officers to have been.

The merits and defects of the proposed constitution have been largely and ably discussed. For myself, I was ready to have embraced any tolerable compromise, that was competent to save us from impending ruin; and I can say there are scarcely any of the amendments, which have been suggested, to which I have much objection, except that which goes to the prevention of direct taxation. And that, I presume, will be more strenuously advocated and insisted upon hereafter, than any other. I had indulged the expectation, that the new government would enable those entrusted with its administration to do justice to the public creditors, and retrieve the national character. But, if no means are to be employed but requisitions, that expectation was vain, and we may as well recur to the old confederation. If the system can be put in operation, without touching much the pockets of the people, perhaps it may be done; but, in my judgment, infinite circumspection and prudence are yet necessary in the experiment. It is nearly impossible for anybody who has not been on the spot, (from any description) to conceive what the delicacy and danger of our situation have been. Though the peril is not past entirely, thank God the prospect is somewhat brightening.

You will probably have heard, before the receipt of this letter, that the general government has been adopted by eleven States, and that the actual Congress have been prevented from issuing their ordinance for carrying it into execution, in consequence of a dispute about the place at which the future Congress shall meet. It is probable, that Philadelphia or New York will soon be agreed upon.

I will just touch on the bright side of our national state, before I conclude; and we may perhaps rejoice, that the people have been ripened by misfortune for the reception of a good government. They are emerging from the gulf of dissipation and debt, into which they had precipitated themselves at the close of the war. Economy and industry are evidently gaining ground. Not only agriculture, but even manufactures, are much more attended to than formerly. Notwithstanding the shackles under which our trade in general labors, commerce to the East Indies is prosecuted with considerable success. Salted provisions and other produce, (particularly from Massachusetts,) have found an advantageous market there. The voyages are so much shorter, and the vessels are navigated at so much less expense, that we may hope to rival and supply, (at least through the West Indies,) some part of Europe with commodities from thence. This year the exports from Massachusetts have amounted to a great deal more than their imports. I wish this was the case everywhere.

*   *   *

Jefferson to Washington, 1788*

Nov. 4, 1788

Sir,

Your favor of Aug. 31. came to hand yesterday; and a confidential conveiance offering, by the way of London, I avail myself of it to acknolege the receipt. I have seen, with infinite pleasure, our new constitution accepted by 11. states, not rejected by the 12th. and that the 13th. happens to be a

*J. P. Boyd, ed., *The Papers of Thomas Jefferson*, Vol. 14, p. 328.

state of the least importance. It is true that the minorities in most of the accepting states have been very respectable, so much so as to render it prudent, were it not otherwise reasonable, to make some sacrifices to them. I am in hopes that the annexation of a bill of rights to the constitution will alone draw over so great a proportion of the minorities, as to leave little danger in the opposition of the residue; and that this annexation may be made by Congress and the assemblies, without calling a convention which might endanger the most valuable parts of the system. Calculation has convinced me that circumstances may arise, and probably will arise, wherein all the resources of taxation will be necessary for the safety of the state. For tho I am decidedly of opinion we should take no part in European quarrels, but cultivate peace and commerce with all, yet who can avoid seeing the source of war in the tyranny of those nations who deprive us of the natural right of trading with our neighbors? The produce of the U.S. will soon exceed the European demand. What is to be done with the surplus, when there shall be one? It will be employed, without question, to open by force a market for itself with those placed on the same continent with us, and who wish nothing better. Other causes too are obvious which may involve us in war; and war requires every resource of taxation and credit. The power of making war often prevents it, and in our case would give efficacy to our desire of peace. If the new government wears the front which I hope it will I see no impossibility in the availing ourselves of the wars of others to open the other parts of America to our commerce, as the price of our neutrality.

*   *   *

Madison to Jefferson, 1788*

Dec. 8, 1788

Dear Sir,

This will be handed to you by Mr. Gouverneur Morris who will embark in a few days for Havre, from whence he will proceed immediately to Paris. He is already well known to you by character; and as far as there may be a defect of personal acquaintance I beg leave to supply it by this introduction.

My two last were of Ocr. 8 & 17th. They furnished a state of our affairs as they then stood. I shall here add the particulars of most consequence, which have since taken place; remembering however that many details will be most conveniently gathered from the conversation of Mr. Morris who is thoroughly possessed of American transactions.

Notwithstanding the formidable opposition made to the New federal Government, first in order to prevent its adoption, and since in order to place its administration in the hands of disaffected men, there is now both a certainty of its peaceable commencement in March next, and a flattering prospect that it will be administered by men who will give it a fair trial. General Washington will certainly be called to the Executive department. Mr. Adams, who is pledged to support him, will probably be the vice president. The enemies to the Government, at the head & the most inveterate, of whom, is Mr. Henry are laying a train for the election of Governor Clinton, but it cannot succeed unless the federal votes be more dispersed than can well happen. Of the seven States which have appointed their Senators, Virginia alone will have anti-federal members in that branch. Those of N. Hampshire are President Langdon & Judge Bartlett—of Massachusetts Mr. Strong and Mr. Dalton— of Connecticut Docr. Johnson and Mr. Elseworth—of N. Jersey Mr. Patterson and Mr. Elmer—of Penna. Mr. R. Morris and Mr. McClay—of Delaware Mr. Geo. Reed and Mr. Basset—of Virginia Mr. R. H. Lee and Col. Grayson. Here is already a majority of the ratifying States on the side of the Constitution. And it is not doubted that it will be reinforced by the appointments of Maryland, S. Carolina and Georgia. As one branch of the Legislature of N. York is attached to the Constitution, it is not improbable that one of the Senators from that State also will be added to the majority. In the House of Representatives the proportion of anti-federal members will of course be greater, but cannot if present appearances are to be trusted, amount to a majority, or even a very formidable minority. The election for this branch has taken place as yet no where except in Penna., and here the returns are not yet come in from all the Counties. It is certain however that seven out of the eight, and probable that the whole eight representatives will bear the federal stamp. Even in Virginia where the enemies to the Government form 2/3 of the legislature it is computed that more than half the number of Representatives, who will be elected by the people, formed into districts for the purpose, will be of the same stamp. By some, it is computed that 7 out of the 10 allotted to that State will be opposed to the politics of the present Legislature.

The questions which divide the public at present relate 1. to the extent of the amendments that ought to be made to the Constitution. 2. to the mode in which they ought to be made. The friends of the Constitution, some from an approbation of particular amendments, others from a spirit of conciliation, are generally agreed that the System should be revised. But they wish the revisal to be carried no farther than to supply additional guards for liberty, without abridging the sum of power transferred from the States to the General Government or altering previous to trial, the particular structure of the latter and are fixed in opposition to the risk of another Convention whilst the purpose can be as well answered, by the other mode provided for introducing amendments. Those who have opposed the Constitution, are on the other hand, zealous for a second Convention, and for a revisal which may either not be restrained at all, or extend at least as far as alterations have been proposed by any State. Some of this class, are no doubt, friends to an effective Government, and even to the substance of the particular Government in question. It is equally certain that there are others who urge a second Convention with the insidious hope, of throwing all things into Confusion, and of subverting the fabric just established, if not the Union itself. If the first Congress embrace the policy which circumstances mark out, they will not fail to propose of themselves, every desirable safeguard for popular rights; and by thus separating the well meaning from the designing opponents fix on the latter their true character, and give to the Government its due popularity and stability.

*　　　　　*　　　　　*

Jefferson to William Carmichael, 1788*

Dec. 25, 1788

Dear Sir,

A sick family has prevented me, for upwards of a month from putting pen to paper but in indispensable cases, and for some time before that I had been waiting to receive American news worth communicating to you. These causes have occasionned my silence since my last which was of the 12th. of August, and my leaving unacknoleged, till now, your several favors of July 24. Aug. 14. Sep. 9. and Nov. 3. That of the 14th. inst. came also to hand the day before yesterday.

You have long ago known that 11. states have ratified our new constitution, and that N. Carolina, contrary to all expectation, has declined either accepting or refusing, but has proposed amendments copied verbatim from those of Virginia. Virginia and Massachussetts had preferred this method of amendment, that is to say, desiring Congress to propose specific amendments to the several legislatures, which is one of the modes of amendment provided in the new constitution. In this way nothing can be touched but the parts specifically pointed out. New York has written circular letters to the legislatures to adopt the other mode of amendment, provided also by the constitution that is to say to assemble another federal convention. In this way the whole fabric could be submitted to alteration. It's friends therefore unite in endeavoring to have the first method adopted, and they seem agreed to concur in adding a bill of rights to the Constitution. This measure will bring over so great a part of the Opposition that what will remain after that will have no other than the good effects of watching, as centinels, the conduct of government, and laying it before the public. Many of the opposition wish to take from Congress the power of internal taxation. Calculation has convinced

*The Papers of Thomas Jefferson, Vol. 14, pp. 385–87.

me this would be very mischievous. The electors are to be chosen the 1st. Wednesday of Jan. the President the 1st. Wed. in Feb., and the new government is to meet at New York the 1st. Wed. in March. The election of Senators has already begun. Pennsylvania has chosen Mr. R. Morris and McClay, Connecticut Dr. Johnson and Elsworth. I have heard of no others. I hope there is no doubt of Genl. Washington's acceptance of the Presidentship. Mr. J. Adams, Mr. Hancock, Mr. Jay, and Genl. Knox are talked of in the Northern and middle states for Vice president; yet it is suggested to me that the two latter will probably prefer their present offices, and the two former divide each other's interest so that neither may be chosen. Remarkeable deaths are Colo. Bannister of Virginia, and John Penn of North Carolina. Genl. Washington writes me word that the great rains had prevented the continuance of their labours on the Patowmac so that they should not be able to bring the navigation this winter to the great falls as he had hoped. It will want little of it, and no doubt remains of their completing the whole. That of James river has some time since been so far completed as to let vessels pass down to Richmond. The crop of wheat in America the last year has been a fine one both for quantity and quality. This country is likely to want. They have offered a premium of 40. sous the quintal on flour of the U.S. and 30. sous on their wheat imported here. They have also opened their islands for our supplies. Much will come here. Views, which bid defiance to my calculations, had induced this court in an Arret of Sep. 28. to comprehend us with the English, in the exclusion of whaleoils from their ports, in flat contradiction to their Arret of Dec. last. This you know would be sentence of banishment to the inhabitants of Nantucket, and there is no doubt they would have removed to Nova Scotia or England in preference to any other part of the world. A temporary order however is now given for our admittance, and a more permanent one under preparation. The internal affairs of this country will I hope go on well. Neither the time, place, nor form of the States general are yet announced. But they will certainly meet in March or April. The clergy and nobility, as clergy and nobility eternally will, are opposed to the giving to the tiers etat so effectual a representation as may dismount them from their backs. The court wishes to give to the unprivileged order an equal number of votes with the privileged, and that they should sit in one house. But the court is timid. Some are of opinion that a majority of the nobles also are on the side of the people. I doubt it when so great a proportion of the Notables, indeed almost an unanimity were against them, and 5. princes of the blood out of 7. If no schism prevents the proceedings of the States general, I suppose they will obtain in their first session 1. the periodical convocation of the states. 2. their participation in the legislature. and 3. their exclusive right to levy and appropriate money: and that at some future day, not very distant they will obtain a habeas corpus law and free press. They have great need of external peace to let them go on quietly with these internal improvements. This seems to be secured to them by the insanity of the K. of England. Regents are generally peaceable, and I think this country will not let itself be diverted from it's object by any other power. There are symptoms which render it suspicious that the two empires may make their peace with the Turks. It seems more eligible to Russia to do this by ceding the Crimea to them, that she may turn to the other side and save Poland which the K. of Prussia is endeavoring to wrest from her. Probably the loss of his principal ally will induce him to adopt a language and a conduct less Thrasonic. The death of the King of Spain contributes to throw into incertainty the future face and fate of Europe. The English count on his successor. We have not yet received from London the decision on the question of regency. It is believed the Prince of Wales will be sole regent and that there will be a total change in the ministry. In this case probably Eden will be recalled. He will have found that the old proverb is not always true 'that a bird in the hand is worth two in the bush.' There is something concerting between your court and our Kentuck[ians]. What is it? It mer[its] your in[vestig]ations.

The necessity of carrying back my family to America, and of arranging my affairs, which I left under expectation of returning to them very soon, have induced me to ask of Congress a leave of 5. or 6. months absence during the next year. I hope to obtain it in time to sail soon after the vernal equinox, and shall return immediately after the autumnal. I shall be happy while there if I can render you any service, and shall hope to receive your commands before my departure, and in the meantime a continuance of your interesting communications, now become more so till we see which way the new administration of your residence will turn itself. I have the honor to be with great and sincere esteem Dear Sir your most obedt. & most humble servt.,

Madison to George Eve, 1789*

Jan. 2, 1789

Sir,

Being informed that reports prevail not only that I am opposed to any amendments whatever to the new federal Constitution, but that I have ceased to be a friend to the rights of Conscience; and inferring from a conversation with my brother William, that you are disposed to contradict such reports as far as your knowledge of my sentiments may justify, I am led to trouble you with this communication of them. As a private Citizen it could not be my wish that erroneous opinions should be entertained, with respect to either of those points, particularly with respect to religious liberty. But having been induced, to offer my services to this district as its representative

*The Writings of James Madison, Vol. 5, p. 319.

in the federal Legislature, considerations of a public nature make it proper that, with respect to both, my principles and views should be rightly understood.

I freely own that I have never seen in the Constitution as it now stands those serious dangers which have alarmed many respectable Citizens. Accordingly whilst it remained unratified, and it was necessary to unite the States in some one plan, I opposed all previous alterations as calculated to throw the States into dangerous contentions, and to furnish the secret enemies of the Union with an opportunity of promoting its dissolution. Circumstances are now changed. The Constitution is established on the ratifications of eleven States and a very great majority of the people of America; and amendments, if pursued with a proper moderation and in a proper mode, will be not only safe, but may serve the double purpose of satisfying the minds of well meaning opponents, and of providing additional guards in favour of liberty. Under this change of circumstances, it is my sincere opinion that the Constitution ought to be revised, and that the first Congress meeting under it ought to prepare and recommend to the States for ratification, the most satisfactory provisions for all essential rights, particularly the rights of Conscience in the fullest latitude, the freedom of the press, trials by jury, security against general warrants &c. I think it will be proper also to provide expressly in the Constitution, for the periodical increase of the number of Representatives until the amount shall be entirely satisfactory, and to put the judiciary department into such a form as will render vexatious appeals impossible. There are sundry other alterations which are either eligible in themselves, or being at least safe, are recommended by the respect due to such as wish for them.

I have intimated that the amendments ought to be proposed by the first Congress. I prefer this mode to that of a General Convention—1st. because it is the most expeditious mode. A Convention must be delayed until 2/3 of the State Legislatures shall have applied for one, and afterwards the amendments must be submitted to the States; whereas if the business be undertaken by Congress the amendments may be prepared and submitted in March next. 2dly. because it is the most certain mode. There are not a few States who will absolutely reject the proposal of a Convention, and yet not be averse to amendments in the other mode.—lastly, it is the safest mode. The Congress who will be appointed to execute as well as to amend the Government, will probably be careful not to destroy or endanger it. A Convention, on the other hand, meeting in the present ferment of parties, and containing perhaps insidious characters from different parts of America, would at least spread a general alarm, and be but too likely to turn everything into confusion and uncertainty. It is to be observed however that the question concerning a General Convention, will not belong to the federal Legislature. If 2/3 of the States apply for one, Congress cannot refuse to call it; if not, the other mode of amendments must be pursued.

Madison to Washington, 1789*

Jan. 14, 1789

Dear Sir,

Your favor of the 2d instant, with the letters attending it never came to hand 'till last evening. I have good reason to believe that the delay happened between Alexanda. & Fredg., rather than at or from the latter place. Mr. F. Maury pays particular attention to all letters which arrive there for me, and forwards them to Orange by opportunities which are frequent & safe. I apprehend there will be no impropriety in committing a confidential letter to that channel. As an additional precaution, I will desire him to be particularly attentive to any letter which may have your name on it.

I have heard from two only of the returns from the Electoral districts; the one in favor of Mr. Gilchrist—the other of General Stephens. He succeeded agst. Col. Cabel by a majority of 82 votes. He owes his success to the coalition between the two parties in Spotsylva. My situation is unfavorable for intelligence from the State at large, and therefore I can say little of the prospects as to the Feby. election.

I fear, from the vague accounts which circulate, that the federal candidates are likely to stand in the way of one another. This is not the case however in my district. The field is left entirely to Monroe & myself. The event of our competition will probably depend on the part to be taken by two or three descriptions of people, whose decision is not known, if not yet to be ultimately formed. I have pursued my pretensions much further than I had premeditated; having not only made great use of epistolary means, but actually visited two Counties, Culpeper & Louisa, and publicly contradicted the erroneous reports propagated agst. me. It has been very industriously inculcated that I am dogmatically attached to the Constitution in every clause, syllable & letter, and therefore not a single amendment will be promoted by my vote, either from conviction or a spirit of accommodation. This is the report most likely to affect the election, and most difficult to be combated with success within the limited period. There are a number of others however which are auxiliaries to it.—With my respectful compliments to Mrs. Washington, & the others of your family,

I remain, Dear Sir, your most obedt & affecte. Servt.

Jefferson to David Humphreys, 1789†

Mar. 18, 1789

Dear Sir,

Your favor of Nov. 29. 1788. came to hand the last month. How it happened that mine of Aug. 1787. was fourteen months on it's way is

*The Writings of James Madison, Vol. 5, p. 318.
†The Papers of Thomas Jefferson, Vol. 14, pp. 676–79.

inconceivable. I do not recollect by what conveyance I sent it. I had concluded however either that it had miscarried or that you had become indolent as most of our countrymen are in matters of correspondence.

The change in this country, since you left it, is such as you can form no idea of. The frivolities of conversation have given way entirely to politicks—men, women and children talk nothing else: and all you know talk a great deal. The press groans with daily productions, which in point of boldness make an Englishman stare, who hitherto has thought himself the boldest of men. A complete revolution in this government has, within the space of two years (for it began with the Notables of 1787) been effected merely by the force of public opinion, aided indeed by the want of money which the dissipations of the court had brought on. And this revolution has not cost a single life, unless we charge to it a little riot lately in Bretagne which begun about the price of bread, became afterwards political and ended in the loss of 4. or 5. lives. The assembly of the states general begins the 27th. of April. The representation of the people will be perfect. But they will be alloyed by an equal number of nobility and clergy. The first great question they will have to decide will be Whether they shall vote by orders or persons. And I have hopes that the majority of the nobles are already disposed to join the tiers etat in deciding that the vote shall be by persons. This is the opinion à la mode at present, and mode has acted a wonderful part in the present instance. All the handsome young women, for example, are for the tiers etat, and this is an army more powerful in France than the 200,000 men of the king. Add to this that the court itself is for the tiers etat, as the only agent which can relieve their wants: not by giving money themselves (they are squeezed to the last drop) but by pressing it from the non-contributing orders. The king stands engaged to pretend no more to the power of laying, continuing or appropriating taxes, to call the States general periodically, to submit letters de cachet to legal restriction, to consent to freedom of the press, and that all this shall be fixed by a fundamental constitution which shall bind his successors. He has not offered a participation in the legislature, but it will surely be insisted on. The public mind is so ripened on all these subjects, that there seems to be now but one opinion. The clergy indeed think separately, and the old men among the Nobles. But their voice is suppressed by the general one of the nation. The writings published on this occasion are some of them very valuable: because, unfettered by the prejudices under which the English labour, they give a full scope to reason, and strike out truths as yet unperceived and unacknoleged on the other side the channel. An Englishman, dozing under a kind of half reformation, is not excited to think by such gross absurdities as stare a Frenchman in the face wherever he looks, whether it be towards the throne or the altar. In fine I beleive this nation will in the course of the present year have as full a portion of liberty dealt out to them as the nation can bear at present, considering how uninformed the mass of their people is. This circumstance will prevent their immediate establishment of the trial by jury. The palsied state of the executive in England is a fortunate circumstance for France, as it will give them time to arrange their affairs internally. The consolidation and funding their debts will give them a credit which will enable them to do what they please. For the present year the war will be confined to the two empires and Denmark against Turkey and Sweden. It is not yet evident whether Prussia will be engaged. If the disturbances of Poland break out into overt acts, it will be a power divided in itself, and so of no weight. Perhaps by the next year England and France may be ready to take the feild. It will depend on the former principally, for the latter, tho she may be then able, must wish still a little time to see her new arrangements well under way. The English papers and English ministry say the king is well. He is better, but not well: no malady requires a longer time to ensure against it's return, than insanity. Time alone can distinguish accidental insanity from habitual lunacy.

The operations which have taken place in America lately, fill me with pleasure. In the first place they realize the confidence I had that whenever our affairs get obviously wrong, the good sense of the people will interpose and set them to rights. The example of changing a constitution by assembling the wise men of the state, instead of assembling armies, will be worth as much to the world as the former examples we had given them. The constitution too which was the result of our deliberations, is unquestionably the wisest ever yet presented to men, and some of the accomodations of interest which it has adopted are greatly pleasing to me who have before had occasions of seeing how difficult those interests were to accomodate. A general concurrence of opinion seems to authorize us to say it has some defects. I am one of those who think it a defect that the important rights, not placed in security by the frame of the constitution itself, were not explicitly secured by a supplementary declaration. There are rights which it is useless to surrender to the government, and which yet, governments have always been fond to invade. These are the rights of thinking, and publishing our thoughts by speaking or writing: the right of free commerce: the right of personal freedom. There are instruments for administering the government, so peculiarly trust-worthy, that we should never leave the legislature at liberty to change them. The new constitution has secured these in the executive and legislative departments; but not in the judiciary. It should have established trials by the people themselves, that is to say by jury. There are instruments so dangerous to the rights of the nation, and which place them so totally at the mercy of their governors, that those governors, whether legislative or executive, should be restrained from keeping such instruments on foot but in well defined cases. Such an instrument is a standing army. We are now allowed to say such a declaration of rights, as a supplement to the constitution where that is silent, is wanting to secure us in these points. The general voice has legitimated this objection. It has not however authorized me to consider as a real defect, what I thought and still think one, the perpetual re-eligibility of the president. But three states out of 11. having declared against this, we must suppose we are wrong according to the fundamental law of every society, the lex majoris partis, to which we are bound to submit. And should the majority change their opinion, and become sensible that this trait in their constitution is wrong, I would wish it to remain uncorrected as long as we can avail ourselves of the services of our great leader, whose talents and whose weight of character I consider as peculiarly necessary to get the government so under way as that it may afterwards be carried on by subordinate characters.

I must give you sincere thanks for the details of small news contained in your letter. You know how precious that kind of information is to a person absent from his country, and how difficult it is to be procured. I hope to receive soon permission to visit America this summer, and to possess myself anew, by conversation with my countrymen, of their spirit and their ideas. I know only the Americans of the year 1784. They tell me this is to be much a stranger to those of 1789. This renewal of acquaintance is no indifferent matter to one acting at such a distance as that instructions cannot be received hot and hot. One of my pleasures too will be that of talking over the old and new with you. In the mean time, and at all times, I have the honor to be with great & sincere esteem Dear Sir Your friend & servant,

Jefferson to John Paul Jones, 1789*

Mar. 23, 1789

Dear Sir,

Your favor of Jan. 20/31 from Petersburg came safe to hand, and is the only proof we have received of your existence since you left Copenhagen. I mention this that, reflecting how and what you have written heretofore, you may know how and what you may write hereafter. I shall put nothing into this letter but what is important to you, and unimportant to any government thro which it may pass.

To begin with your private affairs, I received three days ago from M. Amoureux: a bill for 1900. livres paiable at three usances which I have delivered to Messrs. Grand & co. and desired them to receive it when due, and hold it subject to your order. This Amoureux mentions as forming, *á une bagatelle près*, the balance due you.

Having been enabled to carry into execution the orders for the Medals, I have contracted with workmen for them, and they are all in hand. Your's is to be executed by Dupré, who is I think the best among them; and it will be done in the course of the summer. My instructions as to these medals are general, to wit; I am to deliver one of gold or

*The Papers of Thomas Jefferson, Vol. 14, pp. 686–89.

silver (as the case may be) to the person who is the subject; to send one of silver to every sovereign and one of copper to every university of Europe (Gr. Britain excepted) 200 copies to Congress and one apeice to La Fayette, Rochambeau, Destaing, and Degrasse. I am at liberty to deliver no others, not even at the orders and expence of the persons who are the subjects of the medals. But your wish will be fulfilled as to the Empress, because I shall send her a suite of the whole medals under the general order. I had lately presented to me a demand for about 4000l. from the French Consul at Bergen, without being told for what. My answer was that I knew of no cause for such an application and could not pay it. I suspect this demand has some connection with a very large packet of official papers I received addressed to you from Denmark or Norway, in the Danish language. By the bye, that business makes no way. Tho' I have written to Count Bernstorff pressing a settlement, and often spoken to their envoy here, I cannot obtain one word of an answer of any kind.—Another word on the subject of your medal. Immediately on the receipt of your letter I wrote to the medallist, cul-de-sac Tetebout (his name is Renaud) and bought a copy of the medal he had made, which I gave to Dupré, with the observations of your letter on it. He will avail himself of so much of the design as is good, and as is permitted by the resolution of the Academie, to whom I applied for devices for all the medals. Gordon's history furnished me a good relation of your engagement, tho' the author has permitted himself an impertinence or two relative to you. Renaud's account is 852l. as you will see by the enclosed state of it. Mr. Grand will pay him on your order so much of it as you find just. Houdon has promised to have the eight busts ready as soon as possible, and I shall have him paid out of the same fund. They will be ready packed against your orders arrive as to the persons to whom they were destined. For you will please to observe that neither your letter of Jan. 20/31 nor the extracts forwarded in that from Oczakow before of 29 Aug. /9 Sep. and Sep. 16/26 mention the name of the persons they were to be sent to. In like manner your letter of Jan. 20/31 says it incloses an extract of the journal of your campaign in 1779. But none such was inclosed. Mr. Short, now in Italy, will be here to receive your orders for the distribution of the busts. I shall be absent in America from the 1st. of May to the end of November, as I have asked leave to go and carry my family home and arrange my affairs, and shall return before the winter sets in. But the busts will be finished and paid for before I go so that nothing will remain for Mr. Short but to forward them. You know my sentiments respecting the Algerines. I shall certainly make them a subject of consultation with our government, while I shall be in America. My favorite project is still to procure a concurrence of the powers at war with them, that that concurrence continue till the strength of those barbarians at sea be totally annihilated, and that the combined force employed in effecting this shall not be disturbed in it's operation by wars or other incidents occurring between the powers composing it.

Our new constitution was acceded to in the course of the last summer by all the states except N. Carolina and Rhode island. Massachusets, Virginia and New York, tho they accepted unconditionally, yet gave it as a perpetual instruction to their future delegates never to cease urging certain amendments. N. Carolina insisted that the amendments should be made before she would accede. The most important of these amendments will be effected by adding a bill of rights; and even the friends of the Constitution are become sensible of the expediency of such an addition were it only to conciliate the opposition. In fact this security for liberty seems to be demanded by the general voice of America, and we may conclude it will unquestionably be added. N. York, Virginia and N. Carolina have also demanded that a term be fixed after which the president shall be no longer eligible. But the public has been silent on this demand; so we may doubt it's success. In the mean time the elections for the new government were going on quietly at the date of our last letters. We have the names of most of the Senators; but not of the representatives. There was no question but Genl. Washington would be elected President; and we know that he would accept it, tho' with vast reluctance. The new Congress was to meet the 1st. Wednesday in this month, at New York. The tickets of election of the President would then be opened, and I presume that General Washington is now at New York, and the new legislature in a course of business. The only competitors for the Vice presidentship were Mr. J. Adams and Mr. Hancock. It was thought the former would be chosen. Tho' the new constitution was adopted in 11. states, yet in those of Massachusets, Virginia and New York it was by very small majorities; and the minorities in the two last are far from the laudable acquiescence of that of Massachusets. Govr. Clinton in New York, and Mr. Henry in Virginia are moving heaven and earth to have a new Convention to make capital changes. But they will not succeed. There has been just opposition enough to produce probably further guards to liberty without touching the energy of the government, and this will bring over the bulk of the opposition to the side of the new government.

In this country, things go on well. The States general are to meet the 27th. of April. The report of Mr. Necker, to the king seems to promise the public 1. That the king will pretend in future to no power of laying a new tax or continuing and old one. 2. That he will not take upon him to appropriate the public monies to be given by the States. Of course they are to appropriate. 3. That the States shall convene at fixed epochs. 4. That the king will concur with them in modifying letters de cachet. 5. And in giving a wholesome liberty to the press. 6. That ministers shall be responsible: and 7. that all this shall be so solemnly fixed that the king nor his successors shall have any power to change it. Nothing has been said about giving to the States a participation in legislation: but it will be insisted on. The States will be composed of about 300. clergy, 300 Nobles, and 600. commoners, and their first question will be whether they shall vote by orders or persons. I think the latter will be decided. If this difficulty be got over, I see no other to a very happy settlement of their affairs. They will consolidate and fund their debts, and this circumstance, as well as the stability which the changes will give to the proceedings of their government, will give them probably the first credit in Europe, and enable them, after the present year to take any part they please in the settlement of it's affairs. You have heard of the insanity of the king of England. His ministers pretend he is recovered. In truth he is better, but not well. Time will be necessary for his perfect recovery, and to produce a confidence that it is not merely a lucid interval. I shall be glad to hear from you as often as possible, and have the honor to be with very great esteem, Dear Sir your most obedient & most humble servt,

Jefferson to Lafayette, 1790*

Apr. 2, 1790

Behold me, my dear friend, dubbed Secretary of state, instead of returning to the far more agreeable position which placed me in the daily participation of your friendship. I found the appointment in the newspapers the day of my arrival in Virginia. I had indeed been asked while in France whether I would accept of any appointment at home, and I had answered that without meaning to remain long where I was, I meant it to be the last office I should ever act in. Unfortunately this letter had not arrived at the time of arranging the new government. I expressed freely to the President my desire to return. He left me free, but still shewing his own desire. This, and the concern of others, more general than I had a right to expect, induced me after 3. months parleying, to sacrifice my own inclinations. I have been here then ten days harnessed in new gear. Wherever I am, or ever shall be, I shall be sincere in my friendship to you and to your nation. I think, with others, that nations are to be governed according to their own interest: but I am convinced that it is their interest, in the long run, to be grateful, faithful to their engagements even in the worst of circumstances, and honorable and generous always. If I had not known that the head of our government was in these sentiments, and that his national and private ethics were the same, I would never have been where I am. I am sorry to tell you his health is less firm than it used to be. However there is nothing in it to give alarm. The opposition to our new constitution has almost totally disappeared. Some few indeed had gone such lengths in their declarations of hostility that they feel it awkward perhaps to come over, but the amendments proposed by Congress, have brought over almost all their followers. If the President can be preserved a few years till habits of authority and obedience can be established, generally, we have nothing to fear. The little vaut-rien, Rhode-island

*The Papers of Thomas Jefferson, Vol. 16, pp. 292–93.

will come over with a little more time. Our last news from Paris is of the 8th. of January. So far it seemed that your revolution had got along with a steady pace: meeting indeed occasional difficulties and dangers, but we are not to expect to be translated from despotism to liberty, in a feather-bed. I have never feared for the ultimate result, tho' I have feared for you personally. Indeed I hope you will never see such another 5th. and 6th. of October. Take care of yourself, my dear friend. For tho' I think your nation would in any event work out her salvation, I am persuaded were she to lose you, it would cost her oceans of blood, and years of confusion and anarchy. Kiss and bless your dear children for me. Learn them to be as you are a cement between our two nations. I write to Madame de la fayette so have only to add assurances of the respect & esteem of your affectionate friend & humble servt,

MADISON INTRODUCES HIS AMENDMENTS,
MAY—JUNE, 1789

Commentary

There is no doubt that Madison, acting in fulfillment of his campaign pledge, was the catalyst in the congressional history of the federal Bill of Rights. President Washington had, it is true, referred, in his first message to Congress, to the widespread demand for amendments to the Constitution. But he had declined to make "particular recommendations on this subject," leaving it to Congress to decide what to do on the matter.

Congress itself was concerned with other subjects during the first part of its session. On May 4, Madison made an announcement (in the midst of a lengthy debate on import and tonnage duties) of his intention "to bring on the subject of amendments to the constitution" on May 25. Madison may have been stimulated to act when he did in order to counter the movement for a Second Convention, which was embodied in the application from the Virginia Legislature for such a Convention, which was introduced by Congressman Bland the very next day, as well as a similar application from New York on May 6. Madison was able to secure the filing of both applications (rather than reference to the Committee of the Whole). When Madison actually introduced his proposed amendments on June 8, that effectively ended any chance the applications for a Second Convention might otherwise have had.

Madison did not bring up the subject of amendments on May 25, as he had announced he would, probably because the House was still in the midst of its debate on import duties. Apparently it was agreed, though the *Annals* are silent on the point, to postpone the subject for two weeks. On June 8, Madison rose at the beginning of the session and reminded the House that this was the day assigned for considering the subject of constitutional amendments. He said he would bring the amendments forward, "and advocate them until they should be finally adopted or rejected by a constitutional majority of this House." He then moved that the House go into Committee of the Whole to consider the matter.

Madison's motion was opposed by other members who objected to interrupting the revenue business upon which the House was engaged. Mr. Jackson of Georgia declared that, "we ought not to be in a hurry with respect to altering the constitution," but even "if gentlemen should think it a subject deserving of attention, they will surely not neglect the more important business which is now unfinished before them . . . . without revenue the wheels of Government cannot move." Madison replied that someone like Jackson, who was unfriendly to amendments, was right in opposing his motion; but the same was not true of those who favored amendments: "if we continue to postpone from time to time, . . . it may occasion suspicions" and the public "may think we are not sincere in our desire to incorporate such amendments in the constitution as will secure those rights, which they consider as not sufficiently guarded." Madison's statement here is a good indication of how widespread the popular demand for a Bill of Rights was, and the need for the Federalists themselves (who had a congressional majority) to act speedily to meet that demand. Other opponents of the motion then spoke, repeating, in Roger Sherman's words, that it would be "imprudent to neglect much more important concerns for this."

Madison then rose and delivered his famous speech explaining his proposed amendments and why they were necessary. This is rightly considered one of the great addresses in our history, for, in it, Madison delivered what was, in effect, the sponsor's statement on the legislative measure that was to become the federal Bill of Rights. He began by apologizing for being "accessary to the loss of a single moment of time by the House." But, he said, prudence itself requires the House not to let its first session pass "without proposing some things to be incorporated into the constitution, that will render it . . . acceptable to the whole people of the United States." It is desirable to quiet the apprehensions felt by many that the Constitution does not adequately protect liberty. "We ought not to disregard their inclination, but, on principles of amity and moderation, conform to their wishes, and expressly declare the great rights of mankind secured under this constitution."

Madison goes on to say that there is everything to gain and nothing to lose if we "provide those securities for liberty which are required by a part of the community." He then refers again to the extent of the popular desire for a Bill of Rights: "the great mass of the people who opposed it, disliked it because it did not contain effectual provisions against encroachments on particular rights, and those safeguards which they have been long accustomed to have interposed between them and the magistrate who exercises the sovereign power."

Madison then read the "amendments which have occurred to me, proper to be recommended by Congress to the State Legislatures." Here we have the crucial first draft of the federal Bill of Rights. The Madison proposals covered all of the articles which were eventually included in the Bill of Rights, including much of the language that was ultimately adopted. The Madison amendments are based directly upon the amendments recommended by the state ratifying conventions, particularly by Virginia. He could write a draft which served as the basis for the final Bill of Rights because he built on the state consensus in the matter. He designedly avoided controversial provisions, saying "I shall not propose a single alteration but is likely to meet the concurrence required by the constitution." Or (as he put it in a letter at the time) "two or three contentious additions would even now prostrate the whole project." (See also letters to Pendleton and Johnston [*infra* pp. 1047, 1048].)

The text of Madison's proposed amendments is contained in his June 8 address to the House (*infra* p. 1026). We have available Madison's own notes for his June 8 speech (*infra* p. 1042), and they tell us that the amendments "relate 1st to private rights." As such, the Madison draft "relates to what may be called a bill of rights." The object of it is "To limit and qualify pow[er] by except[ing] from grant cases in wh[ich] it shall not be exercised or ex[pressed] in a particular manner." Its primary purpose is to guard "against the legislative, for it is the most powerful, and most likely to be abused,"—as well as to guard against abuses by the executive and "the body of the people, operating by the majority against the minority."

When we look at the text of the Madison amendments, the first thing we notice is that they are drawn up as insertions into the body of the original Constitution. As his letter to Jefferson of May 27 shows, Madison had decided by then to incorporate his Bill of Rights into the text of the Constitution. As we shall see, this was changed during the congressional debate to the present form of a series of separate amendments to be added at the end of the Constitution.

If we analyze the amendments introduced by Madison, we find that they cover all of the articles which eventually became the federal Bill of Rights. Four of Madison's amendments were eliminated during the congressional debate: his Article 1, containing the general declaration of the theory of popular government; Article 5, prohibiting state violations of freedom of conscience, the press, and trial by jury; Article 6, limiting appeals; and Article 8, separation of powers. Two failed of ratification: his Articles 2 and 3, dealing with congressional size and compensation. The other Madison amendments have survived substantially in their original form as the federal Bill of Rights itself. Every provision of the Bill of Rights is based directly upon Madison's original draft. Where changes were made during the congressional debate, they relate to form rather than substance.

The extent of Madison's achievement in this respect is not lessened by the fact that he based his draft upon the state recommendatory amendments, especially those of Virginia. It was Madison who chose which among the pyramid of state proposals should be acted upon by Congress and (with the perspective of two centuries of subsequent constitutional development) we can say that he chose remarkably well, including in his list all of the great rights which are appropriate for constitutional protection (except for equal protection, which was not even thought of as a basic right at the time). It was Madison who also tightened the constitutional language, substituting the imperative "shall" for the flaccid "ought" and "ought nots" of the state proposals. We can see his contribution in this respect in the following sequence:

Bill of Rights, 1689: "That excessive bail *ought not* to be required, nor excessive fines imposed; nor cruel and unusual punishments inflicted."

Virginia Declaration of Rights, 1776: "That excessive bail *ought not* to be required, nor excessive fines imposed, nor cruel and unusual punishments inflicted."

Virginia Proposed Amendments, 1788: "That excessive bail *ought not* to be required, nor excessive fines imposed, nor cruel and unusual punishments inflicted."

Amendment proposed by Madison, June 8, 1789: "Excessive bail *shall not* be required, nor excessive fines imposed, nor cruel and unusual punishments inflicted."

In addition, it was Madison who followed the New York, rather than the Virginia precedent, and drafted his version of section 39 of Magna Carta in terms of "due process of law," instead of "the law of the land." As seen [*supra* p. 856) this change, which was the origin of the Due Process Clause of the Fifth, and later of the Fourteenth Amendment, was of seminal significance for our subsequent constitutional development—though it may be doubted that Madison, any more than Lansing and Hamilton in New York before him (*supra* p. 856) realized anything like the full import of what he was doing in writing the Due Process Clause into the Constitution.

The remainder of Madison's June 8 speech seeks to explain his amendments and the need for them. There is little new here, though Madison's statement is now considered the classic presentation of the case for a Bill of Rights in a system such as ours. Of particular interest to us is his recognition that a Bill of Rights would be effective because it would be enforced by the courts: "independent tribunals of justice will consider themselves in a peculiar manner the guardians of those rights." Madison concludes by withdrawing his motion for consideration by the Committee of the Whole (since the other speakers had opposed it) and moving that a select committee be appointed to consider his proposals. Now, however, the other speakers opposed the appointment of a select committee and a motion to refer Madison's proposals to the House acting as a Committee of the Whole was adopted. This ended the debate of June 8.

First Annual Message of President Washington, 1789*

The President, having returned to his seat, after a short pause arose, and addressed the Senate and House of Representatives as follows:

Fellow Citizens of the Senate, and of the House of Representatives:

Among the vicissitudes incident to life, no event could have filled me with greater anxieties than that of which the notification was transmitted by your order, and received on the 14th day of the present month. On the one hand,

Annals of Congress, Vol. 1, pp. 27–30.

I was summoned by my country, whose voice I can never hear but with veneration and love, from a retreat which I had chosen with the fondest predilection, and, in my flattering hopes, with an immutable decision, as the asylum of my declining years: a retreat which was rendered every day more necessary, as well as more dear to me, by the addition of habit to inclination, and of frequent interruptions in my health, to the gradual waste committed on it by time. On the other hand, the magnitude and difficulty of the trust to which the voice of my country called me, being sufficient to awaken in the wisest and most experienced of her citizens a distrustful scrutiny into his qualifications, could not but overwhelm with despondence one, who, inheriting inferior endowments from nature, and unpractised in the duties of civil administration, ought to be peculiarly conscious of his own deficiencies. In this conflict of emotions, all I dare aver is, that it has been my faithful study to collect my duty from a just appreciation of every circumstance by which it might be effected. All I dare hope is, that if, in executing this task, I have been too much swayed by a grateful remembrance of former instances, or by an affectionate sensibility to this transcendant proof of the confidence of my fellow-citizens, and have thence too little consulted my incapacity as well as disinclination for the weighty and untried cares before me, my error will be palliated by the motives which misled me, and its consequences be judged by my country, with some share of the partiality in which they originated.

Such being the impressions under which I have, in obedience to the public summons, repaired to the present station, it would be peculiarly improper to omit, in this first official act, my fervent supplications to that Almighty Being, who rules over the universe—who presides in the councils of nations—and whose providential aids can supply every human defect—that his benediction may consecrate to the liberties and happiness of the people of the United States, a Government instituted by themselves, for these essential purposes: and may enable every instrument employed in its administration to execute with success the functions allotted to his charge. In tendering this homage to the Great Author of every public and private good, I assure myself that it expresses your sentiments not less than my own, nor those of my fellow-citizens at large less than either. No people can be bound to acknowledge and adore the invisible hand which conducts the affairs of men, more than the people of the United States. Every step by which they have advanced to the character of an independent nation, seems to have been distinguished by some token of providential agency; and in the important revolution just accomplished in the system of their united Government, the tranquil deliberations and voluntary consent of so many distinct communities from which the event has resulted, cannot be compared with the means by which most Governments have been established, without some return of pious gratitude, along with an humble anticipation of the future blessings which the past seems, to presage. These reflections, arising out of the present crisis, have forced themselves too strongly on my mind to be suppressed. You will join with me, I trust, in thinking, that there are none under the influence of which the proceedings of a new and free Government can more auspiciously commence.

By the article establishing the executive department, it is made the duty of the President "to recommend to your consideration such measures as he shall judge necessary and expedient." The circumstances under which I now meet you will acquit me from entering into that subject, further than to refer to the great constitutional charter under which you are assembled, and which, in defining your powers, designates the objects to which your attention is to be given. It will be more consistent with those circumstances, and far more congenial with the feelings which actuate me, to substitute, in place of a recommendation of particular measures, the tribute that is due to the talents, the rectitude, and the patriotism, which adorn the characters selected to devise and adopt them. In these honorable qualifications, I behold the surest pledges, that, as on one side no local prejudices or attachments, no separate views, nor party animosities, will misdirect the comprehensive and equal eye which ought to watch over this great assemblage of communities and interests; so, on another, that the foundations of our national policy will be laid in the pure and immutable principles of private morality, and the pre-eminence of free Government be exemplified by all the attributes which can win the affections of its citizens, and command the respect of the world. I dwell on this prospect with every satisfaction which an ardent love for my country can inspire: since there is no truth more thoroughly established, than that there exists, in the economy and course of nature, an indissoluble union between virtue and happiness; between duty and advantage; between the genuine maxims of an honest and magnanimous policy, and the solid rewards of public prosperity and felicity: since we ought to be no less persuaded that the propitious smiles of Heaven can never be expected on a nation that disregards the eternal rules of order and right, which Heaven itself has ordained; and since the preservation of the sacred fire of liberty, and the destiny of the republican model of Government, are justly considered as deeply, perhaps as finally, staked, on the experiment entrusted to the hands of the American people.

Besides the ordinary objects submitted to your care, it will remain with your judgment to decide how far an exercise of the occasional power delegated by the fifth article of the Constitution, is rendered expedient at the present juncture, by the nature of objections which have been urged against the system, or by the degree of inquietude which has given birth to them. Instead of undertaking particular recommendations on this subject, in which I could be guided by no lights derived from official opportunities, I shall again give way to my entire confidence in your discernment and pursuit of the public good: for, I assure myself, that whilst you carefully avoid every alteration which might endanger the benefits of a united and effective Government, or which ought to await the future lessons of experience; a reverence for the characteristic rights of freemen, and a regard for the public harmony, will sufficiently influence your deliberations on the question, how far the former can be more impregnably fortified, or the latter be safely and advantageously promoted.

To the preceding observations I have one to add, which will be most properly addressed to the House of Representatives. It concerns myself, and will, therefore, be as brief as possible. When I was first honored with a call into the service of my country, then on the eve of an arduous struggle for its liberties, the light in which I contemplated my duty required that I should renounce every pecuniary compensation. From this resolution I have in no instance departed. And being still under the impressions which produced it, I must decline, as inapplicable to myself, any share in the personal emoluments which may be indispensably included in a permanent provision for the executive department; and must accordingly pray that the pecuniary estimates for the station in which I am placed may, during my continuance in it, be limited to such actual expenditures as the public good may be thought to require.

Having thus imparted to you my sentiments, as they have been awakened by the occasion which brings us together, I shall take my present leave; but not without resorting once more to the benign Parent of the human race, in humble supplication, that, since He has been pleased to favor the American people with opportunities for deliberating in perfect tranquillity, and dispositions for deciding with unparalleled unanimity on a form of Government for the security of their union, and the advancement of their happiness, so his divine blessing may be equally conspicuous in the enlarged views, the temperate consultations, and the wise measures, on which the success of this Government must depend.

House of Representatives Debates, May—June, 1789*

[Monday, May 4]

Before the House adjourned, Mr. Madison gave notice, that he intended to bring on the subject of amendments to the constitution, on the 4th Monday of this month.

[Tuesday, May 5]

. . . Mr. Madison, from the committee appointed to prepare an address on the part of this House to the President of the United States, in answer to his speech to both Houses of Congress, reported as followeth:

*Annals of Congress, Vol. 1, pp. 257–468.

The Address of the House of Representatives to George Washington, President of the United States

Sir: The Representatives of the People of the United States present their congratulations on the event by which your fellow-citizens have attested the pre-eminence of your merit. You have long held the first place in their esteem. You have often received tokens of their affection. You now possess the only proof that remained of their gratitude for your services, of their reverence for your wisdom, and of their confidence in your virtues. You enjoy the highest, because the truest honor, of being the First Magistrate, by the unanimous choice of the freest people on the face of the earth.

*   *   *

The question arising out of the fifth article of the Constitution will receive all the attention demanded by its importance; and will, we trust, be decided, under the influence of all the considerations to which you allude.

*   *   *

All that remains is, that we join in your fervent supplications for the blessings of heaven on our country, and that we add our own for the choicest of these blessings on the most beloved of our citizens.

*   *   *

Mr. Bland presented to the House the following application from the Legislature of Virginia, to wit:

Virginia, to wit:

In General Assembly, Nov. 14, 1788

Resolved, That an application be made in the name and on behalf of the Legislature of this Commonwealth to the Congress of the United States, in the words following, to wit:

The good People of this Commonwealth, in Convention assembled, having ratified the Constitution submitted to their consideration, this Legislature has in conformity to that act, and the resolutions of the United States in Congress assembled, to them transmitted, thought proper to make the arrangements that were necessary for carrying it into effect. Having thus shown themselves obedient to the voice in their constituents, all America will find that, so far as it depended on them, that plan of Government will be carried into immediate operation.

But the sense of the People of Virginia would be but in part complied with, and but little regarded, if we went no farther. In the very moment of adoption, and coeval with the ratification of the new plan of Government, the general voice of the Convention of this State pointed to objects no less interesting to the People we represent, and equally entitled to our attention. At the same time that, from motives of affection to our sister States, the

Convention yielded their assent to the ratification, they gave the most unequivocal proofs that they dreaded its operation under the present form.

In acceding to the Government under this impression, painful must have been the prospect, had they not derived consolation from a full expectation of its imperfections being speedily amended. In this resource, therefore, they placed their confidence, a confidence that will continue to support them, whilst they have reason to belive that they have not calculated upon it in vain.

In making known to you the objections of the People of this Commonwealth to the new plan of Government, we deem it unnecessary to enter into a particular detail of its defects, which they consider as involving all the great and unalienable rights of freemen. For their sense on this subject, we beg leave to refer you to the proceedings of their late Convention, and the sense of the House of Delegates, as expressed in their resolutions of the thirtieth day of October, one thousand seven hundred and eighty-eight.

We think proper, however, to declare, that, in our opinion, as those objections were not founded in speculative theory, but deduced from principles which have been established by the melancholy example of other nations in different ages, so they will never be removed, until the cause itself shall cease to exist. The sooner, therefore, the public apprehensions are quieted, and the Government is possessed of the confidence of the People, the more salutary will be its operations; and the longer its duration.

The cause of amendments we consider as a common cause; and, since concessions have been made from political motives, which, we conceive, may endanger the Republic, we trust that a commendable zeal will be shown for obtaining those provisions, which experience has taught us are necessary to secure from danger the unalienable rights of human nature.

The anxiety with which our countrymen press for the accomplishment of this important end, will all admit of delay. The slow forms of Congressional discussion and recommendation, if, indeed, they should ever agree to any change, would, we fear, be less certain of success. Happily for their wishes, the Constitution hath presented an alternative, by admitting the submission to a convention of the States. To this, therefore, we resort as the source from whence they are to derive relief from their present apprehensions.

We do, therefore, in behalf of our constituents, in the most earnest and solemn manner, make this application to Congress, that a convention be immediately called, of deputies from the several States, with full power to take into their consideration the defects of this constitution that have been suggested by the State Conventions, and report such amendments thereto as they shall find best suited to promote our common interests, and secure to ourselves and our latest posterity the great and unalienable rights of mankind.

John Jones, Speaker Senate.
Thomas Mathews, Speaker Ho. Del.

After the reading of this application,

Mr. Bland moved to refer it to the Committee of the whole on the state of the Union.

Mr. Boudinot: According to the terms of the Constitution, the business cannot be taken up until a certain number of States have concurred in similar applications; certainly the House is disposed to pay a proper attention to the application of so respectable a State as Virginia, but if it is a business which we cannot interfere with in a constitutional manner, we had better let it remain on the files of the House until the proper number of applications come forward.

Mr. Bland thought there could be no impropriety in referring any subject to a committee, but surely this deserved the serious and solemn consideration of Congress. He hoped no gentleman would oppose the compliment of referring it to a Committee of the whole; beside, it would be a guide to the deliberations of the committee on the subject of amendments, which would shortly come before the House.

Mr. Madison said, he had no doubt but the House was inclined to treat the present application with respect, but he doubted the propriety of committing it, because it would seem to imply that the House had a right to deliberate upon the subject. This he believed was not the case until two-thirds of the State Legislatures concurred in such application, and then it is out of the power of Congress to decline complying, the words of the Constitution being express and positive relative to the agency Congress may have in case of applications of this nature. "The Congress, wherever two-thirds of both Houses shall deem it necessary, shall propose amendments to this Constitution; or, on the application of the Legislatures of two-thirds of the several States, shall call a convention for proposing amendments." From hence it must appear, that Congress have no deliberative power on this occasion. The most respectful and constitutional mode of performing our duty will be, to let it be entered on the minutes, and remain upon the files of the House until similar applications come to hand from two-thirds of the States.

Mr. Boudinot hoped the gentleman who desired the commitment of the application would not suppose him wanting in respect to the State of Virginia. He entertained the most profound respect for her—but it was on a principle of respect to order and propriety that he opposed the commitment; enough had been said to convince gentlemen that it was improper to commit—for what purpose can it be done? what can the committee report? The application is to call a new convention. Now, in this case, there is nothing left for us to do, but to call one when two-thirds of the State Legislatures apply for that purpose. He hoped the gentleman would withdraw his motion for commitment.

Mr. Bland: The application now before the committee contains a number of reasons why it is necessary to call a convention. By the fifth article of the

Constitution, Congress are obliged to order this convention when two-thirds of the Legislatures apply for it; but how can these reasons be properly weighed, unless it be done in committee? Therefore, I hope the House will agree to refer it.

Mr. Huntington thought it proper to let the application remain on the table, it can be called up with others when enough are presented to make two-thirds of the whole States. There would be an evident impropriety in committing, because it would argue a right in the House to deliberate, and, consequently, a power to procrastinate the measure applied for.

Mr. Tucker thought it not right to disregard the application of any State, and inferred, that the House had a right to consider every application that was made; if two-thirds had not applied, the subject might be taken into consideration, but if two-thirds had applied, it precluded deliberation on the part of the House. He hoped the present application would be properly noticed.

Mr. Gerry. The gentleman from Virginia (Mr. Madison) told us yesterday, that he meant to move the consideration of amendments on the fourth Monday of this month; he did not make such motion then, and may be prevented by accident, or some other cause, from carrying his intention into execution when the time he mentioned shall arrive. I think the subject however is introduced to the House, and, perhaps, it may consist with order to let the present application lie on the table until the business is taken up generally.

Mr. Page thought it the best way to enter the application at large upon the Journals, and do the same by all that came in, until sufficient were made to obtain their object, and let the original be deposited in the archives of Congress. He deemed this the proper mode of disposing of it, and what is in itself proper can never be construed into disrespect.

Mr. Bland acquiesced in this disposal of the application. Whereupon, it was ordered to be entered at length on the Journals, and the original to be placed on the files of Congress.

*   *   *

[Wednesday, May 6]

Mr. Lawrence, from New York, presented to the House an application, in the name and behalf of the Legislature of that State, addressed to the Congress of the United States; which being read, was ordered to be filed.

*   *   *

[Monday, June 8]

*   *   *

Amendments to the Constitution

Mr. Madison rose, and reminded the House that this was the day that he had heretofore named for bringing forward amendments to the constitution, as contemplated in the fifth article of the constitution, addressing the Speaker as follows: This day, Mr. Speaker, is the day assigned for taking into consideration the subject of amendments to the constitution. As I considered myself bound in honor and in duty to do what I have done on this subject, I shall proceed to bring the amendments before you as soon as possible, and advocate them until they shall be finally adopted or rejected by a constitutional majority of this House. With a view of drawing your attention to this important object, I shall move that this House do now resolve itself into a Committee of the whole on the state of the Union; by which an opportunity will be given, to bring forward some propositions, which I have strong hopes will meet with the unanimous approbation of this House, after the fullest discussion and most serious regard. I therefore move you, that the House now go into a committee on this business.

Mr. Smith was not inclined to interrupt the measures which the public were so anxiously expecting, by going into a Committee of the whole at this time. He observed there were two modes of introducing this business to the House. One by appointing a select committee to take into consideration the several amendments proposed by the State conventions; this he thought the most likely way to shorten the business. The other was, that the gentleman should lay his propositions on the table, for the consideration of the members; that they should be printed, and taken up for discussion at a future day. Either of these modes would enable the House to enter upon business better prepared than could be the case by a sudden transition from other important concerns to which their minds were strongly bent. He therefore hoped that the honorable gentleman would consent to bring the subject forward in one of those ways, in preference to going into a Committee of the whole. For, said he, it must appear extremely impolitic to go into the consideration of amending the Government, before it is organized, before it has begun to operate. Certainly, upon reflection, it must appear to be premature. I wish, therefore, gentlemen would consent to the delay: for the business which lies in an unfinished state—I mean particularly the collection bill—is necessary to be passed; else all we have hitherto done is of no effect. If we go into the discussion of this subject, it will take us three weeks or a month; and during all this time, every other business must be suspended, because we cannot proceed with either accuracy or despatch when the mind is perpetually shifted from one subject to another.

Mr. Jackson: I am of opinion we ought not to be in a hurry with respect to altering the constitution. For my part, I have no idea of speculating in this serious manner on theory. If I agree to alterations in the mode of administering this Government, I shall like to stand on the sure ground of experience, and not be treading air. What experience have we had of the good or bad qualities of this constitution? Can any gentleman affirm to me one proposition that is the certain and absolute amendment? I deny that he can. Our constitution, sir, is like a vessel just launched, and lying at the wharf; she is untried, you can hardly discover any one of her properties. It is not known how she will answer her helm, or lay her course; whether she will bear with safety the precious freight to be deposited in her hold. But, in this state, will the prudent merchant attempt alterations? Will he employ workmen to tear off the planking and take asunder the frame? He certainly will not. Let us, gentlemen, fit out our vessel, set up the masts, and expand her sails, and be guided by the experiment in our alterations. If she sails upon an uneven keel, let us right her by adding weight where it is wanting. In this way, it may remedy her defects to the satisfaction of all concerned; but if we proceed now to make alterations, we may deface a beauty, or deform a well proportioned piece of workmanship. In short, Mr. Speaker, I am not for amendment at this time; but if gentlemen should think its subject deserving of attention, they will surely not neglect the more important business which is now unfinished before them. Without we pass the collection bill we can get no revenue and without revenue the wheels of Government cannot move. I am against taking up the subject at present, and shall therefore be totally against the amendments, if the Government is not organized, that I may see whether it is grievous or not.

When the propriety of making amendments shall be obvious from experience, I trust there will be virtue enough in my country to make them. Much has been said by the opponents to this constitution, respecting the insecurity of jury trials, that great bulwark of personal safety. All their objections may be done away, by proper regulations on this point, and I do not have but such regulations will take place. The bill is now before the Senate, and a proper attention is shown to this business. Indeed, I cannot conceive how it could be opposed; I think an almost omnipotent Emperor would not be hard enough to set himself against it. Then why should we fear a power which cannot be improperly exercised?

We have proceeded to make some regulations under the constitution; but have met with an inaccuracy, unless it may be said that the clause respecting vessels bound to or from one State be obliged to enter, clear, or pay duties in another, is somewhat obscure; yet that is not sufficient, I trust, in any gentleman's opinion to induce an amendment. But let me see what will be the consequence of taking up the subject? Are we going to finish it in an hour; believe not; it will take us more than a day, a week, a month—it will take a year to complete it! And will it be doing our duty to our country, to neglect or delay putting the Government in motion, when every thing depends upon its being speedily done?

Let the constitution have a fair trial; let it be examined by experience, discover by that test what its errors are, and then talk of amending; but to attempt it now is doing it at a risk, which is certainly imprudent. I have the honor of coming from a State that ratified the constitution by the unanimous vote of a numerous convention: the people of Georgia have manifested their attachment to it, by adopting a State constitution framed upon the same plan as this. But although they are thus satisfied, I shall not be against such amendments as will gratify the inhabitants of other States, provided they are judged of by experience and not merely on theory. For this reason, I wish the consideration of the subject postponed until the 1st of March, 1790.

Mr. Goodhue: I believe it would be perfectly right in the gentleman who spoke last, to move a postponement to the time he has mentioned; because he is opposed to the consideration of amendments altogether. But I believe it will be proper to attend to the subject earlier; because it is the wish of many of our constituents, that something should be added to the constitution, to secure in a stronger manner their liberties from the inroads of power. Yet I think the present time premature; inasmuch as we have other business before us, which is incomplete, but essential to the public interest. When that is finished, I shall concur in taking up the subject of amendments.

Mr. Burke thought amendments to the constitution necesssary, but this was not the proper time to bring them forward. He wished the Government completely organized before they entered upon this ground. The law for collecting the revenue is immediately necessary; the Treasury Department must be established; till this, and other important subjects are determined, he was against taking this up. He said it might interrupt the harmony of the House, which was necessary to be preserved in order to despatch the great objects of legislation. He hoped it would be postponed for the present, and pledged himself to bring it forward hereafter, if nobody else would.

Mr Madison: The gentleman from Georgia (Mr. Jackson) is certainly right in his opposition to my motion for going into a Committee of the whole, because he is unfriendly to the object I have in contemplation; but I cannot see that the gentlemen who wish for amendments to be proposed at the present session, stand on good ground when they object to the House going into committee on this business.

When I first hinted to the House my intentions of begging their deliberations to this object, I found the pressure of other important matters had submitted the propriety of postponning this till the more urgent business was despatched; but finding that business not despatched, when the order of the day for considering amendments arrived, I thought it a good reason for a farther delay; I moved the postponement accordingly. I am sorry the same reason still exists in some degree, but operates with less force, when it is considered that it is not now proposed to enter into a full and minute discussion of every part of the subject, but merely to bring it before the House, that our constituents may see we pay a proper attention to a subject they have much at heart; and if it does not give that full gratification which is to be wished, they will discover that it proceeds from the urgency of business of a very important nature. But if we continue to postpone from time to time, and refuse to let the subject come into view, it may occasion suspicions, which, though not well founded, may tend to inflame or prejudice the public mind against our decisions. They may think we are not sincere in our desire to incorporate such amendments in the constitution as will secure those rights, which they consider as not sufficiently guarded. The applications for amendments come from a very respectable number of our constituents, and it is certainly proper for Congress to consider the subject, in order to quiet that anxiety which prevails in the public mind. Indeed, I think it would have been of advantage to the Government, if it had been practicable to have made some proposition for amendments the first business we entered upon; it would have stifled the voice of complaint,' and made friends of many who doubted the merits of the constitution. Our future measures would then have been more generally agreeably supported; but the justifiable anxiety to put the Government into operation prevented that; it therefore remains for us to take it up as soon as possible. I wish then to commence the consideration at the present moment; I hold it to be my duty to unfold my ideas, and explain myself to the House in some form or other without delay. I only wish to introduce the great work, and, as I said before, I do not expect it will be decided immediately; but if some step is taken in the business, it will give reason to believe that we may come to a final result. This will inspire a reasonable hope in the advocates for amendments, that full justice will be done to the important subject; and I have reason to believe their expectation will not be defeated. I hope the House will not decline my motion for going into a committee.

Mr. Sherman: I am willing that this matter should be brought before the House at a proper time. I suppose a number of gentlemen think it their duty to bring it forward; so that there is no apprehension it will be passed over in silence. Other gentlemen may be disposed to let the subject rest until the more important objects of Government are attended to; and I should con-clude, from the nature of the case, that the people expect the latter from us in preference to altering the constitution; because they have ratified that instrument, in order that the Government may begin to operate. If this was not their wish, they might as well have rejected the constitution, as North Carolina has done, until the amendments took place. The State I have the honor to come from adopted this system by a very great majority, because they wished for the Government; but they desired no amendments. I suppose this was the case in other States; it will therefore be imprudent to neglect much more important concerns for this. The executive part of the Govern-ment wants organization; the business of the revenue is incomplete, to say nothing of the judiciary business. Now, will gentlemen give up these points to go into a discussion of amendments, when no advantage can arise from them? For my part, I question if any alteration which can be now proposed would be an amendment, in the true sense of the word; but nevertheless, I am willing to let the subject be introduced. If the gentleman only desires to go into committee for the purpose of receiving his propositions, I shall consent; but I have strong objections to being interrupted in completing the more important business; because I am well satisfied it will alarm the fears of twenty of our constituents where it will please one.

Mr. White: I hope the House will not spend much time on this subject, till the more pressing business is despatched; but, at the same time, I hope we shall not dismiss it altogether, because I think a majority of the people who have ratified the constitution, did it under the expectation that Congress would, at some convenient time, examine its texture and point out where it was defective, in order that it might be judiciously amended. Whether, while we are without experience, amendments can be digested in such a manner as to give satisfaction to a constitutional majority of this House. I will not pretend to say; but I hope the subject may be considered with all convenient speed. I think it would tend to tranquillize the public mind; therefore, I shall vote in favor of going into a Committee of the whole, and, after receiving the subject, shall be content to refer it to a special committee to arrange and report. I fear, if we refuse to take up the subject, it will irritate many of our constituents, which I do not wish to do. If we cannot, after mature consideration, gratify their wishes, the cause of complaint will be lessened, if not removed. But a doubt on this head will not be a good reason why we should refuse to inquire. I do not say this as it affects my immediate constituents, because I believe a majority of the district which elected me do not require alterations; but I know there are people in other parts who will not be satisfied unless some amendments are proposed.

Mr. Smith, of South Carolina, thought the gentleman who brought forward the subject had done his duty: he had supported his motion with ability and candor, and if he did not succeed, he was not to blame. On considering what had been urged for going into a committee, he was induced to join the gentleman; but it would be merely to receive his propositions, after which he would move something to this effect: That, however desirous this House may be to go into the consideration of amendments to the constitution, in order to establish the liberties of the people of America on the securest foundation, yet the important and pressing business of the Government prevents their entering upon that subject at present.

Mr. Page: My colleague tells you he is ready to submit to the Committee of the whole his ideas on this subject. If no objection had been made to his motion, the whole business might have been finished before this. He has done me the honor of showing me certain propositions which he has drawn up; they are very important, and I sincerely wish the House may receive them. After they are published, I think the people will wait with patience till we are at leisure to resume them. But it must be very disagreeable to them to have it postponed from time to time, in the manner it has been for six weeks past; they will be tired out by a fruitless expectation. Putting myself into the place of those who favor amendments, I should suspect Congress did not mean seriously to enter upon the subject; that it was vain to expect redress from them. I should begin to turn my attention to the alternative contained in the fifth article, and think of joining the Legislatures of those States which have applied for calling a new convention. How dangerous such an expedient would be I need not mention; but I venture to affirm, that unless you take early notice of this subject, you will not have power to deliberate. The people will clamor for a new convention; they will not trust the House any longer. Those, therefore, who dread the assembling of a convention, will do well to acquiesce in the present motion, and lay the foundation of a most important work. I do not think we need consume more than half an hour in the Committee of the whole; this is not so much time but we may conveniently spare it, considering the nature of the business. I do not wish to divert the attention of Congress from the organization of the Government, nor do I think it need be done, if we comply with the present motion.

Mr. Vining: I hope the House will not go into a Committee of the whole. It strikes me that the great amendment which the Government wants is expedition in the despatch of business. The wheels of the national machine cannot turn, until the impost and collection bill are perfected; these are the desiderata which the public mind is anxiously expecting. It is well known, that all we have hitherto done amounts to nothing, if we leave the business in its present state. True; but, say gentlemen, let us go into committee; it will take up but a short time; yet may it not take a considerable proportion of our time? May it not be procrastinated into days, weeks, nay, months? It is not the most facile subject that can come before the Legislature of the Union. Gentlemen's opinions do not run in a parallel on this topic; it may take up more time to unite or concentre them than is now imagined. And what object is to be attained by going into a committee? If information is what we seek after, cannot that be obtained by the gentleman's laying his propositions on the table; they can be read, or they can be printed. But I have two other reasons for opposing this motion; the first is, the uncertainty with which we must decide on questions of amendment, founded merely on speculative theory; the second is a previous question, how far it is proper to take the subject of amendments into consideration, without the consent of two-thirds of both Houses? I will submit it to gentlemen, whether the words of the constitution, "the Congress, whenever two-thirds of both Houses shall deem it necessary, shall propose amendments," do not bear my construction, that it is as requisite for two-thirds to sanction the expediency of going into the measure at present, as it will be to determine the necessary of amending at all. I take it that the fifth article admits of this construction, and think that two-thirds of the Senate and House of Representatives must concur in the expediency, as to the time and manner of amendments, before we can proceed to the consideration of the amendments themselves. For my part, I do not see the expediency of proposing amendments. I think, sir, the most likely way to quiet the perturbation of the public mind, will be to pass salutary laws; to give permanency and stability to constitutional regulations, founded on principles of equity and adjusted by wisdom. Although hitherto we have done nothing to tranquillize that agitation which the adoption of the constitution threw some people into, yet the storm has abated and a calm succeeds. The people are not afraid of leaving the question of amendments to the discussion of their representatives; but is this the juncture for discussing it? What have Congress done towards completing the business of their appointment? They have passed a law regulating certain oaths; they have passed the impost bill; but are not vessels daily arriving, and the revenue slipping through our fingers? Is it not very strange that we neglect the completion of the revenue system? Is the system of jurisprudence unnecessary? And here let me ask gentlemen how they propose to amend that part of the constitution which embraces the judicial branch of government, when they do not know the regulations proposed by the Senate, who are forming a bill on this subject?

If the honorable mover of the question before the House does not think he discharges his duty without bringing his propositions forward, let him take the mode I have mentioned, by which there will be little loss of time. He knows, as well as any gentleman, the importance of completing the business on your table, and that it is best to finish one subject before the introduction of another. He will not, therefore, persist in a motion which tends to distract our minds, and incapacitates us from making a proper decision on any subject. Suppose every gentleman who desires alterations to be made in the constitution were to submit his propositions to a Committee of the whole; what would be the consequence? We should have strings of them contradictory to each other, and be necessarily engaged in a discussion that would consume too much of our precious time.

Though the State I represent had the honor of taking the lead in the adoption of this constitution, and did it by a unanimous vote; and although I have the strongest predilection for the present form of Government, yet I am open to information, and willing to be convinced of its imperfections. If this be done, I shall cheerfully assist in correcting them. But I cannot think this a proper time to enter upon the subject, because more important business is suspended; and, for want of experience, we are as likely to do injury by our prescriptions as good. I wish to see every proposition which comes from that worthy gentleman on the science of Government; but I think it can be presented better by staying where we are, than by going into committee, and therefore shall vote against his motion.

Mr. Madison: I am sorry to be accessary to the loss of a single moment of time by the House. If I had been indulged in my motion, and we had gone into a Committee of the whole, I think we might have rose and resumed the consideration of other business before this time; that is, so far as it depended upon what I proposed to bring forward. As that mode seems not to give satisfaction, I will withdraw the motion, and move you, sir, that a select committee be appointed to consider and report such amendments as are proper for Congress to propose to the Legislatures of the several States, conformably to the fifth article of the constitution.

I will state my reasons why I think it proper to propose amendments, and state the amendments themselves, so far as I think they ought to be proposed. If I thought I could fulfil the duty which I owe to myself and my constituents, to let the subject pass over in silence, I most certainly should not trespass upon the indulgence of this House. But I cannot do this, and am therefore compelled to beg a patient hearing to what I have to lay before you. And I do most sincerely believe, that if Congress will devote but one day to this subject, so far as to satisfy the public that we do not disregard their wishes, it will have a salutary influence on the public councils, and prepare the way for a favorable reception of our future measures. It appears to me that this House is bound by every motive of prudence, not to let the first session pass over without proposing to the State Legislatures some things to be incorporated into the constitution, that will render it as acceptable to the whole people of the United States, as it has been found acceptable to a majority of them. I wish, among other reasons why something should be done, that those who have been friendly to the adoption of this constitution may have the opportunity of proving to those who were opposed to it that they were as sincerely devoted to liberty and a Republican Government, as those who charged them with wishing the adoption of this constitution in order to lay the foundation of an aristocracy or despotism. It will be a desirable thing to extinguish from the bosom of every member of the community, any apprehensions that there are those among his countrymen who wish to deprive them of the liberty for which they valiantly fought and honorably bled. And if there are amendments desired of such a nature as will not injure the constitution, and they can be ingrafted so as to give satisfaction to the doubting part of our fellow-citizens, the friends of the Federal Government will evince that spirit of deference and concession for which they have hitherto been distinguished.

It cannot be a secret to the gentlemen in this House, that, notwithstanding the ratification of this system of Government by eleven of the thirteen United States, in some cases unanimously, in others by large majorities; yet still there is a great number of our constituents who are dissatisfied with it; among whom are many respectable for their talents and patriotism, and respectable for the jealousy they have for their liberty, which, though mistaken in its object, is honorable in its motive. There is a great body of the people falling under this description, who at present feel much inclined to join their support to the cause of Federalism, if they were satisfied on this one point. We ought not to disregard their inclination, but, on principles of amity and moderation, conform to their wishes and expressly declare the great rights of mankind secured under this constitution. The acceptance which our fellow-citizens show under the Government, calls upon us for a like return of moderation. But perhaps there is a stronger motive than this for our going into a consideration of the subject. It is to provide those securities for liberty which are required by a part of the community: I allude in a particular manner to those two States that have not thought fit to throw themselves into the bosom of the Confederacy. It is a desirable thing, on our part as well as theirs, that a re-union should take place as soon as possible. I have no doubt, if we proceed to take those steps which would be prudent and requisite at this juncture, that in a short time we should see that disposition prevailing in those States which have not come in, that we have seen prevailing in those States which have embraced the constitution.

But I will candidly acknowledge, that, over and above all these considerations, I do conceive that the constitution may be amended; that is to say, if all power is subject to abuse, that then it is possible the abuse of the powers of the General Government may be guarded against in a more secure manner than is now done, while no one advantage arising from the exercise of that power shall be damaged or endangered by it. We have in this way something to gain, and, if we proceed with caution, nothing to lose. And in this case it is necessary to proceed with caution; for while we feel all these inducements to go into a revisal of the constitution, we must feel for the constitution itself, and make that revisal a moderate one. I should be unwilling to see a door opened for a reconsideration of the whole structure of the Government—for a re-consideration of the principles and the substance of the powers given; because I doubt, if such a door were opened, we should be very likely to stop at that point which would be safe to the Government itself. But I do wish to see a door opened to consider, so far as to incorporate those provisions for the security of rights, against which I believe no serious objection has been made by any class of our constituents: such as would be likely to meet with the concurrence of two-thirds of both Houses, and the approbation of three-fourths of the State Legislatures. I will not propose a single alteration which I do not wish to see take place, as intrinsically proper in itself, or proper because it is wished for by a respectable number of my fellow-citizens; and therefore I shall not propose a single alteration but is likely to meet the concurrence required by the constitution. There have been objections of various kinds made against the constitution. Some were levelled against its structure because the President was without a council; because the Senate, which is a legislative body, had judicial powers in trials on impeachments; and because the powers of that body were compounded in other respects, in a manner that did not correspond with a particular theory; because it grants more power than is supposed to be necessary for every good purpose, and controls the ordinary powers of the State Governments. I know some respectable characters who opposed this Government on these grounds; but I believe that the great mass of the people who opposed it, disliked it because it did not contain effectual provisions against encroachments on particular rights, and those safeguards which they have been long accustomed to have interposed between them and the magistrate who exercises the sovereign power; nor ought we to consider them safe, while a great number of our fellow-citizens think these securities necessary.

It is a fortunate thing that the objection to the Government has been made on the ground I stated, because it will be practicable, on that ground, to obviate the objection, so far as to satisfy the public mind that their liberties will be perpetual, and this without endangering any part of the constitution, which is considered as essential to the existence of the Government by those who promoted its adoption.

The amendments which have occurred to me, proper to be recommended by Congress to the State Legislatures, are these:

First, That there be prefixed to the constitution a declaration, that all power is originally rested in, and consequently derived from, the people.

That Government is instituted and ought to be exercised for the benefit of the people; which consists in the enjoyment of life and liberty, with the right of acquiring and using property, and generally of pursuing and obtaining happiness and safety.

That the people have an indubitable, unalienable, and indefeasible right to reform or change their Government, whenever it be found adverse or inadequate to the purposes of its institution.

Secondly, That in article 1st, section 2, clause 3, these words be struck out, to wit:

"The number of Representatives shall not exceed one for every thirty thousand, but each State shall have at least one Representative, and until such enumeration shall be made;" and that in place thereof be inserted these words, to wit: "After the first actual enumeration, there shall be one Representative for every thirty thousand, until the number amounts to——, after which the proportion shall be so regulated by Congress, that the number shall never be less than——, nor more than——, but each State shall, after the first enumeration, have at least two Representatives; and prior thereto."

Thirdly, That in article 1st, section 6, clause 1, there be added to the end of the first sentence, these words, to wit: "But no law varying the compensation last ascertained shall operate before the next ensuing election of Representatives."

Fourthly, That in article 1st, section 9, between clauses 3 and 4, be inserted these clauses, to wit: The civil rights of none shall be abridged on account of religious belief or worship, nor shall any national religion be established, nor shall the full and equal rights of conscience be in any manner, or on any pretext, infringed.

The people shall not be deprived or abridged of their right to speak, to write, or to publish their sentiments; and the freedom of the press, as one of the great bulwarks of liberty, shall be inviolable.

The people shall not be restrained from peaceably assembling and consulting for their common good; nor from applying to the Legislature by petitions, or remonstrances, for redress of their grievances.

The right of the people to keep and bear arms shall not be infringed; a well armed and well regulated militia being the best security of a free country; but no person religiously scrupulous of bearing arms shall be compelled to render military service in person.

No soldier shall in time of peace be quartered in any house without the consent of the owner; nor at any time, but in a manner warranted by law.

No person shall be subject, except in cases of impeachment, to more than one punishment or one trial for the same offence; nor shall be compelled to be a witness against himself; nor be deprived of life, liberty, or property, without due process of law; nor be obliged to relinquish his property, where it may be necessary for public use, without a just compensation.

Excessive bail shall not be required, nor excessive fines imposed, nor cruel and unusual punishments inflicted.

The rights of the people to be secured in their persons; their houses, their papers, and their other property, from all unreasonable searches and seizures, shall not be violated by warrants issued without probable cause, supported by oath or affirmation, or not particularly describing the places to be searched, or the persons or things to be seized.

In all criminal prosecutions, the accused shall enjoy the right to a speedy and public trial, to be informed of the cause and nature of the accusation, to be confronted with his accusers, and the witnesses against him; to have a compulsory process for obtaining witnesses in his favor; and to have the assistance of counsel for his defence.

The exceptions here or elsewhere in the constitution, made in favor of particular rights, shall not be so construed as to diminish the just importance of other rights retained by the people, or as to enlarge the powers delegated by the constitution; but either as actual limitations of such powers, or as inserted merely for greater caution.

Fifthly, That in article 1st, section 10, between clauses 1 and 2, be inserted this clause, to wit:

No State shall violate the equal rights of conscience, or the freedom of the press, or the trial by jury in criminal cases.

Sixthly, That, in article 3d, section 2, be annexed to the end of clause 2d, these words, to wit:

But no appeal to such court shall be allowed where the value in controversy shall not amount to——dollars: nor shall any fact triable by jury, according to the course of common law, be otherwise re-examinable than may consist with the principles of common law.

Seventhly, That in article 3d, section 2, the third clause be struck out, and in its place be inserted the clauses following, to wit:

The trial of all crimes (except in cases of impeachments, and cases arising in the land or naval forces, or the militia when on actual service, in time of war or public danger) shall be by an impartial jury of freeholders of the vicinage, with the requisite of unanimity for conviction, of the right of challenge, and other accustomed requisites; and in all crimes punishable with loss of life or member, presentment or indictment by a grand jury shall be an essential preliminary, provided that in cases of crimes committed within any county which may be in possession of an enemy, or in which a general insurrection may prevail, the trial may by law be authorized in some other county of the same State, as near as may be to the seat of the offence.

In cases of crimes committed not within any county, the trial may by law be in such county as the laws shall have prescribed. In suits at common law, between man and man, the trial by jury, as one of the best securities to the rights of the people, ought to remain inviolate.

Eighthly, That immediately after article 6th, be inserted, as article 7th, the clauses following, to wit:

The powers delegated by this constitution are appropriated to the departments to which they are respectively distributed: so that the legislative department shall never exercise the powers vested in the executive or judicial nor the executive exercise the powers vested in the legislative or judicial, nor the judicial exercise the powers vested in the legislative or executive departments.

The powers not delegated by this constitution, nor prohibited by it to the States, are reserved to the States respectively.

Ninthly, That article 7th be numbered as article 8th.

The first of these amendments relates to what may be called a bill of rights. I will own that I never considered this provision so essential to the federal constitution, as to make it improper to ratify it, until such an amendment was added; at the same time, I always conceived, that in a certain form, and to a certain extent, such a provision was neither improper nor altogether useless. I am aware, that a great number of the most respectable friends to the Government, and champions for republican liberty, have thought such a provision, not only unnecessary, but even improper; nay, I believe some have gone so far as to think it even dangerous. Some policy has been made use of, perhaps, by gentlemen on both sides of the question: I acknowledge the ingenuity of those arguments which were drawn against the constitution, by a comparison with the policy of Great Britain, in establishing a declaration of rights; but there is too great a difference in the case to warrant the comparison: therefore, the arguments drawn from that source were in a great measure inapplicable. In the declaration of rights which that country has established, the truth is, they have gone no farther than to raise a barrier against the power of the Crown; the power of the Legislature is left altogether indefinite. Although I know whenever the great rights, the trial by jury, freedom of the press, or liberty of conscience, come in question in that body, the invasion of them is resisted by able advocates, yet their Magna Charta does not contain any one provision for the security of those rights, respecting which the people of America are most alarmed. The freedom of the press and rights of conscience, those choicest privileges of the people, are unguarded in the British constitution.

But although the case may be widely different, and it may not be thought necessary to provide limits for the legislative power in that country, yet a different opinion prevails in the United States. The people of many States have thought it necessary to raise barriers against power in all forms and departments of Government, and I am inclined to believe, if once bills of rights are established in all the States as well as the federal constitution, we shall find that although some of them are rather unimportant, yet, upon the whole, they will have a salutary tendency.

It may be said, in some instances, they do no more than state the perfect equality of mankind. This, to be sure, is an absolute truth, yet it is not absolutely necessary to be inserted at the head of a constitution.

In some instances they assert those rights which are exercised by the people in forming and establishing a plan of Government. In other instances, they specify those rights which are retained when particular powers are given up to be exercised by the Legislature. In other instances, they specify positive rights, which may seem to result from the nature of the compact. Trial by jury cannot be considered as a natural right, but a right resulting from a social compact which regulates the action of the community, but is as essential to secure the liberty of the people as any one of the pre-existent rights of nature. In other instances, they lay down dogmatic maxims with respect to the construction of the Government; declaring that the legislative, executive, and judicial branches shall be kept separate and distinct. Perhaps the best way of securing this in practice is, to provide such checks as will prevent the encroachment of the one upon the other.

But whatever may be the form which the several States have adopted in making declarations in favor of particular rights, the great object in view is to limit and qualify the powers of Government, by excepting out of the grant of power those cases in which the Government ought not to act, or to act only in a particular mode. They point these exceptions sometimes against the abuse of the executive power, sometimes against the legislative, and, in some cases, against the community itself; or, in other words, against the majority in favor of the minority.

In our Government it is, perhaps, less necessary to guard against the abuse in the executive department than any other; because it is not the stronger branch of the system, but the weaker. It therefore must be levelled against the legislative, for it is the most powerful, and most likely to be abused, because it is under the least control. Hence, so far as a declaration of rights can tend to prevent the exercise of undue power, it cannot be doubted but such declaration is proper. But I confess that I do conceive, that in a Government modified like this of the United States, the great danger lies rather in the abuse of the community than in the legislative body. The prescriptions in favor of liberty ought to be levelled against that quarter where the greatest danger lies, namely, that which possesses the highest prerogative of power. But it is not found in either the executive or legislative departments of Government, but in the body of the people, operating by the majority against the minority.

It may be thought that all paper barriers against the power of the community are too weak to be worthy of attention. I am sensible they are not so strong as to satisfy gentlemen of every description who have seen and examined thoroughly the texture of such a defence; yet, as they have a tendency to impress some degree of respect for them, to establish the public opinion in their favor, and rouse the attention of the whole community, it may be one means to control the majority from those acts to which they might be otherwise inclined.

It has been said, by way of objection to a bill of rights, by many respectable gentlemen out of doors, and I find opposition on the same principles likely to be made by gentlemen on this floor, that they are unnecessary articles of a Republican Government, upon the presumption that the people have those rights in their own hands, and that is the proper place for them to rest. It would be a sufficient answer to say, that this objection lies against such provisions under the State Governments, as well as under the General Government: and there are, I believe, but few gentlemen who are inclined to push their theory so far as to say that a declaration of rights in those cases is either ineffectual or improper. It has been said, that in the Federal Government they are unnecessary, because the powers are enumerated, and it follows, that all that are not granted by the constitution are retained; that the constitution is a call of powers, the great residuum being the rights of the people; and, therefore, a bill of rights cannot be so necessary as if the residuum was thrown into the hands of the Government. I admit that these arguments are not entirely without foundation; but they are not conclusive to the extent which has been supposed. It is true, the powers of the General Government are circumscribed, they are directed to particular objects; but even if Government keeps within those limits, it has certain discretionary powers with respect to the means, which may admit of abuse to a certain extent, in the same manner as the powers of the State Governments under their constitutions may to an indefinite extent; because in the constitution of the United States, there is a clause granting to Congress the power to make all laws which shall be necessary and proper for carrying into execution all the powers vested in the Government of the United States, or in any department or officer thereof; this enables them to fulfil every purpose for which the Government was established. Now, may not laws be considered necessary and proper by Congress, for it is for them to judge of the necessity and propriety to accomplish those special purposes which they may have in contemplation, which laws in themselves are neither necessary nor proper; as well as improper laws could be enacted by the State Legislatures, for fulfilling the more extended objects of those Governments. I will state an instance, which I think in point, and proves that this might be the case. The General Government has a right to pass all laws which shall be necessary to collect its revenue; the means for enforcing the collection are within the direction of the Legislature: may not general warrants be considered necessary for this purpose, as well as for some purposes which it was supposed at the framing of their constitutions the State Governments had in view? If there was reason for restraining the State Governments from exercising this power, there is like reason for restraining the Federal Government.

It may be said, indeed it has been said, that a bill of rights is not necessary, because the establishment of this Government has not repealed those declarations of rights which are added to the several State constitutions; that those rights of the people, which had been established by the most solemn act, could not be annihilated by a subsequent act of that people, who meant, and declared at the head of the instrument, that they ordained and established a new system, for the express purpose of securing to themselves and posterity the liberties they had gained by an arduous conflict.

I admit the force of this observation, but I do not look upon it to be conclusive. In the first place, it is too uncertain ground to leave this provision upon, if a provision is at all necessary to secure rights so important as many of those I have mentioned are conceived to be, by the public in general, as well as those in particular who opposed the adoption of this constitution. Besides, some States have no bills of rights, there are others provided with very defective ones, and there are others whose bills of rights are not only defective, but absolutely improper; instead of securing some in the full extent which republican principles would require, they limit them too much to agree with the common ideas of liberty.

It has been objected also against a bill of rights, that, by enumerating particular exceptions to the grant of power, it would disparage those rights which were not placed in that enumeration; and it might follow, by implication, that those rights which were not singled out, were intended to be assigned into the hands of the General Government, and were consequently insecure. This is one of the most plausible arguments I have ever heard urged against the admission of a bill of rights into this system; but, I conceive, that it may be guarded against. I have attempted it, as gentlemen may see by turning to the last clause of the fourth resolution.

It has been said, that it is unnecessary to load the constitution with this provision, because it was not found effectual in the constitution of the particular States. It is true, there are a few particular States in which some of the most valuable articles have not, at one time or other, been violated; but it does not follow but they may have, to a certain degree, a salutary effect against the abuse of power. If they are incorporated into the constitution, independent tribunals of justice will consider themselves in a peculiar manner the guardians of those rights; they will be an impenetrable bulwark against every assumption of power in the legislative or executive; they will be naturally led to resist every encroachment upon rights expressly stipulated for in the constitution by the declaration of rights. Besides, this security, there is a great probability that such a declaration in the federal system would be enforced; because the State Legislatures will jealously and closely watch the operations of this Government, and be able to resist with more effect every assumption of power, than any other power on earth can do; and the greatest opponents to a Federal Government admit the State Legislatures to be sure guardians of the people's liberty. I conclude, from this view of the subject, that it will be proper in itself, and highly politic, for the tranquillity of the public mind, and the stability of the Government, that we should offer something, in the form I have proposed, to be incorporated in the system of Government, as a declaration of the rights of the people.

In the next place, I wish to see that part of the constitution revised which declares that the number of Representatives shall not exceed the proportion of one for every thirty thousand persons, and allows one Representative to every State which rates below that proportion. If we attend to the discussion of this subject, which has taken place in the State conventions, and even in the opinion of the friends to the constitution, an alteration here is proper. It is the sense of the people of America, that the number of Representatives ought to be increased, but particularly that it should not be left in the discretion of the Government to diminish them, below that proportion which certainly is in the power of the Legislature as the constitution now stands; and they may, as the population of the country increases, increase the House of Representatives to a very unwieldy degree. I confess I always thought this part of the constitution defective, though not dangerous; and that it ought to be particularly attended to whenever Congress should go into the consideration of amendments.

There are several minor cases enumerated in my proposition, in which I wish also to see some alteration take place. That article which leaves it in the power of the Legislature to ascertain its own emolument, is one to which I allude. I do not believe this is a power which, in the ordinary course of Government, is likely to be abused. Perhaps of all the powers granted, it is least likely to abuse; but there is a seeming impropriety in leaving any set of men without control to put their hand into the public coffers, to take out money to put in their pockets; there is a seeming indecorum in such power, which leads me to propose a change. We have a guide to this alteration in several of the amendments which the different conventions have proposed. I have gone, therefore, so far as to fix it, that no law, varying the compensation shall operate until there is a change in the Legislature, in which case it cannot be for the particular benefit of those who are concerned in determining the value of the service.

I wish also, in revising the constitution, we may throw into that section, which interdict the abuse of certain powers in the State Legislatures, some other provisions of equal, if not greater importance than those already made. The words, "No State shall pass any bill of attainder, ex post facto law," &c. were wise and proper restrictions in the constitution. I think there is more danger of those powers being abused by the State Governments than by the Government of the United States. The same may be said of other powers which they possess, if not controlled by the general principle, that laws are unconstitutional which infringe the rights of the community. I should therefore wish to extend this interdiction, and add, as I have stated in the 5th resolution, that no State shall violate the equal right of conscience, freedom of the press, or trial by jury in criminal cases; because it is proper that every Government should be disarmed of powers which trench upon those particular rights. I know, in some of the State constitutions, the power of the Government is controlled by such a declaration; but others are not. I cannot see any reason against obtaining even a double security on those points; and nothing can give a more sincere proof of the attachment of those who opposed this constitution to these great and important rights, than to see them join in obtaining the security I have now proposed; because it must be admitted, on all hands, that the State Governments are as liable to attack the invaluable privileges as the General Government is, and therefore ought to be as cautiously guarded against.

I think it will be proper, with respect to the judiciary powers, to satisfy the public mind of those points which I have mentioned. Great inconvenience has been apprehended to suitors from the distance they would be dragged to obtain justice in the Supreme Court of the United States, upon an appeal on an action for a small debt. To remedy this, declare that no appeal shall be made unless the matter in controversy amounts to a particular sum; this, with the regulations respecting jury trials in criminal cases, and suits at common law, it is to be hoped, will quiet and reconcile the minds of the people to that part of the constitution.

I find, from looking into the amendments proposed by the State conventions, that several are particularly anxious that it should be declared in the constitution, that the powers not therein delegated should be reserved to the several States. Perhaps words which may define this more precisely than the whole of the instrument now does, may be considered as superflous. I admit they may be deemed unnecessary: but there can be no harm in making such a declaration, if gentlemen will allow that the fact is as stated. I am sure I understand it so, and do therefore propose it.

These are the points on which I wish to see a revision of the constitution take place. How far they will accord with the sense of this body, I cannot take upon me absolutely to determine; but I believe every gentleman will readily admit that nothing is in contemplation, so far as I have mentioned, that can endanger the beauty of the Government in any one important feature, even in the eyes of its most sanguine admirers. I have proposed nothing that does not appear to me as proper in itself, or eligible as patronized by a respectable number of our fellow-citizens; and if we can make the constitution better in the opinion of those who are opposed to it, without weakening its frame, or abridging its usefulness, in the judgment of those who are attached to it, we act the part of wise and liberal men to make such alterations as shall produce that effect.

Having done what I conceived was my duty, in bringing before this House the subject of amendments, and also stated such as I wish for and approve, and offered the reasons which occurred to me in their support, I shall content myself, for the present, with moving "that a committee be appointed to consider of and report such amendments as ought to be proposed by Congress to the Legislatures of the States, to become, if ratified by three-fourths thereof, part of the constitution of the United States." By agreeing to this motion, the subject may be going on in the committee, while other important business is proceeding to a conclusion in the House. I should advocate greater despatch in the business of amendments, if I were not convinced of the absolute necessity there is of pursuing the organization of the Government; because I think we should obtain the confidence of our fellow-citizens, in proportion as we fortify the rights of the people against the encroachments of the Government.

Mr. Jackson: The more I consider the subject of amendments, the more I am convinced it is improper. I revere the rights of my constituents as much as any gentleman in Congress, yet I am against inserting a declaration of rights in the constitution, and that for some of the reasons referred to by the gentleman last up. If such an addition is not dangerous or improper, it is at least unnecessary: that is a sufficient reason for not entering into the subject at a time when there are urgent calls for our attention to important business. Let me ask gentlemen, what reason there is for the suspicions which are to be removed by this measure? Who are Congress, that such apprehensions should be entertained of them? Do we not belong to the mass of the people? Is there a single right that, if infringed, will not affect us and our connexions as much as any other person? Do we not return at the expiration of two years into private life? and is not this a security against encroachments? Are we not sent here to guard those rights which might be endangered, if the Government was an aristocracy or a despotism? View for a moment the situation of Rhode Island, and say whether the people's rights are more safe under State Legislatures than under a Government of limited powers? Their liberty is changed to licentiousness. But do gentlemen suppose bills of rights necessary to secure liberty? If they do, let them look at New York, New Jersey, Virginia, South Carolina, and Georgia. Those States have no bill of rights, and is the liberty of the citizens less safe in those States, than in the other of the United States? I believe it is not.

There is a maxim in law, and it will apply to bills of rights, that when you enumerate exceptions, the exceptions operate to the exclusion of all circumstances that are omitted; consequently, unless you except every right from the grant of power, those omitted are inferred to be resigned to the discretion of the Government.

The gentleman endeavors to secure the liberty of the press; pray how is this in danger? There is no power given to Congress to regulate this subject as they can commerce, or peace, or war. Has any transaction taken place to make us suppose such an amendment necessary? An honorable gentleman, a member of this House, has been attacked in the public newspapers on account of sentiments delivered on this floor. Have Congress taken any notice of it? Have they ordered the writer before them, even for a breach of privilege, although the constitution provides that a member shall not be questioned in any place for any speech or debate in the House? No, these things are offered to the public view, and held up to the inspection of the world. These are principles which will always prevail. I am not afraid, nor are other members I believe, our conduct should meet the severest scrutiny. Where, then, is the necessity of taking measures to secure what neither is nor can be in danger?

I hold, Mr. Speaker, that the present is not a proper time for considering of amendments. The States of Rhode Island and North Carolina are not in the Union. As to the latter, we have every presumption that she will come in. But in Rhode Island I think the anti-federal interest yet prevails. I am sorry for it, particularly on account of the firm friends of the Union, who are kept without the embrace of the confederacy by their countrymen. These persons are worthy of our patronage; and I wish they would apply to us for protection; they should have my consent to be taken into the Union upon such application. I understand there are some important mercantile and manufacturing towns in that State, who ardently wish to live under the laws of the General Government; if they were to come forward and request us to take measures for this purpose, I would give my sanction to any which would be likely to bring about such an event.

But to return to my argument. It being the case that those States are not yet come into the Union, when they join us, we shall have another list of amendments to consider, and another bill of rights to frame. Now, in my judgment, it is better to make but one work of it whenever we set about the business.

But in what a situation shall we be with respect to those foreign Powers with whom we desire to be in treaty? They look upon us as a nation emerging into figure and importance. But what will be their opinion, if they see us unable to retain the national advantages we have just gained? They will smile at our infantine efforts to obtain consequence, and treat us with the contempt we have hitherto borne by reason of the imbecility of our Government. Can we expect to enter into a commercial competition with any of them, while our system is incomplete? And how long it will remain in such a situation, if we enter upon amendments, God only knows. Our instability will make us objects of scorn. We are not content with two revolutions in less than fourteen years; we must enter upon a third, without necessity or propriety. Our faith will be like the *punica fides* of Carthage; and we shall have none that will repose confidence in us. Why will gentlemen press us to propose amendments, while we are without experience? Can they assure themselves that the amendments, as they call them, will not want amendments, as soon as they are adopted? I will not tax gentlemen with a desire of amusing the people; I believe they venerate their country too much for this; but what more can amendments lead to? That part of the constitution which is proposed to be altered, may be the most valuable part of the whole; and perhaps those who now clamor for alterations may, ere long, discover that they have marred a good Government, and rendered their own liberties insecure. I again repeat it, this is not the time for bringing forward amendments; and, notwithstanding the honorable gentleman's ingenious arguments on that point, I am now more strongly persuaded it is wrong.

If we actually find the constitution bad upon experience, or the rights and privileges of the people in danger, I here pledge myself to step forward among the first friends of liberty to prevent the evil; and if nothing else will avail, I will draw my sword in the defence of freedom, and cheerfully immolate at that shrine my property and my life. But how are we now proceeding? Why, on nothing more than theoretical speculation, pursuing a mere *ignis fatuus,* which may lead us into serious embarrassments. The imperfections of the Government are now unknown; let it have a fair trial, and I will be bound they show themselves; then we can tell where to apply the remedy, so as to secure the great object we are aiming at.

There are, Mr. Speaker, a number of important bills on the table which require despatch; but I am afraid, if we enter on this business, we shall not be able to attend to them for a long time. Look, sir, over the long list of amendments proposed by some of the adopting States, and say, when the House could get through the discussion; and I believe, sir, every one of those amendments will come before us. Gentlemen may feel themselves called by duty or inclination to oppose them. How are we then to extricate ourselves from this labyrinth of business? Certainly we shall lose much of our valuable time, without any advantage whatsoever. I hope, therefore, the gentleman will press us no further; he had done his duty, and acquitted himself of the obligation under which he lay. He may now accede to what I take to be the sense of the House, and let the business of amendments lie over until next spring; that will be soon enough to take it up to any good purpose.

Mr. Gerry: I do not rise to go into the merits or demerits of the subject of amendments; nor shall I make any other observations on the motion for going into a Committee of the whole on the state of the Union, which is now withdrawn, than merely to say, that, referring the subject to that committee, is treating it with the dignity its importance requires. But I consider it improper to take up this business, when our attention is occupied by other important objects. We should despatch the subjects now on the table, and let this lie over until a period of more leisure for discussion and attention. The gentleman from Virginia says it is necessary to go into a consideration of this subject, in order to satisfy the people. For my part, I cannot be of his opinion. The people know we are employed in the organization of the Government, and cannot expect that we should forego this business for any other. But I would not have it understood, that I am against entering upon amendments when the proper time arrives. I shall be glad to set about it as soon as possible, but I would not stay the operations of the Government on this account. I think with the gentleman from Delaware, (Mr. Vining,) that the great wheels of the political machine should first be set in motion; and with the gentleman from Georgia, (Mr. Jackson,) that the vessel ought to be got under way, lest she lie by the wharf till she beat off her rudder, and run herself a wreck on shore.

I say I wish as early a day as possible may be assigned for taking up this business, in order to prevent the necessity which the States may think themselves under of calling a new convention. For I am not, sir, one of those blind admirers of this system, who think it all perfection; nor am I so blind as not to see its beauties. The truth is, it partakes of humanity; in it is blended virtue and vice, errors and excellence. But I think, if it is referred to a new convention, we run the risk of losing some of its best properties; this is a case I never wish to see. Whatever might have been my sentiments of the ratification of the constitution without amendments, my sense now is, that the salvation of America depends upon the establishment of this Government, whether amended or not. If the constitution which is now ratified should not be supported, I despair of ever having a government of these United States.

I wish the subject to be considered early for another reason. There are two States not in the union; it would be a very desirable circumstance to gain them. I should therefore be in favor of such amendments as might tend to incite them and gain their confidence; good policy will dictate to us to expedite that event. Gentlemen say, that we shall not obtain the consent of two-thirds of both Houses to amendments. Are gentlemen willing then to throw Rhode Island and North Carolina into the situation of foreign nations? They have told you that they cannot accede to the Union, unless certain amendments are made to the constitution; if you deny a compliance with their request in that particular, you refuse an accommodation to bring about that desirable event, and leave them detached from the Union.

I have another reason for going early into this business. It is necessary to establish an energetic Government. My idea of such a Government is, that due deliberation be had in making laws, and efficiency in the execution. I hope, in this country, the latter may obtain without the dread of despotism. I would wish to see the execution of good laws irresistible. But from the view which we have already had of the disposition of the Government, we seem really to be afraid to administer the powers with which we are invested, lest we give offence. We appear afraid to exercise the constitutional powers of the Government, which the welfare of the State requires, lest a jealousy of our powers be the consequence. What is the reason of this timidity? Why, because we see a great body of our constituents opposed to the constitution as it now stands, who are apprehensive of the enormous powers of Government. But if this business is taken up, and it is thought proper to make amendments, it shall remove this difficulty. Let us deal fairly and candidly with our constituents, and give the subject a full discussion; after that, I have no doubt but the decision will be such as, upon examination, we shall discover to be right. If it shall then appear proper and wise to reject the amendments, I dare to say the reasons for so doing will bring conviction to the people out of doors, as well as it will to the members of this House; and they will acquiesce in the decision, though they may regret the disappointment of their fondest hopes for the security of the liberties of themselves and their posterity. Thus, and thus only, the Government will have all due energy, and accomplish the end for which it was instituted.

I am against referring the subject to a select committee, because I conceive it would be disrespectful to those States which have proposed amendments. The conventions of the States consisted of the most wise and virtuous men of the community; they have ratified this constitution, in full confidence that their objections would at least be considered; and shall we, sir, preclude them by the appointment of a special committee, to consider of a few propositions brought forward by an individual gentleman? Is it in contemplation that the committee should have the subject at large before them, or that they should report upon the particular amendments just mentioned, as they think proper? And are we to be precluded from the consideration of any other amendments but those the committee may report? A select committee must be considered improper, because it is putting their judgments against that of the conventions which have proposed amendments; but if the committee are to consider the matter at large, they will be liable to this objection, that their report will only be waste of time. For if they do not bring forward the whole of the amendments recommended, individual members will consider themselves bound to bring them forward for the decision of the House. I would therefore submit, if gentlemen are determined to proceed in the business at this time, whether it is not better that it should go, in the first instance, to a Committee of the whole, as first proposed by the gentleman from Virginia?

Some gentlemen consider it necessary to do this to satisfy our constituents. I think referring the business to a special committee will be attempting to amuse them with trifles. Our fellow-citizens are possessed of too much discernment not to be able to discover the intention of Congress by such procedure. It will be the duty of their representatives to tell them, if they were not able to discover it of themselves, they require the subject to be fairly considered; and if it be found to be improper to comply with their reasonable expectations, to tell them so. I hope there is no analogy between federal and punic faith; but unless Congress shall candidly consider the amendments which have been proposed in confidence by the State conventions, federal faith will not be considered very different from the *punica fides* of Carthage. The ratification of the constitution in several States would never have taken place, had they not been assured that the objections would have been duly attended to by Congress. And I believe many members of these conventions would never have voted for it, if they had not been persuaded that Congress would notice them with that candor and attention which their importance requires. I will say nothing respecting the amendments themselves; they ought to stand or fall on their own merits. If any of them are eligible, they will be adopted; if not, they will be rejected.

Mr. Livermore was against this motion; not that he was against amendments at a proper time. It is enjoined on him to act a rational part in procuring certain amendments, and he meant to do so; but he could not say what amendments were requisite, until the Government was organized. He supposed the judiciary law would contain certain regulations that would remove the anxiety of the people respecting such amendments as related thereto; because he thought much of the minutiae respecting suits between citizens of different States, &c. might be provided for by law. He could not agree to make jury trials necessary on every occasion; they were not practised even at this time, and there were some cases in which a cause could be better decided without a jury than with one.

In addition to the judiciary business, there is that which relates to the revenue. Gentlemen had let an opportunity go through their hands of getting a considerable supply from the impost on the spring importations. He reminded them of this; and would tell them now was the time to finish that business; for if they did not sow in seed-time, they would be beggars in harvest. He was well satisfied in his own mind, that the people of America did not look for amendments at present; they never could imagine it to be the first work of Congress.

He wished the concurrence of the Senate upon entering on this business, because if they opposed the measure, all the House did would be mere waste of time; and there was some little difficulty on this point, because it required the consent of two-thirds of both Houses to agree to what was proper on this occasion. He said, moreover, it would be better to refer the subject generally, if referred to them at all, than to take up the propositions of individual members.

Mr. Sherman: I do not suppose the constitution to be perfect, nor do I imagine if Congress and all the Legislatures on the continent were to revise it, that their united labors would make it perfect. I do not expect any perfection on this side the grave in the works of man; but my opinion is, that we are not at present in circumstances to make it better. It is a wonder that there has been such unanimity in adopting it, considering the ordeal it had to undergo; and the unanimity which prevailed at its formation is equally astonishing; amidst all the members from the twelve States present at the federal convention, there were only three who did not sign the instrument to attest their opinion of its goodness. Of the eleven States who have received it, the majority have ratified it without proposing a single amendment. This circumstance leads me to suppose that we shall not be able to propose any alterations that are likely to be adopted by nine States; and gentlemen know, before the alterations take effect, they must be agreed to by the Legislatures of three-fourths of the States in the Union. Those States which have not recommended alterations, will hardly adopt them, unless it is clear that they tend to make the constitution better. Now how this can be made out to their satisfaction I am yet to learn; they know of no defect from experience. It seems to be the opinion of gentlemen generally, that this is not the time for entering upon the discussion of amendments, our only question therefore is, how to get rid of the subject. Now, for my own part, I would prefer to have it referred to a Committee of the whole, rather than a special committee, and therefore shall not agree to the motion now before the House.

Mr. Gerry moved, that the business lie over until the 1st day of July next, and that it be the order for that day.

Mr. Sumter: I consider the subject of amendments of such great importance to the Union, that I shall be glad to see it undertaken in any manner. I am not, Mr. Speaker, disposed to sacrifice substance to form; therefore, whether the business shall originate in a Committee of the whole, or in the House, is a matter of indifference to me, so that it be put in train. Although I am seriously inclined to give this subject a full discussion, yet I do not wish it to be fully entered into at present, but am willing it should be postponed to a future day, when we shall have more leisure. With respect to referring to a select committee, I am rather against it; because I consider it as treating the applications of the State conventions rather slightly; and I presume it is the intention of the House to take those applications into consideration as well as any other. If it is not, I think it will give fresh cause for jealousy; it will rouse the alarm which is now suspended, and the people will become clamorous for amendments. They will decline any further application to Congress, and resort to the other alternative pointed out in the constitution. I hope, therefore, this House, when they do go into the business, will receive those propositions generally. This I apprehend will tend to tranquillize the public mind, and promote that harmony which ought to be kept up between those in the exercise of the powers of Government, and those who have clothed them with the authority, or, in other words, between Congress and the people. Without a harmony and confidence subsist between them, the measures of Government will prove abortive, and we shall have still to lament that imbecility and weakness which have long marked our public councils.

Mr. Vining found himself in a delicate situation respecting the subject of amendments. He came from a small State, and therefore his sentiments would not be considered of so much weight as the sentiments of those gentlemen who spoke the sense of much larger States. Besides, his constituents had prejudged the question, by a unanimous adoption of the constitution, without suggesting any amendments thereto. His sense accorded with the declared sense of the State of Delaware, and he was doubly bound to object to amendments which were either improper or unnecessary. But he had good reasons for opposing the consideration of even proper alterations at this time. He would ask the gentleman who pressed them whether he would be responsible for the risk the Government would run of being injured by in *interregnum?* Proposing amendments at this time, is suspending the operations of Government, and may be productive of its ruin.

He would not follow the gentleman in his arguments, though he supposed them all answerable, because he would not take up the time of the House; he contented himself with saying, that a bill of rights was unnecessary in a Government deriving all its powers from the people; and the constitution enforced the principle in the strongest manner by the practical declaration prefixed to that instrument; he alluded to the words, "We the people do ordain and establish."

There were many things mentioned by some of the State conventions which he would never agree to, on any conditions whatever; they changed the principles of the Government, and were therefore obnoxious to its friends. The honorable gentleman from Virginia had not touched upon any of them; he was glad of it, because he could by no means bear the idea of an alteration respecting them; he referred to the mode of obtaining direct taxes, judging of elections, &c.

He found he was not speaking to the question; he would therefore return to it, and declare he was against committing the subject to a select committee; if it was to be committed at all, he preferred a Committee of the whole, but hoped the subject would be postponed.

Mr. Madison found himself unfortunate in not satisfying gentlemen with respect to the mode of introducing the business; he thought, from the dignity and peculiarity of the subject, that it ought to be referred to a Committee of the whole. He accordingly made that motion first, but finding himself not likely to succeed in that way, he had changed his ground. Fearing again to be discomfited, he would change his mode, and move the propositions he had stated before, and the House might do what they thought proper with them. He accordingly moved the propositions by way of resolutions be adopted by the House.

Mr. Livermore objected to these propositions, because they did not take up the amendments of the several States.

Mr. Page was much obliged to his colleague for bringing the subject forward in the manner he had done. He conceived it to be just and fair. What was to be done when the House would not refer it to a committee of any sort, but bring the question at once before them? He hoped it would be the means of bringing about a decision.

Mr. Lawrence moved to refer Mr. Madison's motion to the Committee of the whole on the state of the Union.

Mr. Lee thought it ought to be taken up in that committee; and hoped his colleague would bring the propositions before the committee, when on the state of the Union, as he had originally intended.

Mr. Boudinot wished the appointment of a select committee, but afterwards withdrew his motion.

At length Mr. Lawrence's motion was agreed to, and Mr. Madison's propositions were ordered to be referred to a Committee of the whole. Adjourned.

*   *   *

Madison's Notes for Amendments Speech, 1789*

Reasons for urging amendts.
1. to prove fedts. friends to liberty.
2. remove remaining inquietudes.
3. bring in N. C. R. Island.
4. to improve the Constitution.
Reasons for moderating the plan.
1. No stop if door opened to theoretic amendts.
2. as likely to make worse as better till tried.
3. insure passage by 2/3 of Congs. & 3/4 of Sts:
Objectns. of 3 kinds vs. the Constn.
1. vs. the theory of its structure.
2. vs. substance of its powers—elections & [illegible].
3. vs. omission of guards in favr. of rights & liberty.
The last most urged & easiest obviated.
Read the amendments—
They relate 1st. to private rights—
Bill of Rights—useful not essential—fallacy in both sides, aspects [?]
as to English Decln. of Rts—
1. mere act of parl:
2. no freedom of press—Conscience Gl. Warrants—Habs. Corpus jury in civil causes—criml. attainders—arms to Protests.
frequent Parlts.—chief trust.
freedom of press & of conscience unknown to Magna Cha—& Pet: Rts.
Contents of Bill of Rhts,
1. assertion of primitive equality &c.
2. do. of rights exerted in formg. of Govts.
3. natural rights. retained as speach [illegible].
4. positive rights resultg. as trial by jury.
5. Doctrinl. artics vs. Depts. distinct electn.
6. moral precepts for the administrn. & natl. character—as justice—economy—&c.
Object of Bill Rhts.

*The Writings of James Madison, Vol. 5, pp. 389–90.

To limit & qualify powr. by exceptg. from grant cases in wch. it shall not be exercised or exd. in a particular manner.
to guard
    1. vs Executive & in Engl. &c—
    2. Legislative as in Sts—
    3. Majority of people.
ought to point as greatest danger which in Rep: is Prerogative of majority— Here proper, tho' less nessary than in small Repubs.
Objectns.—vs—Bill of Rhts.
    1. in Elective Govts. all power in people hence unnecessary & improper— This vs Sts.
    2. In fedl. Govt. all not given retained—Bill of powers—need no Bill of Rhts—
    sweeping clause—Genl. Warrants &c.
    3. St: Bills not repeald.
too uncertain
Some Sts have not bills—others defect: —others—injurious [illegible].
    4. disparge other rights—or constructively enlarge—
The first goes vs. St: Bills—
both guarded vs. by amendts.
    5. Not effectl.—vs Sts also—but some check.
Courts will aid—also Ex: also Sts Legisls: watch
Time sanctify—incorporate public Sentiment
Bill of Rts ergo proper.
II increase of Reps.—2 for each St.
III pay of Congs.
IV Interdict to Sts as to Conscience—press—& jury—
This more necsy. to Sts—ye. Congs.
V Check on appeals—comn law
VI partn. as to 3 Depts.—& do. as to Genl. & St Govts.

Madison to Randolph, 1789*

Apr. 12, 1789
    On the subject of amendments nothing has been publickly, and very little privately said. Such as I am known to have espoused will as far as I can gather, be attainable from the federalists, who sufficiently predominate in both branches; though with some, the concurrence will proceed from a spirit of conciliation rather than conviction. Connecticut is least inclined though I presume not inflexibly opposed, to a moderate revision. A paper wch. will probably be republished in the Virga. Gazettes, under the signature of a

*The Writings of James Madison, Vol. 5, p. 346.

Citizen of New Haven, unfolds Mr. Sherman's opinions. Whatever the amendments may be it is clear that they will be attempted in no other way than through Congress. Many of the warmest of the opponents of the Govt. disavow the mode contended for by Virga.

I wish I could see an equal prospect of appeasing the disquietude on the two other points you mention—British debts and taxes. With respect to the first, you know my sentiments. It will be the duty of the Senate in my opinion to promote regulations with G. B. as speedily as circumstances will admit, and the aspect of the Goverut. seems likely to command a respectful attention to its measures. I see nothing else that can be done. As to the taxes I see nothing that can be done, more than the ordinary maxims of policy suggest. They may certainly be diminished in consequence of the revolution in the federal Gov [torn out], since the public wants will be little if at all increased, [torn out] be supplied in greater proportion out of commerce.

Madison to Jefferson, 1789*

May 27, 1789

Dear Sir,

Since my last which was written on Sunday last and included an introduction of young Mr. Colden who is to be the bearer of it from Scotland where he now resides, I have had the pleasure of yours of March 15. My former letters will have made known to you the obstacles to a licence for your visit to America. The new authority has not yet taken up your application. As soon as the auxiliary offices to the President shall be established and filled which will probably not be long delayed, I hope the subject will be decided on, and in the manner you wish. It is already agreed in the form of resolutions that there shall be three departments one for finance, another for foreign affairs, and the third for war. The last will be continued in the hands of General Knox. The second will remain with Mr. Jay if he chooses to keep it. The first is also to be under one head, though to be branched out in such a manner as will check the administration. Chancellor wishes this department but will not succeed. It will be given I think to Jay or Hamilton. The latter is perhaps best qualified for that species of business and on that account would be prefered by those who know him personally. The former is more known by character throughout the U.S.

I have been asked whether any appointment at home would be agreeable to you. Being unacquainted with your mind I have not ventured on an answer.

*The Papers of Thomas Jefferson, Vol. 15, pp. 153–54.

The Bill of rates which passed the House of Representatives a few days ago is not yet come down from the Senate. The duties will it is said be pretty much reduced. In a few instances perhaps the reductions may not be improper. If they are not generally left as high as will admit of collection, the dilemma will be unavoidable, of either maiming our public credit in its birth, or resorting to other kinds of taxation for which our constituents are not yet prepared. The Senate is also abolishing the discriminations in favor of nations in treaty whereby Britain will be quieted in the enjoyment of our trade as she may please to regulate it and France discouraged from her efforts at a competition which it is not less our interest than hers to promote. The question was agitated repeatedly in the house of representatives and decided at last almost unanimously in favor of some monitory proof that our new government is able and not afraid to encounter the restrictions of Britain. Both the senators from Virginia particularly Lee go with the majority of the senate. In this I suspect the temper of the party which sent them is as little consulted as in the conduct of Lee in the affair of titles and his opinion in relation to the western country.

I have already informed you that Madam Brehan is every day recovering from the disesteem and neglect into which reports had thrown her and that Moustier is also becoming more and more acceptable or at least less and less otherwise. His commercial ideas are probably neither illiberal nor unfriendly to this country. The contrary has been supposed. When the truth is ascertained and known, unfavorable impressions will be still more removed.

The subject of amendments was to have been introduced on Monday last; but is postponed in order that more urgent business may not be delayed. On Monday sevennight it will certainly come forward. A Bill of rights, incorporated perhaps into the Constitution will be proposed, with a few other alterations most called for by the opponents of the Government and least objectionable to its friends.

As soon as Mr. Brown arrives who is the Representative of Kentucky, the admission of that district to the character of a State and a member of the union, will claim attention. I foresee no difficulty, unless local jealousy should couple the pretensions of Vermont with those of Kentucky: and even then no other delay than what may be necessary to open the way for the former through the forms and perhaps the objections of this State, which must not be altogether disregarded.

The proceedings of the new Congress are so far marked with great moderation and liberality; and will disappoint the wishes and predictions of many who have opposed the Government. The spirit which characterises the House of Representatives in particular is already extinguishing the honest fears which considered the system as dangerous to republicanism. For myself I am persuaded that the biass of the federal is on the same side with that of the State Governments tho' in a much less degree. Yrs. truly,

Benjamin Hawkins to Madison, 1789*

June 1, 1789

*   *   *

A circumstance trivial indeed, but from its effect here, important, deserves to be told. The opponents had predicted that Congress being once possessed with power, the friends to the new Government would never consent to make any amendments, your motion on that great and delicate subject directly contradicts it. And they swear that they will never forget Bland, Grayson and their other friends for suffering any business however important to be done in Congress prior to the subject of amendments, and moreover for suffering this important prophecy by their tardiness to be contradicted.

If you can do something by way of amendment without any material injury to the system, I shall be much pleased, and as far as I can learn it will be pleasing to my countrymen, or a majority of them I mean, we certainly are more friendly than we were at the meeting of our Convention, several counties who were much opposed to it, are now decidedly very friendly, and I count ["pretty certainly" stricken out] on its being adopted at our next convention.

*   *   *

Tench Coxe to Madison, 1789†

June 18, 1789

I observe you have brought forward the amendments you proposed to the federal Constitution. I have given them a very careful perusal, and have attended particularly to their reception by the public. The most decided friends of the constitution admit (generally) that they will meliorate the government by removing some points of litigation and jealousy, and by heightening and strengthening the barriers between necessary power and indispensible liberty. In short the most ardent & irritable among our friends are well pleased with them. On the part of the opposition I do not observe any unfavorable animadversion. Those who are honest are well pleased at the footing on which the press, liberty of conscience, original right & power, trial by jury &ca. are rested—Those who are not honest have hitherto been silent, for in truth they are stript of every rational, and most of the popular arguments they have heretofore used. I will not detain you with further remarks, but feel very great satisfaction in being able to assure you general-ly, that the proposed amendments will greatly tend to promote harmony

*Documentary History of the Constitution of the United States (1905), Vol. 5, p. 175.

†Documentary History of the Constitution of the United States, Vol. 5, pp. 178–79.

among the late contending parties and a general confidence in the patriotism of Congress. It has appeared to me that a few well tempered observations on these propositions might have a good effect. I have therefore taken an hour from my present Engagements, which on account of my absence are greater than usual, and have thrown together a few remarks upon the first part of the Resolutions. I shall endeavour to pursue them in one or two more short papers. It may perhaps be of use in the present turn of the public opinions in New York state that they should be republished there. It is in fed. Gazette of 18th. instant—

At some future day I should wish the powers of the general government extended to the declaring in what places canals may be cut, without giving them the power of providing for the expence, but at present this would be a dangerous Idea. I much doubt whether the federalists of N. Cara. would consent to adopt the constitution, if it contained such a power. You will see however infinite advantages, both pecuniary & political in a canal at the dismal Swamp in Virginia, and another at the head of the Delaware peninsula.

*   *   *

Madison to Pendleton, 1789*

June 21, 1789

Dear Sir,

 . . . The papers now covered contain a sketch of a very interesting discussion which consumed great part of the past week. The Constitution has omitted to declare expressly by what authority removals from office are to be made. Out of this silence four constructive doctrines have arisen. 1. that the power of removal may be disposed of by the Legislative discretion. To this it is objected that the Legislature might then confer it on themselves, or even on the House of Reps., which could not possibly have been intended by the Constitution. 2. that the power of removal can only be exercised in the mode of impeachment. To this the objection is that it would make officers of every description hold their places during good behavior, which could have still less been intended. 3. that the power of removal is incident to the power of appointment. To this the objections are that it would require the constant Session of the Senate, that it extends the mixture of Legislative & Executive power, that it destroys the responsibility of the President by enabling a subordinate Executive officer to intrench himself behind a party in the Senate, and destroys the utility of the Senate in their Legislative and Judicial characters, by involving them too much in the heats and cabals inseparable from questions of a personal nature; in fine, that it transfers the trust in fact

*The Writings of James Madison, Vol. 5, pp. 405–06.

from the President who being at all times impeachable as well as every 4th year eligible by the people at large, may be deemed the most responsible member of the Government, to the Senate who from the nature of that institution, is and was meant after the Judiciary & in some respects without that exception to be the most irresponsible branch of the Government. 4. that the Executive power being in general terms vested in the President, all power of an Executive nature, not particularly taken away must belong to that department, that the power of appointment only being expressly taken away, the power of Removal, so far as it is of an Executive nature must be reserved. In support of this construction it is urged that exceptions to general positions are to be taken strictly, and that the axiom relating to the separation of the Legislative & Executive functions ought to be favored. To this are objected the principle on which the 3d construction is founded & the danger of creating too much influence in the Executive Magistrate.

The last opinion has prevailed, but is subject to various modifications, by the power of the Legislature to limit the duration of laws creating offices, or the duration of the appointments for filling them, and by the power over the salaries and appropriations. In truth, the Legislative power is of such a nature that it scarcely can be restrained either by the Constitution or by itself. And if the federal Government should lose its proper equilibrium within itself, I am persuaded that the effect will proceed from the Encroachments of the Legislative department. If the possibility of encroachments on the part of the Ex or the Senate were to be compared, I should pronounce the danger to lie rather in the latter than the former. The mixture of Legislative, Executive & Judiciary authorities, lodged in that body, justifies such an inference; At the same [time], I am fully in the opinion that the numerous and immediate representatives of the people, composing the other House, will decidedly predominate in the Government.

Mr. Page tells me he has forwarded to you a copy of the amendments lately submitted to the H. of Reps. They are restrained to points on which least difficulty was apprehended. Nothing of a controvertible nature ought to be hazarded by those who are sincere in wishing for the approbation of 2/3 of each House, and 3/4 of the State Legislatures.

Madison to Samuel Johnston, 1789*

June 21, 1789

Dear Sir,

I lost no time in handing to the President the address inclosed in your favor of the 22 of May, and have postponed an acknowledgement of the latter in expectation of being able at the same time to cover the President's

*The Writings of James Madison, Vol. 5, pp. 409–10.

answer. This has been and continues to be delayed by a very serious indisposition, we hope he is not in much danger, but are by no means without our fears also. His disorders commenced in a fever which has greatly reduced him, and is terminating in a very large tumor which, unless it degenerate itself into a dangerous malady, will probably be remedial.

In the enclosed paper is a copy of a late proposition in Congress on the subject of amending the Constitution. It aims at the two-fold object of removing the fears of the discontented and of avoiding all such alterations as would either displease the adverse side, or endanger the success of the measure. I need not remark to you the hazard of attempting anything of a controvertible nature which is to depend on the concurrence of 2/3 of both Houses here, and the ratification of 3/4 of the State Legislatures. It will be some time before the proposed amendments will become a subject of discussion in Congress. The bills relating to revenue, and the organization of the Judiciary and Executive Departments, being likely to remain for some time on hand. This delay proceeds from the intricacy and partly from the novelty of the business. At every step difficulties from one or another of these sources arrest our progress. After the first essays the work will become every day more easy.

Among other difficulties, the exposition of the Constitution is frequently a Copious Source, and must continue so untill its meaning on all great points shall have been settled by precedents. The greatest part of the week past has been consumed in deciding a question as to the power of removal from offices held during pleasure. Four Constructive doctrines have been maintained 1, that the power is subject to the disposal of the Legislature. 2 that no removal can take place otherwise than by impeachment. 3 that the power is incident to that of appointment and therefore belongs to the President & Senate. 4 that the Executive power being generally vested in the President every power of an Executive Nature, not expressly excepted is to be referred thither, and consequently the power of removal, the power of appointment only being taken away.

In support of each of these constructions the Argumenta ab inconvenientibus have been elaborately dealt out against the others. The decision in a Committee of the whole on the Office of Foreign Affairs has adopted the 4th opinion as most consonant to the frame of the Constitution, to the policy of mixing the Legislature & Executive honors as little as possible, and to the responsibility necessary in the head of the Executive Department.

*   *   *

SELECT COMMITTEE AND COMMITTEE OF THE WHOLE, JULY—AUGUST, 1789

Commentary

On July 21, six weeks after he introduced his proposed amendments, Madison again rose and "begged the House to indulge him in the further consideration of amendments." He moved that the House go into Committee of the Whole, in accordance with the motion agreed to at the end of the June 8 debate. The House instead voted to send Madison's motion, as well as the amendments proposed by the various states, to a select committee, "to consist of a member from each state," with instructions to consider the subject of amendments, "and to report thereupon to the House." A Committee of Eleven (North Carolina and Rhode Island had not yet ratified) was appointed, of which Madison himself was a member (the only other well-known member was Roger Sherman, who had been a consistent opponent of a Bill of Rights).

The select committee did its job rapidly and, a week later, on July 28, John Vining of Delaware, who acted as Chairman, "made a report which was ordered to lie on the table." The amendments as rewritten by the Committee of Eleven are given *infra* p. 1055. It is fair to say that the Committee version made no substantial alteration in the original Madison draft. The Committee did, however, make certain stylistic changes which brought the amendments closer to the final Bill of Rights version. The most important of these are: the direct use of the term "freedom of speech, and of the press"; the change to what was to be language of the Just Compensation Clause of the Fifth Amendment; the use of almost the exact language ultimately contained in the Ninth Amendment; and the adoption of the substance of what was to be the language of the Seventh Amendment. These changes scarcely alter the fact that the Committee version was a virtual restatement of the amendments proposed by Madison.

Again Madison had to stir his colleagues to action. On August 3, he moved that the amendments recommended by the Committee of Eleven be made the order of business for August 12. The House agreed, resolving to go into Committee of the Whole on that day to consider the matter. On August 12, the House was busy on other matters and it was not until the next day that the House actually began to consider the amendments in Committee of the Whole. The debate lasted until August 24 with the House sitting in Committee of the Whole through August 18, and as the House itself from then on.

The August 13 debate began with a discussion of whether the House should devote the time needed for consideration of the proposed amendments. To the present-day observer, it is amazing that members could believe that "there were several matters before them of more importance than the present" or that "the discussion would take up more time than the House could now spare." We should remember, however, that even as late as 1886 so discerning an observer as Sir Henry Maine could refer to the federal Bill of Rights as "a certain number of amendments on comparatively unimportant points." To the Federalist majority in the first Congress, the Madison amendments seemed less pressing than setting up the details of the new governmental system. To get the motion to consider carried, Madison had to stress how necessary it was to reconcile those who had opposed the new system on the Bill of Rights issue: "Is it desirable to keep up a division among the people of the United States on a point in which they consider their most essential rights are concerned?"

During the August 13 debate, Roger Sherman urged that the Madison-Committee approach of inserting the amendments into the body of the Constitution was not the proper one: "We might as well endeavor to mix brass, iron, and clay, as to incorporate such heterogenous articles." Sherman moved that the amendments be adopted as a series of separate articles to be added at the end of the Constitution. Madison replied that "there is a neatness and propriety in incorporating the amendments into the constitution itself"—something which we should say today was rather true of the Sherman proposal. At this stage of the debate, a majority supported Madison on the form of the amendments, and the Sherman motion was defeated, only to be revived on August 19 when it was carried. Probably, at this point, the majority believed with Elbridge Gerry that to spend time on the question of form was "to be trifling about matters of little consequence"—or (as another member put it) "the time of the House was too precious to be squandered away in discussing mere matter of form."

From August 14 to 18, the House considered the amendments reported by the Committee of Eleven in Committee of the Whole. On August 14, members discussed and adopted the provisions on congressional representation and salary increases. On August 15, some of the most important provisions of the proposed amendments were dealt with. First came the discussion of freedom of religion, which was (as Irving Brant tells us in his leading biography of Madison) "Madison's first concern, both in drafting his amendments and in the deliberations which now ensued." Members objected to the provision on religious freedom on the ground that it might be "hurtful to the cause of religion." (One went so far as to assert that it might "have a tendency to abolish religion altogether").

Madison answered by giving his interpretation of the provision: "that Congress should not establish a religion, and enforce the legal observation of it by law, nor compel men to worship God in any manner contrary to their conscience." The purpose was to prevent Congress from making "laws of such a nature as might infringe the rights of conscience, and establish a national religion." To make this plain, Madison suggested that the word "national" be inserted before "religion." Other members objected, and Madison withdrew his suggestion. Samuel Livermore of New Hampshire then moved that the wording of the provision be changed to that proposed by his state's recommendatory amendment on the matter: "Congress shall make no laws touching religion or infringing the rights of conscience." This change was voted, and the proposed amendments now included, for the first time, the actual introductory language of the First Amendment.

The House then considered the guarantee of freedom of speech, press, assembly, and petition (also ultimately to be included in the First Amendment). Mr. Sedgwick moved to strike out the words "assemble and," saying it was implied and also trifling compared to the other rights covered. If it were covered, why not also the right to wear one's hat as he pleases or to go to bed when one chooses? Other members disagreed, stressing that the right to assemble was important, and Sedgwick's motion "lost by a considerable majority." Thomas Tucker of South Carolina then moved to insert expressly the people's right "to instruct their Representatives." The motion was opposed on the ground it would interfere unduly with the discretion and conscience of legislators, though Gerry supported it because sovereignty was ultimately in the people.

Madison now made an important reply to the Tucker motion. He warned against enumerating other than "simple, acknowledged principles" in the provisions to be adopted. "Amendments of a doubtful nature will have a tendency to prejudice the whole system; and the proposition now suggested partakes highly of this nature." With freedom of speech and press protected, the people can freely advise their representatives. To do more would be dangerous. To Gerry's assertion of sovereignty in the people, Madison replied: "My idea of sovereignty of the people is, that the people can change the constitution if they please; but while the constitution exists, they must conform themselves to its dictates."

Madison was making a basic point—that the House should consider the amendments before it and not add others "of a doubtful nature." Gerry could chide him: "It is natural, sir, for us to be fond of our own work. We do not like to see it disfigured by other hands." But Madison was plainly right. Let the proposed Bill of Rights be opened to all sorts of irrelevant amendments and "it obliges us to run the risk of losing the whole system."

Eventually, the Tucker motion was resoundingly defeated, and the provision on speech, press, assembly, and petition adopted as reported by the Committee of Eleven. By this point, Gerry could refer to the fact that the temper of the debate matched the weather itself: "Gentlemen now feel the weather warm, and the subject is warm; no wonder it produces some degree of heat."

On August 17, the debate began with consideration of the right to bear arms. There was an attempt to strike out the exemption for conscientious objectors, as well as to require a two-thirds vote for a standing army. Both attempts were defeated, and the provision carried as reported. The same was true of the provision prohibiting the quartering of soldiers. The debate then turned to the provision that was to become the Fifth Amendment: prohibition of double jeopardy and self-incrimination, and guarantee of due process and just compensation. John Laurence of New York moved to confine the self-incrimination guarantee to criminal cases, and his motion carried. The provision as reported was then agreed to unanimously.

The provision governing bail, fines, and punishments, was next agreed to, despite the objection that it was both indefinite and too strict. Conceptions of penology strikingly different from our own may be seen in Livermore's plaint that "villains often deserve whipping, and perhaps having their ears cut off; but are we in future to be prevented from inflicting these punishments because they are cruel?" The provision on searches and seizures was considered next and speedily approved, after adoption of a Gerry amendment that corrected a mistake in wording. Then the provision that was to become the Ninth Amendment was quickly approved.

The House next considered the provision prohibiting the states from infringing on freedom of conscience, speech, and press, and trial by jury in criminal cases. This provision was approved, as restated in affirmative form by Mr. Livermore. The debate here is important because of Madison's famous statement that he "conceived this to be the most valuable amendment in the whole list." This provision was to be eliminated by the Senate. Hence, the Bill of Rights as adopted was to impose restrictions only upon the Federal Government. Not until after the amendments added in the post Civil War period was the Constitution to contain significant limitations upon state power to infringe upon individual liberties.

The only thing of importance considered in the rest of the August 17 debate was the provision that became the first part of the Sixth Amendment. Livermore moved that the right to trial in the state where the offense was committed be added and this was adopted.

When the proposed amendments were considered the next day (August 18), Gerry moved that the House consider all of the amendments recommended by the different states, not just those reported by the Committee of Eleven. Madison and Vining (the Chairman of the reporting Committee) both objected, and Gerry's motion was defeated. The remaining provision on criminal procedure (trial by jury of vicinage and indictment) was then approved. Mr. Burke of South Carolina moved to change "vicinage" into "district or county in which the offense had been committed." The motion lost, though the Sixth Amendment was ultimately to contain language closer to that proposed by Burke. The provision on jury trial in civil cases, as well as that on separation of powers, were next adopted.

When the provision on reserved powers was taken up, Tucker moved to add the word "expressly," so that "the powers not *expressly* delegated" to the Federal Government would be reserved to the states. Madison was quick to oppose, objecting that "it was impossible to confine a Government to the exercise of express powers; there must necessarily be admitted powers by implication, unless the constitution descended to recount every minutia." Here we have the first statement of the seminal constitutional doctrine of implied powers (compare *supra* p. 854)—two years before Hamilton relied on the doctrine in his opinion on the constitutionality of the Bank of the United States and three decades before Marshall was to elevate the doctrine to the constitutional plane in *McCulloch* v. *Maryland.* Had Madison not persuaded his colleagues to defeat Tucker's motion, the landmark *McCulloch* opinion could never have been written.

The report of the Committee of Eleven (as amended in Committee of the Whole) was then reported to the House. Tucker moved to refer seventeen additional amendments to the Committee of the Whole. Fortunately the Tucker motion was defeated and the House could now proceed to final consideration of the amendments.

House of Representatives Journal, June—August, 1789*

The first action of Congress upon this subject was on the 8th of June, when a motion was made in the House of Representatives, that the house do come to a resolution, stating certain specific amendments proper to be proposed by Congress to the legislatures of the states, to become, if ratified by three-fourths thereof, part of the Constitution of the United States, which motion was referred to the consideration of the committee of the whole house on the state of the Union. On the 21st of July, the house, on motion, ordered that the committee of the whole house on the state of the Union be discharged from proceeding on this motion; and that the said motion, together with the amendments to the said Constitution, as proposed by the several states, be referred to a committee, to consist of a member from each state, with instruction to take the subject of amendments to the Constitution of the United States, generally, into their consideration, and to report thereupon to the house: and the following committee was appointed: Messrs. Vining, Madison, Baldwin, Sherman, Burke, Clymer, Benson, Gilman, Goodhue, Boudinot, and Gale. Mr. Vining made a report from this committee on the 28th of July, which was read and ordered to lie on the table. And, on the 3d of August, the house resolved, that it would, on Wednesday the 12th, resolve itself into a committee of the whole house to take the subject into consideration. On the 13th, the house went into committee of the whole on the report, which occupied the committee daily until the 18th, on which day the committee reported several amendments. Previously to the house going into committee on the 18th, the following motion was submitted:

History of Congress Exhibiting a Classification of the Proceedings of the Senate and House of Representatives from March 4, 1789 to March 4, 1793 (1843), pp. 152–55.

> That such of the amendments to the Constitution, proposed by the
> several states, as are not in substance comprised in the report of the select
> committee appointed to consider amendments, be referred to a committee
> of the whole house; and that all the amendments which shall be agreed to
> by the committee last mentioned, be included in one report.

The previous question having been demanded by five members—"Shall
the main question, to agree to the said order, be now put?"—on the question, "Shall the main question be now put?"—the ayes and noes being
required, it was decided as follows:

Ayes—Messrs. Burke, Coles, Floyd, Gerry, Griffin, Grout, Hathorn, Livermore, Page, Parker, Van Rensselaer, Sherman, Stone, Sturges, Sumpter,
Tucker.—16.

Noes—Messrs. Ames, Baldwin, Benson, Boudinot, Brown, Cadwalader,
Carroll, Clymer, Fitzsimons, Foster, Gilman, Goodhue, Hartley, Heister,
Huntington, Lawrance, Lee, Madison, jr., Moore, Muhlenberg, Partridge,
Schureman, Scott, Sedgwick, Seney, Silvester, Sinnickson, Smith, of Mary-
land, Smith, of South Carolina, Thatcher, Trumbull, Vining, Wadsworth,
Wynkoop.—34.

On the 18th, it was moved that the following propositions of amendment
to the Constitution of the United States be referred to a committee of the
whole house; to wit:

"Article 1, Section 2, Clause 2.—At the end, add these words: 'nor shall
any person be capable of serving as a representative more than six years, in
any term of eight years.'

"Clause 3.—At the end, add these words: 'from and after the commencement of the year 1795, the election of senators for each state shall be
annual: and no person shall be capable of serving as a senator more than
five years, in any term of six years.'

"Section 4, Clause 1.—Strike out the words, 'But the Congress may, at
any time, by law, make or alter such regulations, except as to the places of
choosing senators.'

"Section 5, Clause 1.—Amend the first part to read thus: 'Each state shall
be the judge (according to its own laws) of the election of its senators and
representatives to sit in Congress, and shall furnish them with sufficient
credentials; but each house shall judge of the qualifications of its own
members. A majority of said houses shall constitute,' &c.

"Clause 2.—Strike out these words: 'and, with the concurrence of two-
thirds, expel a member;' and insert the word 'and,' after the word 'proceedings.'

"Section 6, Clause 2.—Amend, to read thus: 'No person, having been
elected, and having taken his seat as a senator or representative, shall,
during the time for which he was elected, be appointed to any civil office
under the authority of the United States; and no person,' &c.

"Article 1, Section 8, Clause 1.—At the end, add these words: 'No direct tax shall be laid, unless any state shall have neglected to furnish, in due time, its proportion of a previous requisition; in which case, Congress may proceed to levy, by direct taxation, within any state so neglecting, its proportion of such requisition, together with interest, at the rate of six per cent. per annum, from the time it ought to have been furnished, and the charges of levying the same.'

"Clause 9.—Strike out the words, 'tribunals inferior to the Supreme Court,' and insert the words, 'Courts of Admiralty.'

"Clause 17.—At the end, add these words: 'Provided, That the Congress shall not have authority to make any law to prevent the laws of the states respectively, in which such district or places may be, from extending to such district or places in all civil and criminal matters, in which any person, without the limits of such district or places, shall be a party aggrieved.'

"Section 9, Clause 7.—Strike out the words, 'without the consent of the Congress;' and amend to read thus: 'shall accept of any present or emolument, or hold any office or title of any kind whatever, from any king, prince, or foreign state: Provided, That this clause shall not be construed to affect the rights of those persons (during their own lives) who are now citizens of the United States, and hold foreign titles.'

"Section 10, Clause 2.—Amend the first sentence to read thus: 'No state shall lay any duties on imports or exports, or any duty of tonnage, except such as shall be uniform in their operation on all foreign nations, and consistent with the existing treaties; and also uniform in their operation on the citizens of all the several states in the Union.'

"Article 2, Section 1, Clause 5.—At the end, add these words: 'nor shall any person be capable of holding the office of President of the United States more than eight years in any term of twelve years.'

"Section 2, Clause 1.—Strike out the words, 'be commander-in-chief,' and insert, 'have power to direct (agreeably to law) the operations."

"Clause 3.—At the end, add these words: "He shall also have power to suspend from his office, for a time not exceeding twelve months, any officer whom he shall have reason to think unfit to be intrusted with the duties thereof; and Congress may, by law, provide for the absolute removal of officers found to be unfit for the trust reposed in them.'

"Article 3, Section 1.—From each sentence strike out the words, 'inferior courts,' and insert the words, 'Courts of Admiralty.'

"Section 2, Clause 1.—Strike out the words, 'between a state and citizens of another state,' &c., to the end, and amend to read thus: 'between a state and foreign states, and between citizens of the United States, claiming the same lands under grants of different states.'

"Article 6, Clause 3.—Between the word 'no,' and the word 'religious,' insert the word, 'other.' "

On the question of the commitment of these propositions, it was decided in the negative.

House of Representatives Debates, July—August, 1789*

[Tuesday, July 21]

Amendments to the Constitution

Mr. Madison begged the House to indulge him in the further consideration of amendments to the constitution, and as there appeared to some degree, a moment of leisure, he would move to go into a Committee of the whole on the subject, conformably to the order of these of last month.

Mr. Ames hoped that the House would be induced, on mature reflection, to rescind the vote of going into a committee on the business and refer it to a select committee. It would certainly tend to facilitate the business. If they had the subject at large before a Committee of the whole, he could not see where the business was likely to end. The amendments proposed were so various, that their discussion must inevitably occupy many days, and that at a time when they can be ill spared; where as a select committee could go through and cull out those of the most material kind, without interrupting the principal business of the House. He therefore moved, that the Committee of the whole be discharged, and the subject referred to a select committee.

Mr. Sedgwick opposed the move 1, for the reasons given by his colleague, observing that the members from the several States proposing amendments would no doubt drag the House through the consideration of every one, whatever their fate might be after they were discussed; now gentlemen had only to reflect on this, and conceive the length of time the business would take up, if managed in this way.

Mr. White thought no time would be saved by appointing a select committee. Every member would like to be satisfied with the reasons upon which the amendments offered by the select committee are grounded, consequently the train of argument which gentlemen have in contemplation to avoid, must be brought forward.

He did not presume to say the constitution was perfect, but it was such as had met with the approbation of wise and good men in the different States. Some of the proposed amendments were also of high value; but he did not expect they would be supported by two-thirds of both Houses, without undergoing a thorough investigation. He did not like to refer any business to a select committee, until the sense of the House had been expressed upon it, because it rather tended to retard than despatch it; witness the collection bill, which had cost them much time, but after all had to be deserted,

Mr. Sherman: The provision for amendments made in the fifth article of the constitution, was intended to facilitate the adoption of those which experience should point out to be necessary. This constitution has been adopted by eleven States, a majority of those eleven have received it without

Annals of Congress, Vol. 1, pp. 685–792.

expressing a wish for amendments; now, is it probable that three-fourths of the eleven States will agree to amendments offered on mere speculative points when the constitution has had no kind of trial whatever? It is hardly to be expected that they will. Consequently we shall lose our labor and had better decline having any thing further to do with it for the present.

But if the House are to go into a consideration, it had better be done in such a way as not to interfere much with the organization of the government.

Mr. Page hoped the business would proceed as heretofore directed. He thought it would be very agreeable to the majority of the Union, he knew it would be to his constituents, to find that the Government meant to give every security to the rights and liberties of the people, and to examine carefully into the grounds of the apprehensions expressed by several of the state conventions; he thought they would be satisfied with the amendments brought forward by his colleague, when the subject was last before the House.

Mr. Partridge knew the subject must be taken up in some way or other, and preferred, for the sake of expedition, doing it by a select committee.

Mr. Jackson was sorry to see the House was to be troubled any further on the subject; he looked upon it as a mere waste of time; but as he always chose the least of two evils, he acquiesced in the motion for referring it to a special committee.

Mr. Gerry asked, whether the House had cognizance of the amendments proposed by the State conventions? If they had not, he would make a motion to bring them forward.

Mr. Page replied, that such motion would be out of order, until the present question was determined.

A desultory conversation ensued, and it was questioned whether the subject generally was to be before the Committee of the whole, or those specific propositions only which had already been introduced.

Mr. Gerry said, that it was a matter of indifference how this question was understood, because no gentleman could pretend to deny another the privilege of bringing forward propositions conformably to his sentiments. If gentlemen, then, might bring forward resolutions to be added, or motions of amendment, there would be no time saved by referring the subject to a special committee. But such procedure might tend to prejudice the House against an amendment neglected by the committee, and thereby induce them not to show that attention to the State which proposed it that would be delicate and proper.

He wished gentlemen to consider the situation of the States; seven out of thirteen had thought the constitution very defective, yet five of them have adopted it with a perfect reliance on Congress for its improvement. Now, what will these States feel if the subject is discussed in a select committee, and their recommendations totally neglected? The indelicacy of treating the application of five States in a manner different from other important subjects, will give no small occasion for disgust, which is a circumstance that this

Government ought carefully to avoid. If, then, the House could gain nothing by this manner of proceeding, he hoped they would not hesitate to adhere to their former vote for going into a Committee of the whole. That they would gain nothing was pretty certain, for gentlemen must necessarily come forward with their amendments to the report when it was brought in. The members from Massachusetts were particularly instructed to press the amendments recommended by the convention of that State at all times, until they had been maturely considered by Congress; the same duties were made incumbent on the members from some other States; consequently, any attempt to smother the business, or prevent a full investigation, must be nugatory, while the House paid a proper deference to their own rules and orders. He did not contend for going into a Committee of the whole at the present moment; he would prefer a time of greater leisure than the present, from the business of organizing the Government.

Mr. Ames declared to the House, that he was no enemy to the consideration of amendments; but he had moved to rescind their former vote, in order to save time, which he was confident would be the consequence of referring it to a select committee.

He was sorry to hear an intention avowed by his colleague, of considering every part of the frame of this constitution. It was the same as forming themselves into a convention of the United States. He did not stand for words, the thing would be the same in fact. He could not but express a degree of anxiety at seeing the system of Government encounter another ordeal, when it ought to be extending itself to furnish security to others. He apprehended, if the zeal of some gentlemen broke out on this occasion, that there would be no limits to the time necessary to discuss the subject; he was certain the cession would not be long enough; perhaps they might be bounded by the period of their appointment, but he questioned it.

When gentlemen suppose themselves called upon to vent their ardor in some favorite pursuit, in securing to themselves and their posterity the inestimable rights and liberties they have just snatched from the hand of despotism, they are apt to carry their exertions to an extreme; but he hoped the subject itself would be limited; not that he objected to the consideration of the amendments proposed, indeed he should move himself for the consideration, by the committee, of those recommended by Massachusetts, if his colleagues omitted to do it; but he hoped gentlemen would not think of bringing in new amendments, such as were not recommended, but went to tear the frame of Government into pieces.

He had considered a select committee much better calculated to consider and arrange a complex business, than a Committee of the whole; he thought they were like the senses to the soul, and on an occasion like the present, could be made equally useful.

If he recollected rightly the decision made by the House on the 8th of June, it was that certain specific amendments be referred to the Committee of the whole; not that the subject generally be referred, and that amendments be made in the committee that were not contemplated, before. This public discussion would be like a dissection of the constitution, it would be defacing its symmetry, laying bare its sinews and tendons, ripping up the whole form, and tearing out its vitals; but is it presumable that such conduct would be attended with success? Two thirds of both Houses must agree in all these operations, before they can have effect. His opposition to going into a Committee of the whole, did not arise from any fear that the constitution would suffer by a fair discussion in this, or any other House; but while such business was going on, the Government was laid prostrate, and every artery ceased to beat. The unfair advantages that might be taken in such a situation, were easier apprehended than resisted. Wherefore, he wished to avoid the danger, by a more prudent line of conduct.

Mr. Tucker would not say whether the discussion alluded to by the gentleman last up would do good or harm, but he was certain it ought to take place no where but in a Committee of the whole; the subject is of too much importance for a select committee. Now, suppose such a committee to be appointed, and that the amendments proposed by the several States, together with those brought forward by the gentleman from Virginia, are referred to them; after some consideration they report, but not one of the amendments proposed by either State; what is the inference? They have considered them, and as they were better capable than the House of considering them, the House ought to reject every proposition coming from the State conventions. Will this give satisfaction to the States who have required amendments? Very far from it. They will expect that their propositions would be fully brought before the House, and regularly and fully considered; if indeed then they are rejected, it may be some satisfaction to them, to know that their applications have been treated with respect.

What I have said with respect to the propositions of the several States, may apply in some degree to the propositions brought forward by the gentleman (Mr. Madison) from Virginia; the select committee may single out one or two, and reject the remainder, notwithstanding the vote of the House for considering them. The gentleman would have a right to complain, and every State would be justly disgusted.

Will it tend to reconcile the Government to that great body of the people who are dissatisfied, who think themselves and all they hold most dear, unsafe under it, without certain amendments are made? Will it answer any one good purpose to slur over this business, and reject the propositions without giving them a fair chance of a full discussion? I think not, Mr. Speaker. Both the Senate and this House ought to treat the present subject with delicacy and impartiality.

The select committee will have it in their power so to keep this business back, that it may never again come before the House; this is an imprudent step for us to take; not that I would insinuate it is an event likely to take place, or which any gentleman has in contemplation. I give every gentleman credit for his declaration, and believe the honorable mover means to save time by this arrangement; but do not let us differ on this point. I would rather the business should lie over for a month, nay, for a whole session, than have it put into other hands, and passed over without investigation.

Mr. Gerry inquired of his colleague, how it was possible that the House could be a federal convention without the Senate, and when two-thirds of both Houses are to agree to the amendments? He would also be glad to find out how a committee was the same to the House as the senses to the soul? What, said he, can we neither see, hear, smell, or feel, without we employ a committee for the purpose? My colleague further tells us, that if we proceed in this way, we shall lay bare the sinews and tendons of the constitution; that we shall butcher it, and put it to death. Now, what does this argument tend to prove? Why, sir, to my mind, nothing more nor less than this, that we ought to adopt the report of the committee, whatever the report may be; for we are to judge by the knowledge derived through our senses, and not to proceed on to commit murder. If these are the arguments to induce the House to refer the subject to a select committee, they are arguments to engage to go further, and give into the hands of select committees the whole legislative power. But what was said respecting a public discussion? Are gentlemen afraid to meet the public ear on this topic? Do they wish to shut the gallery doors? Perhaps nothing would be attended with more dangerous consequences. No, sir, let us not be afraid of full and public investigation. Let our means, like our conclusions, be justified; let our constituents see, hear, and judge for themselves.

The question on discharging the Committee of the whole on the state of the Union from proceeding on the subject of amendments, as referred to them, was put, and carried in the affirmative—the House divided, 34 for it, and 15 against it.

It was then ordered that Mr. Madison's motion, stating certain specific amendments, proper to be proposed by Congress to the Legislatures of the States, to become, if ratified by three-fourths thereof, part of the constitution of the United States, together with the amendments to the said constitution, as proposed by the several States, be referred to a committee, to consist of a member from each State, with instruction to take the subject of amendments to the constitution of the United States generally into their consideration, and to report thereupon to the House.

The committee appointed were, Messrs. Vining, Madison, Baldwin, Sherman, Burke, Gilman, Clymer, Benson, Goodhue, Boudinot, and Gale.

Then the House adjourned.

*   *   *

[Tuesday, July 28]

Mr. Vining, from the committee to whom it was referred to take the subject of amendments to the constitution generally into their consideration, and to report thereon, made a report, which was ordered to lie on the table.

*   *   *

[Monday, August 3]

*   *   *

The report of the committee on amendments to the constitution was, on motion of Mr. Madison, made the order of the day for Wednesday sennight.

*   *   *

[Thursday, August 13]

*   *   *

Amendments to the Constitution

Mr. Lee moved that the House now resolve itself into a Committee of the whole, on the report of the committee of eleven, to whom it had been referred to take the subject of amendments to the constitution of the United States generally into their consideration.

Mr. Page hoped the House would agree to the motion of his colleague without hesitation, because he conceived it essentially necessary to proceed and finish the business as speedily as possible; for whatever might be the fact with respect to the security which the citizens of America had for their rights and liberties under the new constitution, yet unless they saw it in that light, they would be uneasy, not to say dissatisfied.

He thought, likewise, that the business would be expedited by the simplicity and self-evidence which the propositions reported possessed, as it was impossible that much debate could take place.

Mr. Sedgwick was sorry that the motion was made, because he looked upon this as a very improper time to enter upon the consideration of a subject which would undoubtedly consume many days; and when they had so much other and more important business requiring immediate attention, he begged gentlemen to recollect that all they had hitherto done was of little or no effect; their impost and tonnage laws were but a dead letter.

Mr. Madison did not think it was an improper time to proceed in this business; the House had already gone through with subjects of a less interesting nature; now if the Judiciary bill was of such vast importance, its consideration ought not to have been postponed for those purposes.

He would remind gentlemen that there were many who conceived amendments of some kind necessary and proper in themselves; while others who are not so well satisfied of the necessity and propriety, may think they are rendered expedient from some other consideration. Is it desirable to keep up a division among the people of the United States on a point in which they consider their most essential rights are concerned? If this is an object worthy the attention of such a numerous part of our constituents, why should we decline taking it into our consideration, and thereby promote that spirit of urbanity and unanimity which the Government itself stands in need of for its more full support?

Already has the subject been delayed much longer than could have been wished. If after having fixed a day for taking it into consideration, we should put it off again, a spirit of jealousy may be excited, and not allayed without great inconvenience.

Mr. Vining, impressed by the anxiety which the honorable gentleman from Virginia had discovered for having the subject of amendments considered, had agreed, in his own mind, to waive, for the present, the call he was well authorized to make, for the House to take into consideration the bill for establishing a Land Office for the disposal of the vacant lands in the Western Territory. In point of time, his motion had the priority; in point of importance, every candid mind would acknowledge its preference; and he conceived the House was bound to pay attention to it as early as possible; as they had given leave for a bill to be brought in, they ought not to neglect proceeding onwards with it.

Mr. Sedgwick hoped the House would not consume their time in a lengthy discussion upon what business should be done first. He was of opinion that there were several matters before them of more importance than the present; and he believed the people abroad were neither anxious nor jealous about it; but if they were, they would be satisfied at the delay, when they were informed of the cause. He begged, therefore, that the question proposed by the gentleman from Virginia (Mr. Lee) might be put without further debate.

Mr. Smith said that the judicial bill was entitled to the preference in point of order, and in point of propriety it deserved the first attention of the House. For his part, he could not conceive the necessity of going into any alterations of the Government until the Government itself was perfected. The constitution establishes three branches to constitute a whole; the legislative and executive are now in existence, but the judicial is uncreated. While we remain in this state, not a single part of the revenue system can operate; no breach of your laws can be punished; illicit trade cannot be prevented. Greater harm will arise from delaying the establishment of the judicial system, than can possibly grow from a delay of the other subject. If gentlemen are willing to let it lie over to a period of greater leisure, I shall join them cheerfully and candidly, said he, in a full discussion of that business.

An honorable gentleman from Virginia observed to us that these propositions were self-evident, that little or no debate could grow out of them. That may be his opinion, but truly, sir, it is not mine; for I think some of them are not self-evident, and some of them will admit of lengthy discussion; and some others, I hope, may be rejected, while their place may be better supplied by others hereafter to be brought forward. Some members are pledged to support amendments, and will, no doubt, support them with all the arguments their fancy or ingenuity can suggest. Viewing it in this light, it is not to be expected that the discussion will be ended in less than a fortnight or three weeks; and let gentlemen consult their own feelings whether they have so much time now to spare.

Mr. Hartley thought the judicial system ought to be finished before any other business was entered upon, and was willing to consider of amendments to the constitution when the House was more disengaged; because he wished very much that the constitution was so modified as to give satisfaction to honest and candid minds. Such would be satisfied with securing to themselves and their posterity all those blessings of freedom which they are now possessed of. As to the artful and designing, who had clamored against the whole work, he had not the smallest desire to gratify them: he hoped and trusted their numbers were but few.

Mr. Gerry thought the discussion would take up more time than the House could now spare; he was, therefore, in favor of postponing the consideration of the subject, until the Judicial bill, and the bill for registering and clearing vessels, and some other bills relating to the revenue business, were gone through. He asked the gentleman from Virginia, if he conceived that the amendments in the report were all that were to be taken into consideration. He thought the community would be little more pleased with them than if they had omitted the subject altogether. Besides, it was absurd to suppose that the members were obliged to confine their deliberations solely to those objects, when it was very well known that the members from Massachusetts and New Hampshire were bound to bring forward and support others. The members from other States may be inclined to do the same with respect to the amendments of their own conventions; this will inevitably produce a more copious debate than the gentleman contemplates. From these considerations it might be hoped that honorable gentlemen would no longer press the motion.

Mr. Lawrence had no objection to consider amendments at a proper time, but did not think that the present was a proper time to enter upon them, nor did he suppose that gentlemen would be precluded from a full discussion of the whole subject whenever it was taken up. Gentlemen would find him ready to acquiesce in every thing that was proper, but he could not consent to let the great business of legislation stand still, and thereby incur an absolute evil in order to rid themselves of an imaginary one; for whether the subject of amendments was considered now or at a more distant period, appeared to his mind a matter of mere indifference. It may further be observed, that few, if any, of the State Assemblies are now in session; consequently the business could not be completed even if Congress had already done their part; but certainly the people in general are more anxious to see the Government in operation, than speculative amendments upon an untried constitution.

Mr. Madison: I beg leave to make one or two remarks more, in consequence of the observations which have fallen from the different sides of the House. Some gentlemen seem to think that additional propositions will be brought forward; whether they will or not, I cannot pretend to say; but if they are, I presume they will be no impediment to our deciding upon those contained in the report. But gentlemen who introduce these propositions will see, that if they are to produce more copious debate than has hitherto taken place, they will consume a great part of the remainder of the session. I wish the subject well considered, but I do not wish to see any unnecessary waste of time; and gentlemen will please to remember that this subject has yet to go before the Senate.

I admit, with the worthy gentleman who preceded me, that a great number of the community are solicitous to see the Government carried into operation; but I believe that there is a considerable part also anxious to secure those rights which they are apprehensive are endangered by the present constitution. Now, considering the full confidence they reposed at the time of its adoption in their future representatives, I think we ought to pursue the subject to effect. I confess it has already appeared to me, in point of candor and good faith, as well as policy, to be incumbent on the first Legislature of the United States, at their first session, to make such alterations in the constitution as will give satisfaction, without injuring or destroying any of its vital principles.

I should not press the subject at this time because I am well aware of the importance of the other business enumerated by the gentlemen who are adverse to the present motion, but from an apprehension that, if it is delayed until the other is gone through, gentlemen's patience and application will be so harassed and fatigued, as to oblige them to leave it in an unfinished state until the next session; besides, were the Judicial bill to pass now, it could not take effect until others were enacted, which probably at this time are not drawn up.

Mr. Smith: The honorable gentleman has concluded his remarks by assigning the best reason in the world why we should go into a consideration of the Judicial bill. He says, that even if it were now passed, it would take some time before it could get into operation; he must admit it to be an essential part of the Government, and, as such, ought not to remain a single instant in a state of torpidity.

Mr. Fitzsimons wished gentlemen would suffer the question to be put, and not consume the time in arguing about what should be done. If a majority was not in favor of considering amendments, they might proceed to some other business.

Mr. Page was positive the people would never support the Government unless their anxiety was removed. They, in some instances, adopted it, in confidence of its being speedily amended; they will complain of being deceived unless their expectations are fulfilled. So much time has elapsed since the subject was first brought forward, said he, that people will not think us serious, unless we now set about and complete it.

He begged gentlemen to consider the importance of the number of citizens, who were anxious for amendments; if these had been added to those who openly opposed the constitution, it possibly might have met a different fate. Can the Government, under these circumstances, possess energy, as some gentlemen suppose? Is not the confidence of the people absolutely necessary to support it?

The question was now put, and carried in the affirmative.

The House then resolved itself into a Committee of the whole, Mr. Boudinot in the chair, and took the amendments under consideration. The first article ran thus: "In the introductory paragraph of the constitution, before the words 'We the people,' add 'Government being intended for the benefit of the people, and the rightful establishment thereof being derived from their authority alone.' "

Mr. Sherman: I believe, Mr. Chairman, this is not the proper mode of amending the constitution. We ought not to interweave our propositions into the work itself, because it will be destructive of the whole fabric. We might as well endeavor to mix brass, iron, and clay, as to incorporate such heterogeneous articles; the one contradictory to the other. Its absurdity will be discovered by comparing it with a law. Would any Legislature endeavor to introduce into a former act a subsequent amendment, and let them stand so connected? When an alteration is made in an act, it is done by way of supplement; the latter act always repealing the former in every specified case of difference.

Besides this, sir, it is questionable whether we have the right to propose amendments in this way. The constitution is the act of the people, and ought to remain entire. But the amendments will be the act of the State Governments. Again, all the authority we possess is derived from that instrument; if we mean to destroy the whole, and establish a new constitution, we remove the basis on which we mean to build. For these reasons, I will move to strike out that paragraph and substitute another.

The paragraph proposed was to the following effect:

Resolved by the Senate and House of Representatives of the United States in Congress assembled, That the following articles be proposed as amendments to the constitution, and when ratified by three-fourths of the State Legislatures shall become valid to all intents and purposes, as part of the same.

Under this title, the amendments might come in nearly as stated in the report, only varying the phraseology so as to accommodate them to a supplementary form.

Mr. Madison: Form, sir, is always of less importance than the substance; but on this occasion, I admit that form is of some consequence, and it will be well for the House to pursue that which, upon reflection, shall appear to be the most eligible. Now it appears to me, that there is a neatness and propriety in incorporating the amendments into the constitution itself; in that case the system will remain uniform and entire; it will certainly be more simple, when the amendments are interwoven into those parts to which they naturally belong, than it will if they consist of separate and distinct parts. We shall then be able to determine its meaning without references or comparison; whereas, if they are supplementary, its meaning can only be ascertained by a comparison of the two instruments which will be a very considerable embarrassment. It will be difficult to ascertain to what parts of the instrument the amendments particularly refer; they will create unfavorable comparisons; whereas, if they are placed upon the footing here proposed, they will stand upon as good foundation as the original work.

Nor is it so uncommon a thing as gentlemen suppose; systematic men frequently take up the whole law, and, with its amendments and alterations, reduce it into one act. I am not, however, very solicitous about the form, provided the business is but well completed.

Mr. Smith did not think the amendment proposed by the honorable gentlemen from Connecticut was compatible with the constitution, which declared, that the amendments recommended by Congress, and ratified by the Legislatures of three-fourths of the several States, should be part of this constitution; in which case it would form one complete system; but according to the idea of the amendment, the instrument is to have five or six suits of improvements. Such a mode seems more calculated to embarrass the people than any thing else, while nothing in his opinion was a juster cause of complaint than the difficulties of knowing the law, arising from legislative obscurities that might easily be avoided. He said, that it had certainly been the custom in several of the State Governments, to amend their laws by way of supplement. But South Carolina had been an instance of the contrary practice, in revising the old code; instead of making acts in addition to acts, which is always attended with perplexity, she has incorporated them, and brought them forward as a complete system, repealing the old. This is what he understood was intended to be done by the committee; the present copy of the constitution was to be done away, and a new one substituted in its stead.

Mr. Tucker wished to know whether the deliberations of the committee were intended to be confined to the propositions on the table. If they were not, he should beg leave to bring before them the amendments proposed by South Carolina. He considered himself as instructed to bring them forward, and he meant to perform his duty by an early and prompt obedience. He wished to have the sense of the House on this point, whether he was in order to bring them forward.

Mr. Livermore was clearly of opinion, that whatever amendments were made to the constitution, they ought to stand separate from the original instrument. We have no right, said he, to alter a clause, any otherwise than by a new proposition. We have well-established precedents for such a mode of procedure in the practice of the British Parliament and the State Legislatures throughout America. I do not mean, however, to assert that there has been no instance of a repeal of the whole law on enacting another; but this has generally taken place on account of the complexity of the original, with its supplements. Were we a mere Legislative body, no doubt it might be warrantable in us to pursue a similar method; but it is questionable whether it is possible for us, consistent with the oath we have taken, to attempt a repeal of the constitution of the United States, by making a new one to substitute in its place; the reason of this is grounded on a very simple consideration. It is by virtue of the present constitution, I presume, that we attempt to make another; now, if we proceed to the repeal of this, I cannot see upon what authority we shall erect another; if we destroy the base, the superstructure falls of course. At some future day it may be asked upon what authority we proceeded to raise and appropriate public moneys. We suppose we do it in virtue of the present constitution; but it may be doubted whether we have a right to exercise any of its authorities while it is suspended, as it will certainly be from the time that two-thirds of both Houses have agreed to submit it to the State Legislatures; so that, unless we mean to destroy the whole constitution, we ought to be careful how we attempt to amend it in the way proposed by the committee. From hence, I presume it will be more prudent to adopt the mode proposed by the gentlemen from Connecticut, than it will be to risk the destruction of the whole by proposing amendments in the manner recommended by the committee.

Mr. Vining disliked a supplementary form, and said it was a bad reason to urge the practice of former ages, when there was a more convenient method of doing the business at hand. He had seen an act entitled an act to amend a supplement to an act entitled an act for altering part of an act entitled an act for certain purposes therein mentioned. If gentlemen were disposed to run into such jargon in amending and altering the constitution, he could not help it; but he trusted they would adopt a plainness and simplicity of style on this and every other occasion, which should be easily understood. If the mode proposed by the gentleman from Connecticut was adopted, the system would be distorted, and, like a careless written letter, have more attached to it in a postscript than was contained in the original composition.

The constitution being a great and important work, ought to be brought into one view, and made as intelligible as possible.

Mr. Clymer was of opinion with the gentleman from Connecticut, that the amendments ought not to be incorporated in the body of the work, which he hoped would remain a monument to justify those who made it; by a comparison, the world would discover the perfection of the original, and the superfluity of the amendments. He made this distinction, because he did not conceive any of the amendments essential, but as they were solicited by his fellow-citizens, and for that reason they were acquiesced in by others; he therefore wished the motion for throwing them into a supplementary form might be carried.

Mr. Stone: It is not a matter of much consequence, with respect to the preservation of the original instrument, whether the amendments are incorporated or made distinct; because the records will always show the original form in which it stood. But in my opinion, we ought to mark its progress with truth in every step we take. If the amendments are incorporated in the body of the work, it will appear, unless we refer to the archives of Congress, that George Washington, and the other worthy characters who composed the convention, signed an instrument which they never had in contemplation. The one to which he affixed his signature purports to be adopted by the unanimous consent of the delegates from every State there assembled. Now if we incorporate these amendments, we must undoubtedly go further, and say that the constitution so formed was defective, and had need of alteration; we therefore purpose to repeal the old and substitute a new one in its place. From this consideration alone, I think we ought not to pursue the line of conduct drawn for us by the committee. This perhaps is not the last amendment the constitution may receive; we ought therefore to be careful how we set a precedent which, in dangerous and turbulent times, may unhinge the whole.

With respect to the observations of the gentleman from South Carolina, I shall just remark, that we have no authority to repeal the whole constitution. The words referred to in that instrument only authorize us to propose amendments to it, which, when properly ratified, are to become valid as a part of the same; but these can never be construed to empower, us to make a new constitution.

For these reasons, I would wish our expressions might be so guarded, as to purport nothing but what we really have in view.

Mr. Livermore: The mode adopted by the committee might be very proper, provided Congress had the forming of a constitution in contemplation; then they, or an individual member, might propose to strike out a clause and insert another, as is done with respect to article 3, section 2. But certainly no gentleman acquainted with legislative business would pretend to alter and amend, in this manner, a law already passed. He was convinced it could not be done properly in any other way than by the one proposed by the gentleman from Connecticut.

Mr. Gerry asked, if the mode could make any possible difference, provided the sanction was the same; or whether it would operate differently in any one instance? If it will not, we are disputing about form, and the question will turn on the expediency. Now one gentleman tells you, that he is so attached to this instrument, that he is unwilling to lose any part of it; therefore, to gratify him, we may throw it into a supplementary form. But let me ask, will not this as effectually destroy some parts, as if the correction had been made by way of incorporation? or will posterity have a more favorable opinion of the original, because it has been amended by distinct acts? For my part, I cannot see what advantage can accrue from adopting the motion of the honorable gentleman from Connecticut unless it be to give every one the trouble of erasing out of his copy of the constitution certain words and sentences, and inserting others. But, perhaps, in our great veneration for the original composition, we may go further, and pass an act to prohibit these interpolations, as it may injure the text.

All this, sir, I take to be trifling about matters of little consequence. The constitution had undoubtedly provided that the amendments shall be incorporated if I understand the import of the words, "and shall be valid to all intents and purposes, as part of the constitution," if it had said that the present form should be preserved, then it would be proper to propose the alterations by way of a supplement. One gentleman has said we shall lose the names that are now annexed to the instrument. They are names, sir, I admit, of high respect; but I would ask that gentleman, if they would give validity to the constitution if it were not ratified by the several States? or if their names were struck out, whether it would be of less force than it is at present? If he answers these questions in the negative, I shall consider it of no consequence whether the names are appended to it or not. But it will be time enough to discuss this point, when a motion is made for striking them out.

If we proceed in the way proposed by the honorable gentleman from Connecticut, I presume the title of our first amendment will be, a supplement to the constitution of the United States; the next a supplement to the supplement, and so on, until we have supplements annexed five times in five years, wrapping up the constitution in a maze of perplexity; and as great an adept as that honorable gentleman is at finding out the truth, it will take him, I apprehend, a week or a fortnight's study to ascertain the true meaning of the constitution.

It is said, if the amendments are incorporated, it will be a virtual repeal of the constitution. I say the effect will be the same in a supplementary way; consequently the objection goes for nothing, or it goes against making any amendments whatever.

It is said that the present form of the amendments is contrary to the 5th article. I will not undertake to define the extent of the word amendment, as it stands in the fifth article; but I suppose if we proposed to change the division of the powers given to the three branches of the Government, and that proposition is accepted and ratified by three-fourths of the State Legislatures, it will become as valid, to all intents and purposes, as any part of the constitution; but if it is the opinion of gentlemen that the original is to be kept sacred, amendments will be of no use, and had better be omitted; whereas, on the other hand, if they are to be received as equal in authority, we shall have five or six constitutions, perhaps differing in material points from each other, but all equally valid; so that they may require a man of science to determine what is or is not the constitution. This will certainly be attended with great inconvenience, as the several States are bound not to make laws contradictory thereto, and all officers are sworn to support it, without knowing precisely what it is.

Mr. Stone asked the gentleman last up, how he meant to have the amendments incorporated? Was it intended to have the constitution republished, and the alterations inserted in their proper places? He did not see how it was practicable to propose amendments, without making out a new constitution, in the manner brought forward by the committee.

Mr. Lawrence could not conceive how gentlemen meant to engraft the amendments into the constitution. The original one, executed by the convention at Philadelphia, was lodged in the archives of the late Congress, it was impossible for this House to take, and correct, and interpolate that without making it speak a different language: this would be supposing several things which never were contemplated. But what would become of the acts of Congress? They will certainly be vitiated, unless they are provided for by an additional clause in the constitution.

What shall we say with respect to the ratifications of the several States? They adopted the original constitution, but they have not thereby enabled us to change the one form of Government for another. It is true, amendments were proposed by some of them; but it does not follow, of necessity, that we should alter the form of the original which they have ratified. Amendments in this way are only proper in legislative business, while the bill is on its passage, as was justly observed before.

Mr. Benson said, that this question had been agitated in the select committee, and determined in favor of the form in which it was reported; he believed this decision was founded in a great degree upon the recommendation of the State conventions, which had proposed amendments in this very form. This pointed out the mode most agreeable to the people of America, and therefore the one most eligible for Congress to pursue; it will likewise be the most convenient way. Suppose the amendments ratified by the several States; Congress may order a number of copies to be printed, into which the alterations will be inserted, and the work stand perfect and entire.

I believe it never was contemplated by any gentleman to alter the original constitution deposited in the archives of the Union, that will remain there with the names of those who formed it, while the Government has a being. But certainly there is convenience and propriety in completing the work in a way provided for in itself. The records of Congress and the several States will mark the progress of the business, and nothing will appear to be done but what is actually performed.

Mr. Madison: The gentleman last up has left me but one remark to add, and that is, if we adopt the amendment, we shall so far unhinge the business, as to occasion alterations in every article and clause of the report.

Mr. Hartley hoped the committee would not agree to the alteration, because it would perplex the business. He wished the propositions to be simple and entire, that the State Legislatures might decide without hesitation, and every man know what was the ground on which he rested his political welfare. Besides, the consequent changes which the motion would induce, were such as, he feared, would take up some days, if not weeks; and the time of the House was too precious to be squandered away in discussing mere matter of form.

Mr. Page was sorry to find the gentlemen stop at the preamble; he hoped they would proceed as soon as the obstruction was removed, and that would be when the motion was negatived.

He thought the best way to view this subject, was to look at the constitution as a bill on its passage through the House, and to consider and amend its defects, article by article; for which reason he was for entering at once upon the main business. After that was gone through, it would be time enough to arrange the materials with which the House intended to form the preamble.

Mr. Livermore insisted, that neither this Legislature, nor all the Legislatures in America, were authorized to repeal a constitution; and that must be an inevitable consequence of an attempt to amend it in a way proposed by the committee. He then submitted to gentlemen the propriety of the alteration.

As to the difficulty which had been supposed in understanding supplemental laws, he thought but little of it; he imagined there were things in the constitution more difficult to comprehend than any thing he had yet seen in the amendments.

Mr. Jackson: I do not like to differ with gentlemen about form; but as so much has been said, I wish to give my opinion; it is this: that the original constitution ought to remain inviolate, and not be patched up, from time to time, with various stuffs resembling Joseph's coat of many colors.

Some gentlemen talk of repealing the present constitution, and adopting an improved one. If we have this power, we may go on from year to year, making new ones; and in this way, we shall render the basis of the superstructure the most fluctuating thing imaginable, and the people will never know what the constitution is. As for the alteration proposed by the committee to prefix before "We the people," certain dogmas, I cannot agree to it; the words, as they now stand, speak as much as it is possible to speak; it is a practical recognition of the right of the people to ordain and establish Governments, and is more expressive than any other mere paper declaration.

But why will gentlemen contend for incorporating amendments into the constitution? They say, that it is necessary for the people to have the whole before them in one view. Have they precedent for this assertion? Look at the constitution of Great Britain; is that all contained in one instrument? It is well known, that *magna charta* was extorted by the barons from King John some centuries ago. Has that been altered since by the incorporation of amendments? Or does it speak the same language now, as it did at the time it was obtained? Sir, it is not altered a little from its original form. Yet there have been many amendments and improvements in the constitution of Britain since that period. In the subsequent reign of his son, the great charters were confirmed with some supplemental acts. Is the habeas corpus act, or the statute *De Tollagio non concedendo* incorporated in *magna charta?* And yet there is not an Englishman but would spill the last drop of his blood in their defence; it is these, with some other acts of Parliament and *magna charta*, that form the basis of English liberty. We have seen amendments to their constitution during the present reign, by establishing the independence of the judges, who are hereafter to be appointed during good behavior; formerly they were at the pleasure of the crown. But was this done by striking out and inserting other words in the great charter? No, sir, the constitution is composed of many distinct acts; but an Englishman would be ashamed to own that, on this account, he could not ascertain his own privileges or the authority of the Government.

The constitution of the Union has been ratified and established by the people; let their act remain inviolable; if any thing we can do has a tendency to improve it, let it be done, but without mutilating and defacing the original.

Mr. Sherman: If I had looked upon this question as mere matter of form, I should not have brought it forward or troubled the committee with such a lengthy discussion. But, sir, I contend that amendments made in the way proposed by the committee are void. No gentleman ever knew an addition and alteration introduced into an existing law, and that any part of such law was left in force; but if it was improved or altered by a supplemental act, the original retained all its validity and importance, in every case where the two were not incompatible. But if these observations alone should be thought insufficient to support my motion, I would desire gentlemen to consider the authorities upon which the two constitutions are to stand. The original was established by the people at large, by conventions chosen by them for the express purpose. The preamble to the constitution declares the act: but will it be a truth in ratifying the next constitution, which is to be done perhaps by the State Legislatures, and not conventions chosen for the purpose? Will gentlemen say it is "We the people" in this case? Certainly they cannot; for, by the present constitution, we, nor all the Legislatures in the Union together, do not possess the power of repealing it. All that is granted us by the 5th article is, that whenever we shall think it necessary, we may propose amendments to the constitution; not that we may propose to repeal the old, and substitute a new one.

Gentlemen say, it would be convenient to have it in one instrument, that people might see the whole at once; for my part, I view no difficulty on this point. The amendments reported are a declaration of rights; the people are secure in them, whether we declare them or not; the last amendment but one provides that the three branches of Government shall each exercise its own rights. This is well secured already; and, in short, I do not see that they lessen the force of any article in the constitution; if so, there can be little more difficulty in comprehending them whether they are combined in one, or stand distinct instruments.

Mr. Smith read extracts from the amendments proposed by several of the State conventions at the time they ratified the constitution, from which, he said, it appeared that they were generally of opinion that the phraseology of the constitution ought to be altered; nor would this mode of proceeding repeal any part of the constitution but such as it touched, the remainder will be in force during the time of considering it and ever after.

As to the observations made by the honorable gentleman from Georgia, respecting the amendments made to the constitution of Great Britain, they did not apply; the cases were nothing like similar, and consequently, could not be drawn into precedent. The constitution of Britain is neither the magna charta of John, nor the habeas corpus act, nor all the charters put together; it is what the Parliament wills. It is true, there are rights granted to the subject that cannot be resumed; but the constitution, or form of Government, may be altered by the authority of Parliament, whose power is absolute without control.

Mr. Seney was afraid the House would consume more time than was at first apprehended in discussing the subject of amendments, if he was to infer any thing from what had now taken place. He hoped the question would soon be put and decided.

Mr. Vining was an enemy to unnecessary debate, but he conceived the question to be an important one, and was not displeased with the discussion that had taken place; he should, however, vote in favor of the most simple mode.

Mr. Gerry: The honorable gentleman from Connecticut, if I understand him right, says that the words "We the people" cannot be retained, if Congress should propose amendments, and they be ratified by the State Legislatures. Now, if this is a fact, we ought most undoubtedly to adopt his motion; because if we do not, we cannot obtain any amendment whatever. But upon what ground does the gentleman's position stand? The constitution of the United States was proposed by a convention met at Philadelphia; but, with all its importance, it did not possess as high authority as the President, Senate, and House of Representatives of the Union. For that convention was not convened in consequence of any express will of the people, but an implied one, through their members in the State Legislatures. The constitution derived no authority from the first convention; it was concurred in by conventions of the people, and that concurrence armed it with power and invested it with dignity. Now the Congress of the United States are expressly authorized by the sovereign and uncontrollable voice of the people, to propose amendments whenever two-thirds of both Houses shall think fit. Now, if this is the fact, the propositions of amendment will be found to originate with a higher authority than the original system. The conventions of the States, respectively, have agreed for the people, that the State Legislatures shall be authorized to decide upon these amendments in the manner of a convention. If these acts of the State Legislatures are not good, because they are not specifically instructed by their constituents, neither were the acts calling the first and subsequent conventions.

Does he mean to put amendments on this ground, that after they have been ratified by the State Legislatures, they are not to have the same authority as the original instrument? If this is his meaning, let him avow it; and if it is well founded, we may save ourselves the trouble of proceeding in the business. But, for my part, I have no doubt but a ratification of the amendments, in any form, would be as valid as any part of the constitution. The Legislatures are elected by the people. I know no difference between them and conventions, unless it be that the former will generally be composed of men of higher characters than may be expected in conventions; and in this case, the ratification by the Legislatures would have the preference.

Now, if it is clear that the effect will be the same in either mode, will gentlemen hesitate to approve the most simple and clear? It will undoubtedly be more agreeable to have it all brought into one instrument, than have to refer to five or six different acts.

Mr. Sherman: The gentlemen who oppose the motion say we contend for matter of form; they think it nothing more. Now we say we contend for substance, and therefore cannot agree to amendments in this way. If they are so desirous of having the business completed, they had better sacrifice what they consider but a matter of indifference to gentlemen, to go more unanimously along with them in altering the constitution.

The question on Mr. Sherman's motion was now put and lost.

Mr. Livermore wished to know whether it was necessary, in order to carry a motion in committee, that two-thirds should agree.

Mr. Hartley mentioned, that in Pennsylvania, they had a council of censors who were authorized to call a convention to amend the constitution when it was thought necessary, but two-thirds were required for that purpose. He had been a member of that body, when they had examined the business in a committee of council; the majority made a report, which was lost for want of two-thirds to carry it through the council.

Some desultory conversation took place on this subject, when it was decided by the chairman of the committee that a majority of the committee were sufficient to form a report.

An appeal being made from the opinion of the chair, it was, after some observations, confirmed by the committee. After which the committee rose and reported progress.

Adjourned.

[Friday, August 14]

Amendments to the Constitution

The House then again resolved itself into a Committee of the whole, on the amendments to the constitution, Mr. Trumbull in the chair; when;

Mr. Smith wished to transpose the words of the first amendment, as they did not satisfy his mind in the manner they stood.

Mr. Gerry said, they were not well expressed; we have it here "government being intended for the benefit of the people;" this holds up an idea that all the Governments of the earth are intended for the benefit of the people. Now, I am so far from being of this opinion, that I do not believe that one out of fifty is intended for any such purpose. I believe the establishment of most Governments is to gratify the ambition of an individual, who, by fraud, force, or accident, had made himself master of the people. If we contemplate the history of nations, ancient or modern, we shall find they originated either in fraud or force, or both. If this is demonstrable, how can we pretend to say that Governments are intended for the benefit of those who are most oppressed by them. This maxim does not appear to me to be strictly true in fact, therefore I think we ought not to insert it in the constitution. I shall therefore propose to amend the clause, by inserting "of right," then it will stand as it ought. I do not object to the principle, sir; it is a good one, but it does not generally hold in practice.

The question on inserting the words "of right" was put, and determined in the negative.

Mr. Tucker: I presume these propositions are brought forward under the idea of being amendments to the constitution; but can this be esteemed an amendment of the constitution? If I understand what is meant by the introductory paragraph, it is the preamble to the constitution; but a preamble is no part of the constitution. It is, to say the best, a useless amendment. For my part, I should as soon think of amending the concluding part, consisting of General Washington's letter to the President of Congress, as the preamble; but if the principle is of importance, it may be introduced into a bill of rights.

Mr. Smith read the amendments on this head, proposed by the conventions of New York, Virginia, and North Carolina, from which it appeared that these States had expressed a desire to have an amendment of this kind.

Mr. Tucker replied, that the words "We the people do ordain and establish this constitution for the United States of America," were a declaration of their action; this being performed, Congress have nothing to do with it. But if it was necessary to retain the principle, it might come in at some other place.

Mr. Sumter thought this was not a proper place to introduce any general principle; perhaps, in going through with the amendments, something might be proposed subversive of what was there declared; wherefore he wished the committee would pass over the preamble until they had gone through all the amendments, and then, if alterations were necessary, they could be accommodated to what had taken place in the body of the constitution.

Mr. Livermore was not concerned about the preamble; he did not care what kind it was agreed to form in the committee; because, when it got before the House, it would be undone if one member more than one-third of the whole opposed it.

Mr. Page thought the preamble no part of the constitution; but if it was, it stood in no need of amendment; the words "We the people," had the neatness and simplicity, while its expression was the most forcible of any he had ever seen prefixed to any constitution. He did not doubt the truth of the proposition brought forward by the committee, but he doubted its necessity in this place.

Mr. Madison: If it be a truth, and so self-evident that it cannot be denied; if it be recognised, as is the fact in many of the State constitutions; and if it be desired by three important States, to be added to this, I think they must collectively offer a strong inducement to the mind desirous of promoting harmony, to acquiesce with the report; at least, some strong arguments should be brought forward to show the reason why it is improper.

My worthy colleague says, the original expression is neat and simple; that loading it with more words may destroy the beauty of the sentence; and others say it is unnecessary, as the paragraph is complete without it. Be it so, in their opinion; yet, still it appears important in the estimation of three States, that this solemn truth should be inserted in the constitution. For my part, sir, I do not think the association of ideas anywise unnatural; it reads very well in this place; so much so, that I think gentlemen, who admit it should come in somewhere, will be puzzled to find a better place.

Mr. Sherman thought they ought not to come in in this place. The people of the United States have given their reasons for doing a certain act. Here we propose to come in and give them a right to do what they did on motives which appeared to them sufficient to warrant their determination; to let them know that they had a right to exercise a natural and inherent privilege, which they have asserted in a solemn ordination and establishment of the constitution. Now, if this right is indefeasible, and the people have recognised it in practice, the truth is better asserted than it can be by any words whatever. The words "We the people" in the original constitution, are as copious and expressive as possible; any addition will only drag out the sentence without illuminating it; for these reasons, it may be hoped the committee will reject the proposed amendment.

The question on the first paragraph of the report was put and carried in the affirmative, twenty-seven to twenty-three.

The second paragraph in the report was read as follows:

Article 1. Section 2. Paragraph 3. Strike out all between the words "direct" and "and until such," and instead thereof, insert "after the first enumeration, there shall be one representative for every thirty thousand, until the number shall amount to one hundred. After which the proportion shall be so regulated by Congress, that the number of representatives shall never be less than one hundred, nor more than one hundred and seventy-five; but each State shall always have at least one representative."

Mr. Vining: The duty, sir, which I owe to my constituents, and my desire to establish the constitution on a policy, dictated by justice and liberality, which will ever secure domestic tranquillity and promote the general welfare, induces me to come forward with a motion, which I rest upon its own merits. Gentlemen who have a magnanimous policy in view, I trust, will give it their support, and concede to what is proper in itself, and likely to procure a greater degree of harmony. I therefore move you, sir, to insert after the words "one hundred and seventy-five," these words: "That where the number of inhabitants of any particular State amounts to forty-five thousand, they shall be entitled to two representatives.

This motion was negatived without a division.

Mr. Ames moved to strike out "thirty thousand," and insert "forty thousand." I am induced to this, said he, because I think my fellow citizens will be dissatisfied with too numerous a representation. The present, I believe, is in proportion to one for forty thousand, the number I move to insert. I believe we have hitherto experienced no difficulty on account of the smallness of our number; if we are embarrassed, I apprehend the embarrassment will arise from our want of knowing the general interest of the nation at large; or for want of local information. If the present number is found sufficient for the purpose of legislation, without any such embarrassment, it ought to be preferred, inasmuch as it is most adequate to its object.

But before we proceed in the discussion, let us consider the effect which a representation, founded on one member for 30,000 citizens, will produce. In the first place, it will give four members for every three now entitled to a seat in this House, which will be an additional burthen to the Union, in point of expense, in the same ratio. Add to this another consideration, that probably before the first census is taken, the number of inhabitants will be considerably increased from what it was when the convention which formed this constitution obtained their information. This will probably increase the expenses of Government to 450,000 dollars annually. Now those who have attended particularly to economy; who, upon the most careful calculation, find that our revenue is likely to fall infinitely short of our expenses, will consider this saving as a considerable object, and deserving their most serious regard.

It may become dissatisfactory to the people as an intolerable burthen. Again, it must be abundantly clear to every gentleman, that, in proportion as you increase the number of Representatives, the body degenerates; you diminish the individual usefulness; gentlemen will not make equal exertions to despatch public business, when they can lean upon others for the arrangement.

By enlarging the representation, we lessen the chance of selecting men of the greatest wisdom and abilities; because small district elections may be conducted by intrigue, but in large districts nothing but real dignity of character can secure an election. Gentlemen ought to consider how essential it is to the security and welfare of their constituents, that this branch of the Government should support its independence and consequence.

Another effect of it, will be an excitement or fermentation in the representative body. Numerous assemblies are supposed to be less under the guidance of reason than smaller ones; their deliberations are confused; they will fall the prey of party spirit; they will cabal to carry measures which they would be unable to get through by fair and open argument. All these circumstances tend to retard the public business, and increase the expense; making Government, in the eyes of some, so odious, as to induce them to think it rather a curse than a blessing.

It lessens that responsibility which is annexed to the representative of a more numerous body of people. For I believe it will be found true, that the representative of 40,000 citizens will have more at risk than the man who represents a part of them. He has more dignity of character to support, and must use the most unremitting industry in their service to preserve it unsullied; he will be more sensible of the importance of his charge, and more indefatigable in his duty.

It is said, that these amendments are introduced with a view to conciliate the affections of the people to the Government. I am persuaded the people are not anxious to have a large representation, or a representation of one for every 30,000; they are satisfied with the representation they now enjoy. The great object which the convention of Massachusetts had in view by proposing this amendment, was to obtain a security that Congress should never reduce the representation below what they conceived to be a point of security. Their object was not augmentation, it was certainty alone they wished for; at the next census, the number of representatives will be seventy or eighty, and in twenty years it will be equal to the desires of any gentleman. We shall have to guard against its growth in less than half a century. The number of proper characters to serve in the Legislature of any country is small; and of those, many are inclined to pursue other objects. If the representation is greatly enlarged, men of inferior abilities will undoubtedly creep in, for although America has as great a proportion of men of sense and judgment as any nation on earth, yet she may not have sufficient to fill a legislative body unduly enlarged. Now if it has been questioned whether this country can remain united under a Government administered by men of the most consummate abilities, the sons of wisdom, and the friends of virtue, how much more doubtful will it be, if the administration is thrown into different hands; and different hands must inevitably be employed, if the representation is too large.

Mr. Madison: I cannot concur in sentiment with the gentleman last up, that one representative for forty thousand inhabitants will conciliate the minds of those to the Government, who are desirous of amendments; because they have rather wished for an increase, than confined themselves to a limitation.

I believe, by this motion, we shall avoid no inconvenience that can be considered of much consequence, for one member for either thirty thousand or forty thousand inhabitants, will, in a few years, give the number beyond which it is proposed Congress shall not go.

Now, if good policy requires that we accommodate the constitution to the wishes of that part of the community who are anxious for amendments, we shall agree to something like what is proposed in the report, for the States of New Hampshire, Massachusetts, New York, Virginia, and North Carolina, have desired an alteration on this head; some have required an increase as far as two hundred at least. This does not look as if certainty was their sole object.

I do not consider it necessary, on this occasion, to go into a lengthy discussion of the advantages of a less or greater representation. I agree that after going beyond a certain point, the number may become inconvenient; that is proposed to be guarded against; but it is necessary to go to a certain number, in order to secure the great objects of representation. Numerous bodies are undoubtedly liable to some objections, but they have their advantages also; if they are more exposed to passion and fermentation, they are less subject to venality and corruption; and in a Government like this, where the House of Representatives is connected with a smaller body, it might be good policy to guard them in a particular manner against such abuse.

But for what shall we sacrifice the wishes of the people? Not for a momentary advantage. Yet the amendments proposed by the gentleman from Massachusetts will lose its efficacy after the second census. I think, with respect to futurity, it makes little or no difference; and as it regards the present time, thirty thousand is the most proper, because it is the number agreed upon in the original constitution, and what is required by several States.

Mr. Sedgwick observed, that the amendment proposed by the convention of Massachusetts was carried there, after a full discussion; since then, the whole of the amendments proposed by the convention had been recommended by the Legislature of that State to the attention of their delegates in Congress. From these two circumstances he was led to believe, that his and his colleague's constituents were generally in favor of the amendment as stated in the report.

He did not expect any advantage would arise from enlarging the number of representatives beyond a certain point; but he thought one hundred and seventy-five rather too few.

Mr. Gerry: My colleague (Mr. Ames) has said, that we experience no inconvenience for want of either general or local knowledge. Sir, I may dispute the fact, from the difficulties we encountered in carrying through the collection bill, and on some other occasions, where we seemed much at a loss to know what are the dispositions of our constituents. But admitting this to be the fact, is information the only principle upon which we are to stand? Will that gentleman pretend to say we have as much security in a few representatives as in many? Certainly he will not. Not that I would insist upon a burthensome representation, but upon an adequate one. He supposes the expenses of the Government will be increased in a very great proportion; but if he calculates with accuracy, he will find the difference of the pay of the additional members not to exceed a fourth. The civil list was stated to cost three hundred thousand dollars, but the House of Representatives does not cost more than a ninth of that sum; consequently the additional members, at the ratio of four for three, could not amount to more than a thirtieth part, which would fall far short of what he seemed to apprehend. Is this such an object as to induce the people to risk every security which they ought to have in a more numerous representation?

One observation which I understood fell from him, was, that multiplying the number of representatives diminished the dignity and importance of the individuals who compose the House. Now I wish to know, whether he means that we should establish our own importance at the risk of the liberties of America; if so, it has been of little avail that we successfully opposed the lordly importance of a British Parliament. We shall now, I presume, be advised to keep the representation where it is, in order to secure our dignity that I hope it will be ineffectual, and that gentlemen will be inclined to give up some part of their consequence to secure the rights of their constituents.

My honorable colleague has said, that large bodies are subject to fermentations; true, sir, but so are small ones also, when they are composed of aspiring and ambitious individuals. Large bodies in this country are likely to be composed, in a great measure, of gentlemen who represent the landed interest of the country; these are generally more temperate in debate than in others, consequently, by increasing the representation we shall have less of this fermentation than on the present establishment. As to the other objections, they are not of sufficient weight to induce the House to refuse adopting an amendment recommended by so large a body of our constituents.

Mr. Livermore was against the alteration, because he was certain his constituents were opposed to it. He never heard a single person but supposed that one member was little enough to represent the interest of thirty thousand inhabitants; many had thought the proposition ought to be one for twenty or twenty-five thousand. It would be useless to propose amendments which there was no probability of getting ratified, and he feared this would be the fate of the one under consideration, if the honorable gentleman's alteration took place.

Mr. Ames begged to know the reasons upon which amendments were founded. He hoped it was not purely to gratify an indigested opinion; but in every part where they retouched the edifice it was with an intention of improving the structure; they certainly could not think of making alterations for the worse. Now that his motion would be an improvement was clearly demonstrable from the advantage in favor of deliberating by a less numerous body, and various other reasons already mentioned; but to those, the honorable gentleman from Virginia (Mr. Madison) replied, by saying we ought to pay attention to the amendments recommended by the States. If this position is true, we have nothing more to do than read over their amendments, and propose them without exercising our judgment upon them. But he would undertake to say, that the object of the people was rather to procure certainty than increase; if so, it was the duty of Congress rather to carry the spirit of the amendment into operation than the letter of it.

The House of Representatives will furnish a better check upon the Senate, if filled with men of independent principles, integrity, and eminent abilities, than if consisting of a numerous body of inferior characters; in this opinion, said he, my colleague cannot but agree with me. Now if you diminish the consequence of the whole you diminish the consequence of each individual; it was in this view that he contended for the importance of the amendment.

He said it could not be the wish of Massachusetts to have the representation numerous, because they were convinced of its impropriety in their own Legislature, which might justly be supposed to require a greater number, as the objects of their deliberation extended to minute and local regulations. But that kind of information was not so much required in Congress, whose power embraced national objects alone. He contended, that all the local information necessary in this House, was to be found as fully among the ten members from Massachusetts, as if there had been one from every town in the State.

It is not necessary to increase the representation, in order to guard against corruption, because no one will presume to think that a body composed like this, and increased in a ratio of four to three, will be much less exposed to sale than we are. Nor is a greater number necessary to secure the rights and liberties of the people for the representative of a great body of people, is likely to be more watchful of its interests than the representative of a lesser body.

Mr. Jackson: I have always been afraid of letting this subject come before the House, for I was apprehensive that something would be offered striking at the very foundation of the constitution, by lessening it in the good opinion of the people. I conceive that the proposition for increasing the ratio of representation will have this tendency; but I am not opposed to the motion only on the principle of expediency, but because I think it grounded on wrong principles. The honorable gentleman's arguments were as much in favor of intrusting the business of legislation to one, two, or three men, as to a body of sixty or a hundred, they would dispatch business with greater facility and be an immense saving to the public; but will the people of

America be gratified with giving the power of managing their concerns into the hands of one man? Can this take place upon the democratic principle of the constitution, I mean the doctrine of representation? Can one man, however consummate his abilities, however unimpeachable his integrity, and however superior his wisdom, be supposed capable of understanding, combining and managing interests so diversified as those of the people of America? It has been complained of, that the representation is too small at one for thirty thousand; we ought not therefore attempt to reduce it.

In a republic, the laws should be founded upon the sense of the community; if every man's opinion could be obtained, it would be the better; it is only in aristocracies, where the few are supposed to understand the general interests of the community better than the many. I hope I shall never live to see that doctrine established in this country.

Mr. Stone supposed the United States to contain three millions of people; these, at one representative for every thirty thousand, would give a hundred members, of which fifty-one were a quorum to do business; twenty-six men would be a majority, and give law to the United States, together with seven in the Senate. If this was not a number sufficiently small to administer the Government, he did not know what was. He was satisfied that gentlemen, upon mature reflection, would deem it inexpedient to reduce that number one-fourth.

Mr. Seney said, it had been observed by the gentleman from Massachusetts, that it would tend to diminish the expense; but he considered this object as very inconsiderable when compared with that of having a fair and full representation of the people of the United States.

Mr. Ames's motion was now put, and lost by a large majority.

Mr. Sedgwick: When he reflected on the country, and the increase of population which was likely to take place, he was led to believe that one hundred and seventy-five members would be a body rather too small to represent such extensive concerns; for this reason he would move to strike out a hundred and seventy-five and insert two hundred.

Mr. Sherman said, if they were now forming a constitution, he should be in favor of one representative for forty thousand, rather than thirty thousand. The proportion by which the several States are now represented in this House was founded on the former calculation. In the convention that framed the constitution, there was a majority in favor of forty thousand, and though there were some in favor of thirty thousand, yet that proposition did not obtain until after the constitution was agreed to, when the President had expressed a wish that thirty thousand should be inserted, as more favorable to the public interest; during the contest between thirty and forty thousand, he believed there were not more than nine States who voted in favor of the former.

The objects of the Federal Government were fewer than those of the State Government; they did not require an equal degree of local knowledge; the only case, perhaps, where local knowledge would be advantageous, was in laying direct taxes; but here they were freed from an embarrassment, because the arrangements of the several States might serve as a pretty good rule on which to found their measures.

So far was he from thinking a hundred and seventy-five insufficient, that he was about to move for a reduction, because he always considered that a small body deliberated to better purpose than a greater one.

Mr. Madison hoped gentlemen would not be influenced by what had been related to have passed in the convention; he expected the committee would determine upon their own sense of propriety; though as several States had proposed the number of two hundred, he thought some substantial reason should be offered to induce the House to reject it.

Mr. Livermore said, he did not like the amendment as it was reported; he approved of the ratio being one for thirty thousand, but he wished the number of representatives might be increased in proportion as the population of the country increased, until the number of representatives amounted to two hundred.

Mr. Tucker said, the honorable gentleman who spoke last had anticipated what he was going to remark. It appeared to him that the committee had looked but a very little way forward when they agreed to fix the representation at one hundred members, on a ratio of one to every thirty thousand upon the first enumeration. He apprehended the United States would be found to comprehended nearly three millions of people, consequently they would give a hundred members. Now, by the amendment, it will be in the power of Congress to prevent any addition to that number; if it should be a prevalent opinion among the members of this House that a small body was better calculated to perform the public business than a larger one, they will never suffer their members to increase to a hundred and seventy-five, the number to which the amendment extended.

Mr. Gerry expressed himself in favor of extending the number to two hundred, and wished that the amendment might be so modified as to insure an increase in proportion to the increase of population.

Mr. Sherman was against any increase. He thought if a future House should be convinced of the impropriety of increasing this number to above one hundred, they ought to have it at their discretion to prevent it; and if that was likely to be the case, it was an argument why the present House should not decide. He did not consider that all that had been said with respect to the advantages of a large representation was founded upon experience; it had been intimated, that a large body was more incorruptible than a smaller one; this doctrine was not authenticated by any proof; he could invalidate it by an example notorious to every gentleman in this House; he alluded to the British House of Commons, which although it consisted of upwards of five hundred members, the minister always contrived to procure votes enough to answer his purpose.

Mr. Lawrence said, that it was a matter of opinion upon which gentlemen held different sentiments, whether a greater or less number than a certain point was best for a deliberate body. But he apprehended that whatever number was now fixed would be continued by a future Congress, if it were left to their discretion. He formed this opinion from the influence of the Senate, in which the small States were represented in an equal proportion with the larger ones. He supposed that the Senators from New Hampshire, Rhode Island, Connecticut, Jersey, and Delaware, would ever oppose an augmentation of the number of representatives; because their influence in the House would be proportionably abated. These States were incapable of extending their population beyond a certain point, inasmuch as they were confined with respect to territory. If, therefore, they could never have more than one representative, they would hardly consent to double that of others, by which their own importance would be diminished. If such a measure was carried by the large States through this House; it might be successfully opposed in the Senate; he would, therefore, be in favor of increasing the number to two hundred, and making its increase gradual till it arrived at that height.

Mr. Gerry: The presumption is, that if provision is not made for the increase of the House of Representatives, by the present Congress, the increase never will be made. Gentlemen ought to consider the difference between the Government in its infancy and when well established. The people suppose their liberties somewhat endangered; they have expressed their wishes to have them secured, and instructed their representatives to endeavor to obtain for them certain amendments, which they imagine will be adequate to the object they have in view. Besides this, there are two States not in the Union; but which we hope to annex to it by the amendments now under deliberation. These are inducements for us to proceed and adopt this amendment, independent of the propriety of the amendment itself, and such inducements as no future Congress will have, the principle of self-interest and self-importance will always operate on them to prevent any addition to the number of representatives. Cannot gentlemen contemplate a difference in situation between this and a future Congress on other accounts. We have neither money nor force to administer the constitution; but this will not be the case hereafter. In the progress of this Government its revenues will increase, and an army will be established; a future Legislature will find other means to influence the people than now exist.

This circumstance proves that we ought to leave as little as possible to the discretion of the future Government; but it by no means proves that the present Congress ought not to adopt the amendment moved by my colleague, Mr. Sedgwick.

Mr. Ames: It has been observed that there will be an indisposition in future Legislatures to increase the number of representatives. I am by no means satisfied that this observation is true. I think there are motives which will influence Legislatures of the best kind to increase the number of members. There is a constant tendency in a republican Government to multiply what it thinks to be the popular branch. If we consider that men are often more attached to their places than they are to their principles, we shall not be surprised to see men of the most refined judgment advocating a measure which will increase their chance of continuing in office.

My honorable colleague has intimated that a future Legislature will be against extending the number of this branch; and that if the people are displeased, they will have it in their power, by force, to compel their acquiescence. I do not see, sir, how the Legislature is strengthened by the increase of an army. I have generally understood that it gave power to the executive arm, but not to the deliberative head: the example of every nation is against him. Nor can I conceive upon what foundation he rests his reasoning. If there is a natural inclination in the Government to increase the number of administrators, it will be prudent in us to endeavor to counteract its baneful influence.

Mr. Livermore now proposed to strike out the words "one hundred," and insert "two hundred."

Mr. Sedgwick suspended his motion until this question was determined; whereupon it was put and lost, there being twenty-two in favor of, and twenty-seven against it.

Mr. Sedgwick's motion was then put, and carried in the affirmative.

Mr. Livermore wished to amend the clause of the report in such a manner as to prevent the power of Congress from deciding the rate of increase. He thought the constitution had better fix it, and let it be gradual until it arrived at two hundred. After which, if it was the sense of the committee, it might be stationary, and liable to no other variation than that of being apportioned among the members of the Union.

Mr. Ames suggested to the consideration of gentlemen, whether it would not be better to arrange the subject in such a way as to let the representation be proportioned to a ratio of one for thirty thousand at the first census, and one for forty thousand at the second, so as to prevent a too rapid increase of the number of members. He did not make a motion of this nature, because he conceived it to be out of order, after the late decision of the committee; but it might be brought forward in the House, and he hoped would accommodate both sides.

Mr. Gerry wished that the gentleman last up would pen down the idea he had just thrown out; he thought it very proper for the consideration of the House.

The question on the second proposition of the report, as amended, was now put and carried, being twenty-seven for, and twenty-two against it.

The next proposition in the report was as follows:

Article 1. Section 6. Between the words "United States," and "shall in all cases," strike out "they," and insert "but no law varying the compensation shall take effect, until an election of representatives shall have intervened. The members."

Mr. Sedgwick thought much inconvenience and but very little good would result from this amendment; it might serve as a tool for designing men; they might reduce the wages very low, much lower than it was possible for any gentleman to serve without injury to his private affairs, in order to procure popularity at home, provided a diminution of pay was looked upon as a desirable thing. It might also be done in order to prevent men of shining and disinterested abilities, but of indigent circumstances, from rendering their fellow-citizens those services they are well able to perform, and render a seat in this House less eligible than it ought to be.

Mr. Vining thought every future Legislature would feel a degree of gratitude to the preceding one, which had performed so disagreeable a task for them. The committee who had made this a part of their report, had been guided by a single reason, but which appeared to them a sufficient one. There was, to say the least of it, a disagreeable sensation, occasioned by leaving it in the breast of any man to set a value on his own work; it is true it is unavoidable in the present House, but it might and ought to be avoided in future; he therefore hoped it would obtain without any difficulty.

Mr. Gerry would be in favor of this clause, if they could find means to secure an adequate representation; but he apprehended that it would be considerably endangered; he should therefore be against it.

Mr. Madison thought the representation would be as well secured under this clause as it would be if it was omitted; and as it was desired by a great number of the people of America, he would consent to it, though he was not convinced it was absolutely necessary.

Mr. Sedgwick remarked once more, that the proposition had two aspects which made it disagreeable to him; the one was to render a man popular to his constituents, the other to render the place ineligible to his competitor.

He thought there was very little danger of an abuse of the power of laying their own wages: gentlemen were generally more inclined to make them moderate than excessive.

The question being put on the proposition, it was carried in the affirmative, twenty-seven for, and twenty against it.

The committee then rose and reported progress, and the House adjourned.

[Saturday, August 15]

Amendments to the Constitution

The House again went into a Committee of the whole on the proposed amendments to the constitution, Mr. Boudinot in the chair.

The fourth proposition being under consideration, as follows:

Article 1. Section 9. Between paragraphs two and three insert "no religion shall be established by law, nor shall the equal rights of conscience be infringed."

Mr. Sylvester had some doubts of the propriety of the mode of expression used in this paragraph. He apprehended that it was liable to a construction different from what had been made by the committee. He feared it might be thought to have a tendency to abolish religion altogether.

Mr. Vining suggested the propriety of transposing the two members of the sentence.

Mr. Gerry said it would read better if it was, that no religious doctrine shall be established by law.

Mr. Sherman thought the amendment altogether unnecessary, inasmuch as Congress had no authority whatever delegated to them by the constitution to make religious establishments; he would, therefore, move to have it struck out.

Mr. Carroll: As the rights of conscience are, in their nature, of peculiar delicacy, and will little bear the gentlest touch of governmental hand; and as many sects have concurred in opinion that they are not well secured under the present constitution, he said he was much in favor of adopting the words. He thought it would tend more towards conciliating the minds of the people to the Government than almost any other amendment he had heard proposed. He would not contend with gentlemen about the phraseology, his object was to secure the substance in such a manner as to satisfy the wishes of the honest part of the community.

Mr. Madison said, he apprehended the meaning of the words to be, that Congress should not establish a religion, and enforce the legal observation of it by law, nor compel men to worship God in any manner contrary to their conscience. Whether the words are necessary or not, he did not mean to say, but they had been required by some of the State Conventions, who seemed to entertain an opinion that under the clause of the constitution, which gave power to Congress to make all laws necessary and proper to carry into execution the constitution, and the laws made under it, enabled them to make laws of such a nature as might infringe the rights of conscience, and establish a national religion; to prevent these effects he presumed the amendment was intended, and he thought it as well expressed as the nature of the language would admit.

Mr. Huntington said that he feared, with the gentleman first up on this subject, that the words might be taken in such latitude as to be extremely hurtful to the cause of religion. He understood the amendment to mean what had been expressed by the gentleman from Virginia; but others might find it convenient to put another construction upon it. The ministers of their congregations to the Eastward were maintained by the contributions of those who belonged to their society; the expense of building meeting-houses was contributed in the same manner. These things were regulated by bylaws. If any action was brought before a Federal Court on any of these cases, the person who had neglected to perform his engagements could not be compelled to do it; for a support of ministers, or building of places of worship might be construed into a religious establishment.

By the charter of Rhode Island, no religion could be established by law; he could give a history of the effects of such a regulation; indeed the people were now enjoying the blessed fruits of it. He hoped, therefore, the amendment would be made in such a way as to secure the rights of conscience, and a free exercise of the rights of religion, but not to patronize those who professed no religion at all.

Mr. Madison thought, if the word national was inserted before religion, it would satisfy the minds of honorable gentlemen. He believed that the people feared one sect might obtain a pre-eminence, or two combine together, and establish a religion to which they would compel others to conform. He thought if the word national was introduced, it would point the amendment directly to the object it was intended to prevent.

Mr. Livermore was not satisfied with that amendment; but he did not wish them to dwell long on the subject. He thought it would be better if it was altered, and made to read in this manner, that Congress shall make no laws touching religion, or infringing the rights of conscience.

Mr. Gerry did not like the term national, proposed by the gentleman from Virginia, and he hoped it would not be adopted by the House. It brought to his mind some observations that had taken place in the conventions at the time they were considering the present constitution. It had been insisted upon by those who were called antifederalists, that this form of Government consolidated the Union; the honorable gentleman's motion shows that he considers it in the same light. Those who were called antifederalists at that time complained that they had injustice done them by the title, because they were in favor of a Federal Government, and the others were in favor of a national one; the federalists were for ratifying the constitution as it stood, and the others not until amendments were made. Their names then ought not to have been distinguished by federalists and antifederalists, but rats and antirats.

Mr. Madison withdrew his motion, but observed that the words "no national religion shall be established by law," did not imply that the Government was a national one; the question was then taken on Mr. Livermore's motion, and passed in the affirmative, thirty-one for, and twenty against it.

The next clause of the fourth proposition was taken into consideration, and was as follows: "The freedom of speech and of the press, and the right of the people peaceably to assemble and consult for their common good, and to apply to the Government for redress of grievances, shall not be infringed.

Mr. Sedgwick submitted to those gentlemen who had contemplated the subject, what effect such an amendment as this would have; he feared it would tend to make them appear trifling in the eyes of their constituents;

what, said he, shall we secure the freedom of speech, and think it necessary, at the same time, to allow the right of assembling? If people freely converse together, they must assemble for that purpose; it is a self-evident, unalienable right which the people possess; it is certainly a thing that never would be called in question; it is derogatory to the dignity of the House to descend to such minutiae; he therefore moved to strike out "assemble and."

Mr. Benson: The committee who framed this report proceeded on the principle that these rights belonged to the people; they conceived them to be inherent; and all that they meant to provide against was their being infringed by the Government.

Mr. Sedgwick replied, that if the committee were governed by that general principle, they might have gone into a very lengthy enumeration of rights; they might have declared that a man should have a right to wear his hat if he pleased; that he might get up when he pleased, and go to bed when he thought proper; but he would ask the gentleman whether he thought it necessary to enter these trifles in a declaration of rights, in a Government where none of them were intended to be infringed.

Mr. Tucker hoped the words would not be struck out, for he considered them of importance; besides, they were recommended by the States of Virginia and North Carolina, though he noticed that the most material part proposed by those States was omitted, which was, a declaration that the people should have a right to instruct their representatives. He would move to have those words inserted as soon as the motion for striking out was decided.

Mr. Gerry was also against the words being struck out, because he conceived it to be an essential right; it was inserted in the constitutions of several States; and though it had been abused in the year 1786 in Massachusetts, yet that abuse ought not to operate as an argument against the use of it. The people ought to be secure in the peaceable enjoyment of this privilege, and that can only be done by making a declaration to that effect in the constitution.

Mr. Page: The gentleman from Massachusetts, (Mr. Sedgwick) who made this motion, objects to the clause, because the right is of so trivial a nature. He supposes it no more essential than whether a man has a right to wear his hat or not; but let me observe to him that such rights have been opposed, and a man has been obliged to pull off his hat when he appeared before the face of authority; people have also been prevented from assembling together on their lawful occasions, therefore it is well to guard against such stretches of authority, by inserting the privilege in the declaration of rights. If the people could be deprived of the power of assembling under any pretext whatsoever, they might be deprived of every other privilege contained in the clause.

Mr. Vining said, if the thing was harmless, and it would tend to gratify the States that had proposed amendments, he should agree to it.

Mr. Hartley observed, that it had been asserted in the convention of Pennsylvania, by the friends of the constitution, that all the rights and powers that were not given to the Government were retained by the States and the people thereof. This was also his own opinion; but as four or five States had required to be secured in those rights by an express declaration in the constitution, he was disposed to gratify them; he thought every thing that was not incompatible with the general good ought to be granted, if it would tend to obtain the confidence of the people in the Government; and, upon the whole, he thought these words were as necessary to be inserted in the declaration of rights as most in the clause.

Mr. Gerry said, that his colleague contended for nothing, if he supposed that the people had a right to consult for the common good, because they could not consult unless they met for the purpose.

Mr. Sedgwick replied that if they were understood or implied in the word consult, they were utterly unnecessary, and upon that ground he moved to have them struck out.

The question was now put upon Mr. Sedgwick's motion, and lost by a considerable majority.

Mr. Tucker then moved to insert these words, "to instruct their Representatives."

Mr. Hartley wished the motion had not been made, for gentlemen acquainted with the circumstances of this country, and the history of the country from which we separated, differed exceedingly on this point. The members of the House of Representatives, said he, are chosen for two years, the members of the Senate for six.

According to the principles laid down in the Constitution, it is presumable that the persons elected know the interests and the circumstances of their constituents, and being checked in their determinations by a division of the Legislative power into two branches, there is little danger of error. At least it ought to be supposed that they have the confidence of the people during the period for which they are elected; and if, by misconduct, they forfeit it, their constituents have the power of leaving them out at the expiration of that time—thus they are answerable for the part they have taken in measures that may be contrary to the general wish.

Representation is the principle of our Government; the people ought to have confidence in the honor and integrity of those they send forward to transact their business; their right to instruct them is a problematical subject. We have seen it attended with bad consequences, both in England and America. When the passions of the people are excited, instructions have been resorted to and obtained, to answer party purposes; and although the public opinion is generally respectable, yet at such moments it has been known to be often wrong; and happy is that Government composed of men of firmness and wisdom to discover, and resist popular error.

If, in a small community, where the interests, habits, and manners are neither so numerous or diversified, instructions bind not, what shall we say of instructions to this body? Can it be supposed that the inhabitants of a single district in a State, are better informed with respect to the general interests of the Union, than a select body assembled from every part? Can it be supposed that a part will be more desirous of promoting the good of the whole than the whole will of the part? I apprehend, sir, that Congress will be the best judges of proper measures, and that instructions will never be resorted to but for party purposes, when they will generally contain the prejudices and acrimony of the party, rather than the dictates of honest reason and sound policy.

In England, this question has been considerably agitated. The representatives of some towns in Parliament have acknowledged, and submitted to the binding force of instructions, while the majority have thrown off the shackles with disdain. I would not have this precedent influence our decision; but let the doctrine be tried upon its own merits, and stand or fall as it shall be found to deserve.

It appears to my mind, that the principle of representation is distinct from an agency, which may require written instructions. The great end of meeting is to consult for the common good; but can the common good be discerned without the object is reflected and shown in every light. A local or partial view does not necessarily enable any man to comprehend it clearly; this can only result from an inspection into the aggregate. Instructions viewed in this light will be found to embarrass the best and wisest men. And were all the members to take their seats in order to obey instructions, and those instructions were as various as it is probable they would be, what possibility would there exist of so accommodating each to the other as to produce any act whatever? Perhaps a majority of the whole might not be instructed to agree to any one point, and is it thus the people of the United States propose to form a more perfect union, provide for the common defence, and promote the general welfare?

Sir, I have known within my own time so many inconveniences and real evils arise from adopting the popular opinions on the moment, that although I respect them as much as any man, I hope this Government will particularly guard against them, at least that they will not bind themselves by a constitutional act, and by oath, to submit to their influence; if they do, the great object which this Government has been established to attain, will inevitably elude our grasp on the uncertain and veering winds of popular commotion.

Mr. Page: The gentleman from Pennsylvania tells you, that in England this principle is doubted; how far this is consonant with the nature of the Government I will not pretend to say; but I am not astonished to find that the administrators of a monarchical Government are unassailable by the weak voice of the people; but under a democracy, whose great end is to form a code of laws congenial with the public sentiment, the popular opinion ought to be collected and attended to. Our present object is, I presume, to secure to our constituents and to posterity these inestimable rights. Our Government is derived from the people, of consequence the people have a right to consult for the common good; but to what end will this be done, if they have not the power of instructing their representatives? Instruction and representation in a republic appear to me to be inseparably connected; but were I the subject of a monarch, I should doubt whether the public good did not depend more upon the prince's will than the will of the people, I should dread a popular assembly consulting for the public good, because, under its influence, commotions and tumults might arise that would shake the foundation of the monarch's throne, and make the empire tremble in expectation. The people of England have submitted the crown to the Hanover family, and have rejected the Stuarts. If instructions upon such a revolution were considered binding, it is difficult to know what would have been the effects. It might be well, therefore, to have the doctrine exploded from that kingdom; but it will not be advanced as a substantial reason in favor of our treading in the same steps.

The honorable gentleman has said, that when once the people have chosen a representative, they must rely on his integrity and judgment during the period for which he is elected. I think, sir, to doubt the authority of the people to instruct their representatives, will give them just cause to be alarmed for their fate. I look upon it as a dangerous doctrine, subversive of the great end for which the United States have confederated. Every friend of mankind, every well-wisher of his country, will be desirous of obtaining the sense of the people on every occasion of magnitude; but how can this be so well expressed as in instructions to their representatives? I hope, therefore, that gentlemen will not oppose the insertion of it in this part of the report.

Mr. Clymer: I hope the amendment will not be adopted; but if our constituents choose to instruct us, that they may be left at liberty to do so. Do gentlemen foresee the extent of these words? If they have a constitutional right to instruct us, it infers that we are bound by those instructions; and as we ought not to decide constitutional questions by implication, I presume we shall be called upon to go further, and expressly declare the members of the Legislature bound by the instruction of their constituents. This is a most dangerous principle, utterly destructive of all ideas of an independent and deliberative body, which are essential requisites in the Legislatures of free Governments; they prevent men of abilities and experience from rendering those services to the community that are in their power, destroying the object contemplated by establishing an efficient General Government, and rendering Congress a mere passive machine.

Mr. Sherman: It appears to me, that the words are calculated to mislead the people, by conveying an idea that they have a right to control the debates of the Legislature. This cannot be admitted to be just, because it would destroy the object of their meeting. I think, when the people have chosen a representative, it is his duty to meet others from the different parts of the Union, and consult, and agree with them to such acts as are for the general benefit of the whole community. If they were to be guided by instructions, there would be no use in deliberation; all that a man would have to do, would be to produce his instructions, and lay them on the table, and let them speak for him. From hence I think it may be fairly inferred, that the right of the people to consult for the common good can go no further than to petition the Legislature, or apply for a redress of grievances. It is the duty of a good representative to inquire what measures are most likely to promote the general welfare, and, after he has discovered them, to give them his support. Should his instructions, therefore, coincide with his ideas on any measure, they would be unnecessary; if they were contrary to the conviction of his own mind, he must be bound by every principle of justice to disregard them.

Mr. Jackson was in favor of the right of the people to assemble and consult for the common good; it had been used in this country as one of the best checks on the British Legislature in their unjustifiable attempts to tax the colonies without their consent. America had no representatives in the British Parliament, therefore they could instruct none, yet they exercised the power of consultation to a good effect. He begged gentlemen to consider the dangerous tendency of establishing such a doctrine; it would necessarily drive the house into a number of factions. There might be different instructions from every State, and the representation from each State would be a faction to support its own measures.

If we establish this as a right, we shall be bound by those instructions; now, I am willing to leave both the people and representatives to their own discretion on this subject. Let the people consult and give their opinion; let the representative judge of it; and if it is just, let him govern himself by it as a good member ought to do; but if it is otherwise, let him have it in his power to reject their advice.

What may be the consequence of binding a man to vote in all cases according to the will of others? He is to decide upon a constitutional point, and on this question his conscience is bound by the obligation of a solemn oath; you now involve him in a serious dilemma. If he votes according to his conscience, he decides against his instructions; but in deciding against his instructions, he commits a breach of the constitution, by infringing the prerogative of the people, secured to them by this declaration. In short, it will give rise to such a variety of absurdities and inconsistencies, as no prudent Legislature would wish to involve themselves in.

Mr. Gerry: By the checks provided in the constitution, we have good grounds to believe that the very framers of it conceived that the Government would be liable to mal-administration, and I presume that the gentlemen of this House do not mean to arrogate to themselves more perfection than human nature has as yet been found to be capable of; if they do not, they will admit an additional check against abuses which this, like every other

Government, is subject to. Instruction from the people will furnish this in a considerable degree.

It has been said that the amendment proposed by the honorable gentleman from South Carolina (Mr. Tucker) determines this point, "that the people can bind their representatives to follow their instructions." I do not conceive that this necessarily follows. I think the representative, notwithstanding the insertion of these words, would be at liberty to act as he pleased; if he declined to pursue such measures as he was directed to attain, the people would have a right to refuse him their suffrages at a future election.

Now, though I do not believe the amendment would bind the representatives to obey the instructions, yet I think the people have a right both to instruct and bind them. Do gentlemen conceive that on any occasion instructions would be so general as to proceed from all our constituents? If they do, it is the sovereign will; for gentlemen will not contend that the sovereign will presides in the Legislature. The friends and patrons of this constitution have always declared that the sovereignty resides in the people, and that they do not part with it on any occasion; to say the sovereignty vests in the people, and that they have not a right to instruct and control their representatives, is absurd to the last degree. They must either give up their principle, or grant that the people have a right to exercise their sovereignty to control the whole Government, as well as this branch of it. But the amendment does not carry the principle to such an extent, it only declares the right of the people to send instructions; the representative will, if he thinks proper, communicate his instructions to the House, but how far they shall operate on his conduct, he will judge for himself.

The honorable gentleman from Georgia (Mr. Jackson) supposes that instructions will tend to generate factions in this House; but he did not see how it could have that effect, any more than the freedom of debate had. If the representative entertains the same opinion with his constituents, he will decide with them in favor of the measure; if other gentlemen, who are not instructed on this point, are convinced by argument that the measure is proper, they will also vote with them; consequently, the influence of debate and of instruction is the same.

The gentleman says further, that the people have the right of instructing their representatives; if so, why not declare it? Does he mean that it shall lie dormant and never be exercised? If so, it will be a right of no utility. But much good may result from a declaration in the constitution that they possess this privilege; the people will be encouraged to come forward with their instructions, which will form a fund of useful information for the Legislature. We cannot, I apprehend, be too well informed of the true state, condition, and sentiment of our constituents, and perhaps this is the best mode in our power of obtaining information. I hope we shall never shut our ears against that information which is to be derived from the petitions and instructions of our constituents. I hope we shall never presume to think that all the wisdom of this country is concentred within the walls of this House. Men, unambitious of distinctions from their fellow-citizens, remain within their own domestic walk, unheard of and unseen, possessing all the advantages resulting from a watchful observance of public men and public measures, whose voice, if we would descend to listen to it, would give us knowledge superior to what could be acquired amidst the cares and bustles of a public life; let us then adopt the amendment, and encourage the diffident to enrich our stock of knowledge with the treasure of their remarks and observations.

Mr. Madison: I think the committee acted prudently in omitting to insert these words in the report they have brought forward; if, unfortunately, the attempt of proposing amendments should prove abortive, it will not arise from the want of a disposition in the friends of the constitution to do what is right with respect to securing the rights and privileges of the people of America, but from the difficulties arising from discussing and proposing abstract propositions, of which the judgment may not be convinced. I venture to say, that if we confine ourselves to an enumeration of simple, acknowledged principles, the ratification will meet with but little difficulty. Amendments of a doubtful nature will have a tendency to prejudice the whole system; the proposition now suggested partakes highly of this nature. It is doubted by many gentlemen here; it has been objected to in intelligent publications throughout the Union; it is doubted by many members of the State Legislatures. In one sense this declaration is true, in many others it is certainly not true; in the sense in which it is true, we have asserted the right sufficiently in what we have done; if we mean nothing more than this, that the people have a right to express and communicate their sentiments and wishes, we have provided for it already. The right of freedom of speech is secured; the liberty of the press is expressly declared to be beyond the reach of this Government; the people may therefore publicly address their representatives, may privately advise them, or declare their sentiment by petition to the whole body; in all these ways they may communicate their will. If gentlemen mean to go further, and to say that the people have a right to instruct their representatives in such a sense as that the delegates are obliged to conform to those instructions, the declaration is not true. Suppose they instruct a representative, by his vote, to violate the constitution; is he at liberty to obey such instructions? Suppose he is instructed to patronize certain measures, and from circumstances known to him, but not to his constituents, he is convinced that they will endanger the public good; is he obliged to sacrifice his own judgment to them? Is he absolutely bound to perform what he is instructed to do. Suppose he refuses, will his vote be the less valid, or the community be disengaged from that obedience which is due to the laws of the Union? If his vote must inevitably have the same effect, what sort of a right is this in the constitution, to instruct a representative who has a right to disregard the order, if he pleases? In this sense the right does not exist, in the other sense it does exist, and is provided largely for.

The honorable gentleman from Massachusetts asks if the sovereignty is not with the people at large. Does he infer that the people can, in detached bodies, contravene an act established by the whole people? My idea of the sovereignty of the people is, that the people can change the constitution if they please; but while the constitution exists, they must conform themselves to its dictates. But I do not believe that the inhabitants of any district can speak the voice of the people; so far from it, their ideas may contradict the sense of the whole people; hence the consequence that instructions are binding on the representative is of a doubtful, if not of a dangerous nature. I do not conceive, therefore, that it is necessary to agree to the proposition now made; so far as any real good is to arise from it, so far that real good is provided for; so far as it is of a doubtful nature, so far it obliges us to run the risk of losing the whole system.

Mr. Smith, of South Carolina: I am opposed to this motion, because I conceive it will operate as a partial inconvenience to the more distant States. If every member is to be bound by instructions how to vote, what are gentlemen from the extremities of the continent to do? Members from the neighboring States can obtain their instructions earlier than those from the Southern ones, and I presume that particular instructions will be necessary for particular measures; of consequence, we vote perhaps against instructions on their way to us, or we must decline voting at all. But what is the necessity of having a numerous representation? One member from a State can receive the instructions, and by his vote answer all the purposes of many, provided his vote is allowed to count for the proportion the State ought to send; in this way the business might be done at a less expense than having one or two hundred members in the House, which had been strongly contended for yesterday.

Mr. Stone: I think the clause would change the Government entirely; instead of being a Government founded upon representation, it would be a democracy of singular properties.

I differ from the gentleman from Virginia, (Mr. Madison) if he thinks this clause would not bind the representative; in my opinion, it would bind him effectually, and I venture to assert, without diffidence, that any law passed by the Legislature would be of no force, if a majority of the members of this House were instructed to the contrary, provided the amendment became part of the constitution. What would follow from this? Instead of looking in the code of laws passed by Congress, your Judiciary would have to collect and examine the instructions from the various parts of the Union. It follows very clearly from hence, that the Government would be altered from a representative one to a democracy, wherein all laws are made immediately by the voice of the people.

This is a power not to be found in any part of the earth except among the Swiss cantons; there the body of the people vote upon the laws, and give instructions to their delegates. But here we have a different form of Government; the people at large are not authorized under it to vote upon the law, nor did I ever hear that any man required it. Why, then, are we called upon to propose amendments subversive of the principles of the constitution, which were never desired?

Several members now called for the question, and the Chairman being about to put the same:

Mr. Gerry: Gentlemen seem in a great hurry to get this business through. I think, Mr. Chairman, it requires a further discusion; for my part, I had rather do less business and do it well, than precipitate measures before they are fully understood.

The honorable gentleman from Virginia (Mr. Madison) stated, that if the proposed amendments are defeated, it will be by the delay attending the discussion of doubtful propositions; and he declares this to partake of that quality. It is natural, sir, for us to be fond of our own work. We do not like to see it disfigured by other hands. That honorable gentleman brought forward a string of propositions; among them was the clause now proposed to be amended: he is no doubt ready for the question, and determined not to admit what we think an improvement. The gentlemen who were on the committee, and brought in the report, have considered the subject, and are also ripe for a decision. But other gentlemen may crave a like indulgence. Is not the report before us for deliberation and discussion, and to obtain the sense of the House upon it; and will not gentlemen allow us a day or two for these purposes, after they have forced us to proceed upon them at this time? I appeal to their candor and good sense on the occasion, and am sure not to be refused; and I must inform them now, that they may not be surprised hereafter, that I wish all the amendments proposed by the respective States to be considered. Gentlemen say it is necessary to finish the subject, in order to reconcile a number of our fellow-citizens to the Government. If this is their principle, they ought to consider the wishes and intentions which the convention has expressed for them; if they do this, they will find that they expect and wish for the declaration proposed by the honorable gentleman over the way, (Mr. Tucker) and, of consequence, they ought to agree to it; and why it, with others recommended in the same way, were not reported, I cannot pretend to say; the committee know this best themselves.

The honorable gentleman near me (Mr. Stone) says, that the laws passed contrary to instruction will be nugatory. And other gentlemen ask, if their constituents instruct them to violate the constitution, whether they must do it. Sir, does not the constitution declare that all laws passed by Congress are paramount to the laws and constitutions of the several States; if our decrees are of such force as to set aside the State laws and constitutions, certainly they may be repugnant to any instructions whatever, without being injured thereby. But can we conceive that our constituents would be so absurd as to instruct us to violate our oath, and act directly contrary to the principles of a Government ordained by themselves? We must look upon them to be absolutely abandoned and false to their own interests, to suppose them capable of giving such instructions.

If this amendment is introduced into the constitution, I do not think we shall be much troubled with instructions; a knowledge of the right will operate to check a spirit that would render instruction necessary.

The honorable gentleman from Virginia asked, will not the affirmative of a member who votes repugnant to his instructions bind the community as much as the votes of those who conform? There is no doubt, sir, but it will; but does this tend to show that the constituent has no right to instruct? Surely not. I admit, sir, that instructions contrary to the constitution ought not to bind, though the sovereignty resides in the people. The honorable gentleman acknowledges that the sovereignty vests there; if so, it may exercise its will in any case not inconsistent with a previous contract. The same gentleman asks if we are to give the power to the people in detached bodies to contravene the Government while it exists. Certainly not; nor does the proposed proposition extend to that point; it is only intended to open for them a convenient mode in which they may convey their sense to their agents. The gentleman therefore takes for granted what is inadmissible, that Congress will always be doing illegal things, and make it necessary for the sovereign to declare its pleasure.

He says the people have a right to alter the constitution, but they have no right to oppose the Government. If, while the Government exists, they have no right to control it, it appears they have divested themselves of the sovereignty over the constitution. Therefore, our language, with our principles, must change, and we ought to say that the sovereignty existed in the people previous to the establishment of this Government. This will be ground for alarm indeed, if it is true; but I trust, sir, too much to the good sense of my fellow-citizens ever to believe that the doctrine will generally obtain in this country of freedom.

Mr. Vining: If, Mr. Chairman, there appears on one side too great an urgency to despatch this business, there appears on the other an unnecessary delay and procrastination equally improper and unpardonable. I think this business has been already well considered by the House, and every gentleman in it; however, I am not for an unseemly expedition.

The gentleman last up has insinuated a reflection upon the committee for not reporting all the amendments proposed by some of the State conventions. I can assign a reason for this. The committee conceived some of them superfluous or dangerous, and found many of them so contradictory that it was impossible to make any thing of them; and this is a circumstance the gentleman cannot pretend ignorance of.

Is it not inconsistent in that honorable member to complain of hurry, when he comes day after day reiterating the same train of arguments, and demanding the attention of this body by rising six or seven times on a question. I wish, sir, this subject discussed coolly and dispassionately, but hope we shall have no more reiterations or tedious discussions; let gentlemen try to expedite public business, and their arguments will be conducted in a laconic and consistent manner. As to the business of instruction, I look upon it inconsistent with the general good. Suppose our constituents were to instruct us to make paper money: no gentleman pretends to say it would be unconstitutional, yet every honest mind must shudder at the thought. How can we then assert that instructions ought to bind us in all cases not contrary to the constitution?

Mr. Livermore was not very anxious whether the words were inserted or not, but he had a great deal of doubt on the meaning of this whole amendment; it provides that the people may meet and consult for the common good. Does this mean a part of the people in a township or district, or does it mean the representatives in the State Legislatures? If it means the latter there is no occasion for a provision that the Legislature may instruct the members of this body.

In some States the representatives are chosen by districts. In such case, perhaps, the instructions may be considered as coming from the district; but in other States, each representative is chosen by the whole people. In New Hampshire it is the case; the instructions of any particular place would have but little weight, but a legislative instruction would have considerable influence upon each representative. If therefore, the words mean that the Legislature may instruct, he presumed it would have considerable effect, though he did not believe it binding. Indeed, he was inclined to pay a deference to any information he might receive from any number of gentlemen, even by a private letter; but as for full binding force, no instructions contained that quality. They could not, nor ought not to have it, because different parties pursue different measures; and it might be expedient, nay, absolutely necessary, to sacrifice them in mutual concessions.

The doctrine of instructions would hold better in England than here, because the boroughs and corporations might have an interest to pursue totally immaterial to the rest of the kingdom; in that case, it would be prudent to instruct their members in Parliament.

Mr. Gerry wished the constitution amended without his having any hand in it; but if he must interfere, he would do his duty. The honorable gentleman from Delaware had given him an example of moderation and laconic and consistent debate that he meant to follow; and would just observe to the worthy gentleman last up, that several States had proposed the amendment, and among the rest New Hampshire

There was one remark which escaped him, when he was up before. The gentleman from Maryland (Mr. Stone) had said that the amendment would change the nature of the Government, and make it a democracy. Now he had always heard that it was a democracy; but perhaps he was misled, and the honorable gentleman was right in distinguishing it by some other appellation; perhaps an aristocracy was a term better adapted to it.

Mr. Sedgwick opposed the idea of the gentleman from New Hampshire, that the State Legislature had the power of instructing the members of this House; he looked upon it as a subornation of the rights of the people to admit such an authority. We stand not here, said he, the representatives of the State Legislatures, as under the former Congress, but as the representatives of the great body of the people. The sovereignty, the independence, and the rights of the States are intended to be guarded by the Senate; if we are to be viewed in any other light, the greatest security the people have for their rights and privileges is destroyed.

But with respect to instructions, it is well worthy of consideration how they are to be procured. It is not the opinion of an individual that is to control my conduct; I consider myself as the representative of the whole Union. An individual may give me information, but his sentiments may be in opposition to the sense of the majority of the people. If instructions are to be of any efficacy, they must speak the sense of the majority of the people, at least of a State. In a State so large as Massachusetts it will behoove gentlemen to consider how the sense of the majority of the freemen is to be obtained and communicated. Let us take care to avoid the insertion of crude and indigested propositions, more likely to produce acrimony than that spirit of harmony which we ought to cultivate.

Mr. Livermore said that he did not understand the honorable gentleman, or was not understood by him; he did not presume peremptorily to say what degree of influence the legislative instructions would have on a representative. He knew it was not the thing in contemplation here; and what he had said respected only the influence it would have on his private judgment.

Mr. Ames said there would be a very great inconvenience attending the establishment of the doctrine contended for by his colleague. Those States which had selected their members by districts would have no right to give them instructions, consequently the members ought to withdraw; in which case the House might be reduced below a majority, and not be able, according to the constitution, to do any business at all.

According to the doctrine of the gentleman from New Hampshire, one part of the Government would be annihilated; for of what avail is it that the people have the appointment of a representative, if he is to pay obedience to the dictates of another body?

Several members now rose, and called for the question.

Mr. Page was sorry to see gentlemen so impatient; the more so, as he saw there was very little attention paid to any thing that was said; but he would express his sentiments if he was only heard by the Chair. He discovered clearly, notwithstanding what had been observed by the most ingenious supporters of the opposition, that there was an absolute necessity for adopting the amendment. It was strictly compatible with the spirit and the nature of the Government; all power vests in the people of the United States; it is, therefore, a Government of the people, a democracy. If it were consistent with the peace and tranquillity of the inhabitants, every freeman would have a right to come and give his vote upon the law; but, inasmuch as this cannot be done, by reason of the extent of territory, and some other causes, the people have agreed that their representatives shall exercise a part of their authority. To pretend to refuse them the power of instructing their agents, appears to me to deny them a right. One gentleman asks how the instructions are to be collected. Many parts of this country have been in the practice of instructing their representatives; they found no difficulty in communicating their sense. Another gentleman asks if they were to instruct us to make paper money, what we would do. I would tell them, said he, it was unconstitutional; alter that, and we will consider on the point. Unless laws are made satisfactory to the people, they will lose their support, they will be abused or done away; this tends to destroy the efficiency of the Government.

It is the sense of several of the conventions that this amendment should take place; I think it my duty to support it, and fear it will spread an alarm among our constituents if we decline to do it.

Mr. Wadsworth: Instructions have frequently been given to the representatives of the United States; but the people did not claim as a right that they should have any obligation upon the representatives; it is not right that they should. In troublesome times, designing men have drawn the people to instruct the representatives to their harm; the representatives have, on such occasions, refused to comply with their instructions. I have known, myself, that they have been disobeyed, and yet the representative was not brought to account for it; on the contrary, he was caressed and reelected, while those who have obeyed them, contrary to their private sentiments, have ever after been despised for it. Now, if people considered it an inherent right in them to instruct their representatives, they would have undoubtedly punished the violation of them. I have no idea of instructions, unless they are obeyed; a discretional power is incompatible with them.

The honorable gentleman who was up last says, if he were instructed to make paper money, he would tell his constituents it was unconstitutional. I believe that is not the case, for this body would have a right to make paper money; but if my constituents were to instruct me to vote for such a measure, I would disobey them, let the consequence be what it would.

Mr Sumter: The honorable gentlemen who are opposed to the motion of my colleague, do not treat it fairly. They suppose that it is meant to bind the representative to conform to his instructions. The mover of this question, I presume to say, has no such thing in idea. That they shall notice them and obey them, as far as is consistent and proper, may be very just; perhaps they ought to produce them to the House, and let them have as much influence as they deserve; nothing further, I believe, is contended for.

I rose on this occasion, not so much to make any observations upon the point immediately under consideration, as to beg the committee to consider the consequences that may result from an undue precipitancy and hurry. Nothing can distress me more than to be obliged to notice what I conceive to be somewhat improper in the conduct of so respectable a body. Gentlemen will reflect how difficult it is to remove error when once the passions are engaged in the discussion; temper and coolness are necessary to complete what must be the work of time. It cannot be denied but that the present constitution is imperfect; we must, therefore, take time to improve it. If gentlemen are pressed for want of time, and are disposed to adjourn the session of Congress at a very early period, we had better drop the subject of amendments, and leave it until we have more leisure to consider and do the business effectually. For my part, I would rather sit till this day twelvemonth, than have this all-important subject inconsiderately passed over. The people have already complained that the adoption of the constitution was done in too hasty a manner; what will they say of us if we press the amendments with so much haste?

Mr. Burke: It has been asserted, Mr. Chairman, that the people of America do not require this right. I beg leave to ask the gentleman from Massachusetts, whether the constitution of that State does not recognise that right, and the gentleman from Maryland, whether their declaration of rights does not expressly secure it to the inhabitants of that State? These circumstances, added to what has been proposed by the State conventions as amendments to this constitution, pretty plainly declare the sense of the people to be in favor of securing to themselves and to their posterity a right of this nature.

Mr. Seney said that the declaration of rights prefixed to the constitution of Maryland secured to every man a right of petitioning the Legislature for a redress of grievances, in a peaceable and orderly manner.

Mr. Burke: I am not positive with respect to the particular expression in the declaration of rights of the people of Maryland, but the constitutions of Massachusetts, Pennsylvania, and North Carolina, all of them recognise, in express terms, the right of the people to give instruction to their representatives. I do not mean to insist particularly upon this amendment; but I am very well satisfied that those that are reported and likely to be adopted by this House are very far from giving satisfaction to our constituents; they are not those solid and substantial amendments which the people expect; they are little better than whip syllabub, frothy and full of wind, formed only to please the palate; or they are like a tub thrown out to a whale, to secure the freight of the ship and its peaceable voyage. In my judgment, the people will not be gratified by the mode we have pursued in bringing them forward. There was a committee of eleven appointed; and out of the number I think there were five who were members of the convention that formed the constitution. Such gentlemen, having already given their opinion with respect to the perfection of the work, may be thought improper agents to bring forward amendments. Upon the whole, I think it will be found that we have done nothing but lose our time, and that it will be better to drop the subject now, and proceed to the organization of the Government.

Mr. Sinnickson inquired of Mr. Chairman what was the question before the committee, for really the debate had become so desultory, as to induce him to think it was lost sight of altogether.

Mr. Lawrence was averse to entering on the business at first; but since they had proceeded so far he hoped they would finish it. He said, if gentlemen would confine themselves to the question when they were speaking, that the business might be done in a more agreeable manner. He was against the amendment proposed by the gentleman from South Carolina, (Mr. Tucker,) because every member on this floor ought to consider himself the representative of the whole Union, and not of the particular district which had chosen him; as their decisions were to bind every individual of the confederated States, it was wrong to be guided by the voice of a single district, whose interests might happen to clash with those of the general good; and unless instructions were to be considered as binding, they were altogether superfluous.

Mr. Madison was unwilling to take up any more of the time of the committee; but, on the other hand, he was not willing to be silent after the charges that had been brought against the committee, and the gentleman who introduced the amendments, by the honorable members on each side of him, (Messrs. Sumter and Burke.) Those gentlemen say that we are precipitating the business, and insinuate that we are not acting with candor. I appeal to the gentlemen who have heard the voice of their country, to those who have attended the debates of the State conventions, whether the amendments now proposed are not those most strenuously required by the opponents to the constitution? It was wished that some security should be given for those great and essential rights which they had been taught to believe were in danger. I concurred, in the convention of Virginia, with those gentlemen, so far as to agree to a declaration of those rights which corresponded with my own judgment, and the other alterations which I had the honor to bring forward before the present Congress. I appeal to the gentlemen on this floor who are desirous of amending the constitution, whether these proposed are not compatible with what are required by our constituents? Have not the people been told that the rights of conscience, the freedom of speech, the liberty of the press, and trial by jury, were in jeopardy? that they ought not to adopt the constitution until those important rights were secured to them?

But while I approve of these amendments, I should oppose the consideration at this time of such as are likely to change the principles of the Government, or that are of a doubtful nature; because I apprehend there is little prospect of obtaining the consent of two-thirds of both Houses of Congress, and three-fourths of the State Legislatures, to ratify proposition of this kind; therefore, as a friend to what is attainable, I would limit it to the plain, simple, and important security that has been required. If I were inclined to make no alteration in the constitution, I would bring forward such amendments as were of a dubious cast, in order to have the whole rejected.

Mr. Burke never entertained an idea of charging gentlemen with the want of candor; but he would appeal to any man of sense and candor, whether the amendments contained in the report were any thing like the amendments required by the States of New York, Virginia, New Hampshire, and Carolina; and having these amendments in his hand, he turned to them to show the difference, concluding that all the important amendments were omitted in the report.

Mr. Smith, of South Carolina, understood his colleague, who had just sat down, to have asserted that the amendment under consideration was contained in the constitution of the State of South Carolina: this was not the fact.

Mr. Burke said he mentioned the State of North Carolina, and there it was inserted in express terms.

The question was now called for from several parts of the House; but a desultory conversation took place before the question was put. At length the call becoming general, it was stated from the chair, and determined in the negative, 10 rising in favor of it, and 41 against it.

The question was now taken on the second clause of the fourth proposition, as originally reported and agreed to.

Mr. Ames moved the committee to rise and report progress; which being agreed to,

Mr. Speaker having resumed the chair,

Mr. Ames moved to discharge the committee from any further proceeding. He was led to make the motion from two considerations: first, that as the committee were not restrained in their discussions, a great deal of time was consumed in unnecessary debate; and, second, that as the constitution required two-thirds of the House to acquiesce in amendments, the decisions of the committee, by a simple majority, might be set aside for the want of the constitutional number to support them in the House. He further observed, that it might have an evil influence if alterations agreed to in committee were not adopted by the House.

Mr. Smith, of South Carolina, was in favor of the motion.

Mr. Gerry thought that the object of the motion was to prevent such a thorough discussion of the business as the nature of it demanded. He called upon gentlemen to recollect the consistency of his honorable colleague, who had proposed to refer the subject to a select committee, lest an open and full examination should lay bare the muscles and sinews of the constitution. He had succeeded on that occasion, and the business was out into the hands of a select committee. He now proposes to curtail the debate, because gentlemen will not swallow the propositions as they stand, when their judgment and their duty require to have them improved. Will this House, said he, agree that an important subject like this shall have less consideration than the most trifling business yet come before us? I hope they will not. If they are tired of it, let it be postponed until another session, when it can be attended to with leisure and good temper. Gentlemen now feel the weather warm, and the subject is warm; no wonder it produces some degree of heat. Perhaps, as our next will be a winter session, we may go through more coolly and dispassionately.

Mr. Sedgwick seconded Mr. Ames's motion, thinking there was little probability of getting through with the business, if gentlemen were disposed to offer motions, and dwell long upon them in committee, when there was no likelihood they would meet the approbation of two-thirds of both Houses, and three-fourths of the State Legislatures.

Mr. Gerry moved to call the yeas and nays on the motion.

Mr. Page begged gentlemen to consider that the motion tended to deprive the members of that freedom of debate which they had heretofore been indulged in, and prevented the Speaker from giving his sentiments. He was sorry to see this hurry, and hoped the subject would be fairly treated, otherwise the people might think they were unjustly dealt by. They would have a right to suppose, with the honorable gentleman from Carolina, (Mr. Burke,) that we meant nothing more than to throw out a tub to the whale.

Mr. Burke would oppose the motion, and join in calling the yeas and nays, because its object must be to preclude debate. He was certain the subject was so variegated, and at the same time so important, that it could not be thoroughly discussed in any other manner than in a Committee of the whole; and unless it was discussed in a satisfactory manner, he apprehended it would occasion a great deal of mischief. He said the people knew, and were sensible, that in ratifying the present constitution, they parted with their liberties; but it was under a hope that they would get them back again. Whether this was to be the case or not, he left it to time to discover, but the spirit which now seemed to prevail in the House was no favorable omen. He begged gentlemen to treat the subject with fairness and candor, and not depart from their usual mode of doing business.

Mr. Smith, of South Carolina, had said he would support the motion, under an impression that it was useless to carry a measure through the committee, with a small majority, which was unlikely to meet the approbation of two-thirds of the House; but as gentlemen appeared so desirous of pursuing the common routine of doing business, he would withdraw his support.

Mr. Tucker was in hopes the honorable mover would have seen the impropriety of his motion, and have withdrawn it; but as he had not, he would presume to ask him upon what principle it was founded? Is it to precipitate the business, and prevent an investigation? or is it because the committee have spent some time on it, and made no progress? He thought the latter was not the case, because the committee had proceeded as far in it as could reasonably be expected for the time. The gentleman says he is apprehensive it may do harm to have propositions agreed to in committee, and rejected by the House. Certainly there is no foundation for this apprehension, or the clause in the constitution requiring the consent of two thirds of the Legislature to amendments is formed on wrong principles. If the propositions are reasonable in themselves, they ought to be admitted; but if they are improper, they ought to be rejected. We would not presume to prevent our constituents from contemplating the subject in their own mind.

Is this haste produced by a desire to adjourn? He was as desirous of adjourning as any member, but he would not sacrifice the duty he owed the public to his own private convenience.

Mr. Livermore hoped the gentleman would withdraw his motion, because it would have a disagreeable aspect to leave the business in the unfinished state it now stood. He thought it had better been altogether let alone.

Mr. Ames withdrew his motion, and laid another on the table, requiring two-thirds of the committee to carry a question; and, after some desultory conversation,

The House adjourned.

[Monday, August 17]

Amendments to the Constitution
The House again resolved itself into a committee, Mr. Boudinot in the chair, on the proposed amendments to the constitution. The third clause of the fourth proposition in the report was taken into consideration, being as follows: "A well regulated militia, composed of the body of the people, being the best security of a free state, the right of the people to keep and bear arms shall not be infringed; but no person religiously scrupulous shall be compelled to bear arms."

Mr. Gerry: This declaration of rights, I take it, is intended to secure the people against the mal-administration of the Government; if we could suppose that, in all cases, the rights of the people would be attended to, the occasion for guards of this kind would be removed. Now, I am apprehensive, sir, that this clause would give an opportunity to the people in power to destroy the constitution itself. They can declare who are those religiously scrupulous, and prevent them from bearing arms.

What, sir, is the use of a militia? It is to prevent the establishment of a standing army, the bane of liberty. Now, it must be evident, that, under this provision, together with their other powers, Congress could take such measures, with respect to a militia, as to make a standing army necessary. Whenever Governments mean to invade the rights and liberties of the people, they always attempt to destroy the militia, in order to raise an army upon their ruins. This was actually done by Great Britain at the commencement of the late revolution. They used every means in their power to prevent the establishment of an effective militia to the eastward. The Assembly of Massachusetts, seeing the rapid progress that administration were making to divest them of their inherent privileges, endeavored to counteract them by the organization of the militia; but they were always defeated by the influence of the Crown.

Mr. Seney wished to know what question there was before the committee, in order to ascertain the point upon which the gentleman was speaking.

Mr. Gerry replied that he meant to make a motion, as he disapproved of the words as they stood. He then proceeded. No attempts that they made were successful, until they engaged in the struggle which emancipated them at once from their thraldom. Now, if we give a discretionary power to exclude those from militia duty who have religious scruples, we may as well make no provision on this head. For this reason, he wished the words to be altered so as to be confined to persons belonging to a religious sect scrupulous of bearing arms.

Mr. Jackson did not expect that all the people of the United States would turn Quakers or Moravians; consequently, one part would have to defend the other in case of invasion. Now this, in his opinion, was unjust, unless the constitution secured an equivalent: for this reason he moved to amend the clause, by inserting at the end of it, "upon paying an equivalent, to be established by law."

Mr. Smith, of South Carolina, inquired what were the words used by the conventions respecting this amendment. If the gentleman would conform to what was proposed by Virginia and Carolina, he would second him. He thought they were to be excused provided they found a substitute.

Mr. Jackson was willing to accommodate. He thought the expression was, "No one, religiously scrupulous of bearing arms, shall be compelled to render military service, in person, upon paying an equivalent."

Mr. Sherman conceived it difficult to modify the clause and make it better. It is well known that those who are religiously scrupulous of bearing arms, are equally scrupulous of getting substitutes or paying an equivalent. Many of them would rather die than do either one or the other; but he did not see an absolute necessity for a clause of this kind. We do not live under an arbitrary Government, said he, and the States, respectively, will have the government of the militia, unless when called into actual service; besides, it would not do to alter it so as to exclude the whole of any sect, because there are men amongst the Quakers who will turn out, notwithstanding the religious principles of the society, and defend the cause of their country. Certainly it will be improper to present the exercise of such favorable dispositions, at least whilst it is the practice of nations to determine their contests by the slaughter of their citizens and subjects.

Mr. Vining hoped the clause would be suffered to remain as it stood, because he saw no use in it if it was amended so as to compel a man to find a substitute, which, with respect to the Government, was the same as if the person himself turned out to fight.

Mr. Stone inquired what the words "religiously scrupulous" had reference to: was it of bearing arms? If it was, it ought so to be expressed.

Mr. Benson moved to have the words "but to person religiously scrupulous shall be compelled to bear arms," struck out. He would always leave it to the benevolence of the Legislature, for, modify it as you please, it will be impossible to express it in such a manner as to clear it from ambiguity. No man can claim this indulgence of right. It may be a religious persuasion, but it is no natural right, and therefore ought to be left to the discretion of the Government. If this stands part of the constitution, it will be a question before the Judiciary on every regulation you make with respect to the organization of the militia, whether it comports with this declaration or not. It is extremely injudicious to intermix matters of doubt with fundamentals.

I have no reason to believe but the Legislature will always possess humanity enough to indulge this class of citizens in a matter they are so desirous of; but they ought to be left to their discretion.

The motion for striking out the whole clause being seconded, was put, and decided in the negative—22 members voting for it, and 24 against it.

Mr. Gerry objected to the first part of the clause, on account of the uncertainty with which it is expressed. A well regulated militia being the best security of a free State, admitted an idea that a standing army was a secondary one. It ought to read, "a well regulated militia, trained to arms;" in which case it would become the duty of the Government to provide this security, and furnish a greater certainty of its being done.

Mr. Gerry's motion not being seconded, the question was put on the clause as reported; which being adopted,

Mr. Burke proposed to add to the clause just agreed to, an amendment to the following effect: "A standing army of regular troops in time of peace is dangerous to public liberty, and such shall not be raised or kept up in time of peace but from necessity, and for the security of the people, nor then without the consent of two-thirds of the members present of both Houses; and in all cases the military shall be subordinate to the civil authority." This being seconded.

Mr. Vining asked whether this was to be considered as an addition to the last clause, or an amendment by itself. If the former, he would remind the gentleman the clause was decided; if the latter, it was improper to introduce new matter, as the House had referred the report specially to the Committee of the whole.

Mr. Burke feared that, what with being trammelled in rules, and the apparent disposition of the committee, he should not be able to get them to consider any amendment; he submitted to such proceeding because he could not help himself.

Mr. Hartley thought the amendment in order, and was ready to give his opinion on it. He hoped the people of America would always be satisfied with having a majority to govern. He never wished to see two-thirds or three-fourths required, because it might put it in the power of a small minority to govern the whole Union.

The question on Mr. Burke's motion was put, and lost by a majority of thirteen.

The fourth clause of the fourth proposition was taken up as follows: "No soldier shall, in time of peace, be quartered in any house, without the consent of the owner, nor in time of war, but in a manner to be prescribed by law."

Mr. Sumter hoped soldiers would never be quartered on the inhabitants, either in time of peace or war, without the consent of the owner. It was a burthen, and very oppressive, even in cases where the owner gave his consent; but where this was wanting, it would be a hardship indeed! Their property would lie at the mercy of men irritated by a refusal, and well disposed to destroy the peace of the family.

He moved to strike out all the words from the clause but "no soldier shall be quartered in any house without the consent of the owner."

Mr. Sherman observed that it was absolutely necessary that marching troops should have quarters, whether in time of peace or war, and that it ought not to be put in the power of an individual to obstruct the public service; if quarters were not to be obtained in public barracks, they must be procured elsewhere. In England, where they paid considerable attention to private rights, they billeted the troops upon the keepers of public houses, and upon private houses also, with the consent of the magistracy.

Mr. Sumter's motion being put, was lost by a majority of sixteen.

Mr. Gerry moved to insert between "but" and, "in a manner" the words "by a civil magistrate," observing that there was no part of the Union but where they could have access to such authority.

Mr. Hartley said those things ought to be entrusted to the Legislature; that cases might arise where the public safety would be endangered by putting it in the power of one person to keep a division of troops standing in the inclemency of the weather for many hours; therefore he was against inserting the words.

Mr. Gerry said either his amendment was essential, or the whole clause was unnecessary.

On putting the question, thirteen rose in favor of the motion, thirty-five against it; and then the clause was carried as reported.

The fifth clause of the fourth proposition was taken up, viz: "No person shall be subject, in case of impeachment, to more than one trial or one punishment for the same offence, nor shall be compelled to be a witness against himself, nor be deprived of life, liberty, or property, without due process of law; nor shall private property be taken for public use without just compensation."

Mr. Benson thought the committee could not agree to the amendment in the manner it stood, because its meaning appeared rather doubtful. It says that no person shall be tried more than once for the same offence. This is contrary to the right heretofore established; he presumed it was intended to express what was secured by our former constitution, that no man's life should be more than once put in jeopardy for the same offence; yet it was well known, that they were entitled to more than one trial. The humane intention of the clause was to prevent more than one punishment; for which reason he would move to amend it by striking out the words "one trial or."

Mr. Sherman approved of the motion. He said, that as the clause now stood, a person found guilty could not arrest the judgment, and obtain a second trial in his own favor. He thought that the courts of justice would never think of trying and punishing twice for the same offence. If the person was acquitted on the first trial, he ought not to be tried a second time; but if he was convicted on the first, and any thing should appear to set the judgment aside, he was entitled to a second, which was certainly favorable to him. Now the clause as it stands would deprive him of that advantage.

Mr. Livermore thought the clause very essential; it was declaratory of the law as it now stood; striking out the words, would seem as if they meant to change the law by implication, and expose a man to the danger of more than one trial. Many persons may be brought to trial for crimes they are guilty of, but for want of evidence may be acquitted; in such cases, it is the universal practice in Great Britain, and in this country, that persons shall not be brought to a second trial for the same offence; therefore the clause is proper as it stands.

Mr. Sedgwick thought, instead of securing the liberty of the subject, it would be abridging the privileges of those who were prosecuted.

The question on Mr. Benson's motion being put, was lost by a considerable majority.

Mr. Partridge moved to insert after "same offence," the words "by any law of the United States." This amendment was lost also.

Mr. Lawrence said this clause contained a general declaration, in some degree contrary to laws passed. He alluded to that part where a person shall not be compelled to give evidence against himself. He thought it ought to be confined to criminal cases, and moved an amendment for that purpose; which amendment being adopted, the clause as amended was unanimously agreed to by the committee, who then proceeded to the sixth clause of the fourth proposition, in these words, "Excessive bail shall not be required, nor excessive fines imposed, nor cruel and unusual punishments inflicted."

Mr. Smith, of South Carolina, objected to the words "nor cruel and unusual punishments;" the import of them being too indefinite.

Mr. Livermore: The clause seems to express a great deal of humanity, on which account I have no objection to it; but as it seems to have no meaning in it, I do not think it necessary. What is meant by the terms excessive bail? Who are to be the judges? What is understood by excessive fines? It lies with the court to determine. No cruel and unusual punishment is to be inflicted; it is sometimes necessary to hang a man, villains often deserve whipping, and perhaps having their ears cut off; but are we in future to be prevented from inflicting these punishments because they are cruel? If a more lenient mode of correcting vice and deterring others from the commission of it could be invented, it would be very prudent in the Legislature to adopt it; but until we have some security that this will be done, we ought not to be restrained from making necessary laws by any declaration of this kind.

The question was put on the clause, and it was agreed to by a considerable majority.

The committee went on to the consideration of the seventh clause of the fourth proposition, being as follows: "The right of the people to be secured in their persons, houses, papers, and effects, shall not be violated by warrants issuing without probable cause, supported by oath or affirmation, and not particularly describing the place to be searched, and the persons or things to be seized."

Mr. Gerry said he presumed there was a mistake in the wording of this clause; it ought to be "the right of the people to be secure in their persons, houses, papers, and effects, against unreasonable seizures and searches," and therefore moved that amendment.

This was adopted by the committee.

Mr. Benson objected to the words "by warrants issuing." This declaratory provision was good as far as it went, but he thought it was not sufficient; he therefore proposed to alter it so as to read "and no warrant shall issue."

The question was put on this motion, and lost by a considerable majority.

Mr. Livermore objected to the words "and not" between "affirmation" and "particularly." He moved to strike them out, in order to make it an affirmative proposition.

But the motion passed in the negative.

The clause as amended being now agreed to,

The eighth clause of the fourth proposition was taken up, which was, "The enumeration in this constitution of certain rights shall not be construed to deny or disparage others retained by the people,"

Mr. Gerry said, it ought to be "deny or impair," for the word "disparage" was not of plain import; he therefore moved to make that alteration, but not being seconded, the question was taken on the clause, and it passed in the affirmative,

The committee then proceeded to the fifth proposition:

Article 1, section 10. between the first and second paragraph, insert "no State shall infringe the equal rights of conscience, nor the freedom of speech or of the right of trial by jury in criminal cases."

Mr. Tucker: This is offered, I presume, as an amendment to the constitution of the United States, but it goes only to the alteration of the constitutions of particular States. It will be much better, I apprehend, to leave the State Governments to themselves, and not to interfere with them more than we already do; and that is thought by many to be rather too much. I therefore move, sir, to strike out these words.

Mr. Madison conceived this to be the most valuable amendment in the whole list. If there was any reason to restrain the Government of the United States from infringing upon these essential rights, it was equally necessary that they should be secured against the State Governments. He thought that if they provided against the one, it was as necessary to provide against the other, and was satisfied that it would be equally grateful to the people.

Mr. Livermore had no great objection to the sentiment, but he thought it not well expressed. He wished to make it an affirmative proposition; "the equal rights of conscience, the freedom of speech or of the press, and the right of trial by jury in criminal cases, shall not be infringed by any State."

This transposition being agreed to, and Mr. Tucker's motion being rejected, the clause was adopted.

The sixth proposition, article 3, section 2, add to the second paragraph, "But no appeal to such court shall be allowed, where the value in controversy shall not amount to one thousand dollars; nor shall any fact, triable by a jury according to the course of the common law, be otherwise re-examinable than according to the rules of the common law."

Mr. Benson moved to strike out the first part of the paragraph respecting the limitation of appeals, because the question in controversy might be an important one, though the action was not to the amount of a thousand dollars.

Mr. Madison: If the gentleman will propose any restriction to answer his purpose, and for avoiding the inconvenience he apprehends, I am willing to agree to it; but it will be improper to strike out the clause without a substitute.

There is little danger that any court in the United States will admit an appeal where the matter in dispute does not amount to a thousand dollars; but as the possibility of such an event has excited in the minds of many citizens the greatest apprehension that persons of opulence would carry a cause from the extremities of the Union to the Supreme Court, and thereby prevent the due administration of justice, it ought to be guarded against.

Mr. Livermore thought the clause was objectionable, because it comprehended nothing more than the value.

Mr. Sedgwick moved to insert three thousand dollars, instead of one thousand; but on the question, this motion was rejected, and the proposition accepted in its original form.

The committee then proceeded to consider the seventh proposition, in the words following:

Article 3, section 2. Strike out the whole of the third paragraph, and insert, "In all criminal prosecutions, the accused shall enjoy the right to a speedy and public trial, to be informed of the nature and cause of the accusation, to be confronted with the witnesses against him, to have compulsory process for obtaining witnesses in his favor, and to have the assistance of counsel for his defence."

Mr. Burke moved to amend this proposition in such a manner as to leave it in the power of the accused to put off the trial to the next session, provided he made it appear to the court that the evidence of the witnesses, for whom process was granted but not served, was material to his defence.

Mr. Hartley said, that in securing him the right of compulsory process, the Government did all it could; the remainder must lie in the discretion of the court.

Mr. Smith, of South Carolina, thought the regulation would come properly in, as part of the judicial system.

The question on Mr. Burke's motion was taken and lost; ayes 9, noes 41.

Mr. Livermore moved to alter the clause, so as to secure to the criminal the right of being tried in the State where the offence was committed.

Mr. Stone observed that full provision was made on the subject in the subsequent clause.

On the question, Mr. Livermore's motion was adopted.

Mr. Burke said, he was not so much discouraged by the fate of his former motions, but that he would venture upon another. He therefore proposed to add to the clause, that no criminal prosecution should be had by way of information.

Mr. Hartley only requested the gentleman to look to the clause, and he would see the impropriety of inserting it in this place.

A desultory conversation arose, respecting the foregoing motion, and after some time, Mr. Burke withdrew it for the present.

The committee then rose and reported progress, after which the House adjourned.

[Tuesday, August 18]

*   *   *

Amendments to the Constitution

Mr. Gerry moved, "That such of the amendments to the constitution proposed by the several States, as are not in substance comprised in the report of the select committee appointed to consider amendments, be referred to a Committee of the whole House; and that all amendments which shall be agreed to by the committee last mentioned be included in one report."

Mr. Tucker remarked, that many citizens expected that the amendments proposed by the conventions would be attended to by the House, and that several members conceived it to be their duty to bring them forward. If the

House should decline taking them into consideration it might tend to destroy that harmony which had hitherto existed, and which did great honor to their proceedings; it might affect all their future measures, and promote such feuds as might embarrass the Government exceedingly. The States who had proposed these amendments would feel some degree of chagrin at having misplaced their confidence in the General Government. Five important States have pretty plainly expressed their apprehensions of the danger to which the rights of their citizens are exposed. Finding these cannot be secured in the mode they had wished, they will naturally recur to the alternative, and endeavor to obtain a federal convention; the consequence of this may be disagreeable to the Union; party spirit may be revived, and animosities rekindled destructive of tranquillity. States that exert themselves to obtain a federal convention, and those that oppose the measure, may feel so strongly the spirit of discord, as to sever the Union asunder.

If in this conflict the advocates for a federal convention should prove successful, the consequences may be alarming; we may lose many of the valuable principles now established in the present constitution. If, on the other hand, a convention should not be obtained, the consequences resulting are equally to be dreaded; it would render the administration of this system of government weak, if not impracticable; for no Government can be administered with energy, however energetic its system, unless it obtains the confidence and support of the people. Which of the two evils is the greatest would be difficult to ascertain.

It is essential to our deliberations that the harmony of the House be preserved; by it alone we shall be enabled to perfect the organization of the Government—a Government but in embryo, or at best but in its infancy.

My idea relative to this constitution, whilst it was dependent upon the assent of the several States, was, that it required amendment, and that the proper time for amendment was previous to the ratification. My reasons were, that I conceived it difficult, if not impossible, to obtain essential amendments by the way pointed out in the constitution; nor have I been mistaken in this suspicion. It will be found, I fear, still more difficult than I apprehended; for perhaps these amendments, should they be agreed to by two-thirds of both Houses of Congress, will be submitted for ratification to the Legislatures of the several States, instead of State conventions, in which case the chance is still worse. The Legislatures of almost all the States consist of two independent, distinct bodies; the amendments must be adopted by three-fourths of such Legislatures; that is to say, they must meet the approbation of the majority of each of eighteen deliberative assemblies. But, notwithstanding all these objections to obtaining amendments after the ratification of the constitution, it will tend to give a great degree of satisfaction to those who are desirous of them, if this House shall take them up, and consider them with that degree of candor and attention they have hitherto displayed on the subjects that have come before them; consider the amendments separately, and, after fair deliberation, either approve or disapprove of them. By such conduct, we answer in some degree the expectations of those citizens in the several States who have shown so great a tenacity to the preservation of those rights and liberties they secured to themselves by an arduous, persevering, and successful conflict.

I have hopes that the States will be reconciled to this disappointment, in consequence of such procedure.

A great variety of arguments might be urged in favor of the motion; but I shall rest it here, and not trespass any further upon the patience of the House.

Mr. Madison was just going to move to refer these amendments, in order that they might be considered in the fullest manner; but it would be very inconvenient to have them made up into one report, or all of them discussed at the present time.

Mr. Vining had no objection to the bringing them forward in the fullest point of view; but his objection arose from the informality attending the introduction of the business.

The order of the House was to refer the report of the Committee of eleven to a Committee of the whole, and therefore it was improper to propose any thing additional.

A desultory conversation arose on this motion, when Mr. Vining moved the previous question, in which, being supported by five members, it was put, and the question was, Shall the main question, to agree to the motion, be now put? The yeas and nays being demanded by one-fifth of the members present, on this last motion, they were taken as follows:

Yeas—Messrs. Burke, Coles, Floyd, Gerry, Griffin, Grout, Hathorn, Livermore, Page, Parker, Van Rensselaer, Sherman, Stone, Sturgis, Sumter, and Tucker.—16.

Nays—Messrs. Ames, Baldwin, Benson, Boudinot, Brown, Cadwalader, Carroll, Clymer, Fitzsimons, Foster, Gilman, Goodhue, Hartley, Heister, Huntington, Lawrence, Lee, Madison, Moore, Muhlenburg, Partridge, Schureman, Scott, Sedgwick, Seney, Sylvester, Sinnickson, Smith, of Maryland, Smith, of South Carolina, Thatcher, Trumbull, Vining, Wadsworth, and Wynkoop.—34.

So the motion was lost.

A message from the Senate informed the House that the Senate had passed the bill providing for expenses which may attend negotiations or treaties with the Indian tribes, and the appointment of commissioners for managing the same, with an amendment, to which they desire the concurrence of the House.

The House again resolved itself into a Committee of the whole on the subject of amendments, and took into consideration the 2d clause of the 7th proposition, in the words following. "The trial of all crimes (except in cases of impeachment, and in cases arising in the land and naval forces, or in the militia when in actual service in the time of war, or public danger,) shall be by an impartial jury of freeholders of the vicinage, with the requisite of unanimity for conviction, the right of challenge, and other accustomed requisites; and no person shall be held to answer for a capital, or otherwise infamous crime, unless on a presentment, or indictment, by a grand jury; but if a crime be committed in a place in the possession of an enemy, or in which an insurrection may prevail, the indictment and trial may by law be authorized in some other place within the same State; and if it be committed in a place not within a State, the indictment and trial may be at such place or places as the law may have directed."

Mr. Burke moved to change the word "vicinage" into "district or county in which the offence has been committed." He said this was conformable to the practice of the State of South Carolina, and he believed to most of the States in the Union; it would have a tendency also to quiet the alarm entertained by the good citizens of many of the States for their personal security; they would no longer fear being dragged from one extremity of the State to the other for trial, at the distance of three or four hundred miles.

Mr. Lee thought the word "vicinage" was more applicable than that of "district, or county," it being a term well understood by every gentleman of legal knowledge.

The question on Mr. Burke's motion being put was negatived.

Mr. Burke then revived his motion for preventing prosecutions upon information, but on the question this was also lost.

The clause was now adopted without amendment.

The 3d clause of the 7th proposition, as follows, "In suits at common law, the right of trial by jury shall be preserved," was considered and adopted.

The 8th proposition in the words following, was considered, "Immediately after art. 6, the following to be inserted as art. 7: "

"The powers delegated by this constitution to the Government of the United States shall be exercised as therein appropriated, so that the Legislative shall not exercise the powers vested in the Executive or Judicial; nor the Executive the power vested in the Legislative or Judicial; nor the Judicial the powers vested in the Legislative or Executive."

Mr. Sherman conceived this amendment to be altogether unnecessary, inasmuch as the constitution assigned the business of each branch of the Government to a separate department.

Mr. Madison supposed the people would be gratified with the amendment, as it was admitted that the powers ought to be separate and distinct; it might also tend to an explanation of some doubts that might arise respecting the construction of the constitution.

Mr. Livermore, thinking the clause subversive of the constitution, was opposed to it, and hoped it might be disagreed to.

On the motion being put, the proposition was carried.

The 9th proposition, in the words following, was considered, "The powers not delegated by the constitution, nor prohibited by it to the States, are reserved to the States respectively."

Mr. Tucker proposed to amend the proposition, by prefixing to it "all powers being derived from the people." He thought this a better place to make this assertion than the introductory clause of the constitution, where a similar sentiment was proposed by the committee. He extended his motion also, to add the word "expressly," so as to read "the powers not expressly delegated by this constitution."

Mr. Madison objected to this amendment, because it was impossible to confine a Government to the exercise of express powers; there must necessarily be admitted powers by implication, unless the constitution descended to recount every minutia. He remembered the word "expressly" had been moved in the convention of Virginia, by the opponents to the ratification, and, after full and fair discussion, was given up by them, and the system allowed to retain its present form.

Mr. Sherman coincided with Mr. Madison in opinion, observing that corporate bodies are supposed to possess all powers incident to a corporate capacity, without being absolutely expressed.

Mr. Tucker did not view the word "expressly" in the same light with the gentleman who opposed him; he thought every power to be expressly given that could be clearly comprehended within any accurate definition of the general power.

Mr. Tucker's motion being negatived,

Mr. Carroll proposed to add to the end of the proposition, "or to the people;" this was agreed to.

The 10th proposition, "Art. 7 to be made Art. 8," agreed to.

The committee then rose, and reported the amendments as amended by the committee.

Mr. Tucker then moved that the following propositions of amendment to the constitution of the United States, be referred to a Committee of the whole House, to wit:

Art. 1. sect. 2. clause 2. at the end, add these words, "Nor shall any person be capable of serving as a Representative more than six years, in any term of eight years."

Clause 3. at the end, add these words, "From and after the commencement of the year 1795, the election of Senators for each State shall be annual, and no person shall be capable of serving as a Senator more than five years in any term of six years."

Sect. 4. clause 1. strike out the words, "But the Congress may at any time, by law, make or alter such regulations, except as to the places of choosing Senators."

Sect. 5. clause 1. amend the first part to read thus, "Each State shall be the judge (according to its own laws) of the election of its Senators and Representatives to sit in Congress, and shall furnish them with sufficient credentials; but each House shall judge of the qualification of its own members: a majority of each House shall constitute," &c.

Clause 2. strike out these words, "And with the concurrence of two-thirds expel a member," and insert the word "and" after the word "proceedings."

Sect. 6. clause 2. amend to read thus, "No person having been elected, and having taken his seat as a Senator or Representative, shall, during the time for which he was elected, be appointed to any civil office under the authority of the United States, and no person," &c.

Art. 1. sect. 8. clause 1. at the end, add these words, "No direct tax shall be laid, unless any State shall have neglected to furnish, in due time, its proportion of a previous requisition; in which case Congress may proceed to levy, by direct taxation, within any State so neglecting, its proportion of such requisition, together with interest, at the rate of six per cent. per annum from the time it ought to have been furnished, and the charges of levying the same."

Clause 9. strike out the words "tribunals inferior to the Supreme Court," and insert the words "courts of admiralty."

Clause 17. at the end, add these words, "Provided that the Congress shall not have authority to make any law to prevent the laws of the States respectively in which such district or places may be, from extending to such district or places in all civil and criminal matters, in which any person without the limits of such district or places shall be a party aggrieved."

Sect. 9. clause 7. Strike out the words "Without the consent of the Congress," and amend to read thus, "Shall accept of any present or emolument, or hold any office or title of any kind whatever from any king, prince, or foreign state; provided that this clause shall not be construed to affect the rights of those persons (during their own lives) who are now citizens of the United States, and hold foreign titles."

Sect. 10. clause 2. amend the first sentence to read thus, "No State shall lay any duties on imports or exports, or any duty of tonnage, except such as shall be uniform in their operation on all foreign nations, and consistent with existing treaties, and also uniform in their operation on the citizens of all the several States in the Union."

Art. 2. sect. 1, clause 5. at the end, add these words, "Nor shall any person be capable of holding the office of President of the United States more than eight years in any term of twelve years."

Sect. 2. clause 1. Strike out the words "be commander in chief," and insert, "have power to direct (agreeable to law) the operations."

Clause 3. at the end, add these words, "He shall also have power to suspend from his office, for a time not exceeding twelve months, any officer whom he shall have reason to think unfit to be entrusted with the duties thereof; and Congress may, by law, provide for the absolute removal of officers found to be unfit for the trust reposed in them."

Art. 3. sect. 1. from each sentence strike out the words "inferior courts" and insert the words "courts of admiralty."

Sect. 2. clause 1. strike out the words "Between a State and citizens of another State," &c. to the end, and amend to read thus, "between a State and foreign States, and between citizens of the United States claiming the same lands under grants of different States."

Article 6. clause 3. Between the word "no" and the word "religious," insert the word "other."

On the question, Shall the said propositions of amendments be referred to the consideration of a Committee of the whole House ? it was determined in the negative.

*   *   *

PASSAGE BY THE HOUSE, AUGUST, 1789

Commentary

On August 19, the House began its consideration of the proposed amendments to the Constitution, as reported by the Committee of the Whole. The debate started with a renewal by Sherman of his motion to add the amendments by way of supplement at the end of the Constitution. This time the Sherman motion was carried by two-thirds of the House and that is why we have the federal Bill of Rights in its present form, as a series of separate amendments following the original Constitution. This change was of the greatest consequence, for it may be doubted that the Bill of Rights itself could have attained its position as the vital center of our constitutional law, if its provisions were diluted throughout the Constitution. Paradoxically, it is to Sherman (himself a consistent opponent of a Bill of Rights) that we owe the fact that we have a separate Bill of Rights.

On August 20, the House adopted (on motion of Fisher Ames of Massachusetts) the following substitute on freedom of religion: "Congress shall make no law establishing religion, or to prevent the free exercise thereof, or to infringe the rights of conscience." Irving Brant states that this was written by Madison and, if so, it meant that Madison was able to get his view of religious freedom written into the Constitution. The Ames amendment is very close to the actual language of the First Amendment's two-fold prohibition—containing both a provision for free exercise (similar to that which Madison had inserted into the Virginia Declaration of Rights [*supra* p. 232]) and the ban against establishment which he emphasized in his August 15 speech (*supra* p. 1088). The August 20 session ended with the House approving the first seven propositions reported.

On August 21, Gerry renewed the motion to add "expressly" to the provision on reserved powers, emphasizing that this was "an amendment of great importance." Again the motion lost. Sherman successfully moved to change the provision's language to that ultimately included in the Tenth Amendment. There was lengthy debate on a Burke motion to add a provision prohibiting Congress from interfering with elections. The Burke amendment was defeated, as were amendments dealing with taxation, courts, merchants' companies, and foreign titles of nobility. Fortunately, the House followed Madison's plea not "to delay the amendments now agreed upon, by entering into the consideration" of new and lesser amendments. On August 22, the remaining amendments reported were approved and the amendments then referred to a three-man committee (including Sherman) "to prepare and report a proper arrangement of . . . the articles of amendment, as they had been agreed to." The task of this committee was essentially to arrange the House amendments as separate amendments to be added at the end of the Constitution, in accordance with the Sherman motion adopted on August 19. The committee reported on August 24. The seventeen proposed amendments reported by it are contained in the extract from the House *Journal* (*infra* below). The amendments in the form thus reported were agreed to by the House the same day, and it was ordered that the Clerk of the House carry to the Senate a copy of the House amendments and desire their concurrence.

House of Representatives Journal, August, 1789*

On the 19th and 20th of August, the house was occupied in the consideration of the amendments made by the committee of the whole house to the report of the committee of eleven; and, on the 20th, the said amendments being partly agreed to, and partly disagreed to, the house proceeded to consider the original report of the committee of eleven, consisting of seventeen articles, as now amended; and the sixteen first articles were agreed to, two-thirds of the members concurring. The articles agreed to are as follows:

1. After the first enumeration, there shall be one representative for every thirty thousand, until the number shall amount to one hundred; after which the proportion shall be so regulated by Congress, that there shall be not less than one hundred representatives, nor less than one representative for every forty thousand persons, until the number of representatives shall amount to two hundred; after which the proportion shall be so regulated, that there shall not be less than two hundred representatives, nor less than one representative for every fifty thousand persons.

2. No law varying the compensation of members of Congress shall take effect until an election of representatives shall have intervened.

3. Congress shall make no law establishing religion, or prohibiting the free exercise thereof; nor shall the rights of conscience be infringed.

4. The freedom of speech, and of the press, and the right of the people peaceably to assemble, and consult for their common good, and to apply to the government for redress of grievances, shall not be infringed.

5. A well regulated militia, composed of the body of the people, being the best security of a free state, the right of the people to keep and bear arms shall not be infringed; but no one religiously scrupulous of bearing arms shall be compelled to render military service in person.

6. No soldier shall, in time of peace, be quartered in any house without the consent of the owner; nor in time of war, but in a manner to be prescribed by law.

*History of Congress Exhibiting a Classification of the Proceedings of the Senate and the House of Representatives from March 4, 1789 to March 3, 1793, pp. 155–59.

7. No person shall be subject, except in case of impeachment, to more than one trial, or one punishment for the same offence; nor shall be compelled, in any criminal case, to be witness against himself; nor be deprived of life, liberty, or property, without due process of law; nor shall private property be taken for public use, without just compensation.

8. Escessive bail shall not be required; nor excessive fines imposed; nor cruel and unusual punishments inflicted.

9. The right of the people to be secure in their persons, houses, papers, and effects, against unreasonable searches and seizures, shall not be violated; qnd no warrants shall issue, but upon probable cause, supported by oath or affirmation, and particularly describing the place to be searched, and the persons or things to be seized.

10. The enumeration in this Constitution of certain rights, shall not be construed to deny or disparage others retained by the people.

11. No state shall infringe the right of trial by jury in criminal cases; nor the rights of conscience; nor the freedom of speech, or of the press.

12. No appeal to the Supreme Court of the United States shall be allowed where the value in controversy shall not amount to one thousand dollars; nor shall any fact, triable by a jury, according to the course of the common law, be otherwise re-examinable than according to the rules of common law.

13. In all criminal prosecutions, the accused shall enjoy the right to a speedy and public trial; to be informed of the nature and cause of the accusation; to be confronted with the witnesses against him; to have compulsory process for obtaining witnesses in his favour; and to have the assistance of counsel for his defence.

14. The trial of all crimes (except in cases of impeachment, and in cases arising in the land or naval forces, or in the militia when in actual service in time of war or public danger,) shall be by an impartial jury of the vicinage, with the requisite of unanimity for conviction, the right of challenge, and other accustomed requisites; and no person shall be held to answer for a capital, or otherwise infamous crime, unless on a presentment or indictment by a grand jury; but if a crime be committed in a place in the possession of an enemy, or in which an insurrection may prevail, the indictment and trial may by law be authorized in some other place within the same state.

15. In suits at common law, the right of trial by jury shall be preserved.

16. The powers delegated by the Constitution to the government of the United States, shall be exercised as therein appropriated; so that the legislature shall never exercise the powers vested in the executive or judicial; nor the executive the powers vested in the legislative or judicial; nor the judicial the powers vested in the legislative or executive.

The 17th article of amendment, reported by the committee, is as follows: —

The powers not delegated by the Constitution, nor prohibited by it to the states, are reserved to the states respectively.

A motion was made to amend this article, by inserting, after the third word, ("not,") the word "expressly." And the ayes and noes being required on this question, it was decided as follows:

Ayes—Messrs. Burke, Coles, Floyd, Gerry, Grout, Hathorn, Jackson, Livermore, Page, Parker, Partridge, Van Rensselaer, Smith, of South Carolina, Stone, Sumpter, Thatcher, Tucker.—17.

Noes—Messrs. Ames, Benson, Boudinot, Brown, Cadwalader, Carroll, Clymer, Fitzsimons, Foster, Gale, Gilman, Goodhue, Hartley, Heister, Lawrance, Lee, Madison, jr., Moore, Muhlenberg, Schureman, Scott, Sedgwick, Seney, Sherman, Sylvester, Sinnickson, Smith, of Maryland, Sturges, Trumbull, Vining, Wadsworth, Wynkoop.—32.

The article was then agreed to in the original form, two-thirds of the members concurring.

It was then moved to add to the others, the following article:

Congress shall not alter, modify, or interfere in, the times, places, or manner of holding elections of senators, or representatives, except when any state shall refuse, or neglect, or be unable, by invasion or rebellion, to make such election.

The question on this motion being required by ayes and noes, it was decided as follows:

Ayes—Messrs. Burke, Coles, Floyd, Gerry, Griffin, Grout, Hathorn, Heister, Jackson, Livermore, Mathews, Moore, Page, Parker, Partridge, Van Rensselaer, Seney, Sylvester, Smith, of South Carolina, Stone, Sumter, Thatcher, Tucker.—23.

Noes—Messrs. Ames, Benson, Boudinot, Brown Cadwalader, Carroll, Clymer, Fitzsimons, Foster, Gale, Gilman, Goodhue, Hartley, Lawrence, Lee, Madison, jr., Muhlenberg, Schureman, Scott, Sedgwick, Sherman, Sinnickson, Smith, of Maryland, Sturges, Trumbull, Vining, Wadsworth, Wynkoop.—28.

The subject being again taken up for consideration on the 22nd of August, a motion was made to add to the amendments already agreed to, the following article:

The Congress shall never impose direct taxes, but where the moneys arising from the duties, imposts, and excise, are insufficient for the public exigencies; nor then, until Congress shall have made a requisition upon the states, to assess, levy, and pay, their respective proportions of such requisitions; and, in case any state shall neglect or refuse to pay its proportion pursuant to such requisition, then Congress may assess and levy such state's proportion, together with interest thereon, at the rate of six per cent, per annum, from the time of payment prescribed by such requisition.

The question on this motion being taken by ayes and noes, it was decided in the negative, by the following vote:

Ayes—Messrs. Burke, Coles, Floyd, Grout, Hathorn, Livermore, Van Rensselaer, Sumter, Tucker.—9.

Noes—Messrs. Ames, Benson, Brown, Cadwalader, Carroll, Clymer,

Fitzsimons, Foster, Gale, Gerry, Gilman, Goodhue, Hartley, Heister, Jackson, Lawrance, Lee, Madison, jr., Mathews, Moore, Muhlenberg, Page, Parker, Partridge, Schureman, Scott, Sedgwick, Seney, Sherman, Sylvester, Sinnickson, Smith, of Maryland, Smith, of South Carolina, Stone, Sturges, Thatcher, Trumbull, Vining, Wadsworth.—39.

It was then moved further to amend the Constitution, as follows:

Article 1, Section 8, Clause 9: Strike out the words 'tribunals inferior to the Supreme Court,' and insert the words "Courts of Admiralty."

But this motion was decided in the negative.

A motion was then made further to amend the Constitution, as follows:

In the third section of the sixth article, insert the word "other" between the word "no" and the word "religious."

This motion was also negatived.

It was then further moved to add the following to the other amendments.

That Congress erect no company of merchants with exclusive advantages of commerce.

This motion was also determined in the negative.

A motion was then made to add the following amendment:

Congress shall at no time consent, that any person holding an office of trust or profit under the United States, shall accept of a title of nobility, or any other title or office, from any king, prince, or foreign state.

This motion was also decided in the negative.

No other proposition to amend being brought forward, the house appointed Messrs. Benson, Sherman, and Sedgwick to be a committee to prepare and report a proper arrangement of, and introduction to, the articles of amendment, as they had been agreed to. This committee, on the 24th, reported an arrangement of the articles of amendment, and a resolution proper to be prefixed to the same, which was agreed to as follows:

> Resolved by the Senate and House of Representatives of the United States of America, in Congress assembled, two-thirds of both houses deeming it necessary—That the following articles be proposed to the legislatures of the several states, as amendments to the Constitution of the United States; all, or any of which articles, when ratified by three-fourths of the said legislatures, to be valid, to all intents and purposes, as part of the said Constitution.

House of Representatives Debates, August, 1789*

[Wednesday, August 19]

Amendments to the Constitution

The House then took into consideration the amendments to the constitution, as reported by the Committee of the whole.

* *Annals of Congress*, Vol. 1, pp. 795–809.

Mr. Sherman renewed his motion for adding the amendments to the constitution by way of supplement.

Hereupon ensued a debate similar to what took place in the Committee of the whole, but, on the question, Mr. Sherman's motion was carried by two-thirds of the House; by consequence it was agreed to.

The first proposition of amendment was rejected, because two-thirds of the members present did not support it.

Mr. Ames then brought forward his motion respecting the representation suggested. A desultory conversation took place, and several amendments of the motion were attempted; but the House adjourned without coming to any determination.

[Thursday, August 20]

*   *   *

Amendments to the Constitution

The House resumed the consideration of the report of the Committee of the whole on the subject of amendment to the constitution.

Mr. Ames's proposition was taken up. Five or six other members introduced propositions on the same point, and the whole were, by mutual consent, laid on the table. After which, the House proceeded to the third amendment, and agreed to the same.

On motion of Mr. Ames, the fourth amendment was altered so as to read "Congress shall make no law establishing religion, or to prevent the free exercise thereof, or to infringe the rights of conscience." This being adopted,

The first proposition was agreed to.

Mr. Scott objected to the clause in the sixth amendment, "No person religiously scrupulous shall be compelled to bear arms." He observed that if this becomes part of the constitution, such persons can neither be called upon for their services, nor can an equivalent be demanded; it is also attended with still further difficulties, for a militia can never be depended upon. This would lead to the violation of another article in the constitution, which secures to the people the right of keeping arms, and in this case recourse must be had to a standing army. I conceive it, said he, to be a legislative right altogether. There are many sects I know, who are religiously scrupulous in this respect; I do not mean to deprive them of any indulgence the law affords; my design is to guard against those who are of no religion. It has been urged that religion is on the decline; if so, the argument is more strong in my favor, for when the time comes that religion shall be discarded, the generality of persons will have recourse to these pretexts to get excused from bearing arms.

Mr. Boudinot thought the provision in the clause, or something similar to it, was necessary. Can any dependence, said he, be placed in men who are conscientious in this respect? or what justice can there be in compelling them to bear arms, when, according to their religious principles, they would rather die than use them? He adverted to several instances of oppression on this point, that occurred during the war. In forming a militia, an effectual defence ought to be calculated, and no characters of this religious description ought to be compelled to take up arms. I hope that in establishing this Government, we may show the world that proper care is taken that the Government may not interfere with the religious sentiments of any person. Now, by striking out the clause, people may be led to believe that there is an intention in the General Government to compel all its citizens to bear arms.

Some further desultory conversation arose, and it was agreed to insert the words "in person" to the end of the clause; after which, it was adopted, as was the fourth, fifth, sixth, seventh, and eighth clauses of the fourth proposition; then the fifth, sixth, and seventh propositions were agreed to, and the House adjourned.

[Friday, August 21]

Amendments to the Constitution

The House proceeded in the consideration of the amendments to the constitution reported by the Committee of the whole, and took up the second clause of the fourth proposition.

Mr. Gerry then proposed to amend it by striking out these words, "public danger," and to insert "foreign invasion;" this being negatived, it was then moved to strike out the last clause, "and if it be committed," &c. to the end. This motion was carried, and the amendment was adopted.

The House then took into consideration the third clause of the seventh proposition, which was adopted without debate.

The eighth proposition was agreed to in the same manner.

The ninth proposition Mr. Gerry proposed to amend by inserting the word "expressly," so as to read "the powers not expressly delegated by the constitution, nor prohibited to the States, are reserved to the States respectively, or to the people." As he thought this an amendment of great importance, he requested the yeas and nays might be taken. He was supported in this by one-fifth of the members present; whereupon they were taken, and were as follows:

Yeas—Messrs. Burke, Coles, Floyd, Gerry, Grout, Hathorn, Jackson, Livermore, Page, Parker, Partridge, Van Rensselaer, Smith, (of South Carolina,) Stone, Sumter, Thatcher, and Tucker.—17.

Nays—Messrs. Ames, Benson, Boudinot, Brown, Cadwalader, Carroll, Clymer, Fitzsimons, Foster, Gale, Gilman, Goodhue, Hartley, Heister, Lawrence, Lee, Madison, Moore, Muhlenburg, Schureman, Scott, Sedgwick, Seney, Sherman, Sylvester, Sinnickson, Smith, (of Maryland,) Sturges, Trumbull, Vining, Wadsworth, and Wynkoop.—32.

Mr. Sherman moved to alter the last clause, so as to make it read, "the powers not delegated to the United States by the constitution, nor prohibited by it to the States, are reserved to the States respectively, or to the people."

This motion was adopted without debate.

Mr. Burke: The majority of this House may be inclined to think all our propositions unimportant, as they seemed to consider that upon which the ayes and noes were just now called. However, to the minority they are important; and it will be happy for the Government, if the majority of our citizens are not of their opinion; but be this as it may, I move you, sir, to add to the articles of amendment the following: "Congress shall not alter, modify, or interfere in the times, places, or manner of holding elections of Senators, or Representatives, except when any State shall refuse or neglect, or be unable, by invasion or rebellion, to make such election."

Mr. Ames thought this one of the most justifiable of all the powers of Congress; it was essential to a body representing the whole community, that they should have power to regulate their own elections, in order to secure a representation from every part, and prevent any improper regulations, calculated to answer party purposes only. It is a solecism in politics to let others judge for them, and is a departure from the principles upon which the constitution was founded.

Mr. Livermore said, this was an important amendment, and one that had caused more debate in the Convention of New Hampshire than any other whatever. The gentleman just up said it was a solecism in politics, but he could cite an instance in which it had taken place. He only called upon gentlemen to recollect the circumstance of Mr. Smith's (of South Carolina) election, and to ask if that was not decided by the State laws? Was not his qualification as a member of the Federal Legislature determined upon the laws of South Carolina? It was not supposed by the people of South Carolina, that the House would question a right derived by their representative from their authority.

Mr. Madison: If this amendment had been proposed at any time either in the Committee of the whole or separately in the House, I should not have objected to the discussion of it. But I cannot agree to delay the amendments now agreed upon, by entering into the consideration of propositions not likely to obtain the consent of either two-thirds of this House or three-fourths of the State Legislatures. I have considered this subject with some degree of attention, and, upon the whole, am inclined to think the constitution stands very well as it is.

Mr. Gerry was sorry that gentlemen objected to the time and manner of introducing this amendment, because it was too important in its nature to be defeated by want of form. He hoped, and he understood it to be the sense of the House, that each amendment should stand upon its own ground; if this was, therefore, examined on its own merits, it might stand or fall as it deserved, and there would be no cause for complaint on the score of inattention.

His colleague (Mr. Ames) objected to the amendment, because he thought no Legislature was without the power of determining the mode of its own appointment; but he would find, if he turned to the constitution of the State he was a representative of, that the times, places, and manner of choosing members of their Senate and Council were prescribed therein.

Why, said he, are gentlemen desirous of retaining this power? Is it because it gives energy to the Government? It certainly has no such tendency; then why retain a clause so obnoxious to almost every State? But this provision may be necessary in order to establish a Government of an arbitrary kind, to which the present system is pointed in no very indirect manner: in this way, indeed, it may be useful. If the United States are desirous of controlling the elections of the people, they will in the first place, by virtue of the powers given them by the 4th sect. of the 1st art. abolish the mode of balloting; then every person must publicly announce his vote, and it would then frequently happen that he would be obliged to vote for a man, or "the friend of a man" to whom he was under obligations. If the Government grows desirous of being arbitrary, elections will be ordered at remote places, where their friends alone will attend. Gentlemen will tell me that these things are not to be apprehended; but if they say that the Government has the power of doing them, they have no right to say the Government will never exercise such powers, because it is presumable that they will administer the constitution at one time or another with all its powers; and whenever that time arrives, farewell to the rights of the people, even to elect their own representatives.

Mr. Stone called upon gentlemen to show what confederated Government had the power of determining on the mode of their own election. He apprehended there were none; for the representatives of States were chosen by the States in the manner they pleased. He was not afraid that the General Government would abuse this power, and as little afraid that the States would; but he thought it was in the order of things that the power should vest in the States respectively, because they can vary their regulations to accommodate the people in a more convenient manner than can be done in any general law whatever. He thought the amendment was generally expected, and therefore, on the principles of the majority, ought to be adopted.

Mr. Smith (of South Carolina) said, he hoped it would be agreed to; that eight States had expressed their desires on this head, and all of them wished the General Government to relinquish their control over the elections. The eight States he alluded to were New Hampshire, Massachusetts, New York, Pennsylvania, Maryland, Virginia, North Carolina, and South Carolina.

Mr. Carroll denied that Maryland had expressed the desire attributed to her.

Mr. Fitzsimons: The remark was not just as it respected Pennsylvania.

Mr. Smith (of South Carolina) said, the Convention of Maryland appointed a committee to recommend amendments, and among them was the one now under consideration.

Mr. Stone replied there was nothing of the kind noticed on the journals of that body.

Mr. Smith (of South Carolina) did not know how they came into the world, but he had certainly seen them. As to Pennsylvania, there was a very considerable minority, he understood one-third, who had recommended the amendment. Now, taking all circumstances into consideration, it might be fairly inferred that a majority of the United States were in favor of this amendment. He had studied to make himself acquainted with this particular subject, and all that he had ever heard in defence of the power being exercised by the General Government was, that it was necessary, in case any State neglected or refused to make provision for the election. Now these cases were particularly excepted by the clause proposed by his honorable colleague; and therefore he presumed there was no good argument against it.

Mr. Sedgwick moved to amend the motion, by giving the power to Congress to alter the times, manner, and places of holding elections, provided the States made improper ones; for as much injury might result to the Union from improper regulations, as from a neglect or refusal to make any. It is as much to be apprehended that the States may abuse their powers, as that the United States may make an improper use of theirs.

Mr. Ames said, that inadequate regulations were equally injurious as having none, and that such an amendment as was now proposed would alter the constitution; it would vest the supreme authority in places where it was never contemplated.

Mr. Sherman observed, that the Convention were very unanimous in passing this clause; that it was an important provision, and if it was resigned it would tend to subvert the Government.

Mr. Madison was willing to make every amendment that was required by the States, which did not tend to destroy the principles and the efficacy of the constitution; he conceived that the proposed amendment would have that tendency, he was therefore opposed to it.

Mr. Smith (of South Carolina) observed, that the States had the sole regulation of elections, so far as it respected the President. Now he saw no good reason why they should be indulged in this, and prohibited from the other. But the amendment did not go so far; it admitted that the General Government might interfere whenever the State Legislature refused or neglected; and it might happen that the business would be neglected without any design to injure the administration of the General Government; it might be that the two branches of the Legislature could not agree, as happened he believed in the Legislature of New York, with respect to their choice of Senators at their late session.

Mr. Tucker objected to Mr. Sedgwick's motion of amendment, because it had a tendency to defeat the object of the proposition brought forward by his colleague, (Mr. Burke.) The General Government would be the judge of inadequate or improper regulations; of consequence they might interfere in any or every law which the States might pass on that subject.

He wished that the State Legislatures might be left to themselves to perform every thing they were competent to, without the guidance of Congress. He believed there was no great danger, but they knew how to pursue their own good, as well when left to their discretion, as they would under the direction of a superior. It seemed to him as if there was a strong propensity in this Government to take upon themselves the guidance of the State Governments, which to his mind implied a doubt of their capacity to govern themselves; now his judgment was convinced that the particular State Governments could take care of themselves, and deserved more to be trusted than this did, because the right of the citizen was more secure under it.

It had been supposed by some States, that electing by districts was the most convenient mode of choosing members to this House; others have thought that the whole State ought to vote for the whole number of members to be elected for that State. Congress might, under like impressions, set their regulations aside. He had heard that many citizens of Virginia (which State was divided into eleven districts) supposed themselves abridged of nine-tenths of their privilege by being restrained to the choice of one man instead of ten, the number that State sends to this House.

With respect to the election of Senators, the mode is fixed; every State but New York has established a precedent; there is, therefore, but little danger of any difficulty on this account. As to New York, she suffers by her want of decision; it is her own loss; but probably they may soon decide the point, and then no difficulty can possibly arise hereafter. From all these considerations, he was induced to hope Mr. Sedgwick's motion would be negatived, and his colleague's agreed to.

Mr. Goodhue hoped the amendment never would obtain. Gentlemen should recollect there appeared a large majority against amendments, when the subject was first introduced, and he had no doubt but that majority still existed. Now, rather than this amendment should take effect, he would vote against all that had been agreed to. His greatest apprehensions were, that the State Governments would oppose and thwart the general one to such a degree as finally to overturn it. Now, to guard against this evil, he wished the Federal Government to possess every power necessary to its existence.

Mr. Burke was convinced there was a majority against him; but, nevertheless, he would do his duty, and propose such amendments as he conceived essential to secure the rights and liberties of his constituents. He begged permission to make an observation or two, not strictly in order; the first was on an assertion that had been repeated more than once in this House, "That this revolution or adoption of the new constitution was agreeable to the public mind, and those who opposed it at first are now satisfied with it." I believe, sir, said he, that many of those gentlemen who agreed to the ratification without amendments, did it from principles of patriotism, but they knew at the same time that they parted with their liberties; yet they had such reliance on the virtue of a future Congress, that they did not hesitate, expecting that they would be restored to them unimpaired, as soon as the Government commenced its operations, conformably to what was mutually understood at the sealing and delivering up of those instruments.

It has been supposed that there is no danger to be apprehended from the General Government of an invasion of the rights of election. I will remind gentlemen of an instance in the Government of Holland. The patriots in that country fought no less strenuously for that prize than the people of America; yet, by giving to the States General powers not unlike those in this constitution, their right of representation was abolished. That they once possessed it is certain, and that they made as much talk about its importance as we do; but now the right has ceased, all vacancies are filled by the men in power. It is our duty, therefore, to prevent our liberties from being fooled away in a similar manner; consequently we ought to adopt the clause which secures to the General Government every thing that ought to be required.

Mr. Madison observed, that it was the State Governments in the Seven United Provinces which had assumed to themselves the power of filling vacancies, and not the General Government; therefore the gentleman's application did not hold.

The question on Mr. Sedgwick's motion for amending Mr. Burke's proposition was put and lost.

The question was then put on Mr. Burke's motion, and the yeas and nays being demanded by the constitutional number, they were taken as follows:

Yeas—Messrs. Burke, Coles, Floyd, Gerry, Griffin, Grout, Hathorn, Heister, Jackson, Livermore, Matthews, Moore, Page, Parker, Partridge, Van Rensselaer, Seney, Sylvester, Smith, (of South Carolina,) Stone, Sumter, Thatcher, and Tucker.—23.

Nays—Messrs. Ames, Benson, Boudinot, Brown, Cadwalader, Carroll, Clymer, Fitzsimons, Foster, Gale, Gilman, Goodhue, Hartley, Lawrence, Lee, Madison, Muhlenberg, Schureman, Scott, Sedgwick, Sherman, Sinnickson, Smith, (of Maryland,) Sturges, Trumbull, Vining, Wadsworth, and Wynkoop.—28.

So it was determined in the negative.

The House then resumed the consideration of the proposition respecting the apportioning of the representation to a certain ratio, proposed by Mr. Ames.

When, after some desultory conversation, it was agreed to, as follows: "After the first enumeration, required by the first article of the constitution, there shall be one representative for every thirty thousand, until the number shall amount to one hundred. After which, the proportion shall be so regulated by Congress that there shall be not less than one hundred representatives, nor less than one representative for every forty thousand persons, until the number of representatives shall amount to two hundred, after which, the proportion shall be so regulated by Congress, that there shall not be less than two hundred representatives, nor less than one representative for fifty thousand persons."

After which the House adjourned.

[Saturday, August 22]

Amendments to the Constitution

The House resumed the consideration of the amendments to the constitution.

Mr. Tucker moved the following as a proposition to be added to the same: "The Congress shall never impose direct taxes but where the moneys arising from the duties, imposts, and excise are insufficient for the public exigencies, nor then until Congress shall have made a requisition upon the States to assess, levy, and pay their respective proportions of such requisitions. And in case any State shall neglect or refuse to pay its proportion, pursuant to such requisition, then Congress may assess, and levy such State's proportion, together with the interest thereon, at the rate of six per cent. per annum, from the time of payment prescribed by such requisition."

Mr. Page said, that he hoped every amendment to the constitution would be considered separately in the manner this was proposed, but he wished them considered fully; it ought to have been referred to the Committee of eleven, reported upon, and then to the Committee of the whole. This was the manner in which the House had decided upon all those already agreed to; and this ought to be the manner in which this should be decided; he should be sorry to delay what was so nearly completed on any account. The House has but little time to sit, and the subject has to go before the Senate, therefore it requires of us all the expedition we can possibly give it. I would prefer putting a finishing hand to what has been already agreed to, and refer this to the Committee of eleven for their consideration.

Mr. Tucker: This proposition was referred to the committee, along with many others in the gross, but the Committee of eleven declined reporting upon it. I understood it to be in any gentleman's power to bring it forward when he thought proper, and it was under this influence that I proposed it, nor do I conceive it to be an improper time. The House is engaged in the discussion of amendments; they have made some progress, and I wish them to go on to complete what they have begun. This may be added without inconvenience, if it meet the sense of the House; but if it does not, I wish my constituents to be acquainted with our decision on the whole subject, and therefore hope it may be decided upon at this time.

Mr. Jackson: The gentleman has an undoubted right to bring forward the proposition; but I differ greatly with respect to its propriety. I hope, sir, the experience we have had will be sufficient to prevent us from ever agreeing to a relinquishment of such an essential power. The requisitions of the former Congress were ineffectual to obtain supplies; they remain to this day neglected by several States. If a sense of common danger, if war, and that a war of the noblest kind, a contest for liberty, were not sufficient to stimulate the States to a prompt compliance, when the means were abundant, by reason of the immense quantities of paper medium, can we ever expect an acquiescence to a requisition in future, when the only stimulus is honesty, to enable the confederation to discharge the debts of the late war?

But suppose requisitions were likely to be, in some degree, complied with, (which, by the by, I never can admit,) in every case where a State had neglected or refused to furnish its quota, Congress must come in, assess, and collect it. Now, in every such case, I venture to affirm that jealousies would be excited, discontent would prevail, and civil wars break out. What less can gentlemen picture to themselves, when a Government has refused to perform its obligations, but that it will support its measures by the point of the bayonet.

Without the power of raising money to defray the expenses of Government, how are we to be secure against foreign invasion? What, can a Government exert itself, with its sinews torn from it? We can expect neither strength nor exertion; and without these are acquired and preserved, our union will not be lasting; we shall be rent asunder by intestine commotion, or exterior assault; and when that period arrives, we may bid adieu to all the blessings we have purchased at the price of our fortunes, and the blood of our worthiest heroes.

Mr. Livermore thought this an amendment of more importance than any yet obtained; that it was recommended by five or six States, and therefore ought to engage their most serious consideration. It had been supposed that the United States would not attempt to levy direct taxes; but this was certainly a mistake. He believed nothing but the difficulty of managing the subject would deter them. The modes of levying and collecting taxes pursued by the several States are so various, that it is an insuperable obstacle to an attempt by the General Government.

He was sensible that the requisitions of the former Congress had not been fully complied with, and the defect of the confederation was, that the Government had no powers to enforce a compliance. The proposition now under consideration obviated that difficulty. Suppose one or two States refused to comply, certainly the force of the others could compel them, and that is all that ought to be required; because it is not to be supposed that a majority of the States will refuse, as such an opposition must destroy the Union. He hoped the States would be left to furnish their quotas in a manner the most easy to themselves, as was requested by more than half of the present Union.

Unless something more effectual was done to improve the constitution, he knew his constitutents would be dissatisfied. As to the amendments already agreed to, they would not value them more than a pinch of snuff; they went to secure rights never in danger.

Mr. Page wished the proposition might be recommitted, for he was certain there was neither time nor inclination to add it to those already agreed upon.

He observed that the warmest friends to amendments differ in opinion on this subject; many of them have ceased urging it, while others have become strenuous advocates for the reverse. The most judicious and discerning men now declare that the Government ought never to part with this power. For his part, experience had convinced him that no reliance was to be had on requisitions, when the States had treated them with contempt in the hour of danger, and had abundant means of compliance. The public credit stood at this moment in the utmost need of support, and he could not consent to throw down one of its strongest props. He thought there was no danger of an abuse of this power, for the Government would not have recourse to it while the treasury could be supplied from any other source; and when they did, they would be studious of adapting their law to the convenience of the States. He hoped, when the gentleman returned home to New Hampshire, his constituents would give him credit for his exertions, and be better satisfied with the amendments than he now supposed them to be.

Mr. Sumter felt himself so sensibly impressed with the importance of the subject, that if he apprehended the proposition would not have a fair discussion at this time, he would second the motion of commitment, and had not a doubt but the House would acquiesce in it.

Gentlemen had said that the States had this business much at heart. Yes, he would venture to say more, that if the power was not relinquished by the General Government, the State Governments would be annihilated. If every resource is taken from them, what remains in the power of the States for their support, or for the extinguishment of their domestic debt?

Mr. Gerry thought if the proposition was referred, that it ought to go to a Committee of the whole, for he wished it to have a full and candid discussion. He would have something left in the power of every State to support itself, independent of the United States, and therefore was not satisfied with the amendment proposed. The constitution, in its original state, gives to Congress the power of levying and collecting taxes, duties, imposts, and excise. The fault here is, that every thing is relinquished to the General Government. Now, the amendment gives the same power, with qualification, that there shall have been a previous requisition. This by no means came up to his idea; he thought that some particular revenue ought to be secured to the States, so as to enable them to support themselves.

He apprehended, when this clause in the constitution was under the consideration of the several State conventions, they would not so readily have ratified it, if they had considered it more fully in the point of view in which he had now placed it; but if they had ratified it, it would have been under a conviction that Congress would admit such amendments as were necessary to the existence of the State Governments. At present, the States are divested of every means to support themselves. If they discover a new source of revenue, after Congress shall have diverted all the old ones into their treasury, the rapacity of the General Government can take that from them also. The States can have recourse to no tax, duty, impost, or excise, but what may be taken from them whenever the Congress shall be so disposed; and yet gentlemen must see that the annihilation of the State Governments will be followed by the ruin of this.

Now, what is the consequence of the amendment? Either the States will or will not comply with the requisitions. If they comply, they voluntarily surrender their means of support; if they refuse, the arms of Congress are raised to compel them, which, in all probability, may lay the foundation for civil war. What umbrage must it give every individual to have two sets of collectors and tax-gatherers surrounding his doors; the people then soured, and a direct refusal by the Legislature, will be the occasion of perpetual discord. He wished to alter this proposition in such a manner as to secure the support of the Federal Government and the State Governments likewise, and therefore wished the amendment referred to a Committee of the whole House.

Mr. Tucker: I do not see the arguments in favor of giving Congress this power in so forcible a light as some gentlemen do. It will be to erect an *imperium in imperio,* which is generally considered to be subversive of all Government. At any time that Congress shall exercise this power, it will raise commotions in the States; whereas, the mode of requisitions will operate in so easy a way, by being consonant to the habits of the people, that the supplies will be sooner realized in the treasury by this means than by any other. It will require a length of time to form a uniform system of taxation, that shall operate equally and justly through all the States; though I doubt the possibility of forming such a system. It has been said, that requisitions have not been complied with in former times, but it is to be hoped that there will not be so much difficulty in future. The supplies from the impost will greatly diminish the requisitions; besides, should any of the States refuse to comply, they will be liable to the exercise of the power of Congress in the very heart of their country. This power will be so disagreeable, that the very dread of it will stimulate the States to an immediate and prompt compliance with the requisitions. This amendment has been proposed by several of the States, and by some of the most important ones. For this and other reasons that have been offered on the subject, I hope the amendment will be adopted.

Several methods were proposed for disposing of this question for the present; but the motion for its lying on the table being put and negatived, Mr. Partridge, referring to his instructions, was solicitous that this amendment should not be too precipitately decided upon, and moved the previous question, which was negatived.

Mr. Sedgwick said, that he believed his mind was as strongly impressed with the force of the instructions he had received from his constituents, as that of other gentlemen. But, sir, a Government entrusted with the freedom and the very existence of the people, ought surely to possess, in a most ample degree, the means of supporting its own existence; and as we do not know what circumstances we may be in, or how necessary it may be for Congress to exercise this power, I should deem it a violation of the oath I have taken to support the constitution were I now to vote for this amendment.

Mr. Sherman remarked, that if Congress should exercise this power, the taxes would be laid by the immediate representatives of the people; neither would it be necessary to adopt one uniform method of collecting direct taxes. The several States might be accommodated by a reference to their respective modes of taxation.

The question upon the paragraph being called for from every part of the House, the yeas and nays were taken.

Yeas—Messrs. Burke, Coles, Floyd, Grout, Hathorn, Livermore, Van Rensselaer, Sumter, and Tucker.—9.

Nays—Messrs. Ames, Benson, Brown, Cadwalader, Carroll, Clymer, Fitzsimons, Foster, Gale, Gerry, Gilman, Goodhue, Hartley, Heister, Jackson, Lawrence, Lee, Madison, Matthews, Moore, Muhlenburg, Page, Parker, Partridge, Schureman, Scott, Sedgwick, Seney, Sherman, Sylvester, Sinnickson, Smith, of Maryland, Smith, of South Carolina, Stone, Sturges, Thatcher, Trumbull, Vining, and Wadsworth.—39.

Mr. Tucker proposed the following amendment to the constitution:

Article 1, section 8, clause 9, strike out the words, "tribunals superior to the Supreme Court," and insert the words "courts of admiralty."

And on the question being put, it passed in the negative.

He then moved for a further amendment to the constitution, as follows:

In the third section of the sixth article insert the word "other" between the word "no" and the word "religious."

And on the question that the House do agree to the said amendment, it passed in the negative.

Mr. Gerry moved to add to the amendments already agreed to the following articles, to wit:

"That Congress erect no company of merchants with exclusive advantages of commerce." And on the question that the House do agree to the said proposed article, it passed in the negative.

He introduced another motion, to add to the amendments already agreed to the following article, to wit:

"Congress shall at no time consent that any person holding an office of trust or profit under the United States shall accept of a title of nobility or any other title or office from any King, Prince, or foreign State."

And on the question being put, it was negatived.

Mr. Benson introduced a resolution to the following purport:

> Resolved by the House of Representatives of the United States in
> Congress assembled, That the following amendments to the constitution of
> the United States having been agreed to by two-thirds of both Houses, be
> submitted to the Legislatures of the several States; which, when ratified, in
> whole or in part, by three-fourths of the said Legislatures, shall be valid to
> all intents and purposes as parts of the said constitution.

This resolution was referred to a committee consisting of Messrs. Benson, Sherman, and Sedgwick, who were directed to arrange the said amendments and make report thereof.

*   *   *

[Monday, August 24]

Mr. Benson, from the committee appointed for the purpose, reported an arrangement of the articles of amendment to the constitution of the United States, as agreed to by the House on Friday last; also, a resolution prefixed to the same, which resolution was twice read and agreed to by the House, as follows:

> Resolved by the Senate and House of Representatives of the United
> States of America in Congress assembled, (two-thirds of both Houses
> deeming it necessary,) That the following articles be proposed to the
> Legislatures of the several States as amendments to the constitution of the
> United States, all or any of which articles, when ratified by three-fourths
> of the said Legislatures, to be valid to all intents and purposes as part of
> the said constitution.

Ordered, That the clerk of this House do carry to the Senate a fair engrossed copy of the said proposed articles of amendment, and desire their concurrence.

*   *   *

Madison to Randolph, 1789*

Aug. 21, 1789

My Dear Friend,

For a week past the subject of amendts. has exclusively occupied the H. of Reps. Its progress has been exceedingly wearisome not only on account of the diversity of opinions that was to be apprehended, but of the apparent views of some to defeat by delaying a plan short of their wishes, but likely to

*The Writings of James Madison, Vol. 5, p. 417.

satisfy a great part of their companions in opposition throughout the Union. It has been absolutely necessary in order to effect anything, to abbreviate debate, and exclude every proposition of a doubtful & unimportant nature. Had it been my wish to have comprehended every amendt. recomended by Virga., I should have acted from prudence the very part to which I have been led by choice. Two or three contentious additions would even now prostrate the whole project.

The Judiciary bill was put off in favr. of the preceding subject. It was evident that a longer delay of that wd. prevent any decision on it at this Session. A push was therefore made, which did not succeed without strenuous opposition. On monday the bill will probably be taken up & be pursued to a final question as fast as the nature of the case will allow.

I find on looking over the notes of your introductory discourse in the Convention at Philada., that it is not possible for me to do justice to the substance of it. I am anxious for particular reasons to be furnished with the means of preserving this as well as the other arguments in that body, and must beg that you will make out & forward me the scope of your reasoning. You have your notes I know & from these you can easily deduce the argument on a condensed plan. I make this request with an earnestness wch. will not permit you either to refuse or delay a compliance.

Madison to Alexander White, 1789*

Aug. 24, 1789

Dear Sir,

The week past has been devoted to the subject of amendments: all that remains is a formal vote on a fair transcript which will be taken this morning; and without debate I hope, as each of the propositions has been agreed to by two thirds of the House. The substance of the report of the Committee of eleven has not been much varied. It became an unavoidable sacrifice to a few who knew their concurrence to be necessary, to the dispatch if not the success of the business, to give up the form by which the amendts. when ratified would have fallen into the body of the Constitution, in favor of the project of adding them by way of appendix to it. It is already apparent I think that some ambiguities will be produced by this change, as the question will often arise and sometimes be not easily solved, how far the original text is or is not necessarily superceded, by the supplemental act. A middle way will be taken between the two modes, of proposing all the amendts. as a single act to be adopted or rejected in the gross, and of proposing them as independent amendts. each of which shall take place or not, as it may be individually decided on. The several propositions will be

*The Writings of James Madison, p. 418.

classed according to their affinity to each other, which will reduce them to the number of 5 or 6 in the whole, to go forth as so many amendts. unconnected with one another.

On Saturday notice was given to the House by Mr. Scott that on Thursday in this week he should bring in the subject of the permanent seat of Congress. [Illegible] & [Illegible] in favr. of Trenton ensued. The like from Lancaster &c. also came forward. I suspect that the motion is the result of some [illegible] of a pretty serious nature. A great push will be made for Trenton which has I fear more partizans than might be wished. It is surmised that a coalition has taken place between Pa. & the East: states. I believe it to be the case in some degree, tho' not fully. As far as I can gather, the coalition for Trenton might be broken, by accepting the Susquehannah, and leaving N.Y. the temporary enjoyment of Congs. This I believe is the ultimate [aim] of the N.Y. party, and will not do for us.

I suspect they begin to despair of a long possession of Congs. and consequently mix the permanent with the temporary considerations. Having given you these facts your own judgment will best decide how far it may be worth while and incumbent on you to hasten your return.

Jefferson to Madison, 1789*

Aug. 28, 1789

Dear Sir,

My last to you was of July 29. Since that I have received yours of May 27. June 13. and 30. The tranquillity of the city has not been disturbed since my last. Dissensions between the French and Swiss guards occasioned some private combats in which five or six were killed. These dissensions are made up. The want of bread for some days past has greatly endangered the peace of the city. Some get a little bread, some none at all. The poor are the best served because they besiege perpetually the doors of the bakers. Notwithstanding this distress, and the palpable impotence of the city administration to furnish bread to the city, it was not till yesterday that general leave was given to the bakers to go into the country and buy flour for themselves as they can. This will soon relieve us, because the wheat harvest is well advanced. Never was there a country where the practice of governing too much had taken deeper root and done more mischeif. Their declaration of rights is finished. If printed in time I will inclose a copy with this. It is doubtful whether they will now take up the finance or the constitution first. The distress for money endangers every thing. No taxes are paid, and no money can be borrowed. Mr. Necker was yesterday to give in a memoir to the Assembly on this subject. I think they will give him leave to put into

* The Papers of Thomas Jefferson, Vol. 15, pp. 364–69.

execution any plan he pleases, so as to debarrass themselves of this and take up that of the constitution. No plan is yet reported; but the leading members (with some small differences of opinion) have in contemplation the following. The Executive power in a hereditary king, with a negative on laws and power to dissolve the legislature, to be considerably restrained in the making of treaties, and limited in his expences. The legislative in a house of representatives. They propose a senate also, chosen on the plan of our federal senate by the provincial assemblies, but to be for life, of a certain age (they talk of 40. years) and certain wealth (4 or 500 guineas a year) but to have no other power as to laws but to remonstrate against them to the representatives, who will then determine their fate by a simple majority. This you will readily perceive is a mere council of revision like that of New York, which, in order to be something, must form an alliance with the king, to avail themselves of his veto. The alliance will be useful to both and to the nation. The representatives to be chosen every two or three years. The judiciary system is less prepared than any other part of their plan. However they will abolish the parliaments, and establish an order of judges and justices, general and provincial, a good deal like ours, with trial by jury in criminal cases certainly, perhaps also in civil. The provinces will have assemblies for their provincial government, and the cities a municipal body for municipal government, all founded on the basis of popular election. These subordinate governments, tho completely dependant on the general one, will be entrusted with almost the whole of the details which our state governments exercise. They will have their own judiciary, final in all but great cases, the Executive business will principally pass through their hands, and a certain local legislation will be allowed them. In short ours has been professedly their model, in which such changes are made as a difference of circumstance rendered necessary and some others neither necessary nor advantageous, but into which men will ever run when versed in theory and new in the practice of government, when acquainted with man only as they see him in their books and not in the world. This plan will undoubtedly undergo changes in the assembly, and the longer it is delayed the greater will be the changes: for that assembly, or rather the patriotic part of it, hooped together heretofore by a common enemy, are less compact since their victory. That enemy (the civil and ecclesiastical aristocracy) begins to raise it's head. The lees too of the patriotic party, of wicked parinciples and desperate fortunes, hoping to pillage something in the wreck of their country, are attaching themselves to the faction of the Duke of Orleans, that faction is caballing with the populace, and intriguing at London, the Hague and Berlin and have evidently in view the transfer of the crown to the D. of Orleans. He is a man of moderate understanding, of no principle, absorbed in low vice, and incapable of abstracting himself from the filth of that to direct any thing else. His name and his money therefore are mere tools in the hands of those who are duping him. Mirabeau is their chief. They may produce a temporary confusion, and even a temporary civil war, supported as they will be by the money of England; but they cannot have success ultimately. The king, the mass of the substantial people of the whole country, the army, and the influential part of the clergy, form a firm phalanx which must prevail. Should those delays which necessarily attend the deliberations of a body of 1200 men give time to this plot to ripen and burst so as to break up the assembly before any thing definitive is done, a constitution, the principles of which are pretty well settled in the minds of the assembly, will be proposed by the national militia (that is by their commander) urged by the individual members of the assembly, signed by the king, and supported by the nation, to prevail till circumstances shall permit it's revision and more regular sanction. This I suppose the pis-aller of their affairs, while their probable event is a peaceable settlement of them. They fear a war from England Holland and Prussia. I think England will give money, but not make war. Holland would soon be afire internally were she to be embroiled in external difficulties. Prussia must know this and act accordingly.

It is impossible to desire better dispositions towards us, than prevail in this assembly. Our proceedings have been viewed as a model for them on every occasion; and tho in the heat of debate men are generally disposed to contradict every authority urged by their opponents, ours has been treated like that of the bible, open to explanation but not to question. I am sorry that in the moment of such a disposition any thing should come from us to check it. The placing them on a mere footing with the English will have this effect. When of two nations, the one has engaged herself in a ruinous war for us, has spent her blood and money to save us, has opened her bosom to us in peace, and receive us almost on the footing of her own citizens, while the other has moved heaven, earth and hell to exterminate us in war, has insulted us in all her councils in peace, shut her doors to us in every part where her interests would admit it, libelled us in foreign nations, endeavored to poison them against the reception of our most precious commodities, to place these two nations on a footing, is to give a great deal more to one than to the other if the maxim be true that to make unequal quantities equal you must add more to the one than the other. To say in excuse that gratitude is never to enter into the motives of national conduct, is to revive a principle which has been buried for centuries with it's kindred principles of the lawfulness of assassination, poison, perjury &c. All of these were legitimate principles in the dark ages which intervened between antient and modern civilisation, but exploded and held in just horror in the 18th century. I know but one code of morality for man whether acting singly or collectively. He who says I will be a rogue when I act in company with a hundred others but an honest man when I act alone, will be believed in the former assertion, but not in the latter. I would say with the poet 'hic niger est, hunc tu Romane caveto.' If the morality of one man produces a just line of conduct in him, acting individually, why should not the morality of 100 men produce a just line of conduct in them acting together? But I indulge myself in these reflections because my own feelings run me into them: with you they were always acknoleged. Let us hope that our new government will take some other occasion to shew that they mean to proscribe no virtue from the canons of their conduct with other nations. In every other instance the new government has ushered itself to the world as honest, masculine and dignified. It has shewn genuine dignity in my opinion in exploding adulatory titles; they are the offerings of abject baseness, and nourish that degrading vice in the people.

I must now say a word on the declaration of rights you have been so good as to send me. I like it as far as it goes; but I should have been for going further. For instance the following alterations and additions would have pleased me. Art. 4. 'The people shall not be deprived or abridged of their right to speak to write or otherwise to publish any thing but false facts affecting injuriously the life, liberty, property, or reputation of others or affecting the peace of the confederacy with foreign nations. Art. 7. All facts put in issue before any judicature shall be tried by jury except 1. in cases of admiralty jurisdiction wherein a foreigner shall be interested, 2. in cases cognisable before a court martial concerning only the regular officers and souldiers of the U.S. or members of the militia in actual service in time of war or insurrection, and 3. in impeachments allowed by the constitution. Art. 8. No person shall be held in confinement more than——days after they shall have demanded and been refused a writ of Hab. corp. by the judge appointed by law nor more than——days after such writ shall have been served on the person holding him in confinement and no order given on due examination for his remandment or discharge, nor more than——hours in any place at a greater distance than——miles from the usual residence of some judge authorised to issue the writ of Hab. corp. nor shall that writ be suspended for any term exceeding one year nor in any place more than—— miles distant from the station or encampment of enemies or of insurgents.— Art. 9. Monopolies may be allowed to persons for their own productions in literature and their own inventions in the arts for a term not exceeding—— years but for no longer term and no other purpose. Art. 10. All troops of the U.S. shall stand ipso facto disbanded at the expiration of the term for which their pay and subsistence shall have been last voted by Congress, and all officers and souldiers not natives of the U.S. shall be incapable of serving in their armies by land except during a foreign war.' These restrictions I think are so guarded as to hinder evil only. However if we do not have them now, I have so much confidence in my countrymen as to be satisfied that we shall have them as soon as the degeneracy of our government shall render them necessary. I have no certain news of P. Jones. I understand only in a general way that some persecution on the part of his officers occasioned his being called to Petersburgh, and that tho protected against them by the empress, he is not yet restored to his station. Silas Deane is coming over to finish his days in America, not having one sou to subsist on elsewhere. He is a wretched monument of the consequences of a departure from right. I will before my departure write Colo. Lee fully the measures I pursued to procure success in his business, and which as yet offer little hope, and I shall leave it in the hands of Mr. Short to be pursued if any prospect opens on him. I propose to sail from Havre as soon after the 1st. of October as I can get a vessel: and shall consequently leave this place a week earlier than that. As my daughters will be with me, and their baggage somewhat more than that of mere voyageures, I shall endeavor if possible to obtain a passage for Virginia directly. Probably I shall be there by the last of November. If my immediate attendance at New York should be requisite for any purpose, I will leave them with a relation near Richmond and proceed immediately to New York. But as I do not foresee any pressing purpose for that journey immediately on my arrival, and as it will be a great saving of time to finish at once in Virginia so as to have no occasion to return there after having once gone on to the Northward, I expect to proceed to my own house directly. Staying there two months (which I believe will be necessary) and allowing for the time I am on the road, I may expect to be at New York in February, and to embark from thence, or some eastern port. You ask me if I would accept any appointment on that side the water? You know the circumstances which led me from retirement, step by step and from one nomination to another, up to the present. My object is a return to the same retirement. Whenever therefore I quit the present, it will not be to engage in any other office, and most especially any one which would require a constant residence from home. The books I have collected for you will go off for Havre in three or four days with my baggage. From that port I shall try to send them by a direct occasion to New York. I am with great & sincere esteem Dr. Sir your affectionate friend and servant,

P.S. I just now learn that Mr. Necker proposed yeaterday to the National assembly a loan of 80. millions, on terms more tempting to the lender than the former, and that they approve it, leaving him to arrange the details in order that they might occupy themselves at once about the constitution.

PASSAGE BY SENATE, SEPTEMBER, 1789

Commentary

Unfortunately, the Senate sat behind closed doors until a resolution in February, 1794, directed that its sessions should be public. This means that there is no report of the Senate debates on the Bill of Rights. All that we have available are the skeleton-like account of the legislative history in the Senate *Journal* and the even skimpier account in the *Annals of Congress.* The pertinent extracts from both these sources follow. They tell us the exact changes made in the House amendments, as well as what further attempted amendments were rejected.

The House amendments were formally read in the Senate on August 25, the day after House approval. At that time, an attempt was made to have Senate consideration postponed until the next session. We know some of the details of this because Senator Maclay of Pennsylvania kept a diary which tells us what went on behind the closed doors of the Senate Chamber. Writing of the introduction of the House amendments on August 25, Maclay writes: "They were treated contemptuously by Izard, Langdon, and Mr. Morris. Izard moved that they should be postponed till next session. Langdon seconded, and Mr. Morris got up and spoke angrily but not well. They, however, lost their motion, and Monday was assigned for taking them up. I could not help observing the six-year class [i.e., of Senators] hung together on this business, or the most of them."

Unhappily, Maclay became ill, and was not present during the actual Senate debates on the Bill of Rights; so we are deprived of the further information which his diary would have afforded. Maclay's diary does, however, tell us the Senate business he discussed with visitors during his illness, and seemingly nothing was mentioned about the proposed constitutional amendments. This tends to confirm the curious point already noted, that the Congress was apparently much less concerned with the Bill of Rights issue than the country at large (if we can judge by the 1787–1788 ratification debates, as well as newspaper and other contemporary writings).

Though Monday, August 31, had been assigned for Senate consideration of the House amendments, the intervention of other business prevented the Senate from taking up the subject until Wednesday, September 2. As already indicated, we do not know what was said during the Senate debates; but we do know what changes the upper House made in the proposed amendments. As a generalization, we can say that the Senate performed the important job of tightening up the language of the House version, striking out surplus wording and provisions.

The most important substantive change made by the Senate was the elimination of the amendment which Madison considered "the most valuable

1145

amendment in the whole lot"—that prohibiting the states from infringing on freedom of conscience, speech, press, and jury trial. The result was that, as the Supreme Court was to hold in the 1833 case of *Barron* v. *Baltimore*, the Bill of Rights as adopted imposed limitations only upon federal (not state) power. In addition, the Senate made a significant change in form, combining the two House amendments covering freedom of religion and freedom of speech, press, assembly and petition into one amendment—the form that was ultimately to be retained in the First Amendment.

When the Senate began consideration of the House amendments on September 2, it first made some minor alterations in the first two, relating to representation and congressional pay. The amendment on religious freedom gave some difficulty on September 3. After debate, in which various alterations were unsuccessfully proposed, the Senate agreed to the House amendment, with the words "nor shall the rights of conscience be infringed" eliminated. (This was to bring the language almost to that contained in the First Amendment, but a later Senate amendment was to change this again.)

The freedom of speech, press, assembly, and petition amendment was then discussed. On September 4, it was approved—an attempt like that in the House to insert "to instruct their representatives" was defeated—with the language brought closer to that ultimately used in the First Amendment. The Senate next adopted the amendment on the right to bear arms, after eliminating the House provision exempting conscientious objectors from service in person. The amendments on quartering of soldiers and search and seizure "were then agreed to; as they came from the House." Next, the Senate rewrote the provision on double jeopardy and that on grand jury indictment (in both cases, putting in language that was to appear in the Fifth Amendment).

The remainder of the Senate debate was concerned with three things: 1) the rejection of other proposed amendments, including a whole series based upon the Virginia-recommended amendments which had not been included by Madison in his proposed amendments; 2) the rejection of several House amendments which included the already-mentioned prohibition upon the states from infringing on freedom of religion, speech, press, and jury trial, as well as the House amendments on appeals to the Supreme Court and separation of powers; and 3) tightening up remaining provisions by changes in language and combining related amendments, particularly in the case of the two House amendments on freedom of religion and freedom of speech, press, assembly, and petition, which were fused on September 9 into the combined prohibition contained in the First Amendment—though with the religious guarantee considerably weakened—a backward step that was to be corrected in the Conference Committee. The Senate also combined the provisions (after improving their language) relating to indictment, double jeopardy, self-incrimination, due process, and just compensation into one amendment—the form it was to retain in the Fifth Amendment—and did the same for the two House provisions bearing on trial by jury in civil cases (inserting the unfortunate $20 limitation that appears in the Seventh Amendment). In the tightening process, the Senate left out (perhaps as Madison tells us in his letter to Pendleton [*infra* p. 1157] because it felt the limitation to juries "of the vicinage" was too restrictive) the express guarantee of trial by jury in criminal cases. This was later corrected by the Conference Committee. There was also apparently the same attempt to insert "expressly" into what became the Tenth Amendment as had been made in the House, and with the same result.

When the Senate finished its debate on the matter, it had reduced the seventeen House amendments to twelve in number. Except for the provision on religious freedom, the language of the House amendments had been substantially improved and brought almost to the final language of the federal Bill of Rights. On September 9, the Senate concurred in the resolution of the House, with the amendments already noted, and ordered communication of this to be made to the House.

Senate Journal, August—September, 1789*

And in this form the resolution was transmitted to the Senate on the 25th of August. The articles having been read *pro forma*, in the Senate, on the same day, an unsuccessful motion was made to postpone their consideration to the next session of Congress. It was then ordered that Monday, the 31st, be assigned for the consideration of the subject. The intervention of other business prevented the Senate from taking up this subject until Wednesday, the 2d of September, when the amendments were brought up for consideration.

The first article being before the Senate, to wit:

After the first enumeration required by the first article of the Constitution, there shall be one representative for every thirty thousand, until the number shall amount to one hundred, &c.

A motion was made to strike out the word "one" before "hundred," and insert the word "two." The yeas and nays being required on this question, it was decided in the negative by the following vote:

Yeas—Messrs. Dalton, Gunn, Grayson, King, Lee, Schuyler.—6.

Nays—Messrs. Bassett, Butler, Carroll, Ellsworth, Elmer, Henry, Johnson, Izard, Morris, Paterson, Read, Wingate.—12.

The article was then amended, by striking out all the language which succeeds in the original proposition, to wit:

After which, the proportion shall be so regulated by Congress, that there

---

*History of Congress Exhibiting a Classification of the Proceedings of the Senate and the House of Representatives from March 4, 1789 to March 3, 1793. pp. 160–68.

shall not be less than one hundred representatives, nor less than one representative for every 40,000 persons, until the number of representatives shall amount to two hundred; after which, the proportion shall be so regulated by Congress, that there shall not be less than two hundred representatives, nor less than one representative for every 50,000 persons;

And by substituting the following clause after the words "one hundred," to wit:

To which number one representative shall be added, for every subsequent increase of forty thousand, until the representatives shall amount to two hundred; to which one representative shall be added for every subsequent increase of sixty thousand persons.

And, in this amended form, it was agreed to.

On the following day, the consideration of the amendments was resumed. The second article, commencing, "No law, varying the compensation to the members of Congress," &c., was amended, by striking out the words, "to the members of Congress," and inserting the words, "for the service of the Senate and House of Representatives of the United States."

The third article, as it passed the house, stand thus: "Congress shall make no law establishing religion, or prohibiting the free exercise thereof; nor shall the rights of conscience be infringed." The first motion to amend this article was by striking out these words: "Religion, or prohibiting the free exercise thereof," and inserting these words: "One religious sect or society in preference to others." This motion was negatived. A motion for reconsideration then prevailed, and it was moved to strike out the third article altogether; but this motion was decided in the negative. An unsuccessful attempt was then made to adopt, as a substitute for the third article, the following: "Congress shall not make any law infringing the rights of conscience, or establishing any religious sect or society." The question was then taken on the adoption of the third article, as it came from the House of Representatives, when it was decided in the negative. Finally, the words, "Nor shall the rights of conscience be infringed," were stricken out; and, in this form, the article was agreed to.

The fourth article was then taken up, namely: "The freedom of speech and of the press, and the right of the people peaceably to assemble and consult for their common good, and to apply to the government for redress of grievances, shall not be infringed." It was moved to insert, after the words "common good," these words: "to instruct their representatives." On this question, the yeas and nays being required, it was decided as follows:

Yeas—Messrs, Grayson and Lee.—2.

Nays—Messrs. Bassett, Carroll, Dalton, Ellsworth, Elmer, Gunn, Henry, Johnson, Izard, King, Morris, Paterson, Read, Wingate.—14.

A motion was then made to insert after the word "press," these words: "in as ample a manner as hath at any time been secured by the common law;" but this motion was unsuccessful; as also was a subsequent motion to strike out the words, "and consult for their common good, and." The further consideration of this article was then postponed until the next day, (the 4th,) when it was adopted in the following form: "That Congress shall make no law abridging the freedom of speech, or of the press, or the right of the people peaceably to assemble and consult for their common good, and to petition the government for a redress of grievances."

The fifth article being under consideration, in its order, a motion was made to subjoin to it the following proposition, namely: "That standing armies, in time of peace, being dangerous to liberty, should be avoided, as far as the circumstances and protection of the community will admit; and that, in all cases, the military should be under strict subordination to, and governed by, the civil power; that no standing army or regular troops shall be raised in time of peace, without the consent of two-thirds of the members present in both houses, and that no soldier shall be enlisted for any longer term than the continuance of the war." The yeas and nays being taken on this question, it was decided as follows:

Yeas—Messrs. Butler, Gunn, Grayson, Henry, Lee, Wingate.—6.

Nays—Messrs. Carroll, Dalton, Ellsworth, Elmer, Johnson, King, Paterson, Read, Schuyler.—9.

The fifth article was then adopted; so amended as to read as follows: "A well regulated militia being the best security of a free state, the right of the people to keep and bear arms shall not be infringed."

The sixth and seventh articles were then agreed to, as they came from the House of Representatives.

The eighth article was then considered, and after a successful motion to strike out these words: "except in case of impeachment, to more than one trial, or one punishment;" and substitute these words: "be twice put in jeopardy of life or limb by any public prosecution;" it was agreed to.

The ninth article was agreed to, as it came from the House of Representatives.

The tenth article was also adopted, after striking out all the clauses, except the following: "No person shall be held to answer for a capital, or otherwise infamous crime, unless on a presentment or indictment by a grand jury."

The eleventh article being taken up for consideration, it was moved to insert, in lieu of it, the following: "The Supreme Judicial Federal Court shall have no jurisdiction of causes between citizens of different states, unless the matter in dispute, whether it concern the realty or personalty, be of the value of three thousand dollars at the least: nor shall the federal judicial powers extend to any action between citizens of different states, where the matter in dispute, whether it concern the realty or personalty, is not of the value of fifteen hundred dollars at the least; and no part, triable by a jury according to the course of the common law, shall be otherwise re-examinable than according to the rules of common law." This motion was determined in the negative, and the article was then adopted, in the following form: "No fact, triable by a jury according to the course of common law, shall be otherwise re-examinable in any court of the United States, than according to the rules of common law."

On Monday, the 7th, the subject being again before the Senate, the twelfth article was agreed to, after the addition of these words: "where the consideration exceeds twenty dollars."

The thirteenth article was then agreed to as it came from the House of Representatives: and the fourteenth article was rejected.

When the fifteenth article was under consideration, a motion was made to add the following to the proposed amendments; to wit: "That the general government of the United States ought never to impose direct taxes but where the moneys arising from the duties, impost, and excise, are insufficient for the public exigencies: nor then, until Congress shall have made a requisition upon the states to assess, levy, and pay their respective proportions of such requisitions; and in case any state shall neglect or refuse to pay its proportion, pursuant to such requisition, then Congress may assess and levy such state's proportion, together with interest thereon, at the rate of six per cent. per annum, from the time of payment prescribed by such requisition." This motion was rejected.

An unsuccessful motion was then made to add the following to the proposed amendments: "That the third section of the sixth article of the Constitution of the United States ought to be amended by inserting the word 'other,' between the words 'no,' and 'religious.' "

It was then moved, with like success, to add the following amendment to the Constitution: "That Congress shall not exercise the powers vested in them by the fourth section of the first article of the Constitution of the United States, but in cases where a state shall neglect or refuse to make regulations therein mentioned, or shall make regulations subversive of the rights of the people, to a free and equal representation in Congress, agreeably to the Constitution."

A motion was then made, and negatived, to subjoin the following to the articles of amendment: "That Congress shall not erect any company of merchants with exclusive advantages of commerce."

A further motion was then made, without success, to add the following to the list of amendments: "That Congress shall at no time consent that any person holding an office of trust or profit under the United States, shall accept of a title of nobility, or any other title or office, from any king, prince, or foreign state."

It was then moved, to subjoin the following to the amendments: "That no person indebted to the United States shall be entitled to a seat in either branch of the legislature;" and this motion also was negatived.

The fifteenth article of amendment was then agreed to; and the sixteenth article was rejected.

The seventeenth article was then considered; and a motion to amend, by inserting the word "expressly" before the word "delegated" having been negatived, the article in the following amended form was agreed to—"The powers not delegated to the United States by the Constitution, nor prohibited by it to the states, are reserved to the states respectively, or to the people."

A motion was then made to amend the preamble: but the further consideration of this motion was postponed until to-morrow. And, on the 8th of September, the consideration was resumed of this motion to amend, by preceding the preamble proposed by the House of Representatives as follows: "The conventions of a number of the states having, at the time of their adopting the Constitution, expressed a desire, in order to prevent misconstruction or abuse of its powers, that further declaratory and restrictive clauses should be added; and, as extending the grounds of public confidence in the government will best ensure the beneficent ends of its institution." The question being taken on this motion to amend, it passed in the affirmative. The preamble was then further amended in the line reading thus: "two-thirds of both houses deeming it necessary," by striking out the words "deeming it necessary" and inserting the word "concurring."

It was then moved to add the following clause to the articles of amendment: "That there are certain natural rights, of which men, when they form a social compact, cannot deprive or divest their posterity; among which are the enjoyment of life and liberty, with the means of acquiring, possessing, and protecting property, and pursuing and obtaining happiness and safety." This motion was determined in the negative.

The following propositions to add new articles of amendment were then successively made and decided in the negative.

1. That all power is naturally vested in, and, consequently, derived from, the people; that magistrates, therefore, are their trustees and agents, and, at all times, amenable to them.

2. That government ought to be instituted for the common benefit, protection, and security of the people; and that the doctrine of non-resistance against arbitrary power and oppression is absurd, slavish, and destructive of the good and happiness of mankind.

3. That no man, or set of men, are entitled to exclusive or separate public emoluments or privileges from the community, but in consideration of public services, which, not being descendible, neither ought the offices of magistrate, legislator, or judge, or any other public officer, to be hereditary.

4. That the legislative, executive, and judicial powers of government should be separate and distinct, and that the members of the two first may be restrained from oppression, by feeling and participating the public burdens: they should, at fixed periods, be reduced to a private station, return into the mass of the people, and the vacancies be supplied by certain and regular elections, in which all or any part of the former members to be eligible or ineligible, as the rules of the constitution of government and the laws shall direct.

5. That every freeman restrained of his liberty, is entitled to a remedy, to

inquire into the lawfulness thereof, and to remove the same, if unlawful, and that such remedy ought not to be denied nor delayed.

6. That every freeman ought to find a certain remedy, by recourse to the laws, for all injuries and wrongs he may receive in his person, property, or character; he ought to obtain right and justice, freely, without sale; completely, and without denial; promptly, and without delay; and that all establishments or regulations contravening these rights, are oppressive and unjust.

7. That the members of the Senate and House of Representatives shall be ineligible to, and incapable of, holding any civil office under the authority of the United States, during the time for which they shall respectively be elected.

8. That the Journals of the proceedings of the Senate and House of Representatives shall be published, at least, once in every year, except such parts thereof relating to treaties, alliances, or military operations, as, in their judgment, require secrecy.

9. That a regular statement and account of the receipts and expenditures of all public money, shall be published at least once in every year.

10. That no commercial treaty shall be ratified without the concurrence of two-thirds of the whole number of the members of the Senate; and no treaty, ceding, contracting, restraining, or suspending the territorial rights or claims of the United States, or any of them, or their, or any of their rights or claims to fishing in the American seas, or navigating the American rivers, shall be but in cases of the most urgent and extreme necessity; nor shall any such treaty be ratified without the concurrence of three-fourths of the whole number of the members of both houses respectively.

11. That no navigation law, or law regulating commerce, shall be passed without the consent of two-thirds of the members present in both houses.

12. That no standing army, or regular troops, shall be raised or kept up in time of peace, without the consent of two-thirds of the members present in both houses.

13. That no soldier shall be enlisted for any longer term than four years, except in time of war, and then for no longer term than the continuance of the war.

14. That each state, respectively, shall have the power to provide for organizing, arming, and disciplining its own militia, whensoever Congress shall omit or neglect to provide for the same; that the militia shall not be subject to martial law, except when in actual service, in time of war, invasion, or rebellion; and when not in the actual service of the United States, shall be subject only to such fines, penalties, and punishments, as shall be directed or inflicted by the laws of its own state.

15. That the exclusive power of legislation given to Congress over the federal town and its adjacent district, and other places purchased or to be purchased by Congress of any of the states, shall extend only to such regulations as respect the police and good government thereof.

16. That no person shall be capable of being President of the United States for more than eight years in any term of sixteen years.

17. That the judicial power of the United States shall be vested in one Supreme Court, and in such Courts of Admiralty as Congress may, from time to time, ordain and establish in any of the different states: the judicial powers shall extend to all cases in law and equity, arising under treaties made, or which shall be made, under the authority of the United States; to all cases affecting ambassadors, other foreign ministers, and consuls; to all cases of admiralty and maritime jurisdiction; to controversies to which the United States shall be a party; to controversies between two or more states; and between parties claiming lands under the grants of different states. In all cases affecting ambassadors, other foreign ministers, and consuls, and those in which a state shall be a party, the Supreme Court shall have original jurisdiction: in all other cases before mentioned, the Supreme Court shall have appellate jurisdiction as to matters of law only, except in cases of equity, and of admiralty and maritime jurisdiction, in which the Supreme Court shall have appellate jurisdiction, both as to law and fact, with such exceptions, and under such regulations, as the Congress shall make. But the judicial power of the United States shall extend to no case where the cause of action shall have originated before the ratification, of this Constitution; except in disputes between states about their territory; disputes between persons claiming lands under the grants of different states, and suits for debts due to the United States."

18. That Congress shall not alter, modify, or interfere in, the times, places, or manner, of holding elections for senators and representatives, or either of them, except when the legislature of any state shall neglect, refuse, or be disabled, by invasion or rebellion, to prescribe the same."

19. That some tribunal, other than the Senate, be provided for trying impeachments of senators."

20. That the salary of a judge shall not be increased or diminished during his continuance in office, otherwise than by general regulations of salary, which may take place on a revision of the subject, at stated periods of not less than seven years, to commence from the time such salaries shall be first ascertained by Congress.

All these propositions to amend having been disposed of, the further consideration of the amendments was postponed until the following day.

On the 9th of September, the subject was resumed. The third article was then amended to read as follows: "Congress shall make no law establishing articles of faith, or a mode of worship, or prohibiting the free exercise of religion, or abridging the freedom of speech, or the press, or the right of the people peaceably to assemble, and petition to the government for the redress of grievances."

The fourth article was then stricken out.

The fifth article was then again made the subject of an amendment. It was moved, to insert the words, "for the common defence," but the motion was not successful. A motion to strike out the words, "the best," in the second line, and to insert, in lieu thereof, the words, "necessary to the," prevailed. The article was then further amended, by striking out the word "fifth," after "article the," and inserting the word "fourth," and by making the article read as follows: "A well regulated militia being [necessary to] the security of a free state, the right of the people to keep and bear arms shall not be infringed."

A motion was then made, and agreed to, to alter article the sixth, so as to stand article the fifth; and article the seventh, so as to stand article the sixth; and article the eighth, so as to stand article the seventh.

The last named article was then amended, so as to read as follows: "No person shall be held to answer for a capital or otherwise infamous crime, unless on a presentment or indictment of a grand jury, except in cases arising in the land or naval forces, or in the militia, when in actual service, in time of war or public danger; nor shall any person be subject to be put in jeopardy of life or limb, for the same offence; nor shall be compelled, in any criminal case, to be a witness against himself; nor be deprived of life, liberty, or property, without due process of law; nor shall private property be taken for public use without just compensation."

The ninth article was then amended, so as to read "eighth." The tenth and eleventh articles were then stricken out; and the twelfth article was so amended as to read "ninth." This article was then so amended as to read as follows: "In suits at common law, where the value in controversy shall exceed twenty dollars, the right of trial by jury shall be preserved; and no fact, tried by a jury, shall be otherwise re-examined in any court of the United States than according to the rules of common law."

A motion was then made to reconsider article the tenth, and to restore the words following: "The trial of all crimes (except in cases of impeachment, and in cases arising in the land or naval forces, or in the militia when in actual service, in time of war or public danger,) shall be by an impartial jury of the vicinage, with the requisite of unanimity for conviction, the right of challenge, and other accustomed requisites." On this question, the yeas and nays being required, it was decided as follows:

Yeas—Messrs. Bassett, Dalton, Grayson, Gunn, Henry, Lee, Paterson, Schuyler.—8

Nays—Messrs. Carroll, Ellsworth, Johnson, Izard, King, Morris, Read, Wingate.—8.

The numbers being equal, the question was lost.

The numbers of the remaining articles were then changed, to correspond with the other changes which had been made; and the concurrence of the Senate in the resolution of the House, with amendments, was then ordered to be communicated to the House of Representatives.

Senate Debates, August—September, 1789*

[Tuesday, August 25]

*   *   *

Also, [proceeded to] the resolve of the House of Representatives, "that certain articles be proposed to the legislatures of the several States, as amendments to the constitution of the United States;" and requested the concurrence of the Senate thereof.

*   *   *

A message was received from the House of Representatives, with seventeen articles to be proposed as additions to, and amendments of the constitution of the United States.

*   *   *

[Wednesday, September 2]

*   *   *

The resolve of the House of Representatives of the 24th of August, 1789, "that certain articles be proposed to the Legislatures of the several States, as amendments to the constitution of the United States," was taken into consideration; and, on motion to amend this clause of the first article proposed by the House of Representatives, to wit: "After the first enumeration required by the first article of the constitution, there shall be one representative for every thirty thousand, until the number shall amount to one hundred," by striking out "one," and inserting "two," between the words "amount to" and "hundred."

The yeas and nays being required by one-fifth of the Senators present, the determination was as follows:

Yeas—Messrs. Dalton, Gunn, Grayson, King, Lee, and Schuyler.—6.

Nays—Messrs. Bassett, Butler, Carroll, Elisworth, Elmer, Henry, Johnson, Izard, Morris, Paterson, Read, and Wingate.—12.

So it passed in the negative.

On motion to adopt the first article proposed by the resolve of the House of Representatives, amended as follows: to strike out these words, "after which the proportion shall be so regulated by Congress, that there shall be not less than one hundred representatives, nor less than one representative for every forty thousand persons, until the number of representatives shall amount to two hundred; after which the proportion shall be so regulated by Congress, that there shall not be less than two hundred representatives, nor

Annals of Congress, Vol. 1, pp. 73–80.

less than one representative for every fifty thousand persons;" and to substitute the following clause after the words "one hundred: " to wit, "to which number one representative shall be added for every subsequent increase of forty thousand, until the representatives shall amount to two hundred, to which one representative shall be added for every subsequent increase of sixty thousand persons: " it passed in the affirmative.

[Friday, September 4]

The Senate proceeded in the consideration of the resolve of the House of Representatives of the 24th of August, on "Articles to be proposed to the Legislatures of the several States, as amendments to the constitution of the United States."

[Monday, September 7]

*   *   *

The Senate resumed the consideration of the resolve of the House of Representatives of the 24th of August, on "Articles to be proposed to the Legislatures of the several States as amendments to the constitution of the United States."

On motion to adopt the twelfth article of the amendments proposed by the House of Representatives, amended by the addition of these words to the article, to wit: "where the consideration exceeds twenty dollars;" it passed in the affirmative.

On motion to adopt the thirteenth article of the amendments proposed by the House of Representatives, it passed in the affirmative.

On motion to adopt the fourteenth article of the amendments proposed by the House of Representatives: it passed in the negative.

In the consideration of the fifteenth article proposed by the House of Representatives, on motion to add the following to the proposed amendments, to wit: "That the General Government of the United States ought never to impose direct taxes but where the moneys arising from the duties, impost, and excise are insufficient for the public exigencies, nor then, until Congress shall have made a requisition upon the States to assess, levy, and pay their respective portions of such requisitions; and in case any State shall neglect or refuse to pay its proportion, pursuant to such requisition, then Congress may assess and levy such State's proportion, together with interest thereon, at the rate of six per cent. per annum, from the time of payment prescribed by such requisition;" it passed in the negative.

On motion to add the following to the proposed amendments, viz: "That the third section of the sixth article of the Constitution of the United States ought to be amended, by inserting the word "other" between the words "no" and "religious: " it passed in the negative.

[Tuesday, September 8]

The Senate proceeded in the consideration of the resolve of the House of Representatives of the 24th of August, "On articles to be proposed to the Legislatures of the several States as amendments to the constitution of the United States." Several amendments were proposed, but none of them were agreed to. The subject was postponed till to-morrow.

*   *   *

[Wednesday, September 9]

The Senate proceeded in the consideration of the resolve of the House of Representatives on the articles to be proposed to the Legislatures of the several States as amendments to the constitution, and agreed to a part of them, and disagreed to others; of which they informed the House.

*   *   *

Madison to Pendleton, 1789*

Sept. 14, 1789

Dear Sir,

I was favd. on saturday with yours of the 2d instant. The Judiciary is now under consideration. I view it as you do, as defective both in its general structure, and many of its particular regulations. The attachment of the Eastern members, the difficulty of substituting another plan, with the consent of those who agree in disliking the bill, the defect of time &c, will however prevent any radical alterations. The most I hope is that some offensive violations of Southern jurisprudence may be corrected, and that the system may speedily undergo a reconsideration under the auspices of the Judges who alone will be able perhaps to set it to rights.

The Senate have sent back the plan of amendments with some alterations which strike in my opinion at the most salutary articles. In many of the States juries even in criminal cases, are taken from the State at large, in others from districts of considerable extent; in very few from the County alone. Hence a [torn out] like to the restraint with respect to vicinage, which has produced a negative on that clause. A fear of inconvenience from a constitutional bar to appeals below a certain value, and a confidence that such a limitation is not necessary, have had the same effect on another article. Several others have had a similar fate. The difficulty of uniting the minds of men accustomed to think and act differently can only be conceived by those who have witnessed it.

*The Writings of James Madison, Vol. 5, pp. 420–21.

A very important question is depending on the subject of a permanent seat for the fedl. Govt. Early in the Session secret negociations were set on foot among the Northern States, from Penna., inclusively. The parties finally disagreeing in their arrangements, both made advances to the Southern members. On the side of N.Y. & N. Engd., we were led to expect the Susquehannah within a reasonable time, if we wd. sit still in N. York, otherwise we were threatened with Trenton. These terms were inadmissible to the friends of Potowmac. On the side of Penna., who was full of distrust and animosity agst. N. Engd. & N. York, the Potowmac was presented as the reward for the temporary advantages if given by the S. States. Some progress was made on this ground, and the prospect became flattering, when a reunion was produced among the original parties by circumstances which it wd. be tedious to explain. The Susquehannah has in consequence been voted. The bill is not yet brought in and many things may yet happen. We shall parry any decision if we can, tho' I see little hope of attaining our own object, the Eastern States being inflexibly opposed to the Potowmac & for some reasons which are more likely to grow stronger than weaker; and if we are to be placed on the Susquehannah, the sooner the better.

CONFERENCE AND FINAL PASSAGE, SEPTEMBER, 1789

Commentary

On September 10, 1789, the House received the Senate's message that it had agreed to the House amendments, "with several amendments; to which they desire the concurrence of this House." The House considered the subject on September 19 and 21. On the latter date, they voted on the Senate changes, "some of which they agreed to, and disagreed to others." The House then resolved that "a committee of conference was desired with the Senate, on the subject matter of the amendments disagreed to." Madison, Sherman, and Vining (the three members who had played the largest part in the House debate) were appointed managers on the part of the House, and Oliver Ellsworth, Charles Carroll, and William Paterson as Senate conferees. Some of the problems dealt with by the conferees may be seen in Madison's letter to Pendleton (*infra* p. 1166).

On September 23, Madison made the Conference Report to the House. It provided that the House would accept all the Senate amendments, and provided for three further changes. The first was a minor alteration in the amendment on representation. The third gave the final form to the Sixth Amendment and reincluded in it the right to a jury trial of the locality (though not restricted to the vicinage) which the Senate had omitted. The second change made by the Conference Committee was of great importance— to replace the weakened Senate version of the religious freedom guarantee by the simple yet strict prohibitions of what are now the Establishment and Free Exercise Clauses of the First Amendment. Without a doubt, this final version of the first guarantee of the First Amendment was written by Madison; it repeats his earlier House version which the Senate had diluted. As Irving Brant puts it, "Of all the versions of the religious guarantee, this most directly covered the thing he was aiming at—absolute separation of church and state and total exclusion of government aid to religion." Madison's success in having the Conference Committee adopt his version of the religious freedom guarantee marked a fitting culmination of his role in the Bill of Rights debate.

On September 24, the House voted 37 to 14 to agree to the Conference Report. On the same day, Ellsworth made the Conference Report to the Senate. The next day, the Senate concurred in the amendments as voted by the House and acquiesced in a House resolution requesting the President to transmit copies of the amendments to the states. September 25 (the day on which the congressional approval was completed) is celebrated as the anniversary of the Bill of Rights. The form in which the amendments finally passed Congress appears (*infra* p. 1164). Apart from the first two Articles (which failed of state ratification), these amendments (renumbered to reflect the non-ratification of the first two) now constitute the federal Bill of Rights.

House of Representatives Journal, September, 1789*

On the 19th of September, the House of Representatives made some progress in the consideration of the amendments made by the Senate: and, on the 21st, the House adopted the following resolutions:

Resolved—That this house doth agree to the second, fourth, eighth, twelfth, thirteenth, sixteenth, eighteenth, nineteenth, twenty-fifth, and twenty-sixth amendments: and doth disagree to the first, third, fifth, sixth, seventh, ninth, tenth, eleventh, fourteenth, fifteenth, seventeenth, twentieth, twenty-first, twenty-second, twenty-third, and twenty-fourth amendments, proposed by the Senate to the said articles, two-thirds of the members present concurring on each vote:

Resolved—That a conference be desired with the Senate on the subject matter of the amendments disagreed to, and that Mr. Madison, Mr. Sherman, and Mr. Vining, be appointed managers of the same on the part of this house.

On receiving these resolutions from the house, the Senate determined to recede from their third amendment, and to insist on all the others: at the same time the Senate passed the following resolution:

Resolved—That the Senate do concur with the House of Representatives in a conference on the subject matter of disagreement on the said articles of amendment, and that Messrs. Ellsworth, Carroll, and Paterson, be managers of the conference on the part of the Senate.

On the 23d, Mr. Madison made a report to the House of Representatives on the subject, which was taken up for consideration on the 24th; whereupon,

Resolved—That this house doth recede from their disagreement to the first, third, fifth, sixth, seventh, ninth, tenth, eleventh, fourteenth, fifteenth, seventeenth, twentieth, twenty-first, twenty-second, twenty-third, and twenty-fourth amendments, insisted on by the Senate: Provided, That the two articles which by the amendments of the Senate are now proposed to be inserted as the third and eighth articles, shall be amended to read as followeth:

Article the third. Congress shall make no law respecting an establishment of religion, or prohibiting the free exercise thereof; or abridging the freedom of speech, or of the press; or the right of the people peaceably to assemble, and to petition the government for a redress of grievances.

Article the eighth. In all criminal prosecutions, the accused shall enjoy the right to a speedy and public trial, by an impartial jury of the state and district wherein the crime shall have been committed; which district shall have been previously ascertained by law, and to be informed of the nature and cause of the accusation; to be confronted with the witnesses against him;

*History of Congress Exhibiting a Classification of the Proceedings of the Senate and the House of Representatives from March 4, 1789 to March 3, 1793, pp. 169–70.

to have compulsory process for obtaining witnesses in his favour; and to have the assistance of counsel for his defence.

And provided, also, That the first article be amended by striking out the word "less," in the last place of the said first article, and inserting, in lieu thereof, the word "more".

The question on agreeing to the alteration and amendment of the eighth article, to make it read as above, being taken by ayes and noes, was determined by the following vote:

Ayes—Messrs. Ames, Baldwin, Benson, Boudinot, Brown, Cadwalader, Carroll, Clymer, Contee, Fitzsimons, Foster, Gale, Gilman, Goodhue, Griffin, Hartley, Lee, Leonard, Madison, jr., Moore, Muhlenberg, Parker, Partridge, Schureman, Scott, Seney, Sherman, Silvester, Sinnickson, Smith, of Maryland, Smith, of South Carolina, Stone, Thatcher, Trumbull, Vining, White, Wynkoop.—37.

Noes—Messrs. Bland, Burke, Coles, Floyd, Gerry, Grout, Hathorn, Jackson, Livermore, Mathews, Page, Van Rensselaer, Sumpter, Tucker.—14.

The house then passed the following resolution:

Resolved—That the President of the United States be requested to transmit to the executives of the several states, which have ratified the Constitution, copies of the amendments proposed by Congress to be added thereto; and like copies to the executives of the states of Rhode Island and North Carolina.

House of Representatives Debates, September, 1789*

[Thursday, September 10]

A message from the Senate informed the House, that the Senate have agreed to the resolution of this House, of the second ultimo, containing certain articles to be proposed by Congress to the Legislatures of the several States, as amendments to the constitution of the United States, with several amendments; to which they desire the concurrence of this House.

*   *   *

[Saturday, September 19]

*   *   *

The House then took into consideration the amendments to the Constitution, as amended by the Senate; and, after some time spent thereon, the business was postponed till to-morrow.

*   *   *

[Monday, September 21]

*   *   *

The House then resumed the consideration of the amendments proposed by the Senate to the several articles of amendments to the Constitution of the United States; some of which they agreed to, and disagreed to others, two-thirds of the members present concurring in each vote: whereupon, a committee of conference was desired with the Senate, on the subject matter of the amendments disagreed to; and Messrs. Madison, Sherman, and Vining were appointed managers on the part of the House.

*   *   *

[Thursday, September 24]

*   *   *

Amendments to the Constitution

The House proceeded to consider the report of a Committee of Conference, on the subject matter of the amendments depending between the two Houses to the seversl articles of amendment to the Constitution of the United States, as proposed by this House: whereupon, it was resolved, that they recede from their disagreement to all the amendments; provided that the two articles, which, by the amendments of the Senate, are now proposed to be inserted as the third and eighth articles, shall be amended to read as follows:

Art. 3. Congress shall make no law respecting an establishment of religion, or prohibiting a free exercise thereof, or abridging the freedom of speech, or of the press, or the right of the people peaceably to assemble, and to petition the Government for a redress of grievances.

Art. 8. In all criminal prosecutions, the accused shall enjoy the right to a speedy and public trial, by an impartial jury of the State and district wherein the crime shall have been committed, which district shall have been previously ascertained by law; and to be informed of the nature and cause of the accusation—to be confronted with the witnesses against him—to have compulsory process for obtaining witnesses in his favor, and to have the assistance of counsel for his defence.

And provided also, that the first article be amended, by striking out the word "less" in the last place of the said article, and inserting, in lieu thereof, "more."

On the question that the House agree to the alteration of the eighth article, in the manner aforesaid, the yeas and nays were called, and are as follow:

Yeas—Messrs. Ames, Baldwin, Benson, Boudinot, Brown, Cadwalader, Carroll, Clymer, Contee, Fitzsimons, Foster, Gale, Gilman, Goodhue, Griffin, Hartley, Lee, Leonard, Madison, Moore, Muhlenberg, Parker, Partridge, Schureman, Scott, Seney, Sherman, Sylvester, Sinnickson, Smith, (of Maryland,) Smith, (of South Carolina,) Stone, Thatcher, Trumbull, Vining, White, and Wynkoop.—37.

Nays—Messrs. Bland, Burke, Coles, Floyd, Gerry, Grom, Harthorn, Jackson, Livermore, Matthews, Page, Van Rensselaer, Sumter, and Tucker.—14.

On motion, it was resolved, that the President of the United States be requested to transmit to the Executives of the several States which have ratified the Constitution, copies of the amendments proposed by Congress, to be added thereto, and like copies to the Executives of the States of Rhode Island and North Carolina.

*   *   *

Senate Journal, September, 1789*

In the Senate, on the 24th, Mr. Ellsworth made the following report:

That it will be proper for the House of Representatives to agree to the said amendments, proposed by the Senate, with an amendment to their fifth amendment, so that the third article shall read as follows: "Congress shall make no law respecting an establishment of religion, or prohibiting the free exercise thereof; or abridging the freedom of speech, or of the press, or the right of the people peaceably to assemble, and petition the government for a redress of grievances:" and, with an amendment to the fourteenth amendment proposed by the Senate, so that the eighth article, as numbered in the amendments proposed by the Senate, shall read as follows: "In all criminal prosecutions, the accused shall enjoy the right to a speedy and public trial, by an impartial jury of the district wherein the crime shall have been committed, as the district shall have been previously ascertained by law, and to be informed of the nature and cause of the accusation; to be confronted with the witnesses against him; and to have compulsory process for obtaining witnesses in his favour; and to have the assistance of counsel for his defence."

The managers were also of opinion that it would be proper for both houses to agree to amend the first article, by striking out the word "less" in the last line but one, and inserting in its place the word "more," and, accordingly, recommend that the said article be reconsidered for that purpose.

This report was ordered to lie for consideration. In the mean time, the resolutions of the House were communicated to the Senate; and on the 25th, the Senate adopted the following resolution:

"Resolved—That the Senate do concur in the amendments proposed by the House of Representatives to the amendments of the Senate."

And on the following day, the Senate acquiesced in the resolution of the

*History of Congress Exhibiting a Classification of the Proceedings of the Senate and the House of Representatives from March 4, 1789, to March 3, 1793, pp. 171–73.

House, requesting the President of the United States to transmit copies of the amendments to the executives of the respective states.

The form in which the amendments finally passed the two houses, is as follows:

Proposed Amendments to the Constitution

> The conventions of a number of the states having, at the time of their adopting the Constitution, expressed a desire, in order to prevent misconstruction or abuse of its powers, that further declaratory and restrictive clauses should be added; and as extending the ground of public confidence in the government will best ensure the beneficent ends of its institution—

Resolved by the Senate and House of Representatives of the United States of America, in Congress assembled, two-thirds of both houses concurring— That the following articles be proposed to the legislatures of the several states, as amendments to the Constitution of the United States, all or any of which articles, when ratified by three-fourths of the said legislatures, to be valid, to all intents and purposes, as part of the said Constitution, viz:

Articles in addition to, and amendment of, the Constitution of the United States of America, proposed by Congress, and ratified by the legislatures of the several states, pursuant to the fifth article of the original Constitution:

Article I. After the first enumeration, required by the first article of the Constitution, there shall be one representative for every thirty thousand, until the number shall amount to one hundred; after which, the proportion shall be so regulated by Congress, that there shall be not less than one hundred representatives, nor less than one representative for every forty thousand persons, until the number of representatives shall amount to two hundred; after which, the proportion shall be so regulated by Congress, that there shall not be less than two hundred representatives, nor more than one representative for every fifty thousand persons.

Art. II. No law, varying the compensation for the services of the senators and representatives, shall take effect until an election of representatives shall have intervened.

Art. III. Congress shall make no law respecting an establishment of religion, or prohibiting the free exercise thereof, or abridging the freedom of speech, or of the press, or the right of the people peaceably to assemble, and to petition the government for a redress of grievances.

Art. IV. A well regulated militia being necessary to the security of a free state, the right of the people to keep and bear arms shall not be infringed.

Art. V. No soldier shall, in time of peace, be quartered in any house, without the consent of the owner, nor in time or war, but in a manner to be prescribed by law.

Art. VI. The right of the people to be secure in their persons, houses, papers, and effects, against unreasonable searches and seizures, shall not be violated; and no warrants shall issue but upon probable cause, supported by oath or affirmation, and particularly describing the place to be searched, and the persons or things to be seized.

Art. VII. No person shall be held to answer for a capital or otherwise infamous crime, unless on a presentment or indictment of a grand jury, except in cases arising in the land or naval forces, or in the militia when in actual service, in time of war or public danger; nor shall any person be subject, for the same offence, to be twice put in jeopardy of life or limb; nor shall be compelled, in any criminal case, to be a witness against himself; nor be deprived of life, liberty, or property, without due process of law; nor shall private property be taken for public use without just compensation.

Art. VIII. In all criminal prosecutions, the accused shall enjoy the right to a speedy and public trial by an impartial jury of the state and district wherein the crime shall have been committed, which district shall have been previously ascertained by law; and to be informed of the nature and cause of the accusation; to be confronted with the witnesses against him; to have compulsory process for obtaining witnesses in his favour; and to have the assistance of counsel for his defence.

Art. IX. In suits at common law, where the value in controversy shall exceed twenty dollars, the right of trial by jury shall be preserved; and no fact, tried by a jury, shall be otherwise re-examined in any court of the United States, than according to the rules of common law.

Art. X. Excessive bail shall not be required, nor excessive fines imposed, nor cruel and unusual punishments inflicted.

Art. XI. The enumeration in the Constitution of certain rights, shall not be construed to deny or disparage others retained by the people.

Art. XII. The powers not delegated to the United States by the Constitution, nor prohibited by it to the states, are reserved to the states respectively, or to the people.

Frederick Augustus Muhlenberg,
Speaker of the House of Representatives
John Adams,
Vice-President of the United States,
and President of the Senate

Attest, John Beckley, Clerk of the House of Representatives
Samuel A. Otis, Secretary of the Senate

Senate Debates, September, 1789*

[Monday, September 21]

*   *   *

A message from the House of Representatives brought up a resolve of the House of this date, to agree to the 2d, 4th, 8th, 12th, 13th, 16th, 18th, 19th, 25th, and 26th amendments, proposed by the Senate, to "Articles of amend-

Annals of Congress, Vol. 1, pp. 85–90.

ment to be proposed to the Legislatures of the several States, as amendments
to the constitution of the United States;" and to disagree to the 1st, 3d, 5th,
6th, 7th, 9th, 10th, 11th, 14th, 15th, 17th, 20th, 21st, 22d, 23d, and 24th
amendments: two-thirds of the members present concurring on each vote;
and "that a conference be desired with the Senate on the subject matter of
the amendments disagreed to," and that Messrs. Madison, Sherman, and
Vining, be appointed managers of the same on the part of the House of
Representatives.

*   *   *

[Friday, September 25]

*   *   *

A message from the House of Representatives informed the Senate that
the House of Representatives had passed a resolve, requesting "the President
of the United States to transmit to the Executives of the several States which
have ratified the constitution, copies of the amendments proposed by Congress to be added thereto; and like copies to the Executives of the States of
Rhode Island and North Carolina;" and that the House requested the
concurrence of the Senate therein.

*   *   *

The Senate proceeded to consider the message from the House of Representatives of the 24th, with amendments to the amendments of the Senate
to "Articles to be proposed to the Legislatures of the several States, as
amendments to the constitution of the United States;" and,
Resolved, That the Senate do concur in the amendments proposed by the
House of Representatives to the amendments of the Senate.

*   *   *

Madison to Pendleton, 1789*

Sept. 23, 1789

Dear Sir,

The pressure of unfinished business has suspended the adjournment of
Congs. till saturday next. Among the articles which required it was the plan
of amendments, on which the two Houses so far disagreed as to require
conferences. It will be impossible I find to prevail on the Senate to concur in
the limitation on the value of appeals to the Supreme Court, which they say
is unnecessary, and might be embarrassing in questions of national or Constitutional importance in their principle, tho' of small pecuniary amount. They
are equally inflexible in opposing a definition of the locality of Juries. The
vicinage they contend is either too vague or too strict a term, too vague if
depending on limits to be fixed by the pleasure of the law, too strict if limited
to the County. It was proposed to insert after the word Juries, "with the

*The Writings of James Madison, Vol. 5, p. 424.

accustomed requisites," leaving the definition to be construed according to the judgment of professional men. Even this could not be obtained. The truth is that in most of the States the practice is different, and hence the irreconcileable difference of ideas on the subject. In some States, jurors are drawn from the whole body of the community indiscriminately; in others, from large districts comprehending a number of Counties; and in a few only from a single County. The Senate suppose also that the provision for vicinage in the Judiciary bill, will sufficiently quiet the fears which called for an amendment on this point. On a few other points in the plan the Senate refuse to join the House of Reps.

The Bill of Rights and the State Ratifying Conventions*

Table Showing which Bill of Rights Guarantees were Contained in State Proposed Amendments

Bill of Rights Guarantees	Penn.	Mass.	Maryland Majority	Maryland Minority	S.C.	N.H.	N.Y.	Va.	N.C.	Total number of states
Religious freedom	x			x		x	x	x	x	6
Free speech	x						x	x		3
Free press	x		x				x	x	x	5
Assembly and petition				x			x	x	x	4
Right to bear arms	x			x	x			x	x	5
Quartering soldiers			x			x	x	x	x	5
Searches and seizures	x		x				x	x	x	5
Grand jury indictment			x			x	x			3
Double jeopardy			x				x			2
Self incrimination	x						x		x	3
Due process	x						x	x	x	4
Just compensation										0
Speedy public trial	x						x	x	x	4
Jury trial	x		x				x	x	x	5
Cause and nature of accusation	x							x	x	3
Confrontation	x							x	x	3
Witnesses	x							x	x	3
Counsel	x							x	x	3
Jury trial (civil)	x	x	x			x	x	x	x	7
Bail	x						x	x	x	4
Fines	x						x	x	x	4
Punishment	x						x	x	x	4
Rights retained by people							x	x	x	3
Reserved powers	x	x	x		x	x	x	x	x	8

*Derived from E. Dumbauld, *The Bill of Rights* (1957), pp. 160–65.

PART EIGHT
RATIFICATION BY THE STATES

RATIFICATION BY THE STATES

Commentary

On October 2, 1789, President Washington officially transmitted the proposed amendments to the states for ratification. (His letter to Governor Huntington of Connecticut [*infra* p. 1172] follows this commentary as an illustration of these transmittal letters). Thus began the process of ratification of the Bill of Rights by the states. The ratification process ended with the official notice sent by Secretary of State Jefferson on March 1, 1792, to the Governors of the several states, announcing that three-fourths of the state legislatures had ratified the first ten amendments.

The Jefferson letter (*infra* p. 1203) may appear to us a singular way of announcing the ratification of what many now consider the most consequential part of the Constitution itself. Yet it bears out the point already made (*supra* p. 1051) about the congressional reluctance to devote the time needed for consideration of the proposed amendments. In addition, it may help explain the lack of materials on the ratification debates in the states.

It is amazing, considering the crucial significance of the Bill of Rights, that we know practically nothing about what went on in the state legislatures during the ratification process. At the time, there was nothing in the states comparable even to the *Annals of Congress*, which reported, however sketchily, proceedings and debates in the federal legislature. Even the contemporary newspapers are virtually silent on the ratification debates in the states. Nor is this to be explained by the fact that ratification was a mere perfunctory matter, since there was virtually no opposition in the state legislatures. The first two of the amendments proposed by Congress were never ratified, being rejected or postponed by five of the states which ratified the Bill of Rights (Delaware, New Hampshire, New Jersey, New York, and Pennsylvania). Certainly, there must have been some sharp debates in those states on the matter.

Even in the states which ratified all twelve proposed amendments, there must have been sharp division and debate. We know this from the fragmentary knowledge we have of the Virginia ratification. The Virginia legislature began its consideration of the amendments in October, 1789, but it was not until December, 1791, that Virginia could announce its ratification. As the letter from Lee to Hamilton (*infra* p. 1186) puts it, "The antifederal gentlemen in our assembly do not relish the amendments," and they were able, as others of the letters reproduced show, to secure the temporary rejection of the amendments. It is unfortunate that we do not have any report of the debates which led to this result, other than the fragmentary glimpses in the newspaper excerpts and letters which follow this commentary.

The materials which are reproduced contain, besides the Washington and Jefferson letters referred to and some letters on the 1789 debates in the Virginia legislature, the official notices of ratification by the states, as well as extracts from contemporary newspapers and legislative materials relating to Massachusetts.

The documents on the action taken by the Massachusetts Legislature (*infra* p. 1174) pose a historical problem. Massachusetts was one of the three states which did not send official notice of ratification to the President. Yet the extracts reproduced from the *Journals* of the Massachusetts Legislature indicate plainly that it approved all but three of the proposed amendments—the first, second, and twelfth. This would mean that the Massachusetts Legislature did adopt what became the first nine amendments. Why then was Massachusetts not included in the states which ratified? The question also puzzled Secretary of State Jefferson, for he wrote Christopher Gore of Boston on August 8, 1791, to inquire what had happened. Gore's answer (*infra* p. 1175) bears out the cryptic account in the Journal extracts. Apparently, the two Houses failed to vote any bill declaring that they had assented to the amendments; indeed, the committee appointed for that purpose did not report any bill. All this raises a nice legal point. When the Constitution, in Article V, requires an amendment to be ratified by a state legislature, it would seem that all that is required is the affirmative vote in favor by the two houses concerned. The further passage of a bill declaring ratification would appear a superfluous formality. If that is the case, Massachusetts did actually ratify the first nine amendments, though official notice was not sent to New York, then the nation's capital.

The state ratifications themselves began with that of Maryland early in 1790. They ended when Virginia became the tenth state to ratify at the end of 1791. Only ten of the amendments were ratified by the required three-fourths of the states. Articles I and II, as already stated, were not ratified. The three states, which had not officially ratified, Connecticut, Georgia, and Massachusetts, belatedly did so in 1939. This had, of course, only symbolic effect; the Bill of Rights officially had become part of the Constitution upon the completion of Virginia's ratification on December 15, 1791.

President Washington to Samuel Huntington, Governor of Connecticut, 1789*

Oct. 2, 1789

In pursuance of the enclosed resolution I have the honor to transmit to your Excellency a copy of the amendments proposed to be added to the Constitution of the United States.

I have the honor to be with due consideration Your Excellency's most obedient Servant.

*Original in private collection. Identical letters were sent to the Governors of all the other states.

Resolution

Congress of the United States, In the House of Representatives,
Thursday, the 24th of September 1789

Resolved by the Senate and the House of Representatives of the United States of America in Congress assembled, that the President of the United States be requested to transmit to the Executives of the several States which have ratified the Constitution, Copies of the Amendments proposed by Congress, to be added thereto; and like Copies to the Executives of the States of Rhode Island and North Carolina.

Attest,

John Beckley, Clerk

United States of America
In Senate, September the 26th 1789

Resolved, that the Senate do concur in this Resolution.

Attest,

Sam. A. Otis, Secy.

[Then followed the text of the twelve proposed amendments.]

Governor John Hancock to
the Massachusetts Legislature, 1790*

Jan. 14, 1970

Gentlemen of the Senate and Gentlemen of the House of Representatives.

Since the adjournment of the General Court I have received the acts of the Congress of the United States of America, passed in their first session, and I have directed the Secretary to lay them before you.

As these acts begin a system of government in which the prosperity of each State in particular, as well as that of all the States in general is concerned, they will command your careful attention.

Amongst the acts of Congress, you will observe one which proposes certain articles of amendments to the constitution of the United States. As it is the ardent wish of every patriot, that the plan may be as compleat as human wisdom can effect it, This resolve, I am confident, will demand your serious and careful attention.

*   *   *

Speech by Governor Hancock to
the Massachusetts Legislature, January 19, 1790†

The acts and proceedings of Congress . . . contain propositions for amendments in the constitution of the United States: these are submitted to your

*D. P. Myers, *Massachusetts and the First Ten Amendments* (1936), p. 9.
†*Massachusetts and the First Ten Amendments*, p. 10.

deliberations, on the part of our Constituents; and there can be no necessity of any other call to awaken your attention, than the interest they have in them.

I shall not be particular in my remarks on these propositions.

As Government is no other than the united consent of the people of a civil community, to be governed in a particular mode, by certain established principles, the more general the union of sentiment is, the more energetic and permanent the government will be. Upon this idea, the adoption of some of the proposed amendments becomes very important; because the people of this Commonwealth felt themselves assured by the proceedings of their Convention, which ratified the Constitution, that certain amendments, amongst which were some of those, would be effected: The seventh, eighth & ninth articles appear to me to be of great consequence. In all free governments, a share in the administration of the laws ought to be vested in, or reserved to the people; this prevents a government from verging towards despotism, secures the freedom of debate, and supports that independence of sentiment which dignifies the citizen, and renders the government permanently respectable. The institutions of Grand and Petit Juries are admirably calculated to produce these happy effects, and to afford security to the best rights of men in civil Society: These articles therefore, I believe, will meet your ready approbation. Some of the others appear to me as very important to that personal security, which is so truly characteristick of a free Government.

Massachusetts Senate and House Journals, 1790*

[Senate, January 28]

Ordered that Friday 10.0 Clock be assigned for taking up the proposed amendments to the Federal Constitution. . . .

[January 29]

The Amendments proposed by Congress to the U.S. Constitution were taken up—and the Senate rejected the 1 & 2 and accepted the 3, 4, 5, 6, 7, 8, 9, 11, & 12, and ordered that Mesrs. Bridge & Lyman, with such to be a Com. to bring in a bill or resolve declaring their adoption—Sent down for concurrence. Came up concurred except the 12. which is rejected & Mesrs. Sponner, Jarvis & Bacon joined—Concurred. . . .

[House, January 29]

The amendments proposed by the Congress of the United States to be added to the Federal Constitution were taken up and considered whereupon

*Massachusetts Senate and House Journals, Vol. 10 (May, 1789–March, 1790).

the Senate rejected the first and second proposed amendment and agree to adopt the third, fourth, fifth, sixth, seventh, eighth, ninth, tenth, eleventh, and twelvth and ordered that Eben Bridge & Wm. Lyman Esqrs. with such as the Hon. House may join be a Committee to report a Bill or Resolve for the purpose of declaring the adoption thereof. Sent down for Concurrence. . . .

[January 30]

The House assigned Tuesday next 11 oClk A M for considering the amendments proposed to be added to the Constitution of the united States. . . .

[February 2]

The House proceeded, according to assignment, to consider the amendments of the constitution of the United States, as recommended by Congress, and the question being taken upon each of them the following were accepted viz The third, fourth, fifth, sixth, seventh, eighth, ninth, tenth & eleventh. The first and second were not accepted. The House then postponed the further consideration of the twelfth article to the afternoon. . . .

The House proceeded to the consideration of the twelfth article in the amendments of the Constitution of the United States, as recommended by Congress, and the question being put whether the House would accept the same, it passed in the negative. The proceedings of the House were then entered on the proceedings of the Senate & Dr. [Charles] Jarvis, Mesrs. Bacon & Spooner were joined to the Committee therein mentioned. Sent up for concurrence. . . .

Christopher Gore to Jefferson, 1791*

Boston, Aug. 18, 1791

Sir—

Immediately on receit of your favor of the 8. inst I applied to the office of the Secretary of the Commonwealth, for a copy of the supposed act, ratifying the amendments proposed by Congress—The Secretary inform'd me, that no such act ever passed the legislature of Massachusetts—The manner in which the business was acted upon, and the state, in which it was left by the General Court, appears, from their journals, to be as follows—The Senate agreed to all the amendments except the 1st & 2d—the House concurr'd except as to the 12th The Senate agreed to the alteration of the house, & appointed two of their body, with such as the house should join, to bring in a bill declaratory of their assent—the house joined one of their members to the

*Massachusetts and the First Ten Amendments, p. 8.

committee—It does not appear that the Committee ever reported any bill—with great respect, I have the honor to be your Excellency's very obed servt.

C. Gore

New York Journal and Weekly Register Account of Actions Taken on Constitutional Amendments, 1789–90

[October 29, 1789]

Providence, Oct. 17 . . . We learn that his Excellency the Governor has received a letter from the President of the United States, enclosing a copy of the proposed amendments to the new constitution; and that the General assembly of this state, now setting at East Greenwich, have ordered them printed, and sent to the several towns for consideration.

[November 19]

The New-Jersey Journal says: We hear from Amboy, that the proposed amendments to the constitution of the United States, have been under consideration of the Legislature, and will be all agreed to except the second article.

[December 10]

In the general assembly of Pennsylvania, on the 30th ult. the committee of the whole went into further consideration of the first and second amendments proposed to be added to the constitution of the United States. A variety of opinion prevailing as to both these articles, it was deemed most proper that the consideration of them should be postponed, that the members might have further time to reflect on them. The committee therefore rose, reported progress, asked, and obtained leave to sit again. As the session is nearly drawing to a close, it is conjectured that nothing will finally be determined in this business, until the house meet again, which will probably be sometime in February next.

*   *   *

Extract of a letter received from Annapolis (Maryland) to a gentleman in Baltimore, dated 21st November:

> . . . The Amendments recommended by Congress, were unanimously adopted by our House on Wednesday last.

[December 24]

The house of delegates of Virginia have agreed to the amendments to the constitution of the United States, which were proposed at the late session of

Congress—It is said, however, that a question of postponement was agitated in the senate, for four of the articles; whether this was agreed to, and concurred by the house of delegates, we have not learnt.

*　　　*　　　*

[January 14, 1790]

Governor George Clinton to the N.Y. Legislature

*　　　*　　　*

The Amendments to the Constitution of the United States, and the other Communications which have been made to me in your Recess by the Direction of Congress, will be submitted to your Consideration with this Message.

*　　　*　　　*

Ordered; that said message of his excellency the Governor, and sundry matters which accompanied the same, be committed to a committee of the whole house.

[January 28]

Legislature of the State of New York
House of Assembly

Jan. 21 . . . Went into committee on the Governor's message; Mr. Watts in the chair.

The committee, after having the proposed amendments to the constitution read, rose, and desired leave to sit again.

*　　　*　　　*

[January 22]

A resolution was agreed to, that it should be the order of the day on Tuesday next, to take up the proposed amendments to the constitution.

[January 26]

The order of the day was then read, when the house resolved itself into a committee of the whole on the amendments proposed by Congress to the Constitution of the United States;

Mr. Watts in the chair.

The several articles having been read and considered, were approved of, excepting the second, which is in the words following:

"Art. 2d. No law varying the compensation for the services of the Senators and Representatives, shall take effect, until an election of Representatives shall have intervened."

The committee divided on the question.

For approving there appeared:

Mr. Speaker,	Mr. Giles,
Mr. King,	Mr. Lewis.—5.
Mr. Scudder,	

Against it:

Mr. Clarkson,	Mr. Barker,
Mr. Will,	Mr. Crane, jun.
Mr. Randall,	Mr. Morgan,
Mr. Post,	Mr. Rowan,
Mr. Childs,	Mr. Savage,
Mr. J. Smith,	Mr. S. V. Rensselaer,
Mr. Landon,	Mr. H. V. Rensselaer,
Mr. Clowse,	Mr. Younglove,
Mr. Cornwell,	Mr. Van Cortlandt,
Mr. J. Brown,	Mr. Sickles,
Mr. Arndt,	Mr. Coe,
Mr. Converse,	Mr. Marvin,
Mr. Gardner,	Mr. Crane,
Mr. Havens,	Mr. Myers,
Mr. Schooumaker,	Mr. M'Mster,
Mr. Clark,	Mr. Tillotson,
Mr. Bruyn,	Mr. Veeder,
Mr. N. Smith,	Mr. Livingston,
Mr. Jones,	Mr. Carpenter,
Mr. Carman,	Mr. Hitchcock,
Mr. Vandervoort,	Mr. Talmon,
Mr. Wynant,	Mr. Tappen,
Mr. Rockwell,	Mr. Gilbert,
Mr. Horton,	Mr. Van Vechter,
Mr. Griffin,	Mr. Seaman.—52.

The committee rose, and the house appointed Messrs. King, Jones, Havens, Livingston, and Gilbert to prepare the form of a ratification.

[January 28]

On the 9th inst. his Excellency the Governor of Massachusetts made a speech to both houses of the Legislature. In this speech his Excellency, among many important matters, mentions the amendments to the Constitution of the United States on which he observes: —"In all free governments, a share in the administration of the laws aught to be vested in, or reserved to the people; this prevents a government from verging towards despotism, se- cures the freedom of debate, and supports that independence of sentiment, which dignifies the citizen, and renders the government permanently respectable. The instutitions of grand and petit Juries are admirably calculated to produce these happy effects, and to afford security to the best rights of men in civil society: These articles, therefore, I believe will meet your ready approbation: Some of the others appear to me as very important to that personal security which is so truly characteristic of a free government. After speaking of the state of the union, he observes: — "Notwithstanding a general government is well established by the free consent of the people, we are to continue to support our own government, with unabating anxiety for its welfare and prosperity: indeed, the general government of the United States is founded in an assemblage of republican governments; and it depends essentially on these, not only for its dignity and energy, but for its very existence in the form it now possesses; therefore, whatever is done to support the commonwealth, has a tendency to advance the interest and honor of all the states. Hence we are called upon in an especial manner, to maintain an equal and regular system of revenue and taxation, to support the faith, and perform the engagements of our republic; to arm and cause our militia to be disciplined according to the mode which shall be provided by Congress; and to see that they are officered with men, who are capable of making the greatest progress in the art military, and who delight in the freedom and happiness of their country. A well regulated and disciplined militia, is at all times a good objection to the introduction of that bane of all free governments—a standing army."

[February 11]

The Legislature of New Hampshire have acceded to all those amendments to the constitution of the United States that were proposed by Congress, except the second, which they totally rejected.

*   *   *

By last Evening's Mail, Boston, Feb. 4 . . . The amendments recommended by the Legislature of the United States, were adopted, except the first and second articles, by the Senate of this Commonwealth, on Friday last.

Tuesday the above Amendments were taken into consideration of the House of Representatives, and after discussion, were adopted, except the 1st, 2d, and 12th.

The Senate afterwards concurred with the House in rejecting the 12th article.

Mr. Thacher, Mr. Austin, Mr. Fowler, of the Senate—Mr. Hill, Mr. Goodman, Mr. Sewall and Mr. Bacon, of the house, are appointed a joint committee, to take into consideration what further amendments to the Federal Constitution are necessary to be proposed to Congress, and report.

[February 18]

The Legislature of Delaware has adopted the amendments proposed by the Congress to the Constitution of the United States, except the first.

[February 25]

Feb. 20 . . . The house went into committee on the bill for ratifying the amendments proposed by Congress to the constitution of the United States. Mr. Gilbert in the chair.

The bill was agreed to, and ordered to be engrossed for a third reading.

*   *   *

Feb. 22 . . . The bill to ratify the amendments proposed by Congress to the Constitution of the United States was read the third time and passed. Adjourned.

[March 4]

A message was received from the senate, that they had passed the bill to ratify certain amendments to the constitution; . . .

[March 25]

The General Assembly of Pennsylvania have ratified all the amendments to the New Constitution proposed by Congress, except the 1st and 2nd.

Pennsylvania Packet and Daily Advertiser Account of Actions Taken on Constitutional Amendments, 1789

[December 29]

New York, Dec. 23 . . . The amendments to the constitution proposed by Congress to the several states, appear to receive that cordial approbation which does honour to the candour and patriotism of the respective state legislatures, to whom they have been submitted. If they do not in every respect meet the ideas of those who never liked the constitution, it ought to be remembered that they are the result of a concession on the part of the majority, who were satisfied with the system in its original form—but from the best motives were induced to aquiesce in amendments to reconcile, if possible, opposition, and to conciliate the doubting.

Maryland Journal & Baltimore Advertiser Account of Actions Taken on Constitutional Amendments, 1789–1790

[November 13, 1789]

Stratford, Oct. 31 . . . The legislature of Connecticut, at their last session, which expired on the 29th inst. took up the subjects of amendments to the Constitution; and a resolve of approbation and ratification of all, except the second article of amendment, passed the house of representatives, by large majorities. The council voted to postpone their determination upon them till the next session, which was agreed to.

[December 4]

The amendments, proposed by the Congress, to the Constitution of the United States, were lately taken into Consideration by the Legislature of New-Jersey, and agreed to, excepting the second Article.

[December 15]

Alexandria, Dec. 10 . . . On Monday, the 30th inst. the twelve amendments to the Constitution of the United States proposed by Congress, were agreed to by the House of Delegates of this State. This circumstance cannot fail to give satisfaction to the community at large, since it proves the sincerity of those who were friends to the government, when they declared in the convention that they would join its adversaries in their endeavours to procure such as were rational and proper, and would serve to remove the scruples and fears of the conscientious and honest; the friends to the federal government favoured these amendments even more than its adversaries. From whence we may fairly conclude that a general union of sentiment in this great question will shortly take place, and that such other amendments as may claim the attention of Congress upon similar principles will be acceded to them and us without opposition. The Senate is yet to decide upon the subject before the adoption on the part of this State is complete—but as they too are the representatives of the people, and no doubt inspired with the same spirit of patriotism, and wishes to quiet the minds of the doubtful and apprehensive amongst their fellow-citizens—it would be indelicate and offensive even to suppose that their votes will be different from that of the House of Delegates.

[January 29, 1790]

New York, Jan. 20 . . . The several State Assemblies which have been, or now are in session, discover a most cordial disposition towards the General

Government. The Amendments to the Constitution have been adopted fully in some of them, and by one branch in others, particularly in Virginia; and what is singular, perhaps, in that State, by the immediate representatives of the people; justly considering those amendments as an earnest of what may still take place, should they be found inadequate.

Congress have discovered so tender a regard for the rights of the people, and there has been such a spirit of candour and fairness in all their proceedings, that there is an universal confidence reposed in them by the wise, judicious and patriotic characters in all the State-Governments; and the honour and dignity of the Union is considered as the glory and happiness of every part of the great Republic, and of every individual citizen.

[February 23]

Boston, Feb. 4 . . . The amendments recommended by the Legislature of the United States were adopted, except the first and second articles, by the Senate of this commonwealth, on Friday last.

Tuesday the above amendments were taken into consideration in the House of Representatives; and after mature discussion, were adopted, except the 1st, 2d, and 12th.

The Senate afterwards concurred with the House in rejecting the 12th article.

Mr. Thatcher, Mr. Austin, Mr. Fowler, of the Senate, Mr. Hill, Mr. Goodman, Mr. Sewall and Mr. Bacon, of the House, are appointed a joint committee, to take into consideration what further amendments to the federal constitution are necessary to be proposed to Congress, and report.

Maryland Gazette Account of Actions
Taken on Constitutional Amendments, 1790

[January 22]

Portsmouth, (N. H.) Dec. 30 . . . Message of His Excellency the President of this State.

Gentlemen of the Honorable Senate and House of Representatives,

It affords me the highest pleasure, to meet you again in Assembly to advise and consult with you upon the affairs of the state at a time when so many important matters will fall under your consideration. The public papers received since the last session, will be laid before you by the Secretary, and among them, you will find many acts and resolves of Congress which will require your deliberations; among others, it is of consequence to consider of the proposal of the Federal Government, to take under their care the support of the Light House upon the conditions therein mentioned, and determine what territory, and whether any shall be ceded to the United States: Also to consider upon the expediency of passing a law empowering the United States to confine their prisoners in the prisons of this state.

Perhaps it may be thought worthy of your attention to take under consideration the present Excise A&T, and determine how long it ought to be continued: And whether the duties may not be lessened, on account of the impost now drawn by the United States.

It may be of importance to have an enquiry, whether any of the existing laws of the state, militate with, or are repugnant to the laws of the United States, or the constitution of the Federal Government.

The amendments proposed by Congress to the constitution of the United States, cannot fail of being considered and determined upon as early as the nature of the business before you will admit. Some other matters of importance will from time to time as they may be in readiness, be communicated by private messages. This being the season for granting the supplies of the present year, that object cannot pass unnoticed.

Gentlemen, I recommend to you unanimity and dispatch, and beg leave to assure you, that I shall be happy in joining with you to promote and carry into execution all those measures which may tend to advance the good of our common country.

Given at the Council Chamber in Portsmouth, the 23d day of Dec. 1789.

John Sullivan

[February 23]

Boston, Feb. 4 . . . The amendments recommended by the legislature of the United States, were adopted, except the first and second articles, by the Senate of this commonwealth on Friday last.

Tuesday the above amendments were taken into consideration in the House of Representatives; and after mature discussion, were adopted, except the 1st, 2d and 12th.

The Senate afterwards concurred with the House in rejecting 12th article.

Mr. Thatcher, Mr. Austin, Mr. Fowler of the Senate—Mr. Hill, Mr. Goodman, Mr. Sewall and Mr. Bacon, of the House are appointed a joint committee, to take into consideration what further amendments to the federal constitution are necessary to be proposed to Congress, and report.

United States Chronicle Account of Actions Taken on Constitutional Amendments, 1790

[February 4]

Portsmouth, Jan. 27 . . . The Hon. Genral Court, after maturely considering the proposed Amendments to the United States Constitution, have acceded to them all, except the second article, which they have rejected in gross.

[March 25]

Jan. 29 . . . Commonwealth of Massachusetts, In Senate, Ordered, that Josiah Thatcher, Benjamin Austin, jun. and Nathan Dane, Esqrs. with such as the Hon. House may join, be a Committee. to consider what further Amendments are necessary to be added to the Federal Constitution, and Sent down for Concurrence.

Thomas Dawes, President, pro tem.

*   *   *

Newport, Mar. 15 . . . We learn from North-Carolina, that the Legislature of that State has agreed to the Amendments proposed by the Congress to the Constitution.

Providence Gazette and Country Journal Account of Actions Taken on Constitutional Amendments, 1790

[February 13]

Boston, Feb. 4 . . . The amendments recommended by the legislature of the United States, were adopted, except the first and second articles, by the Senate of the Commonwealth, last Friday fe'nnight. And, on Tuesday last the above amendments were taken into consideration in the House of Representatives, and after mature discussion were adopted, except the 1st, 2d and 12th.

Hardin Burnley to Madison, 1789*

Nov. 5, 1789

Since the date of my letter to you which I wrote a few days ago the resolutions of the Committee on the amendments proposed by Congress have been reported. Those which respected the ten first were agreed to with even less opposition than they experienced in the Committee, & that wh. passed on the 11th & 12th was rescinded by a majority of about twelve. The amendments with the resolutions on them are now with the Senate, where from the best information which I have been able to collect there is such a division in opinion as not to furnish a ground for probable conjecture as to their decision. Some of that body I am informed propose rejection in toto, others adoption, & others again wish to postpone a decision on them 'till next session of assembly. I believe it may be said with certainty that the greater part of those who wish either to postpone or reject, are not dissatisfied with

*Documentary History of the Constitution of the United States, Vol. 5, p. 214.

the amendments so far as they have gone, but are apprehensive that the adoption of them at this time will be an obstacle to the chief object of their persuit, the amendment on the subject of direct taxation. It is confidently said in this city that the Convention of North Carolina has adopted the Constitution by a very decided majority.

Madison to President Washington, 1789*

Nov. 20, 1789

*   *   *

I hear nothing certain from the Assembly. It is said that an attempt of Mr. H. to revive the project of commutables has been defeated, that the amendments have been taken up, and are likely to be put off to the next Session, ["the" stricken out] the present house having been elected prior to the promulgation of them. This reason would have more force, if the amendments did not so much correspond as far as they go with the propositions of the State Convention, which were before the public long before the last Election. At any rate, the Assembly might pass a vote of approbation along with the postponement, and assign the reason of referring the ratification to their successors. It is probably that the ["difficulty" stricken out] scruple has arisen with the disaffected party. If it be construed by the public into a latent hope of some contingent opportunity for prosecuting the war agst. the Genl. Government, I am of opinion the experiment will recoil on the authors of it. As far as I can gather, the [illegible words stricken out] great bulk of the late opponents are entirely at rest, and more likely to confine a further opposition to the Govt. as now Administred than the Government itself. One of the principal leaders of the Baptists lately sent me word that the amendments had entirely satisfied the disaffected of his Sect, and that it would appear in their subsequent conduct.

*   *   *

Henry Lee to Hamilton, 1789†

Nov. 16, 1789

My dear sir,

The letr. sent to your care, be pleased to return.

Your undertaking is truely arduous but I trust as you progress in the work, difficulty will vanish.

From your situation you must be able to form with some certainty an opinion concerning the domestic debt. Will it speedily rise, will the interest

*Documentary History of the Constitution of the United States, p. 215.
†The Papers of Alexander Hamilton, Vol. 5, p. 517.

accruing command specie or any thing nearly as valuable, what will become of the indents already issued?

These querys are asked for my private information, perhaps they may be improper, I do not think them so, or I would not propound them—of this you will decide & act accordingly. Nothing can induce me to be instrumental in submitting my friend to an impropriety. I wrote G. Knox some time ago enclosing a let. for Governor St. Clair.

Will you before you answer me know whether my letr. was received.

The antefederal gentlemen in our assembly do not relish the amendments proposed by Congress to the constitution.

Yours always & affy

Randolph to President Washington, 1789*

Nov. 26, 1789

Since my last, written ["about" stricken out] five days ago, the committee of the whole house have been engaged in the amendments from congress. Mr. Henry's motion, introduced about three weeks past, for postponing the consideration of them, was negatived by a great majority. The first ten were easily agreed to. The eleventh and twelfth were rejected 64 against 58. I confess, that I see no propriety in adopting the two last. But I trust that the refusal to ratify will open the road to such an expression of foederalism, as will efface the violence of the last year, and the intemperance of the inclosed letter, printed by the enemies to the constitution, without authority. However our final measures will depend on our strength, which is not yet ascertained—

*   *   *

Virginia Senators to the Governor of Virginia, 1789†

Sept. 28, 1789

Sir,

We have long waited in anxious expectations, of having it in our power to transmit effectual Amendments to the Constitution of the United States, and it is with grief that we now send forward propositions inadequate to the purpose of real and substantial Amendments, and so far short of the wishes of our Country. By perusing the Journal of the Senate, your Excellency will see, that we did, in vain, bring to view the Amendments proposed by our Convention, and approved by the Legislature. We shall transmit a complete set of the Journals of both Houses of Congress to your address, which with a letter accompanying them, we entreat your Excellency will have the goodness to lay before the Honorable Legislature of the ensuing meeting.

*Documentary History of the Constitution of the United States, Vol. 5, p. 216.
† New York Journal and Weekly Register, January 7, 1790.

We have the honor, of every sentiment of respect,
To be, Sir, your Excellency's most obedient,
And very humble servants,

Richard Henry Lee
William Grayson

Virginia Senators to the Speaker of the House of Representatives in Virginia, 1789*

Sept. 28, 1789

Sir,

We have now the honor of enclosing the proposition of Amendments to the Constitution of the United States that has been finally agreed upon by Congress. We can assure you sir, that nothing on our part has been omitted, to procure the success of those radical amendments proposed by the Convention, and approved by the Legislature of our Country, which as our constituent we shall always deem it our duty with respect and reverence to obey. The Journal of the Senate herewith transmitted, will at once shew exact and how unfortunate we have been in this business. It is impossible for us not to see the necessary tendency to consolidated empire in the natural operation of the Constitution, if no further amended than as now proposed; and it is equally impossible for us not to be apprehensive for Civil Liberty, when we know of no instance in the records of history, that shew a people ruled in freedom when subject to one undivided Government, and inhabiting a territory so extensive as that of the United States; and when, as it seems to us, the nature of man, and of things join to prevent it. The impracticability in such case, of carrying representation on sufficiently near to the people for procuring their confidence and consequent obedience, compels a resort to fear resulting from great force and excessive power in government. Confederated republics, where the Federal Hand is not possessed of absorbing power, may permit the existence of freedom, whilst it preserves union, strength, and safety. Such amendments therefore as may secure against the annihilation of the state governments we devoutly wish to see adopted.

If a persevering application to Congress from the states that have desired such amendments, should fail of its object, we are disposed to think, reasoning from causes to effects, that unless a dangerous apathy should invade the public mind, it will not be many years before a constitutional number of Legislatures will be found to demand Convention for the purpose.

We have sent a complete set of the Journals of each House of Congress, and through the appointed channel will be transmitted the Acts that have passed this session, in these will be seen the nature and extent of the

---

New York Journal and Weekly Register, January 7, 1790.

judiciary, the estimated expences of the government, and the means so far adopted for defraying the latter.

We beg sir, to be presented with all duty to the Honorable House of Representatives, and to assure you that we are with every sentiment of respect and esteem,

Sir your most obedient and very humble servants,

Richard Henry Lee
William Grayson

Burnley to Madison, 1789*

Nov. 28, 1789

*   *   *

The fate of the amendments proposed by Congress to the General Government is still in suspense. In a committee of the whole house the first ten were acceeded to with but little opposition for on a question taken, on each seperately, there was scarcely a dissenting voice. On the two last a debate of some lenght took place, which ended in rejection. Mr. E. Randolph who advocated all the others stood in this contest in the front of opposition. His principal objection was pointed against the word retained in the eleventh proposed amendment, and his agument if I understood it was applied in this manner, that as the rights declared in the first ten of the proposed amendments were not all that a free people would require the exercise of; and that as there was no criterion by which it could be determined whither any other particular right was retained or not, it would be more safe, & more consistant with the spirit of the 1st. & 17th. amendments proposed by Virginia, that this reservation against constructive power, should operate rather as a provision against extending the powers of Congress by their own authority, than as a protection to rights reducable to no definitive certainty. But others among whom I am one see not the force of the distinction, for by preventing an extension of power in that body from which danger is apprehended safety will be insured if its powers are not too extensive already, & so by protecting the rights of the people & of the States, an improper extension of power will be prevented & safety made equally certain. If the house should agree to the resolution for rejecting the two last I am of opinion that it will bring the whole into hazzard again, as some who have been decided friends to the ten first think it woud be unwise to adopt them without the 11th. & 12th.. Whatever may be the fate of the amendments submitted by Congress it is probable that an application for further amendments will be made by this assembly, for the opposition to the Foederal Consitution is in my opinion reduced to a single point, the power of direct taxation, ["and" stricken out] those who wish the change are desirous of repeating the application whilst those who wish it not are indifferent on the subject, supposing that Congress will not propose a change which would take from them a power so necessary for the accomplishment of those objects which are confided to their care.

* * *

D. Stuart to President Washington, 1789*

Dec. 13, 1789

* * *

During the time of my continuance in Richd on the above business, the Session of our Assembly commenced—A very extraordinary letter from our Senators in Congress, complaining of the inefficacy of the proposed amendments, and expressive of their fears, that the State governments would be annihilated; with a strong hint of the insufficiency of one government for so extensive a country, was recieved and read—I was happy in hearing much indignation expressed at it, by many who were strong Antifederalists, and had voted against the constitution in the Convention— It was generally attributed to an aim at popularity. My belief is, that it was meant by Mr. R. H: Lee to serve his Brother, who is a Candidate for a Judge's seat in this State, and will no doubt assume the merit with his party, of having been neglected on account of his principles— Grayson's short draft would be a sufficient motive with him to affix his signature to it— The letter was evidently in Mr Lee's hand— Mr Henry appears to me by no means content— But if the people continue as much satisfyed, as they at present appear to be, he will be soon alone in his sentiments— He however tried to feel the pulse of the House with respect to the Constitution, in two or three instances, and recieved at length I, understood, a very spirited reply from Col. Lee—

* * *

Madison to President Washington, 1789†

Dec. 5, 1789

Since my last I have been furnished with the inclosed copy of the letter from the Senators of this State to its Legislature. It is well calculated to keep alive the disaffection to the Government, and is accordingly applied to that use by the violent partizans. I understand the letter was written by the first subscriber of it, as indeed is pretty evident from the stile and strain of it. The other, it is said, subscribed it with reluctance. I am less surprized that this should have been the case, than that he should have subscribed at all.

*Documentary History of the Constitution of the United States, p. 220.
†Documentary History of the Constitution of the United States, p. 221.

My last information from Richmond is contained in the following extract from a letter of the 28th. Novr. from an intelligent member of the H. of ["Reps." stricken out] Delegates. [printed *supra* p. 1188]

*   *   *

The difficulty started agst. the amendments is really unlucky, and the more to be regretted as it springs from a friend to the Constitution. It is a still greater cause of regret, if the distinction be, as it appears to me, altogether fanciful. If a line can be drawn between the powers granted and the rights retained, it would seem to be the same thing, whether the latter be secured, ["whether" stricken out] by declaring that they shall ["be not be abridged violated" stricken out], or that the former shall not be extended. If no line can be drawn, a declaration in either form would amount to nothing. If the distinction were just it does not seem to be of sufficient importance to justify the risk of losing the amendts of furnishing a handle to the disaffected, and of arming N.C. with a pretext, if she be disposed, to prolong her exile from the Union.

Randolph to President Washington, 1789*

Dec. 6, 1789

When I had the honor of writing to you last, the amendments had, I believe, been under consideration in a committee of the whole, and ten were adopted, and the two last rejected. Upon the report being made to the house, and without ["a" written upon "no"] debate of any consequence, the whole twelve were ratified. They are now with the senate, who were yesterday employed about them. That body will attempt to postpone them; for a majority is unfriendly to the government. But an effort will be made against this destructive measure.

In the house of delegates, it was yesterday moved to declare the remainder of the amendments, proposed by our convention, essential to the rights and liberties of the people. An amendment was offered, saying, that in pursuance of the will of the people, as expressed by our convention, the general assembly ought to urge congress to a reconsideration of them. The amendment was carried by the speaker, giving a casting vote. This shews the strength of the parties, and that in the house of delegates the antifoederal force has diminished much since the last year. A representation is to be prepared, and the inclosed speaks the temper, which we wish to exhibit in it. Whether we shall succeed in our attempt to carry such a remonstrance through, is with me very doubtful. It will be pushed; because it seems to discountenance any future importunities for amendments; which in my opin-

---

Documentary History of the Constitution of the United States, pp. 222–23.

ion is now a very important point. I should have been sanguine in my belief of carrying the representation thro' in its present form, if the friends would have joined the enemies of the constitution, in suspending the ratification of the eleventh amendment; which is exceptionable to me, in giving a handle to say, that congress have endeavoured to administer an opiate, by an alteration, which is merely plausible.

The twelfth amendment does not appear to me to have any real effect, unless it be to excite a dispute between the United States, and every particular state, as to what is delegated. It accords pretty nearly with what our convention proposed; but being once adopted, it may produce new matter for the cavils of the designing.

P. S. I shall do myself the honor of replying to your official letter, as soon as the assembly rises.

Randolph to President Washington, 1789*

Dec. 15, 1789

*   *   *

The senate, as I mentioned in my last, rejected the 3d. 8th. 11th. & 12th. amendments, and adopted the rest. It has been thought best by the mo[mutilated] zealous friends to the constitution to let the whole of them rest. I have submitted to their opinion; not choosing to rely upon my own judgment in so momentous an affair. The ground of their opinion is a resolution to throw the odium of rejection o["n" written upon "f"] the senate.

Edward Carrington to Madison, 1789†

Dec. 20, 1789

*   *   *

. . . during the session, there has been much less intemperance than prevailed last year. Mr. H—— was disposed to do some antifederal business, but having felt the pulse of the House on several points ["he at" stricken out] and finding that it did not beat with certainty in unison with his own, he at length took his departure about the middle of the session without pushing any thing to its issue. his first effort was to procure an address of thanks, or in some other mode the acknowledgements of the House, for the great vigilance of our senators manifested in their letter upon the subject of our forlorn prospect ["situation" stricken out] in regard to such amendments as will se-

---

*Documentary History of the Constitution of the United States, p. 225.

†Documentary History of the Constitution of the United States, pp. 227–30.

cure our liberties under the Government. upon this point he made a speach to the house, but it not appearing to take well, it was never stirred again. this letter was considered by some of the most violent of the Anti's as seditious and highly reprehensible. his next effort was to refer the amendments sent forward by Congress, to the next session of Assembly, in order that the people might give their sentiments whether they were satisfactory, alledging that in his opinion they were not. to this purpose he proposed a resolution, but finding the disposition of the house to be otherwise, he moved that it might lie on the Table, and went away without even calling it up again. somewhat later in the session the subject of the amendments was ["were" stricken out] taken up—the ten first were, with the ["an" stricken out] exception of perhaps not more than ten members, unanimously agreed to— on the eleventh and twelfth some difficulty arose, from Mr. E. Randolphs objecting to them as unsatisfactory—after much debate ["however" stricken out] they were rejected in the Committee of the whole but the report being defered a few days they were accepted in the House by a pretty good majority thus the whole were adopted in the lower house—they went to the senate in one resolution where they remained long—["they" stricken out] the resolution at length returned with a proposition ["s" stricken out] to amend by stricking out the 3d. 8th. 11th. & 12, these to be refered to the consideration of the people. to this amendment the lower house disagreed and requested a conference—the senate insisted, and assented to the conference, this was, however, productive of conviction on neither side, the Committee on the part of the senate returned with S. T. Mason at their head, to their House, which upon his motion, immediately adhered before any thing further passed between the two Houses; ["this" stricken out] the delegates could in no stage have seen cause to recede from their disagreement; but under this intemperate and unprecedented conduct they were left without a choice of any thing but to adhere also, and thus the whole amendments have fallen. the sense of the house of delegates was fairly & fully passed on the propriety of adopting them, and the intemperance manifested in the conduct of the senate, will doubtless shew the people ["that" stricken out] whether this fate of the amendments, was produced from a want of merit in them, or in the senate. through the whole course of the business in that house there was on the several questions equal divisions of the members, so, as to leave the decision to the chair. notwithstanding the unequivocal decision in the house of delegates for adopting the amendments, yet in the course of the discussion some intemperance was generated—this led to propositions which in the earlier parts of the session none would have thought of, and it was with difficulty that a proposition for demanding a compliance with the amendments proposed by our convention, so far as they have not been agreed to, by Congress was prevented from passing. this proposition was presented to the house as often as three times, at first it was rejected by a great majority, at the next attempt it was rejected by a less majority, and at the third by the vote of the speaker. ["a very small one." stricken out] had Mr. Henry ["had any" stricken out] conceived that such would have been the temper in the latter stages of the session, he would not have left us. my information from the various parts of the Country is that the people are at ease on the subject of amendments, expecting nothing but that those sent on would be adopted and that others ["would" stricken out] will be supplied as further deliberation and experience shall discover the want of them. this I think I am warranted in supposing to be true, because the heats which have appeared in the latter part ["s" stricken out] of the session would have shewn themselves sooner had they been amongst the people when their representatives came from their Counties, but they have been generated here in the course of the discussions upon the amendments.

*   *   *

Madison to President Washington, 1790*

Jan. 4, 1790

. . . You will probably have seen by the papers that the contest in the Assembly on the subject of the amendments ended ["in" written upon "the"] the loss of them. The House of Delegates got over the objections to the 11 & 12, but the Senate revived them with an addition of the 3 & 8 articles, and by a vote of adherence prevented a ratification. On some accounts this event is no doubt to be regretted. But it will do no injury to the Genl. Government. On the contrary it will have the effect ["of" stricken out] with many ·of turning their distrust towards their own Legislature. The miscarriage of the 3d. art: particularly, will have this effect.

*   *   *

Official Notices of State Ratifications, 1790-1791†

On the 25th of January, 1790, the first ratification of the amendments was transmitted to the two houses by the President of the United States, accompanied by the following message:

January 25, 1790

Gentlemen of the Senate, and House of Representatives:

    I have received from his Excellency John E. Howard, Governor of the state of Maryland, an act of the legislature of Maryland, to ratify certain articles in addition to, and amendment of, the Constitution of the United States of America, proposed by Congress to the legislatures of the several states; and have directed my secretary to lay a copy of the same before you, together with a copy of a letter accompanying the above act, from his Excellency, the Governor of Maryland, to the President of the United States.

    The originals will be deposited in the office of the secretary of state.

G. Washington

*Documentary History of the Constitution of the United States, p. 230.

†History of Congress Exhibiting a Classification of the Proceedings of the Senate and House of Representatives from March 4,1789 to March 3,1793, pp. 174-87.

The letter of the governor of Maryland encloses the following act of the legislature of that state:

An Act to ratify certain articles in addition to, and amendment of, the Constitution of the United States of America, proposed by Congress to the Legislatures of the several States.

Whereas it is provided, by the fifth article of the Constitution of the United States of America, that Congress, whenever two-thirds of both houses shall deem it necessary, shall propose amendments to the said Constitution, or, on the application of the legislatures of two-thirds of the several states, shall call a convention, for proposing amendments; which, in either case, shall be valid to all intents and purposes as part of the said Constitution, when ratified by the legislatures of three-fourths of the several states; or by conventions in three-fourths thereof, as the one or the other mode of ratification may be proposed by the Congress. And whereas, at a session of the United States, begun and held at the city of New York, on Wednesday, the fourth day of March, in the year of our Lord one thousand seven hundred and eighty-nine, it was resolved, by the Senate and House of Representatives of the said United States in Congress assembled, two-thirds of both houses concurring, that the following articles be proposed to the legislatures of the several states as amendments to the Constitution of the United States, all, or any of which articles, when ratified by three-fourths of the said legislatures, to be valid to all intents and purposes as part of the said Constitution. [Here follow the several articles of amendment in the words agreed to by Congress.]

Be it enacted, by the General Assembly of Maryland—That the aforesaid articles, and each of them, be, and they are hereby, confirmed and ratified,

By the House of Delegates, December 17, 1789. Read, and assented to.

By order: W. Hardwood, Clerk.

By the Senate, December 19, 1789. Read, and assented to.

By order: H. Ridgely, Clerk
I. E. Howard, (Seal appendant.)

On the 15th of February, the action of the legislature of New Hampshire was communicated by the following message from the President of the United States:

February 15, 1790

Gentlemen of the Senate, and House of Representatives:

I have directed my secretary to lay before you the copy of a vote of the legislature of the state of New Hampshire, to accept the articles proposed in addition to, and amendment of, the Constitution of the United States of America, except the second article: at the same time will be delivered to you the copy of a letter from his Excellency the Governor of the State of New Hampshire, to the President of the United States.

The originals of the above-mentioned vote and letter will be lodged in the office of the secretary of state.

G.   Washington

Durham, New Hampshire January 29, 1790

The President of the United States

Sir: I have the honour to enclose you, for the information of Congress, a vote of the assembly of this state, to accept all the articles of amendment to the Constitution of the United States, except the second, which was rejected.

I have the honour to be, with the most profound respect, Sir, your most obedient and very humble servant,

John Sullivan

State of New Hampshire

January 25, 1790

Upon reading and maturely considering the proposed amendments to the federal Constitution,

Voted—To accept the whole of said amendments, except the second article; which was rejected.

Sent up for concurrence.

Thomas Bartlett, Speaker

In Senate, the same day, read and concurred.

I. Pearson, Secretary

On the 20th of February, the members from South Carolina presented to the House of Representatives an act "for ratifying, on the part of that state, the several articles of amendment to the Constitution of the United States, proposed by Congress; and, on the 1st of April, the following message was sent to the two houses by the President of the United States:

April 1, 1790

Gentlemen of the Senate, and House of Representatives:

I have directed my private secretary to lay before you a copy of the adoption, by the legislature of South Carolina, of the articles proposed by Congress to the legislatures of the several states, as amendments to the Constitution of the United States, together with the copy of a letter from the Governor of the state of South Carolina to the President of the United States, which have lately come to my hands.

The originals of the foregoing will be lodged in the office of the secretary of state.

G. Washington

January 28, 1790

To the President of the United States

Sir: I have the honour to transmit you the entire adoption, by the legislature of this state, of the amendments proposed to the Constitution of the United States.

I am, with the most perfect esteem and respect, your most obedient servant,

Charles Pinckney

January 18, 1790

The house took into consideration the report of the committee, to whom was referred the resolution of the Congress of the United States, of the fourth day of March, one thousand seven hundred and eighty-nine, proposing amendments to the Constitution of the United States, viz: [Here follow the several articles of amendment, in the words agreed to by Congress,] which was being read through, was agreed to; whereupon,

Resolved—That this house do adopt the several articles; and that they become a part of the Constitution of the United States.

Resolved—That the resolutions be sent to the Senate for their concurrence.

By order of the House
Jacob Read
Speaker of the House of Representatives

Resolved—That this house do concur with the House of Representatives in the foregoing resolutions.

By order of the Senate.
D. De Sausure
President of the Senate

On the 8th of March, the President of the United States communicated to the two houses the ratification of the state of Delaware, as follows:

March 8, 1790

Gentlemen of the Senate, and House of Representatives:

I have received from his Excellency Joshua Clayton, Governor of the state of Delaware, the articles proposed by Congress to the legislatures of the several states, as amendments of the Constitution of the United States; which articles were transmitted to him for the consideration of the legislature of Delaware, and are now returned with the following resolutions annexed to them; namely,

The General Assembly of Delaware

Having taken into their consideration the above amendments, proposed by Congress to the respective legislatures of the several states,

Resolved—That the first article be postponed.

Resolved—That the general assembly do agree to the second, third, fourth, fifth, sixth, seventh, eighth, ninth, tenth, eleventh, and twelfth articles; and we do hereby assent to ratify, and confirm the same, as part of the Constitution of the United States.

In testimony whereof, we have caused the great seal of the state to be hereunto affixed, this twenty-eighth day of January, in the year of our Lord one thousand seven hundred and ninety, and in the fourteenth year of the Independence of the Delaware state.

Signed by order of the Council,
George Mitchell, Speaker
Signed by order of the House of Assembly,
Jehu Davis, Speaker

I have directed a copy of the letter which accompanied the said articles, from his Excellency Joshua Clayton, to the President of the United States, to be laid before you.

The above-mentioned articles, and the original of the letter, will be lodged in the office of the secretary of state.

G. Washington

February 19, 1790

His Excellency, George Washington
President of the United States

Sir: Agreeably to the directions of the General Assembly of this state, I do myself the honour to enclose your Excellency the ratification of the articles proposed by Congress to be added to the Constitution of the United States, and am, with every sentiment of esteem, Sir, your Excellency's most obedient, humble servant,

Joshua   Clayton

On the 16th of March, the following message from the President of the United States was communicated to the two houses:

March 16, 1790

Gentlemen of the Senate, and House of Representatives:

I have directed my secretary to lay before you the copy of an act, and the form of ratifications of certain articles of amendment to the Constitution of the United States, by the legislature of the state of Pennsylvania; together with the copy of a letter which accompanied the said act, from the speaker of the House of Assembly, of Pennsylvania, to the President of the United States. The originals of the above will be lodged in the office of the secretary of state.

G.   Washington

[The letter of the speaker, referred to in the above message, is merely to certify that the following is "an exact and true exemplification of the act whereof it purports to be a copy."]

An Act declaring the assent of this state to certain Amendments to the Constitution of the United States.

Section 1. Whereas, in pursuance of the fifth article of the Constitution of the United States, certain articles of amendment to the said Constitution have been proposed by the Congress of the United States, for the consideration of the legislatures of the several states; and whereas this house, being the legislature of the state of Pennsylvania, having maturely deliberated thereupon, have resolved to adopt and ratify the articles hereafter enumerated, as part of the Constitution of the United States:

Section 2. Be it enacted, therefore, and it is hereby enacted by the representatives of the freemen of the commonwealth of Pennsylvania, in General Assembly met, and by the authority of the same, That the following amendments to the Constitution of the United States, proposed by the Congress thereof, namely:

[Here follow the third, fourth, fifth, sixth, seventh, eighth, ninth, tenth, eleventh, and twelfth articles, which were proposed by Congress to the legislatures of the several states, as amendments to the Constitution of the United States.]

"Be, and they are hereby ratified, in behalf of this state, to become, when ratified by the legislatures of three-fourths of the several states, part of the Constitution of the United States.

Signed by order of the House:
Richard Peters, Speaker

Enacted into a law, at Philadelphia, on Wednesday, the tenth day of March, in the year of our Lord one thousand seven hundred and ninety.

Peter   Zachary   Lloyd
Clerk of the General Assembly

The usual certificates were appended.

On the 5th of April, the President of the United States transmitted to Congress the ratification of the legislature of New York, as follows:

The people of the state of New York, by the grace of God free and independent,

To all to whom these presents shall come, or may concern, Greeting:

Know ye, that we, having inspected the records remaining in our secretary's office, do find there a certain act of our legislature, in the words and figures following: "An act ratifying certain articles in addition to, and amendment of, the Constitution of the United States of America, proposed by the Congress: Whereas, by the fifth article of the Constitution of the United States of America, it is provided that the Congress, whenever two-thirds of both houses shall deem it necessary, shall propose amendments to the said Constitution; which shall be valid, to all intents and purposes, as part of the said Constitution, when ratified by the legislatures of three-fourths of the several states, or by conventions in three-fourths thereof; as the one or the other mode of ratification may be proposed by the Congress: And whereas, in the session of the Congress of the United States of America, begun and held at the city of New York, on Wednesday, the fourth of March, one thousand seven hundred and eighty-nine, it was resolved by the Senate and House of Representatives of the United States of America, in Congress assembled, two-thirds of both houses concurring, that the following articles be proposed to the legislatures of the several states, as amendments to the Constitution of the United States, all or any of which articles, when ratified by three-fourths of the said legislatures, to be valid, to all intents and purposes, as part of the said Constitution, namely: Articles in addition to, and amendment of, the Constitution of the United States of America, proposed by Congress, and ratified by the legislatures of the several states, pursuant to the fifth article of the original Constitution:

[Here follow the several articles.] And whereas the legislature of this state have considered the said articles, and do agree to the same, except the second article:

Therefore be it enacted by the people of the state of New York, represented in Senate and Assembly, and it is hereby enacted by the authority of the same, that the said articles, except the second, shall be, and hereby are ratified by the legislature of this state.

February 22, 1790

This bill having been read the third time: —Resolved—That the bill do pass.

By order of the assembly,
Gulian Verplanck, Speaker

February 24, 1790

This bill having been read a third time: —Resolved—That the bill do pass.

By order of the Senate
Issac Roosevelt
President, *pro hav vice*

Council of Revision
February 27, 1790

Resolved—That it does not appear improper to the council, that this bill, entitled "An act ratifying certain articles in addition to, and amendment of, the Constitution of the United States of America, proposed by the Congress, should become a law of this state.

George Clinton

On the 11th of June, the ratification of the state of North Carolina was communicated to Congress in the following manner, by the President of the United States.

Gentlemen of the Senate, and House of Representatives:

I have directed my secretary to lay before you a copy of the ratification of the amendments to the Constitution of the United States by the state of North Carolina, together with an extract from a letter accompanying said ratification, from the governor of the state of North Carolina to the President of the United States.

G. Washington

Extract of a Letter from his Excellency Alexander Martin, Governor of the State of North Carolina, to the President of the United States

May 25, 1790

Sir: I do myself the honour to transmit you, herewith enclosed, an act of the General Assembly of this state, passed at their last session, entitled "An act to ratify the amendments to the Constitution of the United States."

An Act to ratify the Amendments to the Constitution of the United States

Whereas the Senate and House of Representatives of the United States of America, in Congress assembled, on the fourth day of March, did resolve, two-thirds of both houses concurring, that the following articles be proposed to the legislatures of the several states, as amendments to the Constitution of the United States, all or any of which articles, when ratified by three-fourths of the said legislatures, to be valid, to all intents and purposes, as part of the said Constitution:

[Here follow the several articles of amendments verbatim, as proposed by Congress to the legislatures of the several states.]

Be it therefore enacted by the General Assembly of the state of North Carolina, and it is hereby enacted by the authority of the same, that the said amendments, agreeably to the fifth article of the original Constitution, be held and ratified on the part of this state, as articles in addition to, and amendment of, the Constitution of the United States of America.

Read three times, and ratified in General Assembly, this 22d day of December, A. D. 1789.

Charles Johnson, S. S.
S. Cabarrus, S. H. C.

It is not deemed essential in this instance, or any case, to give the formal certificates which accompany the letters and acts to attest their authenticity.

The President of the United States, on the 30th of June, by the following message, informed the two houses of the ratification of the amendments by the state of Rhode Island:

Gentlemen of the Senate, and House of Representatives:

An act of the legislature of the state of Rhode Island and Providence Plantations, for ratifying certain articles as amendments to the Constitution of the United States, was yesterday put into my hands; and I have directed my secretary to lay a copy of the same before you.

G. Washington

State of Rhode Island and Providence Plantations

General Assembly, June session

An act for ratifying certain articles as amendments to the Constitution of the United States of America, and which were proposed by the Congress of the said states at their session in March, A. D. 1789, to the legislatures of the several states, pursuant to the fifth article of the aforesaid Constitution.

Be it enacted by this General Assembly, and by the authority thereof, it is hereby enacted, that the following articles, proposed by the Congress of the United States of America, at their session in March, A. D., 1789, to the legislatures of the several states, for ratification, as amendments to the Constitution of the said United States, pursuant to the fifth article of the said Constitution, be, and the same are hereby, fully assented to and ratified on the part of this state: to wit:

[Here follow all the articles, except the second.]

It is ordered, That his Excellency the governor be, and he is hereby, requested to transmit to the President of the said United States, under the seal of this state, a copy of this act, to be communicated to the Senate and House of Representatives of the Congress of the said United States.

A true copy, duly examined.

Witness, Henry Ward, Secretary

On the 6th of August, the President of the United States, by the following message, communicated to Congress the ratification of the state of New Jersey.

Gentlemen of the Senate, and House of Representatives:

I have directed my secretary to lay before you a copy of an exemplified copy of a law to ratify, on the part of the state of New Jersey, certain amendments to the Constitution of the United States, together with a copy of a letter which accompanied said ratification, from the Hon. Elisha Lawrence, Esq., Vice-President of the state of New Jersey, to the President of the United States.

G.   Washington

August 4, 1790

The President of the United States

Sir: I have the honour to transmit an exemplified copy of a law of the state of New Jersey, ratifying certain amendments to the Constitution of the United States.

I have the honour to be,

Your most obedient, humble servant,

Elisha   Lawrence

State of New Jersey

An Act to ratify, on the part of this State, certain Amendments to the Constitution of the United States

Whereas the Congress of the United States, begun and held at the city of New York, on Wednesday, the fourth day of March, one thousand seven hundred and eighty-nine, resolved, two-thirds of both houses concurring, that sundry articles be proposed to the legislatures of the several states, as amendments to the Constitution of the United States, all, or any of which articles, when ratified by three-fourths of the said legislatures, to be valid, to all intents and purposes, as part of the said

Constitution; and whereas, the President of the United States did, in pursuance of a resolve of the Senate and House of Representatives of the United States of America in Congress assembled, transmit to the governor of this state the amendments proposed by Congress, which were by him laid before the legislature, for their consideration: wherefore,

1. Be it enacted by the Council and General Assembly of this state, and, by the authority of the same, it is hereby enacted, that the following articles proposed by Congress, in addition to, and amendment of, the Constitution of the United States; to wit: [Here follow, verbatim, the first, third, fourth, fifth, sixth, seventh, eighth, ninth, tenth, eleventh, and twelfth articles of the said amendments proposed by Congress to the legislatures of the several states,] be, and the same are, hereby ratified and adopted by the state of New Jersey.

November 20, 1789

This bill having been three times read in council, resolved that the same do pass.

By order of the house
William Livingston, President

November, 18, 1789

This bill having been three times read in this house, resolved that the same do pass.

By order of the house
John Beatty, Speaker

It appears, therefore, that the ratifications of the amendments, by the following nine states; namely, Maryland, New Hampshire, South Carolina, Delaware, Pennsylvania, New York, North Carolina, Rhode Island, and New Jersey, were received by the first Congress; that the first article was rejected by two of the states; namely, Delaware and Pennsylvania; and that the second article was rejected by five of the states; namely, New Hampshire, Pennsylvania, New York, Rhode Island, and New Jersey. No ratifications had been received from the states of Massachusetts, Connecticut, Virginia, or Georgia.

*   *   *

On the 14th of November, [1791] a message from the President of the United States, was received by the two houses, announcing the ratification of the first article of the amendments by the General Assembly of Virginia. The resolution of the state of Virginia is as follows:

Resolved—That the first article of the amendments proposed by Congress to the Constitution of the United States, be ratified by this Commonwealth.

Charles Hay, C. H. D.
H. Brooke, C. S.

November 3, 1791,—agreed to by the Senate.

On the 30th of December, the following message from the President of the United States, communicated the entire ratification of the state of Virginia.

December 30, 1791

Gentlemen of the Senate, and of the House of Representatives:

I lay before you a copy of the ratification, by the commonwealth of Virginia, of the articles of amendment proposed by Congress to the Constitution of the United States; and a copy of a letter which accompanied said ratification from the governor of Virginia.

G. Washington

The following are the papers referred to in the message:

December 22, 1791

The President of the United States

Sir: The General Assembly, during their late session, have adopted, on the part of this commonwealth, all the amendments proposed by Congress to the Constitution of the United States; their ratification whereof I do myself the honour herewith to transmit.

I have the honour to be, &c

Henry Lee

Virginia

General Assembly, begun and held at the Capitol, in the city of Richmond, on Monday, the 17th day of October, in the year of our Lord 1791.

December 5, 1791

Resolved—That the second, third, fourth, fifth, sixth, seventh, eighth, ninth, tenth, eleventh, and twelfth articles of the amendments proposed by Congress to the Constitution of the United States, be ratified by this commonwealth.

John Pride, S. S.
Thomas Matthews, S. H. D.

December 15, 1791,—agreed to by the Senate.

On the 18th of January, 1792, the President of the United States, in the following message, communicated the ratification of the state of Vermont, which state had been admitted into the Union during the third session of the first Congress:

January 18, 1792

Gentlemen of the Senate, and of the House of Representatives:

I lay before you a copy of an exemplified copy of an act of the legislature of Vermont, ratifying, on behalf of that state, the articles of amendment proposed by Congress to the Constitution of the United States, together with a copy of a letter which accompanied said ratification.

G. Washington

An Act ratifying certain Articles proposed by Congress as Amendments to the Constitution of the United States

Whereas the Congress of the United States, begun and held at the city of New York, on Wednesday the fourth of March, one thousand seven hundred and eighty-nine, resolved, that certain articles, to the number of twelve, be proposed to the legislatures of the several states, as amendments to the Constitution of the United States, which articles, when ratified by three-fourths of the said legislatures, should be valid, to all intents and purposes, as part of the said Constitution: Therefore,

It is hereby enacted by the General Assembly of the state of Vermont, that all and every of said articles, so proposed as aforesaid, be, and the same are, hereby ratified and confirmed by the legislature of this state.

A certifying letter from Ros. Hopkins, Secretary, accompanies this act.

At the close of the second Congress, the ratifications of eleven states had been received, Massachusetts, Connecticut, and Georgia, having not yet sent in their acquiescence.

The ratifications of the articles of amendment to the Constitution of the United States, proposed by the resolution of Congress, at their first session under the said Constitution, may be seen at one view by the following tabular arrangement:

The States in alphabetical order	Ratifies the whole	Postpones or rejects	Postpones or rejects
1. Delaware		the 1st	
2. Maryland	1 to 12		
3. New Hampshire			the 2d
4. New Jersey			the 2d
5. New York			the 2d
6. North Carolina	1 to 12		
7. Pennsylvania		the 1st	
8. Rhode Island	1 to 12		
9. South Carolina	1 to 12		
10. Vermont	1 to 12		
11. Virginia	1 to 12		

Official Notice of Ratification, 1792*

Sir,   Mar. 1, 1792

I have the honor to send you herein enclosed, two copies duly authenticated, of an Act concerning certain fisheries of the United States, and for the regulation and government of the fishermen employed therein; also of an Act to establish the post office and post roads within the United States; also the ratifications by three fourths of the Legislatures of the Several States, of certain articles in addition and amendment of the Constitution of the United States, proposed by Congress to the said Legislatures, and of being with sentiments of the most perfect respect, your Excellency's &.

Th. Jefferson

---

*"First Things First," *Harper's*, (June, 1963), p. 43. This letter officially announcing ratification of the Bill of Rights was sent by Jefferson as Secretary of State to the governors of the several states.

Sources of Bill of Rights

Bill of Rights Guarantees	First Document Protecting	First American Guarantee	First Constitutional Guarantee
Establishment of religion	Rights of the Colonists (Boston)	Same	N.J. Constitution, Art. XIX
Free exercise of religion	Md. Act Concerning Religion	Same	Va. Declaration of Rights, S. 16
Free speech	Mass. Body of Liberties, S. 12	Same	Pa. Declaration of Rights, Art. XII
Free press	Address to Inhabitants of Quebec	Same	Va. Declaration of Rights, S.12
Assembly	Declaration and Resolves, Continental Congress	Same	Pa. Declaration of Rights, Art. XVI
Petition	Bill of Rights (1689)	Declaration of Rights and Grievances, (1765). S. XIII	Pa. Declaration of Rights, Art. XVI
Right to bear arms	Bill of Rights (1689)	Pa. Declaration of Rights, Art. XIII	Same
Quartering soldiers	N.Y. Charter of Liberties	Same	Del. Declaration of Rights, S. 21
Searches	Rights of the Colonists (Boston)	Same	Va. Declaration of Rights, S. 10
Seizures	Magna Carta, c. 39	Va. Declaration of Rights, S. 10	Same
Grand jury indictment	N.Y. Charter of Liberties	Same	N.C. Declaration of Rights, Art. VIII
Double jeopardy	Mass. Body of Liberties, S. 42	Same	N.H. Bill of Rights, Art. XVI
Self-incrimination	Va. Declaration of Rights, S. 8	Same	Same
Due process	Magna Carta, c. 39	Md. Act for Liberties of the People	Va. Declaration of Rights, S. 8
Just compensation	Mass. Body of Liberties, S. 8	Same	Vt. Declaration of Rights, Art. II
Speedy trial	Va. Declaration of Rights, S. 8	Same	Same
Public trial	West N.J. Concessions, c. XXIII	Same	Pa. Declaration of Rights, Art. IX
Jury trial	Magna Carta, c. 39	Mass. Body of Liberties, S. 29	Va. Declaration of Rights, S. 8
Cause and nature of accusation	Va. Declaration of Rights, S. 8	Same	Same
Witnessess	Pa. Charter of Privileges, Art. V	Same	N.J. Constitution, Art. XVI
Counsel	Mass. Body of Liberties, S. 29	Same	N.J. Constitution, Art. XVI
Jury trial (civil)	Mass. Body of Liberties, S. 29	Same	Va. Declaration of Rights, S. 11
Bail	Mass. Body of Liberties, S. 18	Same	Va. Declaration of Rights, S. 9
Fines	Pa. Frame of Government, S. XVIII	Same	Va. Declaration of Rights, S. 9
Punishment	Mass. Body of Liberties, S. 43, 46	Same	Va. Declaration of Rights, S. 9
Rights retained by people	Va. Convention, proposed amendment 17	Same	Ninth Amendment
Reserved Powers	Mass. Declaration of Rights, Art. IV	Same	Same

INDEX

A

abuse of power, checks against in federal government, 480, 566, 686–687, 689
accusation, right to know, cause and nature of
   Antifederalist writings: want of, in Constitution, 508
   Delaware Declaration of Rights (1776), 276, 278
   final agreement on amendment covering, in First Congress, 1160, 1162–1163, 1165
   First Congress debates on, 1027, 1114, 1123
   Maryland Declaration of Rights (1776), 279, 282
   Massachusetts Ratifying Convention amendment on, 690
   New Hampshire Bill of Rights (1783), 377
   New York amendment to Constitution, 913
   North Carolina amendment to Constitution, 967
   North Carolina Declaration of Rights (1776), 286–287
   Pennsylvania amendment to Constitution, 628, 658, 665
   Pennsylvania Declaration of Rights (1776), 262, 265
   Vermont Declaration of Rights (1777), 323
   Vermont Ratifying Convention on, 765, 805, 841
   Virginia Declaration of Rights (1776), first guarantee of, 233, 235, 238, 242
Act of Assembly, 410
Act for the Better preserving his Majesty's Dock Yards, Magazines, Ships, Ammunition and Stores, 209
Adams, John, 17, 50, 196, 262–263, 474, 609
   as ambassador, 603–604
   on Lechmere's case, 183–184, 186, 192–193, 195
   at Massachusetts Declaration of Rights, 337–338, 358–359
   at Second Continental Congress, 228–229
   signs Declaration of Independence, 254
   as vice-president, 615, 993, 995, 1003, 1165
Adams, Samuel, 199, 212, 214, 254, 262, 337, 360–361, 364, 615
   proposed amendments at Massachusetts Ratifying Convention, 675–676, 694, 696, 707, 724, 727
Address to the Inhabitants of Quebec, 221–227
Address to a Meeting of the Citizens of Philadelphia, An, 528–532
Address to the People of New York on the Constitution, 554–566
Address to the People of New York on the Necessity of Amendments to the Constitution, 566–577
Address on the Proposed Plan of a Federal Government, 540–546
Address and Reasons of Dissent of the Minority of the Convention of the State of Pennsylvania, 662–673
admiralty, courts of,
   federal judiciary to be limited to, 659, 666, 844, 871, 917, 1056, 1119–1120, 1125, 1137, 1153
   no jury trial in, 454, 462, 530, 550, 670, 740, 742, 787, 806, 897, 941, 1143
   in states, 114, 332
Agreement of the People, 22–29
amendments
   as appendix to Constitution, 1051, 1121, 1139
   to colonial charters, 130, 169, 171
   conditional, 887–891
   difficulty of making under Constitution, 475
   eight states propose, 983
   form of making, 1070–1072, 1074–1075
   House of Representatives debates on, 984, 1022–1023, 1026–1027, 1032, 1035–1043, 1045–1046, 1048–1049, 1057–1120
   James Madison on, 984
   of Maryland Ratifying Convention, 729–735
   of Massachusetts Ratifying Convention, 572, 674–680, 694–704, 706–708, 710–713, 722, 729
   of New Hampshire Ratifying Convention, 758
   of New York Ratifying Convention, 874–876, 880, 882–885, 894, 897–904, 914–915
   of North Carolina Convention, 933–934, 953, 956–957, 966–971, 979
   of Pennsylvania Ratifying Convention, 628, 658–660
   popular demand for, 444, 502, 573, 1006, 1020
   prior, 477–479, 504, 569–571, 592, 763–764, 769–770, 782, 785, 791, 794, 808, 814, 823, 825–827, 839, 850, 877, 926–952, 966, 978
   prior versus subsequent, 443, 518, 554, 566–568, 578
   ratification of, by states, 1171
   of South Carolina Ratifying Convention, 739, 756–757
   to state constitutions, 263–264, 275, 280–281, 300
   subsequent, 465, 554, 588–590, 802, 814–818, 828, 830–832, 964
   system of making, under Constitution, 536, 590, 780, 795, 994, 1066–1069
   of Virginia Ratifying Convention, 762, 781–782, 786, 789, 793, 796, 816, 819, 821, 824, 840–845
   James Winthrop suggests, 518–519

M

Q